Social Psychology

Social Psychology

Exploring Universals Across Cultures

Fathali M. Moghaddam
Georgetown University

 W. H. Freeman and Company • New York

To Mariam

ACQUISITIONS EDITOR: Susan Finnemore Brennan
DEVELOPMENT EDITOR: Jeannine Ciliotta
PROJECT EDITOR: Mary Louise Byrd
TEXT AND COVER DESIGNER: Diana Blume
ILLUSTRATION COORDINATOR: Susan Wein
ILLUSTRATIONS: Hadel Studio
PHOTO EDITORS: Elyse Rieder, Kathy Bendo
PRODUCTION COORDINATOR: Paul W. Rohloff
COMPOSITION: Digitype
MANUFACTURING: RR Donnelley & Sons Company
MARKETING MANAGER: Kate Steinbacher

Library of Congress Cataloging–in–Publication Data

Moghaddam, Fathali M.
    Social psychology : exploring universals across cultures /
    Fathali M. Moghaddam.
        p.   cm.
    Includes bibliographical references and index.
    ISBN 0–7167–2849–4 (alk. paper)
    1. Social psychology.   I. Title
HM251.M584   1998   97–25255
309—dc21   CIP

Cover painting: *Peopled Wall II*, 1993, by Karen Poulson. Acrylic collage on paper, 30" × 40". Courtesy of the artist.

Printed in the United States of America

First printing, 1998

Brief Contents

Contents

Preface

*D*uring my student days in England, I used to return annually to
Iran, where I was born, and travel to different parts of the country.
Each trip brought new opportunities to assess the teachings of Western
social psychology in another cultural context. Some of the explanations offered by Western theories worked well, but many did not, such
as those that assume the self to be independent, individualism to be
the norm, and consistency in cognitions and behavior to be the desired end state.

At the same time that I became committed to a career in social
psychology, I recognized that the discipline would better fulfill its
promise as a science of social behavior if it became more international.
An international social psychology could incorporate cultural diversity
and provide more accurate explanations of human behavior, rather
than just the behavior of a tiny segment of humanity: young, white,
middle–class males in the United States. Social behavior varies in important ways across cultures, and social psychology can only fulfill its
promise as a science by addressing such variations.

As I learned more about other societies around the world and
taught social psychology to students with different cultural backgrounds, I recognized the need for a social psychology text that takes
as its subject the social behavior of *humankind.* But I was not the only
one who saw such a need. Many colleagues and students pointed to it.
As teachers and students in social psychology classes, they recognized
that traditional texts do not seriously address cultural diversity.

Even if we consider only the situation in the United States, the
days when the great majority of college students were males of Western European descent are past. Women and ethnic minority students
now make up the numerical majority in social psychology classes, and
the texts they use should incorporate this historic change. Gender, ethnicity, and cultural diversity are central themes in this text.

This text also makes social psychology more useful to those students, the majority by far, who will not become professional social
psychologists, but who need to use social psychological knowledge in
future careers as managers, lawyers, social workers, doctors, teachers,
engineers, nurses, and so on. The global village has become a reality,
making it necessary for everyone to learn about the social behavior of
groups both within and outside the American mainstream.

The goal of helping social psychology make progress as a science
has remained foremost in my mind. Our young science is evolving,
and it is important that students think critically about the alternative

models offered by the field, by assessing the mainstream model alongside a cultural one. Thus, this text is designed to engage students, to get them to analyze on their own the merits of alternative viewpoints.

The Book: Themes and Approaches

In writing this book I have looked back to the past but also ahead to the promise of the future. I have been careful to include historically important topics, as well as classic studies. Cutting–edge research and innovative ideas are also strongly represented in the text. Discussions of research from Europe, Asia, Africa, South America, and Australia are integrated into the main narrative as well. To better represent international social psychology, there is in–depth coverage of several topics, including gender, intergroup relations, minority influence, social representations, and social psychological research on multiculturalism. These topics are given more importance in research outside the United States, and deserve more attention in a text concerned with the social behavior of humankind.

In-Depth Coverage of Mainstream Topics

This book provides thorough and up-to-date coverage of the most important topics in mainstream social psychology; to this foundation is added a rich cross–cultural perspective. A cross-cultural perspective inspires us to achieve a genuinely different view of the world. Research in other cultures can act as a mirror, helping us to better see and understand social behavior in our own cultures.

A Cross-Cultural Perspective

The cross–cultural perspective of this book has three major features. First, it involves making cross–cultural comparisons to assess the extent to which research studies give the same results when repeated in more than one culture. For example, do studies on obedience to authority replicate across cultures? But this is only a first step, in part because a large number of studies have yet to be adequately repeated in more than one culture.

Second, it involves assessing the influence of culture on the theories and findings of social psychology. Theories of social behavior and the studies designed to test them do not evolve in a vacuum; they are necessarily influenced by culture. Similarly, how we interpret research findings is often influenced by culture. For example, the idea of humans as rational beings has influenced theories such as cognitive dissonance. Similarly, the individualism pervasive in U.S. society has often influenced the interpretation of social behavior as caused by stable cognitive factors. By identifying such influences, we can better distinguish between explanations and interpretations that work at the local level and those that generalize to people in several and perhaps all cultures.

The cross–cultural perspective of this book also offers an alternative theoretical approach to explaining social behavior, one that is normative rather than causal. A major goal in mainstream social psychology has been to identify causes for social behavior, deemed to be dispositional (internal to the person), situational (external to the person), or both. Since the 1970s there has been a focus on cognitive mechanisms, such as stereotyping and categorization, as causal agents determining prejudice and other behaviors. Such elements of social cognition are assumed, sometimes explicitly, to be universal features of human behavior, operating independently of culture.

A normative account assumes that social behavior, including social cognition, is in fundamental ways influenced by culture. For example, stereotyping and prejudice are assumed to arise from certain cultural conditions. But the relationship between culture and behavior is not deterministic; culture does not cause behavior. Most individuals in most situations behave in ways that are correct from the perspective of their culture, but they also have and use the freedom to do otherwise. This freedom means that some people behave differently from the majority, both inside and outside the psychology laboratory.

Critical Thinking

Throughout the 15 chapters of this book, each topic is presented as a balanced dialogue between the findings and the theories of mainstream social psychology and a supportive but questioning cross-cultural voice. Hence *Social Psychology* comprises the dialogue between findings from mainstream social psychological research and cross-cultural research; the dialogue between causal and normative explanations of social behavior; and the dialogue between possible universals in social behavior and possible local features.

These dialogues are designed to develop students' critical thinking skills. Alternative perspectives are presented alongside in-depth discussions of mainstream literature on topics such as attributions, the self, and persuasion. Culture is not treated as "another variable," but as a framework through which the reader can critically evaluate a topic. Consequently, students learn to think through research questions on the basis of a solid grounding in mainstream social psychology as well as an innovative cultural alternative.

A Balanced Coverage

Special attention has been given to achieving the right balance of coverage. Although a cross-cultural perspective runs through the book, the focus remains on the theories, methods, and findings of mainstream social psychology. But I have avoided doing things differently just for the sake of being different. The book follows the same organization as mainstream social psychology texts. The chapter headings and the number of chapters are the same. The sequence of topics is also the same, starting with the self and major topics in social cognition, moving to interpersonal processes, and ending with group dynamics and intergroup relations. Research methods are discussed at the start and applied topics at the end.

The Book: Teaching and Learning Features

The cross-cultural, critical thinking perspective that underlies the text is integrated into the features as well. The summary statement at the end of each chapter section, and the conclusion and review at the end of each chapter, direct attention to key questions, as well as advances already achieved, in each research domain. Critical thinking is again the focus of the questions at the end of each main section and of the broader questions at the end of each chapter.

Concepts and Issues

Each major section of a chapter is followed by a restatement of the major point or points, along with three to four questions specific to that topic or section. The questions are designed to help students focus on and articulate the important issues raised in the text.

For Review, For Discussion

Each chapter ends with *For Review*, a summary of the chapter in paragraph form, followed by *For Discussion*, which are broader, more conceptual questions that can be used for group discussions or for written assignments.

Glossary

Each major concept and term is boldfaced in the text at its introduction/definition, then repeated in the margin. The marginal running glossary is supplemented by a full alphabetical listing at the end of the book.

Annotated Readings and Bibliography

Annotated readings appear at the end of each chapter to point the interested reader to some of the best current work on the topics and issues in the chapter. A full alphabetical listing of text citations appears at the end of the book. The list includes approximately 1,600 items, of which about 40 percent are from 1990 or later.

Photo Essays

Four photo essays further our goal of illuminating major topics in social psychology through a cross-cultural perspective. The topics—Self, Conformity, Altruism, and Gender—lend themselves especially well to a visual presentation of the underlying thesis of the book: that a social psychology of humankind requires us to look beyond our own society in forming and evaluating theories of social behavior.

Photo Program

Each of the 100 or so photographs in the text is accompanied by a caption that ties the photo to major themes and ideas in the chapter. Photos and captions are thus another feature that serves to reinforce the cross-cultural, critical thinking perspective of this text.

Teaching and Study Supplements

Each component of the supplements package for reinforces the themes of the text: cross-cultural exploration and critical thinking.

▶ The *Instructor's Resource Manual* includes a plethora of suggestions for enriching classroom presentation, including strategies for bring ing culture into the classroom, lecture outlines, sample syllabi, discussion topics, critical thinking exercises, and audiovisual resources. An innovative resource for engaging students' interest in cross-cultural thinking is the *Global Film Festival Program Guide*, which includes suggestions on how to incorporate popular films with cross-cultural themes into lectures and assignments.

▶ The *Study Guide* contains resources for students to reinforce their understanding of cross-cultural issues and help them hone their critical thinking skills; it includes chapter outlines, chapter overviews, learning objectives, critical thinking exercises, and practice tests.

▶ The extensive *Testbank* is available in printed and computerized (IBM or Macintosh) formats.

▶ A *Social Psychology Website* supports and enhances the other supplements by expanding on, enriching, and updating their offerings.

Acknowledgments

The international perspective of this book has been influenced by many colleagues and former students around the world. Foremost among these are my friends Donald Taylor and Wallace Lambert (McGill University, Canada).

Among other scholars who have influenced the ideas in this book are John Adair (University of Manitoba, Canada), Yehuda Amir (Bar-Ilan University, Israel), Ximena Arriago (Claremont College, U.S.A.), Mahzarin Banaji (Yale University, U.S.A.), Deborah Best (Wake Forest University, U.S.A.), Mick Billig (Loughborough University, U.K.), Michael Bond (Chinese University in Hong Kong), Francis Cherry (Carlton University, Canada), Richard Clement (University of Ottawa, Canada), Faye Crosby (Smith College, U.S.A.), Ken Dion (University of Toronto, Canada), Willem Doise (University of Geneva, Switzerland), Uwe Geilen (St. Francis College, U.S.A.), Howard Giles (University of California, Santa Barbara, U.S.A.), Peter Grant (University of Saskatchewan, Canada), Carolyn Hafer (Brock University, Canada), Rom Harré (Oxford University, U.K.), Geert Hofstede (University of Limburg, Netherlands), Gui-Young Hong (University of Tennessee, Chattanooga, U.S.A.), Çigdem Kağitçibaşi (Bogazici University, Turkey), Richard Lalonde (York University, Canada), and Yueh-Ting Lee (Westfield State College, U.S.A.).

Also, Joan Miller (Yale University), Maritza Montero (Universidad Central de Venezuela), Serge Moscovici (Ecoles des Hautes Etudes en Sciences Sociales, France), David Myers (Hope College, U.S.A.), Charlan Nemeth (University of California at Berkeley, U.S.A.), Stuart Oskamp (Claremont College, U.S.A.), Al Pepitone (University of Pennsylvania, U.S.A.), Karen Ruggiero (Harvard University, U.S.A.), Robert Serpell

(University of Maryland, Baltimore County, U.S.A.), Jal Sinha (A.N.S. Institute of Social Studies, India), Charles Stangor (University of Maryland, College Park, U.S.A.), John Turner (Australian National University), Colleen Ward (University of Canterbury, New Zealand), Sue Widdicombe (University of Edinburgh, Scotland), John Williams (Wake Forest University, U.S.A.), Durhane Wong–Rieger (University of Windsor, Canada), Stephen Worchel (Texas A&M University, U.S.A.), and Steve Wright (University of California, Santa Cruz, U.S.A.).

I have greatly benefited from discussions at Georgetown University with Norm Finkel, Rom Harré, Jim Lamiell, Jerry Parrott, and Dan Robinson. Darlene Howard provided insightful commentary on the self chapter.

The following provided constructive reviews of the manuscript in its earlier drafts: Assaad Azzi (Yale University), Mary Leary (Wake Forest University), Galen Bodenhausen (Michigan State University), John Berry (Queens University), Russell Cropanzano (Colorado State University), and Harry Reis (University of Rochester) reviewed the proposal and Chapter 1. William Buskist (Auburn University), Uwe Geilen (St. Francis College), Lauren Perdue (Central Connecticut State University), Tod Sloan (University of Tulsa), and Tatiana Wanchula (Bowling Green State University) reviewed Chapters 2, 6, and 7. Deborah Prentice (Princeton University), Frank Bernieri (Oregon State University), and Mark Alicke (Ohio State University), reviewed Chapters 3, 4, and 5. Lauren Perdue (Central Connecticut State University), Jeffrey Scott Mio (Cal–Poly Pomona), Mary Alice Gordon (Southern Methodist University), Tod Sloan (University of Tulsa), William Buskist (Auburn University), and Uwe Geilen (St. Francis College) reviewed Chapters 9 through 15. Mark Snyder (University of Minnesota) reviewed selected parts of earlier drafts. John T. Jost (Stanford University), Lauren Perdue (Central Connecticut State University), Judith Gibbons (St. Louis University), Ted Singelis (California State University, Chico), and Cheryl Drout (SUNY, Fredonia) reviewed the full manuscript in final revision.

Now for a surprise. Along with the agony of writing, there has been ecstasy. Writing and preparing this book for publication has been an exciting and enjoyable experience, in part because of the wonderful collaboration and support provided by our book team at W. H. Freeman and Company. I am particularly indebted to Susan Brennan, who initiated the project and guided it to fruition, and to Mary Shuford and Mary Louise Byrd, who kept our team focused and kept me pointed in the right direction. I also benefited a great deal from discussions with Melissa Wallerstein, Kate Steinbacher, and Kathy Bendo.

I was privileged to have Jeannine Ciliotta as an editor. She was born an editor. She was already reading text, suggesting improvements, and writing "why," "explain," and "needs clarification" in exactly the right places by the age of three.

Writing this book has had it costs also, because it has meant less time spent with my family. My wife, Dr. Mariam Monshipouri, has always been the strongest supporter of my work and continues to be its most constructive critic. The successful completion of this project owes much to her.

About the Author

*F*athali M. Moghaddam is an Iranian–born, British–educated social psychologist who moved from McGill University, Montreal, Canada, to Georgetown University, Washington, D.C., U.S.A., in 1990, where he is currently Professor of Psychology. His most recent books are *The Specialized Society: The Plight of the Individual in an Age of Individualism* (1997) and *Theories of Intergroup Relations: International Social Psychological Perspectives* (with D. M. Taylor, 1994). His numerous research papers have appeared in American, European, and international scientific journals. Dr. Moghaddam has done research in various Western and non–Western societies; and within North America he has conducted studies with women and men participants from many cultural groups, including white, African-American, Hispanic, Jewish, Arab, Chinese, Greek, Iranian, and Haitian populations. He has worked on United Nations national development projects in such areas as refugee resettlement, rural health, and technical training, and he once lectured on social psychology in a nomad tent. Before climbing back over the campus wall to resume life in academia, Dr. Moghaddam worked briefly as a freelance writer. His current home is in Maryland, U.S.A., where he lives with his wife, Mariam, a bioengineer, and their daughter, Nikoo, and son, Guilan.

Social Psychology

CHAPTER *1*

The Challenge of Social Psychology

◀ Social psychology is the scientific study of individuals in social contexts. Social psychologists explore how people think about themselves and others, how they explain and evaluate events, and people's experiences as group members. Much of our personal experience is associated with our membership in groups: At the heart of social psychology is the issue of the relationship between individuals and groups. These young people training for a summer jobs program in San Francisco are to some extent unique individuals, but they are also sharing a common experience as part of a collectivity.

*T*he waters of the Persian Gulf looked calm as we waited for the small wooden fishing boat to take us out to sea. We had been scheduled to go out by eight o'clock in the morning, and it was now almost noon. The four of us impatiently waiting at the harbor front were working on a fisheries project with the United Nations Food and Agriculture Organization (FAO), and part of our mission was to survey local working conditions, fishing techniques, and know-how. It quickly became obvious that the local people were wonderfully skillful in traditional crafts, such as the constructing of the vessel on which we were supposed to have been taken out. However, an efficient modern fishing vessel, operated by just a few individuals, could catch a lot more fish than the entire traditional fleet of a whole village community. The introduction of a single modern vessel could transform traditional lifestyles overnight. Such changes would surely increase incomes over the long term; of course, overfishing could destroy the entire fishing industry forever.

All this was on our minds as we waited that morning. But, as the Canadian fisheries expert in our group kept reminding us, there seemed to be no sign of anything happening. For almost 4 hours now, the captain and his crew had served us tea and all kinds of delicacies. They had shown us around the port and we had inspected the boat no less than three times. The captain was a large, jovial man, and he told his many wondrous and amusing stories in a mixture of broken English and French, at the same time encouraging us to recount our own experiences, which we did with some enthusiasm, at least initially. However, as time ticked by, we became more and more impatient. We had a job to do and standing around swapping stories was not the way to do it.

We expressed our concerns to the captain several times, but to no avail. Captain and crew seemed to be sailing on another, much different course—one we had not been told about. Around noon, food and drinks were brought and everyone settled down to a relaxing lunch—everyone except the four of us, that is. By this time, my colleagues were completely exasperated. They thought the day was lost.

Lunch seemed to move along at a snail's pace, but immediately afterward events took a surprising turn. The crew all went to work on board, the captain then surprised us by reporting that all was ready, and the boat soon moved out of the harbor and into open water. We visited several islands, inspected fishing nets and other equipment, and came back very late in the evening. The other members of the United Nations team still believed the day had been 50 percent disastrous, and could not understand it when the captain turned in his own report, which stated that the day had been a success.

"You are the psychologist here," one of my team members said to me in a complaining tone, "you make sense of this behavior. Why does the captain tell us to be ready to sail at eight in the morning, then make us wait until almost two in the afternoon before setting out to sea?" "Yes, and what do you make of the captain's report?" asked another. "He claims the day was a complete success, when in fact at least half of it was a total loss." "It really is hard working with these people," added the third team member, "they say one thing, and then do something very different. Their actions don't follow their words. What do you psychologists have to say about that?"

Such questions are at the heart of social psychology, a field of study that has developed over the course of the twentieth century as a discipline devoted to understanding social behavior.

Social Psychology: An Overview

Social psychology is the scientific study of individuals in social contexts. The relationships that are the topic of social psychology can be both interpersonal, such as a relationship between two lovers, and intergroup, such as relationships between men and women (Taylor & Moghaddam, 1994). However, the focus of social psychology is always on individuals, even when social psychologists study intergroup relations. For example, prejudice against minorities is studied with a focus on the perceptions and attitudes of individual members of different ethnic groups (this is discussed further in Chapters 10–14).

social psychology the scientific study of individuals in social contexts.

Social psychology is a vitally important science, because with the approach of the twenty-first century we face our most complex, difficult, and significant issues in the realm of social behavior. Breathtaking developments in physics, chemistry, and other pure sciences have allowed humans to walk on the moon and make other serious progress in space exploration—but people are afraid to walk around city centers on earth. Advances in biochemistry, bioengineering, and other new hybrid sciences have allowed amazing feats that until very recently were only found in the world of science fiction, such as extending the shelf life of a tomato to 6 months, but we have not been able to solve the "simple" drug problems that threaten our teenagers. Environmental studies, ethology, and other related disciplines have given us a rich understanding of animal and plant life—yet we often find it impossible to understand other human beings, even our own roommates.

Everywhere we look, social behavior presents puzzles that need to be unraveled through social psychological research. For example, at the end of the twentieth century, people in Western societies are enjoying unprecedented wealth and technological advances, but they also seem to be worried about their circumstances. Consider the following report in the *Washington Post* concerning how Americans see their society in the late 1990s:

> The average American thinks the number of jobless is four times higher than it actually is. Nearly 1 in 4 believes the current unemployment rate tops 25 percent—the proportion of Americans who were estimated to be out of work at the worst of the Great Depression. They believe that prices are rising four times faster than they really are and that the federal budget is higher, not lower, than it was five years ago. (Morrin & Berry, 1996, p. A1)

In assessing the health of the economy, are we to rely on "official statistics," such as the low unemployment and inflation rates, or are we to rely on how people actually feel about the economy? It would be foolhardy to neglect how people actually experience the situation. Such

Humankind has made tremendous progress in technology during the last few decades. We have landed people on the moon, built computers that can defeat even the best chess champions, and used genetic engineering to achieve feats that were once thought possible only in the science fiction world of *Star Trek*—increasing the shelf life of tomatoes and cloning animals are just two examples. Our "smart weapons" can pinpoint and knock out targets hundreds of miles away. Yet we still have not solved some serious and basic social problems, such as violent crime, drugs, racism, sexism, child abuse, and war. We produce surplus food that ends up being destroyed, while millions suffer from hunger and malnutrition. The major challenges facing us are no longer technological, they are social psychological.

large rifts between social perceptions and actual events can pose monumental problems for politicians and economists, as well as for the general public.

That day in 1982 when colleagues challenged me to explain the behavior of the Persian Gulf boat captain reminded me of this enormously important task. The behavior of the captain and his crew had seemed contradictory and incomprehensible to my colleagues. But a closer look at local ideas about correct behavior led to a different conclusion. I spoke at length with the captain, and he explained that he was brought up to believe that the most important part of any business is first to get to know who one is dealing with. The parties in a business arrangement must first get to know one another personally, to develop trust and understanding. Only then can they move ahead with official business. In other words, from his point of view the morning had been spent completing the most important part of our business and laying the foundation of the entire working relationship. Once that was done, then the rest would proceed successfully—which it did.

But what about his insistence that we be at the harbor ready to board at eight o'clock? The captain was puzzled by this question and said that we were obviously having communication problems. Wanting us there at eight o'clock simply meant we would have more time to get to know one another before we set out to sea. "Surely, you do not expect me to work with people before I have had the opportunity to get to know them personally?" asked the captain. The answer to this question is one thing if one is working in the context of Western societies, where behavior is guided by such rules as "business before pleasure" and "business and pleasure do not mix," and something else again if one is from the same culture as the captain. The encounter is a reminder of the complexities of social behavior each of us experience, particularly in a culturally diverse world.

Cultural diversity is important for social psychology because it is associated with different patterns of social behavior. Women and men, the members of different ethnic groups, and, of course, the members of different socioeconomic classes are socialized to behave in ways that are culturally correct. For example, there has been a tradition for men to be socialized to "act tough" and women to "provide sympathy" and "be supportive" (for more on gender differences, see Chapter 12). Wallace Lambert (1987) has argued that social class can be even a more important grouping than gender and ethnicity because similarities within social class can be the most important ones. In a cross-national study of child-rearing values, Lambert found that

> social class turned out to have a much more powerful effect on parental values than ethnicity . . . working-class parents from Italy, for example, are more similar to Japanese working-class parents in their child-rearing values than they are to Italian parents of middle-class socioeconomic standing, just as Japanese middle-class parents are more like Greek middle-class parents than they are like other Japanese from a different socioeconomic stratum. (p. 12)

Thus, social class helps to create certain similarities (within social classes) in behavior across societies, but also some differences (across social classes) within each society. (For broader discussions, see Argyle, 1994, and Joyce, 1995.)

The Practice of Social Psychology

In our everyday lives, we are continuously engaged in the task of trying to understand and explain social behavior better. We each have our own explanations for why people express certain views and why they behave as they do. We constantly ask questions about social life: "Why does Joe hold such negative attitudes toward minorities?" "Why does Clara put so much time and effort into helping homeless people?" "Why does Mrs. Jones blame the unemployed in her town for being out of work?" "Will our work group perform more efficiently if we have a democratic leader or if we have an authoritarian leader?" A number of

In our everyday lives we act as amateur scientists, developing and testing our explanations of the world. Look at this skateboarder, a member of an elite demonstration team. Why is it desirable to be part of such a team, given the obvious risks? What benefits do individuals derive from being associated with high–status groups? Social psychologists also address these kinds of questions, but they try to do so in a scientific manner: Their explanations are systematic and their research methods are carefully designed to be objective.

important social psychologists have argued that in trying to answer these types of questions during the course of our everyday lives, we act as amateur scientists (Heider, 1958; Kelley, 1972; Kelly, 1955). We gather information and test our explanations. For example, I may assume that Joe holds negative views about minorities because he was socialized to behave in this way, and my hunch may be confirmed when I meet his family and friends and learn about their prejudices.

Social psychologists also develop explanations of such social events, and they also test alternative explanations. However, their theories are more formally stated, and their methods of research are more systematic and objective. In order to achieve greater objectivity, social psychologists have developed a range of research methodologies. These include laboratory experiments, which allow more precise control and measurement of behavior, and also survey and observational methods, which enable researchers to investigate aspects of behavior in everyday life. A major objective is to use research methods that allow studies to be conducted by others using exactly the same methodology. (The topic of research methods is discussed in more detail in Chapter 2.)

As a science of *human* social behavior, social psychology faces the challenge of describing and explaining the behavior of different people around the world. After all, more than three-quarters of the world population live outside industrialized societies. However, although the historical origins of social psychology are almost entirely European (Collier, Minton, & Reynolds, 1991), the vast majority of social psychologists presently active in research live in the industrialized societies, and most in the United States. Given that it is more feasible for social psychologists to study people in their own societies than it is to study people in other societies, it is easy to see why most of our social psychological knowledge is based on studies conducted by North American researchers, and have involved North American participants. Social psychology faces a particularly important challenge in becoming a science of human behavior, of testing ideas in different cultural contexts around the globe.

The Historical Development of Social Psychology

The formal launch of social psychology is taken to be the publication of the first social psychology textbooks almost a century ago, by a U.S. psychologist (McDougall, 1908) and a U.S. sociologist (Ross, 1908). However, even before this event, there were experimental studies that are clearly social psychological. In the last decade of the nineteenth century Norman Triplett (1898) noticed that cyclists achieve better times when they race in the company of others than when they race alone. This insight led him to conduct one of the first social psychological experiments, demonstrating that children are faster at winding up fishing line when they are with others than when on their own.

My personal experience of this kind of increased performance as a result of the mere presence of others, termed **social facilitation,** came when I participated in a study on performance in cold environments. We lived in an environmental chamber for several days, with the temperature kept very low. Every few hours we were asked to perform a number of sensorimotor tasks, such as keeping a pointer on a rotating target. In theory, we should have achieved our lowest scores at the end of the session, after being kept in the cold and sleep-deprived. However, the presence of other students created a sense of competition, and we were breaking records until the final minutes of the study.

social facilitation increased performance as a result of the mere presence of others.

Although many of the seminal ideas of social psychology have their roots in the scholarship of Europe (Allport, 1985; Robinson, 1995), it was in the United States that social psychology developed its modern characteristics (Moghaddam, 1987). A look back over the history of social psychology shows that the United States has been the most important influence on the discipline (Cartwright, 1979; Collier, Minton, & Reynolds, 1991; Jackson, 1988). Selections of classic contributions by major figures in the field also reveal the overwhelming influence of American researchers (Evans, 1980; Halberstadt & Ellyson, 1990; Hollander & Hunt, 1972). The vast majority of social psychological studies have addressed questions generated by U.S. researchers, have involved U.S. participants (typically undergraduate students), and have used research methods developed in the United States.

The United States, the "first world" of psychology, is the major producer of social psychological knowledge and the main exporter of such knowledge to the "second world," made up of the other industrialized nations (e.g., members of the European Union, Russia, Japan), and the "third world," made up of the developing societies (e.g., India, Nigeria). "Third world" countries import almost all of their psychological knowledge from the "first and second worlds." The major social psychology publications are written and edited predominantly by Americans (Gielen, 1994), and the tests and measures most widely used in social psychological research have been developed in the United States (Robinson, Shaver, & Wrightsman, 1991). In brief, the United States is the superpower of social psychology.

Concepts and Issues

The major objective of social psychology is to use scientific methods to study individual behavior in social contexts. Although many of the seminal ideas of social psychology have their roots outside the United States, the discipline has come to fruition in North America. The tremendous productivity of U.S. researchers has meant that American social psychology is exported all over the world, and social behavior outside white male North American middle-class circles has been neglected. Particular care has to be taken, then, to establish social psychology as a universal science of human behavior by giving proper attention to the role of culture.

1. In a few sentences, explain the main purpose of social psychology.
2. In what ways do we act as amateur scientists in our everyday lives?
3. What are a few of the obstacles we face in trying to establish social psychology as a science of human social behavior?

The Goals of Social Psychology

The historical development of social psychology and the unique influence of the United States on the discipline in no way undermine the scientific goal of social psychological research: to explain social behavior. However, it does mean that we must make a special effort to look beyond the United States to consider social behavior in a global context (Moghaddam, 1990, 1996). An ultimate goal of social psychology is to discover universals, or **etics,** behaviors that are common to most or all societies, as well as **emics,** behaviors that are found in only one or a few societies.

emic   a characteristic that is specific to one or a few cultural groups and not universal.

etics   behaviors that are found in all or most societies.

Universals (Etics) and Social Psychology

A major challenge in social psychology is to examine empirically possible universals in various domains of social behavior. Throughout the following discussions, we shall review the classic studies, almost all of which have been conducted in the United States or other Western societies using students as participants. We shall take the further step of evaluating these findings in a global context. Thus, a cross-cultural perspective will be used to enrich social psychology and help to move us closer to the goal of achieving a science of human social behavior.

At some fundamental level, certain universals in social behavior must exist in order for there to be a human form of life at all (Holliday, 1988) (a relevant slogan here might be "It's a human thing, of course you understand," in contrast to slogans such as "It's a Black thing, you wouldn't understand"). What might such universals be? Let us begin by identifying three social norms that are strong candidates: the norm of trust, the norm of truth, and the norm of turn-taking in dialogue. A **norm** is a prescription for social behavior, a guide to correct behavior in any given setting. These norms are strong candidates for universals, because without them human social life would be impossible.

norm a guide to correct behavior in a given setting.

The Norm of Trust.   In all human societies, there is a **norm of trust**—people in general trust one another, and function on the assumption that others should generally be trusted. This tendency to trust exists in both private and public spheres, although there will of course be exceptions (there are always some individuals whom we learn to distrust). To realize that this must be so, we need only imagine what the situation would be like if the opposite were true and people generally did not trust one another. The following are some everyday consequences of living without a norm of trust:

norm of trust the norm that others should generally be trusted.

▶   I buy a ticket for a two o'clock train, but do not have trust in the people who provided me with travel information. Consequently, I spend all my time cross-examining different employees at the train station, the tourist office, and various other information centers to double-check everything I am told. During the train journey, my mind is plagued by questions: Will the train really stop at my destination? Did the ticket clerk charge the correct fare? Did the porter really put my bicycle on board?

▶   I go for a job interview, but do not trust the interviewer. When at the end of the interview she shakes my hand and says, "Glad to have you with us," I do not believe her. Nor do I have trust in her information about the salary and benefits her company offers. Can I even trust the contract she shows me? No, in a world in which the norm is "distrust others," I would generally disbelieve rather than believe most things I am told. A society organized in such a manner would not be functional.

The Norm of Truth.   Whereas the norm of trust places the burden on the receiver of information, the norm of truth places the burden on the provider. Life as we know it is only possible if people adhere to a **norm of truth,** if they generally tell the truth. A society would very quickly collapse if it functioned on the norm of falsehood. Imagine two episodes in a "falsehood-as-norm" society:

norm of truth the norm that people should generally tell the truth.

▶   A professor announces at the start of the semester that there will be no final examination for the course. On the final day of class, however, he tells the class to study both the class notes and the main course text for the final examination, which will be held the following morning. When the students protest, the professor simply responds, "Well, I did not tell the truth."

▶ You are having dental surgery and your dentist informs you that 80 percent of the cost will be met by your insurance company. When the treatment is completed and you receive the bill, you are horrified to find that the insurance company covers hardly any of the costs. Your dentist explains, "I did not tell the truth."

The Norm of Turn-Taking in Dialogue.   A third example of a universal in human social behavior is the **norm of turn-taking in dialogue,** which requires that each of the parties in an exchange takes turns to listen to the other, as well as to respond to what is said by the other. Dialogue breaks down if one or both parties stop listening to the other, do not allow the other to take turns to express him- or herself, or do not respond to what the other has said. Some dictatorial governments behave in this way, and in such cases there is a breakdown of dialogue between the people and those who hold the reins of power. You may also know of some individuals who behave in this way, such as parents and children who fail to hold dialogues with one another. The consequence is that the relationship deteriorates.

Dialogue requires more than just mechanical turn-taking; to be successful there must be mutual respect. Thus, a more general norm governing dialogue is that the parties must display at least a minimal level of respect for one another. Although in all societies there will be instances when dialogue breaks down, society can continue to function only if these are the exceptions rather than the rule.

norm of turn-taking in dialogue
the norm that parties in a dialogue should display a minimal level of respect by taking turns to listen to the other as well as to respond to what is being said by the other.

Turn-taking in dialogue is an example of a human universal. Even when two people do not speak the same language, there must be turn-taking in order for there to be dialogue. This tourist in an Istanbul market has to listen to the seller; then if she does not agree with the price, she can, according to local culture, bargain and suggest a lower one. The seller must in turn listen to the customer's offer, then either agree or make a counteroffer. A skillful seller realizes that he can achieve a sale only if dialogue continues. If he dictates terms without listening to the customer, or if the customer refuses to listen to the seller, dialogue ends and there is no deal.

Conformity is a human universal, although conformity takes place according to local rules and norms. For some, the rules and norms may be those of a rebel group, like these young Japanese women dressed in counterculture punk "uniforms." Conformity to the rules and norms of rebel groups can be just as strong as conformity to mainstream rules and norms. The three Parisian models wearing the latest styles for Fall 1929 are also conforming, but to a style that has long since vanished. And the Masai women attending a wedding in Kenya are conforming, in dress and behavior, to the norms and rules of their culture. There is considerable cross-cultural diversity in the variety of lifestyles individuals may choose, but once the choice is made, conformity to group norms and rules is universal.

More Similarities.   Here are some other basic similarities we find across cultures:

▶ In all human societies people behave according to the belief that each human body only has one self residing in it, even though they may not have terms that correspond well with "I" and "me." Without this assumption concerning a singular self, social life would be chaotic, and our explanations, to say the least, controversial, "Yes, you did see my body driving away with your car without your permission, but it was my other self that occupied my body at the time" (Chapter 3).

▶ People everywhere evaluate the world in negative and positive terms, and these evaluations are an integral part of both personal life and the larger culture (Chapter 4).

▶ The search for causes of at least some external events seems to be universal. When humans witness changes in the social and physical environment, they make assumptions about the causes of these changes (Chapter 5).

▶ Inequalities in status exist to some degree in all societies, and those who enjoy higher status and are seen to be more credible tend to be particularly effective at persuasion (Chapter 6).

▶ All societies involve some level of conformity to social norms and rules, and some measure of obedience to authority figures. Under certain conditions, at least some members of the population will obey orders to do harm to others (Chapter 7).

▶ Similarity and attraction are paired in the vast majority of circumstances around the world, so that all people are more likely to like and to love those who are more similar to themselves, although in a few situations opposites are also attracted. Physical proximity, and particularly a location that leads to frequent interaction, facilitates interpersonal attraction (Chapter 8).

▶ Helping behavior is observed among all people, but the specific conditions in which help is sought, accepted, and offered depend on local norms and rules. In many societies, women tend to be more prosocial, and also to be offered more help (Chapter 9).

▶ Awareness of the existence of other people seems to lead to a categorization of the social world into "us" and "them." A consequence of this categorization is often favoritism toward "us." Negative evaluations of groups are often used to legitimize status inequalities, as in "they are less intelligent than we, so they deserve to have fewer opportunities and less money" (Chapter 10).

▶ Aggression, defined as behavior intended to harm another, is found in all human societies, although in some societies collective aggression is relatively rare, and even individual aggression tends to be channeled and verbal, rather than random and physical (Chapter 11).

▶ In most societies women tend to show less physical aggression, but to display more empathy than men (Chapter 12).

▶ Social groups are common to all human societies, as is leadership (Chapter 13).

▶ Perceptions of injustice seem to be associated with intergroup conflicts around the world. Intergroup conflicts are more likely to arise when members of one or more groups feel that they are not receiving a fair share of "resources," such as social status, moral support, material wealth, and so on (Chapter 14).

▶ The concept of fairness and a distinction between just and unjust seem to be present and influential on behavior in all societies (Chapter 15).

These very basic similarities are part of a profile of human social behavior. Even though we may find exceptions, they are still fairly accurate descriptors of most humans. Of course, this by no means implies that the sources of such similarities are biological: The same environmental conditions can lead humans to organize their societies in similar ways in many different places around the world, although alternative systems are always possible. For example, during the twentieth century we have witnessed enormous changes in relationships between women and men in many societies. What used to be thought of as the "natural" role of women ("be obedient to her husband, stay out of politics, business, and education, keep the home and the children clean and in order") has been swept aside, together with "biological" explanations of the traditional role of women (see Chapter 12).

Specific Behaviors (Emics) and Social Psychology

A search for social psychological universals also allows us to identify characteristics that are specific to one or more cultural groups. This is also an important task for social psychologists, to map out the particular characteristics of social behavior in their own and in other cultures. It *is* important to know that people in the United States tend to be much more individualistic than people in other major societies, meaning that Americans place greater emphasis on personal independence, personal rights, self-help, individual responsibility, and personal goals. Many of the differences across cultures are associated with individualism, the extent to which emphasis is placed on personal independence, rights, and freedoms, rather than collectivism, where emphasis is more on collective rights and the duties of individuals to groups (Triandis, 1995).

Here are some other examples of emics in social behavior that we discuss in later chapters:

▶ The major research methods of social psychology, the laboratory procedure and survey methods, are not suitable for many parts of the world. This is in part because such methods require participants to be literate (of the roughly billion adults aged 15 years and over in the world who are illiterate, about 97 percent are in the developing countries [United Nations, 1994, p. 169]), but more important because such methods require familiarity with the idea and culture of research. The very research methods of social psychology have local rather than universal applicability (see Chapter 2).

▶ Research on the self has shown that in some cultures, such as those of India and China, people see the boundaries of the self as more fluid and merged with the larger community. In contrast, people in the United States and some other Western societies see the self as more rigidly bounded and independent of groups (see Chapter 3).

▶ The very idea that people should be consistent in their expressed attitudes or evaluation of the world and in their behavior reflects a Western ideal. In some societies greater emphasis is placed explicitly on training the young to cope with contradictions in thought and action (see Chapter 4).

▶ Members of ethnic minorities in the United States have experienced many external limitations and consequently make attributions that allow their self-esteem to remain positive. Some self-protective attributions, such as those referring to a history of slavery unique to the United States, are local (see Chapter 5).

▶ Researchers have traditionally focused on how independent individuals change their minds as a result of exposure to certain messages. This individualistic approach to persuasion is less appropriate in cultures where behavior is more social and collective (see Chapter 6).

▶ The results of studies on conformity in societies such as that of Japan showed, perhaps surprisingly, low rather than high levels of conformity compared to North Americans. This puzzling finding seems to be explained by the Japanese norm of nonconformity to strangers, such as those Japanese respondents would encounter in a typical psychology experiment, but higher conformity to family, peers, local community, and other familiar groups (see Chapter 7).

▶ In many parts of the world, marriage is still a joining of two families or communities, rather than just two individuals, and friendships are formed primarily through family and community networks. This contrasts sharply with the Western notion of individuals freely selecting friends and lovers on the basis of personal preference (see Chapter 8).

▶ Prosocial or helping behavior is used by people in some cultures as a means of creating obligations and debts, and in this way extending social networks and relations. This suggests that the same altruistic act can have very different meanings, depending on cultural context (see Chapter 9).

▶ There are fundamental differences in the experiences of majority groups, such as white males, and minority groups, such as women and ethnic minorities, with respect to prejudice. In some cases, minority group members may show a bias against their own group (see Chapter 10).

▶ Socialization processes have led to enormous variation in physical aggressivity across cultures, from societies in which there is minimal aggression to those in which it is a routine part of everyday life (see Chapter 11).

How people decide to get married and the nature of their wedding ceremonies are symbolic of cross-cultural differences in the relationship between individuals and groups. In Western societies, marriage in most cases is an individual decision that happens when two people decide they have fallen in love. Their wedding ceremony may be witnessed and celebrated by others, but the focus is on the joining of two independent persons. In contrast, in many non-Western societies, marriage is a joining of two communities, and groups of people (family, friends, neighbors) are involved in the decision-making process. The wedding ceremony is a family and community event, with the bride and groom at the center of a new circle of related people.

▶ There are fundamental differences in most aspects of the social behavior of men and women across cultures. In terms of gender relations, they vary from relatively egalitarian, such as those found in Western societies, to being unequal in major ways, such as those found in some Islamic countries (see Chapter 12).

▶ Social loafing, a tendency for people to exert more effort when working on a task individually than when working as part of a group, is more in evidence in individualistic cultures, such as the United States, than in collectivistic cultures, such as China (Chapter 13).

▶ The behavior of disadvantaged group members in the face of perceived inequalities and injustices varies across cultures. In the mainstream culture of the United States and other individualistic societies, the emphasis is on individual mobility and personal efforts to move up through the social hierarchy. In some other cultures, passive acceptance or collective action is more normative (see Chapter 14).

▶ White juries have been found to treat black defendants more harshly than they do white defendants, particularly when the case is ambiguous (see Chapter 15).

Thus, in each of the major domains discussed in the following chapters, the search for universals in human social behavior will also lead us to identify local, or emic, characteristics.

Manufactured Differences

Historians may well describe our era as the age of diversity and intergroup differences. A wide variety of collective movements, including women's liberation and the civil rights and gay rights movements, as well as numerous ethnic movements at the national and international levels, have emphasized the rights and distinctive characteristics of different groups. Several slogans printed on T-shirts worn by two of my students capture the spirit of these movements very well. The first emphatically declared, "We ARE different." The second said: "It's a Black thing, you wouldn't understand." Such powerful sentiments highlight assumed intergroup differences. However, we might wonder to what extent there really are such deep differences across ethnic, gender, and other groups.

Social psychologists are interested in how we perceive and manufacture such differences, in how, for example, we exaggerate or deny them. I was reminded of this when some years ago I was invited to be part of a panel to discuss North American immigrant cultures and family life. During the proceedings, representatives from several immigrant communities were invited to describe the role of the mother in their culture. Thus, we had presentations of the role of the mother in Greek culture, the role of the mother in Italian culture, and so on. Each presenter took her main task to be to distance herself from the "American mother," who was stereotyped as career-oriented and neglectful of her children.

Each presentation was peppered with statements such as "Mothers in my culture are not like American mothers. We give priority to the family and children, we love to cook our traditional foods and have everyone over to our home for all the special occasions." I am not suggesting, of course, that the role of the mother is not different across cultures. However, the kinds of differences being presented that evening focused almost exclusively on the distinction between "good" immigrant mothers and "bad" American mothers, by which was meant White Anglo-Saxon Protestant (WASP) mothers. Several people in the audience pointed out that the vast majority of WASPs do not fit the stereotype, and that the particular differences they were suggesting do not really exist. The ensuing discussion led us to think about the many similarities in the role of mother across cultures.

Concepts and Issues

Social psychological research strives to identify etics, or universals, as well as behaviors that are specific to one or a few cultures (emics). In order to achieve this goal, social psychologists must go beyond their own borders and study humankind.

1. What are emics and etics? Provide examples of each.
2. Give three examples of universal norms.
3. Why should people manufacture or exaggerate differences between groups?

Explanations in Social Psychology

Social psychologists have developed a wide variety of explanations for social behavior (Doise, 1986; Jackson, 1988; Shaw & Costanzo, 1982). A useful way of thinking about these explanations is in terms of two basic types: causal and normative. Causal explanations seek to establish cause–effect relations in social behavior, whereas normative explanations focus on how individuals use aspects of culture as guides to behavior. Both approaches have led to fruitful research, but the social nature of humankind is more strongly affirmed by normative accounts.

Causal Explanations

causal (explanation) explanations that assume human behavior to be causally determined by factors within persons or within the environment.

By far the most widely used explanations in social psychology are **causal,** meaning that they assume human behavior to be determined by factors either within persons or in the environment (see Figure 1–1). For example, social psychologists have explained aggression as being caused by personality characteristics of individuals, or by environmental conditions such as those that lead individuals to experience frustration (see Chapter 11). These kinds of explanations assume cause–effect relations: If environmental conditions create frustration, then this will cause aggressivity.

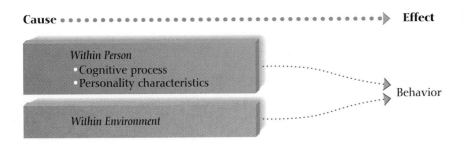

Figure 1-1 Schematic representation of causal accounts of social behavior.

The pervasiveness of the causal model is reflected in the most in-fluential schools of psychology—behaviorism and cognitive psychology. For about half a century, from early in the 1900s to the 1960s, the most influential school of psychology was behaviorism. The behaviorists focused on relations between stimuli (assumed causes) and responses (assumed effects) in behavior. A major assumption was that the causes of behavior are in the external environment. The behaviorist school be-gan to decline in the late 1950s, and by the 1960s the most influential school was cognitive psychology. Cognitive psychology still dominates in most departments of psychology in colleges and universities.

The focus of **cognitive psychology** is thinking and the mental processes inside the person. The influence of the cognitive school is ev-ident in modern social psychology and particularly in areas such as at-titudes, evaluations, and attributions, the way people account for events in the world (see Chapters 4 and 5). Whereas the behaviorists focused exclusively on directly observable stimuli and responses, and neglected anything to do with the "mind" and all that cannot be directly ob-served, cognitive psychologists turned the research spotlight inward on the interior world.

Cognitive psychology assumes that mental processes or mechanisms cause people to behave in certain ways (Moghaddam, 1997a; Moghaddam & Harré, 1995). One of the most influential ideas in cognitive social psy-chology has been that when people hold contradictory attitudes and be-haviors, they feel discomfort (dissonance). This dissonance causes them to change an attitude or behavior so as to reach "balance" again (see Chapter 4). Indeed, in most mainstream discussions of social psychology research methods and cognitive social psychology, it is explicitly stated that a goal of social psychology is to discover the causes of behavior.

A second major assumption of cognitive psychology is that the mental processes or mechanisms that cause behavior are independent of culture (Kegan, 1996). That is, the cognitions or thought processes that cognitive psychologists study are assumed to be universal charac-teristics of all human beings (Kipnis, 1997). This line of thinking has im-portant implications for research methods. For example, if we assume that the basic processes of human thinking are universal, we can con-duct our research using only U.S. male undergraduates as participants and then generalize to all humankind, both male and female. This tended to be the approach taken by many social psychologists before the 1970s. But since then, there has emerged a greater sensitivity to the issue of gender specifically (see Chapter 12) and culture more broadly.

cognitive psychology a branch of psychology that focuses on thinking and on mental processes inside the person.

Normative Explanations

normative explanation
explanations of behavior that assume people are intentional agents who behave in a manner they see as correct in a given context.

An alternative to explaining human behavior as caused by factors inside or outside persons is the **normative explanation**—conceiving of people as *intentional agents* who behave in a manner they see as correct in given contexts (Moghaddam & Studer, 1997a). Through socialization by families, peers, and the larger society, individuals become skilled in recognizing, influencing, and following cultural norms and rules. For example, when children are taken to places of worship—church, synagogue, mosque—they are taught the skills of behaving according to the norms ("dress appropriately," "do not laugh or shout") and rules ("follow the instructions of the priest," "show respect for the church elders") appropriate for the context. A broad way to define culture is everything that is influenced by humans, including the landscapes we create, our cities, art, language, fashions, values, and norms. More specifically, **culture** as pertaining to the domain of social behavior consists of a normative system that prescribes how one should behave in given contexts (see Figure 1–2). **Normative systems** are composed of related norms (general prescriptions for behavior) and **rules** (prescriptions for the behavior of individuals in particular role relationships). Rules prescribe, for example, how doctors and patients and teachers and students should behave toward one another.

culture a normative system that prescribes how individuals should behave in a given context.

normative system networks of related norms and rules.

rule prescription for how people in particular role relationships should behave.

Norms and rules do not "cause" the behavior of individuals; people can and sometimes do behave in ways that contradict the norms and rules of a culture. This is in part what happens when countercultures arise, new fashions gain influence, alternative lifestyles emerge, and change comes about. Groups can establish normative systems with distinct characteristics, and in this way create greater diversity of cultures and behaviors in society. The availability of groups with alternative normative systems makes it possible for individuals to change their own behavior style by leaving one group and joining another.

I came across an interesting example of this possibility during a recent visit to the Amish community of Pennsylvania. The Old Order

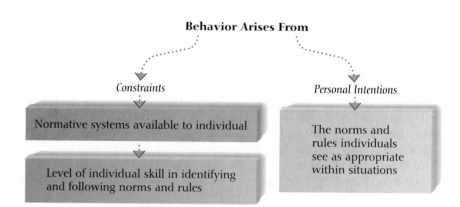

Figure 1–2 Schematic representation of normative accounts of social behavior.

Culture is not a cause of behavior but a guide that teaches individuals how they should behave in different contexts. Most people accept the norms and rules of their cultures and act according to those rules and norms most of the time. The children of this Pennsylvania Amish family are being taught correct behavior according to the norms and rules of their culture. But people can also behave "incorrectly," and some may opt to leave the group altogether if they cannot follow the rules.

Amish still retain a very simple farming life, shunning modern ways, such as the use of electricity and automobiles. Men and boys wear dark suits fastened with hooks and eyes, suspenders to hold up their trousers, broad-brimmed hats, and beards when they are married. Women and girls wear dresses with long skirts, and dark shoes and stockings; their hair is pulled back in a bun and covered with a cap. Neither men nor women wear jewelry. As my Amish guide drove me in a horse-drawn buggy through small winding roads and pointed out typical Amish farms, he also explained that two of his six children had decided to leave the community. "They could not act correctly according to our rules," he explained.

Affirming the Social Nature of Humankind

As Aristotle and others pointed out more than 2,500 years ago (Robinson, 1989), human beings are first and foremost social beings; through participation in social life we take on human characteristics, such as language and complex creative abilities. Studying individuals as social beings is an important and difficult challenge. It is important because a scientific study of our social lives will be successful only if our social nature is fully considered. But it is difficult because it is far easier to study individuals and their assumed thought processes in isolation. By isolating individuals in laboratories, we can more accurately measure their characteristics, but we may lose essential aspects of human social life that reveal themselves only when humans are engaged in group life.

Several avenues have been proposed to make social psychology more social. One is to place greater emphasis on group and intergroup behavior (Doise, 1978; Moscovici, Mucchi-Faina, & Maass, 1994; Tajfel, 1984). Social groups are common to all human societies, and individuals in each society spend a great deal of their time with others in groups, such as the family, play groups, and work groups. Some of the most important groups to which individuals belong, such as sex groups and ethnic groups, are *closed* rather than *open*, in the sense that it is not possible to exit from them (e.g., for most people, it is not possible to change one's ethnic group from black to white or one's sex group from female to male).

Despite the central importance of groups in everyday life, the topic of intergroup relations remains relatively neglected (Taylor & Moghaddam, 1994). Although more attention has been given to gender and ethnic relations since the 1970s, in part because there are now more minority researchers, these topics still tend to be marginal in mainstream social psychology. Thus, for several decades those who have advocated a move toward a more social social psychology have also advocated more research on group and intergroup behavior (Taylor & Brown, 1979).

A second and equally important goal of researchers calling for a more social social psychology has been to highlight the role of discourse in social life (Billig, 1995; Bruner, 1990; Edwards & Potter, 1992; Harré, 1994; Rogers, Stenne, Gleeson, & Rogers, 1995). In this context, **discourse** refers to all kinds of communication, including spoken language. An emphasis on discourse leads us to look closely at relationships between people, between the media and the general public, between different groups, and so on. Michael Billig (1995) examined how ideas about nationalism are conveyed to the general public through countless messages embedded in everyday social life but seldom identified as explicitly nationalistic. His study portrayed nationalism as a feature of a society rather than an individual personality characteristic. In such studies, the social world "out there" becomes the focus rather than thought processes assumed to be going on in individual minds.

discourse   all kinds of communication, including spoken language.

Concepts and Issues

Explanations in social psychology can be grouped as causal, which assume human behavior to be determined by factors either within persons or in the environment, or as normative, which assume humans to behave intentionally in a way they see to be correct for given social contexts. The major schools of psychology have adopted causal models. The normative model assumes that cultural rules and norms act not as "causes" of behavior but as guidelines that can be transgressed. Human behavior is social, deriving many of its characteristics from group life. As a means of achieving a more social social psychology, some scholars give more attention to group and intergroup processes, and to discourse and social behavior.

1. What does the term *causal explanation* mean? Use examples to clarify your answer.
2. Does a normative explanation suggest that norms and rules cause behavior? Explain.

Conclusion

Social psychology, the scientific study of individual social behavior, is rooted in ideas from outside the United States, but owes its distinct contemporary characteristics in large part to American researchers. The United States is the superpower of social psychology, exporting social psychological knowledge to other societies. Much of this knowledge is gained through research on U.S. college undergraduates, using laboratory procedures. This makes it particularly challenging to achieve a science of human behavior and to identify universals in social behavior. Alongside the traditional causal models adopted by psychologists, depicting behavior as caused by factors inside or outside persons, there have emerged cultural accounts that assume a normative model and that portray people as able and willing, for the most part, to behave correctly according to the norms and rules of the local culture.

For Review

Social psychology is the scientific study of individuals in all social contexts. Complex and vitally important social challenges confront humankind at the approach of the twenty-first century, making social psychology important both as an academic and an applied discipline.

All of us act as amateur social psychologists in everyday life, through efforts to explain behavior, attribute causes to events, reduce conflict among friends and family, and so on. Although social psychologists address many of the same issues, their goal is to understand and explain human behavior by asking scientific questions and applying scientific research methods.

Although many of the seminal ideas in social psychology originated in Europe, it is in the United States that the discipline has come to maturity in its current form. It is from the United States that social psychological knowledge is exported to other industrialized societies and to developing societies as well. Many research ideas in social psychology are influenced by the culture of the United States.

Certain universal characteristics, or etics, must be present in order for a human social life to exist. For example, there must be a minimal level of trust and honesty in relationships, as well as turn-taking and respect in dialogue. Research suggests a variety of other possible universals, such as the belief that each human body houses only one self.

Research also shows numerous characteristics that are peculiar to one or a few societies (emics). Searching for these characteristics is also a legitimate goal of social psychology.

Explanations in social psychology can usefully be classified as being causal or normative. The first assumes that social behavior is causally determined by factors inside or outside persons; the second that social behavior involves individuals intentionally following certain norms and rules as guides for action. Normative explanations better match a conception of humans as beings with some measure of free will.

Some scholars have argued for a more social social psychology. One avenue to achieving this goal is to focus more on group and intergroup relations. Another strategy is to place greater emphasis on discourse and communications.

For Discussion

1. Why is it important to study social psychology?
2. What are the benefits of giving more importance to the role of culture and considering normative explanations of social behavior, alongside traditional causal explanations?

Key Terms

Causal
  (explanation)   16
Cognitive
  psychology   17
Culture   18
Discourse   20
Emic   8
Etics   8

Norm   9
Norm of trust   9
Norm of truth   9
Norm of turn–taking
  in dialogue   10
Normative
  explanation   18

Normative
  system   18
Rule   18
Social facilitation
  7
Social psychology
  3

Annotated Readings

The best sources of traditional research are the *Journal of Personality and Social Psychology* and *Personality and Social Psychology Bulletin*, in the United States; and the *European Journal of Social Psychology* and the *British Journal of Social Psychology*, in Europe. The best sources for research that gives more attention to international views are the *Journal of Cross-Cultural Psychology*, the *International Journal of Psychology*, the *Journal of Social Psychology*, *World Psychology*, the *International Journal of Intercultural Relations*, and *Culture and Psychology*.

Personal accounts of their research lives by leading social psychologists and cross–cultural psychologists include G. G. Brannigan and M. R. Merrens, eds., *The social psychologists: Research adventures* (New York: McGraw–Hill, 1995); and M. H. Bond, ed., *Working at the interface of cultures: 20 lives in social science* (London: Routledge, 1997).

An interesting collection of classic and contemporary Western research is found in W. A. Lesko, ed., *Readings in social psychology: General, classic, and contemporary selections*, 3rd ed. (Boston: Allyn & Bacon, 1997).

A good general reference source is E. T. Higgins and A. W. Kruglanski, *Social psychology: Handbook of basic principles* (New York: Guilford, 1996).

Two collections that give a picture of the study of social behavior in developing countries are G. Misra, ed., *Applied social psychology in India* (New Delhi: Sage, 1990); and J. Pandey, D. Sinha, and D. P. S. Bhawuk, *Asian contributions to cross-cultural psychology* (Thousand Oaks, CA: Sage, 1996).

An outline of social psychology from a "new wave" discursive perspective can be found in R. S. Rogers, P. Stenne, K. Gleeson, and W. S. Rogers, *Social psychology: A critical agenda* (Oxford: Polity Press, 1995).

An innovative account of cultural psychology is provided in M. Cole, *Cultural psychology: A once and future discipline* (Cambridge, MA: Harvard University Press, 1996).

For more personalized accounts of social psychology, see E. Aronson, *Social animal*, 7th ed. (New York: W. H. Freeman, 1995), for insightful words from a researcher at the heart of traditional American social psychology. R. Harré, *Social being*, 2nd ed. (Oxford: Blackwell, 1993), provides an outline of social life by one of the leaders of "new wave" social psychology. F. Cherry, *The "stubborn particulars" of social psychology: Essays on the research process* (London: Routledge, 1995), is a colorful account of some classic studies from a feminist perspective.

CHAPTER **2**

Doing Social Psychology

◄ Imagine that these people were lining up to take part in a social psychological study conducted by you. How will you conduct this study? What methods will you use? Most social psychological studies have been carried out in the laboratory. This method allows for precise measurement but may lack the social interactions that are part of everyday life. Most social psychological studies have also used only college undergraduates as participants. Look carefully at each of the people in this line; they are a cross section of people you might meet on a city street in North America. Do you expect them to behave the same way as college undergraduates? As these questions suggest, the topic of research methods in social psychology is full of controversy and excitement.

Marilyn Brewer, a leading U.S. social psychologist, sat thinking about an intriguing issue. People everywhere seem to feel positive about belonging to social groups, to be part of something bigger—a family, a college, a corporation, an ethnic or gender group. At the same time, they want to be separate, independent individuals. It was the early 1990s, and Brewer herself would soon be moving from the University of California, Los Angeles, to Ohio State University. She would have opportunities to join new groups and communities in Ohio, but, like most of us, she would not want to be completely engulfed by them. Brewer wondered how this behavior might be explained. As an experimental social psychologist, she also wondered how her explanation could then be tested.

Two social psychologists, John Darley and Bib Latané, were engrossed in conversation over dinner in 1964. The topic of discussion was a terrifying event that had occurred only a few days earlier in New York City and had already gained notoriety as the "Genovese affair." A young woman, Kitty Genovese, had been attacked and stabbed to death as she came home late one night to her apartment in Kew Gardens in Queens. Investigators were horrified to learn that almost 40 people had been aware of the attack, but the young woman's cries for help had gone unheeded. Some people had looked out of their windows and actually seen what was happening, and some had heard the victim's cries. But nobody had done anything—not even made a telephone call to the police. The incident seemed to illustrate our worst fears about living in large urban centers.

Asking Questions and Forming Explanations

Brewer and her associates (Brewer, 1993; Brewer, Manzi, & Shaw, 1993; Brewer & Weber, 1994) arrived at a compelling explanation for the behavior she had observed: People attempt to achieve an optimal balance between "blending in and standing out," being merged in groups and being separate as individuals. In situations in which individuals become too merged in groups or stand out too far from groups, they will feel threatened. Brewer's next challenge was to design a method for testing her explanation. The **scientific method** is the term we use to describe the systematic procedures social psychologists try to follow in order to do research: to gather and analyze data in order to test hypotheses about social behavior (for an overview, see Shaughnessy & Zechmeister, 1997). And as scientists, social psychologists continue to debate a key issue: What research methods are best suited for studying social behavior?

Notice that the phenomenon Brewer was pondering, that of how far people want to be merged into groups, concerns a real–life situation of considerable complexity and social significance. One approach adopted by Brewer and her associates has been to separate aspects of this complex real–life situation systematically and then study each aspect in laboratory experiments (Brewer's research is discussed further in Chapter 14).

scientific method   the systematic procedures social psychologists try to follow to gather and analyze data in order to test hypotheses about social behavior.

During their dinner conversation, Darley and Latané (1968) analyzed the Genovese affair in social psychological terms. They wondered what it was about that situation that might lead *anybody* in the same circumstances to act in the same manner. When an individual comes across a situation, such as a man slumped by the side of a road, a number of logical explanations are possible, not all of which require intervention. For example, the person may be drunk. If there are other people passing by, we may ask ourselves, "Why should I do something to help? Maybe all those other people passing by know the situation better and have good reasons *not* to intervene." The theoretical explanation Darley and Latané developed involves a multistep model, the first step being the definition of a situation and the second step a diffusion of responsibility.

In recounting his dinner conversation, Darley (see Evans, 1980) explained that by the end of it two things had become clear in their minds:

> First, that we were talking about a cascading phenomenon in which two or three specific processes were fitting together to lead to a very counterintuitive result: no one helping. Second, we were both trained as experimental social psychologists and we wanted to conduct experiments in order to isolate each process and demonstrate its function in relative independence of the other. (p. 217)

Hundreds of studies have been conducted by these researchers and others, systematically manipulating the sex, age, ethnicity, and other characteristics of victims and bystanders.

Like Brewer, these researchers had arrived at hypotheses about a rather complex and important event in the real world. (A **hypothesis** is a proposition that serves as a tentative explanation of certain facts.) The next challenge they confronted was testing their explanation. They believed the best way to do this was to isolate aspects of the complex situation and study each aspect in a laboratory. Careful scrutiny shows that again and again in social psychology researchers first observe a social interaction that intrigues them, often a highly complex and important kind of real-life interaction, and then develop an explanation that they set out to test by separating aspects of the interaction that can be studied in isolation in the laboratory.

hypothesis a proposition that serves as a tentative explanation of certain facts.

Concepts and Issues

As scientists, social psychologists systematically gather and analyze data to test hypotheses about social behavior. They typically begin their research by examining an important but puzzling issue in everyday life and isolating aspects of that situation for more detailed exploration.

1. What real-life situation led John Darley and Bib Latané to study bystander intervention?
2. Give an example of a situation you have experienced that could provide questions for social psychological research.

Research Techniques

laboratory a separate space, such as a room or set of rooms, where all the variables in the context can be controlled by the experimenters.

control the regulation of variables in a situation so that hypothesized causal factors can be unambiguously identified.

variable any characteristic that can have different values for a group of people or category of events, but has only one value at a given time.

experimental method social psychological method concerned with manipulating causes to test for effects.

correlational method social psychological method involving examination of associations between variables.

independent variable hypothesized cause in experimental research.

dependent variable the variable that is measured by experimental research.

field experiment studies involving the manipulation of independent variables in the field.

positive correlation relationship that exists when two or more factors change in the same direction.

negative correlation relationship that exists when two or more factors change in opposite directions.

The wide array of research methods available to social psychologists can be classified in two main ways. First, on the basis of *place*: Research can be conducted either inside or outside a laboratory, the latter being referred to as *in the field*. A social psychology **laboratory** consists of a separate space, such as a room or a set of rooms, where all the variables in the context can be controlled by the experimenters. **Control** refers to the regulation of variables in a situation, so that hypothesized causal factors can be unambiguously identified. The major research methods vary in the level of control they allow, from a high level (laboratory experiment) to almost no control (observation study) (see Figure 2–1). A **variable** is any characteristic that can have different values for a group of people or category of events, but has only one value at a given time. For example, "fear" is a feeling that a group of people may experience to different degrees, some more and some less, but which can have only one value for each person at any one time. Levels of fear can be isolated and measured in a laboratory, as can assumed causes of fear.

Second, social psychological research methods can be classified as **experimental methods,** concerned with manipulating causes in order to test for effects, or **correlational methods,** involving examinations of associations between variables. The manipulation of causes requires some degree of control by experimenters. In experimental research, hypothesized causes are referred to as **independent variables,** and the effects are measured in **dependent variables.** For example, an experimenter may manipulate the number of people in a group (independent variable) and test the effect of this manipulation on the level of participation in group activities shown by each person (dependent variable). As a broad generalization, we can describe laboratory research as experimental, and field research (with the exception of **field experiments,** which are studies involving the manipulation of independent variables in the field) as correlational. We shall begin by discussing correlational techniques (the terms *correlation* and *association* are synonymous).

Correlational Techniques

A correlation exists between two variables when if one changes, so does the other (see Figure 2–2). A **positive correlation** exists when two or more factors change in the same direction. For example, among children age is positively associated with physical size: As children get older, they grow larger. A **negative correlation** exists when changes in two or more factors are in opposite directions. For example,

Low Control					**High Control**
Observation study	Simulation	Survey, Interview	Natural experiment	Field experiment	Laboratory experiment

Figure 2–1 Major research methods and level of control.

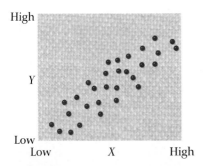

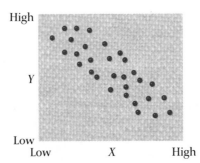

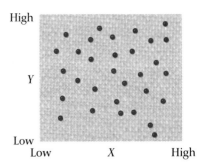

(a) Positive correlation: As the value of X increases, the value of Y also increases.

(b) Negative correlation: As the value of X increases, the value of Y decreases.

(c) Zero correlation: No relationship between X and Y.

Figure 2–2 Correlation: (a) positive, (b) negative, (c) none.

the more alcohol a person has consumed, the less safe a driver that person becomes.

But we have to be careful not to confuse correlation with causation. If our research shows that less educated people are more likely to be in prison, does that finding demonstrate that a lack of education "causes" people to commit crime? The answer is no, because a multitude of other factors could be involved. For example, less educated people tend to have lower incomes, experience more unemployment, suffer from poorer health, and endure worse housing and living conditions. Any or all of these factors might also influence criminal behavior.

Although the relation of factor A to B might not be causal, this does not mean that of B to A cannot be causal. For example, consider the case of an association between the number of people waiting (factor A) on a station platform and the arrival (factor B) of a train. When I get to the station to wait for the train in the morning, the number of people waiting on the platform is associated with the likelihood of a train arriving. As time passes, more people arrive on the platform and also the arrival time of the train grows closer. By the time the train arrives, the platform tends to be packed and there is a rush to get on board. However, increases in the number of people waiting do not *cause* the train to arrive: This is a correlational rather than causal relation.

On the other hand, the arrival of the train causes a change in the number of people waiting on the platform. Thus, in this example the relation of A to B is correlational (as the number of people increases, the likelihood of the train arriving increases), but that of B to A is causal (the arrival of the train causes there to be fewer people waiting on the platform, because they move from the platform to the train).

Correlational studies are particularly suitable for situations in which variables can be observed but not manipulated. Consider, for example, a study of the relationship between aggression and environmental factors. Some features of the environment can be manipulated in the laboratory without participants noticing or "seeing through" the cover of the study. For example, meteorological disturbances, such as lightning and strong winds, cause air molecules to split into positively

One of the most common mistakes in social psychological research is to assume causation on the basis of an association. A positive association between aggression and time spent in prison might lead us to assume that these men are in a prison chain gang because they are aggressive. An alternative explanation is that life conditions in prison have led these men to behave aggressively. Although we may speculate about possible causes of aggression, associations between other factors and aggression could not serve to demonstrate causality.

and negatively charged ions. The concentration of negative and positive ions is known to be associated with a wide range of behaviors, including aggression (Baron, Russell, & Arms, 1985; Charry & Hawkinshire, 1981). Because changes in atmospheric electricity are not noticed, researchers have been able to manipulate electricity levels in laboratories to examine the impact of such changes on social behavior. Increased levels of negative ions have been shown to intensify the similarity-attraction link, so that similar others are liked more and dissimilar others are liked even less (Baron, 1987).

But the laboratory is not suitable for studying the impact of some other environmental characteristics, such as that of extreme temperature, on social behavior. A first reason is ethical: Extreme temperatures are likely to be uncomfortable for research participants. A second reason has to do with the meaning of the findings. Imagine you are a volunteer in a laboratory experiment, and after 20 minutes of activity the temperature in the laboratory is increased until it becomes very hot. You are not only likely to notice such a change but also to suspect it has something to do with the purpose of the experiment. This is one reason why Craig Anderson (1987) and others have studied the relationship between temperature and aggression through correlational field studies rather than laboratory studies (Baron, 1979). Anderson found an increase in violent crime (murder, rape, assault), and a smaller increase in nonviolent crime, during the hotter parts of the year over a 10-year period (this research is discussed further in Chapter 11).

Field Methods

The term **field research** refers loosely to any study conducted outside the laboratory. Only a minority of social psychological studies are conducted in the field. This is in part because researchers have far less control of variables in the field, and thus the possibility of testing causal relations between independent and dependent variables is relatively limited. Among the various field research methods available, the highest level of control is possible through the field experiment. The field experiment involves the manipulation of independent variables, such as the age of a person asking for help, in order to test their effect on dependent variables, how much help is offered by passersby, in the field. The **natural experiment** also involves the manipulation of variables, but under the control of nature rather than experimenters. An earthquake could serve as the independent variable, and the coping behavior of residents in affected areas as the dependent variable.

Most research conducted in the field, however, is correlational rather than experimental; it involves assessments of associations between factors, rather than their experimental manipulation. The most important methods are the survey and the interview. Both typically involve the use of questionnaires.

Survey and Interview. The horrors of war and "ethnic cleansing" in postcommunist Eastern Europe during the 1990s have led many thinking people to ask, "How could this have happened?" "What led to these atrocities?" "Can we prevent such terrible things from happening again?" Perhaps most disturbing of all for many people is the fact that Europe, and the world, seem threatened once again by war. How can democracy be safeguarded in the future?

Similar questions were being asked in 1945, after World War II, and they led to a greater interest in the "type" of person who held profascist attitudes and might be a potential supporter of fascism. Historically, measures developed to assess "fascist attitudes" have used survey and interview techniques. The earlier measures (e.g., Edwards, 1941; Newcomb, 1943; Stagner, 1936) consisted of questionnaires that included questions very specific to the particular historical conditions of the time. For example, in reference to the Great Depression of the time, Stagner (1936) asked people to rate their agreement with such statements as "The average person is not intelligent enough to vote his way out of the Depression." The most influential measure of "profascist tendencies" came out of the work of researchers at Berkeley, initiated in the 1940s by a concern about anti-Semitism, and eventually published under the title of *The Authoritarian Personality* (Adorno, Frenkel-Brunswik, Levinson, & Sanford, 1950).

Adorno and associates began by surveying anti-Semitism among a sample of 2,000 white, middle-class, non-Jewish, native-born-American

field research any study conducted outside the laboratory.

natural experiment an experiment that involves the manipulation of variables, but under the control of nature rather than experimenters.

residents of California. Next, they examined the relationship between anti–Semitism and attitudes toward African–Americans and other minorities. They found that prejudiced individuals tend to be consistently prejudiced against all minorities. Through in–depth interviews of both individuals who were high and individuals who were low on ethnocentrism, they tried to identify the roots of prejudice. The culmination of their research was the development of the famous F-Scale, or Potentiality for Fascism Scale. Since then, other researchers, such as the Canadian Bob Altemeyer (1981, 1988a, 1988b, 1994), have attempted to develop measures of authoritarianism that improve on the reliability and validity of the F–Scale.

A review of the various attempts to use survey and interview methods to assess authoritarianism (see Christie, 1991) raises several questions. First, how culture-specific are the results of this research? Second, are any possible universals revealed? If so, what are they? With regard to the first point, it is apparent that ideology and culture have deeply influenced the development of the available measures of authoritarianism. The profile of persons who would score low on authoritarianism matches the stereotype of the liberal, Western–educated humanist. Such a person is likely to score low on religiosity and be slightly to the left on the political spectrum in Western societies. But consider how various "freedom fighters" and separatist groups around the world would fare on this measure. The communist empire of the former U.S.S.R. was brought crashing down in large part by organizations working through the Church, and described as "right wing" by the communist governments of the time.

And what of the finding that anti–Semites are also prejudiced against African–Americans? This might make sense in the context of many parts of North America, but it makes little sense elsewhere in the world. Individuals high on anti–Semitism in the Middle East may well see African–Americans and other North American ethnic minorities as allies in their fight against what they would see as the "white establishment" of the United States. We are reminded of the idea that those who are "terrorists" in the eyes of some people are "freedom fighters" in the eyes of others.

But despite such limitations, the survey and interview research on authoritarianism seems to have yielded an important general principle that may have universal applicability. This is the idea that in all societies in which there are power disparities, some individuals will be submissive toward those in power and status positions, but punitive and prejudiced against minorities and "deviants."

The measures we use to identify such tendencies must be culturally sensitive. For example, in the climate of the 1990s, people in Western societies are well aware that they are legally obliged not to make sexist or racist statements. Prejudices based on sex and ethnicity now tend to be expressed indirectly rather than directly. In response to what David Sears (1988) and others have termed the "symbolic" expression of prejudices, researchers have developed new ways to assess racial attitudes (this issue is discussed in greater detail in Chapter 10).

Nicaraguan guerrillas. Research in the West has led to some useful insights into the characteristics of authoritarian individuals, who tend to be prejudiced against all minorities, to be particularly supportive of rigid hierarchies, and prone to perceive conspiracies. Such people are often found in militias. Those who score low on authoritarianism tend to be liberal, pro-individual freedom, and low on religiosity. However, in some respects the findings from this research are less valid outside Western societies. In some societies, revolutionaries work through the Church (as in Poland, before the collapse of communism), and in other societies revolutionaries are not supportive of individual liberties as understood in the West (for example, communists in China).

Alternative Field Methods.   You are relaxing at home. The phone rings. You pick up the receiver and hear someone who sounds like an African–American male caller say, "Hello . . . Ralph's Garage? This is George Williams. Listen, I'm stuck out here on the parkway, and I'm wondering if you'd be able to come out here and take a look at my car?"

You say: "This isn't Ralph's Garage. You have the wrong number."

Caller: "This isn't Ralph's Garage? Listen, I'm terribly sorry to have disturbed you, but listen, I'm stuck out here on the highway, and that was the last quarter I had! I have bills in my pocket, but no more change to make another call. Do you think you could call the garage and let them know where I am?"

You would have had this conversation if you had been one of the participants contacted by telephone in a study by Samuel Gaertner and Leonard Bickman (1971) using the so-called "wrong number technique." In this experiment, the caller gives the naive participant (the call receiver) the telephone number of Ralph's Garage, which is actually a number being monitored by the researchers to check how many participants do make the call. By manipulating the voice of the caller (black/white, male/female) and the characteristics of the person telephoned, it is possible to examine the relation between race, sex, and helping behavior. In this case, the researchers discovered that African-Americans helped white and black callers equally, whereas white participants helped black callers less than they helped white callers. Males generally helped more often than did females.

Another innovative behavioral field method is the "lost-letter technique" developed by Stanley Milgram (1972a). This technique involves preparing letters with contents that express obvious prejudices, such as racist views, and then dropping hundreds of such "ready-to-mail" letters (in envelopes that were stamped but not sealed) in different neighborhoods of a city. The dependent measure in such research is the percentage of letters that are actually mailed by the respondents (who accidentally find the letters). Such techniques require a detailed knowledge of the local culture and help provide information about norms of behavior. Among the advantages of such techniques are that they *directly* measure behavior in naturalistic settings (see also Milgram, 1972b, and Moghaddam & Vuksanovic, 1990).

Meta-Analysis: The Analysis of Analyses

The research strategy of meta-analysis is gaining popularity among many social psychologists (Glass, McGraw, & Smith, 1981; Rosenthal & Rosnow, 1984; Schmidt, 1992; Wachter & Straf, 1990) but is frowned upon by some others. Hans Eysenck (1978) has even referred to it as "an exercise in mega-silliness." What is this technique that has caused so much controversy?

meta-analysis   technique for statistically combining and integrating findings from many different studies.

Meta-analysis is a way of statistically combining and integrating findings from many different studies. Because single studies rarely provide definitive answers to research questions, researchers look for general trends by using the findings of many studies. The traditional way to identify such trends has been for a researcher to review the literature by carefully reading many studies and coming to broad conclusions. The traditional narrative reviews obviously depend a great deal on the subjective biases of the reviewer. The objective of meta-analysis is to minimize these subjective biases by combining the statistical findings of many studies to compute a general quantitative index of the trend. To compute this general index, each data point in the analysis is obtained from an individual study rather than from an individual participant, as is typically the case in traditional research.

Some critics argue that meta-analysis involves combining studies that measure "apples" with those that measure "oranges." But one response to this criticism has been that apples and oranges are good things to mix if you are trying to generalize about fruit. Others have criticized meta-analysis as involving just as much subjective bias as the traditional review (for example, personal preferences of "reviewers" still influence the choice of studies included in meta-analysis) and of leaving less room for "good" insights from well-designed studies.

Despite the controversy, meta-analysis is increasingly used, particularly in making broad statements about topics, such as gender differences, in social behavior (see Chapter 12).

Experimental Techniques

Although some fascinating correlational research has been carried out by social psychologists, it is experimental research that serves as the methodological hallmark of the discipline (Aronson, Brewer, & Carlsmith, 1985; Aronson & Carlsmith, 1968; Moghaddam & Harré, 1992). This is because experimental techniques are seen as a more direct way of testing causal explanations. *Laboratory studies* involve testing hypothesized causal relations between independent and dependent variables in a separated and controlled environment. *Field studies* also involve testing hypothesized causal relations between independent and dependent variables, but not in environments controlled completely by experimenters. Field experiments allow for less control of variables than laboratory experiments, and this is one reason why they are used less often. Nevertheless, some of the most influential studies in social psychology, including the one by Sherif (1966), which we consider next, were conducted in the field.

Imagine a typical scene during the first day of summer camp, involving a group of 11- to 12-year-old boys and their camp counselors. After the boys get to know each other and select friends, they are assigned to two different cabin groups. Unfortunately, each boy finds that most of his best friends are in the other cabin. From this moment on, as everyone becomes engrossed in camp activities, the ties within each group become stronger and intergroup rivalries grow more intense.

After several intergroup competitions, each group of boys has come to dislike the other. Having arrived at this stage of intergroup hostilities, is it now possible to return the boys to peaceful relationships? This important research question is of interest to social psychologists. The boys attending this particular summer camp were participating in a field experiment on intergroup relations conducted by two famous social psychologists, Muzafer and Caroline Sherif (Sherif, 1966). The Sherifs tested the proposition that intergroup conflicts arise out of competition for resources (see Chapter 14 for further details of this research).

The Sherifs conducted their study in a naturalistic setting to benefit from the advantages such situations offer. The experiments in real summer camps spanned several weeks, rather than the few hours typical of laboratory research (see Table 2–1). This longer time period allowed for a fuller examination of the group processes leading to conflict and cooperation.

But notice that the context of the Sherifs' study was highly culture-specific, in the sense that the summer camp experience is one that is peculiar to a small number of Western societies. Indeed, the kind of summer camp used by the Sherifs may be peculiar to the United States,

Table 2–1	Characteristics of Major Research Methods		
Research Method	**How Carried Out?**	**Where?**	**How Much Time Does a Typical Study Take to Complete?**
Laboratory experiment	Independent variable manipulated to assess hypothesized effect on dependent variable	Controlled laboratory conditions	About an hour
Field experiment		Field	Several days or weeks
Natural experiment	Natural event serves as manipulation of independent variable	Field	Several days or weeks
Survey, Interview	Participants answer questions posed by questionnaire/ interviewer	Field	Several hours
Simulation	Attempt to reproduce behavior on a smaller scale	Laboratory or field	Several hours or a few days
Observation study	Behavior observed and recorded	Field	Several weeks

and then only to middle–class, urban America. The subjects were all white, middle–class Protestants. At least one serious attempt was made to replicate this study in a non–Western culture, using 11–year–old boys in Lebanon (Diab, 1970). But this try at **replication** (a subsequent study that attempts to reproduce an earlier study) was not successful, proba- bly because of cultural differences (see Chapter 14).

replication a subsequent study that attempts to reproduce an earlier study.

Concepts and Issues

Most social psychological studies are experimental, involving manipulation of variables to examine causal relations, and conducted in the laboratory. The field experiment also involves manipulation of variables, but most other types of field research are correlational, involving an examination of associa- tions between variables. In recent years, researchers have used meta–analysis, a technique for statistically combining and integrating findings from many studies, to summarize results on specific research questions.

1. Are correlational or experimental methods more suitable for studying causal relations? Explain your answer.
2. Explain how meta–analysis is different from traditional research review methods.
3. Describe the different types of variables.

Why the Laboratory Is Considered Better

Social psychologists have concluded that in most cases it is not enough simply to ask people what they do and why they behave in particular ways, because the explanations participants provide are very often inadequate, if not downright misleading. Neither is it sufficient to study social behavior as it occurs in the real world, because often the complexities involved are too great to allow for any kind of reasonable synthesis. The explanations developed by Brewer with respect to individuals balancing "standing in and standing out" in relation to groups, and by Darley and Latané with respect to bystander apathy, involve many different elements. Researchers want to reduce this kind of complexity and to isolate aspects of the situation. This is one important reason why the vast majority of social psychological research has historically been, and continues to be, carried out in the laboratory (Adair, Dushenko, & Lindsay, 1985; Aronson, Ellsworth, Carlsmith, & Gonzales, 1990; Christie, 1965).

In the laboratory, each aspect of a complex situation can be studied independently of all other aspects. In what has come to be perhaps the most well-publicized series of social psychological experiments in the history of the field, Stanley Milgram (1974) examined obedience to authority. Milgram considered such questions as: Will an isolated individual obey an authority figure more than when the same individual is part of a group? To address this kind of question, in his research Milgram varied the number of people in the laboratory experiment while keeping all other aspects of the situation constant (the details of Milgram's research are discussed in Chapter 7). Such control over the situation, so that one or several aspects can be varied while everything else is held constant, can be achieved very effectively in the laboratory.

In order to appreciate better the characteristics of laboratory research and its limitations, we need to become more familiar with the terminology and philosophy with which it is associated.

The Participants: Who We Study

"Most of the subjects were white and middle class"—this is the title of a thought-provoking discussion by Sandra Graham (1992) on the **participants** (subjects) used in psychological research. The term **population** refers to all those who could possibly be included in social psychological research. The largest population includes all humanity, but researchers typically confine themselves to more manageable populations, such as women who work for Mitsubishi in the United States, people who join extremist paramilitary groups, or, more typically, undergraduate students at their own colleges. **Sample** refers to the group selected for study from among the population. (See Figure 2–3.) Graham's research provides evidence that the samples selected for study by psychologists are extremely restricted in terms of such characteristics as age, social class, and ethnicity (Jones, 1983; McLoyd & Randolph, 1984, 1985; Ponterotto, 1988; Sears, 1986). Let us consider just a few ways in which such samples are restricted.

participant   subject in psychological research.

population   all those who could possibly be included in social psychological research.

sample   the group selected for study from among the population.

Figure 2–3 Research population and sample.

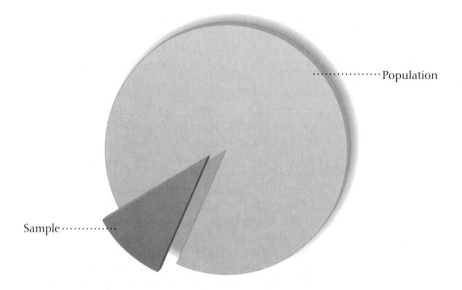

A review of the major research journals since the 1960s led David Sears (1986) to conclude that the majority of social psychological studies have been conducted using college undergraduates in the United States, mostly psychology majors, as participants. He argues that this "narrow data base" has had a profound influence on the view social psychology offers of social behavior and on the research methods adopted by social psychologists. For example, modern social psychology offers a model of humans as rational, cognitive beings who can best be understood through pencil-and-paper testing (laboratory) situations. In many ways the laboratory experiment resembles the exam situation and is designed for people who are used to performing in such a setting.

Now that social psychology has almost a century of research tradition using laboratory procedures with a restricted population, the most convenient approach might seem to be to continue along the same path. Perhaps this explains the continued neglect of ethnic minorities by researchers so that, as Graham notes (1992), the majority of our research papers report "most of the subjects were white and middle class." There has actually been a decline in the representation of African-Americans in psychological research generally, and social psychological research specifically, since 1970 (Graham, 1992). Whereas from 1970 to 1974 just 3.1 percent of the studies published in the *Journal of Personality and Social Psychology* were on African-Americans, in the period 1985–1989 this percentage went down to a mere 0.3. Other ethnic minorities are also nearly absent from the sample pools selected for social psychological research.

Until recently, social psychology was "womanless" (Crawford & Marecek, 1989; Scarr, 1988); social psychologists either did not include women in their samples or did not pay attention to possible gender differences in social behavior. As the number of female social psychologists grew, and as more women were included in research samples, there emerged a small but influential literature on gender and social behavior (see the discussion of this literature in Chapter 12). Now that gender is a topic of study, there is competition between different groups in the research community to "reconstruct" the picture of female social behavior—that is, defining the limits of sex (the biological characteristics that differentiate between females and males) and gender (the social roles assigned to males and females by society).

The Causal Model and Laboratory Research

Another important reason why the laboratory experiment is the most widely used research method in social psychology has to do with the compatibility of this method with the causal model (Aronson, Ellsworth, Carlsmith, & Gonzales, 1990, p. 9). The majority of social psychologists assume that social behavior is the result of certain causes

Test of fear learning in individuals, Yale University. Almost all the participants in most social psychological research continue to be white, and until very recently they were mostly male. The isolated conditions of laboratory participants, as well as their selection from a tiny section of the entire human population, have implications for the findings of traditional social psychology.

and that the goal of social psychology is to discover relationships between causes and effects. That is, they have assumed a causal model. Brewer assumes that the identifications individuals make with groups are caused by two needs, those of belonging to groups and those of being differentiated ("standing in and standing out").

The laboratory procedure allows for a precise examination of assumed causes and effects through the manipulation and measurement of variables.

Variables in the Laboratory Context.   In the terminology of laboratory research, causes are independent variables and effects are dependent variables. Researchers manipulate independent variables (assumed causes) in order to examine their influence on dependent variables (assumed effects). For example, in bystander intervention studies, researchers have varied the sex of the person seeking help (an independent variable) to measure the effect of this variation on level of assistance offered (dependent variable) by bystanders.

nuisance variable   a variable that if not controlled may influence the dependent variables and prevent researchers from isolating the influence of independent variables.

A third category of variables is "noise" or **nuisance variables,** so called because if not controlled they may also influence the dependent variables and prevent the researchers from isolating the influence of independent variables. For example, when researchers recruit participants, they often screen potential participants by administering standard personality tests and include only those who prove to be psychologically "normal." This is because in some studies, abnormalities in the personality characteristics of participants, such as extreme levels of anxiety or paranoia, could influence the results.

Internal and External Causes.   Causes can be thought of as being of different kinds. One very broad way of categorizing causes of social behavior is to distinguish between causes that are internal and those that are external to the individual. For example, if we observe Dave helping another student, we may interpret this as being due to Dave's prosocial personality (internal cause), or conclude that Dave helped the other student because their professor was observing the scene and most other people would have done the same (that is, the cause was external to Dave). One important category of internal causes has to do with the way Dave thinks about social events.

The Laboratory Method and Cognitive Social Psychology

The laboratory method is well adapted to a theoretical approach that views cognitive processes as causal influences in social behavior. This theoretical approach is dominant in social psychology (Sears, 1986). That is, the main orientation for explaining social behavior has been to look for answers in processes that have to do with how people think and how they think they think (see Fiske & Taylor, 1991, p. 2).

This cognitive approach to social behavior is better than a behaviorist explanation because the "thinker" inside the "black box" is now taken into account. But although the cognitive approach does take into consideration what is assumed to be going on inside the individual's head, the focus of this approach is very much on separate individuals, not on relations between individuals and not on groups. This has direct implications for methodology in social psychology.

Since cognition is assumed to take place in an individual head, the causal role of cognitive processes can legitimately be studied through laboratory experiments involving isolated individuals. Of course, cognitive social psychology studies are not conducted only in the laboratory setting. But the vast majority of studies are, and one reason for this is the assumption that the isolated "thinker" is the correct object of study.

Another reason for the tendency to study individuals in isolation in laboratories has been the assumption that major cognitive processes are universal. Since the 1960s there has been a shift from defining psychology as the "science of behavior," as behaviorists would have it, to the "science of mental life," as cognitive psychologists prefer. What has remained the same, however, is the search for universals.

Social psychological research in the 1990s continues to search for universals in social thinking: in the way people evaluate phenomena (Chapter 4) and attribute causes to events (Chapter 5), for example. Social thinking involving attributions, attitudes, and the like is assumed to take place inside individual heads. In this sense, social thinking can be conceived of as individualistic and "portable," so that it can be studied by focusing on individual persons in laboratories.

The "Self-Contained" Computer.

The metaphor of humans as computers further clarifies the model of human behavior employed in social psychology. Cognitive psychologists have used computers to simulate human thinking, so that, for example, there are now computers capable of defeating even excellent chess players (*Deep Blue* is a new kind of computer chess player that can defeat grandmasters and world champions). They have used computer simulations, for example, to investigate how individuals perceive the characteristics of the groups to which they belong (their *in-groups*) and those to which they do not belong (their *out-groups*) (Linville, Fischer, & Salovey, 1989). **Computer simulation** involves an attempt to program the computer to behave in a way analogous to human behavior.

computer simulation an attempt to program the computer to behave in a way analogous to human behavior.

The metaphor of humans as computers, as "thinking machines," is both powerful and telling, because whatever leads a computer to respond in a particular way to the external world is already present inside the computer. In this sense, the computer is a "self-contained" individual entity. The characteristics of the computer do not change when it is moved from room to room, or city to city, or country to country.

Because the computer retains its particular characteristics independent of context, we can find out about its behavior by taking it to a computer laboratory and having it examined. The computer can be "asked" to do various things, to show us "how it thinks" by retrieving some information, or by categorizing the world. Since the way a computer "behaves" is dependent only on things inside the computer, the presence of other computers would not add anything essential to the

The defeat of chess champion Gary Kasparov by IBM's "Deep Blue" in May 1997 served to highlight the growing power of computers to tackle even the most complex problems at breathtaking speed. But the computer is not a social being in the same way that humans are social. If a group of computers were given the opportunity to interact and develop a society, their culture would not be a human culture. This is an important point: The difference between humans and computers lies in the kind of social life humans have and the nature of their social relationships, and not necessarily in how individual minds (of chess players or anyone else) think and solve problems.

research findings. Similarly, the person as social thinker can be studied in isolation, without any need to complicate the situation by including additional persons. If how people think about social life is exclusively dependent on "things inside the head," then the laboratory is appropriate for conducting such an investigation.

Selecting Cultural Variables for Laboratory Research

A traditional strategy for incorporating culture in the laboratory setting is through the inclusion of variables external to individuals. A **situational variable** is an aspect of culture that is selected from all possible cultural characteristics, and it usually serves as an independent variable in laboratory studies. In particular, aspects of normative systems of culture are used. Stanley Milgram (1974) used a scientist as the authority

situational variable an aspect of culture selected from all possible cultural characteristics, usually to serve as an independent variable in laboratory studies.

figure in his study of obedience to authority, and the presence or absence of the scientist served as an independent variable. In Western societies, at least, scientists are symbols of authority, and it is normative for people to be guided by them.

A major goal of laboratory studies has been to achieve the highest possible degree of control over situational variables, so that only selected aspects of culture are included in the laboratory study. Through such control, the exact influence of an aspect of culture can be precisely measured. The selection and inclusion of an aspect of culture in a laboratory study poses a number of challenges, the first having to do with its appropriateness for the task the researchers have in mind. For example, if we want to study the influence of "authority" on obedience, what aspect of culture do we take as the symbol of authority? The answer we give to this question depends to a large extent on the culture we are studying, and the Milgram studies provide an example.

The role of scientist has particular meanings within Western culture, and it was with such meanings in mind that Milgram chose to use the scientist as the symbol of authority in his study. If Milgram had conducted his study in a traditional African village, he might have used a village elder. If he had conducted his study in the United States in the 1760s (instead of the 1960s), he might have used a minister or a town sheriff. Thus, the particular symbol of authority selected by Milgram was matched to the characteristics of the culture within which he was working.

Concepts and Issues

The laboratory procedure has been the preferred research method in social psychology because it is assumed to allow greater control and a more direct measurement of causal relations. But control has costs: Participants are typically tested in isolation, leaving social psychology open to the criticism that it treats people as isolated "thinking machines." For the most part, participants have been college undergraduates in Western societies, a group that is not representative of human diversity.

1. What are the main characteristics of a social psychology laboratory experiment?
2. Why is the laboratory procedure used so often?

Challenges and Solutions in Laboratory Research

The widespread use of the laboratory procedure does not mean that social psychologists have remained unaware of limitations to this research method. Much of the discussion on such limitations has focused on two issues. First, the repeatability of results: How effective is the laboratory method for achieving the same results again and again? Second, the meaning of behavior: Does behavior in the laboratory mean the same as in the outside world? In examining these questions, researchers have moved toward new and perhaps more fruitful ways of thinking about the laboratory method, such as conceptualizing the experiment as drama and the experimenter as dramatist.

Reliability and Validity

If you roam around antique shops enough, you will very likely come across an example of the model plaster skulls used by phrenologists in the latter part of the nineteenth century. Such a skull will have what look likes a jigsaw puzzle sketched on it, with an identification number or letter in each part. Phrenologists marked sections of their model skulls because they believed that mental characteristics were located in distinct parts of the brain and could be assessed by feeling bumps on the outside of the head. Thus, for example, a bump in section 11 of the skull might indicate imaginativeness.

The measurements taken by phrenologists were highly reliable, meaning that repeated measurement would yield identical results. **Reliability** has to do with consistency in measurement, and clearly

reliability consistency in measurement.

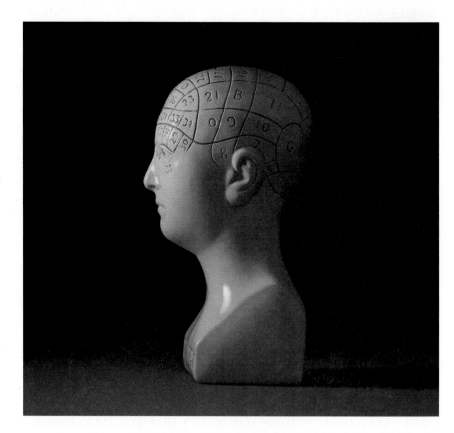

By the mid-nineteenth century, the "science" of phrenology had attracted a lot of attention and some serious supporters. Phrenologists proposed that mental characteristics revealed themselves in the contours of the skull. They divided the skull into sections and studied the relationship between sections and psychological characteristics. For example, section 21 might represent creativity, so that a bump at location 21 would mean high creativity. Their measurements were reliable, because they showed the same results consistently. However, they were not valid, because the inferences made about skull shape and mental characteristics were wrong.

the same bump can be consistently measured with considerable accuracy.

Why, then, has the "science" of phrenology been totally discredited? The answer has to do with the failure of phrenology to meet the essential test of **validity,** which concerns the *meaning* of a measurement, the inferences that can be made on the basis of a measurement. Phrenologists were wrong to assume that the measurement of a bump on a skull can be used to infer something about the mental characteristics of a person. Thus, although the measures taken by phrenologists were reliable, they were not valid.

In order to clarify the issue of validity in laboratory studies, it is useful to distinguish between two types of validity: internal and external (Campbell, 1957). **Internal validity** concerns the degree of control that has been achieved in the laboratory experiment: Have all the nuisance variables been isolated to leave less room for error? Is the manipulation of independent variable(s) effective? Is the measurement of changes in the dependent variable(s) efficient? In short, if we can be certain that the change detected in the dependent variable(s) is exclusively the result of manipulations of the independent variable(s), then the experiment has high internal validity.

Internal validity allows researchers to make correct inferences about *events inside the laboratory* and is concerned only with the meaning of events in that context. For example, high internal validity means that correct inferences can be made about relationships between an independent variable and a dependent variable (such as the relationship between the presence of the scientist and level of obedience, as in Milgram's obedience study).

External validity concerns the relationship between the results of the laboratory study and the external world, the inferences made from the results to social behavior outside the laboratory. When assessing external validity, researchers must address this question: How correct is it to generalize from the results we have obtained in the laboratory context to situations in the real social world outside the laboratory? It is immediately apparent that external validity is a much more challenging issue than internal validity, because the world outside the laboratory is much more complicated than inside it.

The controversy over external validity can be better understood by considering two issues. First is the criticism that by separating aspects of behavior for study in laboratories, researchers are losing essential features of the whole picture. Second is the question of realism in laboratory research: Are laboratory studies realistic?

Validity and Part-Whole Relations. One influential line of criticism leveled at laboratory research is associated with the Gestalt principle that *the whole is more than the sum of its parts.* This general principle has implications for how we go about the business of doing research: We should take great care when we break up a social event into sections and study isolated parts, because the characteristics of the many parts taken separately are not equivalent to the characteristics of the whole.

validity the inferences that can be made on the basis of a measurement.

internal validity the degree of control achieved in a laboratory experiment.

external validity the relationship between the results of the laboratory study and the external world.

Related to this are a number of ideas developed by Kurt Lewin (see Lewin, 1935; Marrow, 1969) that lead us to view behavior and culture as an integrated whole, with each part having a role in relation to other parts. The meaning of each aspect of behavior is derived in large part from its place in a larger social context. Consider the role of "scientist" in Western societies. This role is made meaningful by the part the scientist plays in science and technology, in academic life, in technological progress, and in many other essential components of modern industrial societies. If we transport a scientist to a remote village in a developing country where neither the role of scientist nor the scientific and technological contexts for this role exist, the culture would not be able to give a Western meaning to the scientist role. The villagers would ask the scientist attempting to be accepted as an authority figure: "Who are you and why should we listen to you? What exactly is a scientist and what do you mean by science, anyway? Do you make rain? Can you talk to the spirits of our ancestors? No!? Well, we would rather trust our own medical experts."

Of course, we may feel that their "experts" have no place in our technologically advanced world. Just as the modern scientist does not have a meaningful role in their culture, their traditional experts do not have a meaningful role in ours. Both roles require a larger cultural context to give them meaning; each seems to be very strange, even meaningless perhaps, when taken out of its context. Thus, an aspect of culture gains an important part of its characteristics from the context in which it exists.

In response to this line of criticism, laboratory researchers generally agree that there is a risk of changing some of the meaning of a phenomenon by separating it and placing it in a laboratory. However, the potential risks are worth taking, because the laboratory method is the only one that enables researchers to achieve a high degree of control, and in this way to identify causal relations.

Validity and Realism.

A second line of criticism concerning the validity of laboratory studies is on the issue of realism. The criticism is sometimes made that laboratory experiments are artificial and unrealistic.

The first criticism is that the laboratory lacks realism, that it is somehow artificial. By this it is generally meant that the laboratory context is different from the context of everyday life, that it is a separate and different situation. In designing the laboratory situation, researchers create settings that are removed from and unlike those found in the world outside. Participants who enter the laboratory leave behind their everyday roles and move to a stage that is divorced from their ordinary life.

A second and different point raised by critical discussions on realism concerns the impact of the study on participants. The laboratory context does not have a real impact on participants because they know very well that they are taking part in a laboratory experiment. What they do and say in the context of a laboratory study will not have consequences for them or others in the outside world.

In response to such criticisms, defenders of laboratory research reply that well-planned and properly implemented laboratory studies do have realism, because they have immediate impact and lead participants to become involved in the situation. In this sense, they are as realistic as any other experience, and any distinction between laboratory situations and the so-called real world is misguided. The impact of the laboratory situation can be as "real" as anything in the real world.

This point is captured well by Elliot Aronson and Merrill Carlsmith (1968), who distinguish between experimental realism and mundane realism. **Experimental realism** refers to the realism of the experimental situation for participants: If it does have realism, it will have a more powerful impact on participants and they will take the experiment more seriously. **Mundane realism** refers to the similarity of events in the experiment to those in the world outside the laboratory. An experiment can have mundane realism but be of little research interest because many events are trivial or not meaningful in terms of scientific research. For example, as I write this sentence I can hear a work crew repairing water pipes on the floor above me (my office has been flooded several times during the last year). This is an event in the real world (I can vouch for that—having water pour down from the ceiling on to papers and books is very real), but not one of much research interest. It has mundane realism (very mundane, routinely mundane, particularly dealing with the flood aftermath). By referring to this kind of realism as "mundane," Aronson and Carlsmith clearly signal that in their opinion experimental realism is more important.

experimental realism   the realism of the experimental situation for participants.

mundane realism   the similarity of events in the experiment to those in the world outside the laboratory.

Cultural Realism.
An alternative view is that what Aronson and his associates (Aronson & Carlsmith, 1968; Aronson, Ellsworth, Carlsmith, & Gonzales, 1990) dismiss as "mundane realism" is part of something larger and of fundamental importance: cultural realism. A laboratory experiment has **cultural realism** if, first, participants identify the situation as one in which a certain type of behavior is correct and, second, that not to behave in the correct way in such a situation would be an important cultural transgression. For example, a participant in Milgram's study must first perceive himself to be in a subordinate position to an authority figure and in a powerful position in relation to the person to whom he is being asked to administer electric shocks. Second, the participant must feel that the "correct" thing to do is to obey the authority figure and that not to obey would mean violating significant cultural norms.

cultural realism   the ability of participants to experience the laboratory situation as realistic and to believe that behavior in this context should be guided by certain norms and rules.

Experimental realism is a necessary but not sufficient condition for cultural realism. In order for there to be cultural realism, it is necessary for participants to experience the laboratory situation as realistic. In addition, however, they must believe that behavior in this context should be guided by certain norms and rules. A participant in Milgram's study will feel: "This is a realistic situation"; but he must also feel: "It is correct for me to obey the scientist in this situation."

Thus, in addition to having an impact on participants and in this way having experimental realism, the laboratory situation must lead participants to bring into effect their ideas about correct behavior and in this way meet the requirements of cultural realism.

Packages of Variables or "Cultural Sets"

One reason for the high cultural realism of laboratory studies such as Milgram's is that such studies incorporate cultural sets rather than just isolated variables. A **cultural set** is a whole package of variables normally experienced together in the real world. In Western societies one can think of a cultural set that includes the following: scientist, laboratory, experiment, research equipment, participants, experimental instructions, results. In Milgram's studies, participants were introduced to a situation involving a scientist (apparently) conducting research in a laboratory setting, using research equipment and methodology to achieve research results.

To say that this cultural set is meaningful implies that we expect to find these elements together in the same situation. Other combinations would be seen as less correct: Scientist, grocery store, bingo equipment, rap music would be a less correct combination. (Although we could, in our wilder moments, imagine a situation in which they would go together. Perhaps a rap-singing scientist who has gone to shop at a grocery store only to find a game of bingo in progress? Maybe it is easier to imagine a bingo game played by scientists in a grocery store, accompanied by rap music.) But "experiments have to have cultural realism," a critic may say, "and cultural realism means that significant cultural norms are seen by the participant as being applicable to the laboratory situation. Then should the results of laboratory studies not be obvious and easily predictable?"

"Can you explain a little more?" we ask.

"Surely," the critic continues. "If what you say about cultural realism is correct, all one has to do is to think of the norms applicable to each laboratory situation and the results would become obvious. For example, in the Milgram experiment, it would be enough to know about the norms applicable to relations between authority figures and subordinates, and the results should be predictable."

"But knowing about the norms applicable to a situation is not enough," we point out, "because to predict what participants are going to do in the situation we also have to know *if participants would feel they would be doing something seriously wrong if they did not behave according to particular norms.* In short, they would have had to predict the experimental realism of the laboratory situation, and the norms they would feel obliged to follow."

"What would be an example?"

cultural set   a whole package of variables that are normally experienced together in the real world.

"Well, if we take the case of Milgram's obedience study, to predict how they would behave participants would have had to recognize that they would see it as an important infraction of norms not to obey the authority figure. In fact, both scientists and laypeople failed to predict the outcome of Milgram's study exactly because they underestimated the impact of norms to obey the authority figure."

The Experimenter as Dramatist

A great deal about the laboratory method is revealed when we conceive of the experimenter as a dramatist (Moghaddam & Harré, 1992). Like a dramatist, the experimenter has to prepare the script, cast the players, set the stage, and supervise the production until the whole play comes across as a polished, thoroughly convincing performance. A convincing performance will ensure experimental realism. Among all the research methods available to social psychologists, the laboratory experiment requires the highest degree of stage management, so that every aspect of the final performance is strictly under the control of the dramatist/experimenter.

An interesting way to clarify this point is to consider the case of Milgram's obedience study compared to a "laboratory study" designed by Hamlet in Shakespeare's play of the same name. Although on the surface Milgram and Hamlet may seem very different as dramatists, they are actually very similar. In Shakespeare's play, Hamlet believes that his father, the king, was murdered by Hamlet's mother and uncle. In order to force the suspects to admit their guilt, Hamlet arranges for a play to be performed before the royal court. In the drama, there is a scene in which the king is murdered by his own brother and wife. Hamlet reasons that seeing their own crime enacted before their very eyes will force the guilty partners to react and in this way demonstrate their guilt:

> I have heard
> That guilty creatures sitting at a play
> Have by the very cunning of the scene
> Been struck so to the soul that presently
> They have proclaimed their malefactions.
>
> (*Hamlet*, act II, scene 2)

In the terminology of laboratory research, then, Hamlet's independent variable is the murder scene in the play. The dependent variable is the reaction of his uncle and mother to the murder scene. The other members of the audience act as a control group, so Hamlet can compare their reactions to those of his mother and uncle. Hamlet's hypothesis is that when the independent variable is manipulated, his mother and uncle (who is now king) will react differently because the murder scene will affect their conscience—"The play's the thing/Wherein I'll catch the conscience of the king."

Movie still from the 1948 *Hamlet* showing Laurence Olivier as Hamlet approaching his mother and uncle, now king and queen. In Shakespeare's Hamlet, the main character designs and conducts a social psychological experiment. Hamlet's hypothesis is that his father, the former king, was murdered by Hamlet's own mother and uncle. Hamlet reasons that by putting on a play with a murder scene, showing exactly how his mother and uncle killed his father, he will trick the guilty partners to react in public and display their guilt in front of others. Like a good experimenter, Hamlet prepares the script for the experiment (play), rehearses his confederates (the actors), and ensures that the drama is convincing (has experimental realism).

Preparing the Script. Notice that in preparing the script for his experiment, Hamlet has orchestrated everyone's parts down to the last detail, and left only one gap; this gap is to be filled by the participants (his mother and uncle). Similarly, Milgram prepared a script that called for three main actors: scientist (authority figure), teacher (the naive participant), and learner (confederate of the experimenter). The scripts for the scientist and the teacher were written in great detail, but the script for the learner was left open.

Thus, both the "experiments" by Hamlet and Milgram are rather like those theatrical performances in which all the players have to keep to a set script except one character, who is allowed to improvise on stage. The research question is: How will the "free" player (the participant) improvise the role?

Setting the Stage.   A major challenge facing the experimenter is to set the stage effectively so that the participants will feel involved. The participants have to be told a convincing cover story as to why they are taking part in the event and what the event is about. In Hamlet's experiment, the participants believe they are there to watch a play being performed. But they do not know that Hamlet has added a murder scene to the play. In Milgram's experiment, the participants believe they are taking part in a study about learning. The naive participant is introduced to another person, supposedly another participant but actually a confederate of the experimenter. The naive participant and the confederate are asked to draw lots to decide which will play the part of teacher and which the learner. The result of the draw is predetermined by Milgram, so that the naive participant always gets to play the part of teacher.

During the learning trials in Milgram's study, the naive participant has the task of teaching the learner word associations. Each time the learner makes a mistake, the naive participant is supposed to administer an electric shock to punish the learner. The level of shock supposedly increases each time the learner makes a mistake. The success of the experiment depends on whether the naive participant "really believes" he is administering high-voltage electric shocks to the learner. Does the learner's performance convince the naive participant?

Realism: One More Time.   After watching a theatrical performance, people often react by saying something about the degree to which they became affected or "got involved in" the spectacle. "I really got into that play," someone will say, whereas another may disagree and assert, "It didn't have any impact on me." The same question is central to the experience of participants in laboratory research.

In Hamlet's experiment, his mother and uncle are strongly affected by the murder scene, so much so that they immediately rush out of the "theater" and hide in their rooms. In research terminology, the manipulation of the independent variable had a powerful impact on the dependent measure. Similarly, in Milgram's experiment the manipulation of the main independent variable, the presence of the authority figure, had a very powerful impact. About two-thirds of the naive participants obeyed the authority figure and administered extremely high voltages of electric shocks to the learners.

Combining Cultural and Dramaturgical Perspectives

The traditional way of looking at laboratory experiments is enriched when we add cultural and dramaturgical perspectives. First, the laboratory experiment is itself a cultural phenomenon, because it can be used effectively only among populations that share basic ideas about what research is, and the role laboratories, participants, data, and the like have in research (imagine trying to conduct research with people who, for example, assume that being selected to be a participant is like winning the lottery, and the laboratory is like a hotel, with the experimenters as servants, where they will sleep, be fed, and receive luxurious treatment for the rest of their lives).

It is in part because of this requirement that the vast majority of laboratory research has been conducted using psychology students as the participants (Sears, 1986). Typically, psychology students are asked to act as participants after they have become familiar with the basics of laboratory methodology, but before they have taken more advanced courses that might allow them to second-guess the experimenters. Thus, laboratory research requires participants who share a basic understanding of the part they are being asked to play, without knowing the details about the exact hypothesis being tested.

Second, the laboratory experiment is cultural in that it serves to spotlight certain social phenomena that had not previously been attended to so much in a particular culture. The Milgram studies served to focus more attention on obedience; that is, they made obedience "an issue," at least in Western societies.

But there is a third function of laboratory experiments related to culture, and this is *interpretive*: Laboratory experiments, some more than others, influence our constructions of social life. Milgram's studies serve to strengthen the view that even among people with "normal" personality profiles, many will yield to the pressure of authority figures when they are told to do harm to others. According to John Kotre (1992), the classic social psychological experiments act as parables, as dramatic restatements of some great lessons about life. They become part of the powerful stories of our culture (Howard, 1991), particularly because they have surprising endings that suggest lessons for life.

The Culture of Research Ethics

One of the most controversial issues in social psychology since the 1960s continues to be the ethics of using deception in research (Fisher & Fyrberg, 1994; Korn, 1997). The literature on this topic has grown considerably, and concerns have led the American Psychological Association to develop ethical principles for researchers considering the use of deceptive methodologies (APA, 1992). It is the responsibility of researchers to inform participants fully about any possible risks involved in a study and to obtain written consent from participants prior to its start. All educational institutions now have ethics committees to screen research studies involving human participants. An important part of the research protocol in social psychology is to ensure that every aspect of a research study meets the required ethical standards.

But there are still certain limitations in the ethical standards that social psychological research must meet, and this arises because of the individualistic nature of how ethics is conceived in traditional psychology. Although the rights of individuals are safeguarded to a considerable degree, the rights of collectivities are very often neglected. Thus, for example, it is not considered an ethical issue that certain groups of people, such as ethnic minorities and the economic underclass, are still not adequately represented in social psychological research. The topics selected for research do not arise from the lives of such underrepresented groups but continue to come from the worlds of a middle–class, white, urban population. There is a need for a broader conception of what is encompassed by the term *ethics*, so that the rights of groups as well as individuals are addressed.

Concepts and Issues

The laboratory method is seen to be high on reliability and also on internal validity. However, criticism is often leveled at the external validity achieved in laboratory studies, implying that it is not meaningful to generalize from laboratory research results to the world outside. Defenders of the laboratory method have argued that although laboratory studies often lack mundane realism, they can achieve high experimental realism, which is more important. An alternative view is that mundane realism is a component of cultural realism, which is fundamentally important. Adequate attention is being given to ethical treatment of individual participants but not to ethical issues concerning collectivities.

1. What is reliability? Is it high or low in laboratory research?
2. What is validity?
3. Describe the difference between experimental and mundane realism.
4. Give an example of a cultural set that could be used in a laboratory experiment.

Conclusion

An essential part of the vitality enjoyed by social psychology is the continuing debate about the merits of various research methods. Social psychological research typically begins with a puzzle or an issue extracted from everyday life and then isolated for more systematic examination. In the majority of cases, such examination takes place in a laboratory, using college students as participants, with the purpose of discovering relations between causes (independent variables) and effects (dependent variables). Critics have pointed out that the meaning of behavior can be largely dependent on context, and so the external validity of laboratory research is suspect. Although this argument has some merit, it does not negate the wider value of laboratory studies, which can also be interpreted as dramas. An alternative to the traditional causal explanation of behavior in laboratory studies is a normative explanation, which depicts the experimenter as dramatist and participants as players with freedom as to how they will act out their roles within an otherwise set script. The behavior of participants in this setting informs us about the norms and rules they see to be appropriate for behavior in the given situation set up in the study.

For Review

Research methods are the systematic procedures scientists use to gather data. A routine procedure in social psychology is to start with a real-life problem of considerable complexity and significance and then reduce it to simpler components in order to study it in the laboratory.

Social psychological research is conducted in the laboratory or in the field, and is either experimental or correlational. A minority of studies have been conducted in the field, where there is less possibility to control variables but greater opportunities to observe behavior in everyday life.

Survey and interview methods are available to map out attitudes and opinions, but they generally rely on verbal responses, which may not match overt behavior. Innovative field research methods, such as the "lost-letter technique," have been used to access behavior directly. Meta-analysis is being used increasingly as a research method to identify general trends in research findings.

The social psychology laboratory consists of a separate space where all the characteristics of a situation can be controlled. The vast majority of studies in social psychology are conducted in the laboratory, using white, middle-class students as subjects.

The supremacy of the laboratory method is in large part explained by the use of a causal model in traditional social psychology. This model assumes that social behavior is the result of certain causes, and a goal of research is to discover relationships between causes and effects. The causes of behavior are traditionally classified as being internal to the individual or situated in the environment.

The laboratory enables researchers to achieve a high level of reliability, but critics have faulted the laboratory procedure on the criterion of validity. Other criticisms of the laboratory procedure are that the meaning of phenomena changes when they are transferred from the outside world to the laboratory, and that the laboratory lacks realism.

A normative model interprets the laboratory experiment as a drama. The stage (the laboratory setting) is set and the players rehearse (the experimenters and their confederates learn their parts), but one vital gap is left open in the drama, to be filled by the participant/player. The performance of the participant/player constitutes what traditional social psychology sees as dependent variables.

For Discussion

1. If you wanted to carry out a social psychological study with a high degree of control, would you use laboratory or field research methods? Why?
2. In what ways is the causal model compatible with the laboratory research method?
3. Describe how culture can influence laboratory research.

Key Terms

Computer simulation *41*

Control *28*

Correlational methods *28*

Cultural realism *47*

Cultural set *48*

Dependent variable *28*

Experimental methods *28*

Experimental realism *47*

External validity *45*

Field experiment *28*

Field research *31*

Hypothesis *27*

Independent variable *28*

Internal validity *45*

Laboratory *28*

Meta–analysis *28*

Mundane realism *47*

Natural experiment *31*

Negative correlation *28*

Nuisance variable *40*

Participant *37*

Population *37*

Positive correlation *28*

Reliability *44*

Replication *36*

Sample *37*

Scientific method *26*

Situational variable *42*

Validity *45*

Variable *28*

Annotated Readings

For a broad introductory overview of research methods in social psychology, see E. Aronson, P. C. Ellsworth, J. M. Carlsmith, and M. H. Gonzales, *Methods of research in social psychology*, 2nd ed. (New York: McGraw-Hill, 1990); and J. J. Shaughnessy and E. B. Zechmeister, *Research methods in psychology*, 4th ed. (New York: McGraw-Hill, 1997).

For a discussion of some of the ethical issues involved in social psychological research, see C. B. Fisher and D. Fyrberg, Participant partners: College students weigh the costs and benefits of deceptive research, *American Psychologist*, 49 (1994):417–427.

The kinds of issues that arise when researchers study behavior in non-Western cultures are discussed in T. S. Sloan, Psychological research methods in developing countries, in *Psychology and the developing world*, ed. S. C. Carr and J. F. Schumaker (Westport, CT: Praeger, 1996), pp. 38–45.

Various alternative research methods are discussed in J. Smith, R. Harré, and L. Van Langenhove, eds., *Rethinking methods in psychology* (Thousand Oaks, CA: Sage, 1995).

CHAPTER **3**

The Self in Culture

◄ The twenty–first century promises to be an exciting age for space exploration, but it may prove to be even more momentous for explorations of the self. Social psychological research is leading to new insights about variations in the self across cultures. In India and some other non–Western cultures, the self has characteristics very different from the self as known in Western societies.

"T"he problem with you," the woman was telling her husband, "is that you really don't know yourself."

The three of us were stuck in an elevator in a department store in downtown New York City, with the fire alarm ringing in our ears. They looked like a retired couple on a holiday trip.

"No, I know myself; it's you who doesn't know me after 43 years of marriage," he retorted.

"Well, if you know yourself, how is it you insist on getting us tickets for a Broadway musical whenever we visit New York, and then walk out halfway through the show every time?" she asked.

"If you knew me after all these years, you'd know the answer to that," he said, in a teasing way.

"Oh, I know the answer," she responded emphatically. "The answer is that there are lots of different you's. You are so many different people bundled up in one body."

"Sure," he said, rather pleased with her response, "doesn't everybody have different selves inside them?"

As the husband raised this question, the elevator doors opened and we stepped out to learn that someone had set off the fire alarm by mistake. There was no fire. We had been stuck in the elevator for 10 minutes as a result of a false alarm.

As I left the store and joined the rhythm of the crowded city streets, the idea of "different selves" stayed in my mind. During recent decades, social psychologists have once more turned their attention to explore the **self,** defined as the totality of personal experiences. The twentieth century is ending with a glorious era of explorations into outer space; perhaps the twenty-first century will see us taking even more fascinating expeditions into inner space.

self   the totality of personal experiences.

The Self in Social Psychology

The self that has been studied by modern social psychologists is very similar to the self described by the American poet Walt Whitman in "Song of Myself." Whitman's self is fiercely independent and determined to travel its own personal path in the world, to seek its own destiny through self-help and individual responsibility. Not only does it seek, it "celebrates itself," presenting a positive picture both to the self and to the external world:

> Nor do I understand who there can be more wonderful than
> myself.

Since the 1970s, social psychologists have developed a number of ingenious research methods for studying this self, and their investigations have led to some fascinating discoveries (Baumeister, 1986, 1993, 1995; Carver & Scheier, 1981; Davis, Conklin, Smith, & Luce, 1996; Grodin & Lindlof, 1996; Harré, 1997; Schlenker, 1985; Suls & Greenwald, 1986; Wicklund & Eckert, 1992; Ziller, 1990). For example, research findings suggest that under some conditions people decide what they believe by observing their own behavior and its situational context rather than by looking within themselves and interpreting how they feel (Bem, 1972; Schlenker & Trudeau, 1990). These kinds of discoveries shed light on such questions as what structure the self has and whether it is multiple or singular. These questions, which have a long history in philosophy, have now become the subject of psychological research.

Concepts of the Self

There has also emerged an exciting body of literature that focuses on a different concept of the self, one that has evolved outside Western culture (Campbell, Trapnell, Heine, & Katz, 1996; Cousins, 1989; Kashima, 1995; Markus & Kitayama, 1991; Triandis, 1989). This different concept of the self is more prevalent in Eastern societies and among minority ethnic groups in the West. Following Hazel Markus and Shinobu Kitayama (1991), I refer to this alternative self as the interdependent self. Compared to the **independent self,** which emphasizes separateness, internal characteristics of people, and uniqueness of individuals, this **interdependent self** is more dependent on social relations, emphasizes group characteristics, and has fuzzier boundaries. The interdependent self has gained prominence as researchers try harder to consider "the native's point of view" (Geertz, 1984) when they study people outside the Western mainstream.

independent self a concept of the self that emphasizes separateness, internal characteristics, and uniqueness of individuals.

interdependent self a concept of the self that emphasizes dependence on social relations and group characteristics, and that has fuzzier boundaries.

The independent and interdependent selves arise out of two different cultural contexts. The independent self evolves in cultures that emphasize personal freedom and individual mobility. In such cultures, a major goal of socialization is to develop independent persons who can be "self-contained" (Sampson, 1977). In contrast, the interdependent self evolves in cultures in which a goal of socialization is to strengthen ties between individuals and various groups, such as the family and the clan.

John Beattie (1980), in his discussion of the Nyoro of Africa's western Uganda, points out that

> even today, a Nyoro peasant asked by another Nyoro who he was would be likely to respond by naming his agnatic clan, that is, the social group (or rather, in Bunyoro, the social category) of which he is a member by birth. He might well add the name of his mother's clan, thus locating himself even more exactly in the genealogical framework of Nyroro society. (p. 314)

The equivalent in Western societies might be if someone you met for the first time introduced herself as "belonging to the Jones clan, and my mother is a Robinson." This would not be normative behavior in the West, where people are identified first and foremost by their individual names. Notice how, in his poem "Song of Myself," Walt Whitman actually introduces himself by his name and tells us about his personal characteristics:

Walt Whitman, a kosmos, of Manhattan the son,
Turbulent, fleshy, sensual, eating, drinking and breeding,
No sentimentalist, no stander above men and women or apart
        from them,
No more modest than immodest.

We should not, however, view independent–interdependent aspects of selves in an all-or-nothing way. Ted Singelis and his colleagues have shown that these two aspects of the self can and do coexist in the same individuals (Singelis, 1994; Singelis & Brown, 1995). The extent to which each of them becomes prominent depends on culture, the independent aspect becoming more prominent in individualistic cultures, the interdependent aspect more preeminent in collectivistic cultures.

Aspects of the Self

In order to identify universal and local aspects of the self better, each of the three main parts of this chapter deals with a major aspect of the self: first, the sense of self; second, self-perception; and third, self-presentation. The sense of self refers to what we experience when we reflect on ourselves. This sense of self simply consists of a feeling that we exist as persons. Although some thinkers, such as the Scottish philosopher David Hume (1711–1776), have cast doubt on the certainty of even this elementary aspect of the self, most of us tend to agree with the commonsense viewpoint of the Scotsman Thomas Reid (1710–1796) when he said that "a man that disbelieves his own existence, is surely as unfit to be reasoned with as a man who believes he is made of glass" (see Robinson & Beauchamp, 1978).

Apart from this sense of self, each individual also develops an evaluative self-perception during the course of life (Jenkins, 1996). Clara, for example, may believe that she is too shy. This second aspect of the self is referred to as *evaluative* because it is associated with positive and negative feelings about oneself. Clara may feel that her shyness causes her all kinds of social difficulties, and she may wish that she could be more outgoing and confident in social settings.

A third aspect of the self is how we present ourselves to others. During an interview for a sales position, Clara may try to present herself as a confident and extroverted person. From a social psychological perspective, a fascinating feature of these aspects of the self is that they can contradict one another. For example, Clara may succeed in presenting herself to the interviewer as highly confident, but at the same time feel that she really is very shy and lacking in confidence.

The first and second aspects of the self, the sense of self and self-perception, are different from the third aspect, self-presentation, with respect to how overt they are. The first two are not directly observable from the outside, whereas the third aspect is public and directly observable. The senior managers interviewing Clara cannot directly observe Clara's sense of self or her self-perception that she is shy, but they can directly observe Clara as she presents herself during the course of the interview.

The way in which we report about the self, in terms of how distinctive we think we are, for example, varies across contexts. In a social situation where there is only one of our kind (for example, if we are the only female), then in response to the request "Tell me about yourself" we are more likely to make gender a salient aspect of ourselves and say something like, "I am a woman manager in a major corporation where most of the managers are men."

The nonobservable nature of some of its important aspects led to the neglect of the self as a topic of study for long periods during the twentieth century. Behaviorism, which focused only on the observable, was the dominant school of thought in psychology for about half a century, from approximately the late 1910s to the 1960s. John Watson (1878–1958), Edward Tolman (1886–1959), Clark Hull (1884–1952), B. F. Skinner (1904–1990), and other behaviorists argued that psychology should be concerned only with observable behavior. In what became known as the "behaviorist manifesto," Watson (1913) wrote: "The time has come when psychology must discard all reference to consciousness" (p. 163).

It was not until the cognitive revolution was well underway during the 1960s that the behaviorist deadlock was broken and the self once again became an acceptable topic of study for scientific psychology. The return of the self to mainstream psychology, and social psychology specifically, is all the more exciting because recent research on the self in Western and non-Western cultures promises to lead to a truly universal explanation. Through contrasting what research studies tell us about the Western independent self and the non-Western interdependent self, we can arrive at more accurate generalizations. We can better decide what is truly universal about the self and what aspects of the self tend to vary across cultures. Also, as Anthony Greenwald and Anthony Pratkanis (1984) point out, social psychologists are now conducting empirical studies on aspects of the self, such as conversations within the self and the relationship of the self and social contexts, that were once thought to be outside the realm of scientific investigation.

Concepts and Issues

With the decline of behaviorism and the rise of cognitive psychology in the 1960s, the self has once again become a focus of social psychological research in Western and non-Western societies. The sense of self is universal, but two other topics for research—self-evaluation and self-presentation—vary considerably across cultures.

1. Why was the self neglected while behaviorism was dominant in psychology?
2. What is meant by the terms *independent* and *interdependent selves*?

The Sense of Self

Imagine if I, the writer, were to jump out of this page and land in front of you, greeting you with the question, "What are you doing?" In response, you might answer, "I am reading this social psychology book written by you." Your answer helps to cast light on several characteristics of the self.

Features of the Self

First, your answer suggests you have a sense of self, a sense of your own being. The sense of self seems to have developed in most people, at least in Western societies, by the time they are 2 years old. We assume this because research with human infants shows that they are capable of recognizing themselves in a mirror between the ages of about 18 to 24 months (Bertenthal & Fischer, 1978; Lewis & Brooks-Gunn, 1979). This research involves putting a colored dot on an infant's nose and then placing a mirror in front of the infant. If the infant touches the spot on its own nose, this is taken as a sign of self-recognition. The only other creatures capable of this feat are the great apes (Gallup, 1977). Presumably, there must be a sense of self in order for one to recognize oneself in a mirror. This awareness seems to be universal in humans.

This sense of self has the important characteristic of being located in one place—one's body. As far as we can tell from cross-cultural research, singularity of location seems to be a universal aspect of the self. That is, it seems to be universally assumed that the self resides in a single body (Harré, 1997). In fact, in most societies a person would be judged mentally ill if the person made the claim that he or she resides in more than one body. So would a person reporting more than one self in a single body. One historical explanation of mental illness is that the mentally ill person has been "possessed" by some evil power, implying that a single body now houses not only a self, the original resident, but also some invader who has taken over control. One goal of the beatings and often barbaric mistreatment given to mentally ill individuals was to make the body too uncomfortable a place for outsiders to live in, to "beat the devil out of them" (Zilboorg & Henry, 1941). The modern world may treat mentally ill individuals with greater tolerance, but the presence of multiple persons in the same body (Abroms, 1993; Prince, 1905/1968) leads as surely now to a diagnosis of madness as it did in past centuries.

A second feature of the sense of selfhood is continuity. As you read these words, you feel that you are the same person who started to read this book an hour ago, just as when you woke up this morning you felt sure about being the same person who went to bed last night. This continuous feature of the self seems to be almost universal, with perhaps some exceptions. Peter Muhlhauser and Rom Harré (1990) point out that the Kawi (old Javanese) language does not involve the same assumption of temporal continuity as exists in many other languages, including English. Because of this, a speaker of Kawi has to introduce temporal continuity through explicit reference. When Bob says to his friend in English, "I am sorry I forgot to call you yesterday, but I had a job interview on my mind," it is implied that the self who is feeling apologetic today is the same self who forgot to call yesterday. But to communicate the same message in Kawi, Bob would have to say, "The I who is here today is sorry that the I of yesterday forgot to call you."

A discussion of the sense of self inevitably leads to long-standing philosophical debates concerning the structure of the self and to theoretically intriguing distinctions, such as that made between the *I* and the *me*. The *I/me* distinction is necessary in order for us to describe our experiences, particularly our past experiences. To arrive at this distinction, imagine yourself responding to my question, "When did you start reading this social psychology book?" When you respond, "I'm not absolutely sure, but it seems to me it was about an hour ago," how is it that you are able to report what you yourself were doing some time ago?

As William James (1890/1983) first suggested, a useful way to describe this experience is to portray the self in terms of an *I* that can move about following a train of thought, to report on a *me*. According to this description, the *I* acts as a narrator of a story, with the *me* being the main figure in one's life story. Thus, the *I* can narrate what the *me* was doing some time ago, as well as what it is doing now and what it might do in the future.

The Self-Confrontational Method

This way of viewing the self has influenced recent empirical studies. For example, Hubert Hermans and his associates (Hermans, 1987, 1989; Hermans & Bonarius, 1991; Hermans, Kempen, & van Loon, 1992) have extended James's argument to propose a multiplicity of positions for the *I* and the *me*, so that in each position an *I* narrates about a different *me*. These narrations act as different voices of characters who "exchange information about their respective *Me*'s and their worlds, resulting in a complex, narratively structured self" (Hermans, Kempen, & van Loon, 1992, p. 29).

In order to explore this narratively structured self, Hermans (1987, 1989, 1991) has developed a self–confrontational method out of valuation theory (a *valuation* is anything that people find to be important when thinking about their lives). For example, Roshani has a very dear memory of her grandmother's ninetieth birthday, and this for her is a valuation. The first step in the **self–confrontational method** is for the participant to make a list of valuations. The second step is to rate the extent to which a particular valuation leads the participant to experience each of 16 affects—such as joy, pride, despondency, and worry—provided by the researcher. The pattern of relationships that emerges between valuations and affects is used to identify motives central to the life of the participant. The results of the research are then discussed with the participant. Such discussions have a self-reflective quality, in the sense that the person confronts previously hidden aspects of the self.

Results of research using the self-confrontational method reveal that most people have imagined conversations with significant others, although actual contact with these individuals may not have occurred for years. Jane may not have seen her grandmother for 10 years, but she imagines the conversation they might have if her grandmother were present to witness her success in a career requiring a great deal of confidence during social interactions. Thus, within the self there are not only conversations between *I*'s and *me*'s but also conversations between the self and imagined others (Hermans, Kempen, & van Loon, 1992).

Discussions of multiple *I*'s and multiple *me*'s seem to imply that the thinker is different from the thought, that the self is many different phenomena rather than a single entity. James (1890/1983, p. 379), however, saw the self as a single entity, and his proposal is in line with Ludwig Wittgenstein's (1889–1951) ideas concerning the relationship between the language we use and the assumptions we make about the world: Although the *I* and the *me* are useful for discussing the self, we must not make the mistake of assuming that they actually *do* refer to entities that exist independently within the self. Similarly, although there can be multiple motives within the self (Sedekides & Strube, 1995), this does not negate the unitary nature of the self. The same self can be motivated to win the spelling contest hands down and to behave modestly.

A clear indication that the *I* and the *me* are the same is that we cannot focus on both at the same moment. As soon as one focuses on the *I*, it becomes the *me*. This so-called problem of the "fleeting *I*" is yet another puzzle that results from conventional language use. The puzzle disappears as soon as we recognize that the *I* and the *me* both refer to the sense of self, that they are one and the same thing. A similar puzzle would arise if we were to look in the eastern sky at sunrise and, seeing Venus, identify it as the morning star, then look at the western sky at sunset and, seeing Venus, call it the evening star, and then conclude that there must be two different stars, a morning star and an evening star.

self-confrontational method a research method in which a pattern of relationships is revealed and used to identify motives central to the life of the participant.

The Structure of the Self: Variations Across Cultures

> At the center of the inner self is the *kokoro* which stands for heart, sentiment, spirit, will, and mind. While the outer self is socially circumscribed, the *kokoro* can be free, spontaneous, and even asocial.
>
> —Takie Lebra, "Self in Japanese Culture"

Takie Lebra's (1992) fascinating exploration of the self in Japanese society is part of a growing literature demonstrating that in some societies the

The distinction between the inner and the outer selves is much more explicitly developed in some cultures than it is in others. This Japanese geisha is preparing the formal presentation of the outer self, following a training that emphasizes finely tuned control. Although the outer self is not presented in as formal a manner in the United States, this does not mean that public face is unimportant in American society. It only means that a different style of self–presentation is followed in the United States.

self is believed to have a fundamentally different, non–Western structure (Rosenberger, 1992). Whereas in Western societies the *I* and the *me* are the essential components of that structure, in Japanese society the major distinction made is between an inner self and an outer self. At the core of the inner self is *kokoro*, a reservoir of truthfulness and purity.

As the reservoir of "real" truth, the inner self takes on special significance in Japanese society. This is indicated by findings from a number of studies comparing the sense of self of Japanese participants with that of participants from other cultures. For example, compared with U.S. participants, Japanese participants were found to have a larger inner self that remains private and is not shared with outsiders (Barnlund, 1975). A study comparing Japanese, Korean, and Chinese participants revealed that the Japanese pay greater attention to the inner self than do the other two groups (see Lebra & Lebra, 1986). The centrality of the inner self in Japan has led to *kokoro* being the most often used word in modern Japanese advertising.

Another indication of variation in the structure of the self emerges from a review of self structures formulated by Western researchers. One formulation influential in recent research is **self as schema** (Markus, 1977), which presents the self as a memory structure composed of a collection of schemata. A **schema** is a cognitive structure that serves to organize experiences in a given domain. A **memory structure** is a set of interconnected memories. An example of schemata that might be important for a woman are "mother," "medical doctor," "gourmet cook," "jogger," "volunteer in a charity," and "political activist" (see Figure 3–1).

A second formulation of the self structure is "self as hierarchical category structure" (Rogers, 1981), which sees the self as an overriding category that embraces other, more specific categories. This system is hierarchical—it starts with the most general category, the self, and moves to the more specific categories, such as "mother," "caring person," "manager," and so on. For example, Carole's self-concept starts with the self, then moves to "police officer" and "basketball player," and then to

self-schema   the self as a memory structure composed of a collection of schemata.

schema   a cognitive structure that serves to organize experiences in a given domain.

memory structure   a set of interconnected memories.

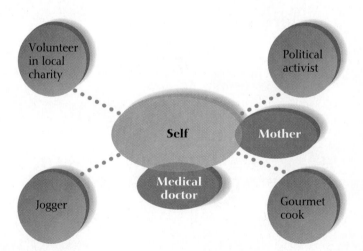

Figure 3–1   A hypothetical structure of the self (after Markus, 1977).

Figure 3–2 Part of a hierarchical model of the self (after Rogers, 1981).

even more specific categories, such as "Democrat," "activist for gun control," and so on (see Figure 3–2).

The Social Origins of the Sense of Self

There is general agreement among researchers with widely differing theoretical orientations that self-awareness evolves in large part through social interactions. Charles Cooley (1902) first coined the phrase **looking–glass self** to indicate that the self is an outcome of people's assumptions about how others view them, "the imagination of our appearance to the other person; the imagination of his judgment of that appearance, and some sort of self-feeling, such as pride or mortification" (p. 152). Sigmund Freud (1921), George Herbert Mead (1934), Jean Piaget (Piaget & Inhelder, 1969) and Lev Vygotsky (1978) are other important thinkers who in their different ways recognize the social origins of self-awareness.

looking-glass self the self as an outcome of people's assumptions about how others view them.

It was only recently, however, that social psychologists began to carry out empirical studies on relations between social experiences and the sense of self. This research, spearheaded by William and Claire McGuire and their associates at Yale University (McGuire & McGuire, 1981; McGuire, McGuire, & Cheever, 1986; McGuire & Padawer–Singer, 1976), has used open-ended, nondirective questions to explore relations between social contexts and the sense of self. In these studies participants are instructed to report whatever comes to mind when asked: "Tell me about yourself." Results show that no fewer than 23 percent of all the noun concepts used in these free descriptions are mentions of other people, indicating that our sense of self is dependent to a considerable extent on our social relationships.

This dependency is further demonstrated through an exploration of the role of "distinctiveness" in forming the sense of self. In a study carried out among children attending a multiethnic school, McGuire and McGuire (1981) found that the likelihood of ethnicity being mentioned as part of the self-concept decreased as the proportional representation of the individual's ethnic group in class increased. This indicates, for example, that if black children are a minority in a classroom, they are more likely to include ethnicity in response to the request "Tell me about yourself" than if they are in the majority. In a situation where everyone in a class is black, then the issue of ethnicity is less likely to be salient for black children, and it will not be used to describe "who I am."

Related to this is a finding that immigrants living in neighborhoods where there were fewer members of ethnic minorities were more likely to use ethnicity as a basis for social comparisons (Moghaddam, 1992a). Presumably, being among the few ethnic minorities in a neighborhood leads ethnic group members to become even more conscious of their ethnicity. Thus, recent social psychological studies support the view that the sense of self evolves through interactions with others, and not in isolation. By this analysis, the sense of self is a social rather than a personal production.

So the first aspect of the self is the sense of self, and it seems to be universal insofar as people in all societies believe the self to be located in one body. In contrast, the experience of the self as continuous is not necessarily universal. In describing the experiences of the self, we find it useful to distinguish between *I* and *me*, or even multiple *I*'s and multiple *me*'s. But the self is just one entity, even though we can think of its various aspects and of our self in different ways.

Concepts and Issues

The sense of self develops by about 2 years of age, and involves the perception that a singular self resides in one body. The sense of self is also continuous in most cultures. Researchers have developed methods to explore dialogues within the self. Studies have also been conducted on how the structure of the self varies across cultures, and how self-perception can be influenced by social context. But the self is singular, even though it can be described from different perspectives.

1. How do we know that the sense of self has developed in most people by about the age of 2?
2. Research using the self-confrontational method shows that conversations go on within the self. Does this prove there are multiple selves within each of us? Explain.
3. What did McGuire and McGuire find when they asked participants to respond to the request "Tell me about yourself"?

Self-Perception

I can't describe to you how surprised I was to find out I loved her, old sport. I even hoped for a while that she'd throw me over, but she didn't, because she was in love with me too. . . . Well, there I was, 'way off my ambitions, getting deeper in love every minute, and all of a sudden I didn't care.

—F. Scott Fitzgerald, *The Great Gatsby*

When Gatsby, the central figure in F. Scott Fitzgerald's uniquely American novel *The Great Gatsby*, reflects on his search for love and success, he is surprised by his own feelings. The experience of being surprised at the result of our own self-perceptions is probably common to people in all societies. But there are aspects of self-perception that vary across cultures. Among the examples we will consider are boundaries of the self, the consequences of making the self a referent in behavior, the sources of information for reflections on the self, and the extent to which attention is given to the self.

Boundaries of the Self

> One's-self I sing, a simple separate person.
> —Walt Whitman, American poet,
> *Song of Myself*

> . . . man forms one body with Heaven–and–earth and all things.
> —Ch'eng Hao, Chinese scholar

In Western societies individuals tend to be perceived as "separate," and the self is perceived to have a clear boundary. Researchers refer to the self in Western contexts as "bounded," "self-contained," and "autonomous" (Johnson, 1985; Sampson, 1989). A major goal of socialization of the young in Western societies is to nurture independence (Cole & Cole, 1993), and an ideal for adults is "self-actualization," which is achieved only by individuals who, among other things, can attain a high degree of autonomy and can resist outside pressures (see Maslow, 1987). The implication is that self-actualized individuals perceive a sharp boundary separating the self and others.

The other side of the coin is that a loss of a sharp self-boundary and the subsequent "diffusion" of the self is often believed to have negative, and even dangerous, consequences. The "diffuse self" has been investigated through research on **deindividuation** (Dipboye, 1977), the loss of one's sense of identity as an independent person. Deindividuation can come about in very different ways. But the different procedures seem to have the same effect: They reduce standards internal to individuals, meaning that they diminish the influence of social norms and rules that have been internalized through socialization and that act as an inner conscience to control behavior. In turn, reduced internal standards often lead to deviant behavior, such as increased aggression while under the influence of alcohol and participation in mob violence. The loss of personal identity and the melting away of individualism within a crowd have been seen as a particularly grave threat to law and order (see Taylor & Moghaddam, 1987, p. 17).

Many non-Western cultures, in contrast, conceive of the self as "boundless" and emphasize the "connectedness" or "fusion" of the self with the social and physical environment (Bond, 1986, 1988; De Vos, 1985; Hsu, 1985; Rosenberger, 1992; Shweder & Bourne, 1984). In such contexts, fulfillment is achieved not by arriving at a sharp boundary

deindividuation   the loss of one's sense of identity as an individual person, associated with lower self-awareness and decreased personal responsibility in group settings.

but by overcoming any such boundaries to merge the self with the surroundings and connect with others (see Figure 3–3).

In some societies, the concept of a "boundless" self is part of a larger vision of the universe (de Bary, 1970; Roland, 1988; Rosenberger, 1992). Such holistic views of the universe influence perceptions in many different areas, for example, as shown by the research of Francis Hsu (1981, 1985). One of Hsu's methods is to present Rorschach inkblots to Chinese, Chinese–American, and Caucasian American participants. (The Rorschach is an unstructured projective test, involving ambiguous stimuli—inkblots—and open-ended responses.) Participants were encouraged to describe freely what they saw in the inkblots. Results showed that the Chinese participants were more holistic in orientation because they focused more on the *entire* inkblot, whereas the Caucasian Americans focused more on *parts* of the whole. Interestingly, the responses of Chinese-Americans, an immigrant group, were a mixture of Chinese- and Caucasian American responses.

Other findings from cross-cultural studies throw additional light on the boundaries of the self in different cultures. For example, Richard Shweder and Edmund Bourne (1984) collected accounts from participants in India and the United States about close acquaintances. Indian participants were more likely to describe others in terms of (1) the behavior ("what was done"), (2) the contexts in which behavior took place ("where action occurred"), and (3) the terms of social relationships ("with whom or to whom the behavior took place"). For example, typical contrasting responses from the two groups would be, Indians: "he shouts curses," Americans: "he is aggressive"; Indians: "she brings cakes to my family on festival days," Americans: "she is friendly." However, Shweder and Bourne's groundbreaking study did suffer from a number of methodological shortcomings, such as the fact that the Indian and American participants did not receive identical instructions (p. 174). Thus, we need to consider its findings in the light of other evidence.

The importance of context is also emphasized by the research of Joan Miller and her associates (Miller, 1984, 1987; Miller, Bersoff, & Harwood, 1990). In one study, Miller (1984) asked participants in India

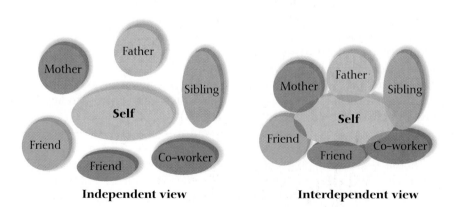

Independent view   **Interdependent view**

Figure 3–3 Two views of the self (Markus & Kitayama, 1991).

Deindividuation involves the loss of one's sense of identity as an independent person. Increasing urbanization and industrialization, associated with increasing population growth, mean that there are more and more situations in which we find ourselves in collectivities, and can become deindividuated. This is perhaps ironic, given that Western societies (at least) are supposed to be entering an era of increasing individualism.

and the United States to explain cases of prosocial and antisocial behavior. Like Shweder and Bourne (1984), she found that Americans were more likely to point to dispositional factors and less likely to identify contextual factors as being responsible for a behavior. For the Indian sample, the social role of individuals and their social relations were relatively more important causal factors. An implication of these findings is that for the Indian sample, the boundary of the self is more diffuse. Causes for "personal" action might lie in the context of social relations rather than within the "bounded, self-contained" individual.

The finding that participants in non–Western societies, such as India (Miller, 1984; Shweder & Bourne, 1984) and central Asia (Luria, 1976), tend to provide more contextualized, concrete descriptions of the self ("He shouts at his son in the presence of the family") might be interpreted to mean that these participants are less capable of abstract representations of the self (as indicated by descriptions such as "He is hostile"). Cousins (1989) tested this "cognitive deficit" explanation against an explanation based on cultural perception. Participants in Japan and the United States completed the Twenty Statements Test (TST), which was presented with the following instructions:

> In the twenty blanks below please make twenty different statements in response to the simple question (addressed to yourself), "Who am I?" Answer as if you are giving the answers to yourself, not to somebody else. Write your answers in the order they occur to you. Don't worry about logic or importance. Go along fairly fast. (Cousins, 1989, p. 126)

In accordance with the standard procedures for the Twenty Statements Test, these instructions were followed by 20 blank lines beginning with the words "I am." In addition to administering the Twenty Statements Test using standard procedures, Cousins (1989) also presented the

Tesuque Pueblo Eagle Dancer, New Mexico. In some non-Western societies, like Native American groups, the self is boundless in the sense that there are no rigid boundaries between the person and the community. Western societies, in contrast, emphasize personal responsibility, self-help, and personal independence and freedom. These values are central to the socialization process in the United States, giving the American self distinct boundaries.

Twenty Statements Test in a *contextualized* form, where the instructions to participants were "Describe yourself in the following situations" followed by the phrases "at home," "at school," and "with close friends."

The results of the standard test replicated previous research, showing that Japanese participants described the self less in abstract terms ("I am shy") and more in contextual ("I am shy at school") and relational ("I am shy with strangers") terms. However, this pattern of results was reversed in response to the contextualized test, where the participants could envisage the context and social relations more specifically. That is, the Japanese participants were more likely to provide more generalized abstract descriptions of the self when the context was already provided. These results suggest that the difference between Western and non-Western participants is not the outcome of different cognitive capabilities, but an outcome of cultural styles. Both groups can provide abstract descriptions of the self, but Westerners and non–Westerners do not provide such descriptions under the same conditions.

Self-Referent Behavior

. . . memory is personal.

—Frederic Bartlett,
Remembering

. . . a book which we read at a certain period does not merely remain for ever conjoined to what existed then around us; it remains also faithfully united to what we ourselves then were and thereafter it can be handled only by the . . . personality that were then ours. . . . If I see something which dates back from another period, it is a young man who comes to life.

—Marcel Proust, *Remembrance of Things Past*

John Locke (1632–1704) and James Mill (1773–1836) are among important philosophers to conceive of links between the self and memory. The experimental study of this link was first undertaken in the twentieth century by the English psychologist Sir Frederic Bartlett. More recently, researchers have investigated the effectiveness of memory under conditions of varying involvement of the self with a given task (Greenwald, 1981; Kaplan, 1986; Klein, Loftus, & Burton, 1989). In these studies, the "involvement" of the self has been achieved by asking participants to memorize and recall material more or less relevant to the sense of self. For example, in two of the most important early studies, participants rated how appropriate a series of about 40 adjectives, such as "shy" or "outgoing," were in describing themselves (Rogers, Kuiper, & Kirker, 1977). When participants were asked to make the ratings in response to the instruction "Indicate whether the word describes you," they recalled the material better than when they made the ratings in response to other instructions, such as "Rate whether you feel the word is long or short" and "Rate whether you feel the word has a rhythmic or lyrical sound."

The findings from this study are in line with a solid body of evidence that has accumulated in support of the **self-reference effect** (see Figure 3–4), the idea that people have more accurate recall of material that has been memorized with reference to the self (Bower & Gilligan, 1979; Hull & Levy, 1979; Lord, 1980; Rogers, 1981). This finding suggests a useful strategy for preparing for tests: personalize the material you need to learn; link it to your own experiences.

Examples of more specific cases of self-reference effects are the self-generation effect (Erdelyi, Buschke, & Finkelstein, 1977; Slamecka & Graf, 1978) and the ego-involvement effect (d'Ydewalle, Degryse, & De Corte, 1981). The **self-generation effect** refers to better retrieval of material that is actively generated by a person than material that is only passively encountered. For example, if Anne has to come up with a list of concepts as part of a solution to a problem, such an "actively generated" list is more easily retrieved by her on a later occasion than if she is provided with the same or a similar list.

self-reference effect the idea that people have more accurate recall of material that has been memorized with reference to the self.

self-generation effect better retrieval of material actively generated by the person than material that is only passively encountered.

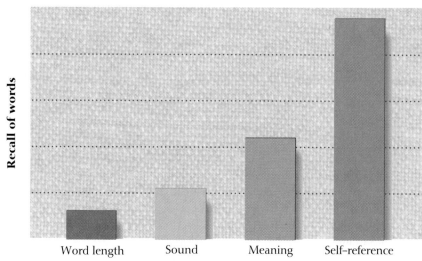

Figure 3–4 The self-reference effect (Rogers, Kuiper, & Kirker, 1977).

ego-involvement effect   better
retrieval of material associated
with an ongoing task than with a
completed task.

encodings   internal representations
of external phenomena.

The importance of active engagement with material to be learned and retrieved is also underlined by research on the **ego–involvement effect,** the better retrieval of material associated with an ongoing task than material associated with a completed task. For example, Anne learns two lists of words, list A and list B, and then completes two tasks associated with those lists. She is more likely to retrieve material accurately from a particular list while she is actively engaged in the task associated with that list than she is to recall material accurately from a list associated with a task already completed.

The self-reference effect has been the subject of some debate among researchers (Kihlstrom, Cantor, Albright, Chew, Klein, & Niedenthal, 1988). What explains the advantage of self-relevant material in memory? A first set of explanations revolves around cognitive processes (Greenwald & Pratkanis, 1984). First, self–relevant material may evoke more personally significant and more elaborate associative **encodings** (internal representations of external phenomena) than other material, such as material relevant to other persons. This is because associations linked to the sense of self are richer and more complex than associations linked to other persons. Second, perhaps self-relevant material is better recalled because it uses already established cognitive structures, principally self-schemas (representations of the self), that can then be used to guide recall. This second explanation employs the well–established rule that we can better remember material when we file it by category.

Because of the highly individualistic orientation of modern Western psychology, there is far more information about a *self*-reference effect than there is about a possible *group*-reference effect. Do people also recall information better if it refers to groups to which they belong—ingroups—as opposed to groups to which they do not belong—outgroups? Theories of intergroup relations lead us to expect this would be the case (see Chapter 14).

How Do I See Myself?

Our deeds determine us, as much as we determine our deeds.

—George Eliot, *Adam Bede*

In her brilliant novel *Adam Bede*, Mary Ann Evans, who published under the pseudonym George Eliot to escape sex discrimination in nineteenth-century England, points out that what people think of themselves to a large extent depends on how they behave, "their deeds." More recently, the U.S. social psychologist Daryl Bem (1972) elaborated on this idea, using the term **self-perception theory,** which proposes that when cues about their internal states seem confused or difficult to interpret, people explain how they feel and what they think by observing their own behavior. For example, Joe realizes that he has forgotten to call his friend and has also misplaced some keys, and these behaviors lead him to conclude that his thoughts must be preoccupied with a job interview scheduled for later that day. After the interview, he finds himself hurriedly drinking water, and concludes that he must have been very thirsty.

We now have empirical evidence to support the idea that under certain conditions people do look to their own behavior to determine beliefs about themselves (Fazio, 1987; Schlenker & Trudeau, 1990). In an intriguing study involving self-esteem, participants in one group were led to talk about themselves in flattering terms, while participants in another group were led to use more modest language for their self-descriptions. The first group scored higher on a subsequent test of self-esteem, suggesting that positive language really can be ego-boosting (Rhodewalt & Agustsdottir, 1986). But two conditions have to be met for this effect to take place. First, the person has to be uncertain about the aspect of the self in question. If Jane is uncertain about her own abilities as a group leader, then giving her the opportunity to talk about her leadership abilities in flattering terms is likely to be ego-boosting. But if she is certain that she is not a fast runner, then giving her an opportunity to talk in flattering terms about her running ability is unlikely to be ego-boosting. Second, the person has to believe that the behavior in question was not forced by the situation (Fazio, 1987).

Bem's self-perception theory is part of a literature that has evolved since the late 1960s in support of the counterintuitive idea that our views of ourselves are generally inaccurate. It seems that there are situations in which we may not, after all, be the ones with the most accurate knowledge about ourselves. Even when we do use our own behavior as the basis for understanding ourselves, argue Robin Vallacher and Daniel Wegner (1985), sometimes it is not our actual behavior, but our interpretations of that behavior that guide us. Such interpretations are highly subjective and can be misleading (Vallacher & Wegner, 1987).

These ideas raise a number of thorny issues, two of which will be considered here. First, what exactly is the role of introspection in self-perception? If we accept that our self-perceptions are influenced by how we interpret our own behavior, surely we also use introspection to know ourselves? People certainly *believe* that introspection into their personal thoughts and feelings yields more information about their true selves than can be achieved by attention to behavior

self-perception theory theory that when cues about their internal states seem confused, people explain how they feel and think by observing their own behavior.

(Anderson, 1987; Anderson & Ross, 1984), but is this belief correct in all situations?

The Role of Introspection in Self-Perception

Richard Nisbett and Timothy Wilson developed the highly controversial idea that we are to a large extent "strangers to ourselves" and that introspection can sometimes hinder self-knowledge (Nisbett & Wilson, 1977). In a series of experiments, these researchers manipulated the factors that (presumably) influenced participants' behavior and then gathered participants' own accounts of what influenced their behavior (Wilson, 1985; Wilson, Hull, & Johnson, 1981; Wilson & Nisbett, 1978; Wilson & Schooler, 1991). In one of their most famous studies, they recruited participants for what was supposed to be a survey of consumer preferences and asked them to select one of four nightgowns on display. Previous research had established that people typically prefer the item at the right to those on the left. Results from this study revealed the same trend, the implication being that participants were affected by the object's position. However, participants themselves offered a variety of other explanations for their choice, such as differences in quality, and were dismissive of the idea that serial position might have influenced their choices.

Nisbett and Wilson proposed that we explain our own behavior in the same way that we explain the behavior of others, by using theories we have about the causes of behavior. The vast majority of such theories are socially derived and shared by a community rather than being limited to one individual, and many such theories are actually correct. For example, after Anne succeeds in landing the job she wanted, she goes out to celebrate and feels euphoric. When a friend asks her what she is so happy about, Anne explains that it is because she has been offered a desirable job. Anne's friend may well share the same theory, that "landing a good job makes people happy," and accept her explanation. However, according to one interpretation this should not lead us to assume that Anne has privileged access to her own internal states. She may simply be interpreting her own feelings by applying generally held ideas about "causes" and behavior.

But can Nisbett and Wilson's proposition be tested directly? Some critics have argued no (Quattrone, 1985); that is, Nisbett and Wilson can claim to be supported both when the participants are wrong about what has influenced them, and when they are right. For example, participants could be correct not because of access to internal cognitive states, but because of some information they have about themselves that is not available to anyone else. Another fatal shortcoming of this research is that it should compare what actually influences behavior in a participant with what that participant believes influenced his or her behavior. Instead, researchers have often compared averages of what influenced a group of participants with averages of perceived influences (Kraut & Lewis, 1982). A further criticism is that the research only highlights biases in behavior, giving the impression that all human behavior must be irrational. We shall expand on this point after considering what motivates individuals to seek information about the self.

Do We Seek Accurate or Self-Enhancing Information?

A second fascinating question raised by self-perception theory concerns the type of information we seek about ourselves and, by implication, our motivation for seeking such information. In seeking this information, are we motivated to "know the truth" about ourselves, or to see ourselves in a better light? Leon Festinger's (1954) **social comparison theory** proposes that individuals evaluate their opinions and abilities by making comparisons with others. Festinger started with the observation that there are many areas of social life where "reality" cannot be adequately measured. For example, how well does Alex respond to the emotional needs of his friends? This question is far more difficult to answer than many others, such as "How tall is Alex?" This is because there are available objective measures of height (Alex is 5'10"), but no such objective measures for "responding to emotional needs of friends." Festinger argued that on issues that have no objective measures available, we attempt to avoid uncertainty by making social comparisons. Our goal, according to Festinger, is to know the self accurately. Studies conducted in the 1960s provided some support for this proposition (Suls & Wills, 1991).

The more recent research of Yaacov Trope (1980, 1983) and other scholars also shows that we often select specific tasks in order to arrive at a more accurate assessment of ourselves (e.g., Sorrentino & Roney, 1986). Particularly in situations in which people are uncertain about their abilities, they will select tasks that are neither too easy nor too difficult, in order to give themselves maximum feedback. If Tracy wants to know how good she is at mountain climbing, she will not tackle the little hill behind her house (too easy) or Mount Everest (much too difficult), but will try to climb a mountain that will test her abilities without being impossibly difficult.

Evidence has also emerged to suggest that in some situations people seek self-enhancing rather than accurate information. This is particularly true when the costs of gaining accurate information far outweigh the benefits (Brown & Dutton, 1995). First, if people are seeking accuracy, they should always prefer objective assessments of their abilities, and evidence suggests this is not the case. Social, "nonobjective" comparisons ("Did I climb faster than Tracy?") are sometimes used as a means of self-evaluation even when objective "reality tests" ("What was my time on the climb?") are available (Suls & Wills, 1991).

Moreover, comparison targets are not only selected to show oneself in a better light, but also to serve as "evidence" that "I deserve better treatment" (Taylor, Moghaddam, & Bellerose, 1989). When employees make demands for higher wages and better working conditions, they often cite cases of employees in other companies who receive better treatment ("We only get 2 weeks' vacation a year, but the employees of these three other major companies enjoy 4 weeks' paid vacation"). On the other hand, management is likely to select alternative comparison targets,

social comparison theory theory that when no objective measures are available, we compare ourselves with others in order to make more accurate self-evaluations.

Research on social comparisons reveals that particularly in situations of uncertainty we are likely to select certain tasks because they help us learn about our own limitations and potentials. A skier is likely to choose a slope that seems neither too easy nor too difficult, in order to get maximum feedback about her abilities. Some of us take the extra precaution of watching other skiers and only going down slopes selected by others who seem to be at the same level as ourselves.

and to highlight information supportive of its position ("We provide better working conditions than two rival companies in this area").

An important factor to keep in mind during this discussion is that "accuracy" tends to be defined subjectively. If Brian sees himself as having an unattractive personality, then he may only accept as "accurate" that information which endorses his own view of himself. Indeed, there is evidence from both laboratory (Swann, Hixon, Stein-Seroussi, & Gilbert, 1990) and field research (Swann, Hixon, & De La Ronde, 1992) that people with deeply held negative views of themselves prefer to interact with others who endorse these negative views.

Laboratory studies on this topic (reviewed by Swann, 1990) may be faulted for using participants who are strangers to one another, and thus may have little commitment to the relationship forged during a brief laboratory study. However, the field research by William Swann and his associates (Swann, Hixon, & De La Ronde, 1992) is particularly convincing because the participants were 95 married couples from 19 to 78 years of age. Participants with negative self-concepts were found to prefer partners who endorsed their own negative self-perceptions.

This line of research is intriguing because it seems to go against the generally accepted proposition that people are motivated to be positively evaluated by others. But another way of interpreting this research is that people positively value being judged correct, even if it means they are judged correct in their negative evaluations of themselves. It may be, after all, that they are presenting themselves positively: They are saying, "You see, I am right! You agree that I have an unattractive personality."

Evaluating Research on Self-Perception

Are we completely strangers to ourselves? Is it truly the case that we do not look within ourselves for information about how we feel and what we think, and when we do we arrive at wrong conclusions? Well, surely not. If our self-perceptions were biased to such an extent, we would be unable to make even simple decisions, such as whether to visit a doctor. It is useful to step back and distance ourselves from research on self-perception and to consider its findings in broader perspective.

The most important achievement of self-perception research has been to alert us to examples of how social thinking can be biased. Since the 1970s, numerous studies of social cognition (Fiske & Taylor, 1991) have contributed to this picture of humans as biased, irrational thinkers. But we should keep in mind that the behaviors reported in this research often depict what can sometimes take place, rather than what ordinarily does take place. For example, the finding that introspection can sometimes hinder self-knowledge (Nisbett & Wilson, 1977) is intriguing, but we should not conclude from this that *as a general rule* introspection hinders self-knowledge. If this were the case, then it would be absurd to ask such questions as "How are you feeling?" or "What do you think?"

Concepts and Issues

Researchers have shown the self in Western cultures to be more autonomous and bounded, as compared to the interdependent self found in some non-Western cultures. There is controversy about the sources of information we use to understand ourselves: Do we learn about ourselves through introspection or by using our own behavior as a guide? We seem to rely more on behavior when we are unsure about our inner experiences. Self-enhancing information is sometimes preferred over accurate information. Research shows that such biases can come about, rather than what ordinarily does happen.

1. Participants in some non-Western societies have been found to provide more contextualized, concrete descriptions of the self. Is this because they are less capable of abstract representations? Explain.
2. What is the self-reference effect?
3. What does self-perception theory propose?
4. Why would we seek self-enhancing rather than accurate information about the self?

Self-Presentation

> Reputation is an idle, and most false imposition;
> oft got without merit, and lost without deserving.
>
> —Iago in *Othello*, act II, scene 3

> Good name in man, and woman, dear my lord,
> Is the immediate jewel of their souls.
>
> —Iago in *Othello*, act III, scene 3

In Shakespeare's tragedy *Othello*, the cunning Iago, who thinks himself a rival to the hero, Othello, argues at one time that reputation is worthless, and at another time that it *is* a person's most important asset. But there *is* consistency in his behavior, in the sense that he changes his argument to suit the situation so that he may always present himself as honest and credible. Although the views he expresses change, his goals in self-presentation remain consistent.

Unlike Iago, who deceives Othello into distrusting his own wife and makes him insanely jealous so he finally kills her, the vast majority of people are not motivated to destroy others. However, most people do attempt to present a particular image of themselves to others, and they also invest a lot of time and energy in developing such an image. Consider the detailed attention people in modern societies give to their appearance. Carol Jackson (1981) is among the numerous consultants who organize classes to teach people how to arrange their self-presentations:

> At these . . . classes, we analyze each client's coloring, give her a packet of fabric swatches in her color palette, and teach her how to use them as a guide for shopping and looking beautiful. We spend one session on in-

A young man practices a job interview; it is videotaped for later review. A lot of professional help is available for people to better manage their self-presentations in public. Before going for an interview for a job or as part of a graduate school application, individuals can practice, using interview scripts. The practice takes place backstage. They can then review their performances and get feedback on how to present themselves more effectively as future lawyers, sales managers, and so on. When people move to the front stage, successful self-presentation requires that they first identify the norms and rules appropriate for a given role.

dividual makeup, another on hair, one on personality and style, and one on wardrobe planning. (pp. 10–11)

From such descriptions, one might imagine that "image consultants" such as Ms. Jackson are preparing people to perform as actors and actresses in a theater, rather than to present themselves in real life. Real life as drama is exactly the metaphor that is used in the **dramaturgical model,** as developed by Ervin Goffman (1959, 1971) and some other researchers and used to explain self-presentation. After reviewing this dramaturgical approach to studying self-presentation, we shall discuss research by Mark Snyder (1974, 1987) and other social psychologists who focus on presentational styles.

dramaturgical model   a model of self-presentation, based on a metaphor of life as drama, which holds that we perform or present ourselves in different ways in different contexts, according to the norms of that context.

The Dramaturgical Model

Imagine a distant relative has arrived in town and invited you for dinner at an exclusive restaurant this evening (we all wish for such relatives!). The limousine will pick you up at eight o'clock sharp. After asking around, you discover that the restaurant is very formal. You rush out and buy a new outfit for the occasion, and arrive at the restaurant that evening looking suitably elegant. The doorman at the restaurant turns out to be a student who had a room on your dormitory floor last year. Whenever he saw you on campus you were wearing jeans and a sweater. The wine steward is also a part-time student who recognizes you. However, they both address you very formally. The headwaiter shows you to your table with proper pomp and respect, and you proceed to review the menu.

Why is it that the doorman does not "give you five" and tell you the latest joke, as had always been his custom when you met him on campus? Why does the wine steward not ask how things are going at school? Why are you sitting at the dinner table as if it were routine for you to dress formally and to review glossy menus written in French as a string quintet plays Mozart in the background?

The explanation, according to the dramaturgical model, is that you are performing on "front stage," in a theatrical piece known in Western culture as "going to a high-status restaurant." The people serving you—the doorman, the wine steward, the busboy—are all part of what Goffman refers to as your "team." They share a working consensus with you, treating you the way you expect to be treated while you play this part. The scenery and props on this stage consist of tables, chairs, fine linens, a small platform for the musicians, and flowers and various other decorations (Figure 3–5).

"Front stage" is where the two groups of players—guests and restaurant personnel—put on their performances. According to Goffman, it is essential that everyone agrees about the definition of the situation because only then can people know which norms should be followed. In this instance, the context is that of a high-status restaurant, and everyone is following the norms that prescribe appropriate behavior in this setting. There is also a "backstage," consisting of the kitchen

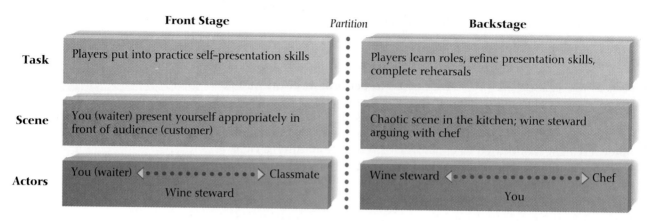

	Front Stage	*Partition*	**Backstage**
Task	Players put into practice self-presentation skills		Players learn roles, refine presentation skills, complete rehearsals
Scene	You (waiter) present yourself appropriately in front of audience (customer)		Chaotic scene in the kitchen; wine steward arguing with chef
Actors	You (waiter) ◀•••••••••••••••▶ Classmate Wine steward		Wine steward ◀•••••••••••••••▶ Chef You

Figure 3–5   High and low self-monitors and dating partners (Snyder & Simpson, 1984).

and all other areas where those preparing and serving the food are honing their performances.

A lot happens backstage that will not be revealed front stage. For example, the wine steward has just had a fight with the head chef, and both of them have set upon an unfortunate busboy who made a remark about the chef being drunk. But as soon as the wine steward is called upon to renew his performance front stage, he straightens up, smooths back his hair, puts on his "I have just inspected our magnificent wine cellar" look, and glides out front stage with sufficient seriousness and pomp so that the guests will continue to be impressed by his carefully chosen words about the best wine to have with their meals this evening.

While you are front stage, the wine steward treats you as an elegantly dressed guest, and you treat him as a sophisticated wine steward. But when you meet him on the way to the washroom, you both stop to talk and catch up with old news. For those few minutes, you are speaking to one another as fellow students, gossiping about mutual friends who were in your class last year. The instant the two of you go back front stage, however, the context of the restaurant takes over and you resume your performances as guest and wine steward.

Performance and Social Norms

All performances, then, take place within particular contexts and follow the social norms of those contexts. For example, your performance in the restaurant took place in line with norms about how one should conduct oneself in high-status restaurants. But we should keep in mind that such norms change over time, and this means that how one should behave in order to present a positive image also changes. John Kasson (1990) has pointed out that during the Middle Ages guides about how to dine in "good company" included such suggestions as "Do not blow your nose with the same hand that you use to hold the meat" (p. 10). But dining had become more genteel by the nineteenth century, so that an etiquette adviser in 1845 suggested to Americans that if it becomes necessary to put a knife in the mouth, the edge should be turned downward (Kasson, 1990, p. 192).

Norms for self-presentation can vary even more dramatically across cultures. Consider the use we make of personal names as an example. While at the restaurant, your relative introduces you to an old friend of his, and this introduction involves an exchange of names. In many societies, particularly those of North America, it is considered essential for people to introduce themselves by their names. The exchange of names, the learning of other people's names, the referring to others and oneself by the use of names, are all aspects of the self-presentation process. We are pleased when our names are remembered, and sometimes go to enormous trouble to publicize our names, to achieve fame. In our societies, a famous name—such as Michael Jordan, Madonna, or Pelé—can be of great economic benefit because it can be used to sell all kinds of products and services.

But consider the experience of Napoleon Chagnon (1992), who spent many years studying the Yanomamo people in South America. During the first 5 months of his stay in a Yanomamo village, Chagnon worked hard to learn the names of all the villagers. What he had not discovered at this early stage in his field research was that the Yanomamo have a strict taboo against mentioning the names of prominent people as well as the names of all dead relatives and friends. An important mark of prestige among the Yanomamo is the respect people show you by *not* mentioning your name publicly.

After the Yanomamo realized that Chagnon was intent on learning their names, which amounted to an attack on their prestige, the entire village participated in a brilliant scheme to teach Chagnon a lesson by giving him false names for each person. It was not until much later, after Chagnon visited another village, that he discovered he had been tricked into learning scores of ridiculous names fabricated especially for him. Imagine the fun the Yanomamo had when they introduced the headman's brother to this troublesome white man as "eagle shit," his son as "asshole," and his daughter as "fart breath," trying hard to control their laughter as they made Chagnon repeat these names.

The Tiwi of North Australia also have a name taboo, which works in the following manner. Whenever a husband dies and a widow remarries, the names given to their children by the earlier husband become taboo and new names are given to all the children by the new husband. Because most women become widows several times, the children acquire several new names over their lives, and each time the former names become taboo (see Hart, Pilling, & Goodale, 1988). Consequently, in Tiwi culture the self is introduced using the most recently given name, and names given by the now deceased fathers or stepfathers are abandoned—even by elders.

Performance style refers to the manner in which individuals present themselves. Although the norms appropriate in a given situation influence individuals, there will still be variation in the ways in which different people perform within the same situation. The style in which you would present yourself in an exclusive restaurant is in some ways

performance style the manner in which individuals present themselves.

different from how your best friends would present themselves. We can think of such performance styles as having three different components: the strategies used for self-presentation, the complexity of the self, and the relative focus on factors internal and external to the self.

Self-Presentation Strategies

Various strategies are available to give an effective "performance" front stage. Edward Jones (1990) has described a range of such strategies (see Table 3–1), from the benign, such as "supplication" (beseech others, so as to be seen as weak), to the more dangerous, such as "intimidation" (threaten others, so as to be seen as dangerous). Jones's research suggests that individuals are able to alter their performances subtly for different strategies, but that some strategies are more difficult to implement than others. For example, in one study (Godfrey, Jones, & Lord, 1986) participants met for two "get-acquainted" conversations about a week apart. Before the second meeting, one set of participants was randomly taken aside and given the task of either promoting themselves or getting the other person to like them. Results showed that the ingratiators did succeed in being liked more by the other participant, and they seemed to do this mainly by speaking less (presumably, this meant they also gave the impression of listening more). But not only did the self-promoters fail to be seen as more competent during the second session, they were also liked less. Thus, at least for these undergraduate participants, ingratiation was an easier strategy to implement than self-promotion. Moreover, the latter strategy seemed to involve greater risks.

Jones has pointed out that each strategy carries risks. Ingratiation and intimidation are perhaps the most direct strategies, but a person who overdoes ingratiation risks being seen as a bootlicker, someone who panders to others and is not to be trusted to give an honest opinion on any subject. An attempt to intimidate others can backfire, with the risk that the person making threats is seen as a windbag. Self-promotion is also a common strategy, but a clumsy performance can lead to a person being seen as a fraud, a big head, rather than competent.

Table 3–1	Self-Presentation Strategies		
Strategy	**Behavior**	**Outcome Sought**	**Risk**
Ingratiation	Be affectionate, flatter, agree	Be seen as likable	Be seen as a bootlicker
Intimidation	Threaten	Be seen as dangerous	Be seen as a blusterer
Self-promotion	Boast	Be seen as competent	Be seen as a fraud
Exemplification	Self-sacrifice	Be seen as morally superior	Be seen as a hypocrite
Supplication	Beseech help	Be seen as helpless	Be seen as undeserving

Source: Jones (1990).

Some celebrities publicize their personal problems, as did the late Princess Diana when she told the world about her battle with bulimia. A consequence of this "coming out" may be self-handicapping (even though it may be an unintended consequence): The celebrity's self-image may be protected by a handy excuse for failure.

More unusual are the strategies of exemplification and supplication. We all know people who don the mantle of saintliness, but such individuals run the risk of being seen as sanctimonious and hypocritical. Finally, when all else fails, people can parade their weaknesses in the hope that others will help them overcome their handicap. Sometimes a handicap may not only result in a person receiving help from others but also in getting additional credit for their efforts and outcomes (Leary & Shepperd, 1986). I recently saw this in action when a student complimented her friend: "That was an amazing feat, getting a D+ and not an F when you had such a hangover from the party last night." Because this strategy can be effective, people sometimes engage in **self-handicapping** (Jones & Berglas, 1978), an attempt to explain poor performance as being due to shortcomings such as drinking rather than to lack of ability. If they drink and then fail, for example, the failure must be due to the drink; if they succeed, then they must be exceptionally

self-handicapping an attempt to explain poor performance as due to shortcomings rather than lack of ability.

talented, because they succeeded despite a handicap. But there is also risk in such strategies, with the possible outcome of the "handicapped" person being seen as lazy and undeserving.

In addition to the individualistic strategies described by Jones, there are also a number of group-related self-presentation strategies. The self derives an important part of its social status through membership in social groups. Consequently, individuals are motivated to be associated with groups that enjoy positive status, to be counted among the "winners" rather than "losers." This leads individuals to associate themselves more with a group when it is winning and less when it is losing. College students bask in the glory of a winning football team by talking about "our team" and how "we" scored the winning touchdown, but tend to distance themselves from a losing team and describe how "they" fumbled the ball at a critical stage in the game (Cialdini & Richardson, 1980).

Self-Complexity and Culture

self-complexity the number of ways in which people think of themselves.

The self also tends to vary across cultures in terms of its complexity. **Self-complexity** refers to the numbers of ways in which people think of themselves (Linville, 1985, 1987). For example, Mariam thinks of herself as an engineer, a mother, a wife, a volunteer in political organizations, a member of the parent-teacher association, and a founding member of a choral group. In contrast, Samantha thinks of herself as a homemaker. In the language of role theory, Mariam sees herself as having many different social roles, whereas Samantha thinks of herself as having only one.

Linville (1985) has provided evidence in support of the proposition that individuals with high levels of self-complexity cope better with stressful life events because if one aspect of their lives is not positive, then that may be compensated for by other aspects. If things do not go well at home for Mariam, who has high self-complexity, she could console herself by concentrating on her successes in other domains, such as in her career as an engineer. For Samantha, who has low self-complexity, it is more difficult to compensate for an unsatisfactory home life because she thinks of herself exclusively as a homemaker. Linville's self-complexity model seems to be supported by research suggesting that professional women who are married and have children are more content than those who devote themselves exclusively to their careers (Roskies & Carrier, 1992).

The variety of roles available to individuals tends to differ across cultures. The range of roles available to women is particularly limited in Islamic societies because the mother role is their major role and they do not have available such roles as engineer or judge. This suggests that self-complexity is also lower for women in Islamic societies compared to Western societies. The same is true for members of cultural minorities that have maintained traditional lifestyles in the United States, such as the Amish (Hostetler, 1980). Linville's proposition that self-complexity can act as a buffer against the negative impact of stressful life events suggests that such a buffer is more available to individuals living in so-cieties in which higher self-complexity is the norm.

The self can also be more or less complex in terms of conceptions of actual and ideal selves. Most, though not all, individuals are able to describe an "ideal" self, reflecting the self they desire to be, as opposed to the "actual" self that they see themselves to be at present (Wojciszke, 1987). Using self-discrepancy theory, Tory Higgins and his associates (Higgins 1987, 1989; Higgins, Tykocinski, & Vookles, 1990; Strauman & Higgins, 1987) have made a further elaboration, identifying not only actual and ideal selves but also an "ought" self, the self we think we should be, and "can" selves, possible future selves we could be. Higgins has examined consequences arising from discrepancies among "actual," "ideal," "ought," and "can" selves. For example, the perception that one cannot close the gap between one's actual self (member of college in-tramural tennis team) and ideal self (nationally ranked tennis player) produced feelings of helplessness. In contrast, the realization that one will not become the company president, as one's parents believe ought to happen, led to anxiety.

Focus of Attention and Self-Presentation

Whereas the dramaturgical model is concerned with the strategies peo-ple use to present themselves, another group of researchers has studied what individuals making self-presentations focus on. Think about your own actions when you are interacting with others: Do you focus on your own feelings and thoughts, or do you focus on the surroundings? A first issue is differences between people who focus more on internal factors and those who focus more on external factors. A second issue is the effect of focusing on factors internal and external to the self during self-presentation.

Self-Monitoring.   The depiction of people as "performers" seems to be more valid when applied to some individuals than others. We can all think of individuals among our friends who are "performers" in the sense that Goffman describes, in that they present themselves very much in accordance with the norms of a given situation and are skillful at changing their performance to suit different situations. We can also think of people we know who "stay themselves," changing very little, if at all, across situations. Such individuals seem unaffected by changes in norms across contexts.

Mark Snyder (1974, 1987) has developed a psychological instrument, a "self-monitoring scale" consisting of 25 questions, to identify these two contrasting types of individuals (an 18-question version of this in-strument is also available; see Snyder & Gangestad, 1986). High self-monitors attempt to say and do things others will like. They even prefer to switch their dating partners to get a better match with the situation (Snyder & Simpson, 1984). Joe, a high self-monitor, knows that Sheila is not very serious or knowledgeable about politics, and decides not to take her to a party given by his activist friends (Figure 3–6). Instead, he

self-monitoring   being aware of how to present the self in a given situation and changing self-presentation to fit the situation.

Figure 3–6 High and low self-monitors and dating partners (Snyder & Simpson, 1984).

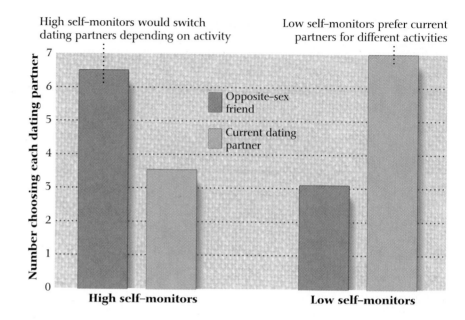

High self-monitors would switch dating partners depending on activity

Low self-monitors prefer current partners for different activities

takes Joan to the party, because she is interested in politics and will fit in much better. Kate, a low self-monitor, takes her boyfriend to the same party even though her boyfriend has no interest in politics. She does not try to find a partner who will fit in with the situation.

Additionally, high self-monitors can talk in an off-the-cuff manner about issues they really know little about, generally put on a show to impress people, sometimes appear to be experiencing deeper emotions than they really are, tend to act like different persons when they are in different situations and with different people, generally do what others expect of them, and are particularly effective at deceiving others. In contrast, low self-monitors find it hard to imitate the behavior of other people, tend to show their true feelings and beliefs by their behavior, are not good entertainers, are not particularly good at making other people like them, and find it difficult to change their behavior to suit different people and different situations. In sum, high self-monitors "act the part" given to them and change with the situation, whereas low self-monitors stay true to themselves and change little with the demands of the situation.

A large body of evidence suggests that high self-monitors are particularly skilled at identifying social cues and adapting their behavior to do what is expected in the given situation (Snyder, 1987). In some contexts, doing what is expected may require nonconformist behavior. For example, in one study students joined discussion groups in settings designed to give the impression that different norms operate (Snyder & Monson, 1975). In the first setting, the discussions were held in a room equipped with videotape cameras and other equipment, and the participants were informed that tapes of the discussions would be shown to undergraduate classes. In this setting, the social cues highlighted the performance of the participants before the wider audience of undergraduates, who presumably favored autonomy in the face of group

Bill Clinton and Al Gore campaigning for president and vice president in 1992. Politicians often act as high self-monitors, changing themselves to fit the norms and rules of the local society. To observers, they may seem to change so much and so often that it is difficult to identify a stable core.

pressure. In the second setting, the discussions took place in a room furnished only with a table and chairs, and only those present would see the performances. In this private setting, social cues seemed to highlight conformity to the norms of the group present. High self-monitors proved to be particularly sensitive to the different cues available in these two situations. They showed autonomy in the public discussions and conformity in the private discussions.

Snyder has suggested that societies which place a high value on rule following and role enactment, such as the Japanese, may also socialize a larger proportion of high self-monitors. However, the relation between self-monitoring and culture is likely to be complicated by the issue of focus of attention.

Inner and Outer Focus of Attention.   While the self-monitoring scale seeks to identify the characteristics of individuals who attend to factors external to themselves, Robert Wicklund and his associates (Wicklund, 1975; Wicklund & Frey, 1980) have focused more generally on the consequences of **objective self-awareness**—the state of self-focused attention. Through a variety of procedures, such as placing mirrors in front of participants while they carried out given tasks, and by using videotapes,

objective self-awareness   the state of self-focused attention.

audiotapes, and live audiences, Wicklund and others have created experimental settings in which participants become objectively self-aware. Wicklund has argued that participants in such situations are influenced because objective self-awareness makes them more conscious of their own internal standards and leads them to try to conform to these standards. For example, dieters who were made to feel that their eating was noticed by researchers ate less than dieters who were not provided this cue (Polivy, Herman, Hackett, & Kuleshnyk, 1986). Thus, perhaps one way to become more successful at dieting is to imagine what relevant others would think and say if they saw you eating.

Wicklund's explanation is appealing because it gives a central place to personal standards, so that objective self-awareness may lead to different behaviors in the same setting. For example, research suggests that women sometimes eat less in front of men in order to present themselves as appropriately feminine (Pliner & Chaiken, 1990). However, presumably a feminist army captain may eat more in front of the men under her command just to behave counter to the stereotype. Although Wicklund's explanation leaves room for different behaviors in the same situation, because it gives importance to personal standards, it has been criticized because it fails to specify which standards will influence behavior (Liebling, Seiler, & Shaver, 1975). This criticism is particularly important because the same individual may hold conflicting standards, leaving us to wonder which standard will be used as a result of objective self-awareness.

Concepts and Issues

How we go about presenting ourselves to others depends largely on cultural norms and rules as well as our personal inclinations. A useful way of conceptualizing this process is in terms of Goffman's dramaturgical model, which depicts real life as drama. Our performance style will vary in terms of the strategies we use, the complexity of the self we present, and our focus on factors internal and external to the self.

1. Using Goffman's dramaturgical model, describe the steps you would take to prepare for a job interview at a law firm.
2. Describe five self-presentation strategies.
3. Will a high or a low self-monitor attempt to say and do things others will like? Explain.
4. How do we know that objective self-awareness makes people more conscious of internal standards?

Conclusion

The truly universal aspect of the self seems to be that in all known human societies it is normal for individuals to believe that they exist as persons within single bodies. Beyond this basic feature, the self seems to vary in fundamental ways across cultures. The bounded, self-contained self of Western societies stands in contrast to the diffuse, interdependent self found in traditional societies. Self-presentation follows the norms present in given contexts and also tends to be heavily influenced by cultural norms. Although some individuals seem to be more skilled than others in following self-presentation norms, the desire to be positively evaluated by others seems to be shared by everyone. Indeed, this desire may itself prove to be a universal feature of social behavior.

For Review

The self is the totality of an individual's personal experiences. A distinction can be made between the independent self, found predominantly in Western societies, and the interdependent self, which is far more prevalent in Eastern societies and among minority communities in the West. The independent self is highly individualistic and self-contained, while the interdependent self is more diffuse and dependent on social relations.

Three aspects of the self can be distinguished: a sense of self, self-perception, and self-presentation. A sense of self and self-perception are subjective and cannot be directly observed from the outside, but self-presentation is observable and, indeed, is manipulated as part of performances for others.

The sense of self is characterized by singularity of personhood within a single body (the feeling that you are a single person existing in one body), as well as continuity of being (the belief that you are the same person who started to read this chapter two hours ago). The former seems to be a true universal, but a few exceptions have been found to the latter. Continuity of the self is not assumed in all societies.

A number of procedures have been used to explore the internal structure of the unitary self. Research suggests that within the self there are conversations between *I*'s and *Me*'s as well as between the self and imagined others.

Both the structure assumed for the self and the sense of self are greatly influenced by culture. Westerners tend to describe themselves as "bounded" independent individuals, whereas non-Westerners describe themselves more as diffuse and interdependent community members.

Daryl Bem asserts in self-perception theory that we know ourselves by observing our own behavior rather than by looking inside ourselves. A great deal of evidence has accumulated to suggest that in some situations "looking inside" in order to know ourselves can lead to incorrect conclusions.

According to Goffman's dramaturgical model, individuals follow social norms to play their roles as parts of teams. They practice their performances backstage, and enjoy the collusion of other team members when they perform front stage.

Performance style refers to how individuals use self-presentational strategies, such as ingratiation, intimidation, self-promotion, exemplification, and supplication. Each strategy involves potential payoffs as well as risks.

Individuals tend to differ in self-complexity (the number of ways they think of themselves); in self-discrepancy (the discrepancies they experience between their actual, ideal, can, and ought selves); and self-monitoring (the extent to which they focus on inner and outer aspects of themselves).

For Discussion

1. "The renewed interest in the self seems to have been made possible by the demise of behaviorism, yet self-perception theory shows the continued influence of behaviorism." Explain and discuss this statement.

2. Describe some ways in which the self varies across cultures, as well as any consistencies in the self across cultures.

3. Imagine you are at a party with two friends who have very different performance styles. Describe how each of them might behave.

Key Terms

Deindividuation 69

Dramaturgical model 81

Ego-involvement effect 74

Encodings 74

Independent self 59

Interdependent self 59

Looking-glass self 67

Memory structure 66

Objective self-awareness 89

Performance style 83

Schema 66

Self 58

Self-complexity 86

Self-confrontational method 64

Self-generation effect 73

Self-handicapping 85

Self-monitoring 87

Self-perception theory 75

Self-reference effect 73

Self-schema 66

Social comparison theory 77

Annotated Readings

For another perspective on traditional research on the self, see R. F. Baumeister, Self and identity: An introduction, in *Advanced social psychology*, ed. A. Tesser (New York: McGraw-Hill, 1995), pp. 51–98.

Two lively, and controversial, treatments of the self are R. Harré, *Singularities of self* (London: Sage, 1997); and R. A. Wicklund and M. Eckert, *The self-knower: A hero under control* (New York: Plenum Press, 1992).

For examples of research on self and culture, see N. R. Rosenberger, ed., *Japanese sense of self* (Cambridge: Cambridge University Press, 1992).

Also of interest is the series of papers in the Special Section on self and culture in the *Journal of Cross Cultural Psychology*, Vol. 26, no. 6 (1995).

The Self

The developing child sets off on a two-pronged journey of discovery and creativity: inward to create and map out a self within; and outward to construct and present a self to others. The journeys are interconnected. Other people act as a mirror, allowing the person to use the reflection to arrive at a detailed picture of the self. This "looking-glass self" begins to emerge from the very first days of life, as mother, father, and others interact with the infant. The 9½-month-old child looking in a mirror is already well along the path of constructing a self. At a much later stage, around 18 months, the infant develops the ability to recognize herself in the reflection of a mirror.

This 9½-month-old infant will be twice as old by the time he can recognize himself in the mirror.

But how we see ourselves, whether in the reflections of a real mirror or in those of a society acting as a mirror for the looking-glass self, is biased. Research in Western societies suggests that individuals exaggerate the positive aspects of the self and minimize the negative aspects. Individuals in some non-Western cultures tend to be less flattering in their self-perceptions. They are less likely to express an "I am number one" attitude, and more likely to point out faults in themselves.

But these are probably surface differences, and underlying them seems to be a more profound similarity. In each case, the self-concept develops and self-presentation strategies evolve in line with norms and rules about correct behavior. In the United States particularly, the correct way to behave is to present the self as positive, active, successful, and happy. The same style of behavior would be considered brash, and even conceited, in some other cultures, where the correct way to present the self is more subdued, even humble.

Miao women of Guizhou, China, in traditional dress that includes intricate silver jewelry indicating wealth and status. The concept of the "looking-glass self" suggests that we come to know ourselves through our assumptions about how others see us.

Correct self-presentation for Muslim women.

Correct self-presentation for Yanomamo women.

95

This difference is related to the tremendous emphasis placed on uniqueness in U.S. culture. Whereas in some non-Western cultures conformity and staying in line is valued (in Japan, for example, "the nail that sticks out is knocked back in"), in the United States being different, achieving a "one-of-a-kind" status, is prized. Countless advertisements encourage Americans to "be different." From one perspective, there seems to be irony in this advertising, because purchasing "brand Z" is often touted as the way to be different—even though several million others also use the same product. But the

Correct formal greeting behavior in the Western style. Note the upright posture, head held high, and the confident and positive face, with hands outstretched and eyes fixed on the other person.

appeal of the message is so powerful that such contradictions are swept aside. Brand Z jeans make Joe feel different, and his car makes him feel like a maverick, even though lots of others around him wear the same brand of jeans and drive the same model car.

More traditional non-Western societies also influence self-presentation, even without modern advertising techniques. By looking across cultures, we discover the enormous variety of normative systems that influence self-presentation. Consider the issue of "proper dress," for example. In Islamic societies, the correct way for women to dress in public is to cover themselves from head to foot, so that only their hands and faces (in some stricter societies, only small parts of their faces) show. This is viewed as the "natural" way to behave. A Muslim woman who reveals her uncovered head in public, or worse, appears on the beach in a bikini, is severely punished. But the Yanomamo of the Amazon jungle also believe they are behaving naturally when they appear in public wearing just a loincloth, apart from intricate tattoos on their bodies. They are in fact almost naked, but dressed correctly according to their norms.

These Japanese women are dressed Western-style but greet one another in traditional manner. Note the bowed heads, eyes looking down, lowered shoulders, and hands tucked neatly back with feet together.

Hispanic men greeting one another in Passaic, New Jersey. Note the close physical embrace, the direct eye contact, the broad smiles. Their behavior suggests the interdependent self, although they now live in an individualistic culture.

Men greeting one another in a Moroccan *souk*. Note the bowed heads and close proximity of the bodies, with the lower-status male kissing the hand of the other.

Important aspects of self–presentation are also captured in greeting behavior. A universal aspect of this situation seems to be that people everywhere greet one another face–to–face. (I know of no society where the norm is for people of equal status to greet one another by turning their backs on one another.) But beyond this basic similarity, there is tremendous variety. Even though at least the affluent sectors of many non–Western societies have adopt-ed Western–style clothing, they have often retained their traditional greeting behavior (as in the case of Japan, for example, or of immigrants in new cultures).

Another possible universal in greeting behavior is a show of deference by the lower–status person toward the higher–status person. This show of deference also varies across cultures. In many Eastern and North African cultures, the practice of men kissing the hand or part of the clothing of a higher–status person is common. In Western societies, higher–status individuals are more likely to initiate, direct, and decide the end of a dialogue.

Another visible cross–cultural difference concerns the amount of physical contact. Physical contact is at a minimum when men meet other men in Western societies, but some ethnic minorities have brought their traditions of high physical contact with them. In neigh-borhoods occupied by Hispanics and other minorities in North America, by Turks in Germany, and by North Africans in France, for example, greetings between men involve a lot of physical contact.

CHAPTER 4

Attitudes

◄ An essential feature of democratic societies is that people are free to demonstrate their attitudes toward issues and to try to persuade others of the correctness of their evaluations. A puzzle for social psychologists is the relationships between attitudes and behavior. Why does person A behave in accordance with her attitude, but person B, who holds similar attitudes, does not?

*T*hings looked pretty bad for me. It was late, it was cold, and it was raining. I was lost, and my car had broken down in what seemed like the middle of nowhere in Vermont (I later learned I had been just south of the Canadian border). After several hours, help arrived in the shape of a tow truck, and before long I found shelter in a small gas station. The driver told me I could wait until morning for the mechanic to arrive, or pay him an extra $100 to fix my car right away. I suggested $50. He hesitated. We eventually settled on $80. It would take about an hour he said, and directed me to what he referred to as "the office," situated next to the garage. The office turned out to be a poky little room stuffed with old files, empty cans, and posters. The walls were covered with fading photographs of classic cars. In one corner was a television set whose picture seemed to be suffering from the hiccups; in another was a middle-aged man who I guessed to be the night attendant. He nodded to me and cleared off newspapers from a chair so I could sit down.

For about 10 minutes neither of us spoke. I tried to adjust my eyes to the random flickering of the television screen. He was watching the final part of *Lonesome Dove*, a series based on Larry McMurtry's best-selling novel about the American West. When it ended, he turned to me and said:

"If only our politicians were like that."

"Like what?" I asked hesitantly.

"True to their word. When Captain Call said he would do something, he kept his word. Our politicians say one thing and then do something else. That's why I never vote for them."

"None of them?"

"Nuh . . . never vote for none of them. They all talk one way before the elections, then act a different way after the elections. What's the use if you can't tell what a person is going to do from what he says?"

I suppose my expression suggested interest in what he was saying, and he went on, "If I say I hate cigarettes and alcohol, my words should tell you what I am going to do. If you find me smoking and drinking, then something is wrong. I am not keeping my word."

He repeated the phrase "keeping my word," then sank back into his chair and proceeded to read his newspaper. His words stayed with me after my car was repaired and on the road again. During the many hours of driving I still had ahead of me that night, I pondered the relationship between expressed attitudes and behavior: our verbal evaluations of something and our actual behavior on the matter. This is one of the most thoroughly examined issues in social psychology; nevertheless, despite considerable progress, a lot of puzzles remain.

The ABCs of Attitudes

Social psychologists have come to a general consensus about some aspects of **attitudes**—evaluations of themselves, other people, events, issues, and material things, with some degree of favor and disfavor (Eagly & Chaiken, 1992; Petty & Cacioppo, 1996; Petty & Krosnick, 1995; Pratkanis, Breckler, & Greenwald, 1989). What do you think of politicians? Do you like hot weather? Do you support stronger gun control

attitude evaluation of oneself, other people, events, issues, and material things, with some degree of favor and disfavor.

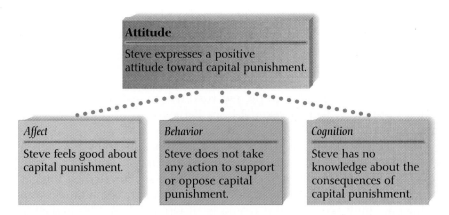

Figure 4–1 The ABCs of attitudes.

legislation? What do you think of the United Nations? In answering these kinds of questions we are expressing our attitudes. Each attitude can be based on feelings or *affects*, "I feel convinced that capital punishment is wrong"; *behaviors*, "I must be against capital punishment because I went on a march to end it"; and *cognitions*, "capital punishment is not an effective deterrent." We can think of these as the *ABCs of attitudes* (see Figure 4–1).

Part of the complexity of attitudes arises from the relationship among affect, behavior, and cognition, which reflects the structure of attitudes (Chaiken & Stangor, 1987; Olson & Zanna, 1993; Petty, 1995; Tesser & Shaffer, 1990). An attitude can be based on one, or two, or all three of the ABCs.

When he hears on the radio that a death sentence is going to be carried out in his state next week, Steve feels good and expresses his positive attitude toward capital punishment. But this attitude may have little to do with behavior (he has never taken any action related to capital punishment, such as signing a petition or joining a march) or cognition (he has no knowledge about issues related to capital punishment, such as whether or not it is an effective deterrent).

Although social psychologists have had differing views about the roles of affect, behavior, and cognition in shaping attitudes, there has been a long history of agreement that attitudes serve important functions (Petty & Cacioppo, 1996). Attitudes serve a *knowledge function*, helping individuals to understand and make sense of the world. As we encounter people, events, issues, and other things in the world every day, our evaluations of what we encounter are immediately available. We do not have to invest time constructing an evaluation each time we come across something. Efficiency is also improved by attitudes giving expression to our values, thus serving a *value-expressive function*. When Steve lets Jane know about his pro–capital punishment attitude, it tells her about the kinds of values he holds. Attitudes also serve an *ego-defensive function*, helping people to achieve a more positive identity (but not always in constructive ways). When Jim expresses negative attitudes toward Hispanics, he makes himself feel superior to them (we discuss this topic in greater detail in Chapter 14).

For some individuals, attitudes serve an important *social-adjustive function*, enabling them to get rewards from other people. When Caroline meets members of her boyfriend's environmental activist group, she expresses proenvironment attitudes and wins their approval. Caroline may be high on self-monitoring (Chapter 3), being a person who changes behavior in order to be rewarded by others. This suggests that when Caroline is with her Republican Party friends, her attitudes are more probusiness and less proenvironment.

Because attitudes serve such important functions, they have been studied extensively by social psychologists. But there is another reason for the attention they have received, and this was indicated by the gas station attendant I encountered: the relationship between attitudes and behavior. Think how useful it would be if we had a way of predicting behavior from attitudes. We could tell how politicians and all kinds of other people would behave from expressed attitudes, and we could influence future behavior by changing attitudes. The Canadian researchers James Olson and Mark Zanna (1993) propose that "the utility of the attitude concept rests on the assumption that attitudes influence behaviors" (p. 131), implying that the concept of attitude would have no purpose if attitudes did not influence behavior.

We begin this chapter by reviewing research attempting to pin down the conditions under which attitudes can predict behavior. We then consider the possibility that the relationship is the other way around, and that behavior determines attitudes. Finally, we examine the relationship between culture and attitudes and consider alternative approaches to understanding attitudes.

Concepts and Issues

Attitudes have been a historically important topic in social psychology because of their knowledge, value-expressive, ego-defensive, social-adjustive, and other functions, as well as their assumed impact on behavior. Attitudes are based on one, two, or all three of affect, behavior, and cognition.

1. What is meant by the ABCs of attitudes?
2. Describe any four functions of attitudes.
3. Complete the following statement: "The utility of the attitude concept rests on the assumption that attitudes influence. . . ."

Attitudes Influence Behavior

From difference in feeling springs difference in conduct.
—Thucydides, *The Peloponnesian War*

The proposition that affect and behavior are associated has a long history, as suggested by the writings of the Greek historian Thucydides (c. 460–c. 400 B.C.). The actual path to establishing an attitude–behavior link has not been smooth (McGuire, 1985). The "infatuation" of modern social psychology with this link arises in part from the causal model of behavior adopted by researchers (discussed in Chapters 1 and 2). The causal model assumes that science progresses by discovering causal relations and that social psychologists should be concerned with discovering the causes of social behavior. The importance of attitudes in social psychology is partly derived from their potential role as "causes" of behavior. If attitudes can be shown to predict behavior, then social psychology will have taken a significant step closer to becoming a science. In this sense, then, the intense focus on predicting behavior from attitudes is pragmatic, because it is seen as a way of establishing the scientific status of social psychology.

Criticisms of an Attitude-Behavior Link

There have been a number of attempts to challenge the idea that attitudes predict behavior. One interesting study was conducted by Robert LaPiere (1934). In the first stage of this study, LaPiere toured the United States in the company of a Chinese couple and visited about 250 hotels, restaurants, and other tourist locations. Only once was the Chinese couple denied service, a surprising outcome considering the reportedly strong anti-Chinese prejudice among the U.S. population at that time. Having established the actual overt behavior of people toward the Chinese couple, in the second stage of the study LaPiere mailed questionnaires to the places they had visited. Only about half of the places responded, and of those about 90 percent reported that they would *not* serve Chinese people.

By the 1960s, the findings of scores of studies seemed to challenge the view that expressed attitudes predict behavior (Wicker, 1969). Many such studies followed LaPiere (1934) and focused specifically on the topic of prejudice. In one study white male college students completed a questionnaire assessing their attitudes toward African-Americans and at a later date participated in a laboratory experiment (Himmelstein & Moore, 1963). When a subject arrived at the laboratory, he would find another participant (a confederate of the experimenter who was black or white, depending on the experimental condition) already seated and waiting for the experiment to begin. During the waiting period, a second confederate (white) would enter the room and ask the first confederate and the subject to sign a petition to extend university library hours. The research question was "Would expressed attitudes toward blacks predict conformity with the (signing/not-signing) behavior of the first black confederate?" The results showed no such association, and current research continues to highlight this gap (Cohen, 1996).

Criticisms of an association between attitudes and behavior have been part of broader criticisms concerning the consistency of behavior (Dudycha, 1936; Mischel, 1968). A central assumption underlying several areas of psychology, particularly social psychology and personality psychology, has been that the behavior of individuals is in important ways consistent across contexts. Such consistency is assumed to arise because of the powerful influence of dispositional characteristics, these being psychological features internal to individuals.

For example, the dispositional feature of "negative attitudes toward minorities" is assumed to persist across contexts, so that a person who manifests such negative attitudes while shopping is also assumed to show them at work, as well as during social interactions at a birthday party. In a similar manner, it is assumed that a person who is shy will be consistently shy in different contexts: shy when meeting people for the first time, shy when asked to make a presentation, shy when offering opinions.

However, what if behavior is not consistent across contexts? What if "negative attitudes toward minorities," "shyness," and other characteristics vary in fundamental ways across contexts? Surely, if behavior is generally inconsistent, then there is little point in trying to use attitudes and other assumed dispositional characteristics as predictors of behavior. As one leading researcher has put it, "Lack of behavioral consistency is an embarrassing problem for personality and social psychologists" (Ajzen, 1988, p. 43).

Attitudes Do Predict Behavior: The Theory of Reasoned Action

Although the literature on attitudes and behavior led some researchers to conclude there is little support for the notion that attitudes predict behavior (Wicker, 1969), a number of other researchers have come to a different conclusion. Icek Ajzen and Martin Fishbein (1977) assessed 109 studies on attitude–behavior relations, and teased apart differences between studies in which attitudes did predict behavior and those where they did not.

Level of Specificity.   One of the important differences found by Ajzen and Fishbein concerned the level of specificity of attitudes and behavior. Studies that showed a weak or no relationship between attitudes and behavior, such as the often-cited one by LaPiere (1934), tended to involve measures of general attitudes and specific behavior. For example, the attitudinal questionnaire used by LaPiere asked, "Will you accept members of the Chinese race as guests in your establishment?" But the behavioral measure used by LaPiere was whether a specific, very presentable Chinese couple accompanied by a white male would receive service at the establishments in question.

theory of reasoned action   theory that specific behavioral intentions are good predictors of specific behaviors.

The **theory of reasoned action** proposes that specific behavioral intentions are good predictors of specific behaviors. Fishbein and Ajzen (1975) argued that in order for attitudes to predict behavior, one condition that needs to be met is that the measures of attitudes and behavior used must be at the same level of specificity. Subsequent research has provided some support for this proposition (Eagly & Chaiken, 1992). In her study of sexually active female teenagers in the United States, Diane Morrison (1989) found that contraception use was effectively predicted by attitudes toward contraception specifically. Effective users of contra-

Efforts are being made to change attitudes toward sex and family planning in many different societies. Success in such efforts, it is hoped, will prevent unwanted pregnancies, slow down the spread of AIDS and various sexually transmitted diseases, and generally improve health. In all such programs, a central issue is the relationship between attitudes toward sex and actual behavior. The attitude–behavior link can be more fully explained if local norms and rules are considered. It may be, for example, that what white middle–class researchers describe as "unwanted" pregnancies are actually highly desired and valued by teenagers like those in this high school class; and a sixth child may be another sign of God's blessing for the family of this Egyptian woman, even though her expressed attitude in a family planning clinic may be different.

ceptives were less likely than ineffective users to agree, for example, that "planning ahead about what kind of birth control to use can spoil the fun of sex," and that "the whole idea of birth control is embarrassing to me." A study of women in India also found that favorable and specific attitudes toward contraception predicted the use of contraceptives (Kumar & Gairola, 1983). A study among students in the United States, Britain, and Sweden found that antiwar activist behavior, such as participating in a march, was better predicted by specific rather than general attitudes toward war (Newcomb, Rabow, & Hernandez, 1992).

Using Multiple Measures. Another reason why some studies fail to find a relationship between attitudes and behavior may be that they only use a single indicator of attitudes and/or behavior (Fishbein & Ajzen, 1974). In the LaPiere (1934) study, one action—refusal to accept Chinese people in restaurants and hotels—was found not to be associated with a single measure of expressed attitude toward serving Chinese people. But a single measure tends to be unreliable, meaning that the results achieved are likely to be inconsistent. Attempts to find relationships between two single measures also tend to be unreliable.

Consider the case of a research team studying the relationship between attitudes toward condom use and actual condom use. If the researchers use a single measure of attitudes—such as the question "Do you feel embarrassed to talk about condoms with your partner?"—and also a single measure of behavior—such as "Did you use condoms when you last had sexual intercourse?"—both measures are likely to be unreliable. The last time the participant had sexual intercourse may have been the only time that he used condoms, despite being sexually active during the last 6 months. He may not have been embarrassed to talk about condoms during the latest episode because his partner introduced the idea and supplied the condoms. Because single measures are heavily influenced by chance factors, a better strategy is to depend on multiple measures. For this reason, Diane Morrison (1989, p. 1443) used 13 different questions to assess attitudes toward contraceptives.

Attitudes and Rationality. Fishbein and Ajzen have gone beyond establishing level of specificity and reliability of measures as requirements and have attempted to formulate a theory that sets out the relationship between attitudes and behavior in some detail. As suggested by its title, the theory of reasoned action assumes that human behavior is rational, as does the more recent adaptation (Ajzen, 1991) of the theory as a **theory of planned behavior.** These theories follow a long tradition in psychology of viewing attitudes as formed by deliberate evaluation of relevant information (Hovland, Janis, & Kelley, 1953; McGuire, 1969). According to this research tradition, human beings form attitudes in a thoughtful way, and such attitudes then lead to behavior.

According to the theory of planned behavior, this rationality manifests itself in a two-stage process (see Figure 4–2). First, three factors combine to influence behavioral intentions: (1) attitudes (Victoria's positive evaluation of marriage); (2) subjective norms, meaning our ideas about what others expect us to do (Victoria's sense that her parents expect her to get married); and (3) perceived control, referring to our view of how much control we have over a particular behavior (Victoria feels all she has to do is name the day, and Charles will make their wedding arrangements). In the second stage, our behavioral intentions determine our behavior (Victoria marries Charles, as she had intended). Thus, Fishbein and Ajzen have placed the attitude–behavior relationship within a much larger and fuller context, with the result that studies have been more successful in pinpointing when attitudes can better predict behavior (Petty, 1995; Petty & Cacioppo, 1996; Sheppard, Hartwick, & Warshaw, 1988).

theory of planned behavior
theory that people form attitudes through a rational two-step process in which three factors combine to influence intent, and intent then determines behavior.

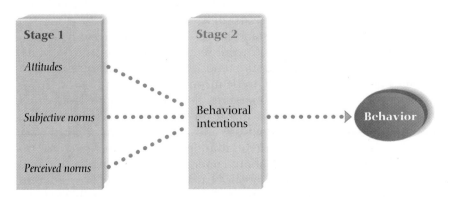

Figure 4–2 Key elements of the theory of planned behavior.

Other Predictors

So far we have identified two conditions that are important in enhancing the power of attitudes to predict behavior: when specific attitudes are used to predict specific behaviors and when the number of behavioral measures is increased and averaged to provide a more reliable index. Other conditions are also suggested by the literature.

The Effect of Direct Experience. One of my friends, an electrical engineer with a doctorate from a prestigious U.S. university, recently experienced being laid off from work. He has found work again, but only after months of desperate searching and worry about the future of his family. One of the first things he said to me when he started his new job was, "I now have very different attitudes toward the unemployed." His newly found "supportive" attitudes came out of his own experience of being unemployed and gaining firsthand knowledge of the hardships and challenges involved.

Social psychological research suggests that my friend is more likely to act on his attitudes toward unemployment, by signing a petition or participating in a march, for example, because his attitudes have been forged through experience and because his own interests are at stake (Fazio & Zanna, 1981). Research shows that on the college campus, students who experienced housing problems themselves were more likely to act on their attitudes—by participating in protests, for example. Another study showed that students are more likely to act on their attitudes toward new legislation on the legal drinking age if their particular year of birth would be affected by the proposed legislation (Sivacek & Crano, 1982). This evidence suggests that attitudes shaped by direct experience and affecting self-interest are more reliable predictors of behavior than are attitudes acquired indirectly and independent of self-interest.

Accessibility. Some attitudes are more easily brought to mind than others (Fazio, 1990), so that the mere mention of a related object will activate the attitude (Bargh, Chaiken, Covender, & Pratto, 1992). For example, I have very negative attitudes toward smoking, in large part because heavy smoking contributed to my father's early death from cancer. The sight or sound of a cigarette advertisement inevitably brings to mind my negative attitudes toward smoking.

Bringing an attitude to mind can lead to better predictions of behavior, but only under some conditions. This is demonstrated by an intriguing study conducted by Eugene Borgida and Bruce Campbell (1982), in which students heard tapes of conversations about plans to expand parking facilities on campus. The taped conversations also brought up the issue of the environmental consequences of expanding parking facilities, such as increased air pollution resulting from more students driving to school. The results showed that bringing environmental attitudes to mind did influence students to show less support for parking expansion, but not if they had experienced serious problems with school parking. Concerns about the environment seemed to be overcome by the more immediate problems of finding parking, so that environmental attitudes did not determine support for parking expansion. Presumably, then, although the accessibility of an attitude is important in determining its influence on behavior (Blasovich et al., 1993), bringing an attitude to mind will have limited impact when self-interest is at risk.

Degree of Knowledge. There is some evidence that more well informed attitudes have a stronger influence on behavior (Kallgren & Wood, 1986). Since the 1980s the public has become better informed about environmental pollution, and attitudes toward the environment tend now to be based on greater knowledge. On the other hand, one can have attitudes about phenomena about which one knows almost nothing (Petty, 1995). For example, Paul may have attitudes toward the Maoris of New Zealand, although he has never met a Maori. Such "weak" attitudes are less likely to influence behavior. When Paul actually arrives in New Zealand and meets some Maori people, his initial attitudes are likely to change dramatically.

Accuracy of Attitude Measure. So far we have seen that attitudes can predict behavior better under conditions where (1) the specificity of attitude–behavior measures correspond; (2) multiple measures are used, so that a more reliable measure of attitudes can be computed; (3) attitudes are shaped by direct experience; (4) attitudes are attended to; and (5) attitudes are based on knowledge. Another important condition concerns the accuracy of the attitude measure. It is so easy for participants to report their attitudes incorrectly. For example, knowing that discrimination on the basis of ethnicity is illegal—and also socially unacceptable in many sectors of contemporary society—even racist participants are likely to be cautious in expressing negative attitudes toward ethnic minorities. How, then, can we get at real attitudes?

An ideal way would be to be able to look directly inside the minds of participants, or to at least have participants believe that the experimenter is capable of doing so, so that attitudes are reported honestly. This is the strategy adopted in a creative study using a so-called bogus-pipeline technique (Jones & Sigall, 1971). The technique involved the use of a machine that supposedly measured attitudes through electrodes sensitive to variations in muscle reactions. When electrodes were attached, participants were led to believe that the machine could access their attitudes directly, independent of their verbal reports. The result was that participants reported more negative attitudes toward African-Americans. They seemed to view the fake machine as a kind of lie detector and consequently decided to report their true attitudes.

Evaluating the Attitude-Behavior Debate

The social psychological study of attitudes has involved a focused and fairly exhaustive attempt to establish attitudes as predictors of behavior. Much of this research has, in recent years, been related to the theory of reasoned action and the newer theory of planned behavior. What has been the outcome of this research, and how successful are the leading attitude theories?

Some progress has been made in identifying more clearly the conditions under which attitudes are more likely to predict behavior. In brief, attitudes are better behavioral predictors when there is correspondence between attitude–behavior specificity, when multiple measures of both are used, and when attitudes are based on direct experience, attended to, based on knowledge, and accurately measured (see Figure 4–3).

When the precautions are followed, the theory of reasoned action has been found to predict intentions or behaviors from attitudes in such areas as seatbelt use (Stasson & Fishbein, 1990) and applying for a nursing program (Strader & Katz, 1990). The revised theory of planned behavior has been shown to be a better predictor of behavior from attitudes (Ajzen, 1991; Madden, Ellen, & Ajzen, 1992). But the fact remains that attitudes do not seem to have a powerful influence on behavior in all, or even most, situations.

Some theorists have attempted to specify the conditions in which the Fishbein and Ajzen model would work. One possibility is suggested by the MODE model, which proposes that the *M*otivation and the *O*pportunity to think about an attitude *D*etermine the *E*ffects of the attitude on behavior (Fazio, 1990). The MODE model implies that the theories of reasoned action and planned behavior explain behavior only when the individual is motivated to think about an attitude and has the opportunity to do so. But such conditions tend to be the exception rather than the norm. This helps to explain why the impact of attitudes on behavior can be spontaneous and powerful in some situations and absent in others.

Indeed, the research of Timothy Wilson and his collaborators depicts attitudes as "temporary constructions" and raises important new challenges to the view of attitudes as stable and persistent over the long term (Wilson, 1990; Wilson & Hodges, 1992; Wilson, Hodges, & LaFleur, 1995). These researchers have investigated the effects of introspection on attitude change. Surprisingly, research has shown that when people are asked to reflect on why they feel the way they do

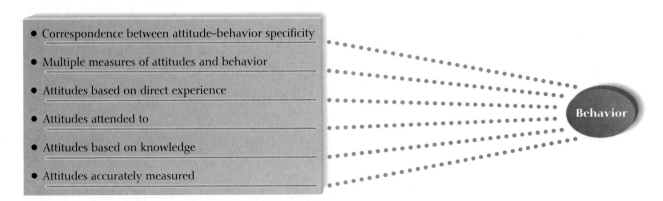

Figure 4–3 Major criteria to be met in order for attitudes to predict behavior.

about dating partners, types of food, or political candidates, among other things, they often change their minds about how they feel. Many attitudes seem to be unstable, changing with the social context and what people are thinking about when they bring an attitude to mind.

priming   the activation of thoughts and experiences that are applicable to presently experienced stimuli.

This suggests that attitudes can be influenced through **priming,** the activation of thoughts and experiences that are applicable to presently experienced stimuli. A friend of mine is closely linked with one of the major political parties in the United States, and he sees everything in terms of party politics. I find that when I am with him, my political attitudes color everything, because he continually activates my political knowledge, feelings, and experiences. This effect gets so overpowering that I can't even watch a movie without interpreting what I am seeing in political terms ("Oh, the actor who just blew up the bridge raises funds for the Republicans in California . . . that actress is prochoice . . . the film director's father was blacklisted because of his left-wing views in the 1950s"). Priming suggests an involuntary or automatic feature to attitudes, and we turn to this next.

Automatic Processes and the Rational Model

In the 1990s social psychologists gave increasing attention to the topic of attitudes and automatic processes, the encoding of often complex material in automatic fashion (Petty & Cacioppo, 1996; Petty & Krosnick, 1995). Among the most important features of automatic processes are their being *involuntary* (they inevitably occur in certain contexts) and *outside awareness* (they occur without a person being conscious of them). This suggests that attitudes could be primed and activated through automatic processes, without a person making intentional efforts or being conscious of this process. Marvin could bring to mind sexist attitudes, and even express and act on them, without intending to or being conscious of doing so.

stereotype   culturally based but often unfounded generalization about groups.

At the same time that research on automatic processes made progress, there was increasing interest in the more subtle forms of sexism and racism (discussed in Chapters 10, 12, and 14). Subtle sexism (Benokraitis, 1997) and subtle racism (Bowser & Hunt, 1996) are different from the traditional sexism and racism in important ways, such as being apparently involuntary and outside awareness. Researchers became particularly intrigued by the ways in which automatic processes are associated with the application of **stereotypes**—culturally based but often unfounded generalizations about groups (discussed in more detail in Chapter 10).

A number of studies suggest that negative attitudes toward minorities can be activated automatically by the manipulation of context, such as showing black and white faces to participants (Fazio, Jackson, Dunton, & Williams, 1995). Studies by Victoria Esses and Mark Zanna (1995) suggest that mood influences automatic activation: Majority group members were more likely to attribute negative stereotypes to minority groups when they experienced negative moods (this relates to the more general topic of relationships between negative experiences, such as frustration and aggression, discussed in Chapter 14).

The current focus on automatic processes is different in orientation from traditional research on whether attitudes cause behavior. More broadly, it moves us away from the rational model of behavior, because central to automatic processes is the assumption of people *not* being aware of what they are doing and *not* being aware of their attitudes toward different groups. Should we now assume that attitudes are "out of our control" and automatically activated by stimuli? No, the research of Irene Blair and Mahzarin Banaji (1996) demonstrates that, although attitudes (such as those on gender issues) can be activated automatically, people are not powerless; they can eliminate this effect. Individuals enjoy some measure of freedom to choose how they behave.

Concepts and Issues

Looking back over the past half-century of attitudinal research, it is clear that the attitude-behavior connection is both complex and dynamic. But it is equally clear that attitudes do not predict behavior in many situations. Given this complexity, it is reasonable to consider an alternative possibility—that behavior could influence attitudes.

1. Give an example of an early study that showed attitudes do not determine behavior.
2. Briefly describe the theory of reasoned action.
3. Explain under what conditions attitudes best predict behavior.

Behavior "Causes" Attitudes

Robert Cialdini (1988) spent several years infiltrating various organizations to find out how sales and fundraising professionals make use of the common wisdom that behavior causes attitudes. A general feature of all the assorted tactics used to get people to buy goods or to make contributions is first to maneuver them into making a commitment, even if it is a very small commitment, such as saying "yes" in response to a seemingly innocuous question. After the initial "foot-in-the-door" has been achieved and a person has been maneuvered to act in a particular way, he or she can be more easily persuaded to make bigger commitments. This topic is discussed in more detail in Chapter 6.

This technique was cleverly demonstrated by Jonathan Freedman and Scott Fraser (1966) in what have become two classic foot-in-the-door experiments. Both experiments were conducted in California and involved researchers making huge demands from participants. In the first experiment, researchers presented themselves as representatives of a consumer group and asked homemakers if they would allow five or six men to have complete freedom in the house for several hours in order to go through all the cupboards and storage spaces to take a complete inventory of the household goods. In the second experiment residents were asked if they would put up a large and awkward "Drive

This sales representative working her trade in a Guatemalan market, dressed in a colorful Mayan gown, is intimately aware of local rules and norms and uses them to sell effectively, but her behavior will in some ways be very familiar to us. She uses the "foot–in–the–door" technique when she offers small "free" samples. The acceptance of such "gifts" opens the door for her to make the real sales pitch, and earn profits.

Carefully" sign in front of their houses. The number of participants agreeing to these large demands increased dramatically in the conditions where a "foot–in–the–door" had already been established by first asking respondents to make a small commitment. Examples of such small commitments were answering a few questions in the first experiment and putting up a very small sign in front of the house in the second. Once people are coaxed into taking a step in a certain direction, it seems to be much easier to get them to go a long way down that road.

Such a step–by–step procedure leading to greater commitments seems to be involved in many conflict situations. Two different examples are the step–by–step escalation of the Vietnam War by the United States in the 1960s and the repeated acquiescence of Britain's Prime Minister Neville Chamberlain in 1938 in the face of Hitler's aggression in the months prior to World War II. In the case of Vietnam, each decision by the United States to escalate the fighting seemed to make it easier to escalate it even more. In the case of Chamberlain, when he took the first step of remaining passive in the face of German aggression, the way was opened for Hitler to attack neighboring European countries, annex territories, and make more promises about peace. But once the war did begin in Europe, attitudes followed the fighting. That is, attitudes toward Germans and others in the enemy camp became extremely hostile. The British and their allies developed negative attitudes toward the "Huns," just as during the Vietnam War attitudes toward the Vietnamese hardened among U.S. citizens.

A number of the classic social psychological studies on conflict show the same trend of hostile attitudes following hostile acts (Taylor & Moghaddam, 1994). When Muzafer Sherif (1966) arranged for boys in a summer camp to join rival groups and take part in intergroup competitions, the boys developed extremely hostile attitudes toward their opponents—this despite the fact that the boys in the competing groups had previously selected one another as good friends. Having created intergroup conflict and hostile intergroup attitudes, Sherif arranged for situations in which the boys in the two groups had to cooperate in order to attain a mutually desired goal, for example, joining together to pull a broken-down truck that was transporting food to their camp. The act of cooperation led to changes in their attitudes so that they once again had positive attitudes toward the members of out-groups. (We discuss Sherif's study in greater detail in Chapter 14.)

In some instances people are placed in roles that by tradition are in conflict, and negative attitudes arise out of their performance in such roles. Consider the roles of "prisoners" and "prison guards," for example. Erving Goffman (1961) proposes that institutionalized norms almost inevitably lead to conflict between people in such roles. A dramatic example is provided by another classic, the Stanford prison simulation study (Zimbardo, Haney, & Banks, 1973). Philip Zimbardo and his colleagues arranged for students to play the roles of prisoners and guards in a makeshift prison. The guards and prisoners acted out their respective roles and also adopted attitudes they saw as appropriate for those roles.

The attitude of the guards toward the prisoners is reflected by remarks such as "I practically considered the prisoners cattle" (Guard M) and "I was tired of seeing the prisoners in their rags and smelling the strong odors of their bodies that filled the cells . . . we were there to show them who was boss" (Guard A). The hostile attitudes of the guards were associated with harsh treatment toward the prisoners—to such an extent that the study had to be abandoned in order to ensure the safety and health of the prisoners. How did these respondents, all "average," middle-class, college-age males with normal personality profiles, come to hold such fierce attitudes? Although this question, and the entire issue of attitudes following behavior, are not novel, the answer provided by dissonance theory was both innovative and highly stimulating for future research.

Cognitive Dissonance

> It is the idea of cognitive invention, cognitive distortion, cognitive change to make your view of the world fit with how you feel or what you are doing; that was the basic idea out of which the formulation of dissonance theory developed.
>
> —Leon Festinger, in discussion with R. I. Evans, *The Making of Social Psychology*

cognitive dissonance a state of discomfort that arises when a person is aware of having incongruent cognitions and is motivated to change one or the other to make them congruent.

The theory of **cognitive dissonance** was formulated by Leon Festinger (1957) to explain situations in which people change their cognitions in order to make them congruent with one another. It is assumed that incongruent cognitions lead to a state of discomfort or dissonance, which will motivate people to make their cognitions congruent. For example, Joan has offers of marriage from Max and Liam. She has a very difficult time choosing between her suitors but finally decides on Max. Not long after making the choice and marrying Max, she has gone through what Festinger refers to as *cognitive invention*. Max seems by far the better man. His good qualities multiply and seem even more important now, whereas, in retrospect, Liam has fewer good qualities and his faults are magnified. How could Joan have put up with his irritating laugh? And as for his relatives and friends, they seemed to be part of the Addams Family!

Why does Joan go to the trouble of "cognitive invention"? According to cognitive dissonance theory, it is because the thoughts "I have married Max" and "I might have been even happier marrying Liam" are incongruent. One of them has to change: Either Joan divorces Max, which she does not wish to do, or she changes her ideas about Liam's suitability, which she can do with less effort.

In many ways cognitive dissonance theory seems obvious, and the situations it explains, such as Joan's predicament, also obvious. To appreciate why cognitive dissonance theory came to be seen as so innovative and became so influential in social psychology, we need to consider three points: first, the particular era in which the theory appeared in the history of social psychology; second, the power of the theory to stimulate experimental research; and third, the relation of cognitive dissonance theory to culture in the United States.

Cognitive Dissonance and the Decline of Behaviorism. Cognitive dissonance theory made its appearance in the late 1950s, at a time when the influence of behaviorism was waning and the cognitive revolution was gaining momentum. Cognitive dissonance theory challenged at least two fundamental tenets of behaviorism: that the concept of "mental life" has no place in a science of psychology and that behavior is shaped by positive and negative reinforcements. A major reason for the rapid success of cognitive dissonance theory and its tremendous influence was that it appeared at a time when researchers were looking for alternative sources of inspiration for experimental studies.

Two Pioneering Experiments on Cognitive Dissonance. Cognitive dissonance theory proved to be extremely effective at stimulating experimental research. In a few years it had inspired dozens of interesting studies (Brehm & Cohen, 1962); within a decade it was the centerpiece of an 84-chapter book (Abelson et al., 1968); within two decades hundreds of experiments attested to its power (Wicklund & Brehm, 1976). And it continues to influence current research (Murphy & Miller, 1997). Moreover, the research stimulated by the theory led to results that seemed to contradict the expectations of behaviorism but were in line with the predictions made by Festinger (1957). Let us look more closely at two examples: a field study and a laboratory experiment.

The field study took advantage of a student riot at Yale University in 1959 (Brehm & Cohen, 1962, pp. 73–77). Police intervention had led to allegations of police brutality, and feelings ran high on campus. Yale social psychologists randomly selected a sample of students and asked them to write an essay in support of the police actions, using the title "Why the New Haven Police actions were justified." Participants were offered $10, $5, $1, or 50 cents for their efforts. Next, participants completed a questionnaire assessing their actual views on police actions. This same questionnaire was administered to a control group consisting of randomly selected students who did not write an essay. The two research questions addressed were "Would writing the essay influence respondents' opinions?" And "If so, would the amount of reward received also have an effect?"

A prediction arising from behaviorism is that the strength of the rewards would shape behavior. Participants who received the highest level of positive reinforcement ($10) should change opinions most, and those who received the lowest level of reinforcement (50 cents) should demonstrate the smallest opinion shift. But cognitive dissonance theory leads to the opposite prediction. Participants who received $10 could justify writing the essay more easily than those who received only 50 cents; the first would look back and say, "I had reason to write that essay—they gave me $10," but the second group had very little justification in terms of monetary rewards. As a consequence, those who received only 50 cents were most likely to experience cognitive dissonance and thus change their attitudes in line with their behavior. This is exactly what happened. Participants who received 50 cents experienced the largest attitude change in support of the police, the next largest change was experienced by those who received $1, whereas those who received $10 and $5 experienced no change.

The second research example involves a laboratory experiment conducted by two of Festinger's students, Elliot Aronson and Judson Mills (1959). Participants were female undergraduates, invited to participate in what ostensibly was a group discussion on sex. Upon arrival, participants were told they would have to pass a screening test to make sure they were the kind of individuals who could discuss the topic frankly. The screening test involved participants reading out loud; the contents of the text they read from depended on the condition to which they were assigned. Participants in the control condition read from a fairly mundane "neutral" text; they had no problems gaining entrance to the discussion group. Those assigned to the "mild initiation" condition read from a text that had a number of fairly embarrassing

Figure 4-4 The price of initiation: resolving cognitive dissonance.

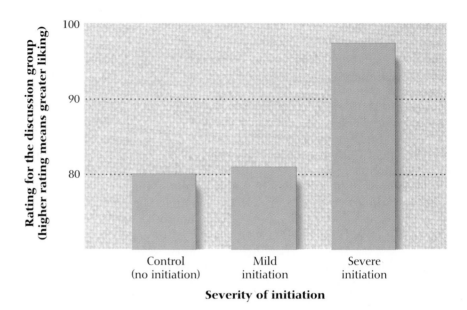

words, and those in the "severe initiation" condition read from a text with extremely obscene words. Aronson (1988) remembers:

> I recall vividly the atmosphere in which Judson Mills and I, as graduate students at Stanford University in 1957, presented the hypothesis and procedure of the initiation experiment to a group of our peers: "Undergoing an embarrassing initiation in order to become a member of a group will increase the attractiveness of that group." The dominant response was that our hypothesis was silly—that it went against common sense. Clearly a stimulus (the group discussion) associated with unpleasantness (the embarrassing initiation) would be liked less through association." (pp. 160–161)

After the "initiation ceremony," participants were told that it was too late for them to take part in this week's group discussion, but they could listen in so that they would be better prepared for the discussion next week. They were taken to a booth, where they put on earphones and listened to an extraordinarily boring group discussion that had actually been pretaped. Finally, they evaluated the group discussion they had just heard. The ratings showed participants in the "severe initiation" condition to be more positively oriented toward the group discussion than those in the "mild initiation" condition. The results confirmed what to some critics had been a "silly" hypothesis (see Figure 4–4).

Two Recent Studies on Cognitive Dissonance. Researchers continue to explore cognitive dissonance, particularly in dealing with problems such as racism (Ruscher & Hammer, 1996). Michael Leippe and Donna Eisenstadt (1994) found that, as predicted by cognitive dissonance theory, white college students in the United States became more favorable to blacks after writing an essay endorsing pro–black policies. It is not clear, however, if such changes in intergroup attitudes are long-lasting. Perhaps the most innovative studies on cognitive dissonance in the 1990s have been conducted by Patricia Murphy and Carol Miller (1997), who explored the relationship between dissonance, consumerism, and the self.

Murphy and Miller argued that, in the United States and in other modern consumer societies, people have internalized the message that their self-worth and identity depend a great deal on appropriate consumption of products. When I ask, "Who is Joe?" part of the response in the U.S. context is likely to be, "Joe is the guy who drives a Jeep, wears Nike stuff, goes to California for his holidays. . . ." Some consumer goods are more important to self-image. More important, for example, are magazines that focus on image (*Cosmopolitan, Vogue, Rolling Stone, Esquire*), compared to those that focus on news (*Newsweek, Life, Time*).

Murphy and Miller asked students to evaluate either five image magazines or five newsmagazines in terms of quality and desirability. After completing other tasks, students were told they could take home either magazine A or magazine B, these being the ones they had rated third and fourth most desirable. After making their choices between magazines A and B, students again rated all five magazines, this time on more specific criteria (usefulness, attractiveness, and so on), as well as on desirability.

Murphy and Miller expected that participants would change their ratings more on the image magazines, giving a higher rating to magazines they could take home, because these are more central to modern self-images than are newsmagazines. This prediction was confirmed. For example, after being told he could take home *Esquire*, his fourth choice, Sam changed his estimate of *Esquire* so that it became his most desirable choice. But after being told he could take home *U.S. News & World Report*, his fourth choice, Tut changed his evaluation only slightly, so this magazine now became his equal third choice.

Murphy and Miller used local image magazines and newsmagazines to repeat their study in Finland, a society with less consumer advertising and consumption than the United States. The self-images of people in Finland presumably are not connected to consumer products to the same degree as are self-images in the United States. Murphy and Miller predicted and found that Finnish participants did not change their ratings of desirability for image magazines or newsmagazines as much as did U.S. participants. This research underscores the profound impact of modern mass communications and consumer advertising on our self-concepts (Gergen, 1991).

Psychological Balance.   But cognitive dissonance theory is concerned with more than just distortions in thinking in order to achieve congruence. Underlying the theory is a rather broad assumption about all social life—that people are motivated to achieve balance in all of their social relations (Abelson et al., 1968; Fiske & Taylor, 1991). For example, if Matthew likes Helen and Helen likes her mother, but Matthew dislikes Helen's mother, then there is going to be trouble because this is an unbalanced relationship. The imbalance will lead to tensions, and steps will have to be taken to try to restore balance. Matthew may decide

Helen's mother is lovable after all, or he may leave Helen because he thinks he really is not that attracted to her.

Although dissonance theory proved to be highly stimulating for experimental social psychology, there were serious challenges. The most inspired of these questioned the assumption that people are motivated to achieve balanced states and, furthermore, came from the very tradition that cognitive dissonance was attempting to replace: behaviorism.

Self-Perception Theory: The Behaviorist Reply

> Inconsistency, they seem to be trying to tell us, motivates belief and attitude change. But I don't believe it. . . . My suspicion is that inconsistency is probably . . . commonplace . . . we academic psychologists . . . probably spend too much time with bright college students who are as eager to achieve a respectable overall unity in their cognitions as we, their instructors, are eager to impress them and ourselves with the same admirable coherence of thought.
>
> —Daryl Bem, *Beliefs, Attitudes, and Human Affairs*

According to self-perception theory, we often know our own attitudes in much the same way as we know other people's—by observations of behavior and the circumstances in which it takes place. When someone asks me if my neighbor likes public transportation, I think about her behavior and recall that I have always seen her using her car and never using public transportation. I infer that she does not like public transportation. I may go through a similar process to infer my own attitude when asked if I like public transportation.

Bem also criticizes the proposition that people strive to achieve balance in their thoughts, actions, and relationships. The "normal" state of affairs, according to Bem, is that social relationships are not balanced and people do not have congruent cognitions. Rather, the balance that Festinger and others have emphasized so much is something that academics and intellectuals value and strive toward.

Interestingly, then, Bem's criticism of the balance theories is cultural, in the sense that he identifies the academic culture as being responsible for the rise of such theories. Balance theories reflect the academic concern for achieving congruent and rational accounts of the world. Logical and consistent thinking are fundamental criteria for evaluating the self and others in academic work. According to Bem, this concern is not shared to the same degree by people in their everyday activities.

Moreover, the idea that people are motivated to achieve congruent cognitions about themselves is wrong, because individuals do not come to know themselves through introspection. According to Bem's self-perception theory, people come to know themselves in the same way that they know others: by looking at their behavior (see Chapter 3). This perspective on attitudes leads to a completely different interpretation of findings from dissonance studies.

Self-perception theory leads to the general prediction that attitudes follow behavior, and individuals come to infer their own attitudes by observing their own behavior. Look again at the Aronson and Mills (1959) study involving female participants who experienced mild or severe group initiation. The cognitive dissonance theory interpretation fits the results, but so does a self-perception interpretation. The participants who went through severe initiation would look at their behavior and decide, quite rationally, that their behavior shows they liked the group discussion very much because they were willing to put up with a lot to become a participant. This interpretation seems much more direct than that provided by cognitive dissonance theory, because it assumes that people observe their own behavior and gain self-knowledge through such observation.

Surrounded by her mentors, a young Apache girl, decorated with eagle feathers and carrying a decorated stick that will be her walking cane in old age, dances as part of a puberty rite lasting four days and four nights. The French girls (at right) wear face paint and costumes as part of a hazing ritual at their university. Initiation ceremonies are found in many different societies. Social psychologists have discovered that difficult rites of passage can serve to increase group cohesion and ties of loyalty. However, not all such rites meet the ethical standards we set for ourselves in modern societies.

To demonstrate his point that people come to know their own attitudes in the same way that they know about the attitudes of others, Bem (1965) conducted a study in which he presented participants with a description of the 1959 student riot and police reactions at Yale. The descriptions indicated that students had agreed to write an essay in support of police actions and that they had been paid $1 or 50 cents for doing so (these were the only two amounts that had induced attitude change in the original study). Participants were then asked to estimate the attitudes of the essay writers toward the police actions. Bem cleverly put the self-perception interpretation to the test by providing a group of "observers" with the same information about the behavior of others as had been available to participants about themselves in the Brehm and Cohen (1962) study. According to self-perception theory, the participant "observers" in Bem's study should use the behavior of the essay writers as their guide and conclude that those who wrote essays for 50 cents must hold attitudes more in line with the essays than those who wrote essays for $1. The results supported this interpretation.

Self-perception theory predicts unexpected findings that are not easily explained by cognitive dissonance theory. Consider the following case: Sam is a 10-year-old boy who likes to play with puzzles. If you ask him, "Sam, why do you play with those puzzles so much?" the response will be, "Because I like to." This liking stems from **intrinsic motivation,** the pleasure that one gets for doing something without receiving external rewards. Now, imagine what would happen if you were to give Sam $10 for every puzzle he completes. According to self-perception theory, Sam now observes his own behavior and concludes, "I play with puzzles for money." His desire to play with puzzles now stems from **extrinsic motivation,** a behavior motivated by external rewards. After a while, if Sam does not receive money for playing, he is likely to abandon the puzzles completely.

Numerous studies support the idea that rewarding people unnecessarily for doing what they already enjoy can lower their motivation for that behavior (Deci & Ryan, 1985). Cognitive dissonance theory does not explain these findings, because being rewarded for doing something is not incongruent and, therefore, there should be no motivation to change either behavior (playing with the puzzles) or attitudes (positive disposition toward playing).

Notice that self-perception theory suggests a two-step process and that the second step brings us back to the process of attribution. The first step involves the person looking back as an observer to past behavior, such as Sam looking back to himself playing with puzzles and receiving rewards. During the second step, the person attributes a cause to the behavior. For example, Sam makes the attribution, "The reason I played with the puzzles was that I got $10 each time I completed one." The attribution that money is the cause of Sam's behavior opens up the possibility of changing that behavior by increasing or decreasing the money offered (see Figure 4–5).

Bem's self-perception theory was described earlier as being in the behaviorist tradition, but we now see that it seems to contradict behaviorism in some ways. Put simply, behaviorism assumes that behavior is

---

intrinsic motivation the pleasure a person gets from performing an activity without receiving any external reward.

extrinsic motivation behavior motivated by external rewards.

Figure 4–5 Schematic representation of self–perception theory.

shaped by positive and negative reinforcements. Behavior that is rewarded is assumed to be more likely to occur. Self-perception theory asserts that the rewarding of behavior can diminish intrinsic motivation, so that there is a decreased likelihood for that behavior to occur. Is there a way to resolve this apparent conflict?

One interpretation of self-perception theory is that rewarding behavior will diminish the occurrence of that behavior only when the reward leads to a changed perception of the cause of behavior (Sansone, 1986). It is only when Sam attributes his playing with puzzles to monetary reward that he stops playing if he is not given money to play. If Sam is given money for improved performance, the rewards will most likely strengthen rather than diminish his behavior (Deci & Ryan, 1985).

As students, if we study hard *only in order to win rewards* (such as money for travel or a car), we run the risk of losing any feeling of enjoyment from studying. Learning then becomes pure drudgery, something boring we have to do in order to get to have fun.

Self-Perception and Cognitive Dissonance in Perspective

Cognitive dissonance and self-perception theories have been the basis of a vast number of research studies, a few of which are considered classics in social psychology. Self-perception theory seems to provide a more direct and simple explanation of attitude–behavior relations. The simplicity of self-perception theory is derived partly from an assumed direct link between observed behavior and inferred attitudes, with the consequence that the whole issue of psychological consistency is avoided. The concern with consistency can be a problem because of the difficulty of defining psychological consistency and predicting exactly what a person will try to change in order to achieve that consistency.

Besides, there are situations in which psychological consistency does not seem to be an issue but attitude change occurs. In one experiment using simple but clever methodology, participants watched cartoons while holding a pen either with their teeth or with their lips (Strack, Martin, & Stepper, 1988). Participants who held the pen with their teeth could smile at the cartoons more easily because holding the pen with their teeth did not prevent them from moving their lips to smile, but those holding the pen with their lips could not smile because they could not move their lips. Which group of respondents found the cartoons funnier? According to self-perception theory, participants would look back at their own behavior and those who smiled more would report that they found the cartoons funnier. This is exactly what the results show. But such instances of people observing their own behavior to infer their attitudes do not require us to include notions of psychological consistency in our explanation.

Do the complexities raised by psychological consistency mean that we should set aside cognitive dissonance theory? Elliot Aronson (1969, 1992) is among those who argue against such a strategy. He has taken up the challenge of identifying the conditions under which cognitive dissonance occurs and suggests that inconsistency becomes important when some aspect of the self is involved. People are most likely to distort events if they are in danger of looking stupid or immoral. For example, participants report positive attitudes toward a boring experiment if they receive only small rewards for participation because otherwise they could look rather silly ("You mean you spent an hour in that stupid experiment and only got 50 cents, when you could have come sailing with us on such a gorgeous afternoon?! There *is* one born every minute!"). Dissonance is also more likely to occur when people *voluntarily* agree to perform a discrepant behavior ("Yes, I chose to be part of that experiment"), when they are *committed* to perform the discrepant behavior ("I am going to finish the essay now that I have gotten involved in the study"), and when they *feel responsible* for aversive outcomes ("My essay helped to persuade the committee to close down the homeless shelter; I feel terrible").

Furthermore, a series of studies has reported that inconsistency is associated with an uncomfortable state of arousal (Elkin & Leippe, 1986; Fazio & Cooper, 1983; Losch & Cacioppo, 1990). While such studies have typically focused on physiological arousal, for example, as indicated by elevated galvanic skin responses (GSRs), ongoing research has demonstrated dissonance also as psychological discomfort (Elliot & Devine, 1993). Thus, there is support for Festinger's original delineation of psychological discomfort and bodily tension or drive state as components of dissonance. If Charles hates his boss but is forced to act positively toward her, he is likely to experience aversive physiological arousal and psychological discomfort if he thinks about the inconsistency between his attitude and his behavior. Such uncomfortable feelings seem to alert us to wrongdoing and to motivate us to change at least how we see the situation. Cognitive dissonance theory predicts such feelings of discomfort arising from inconsistency, but self-perception theory does not.

Common Implications of Dissonance and Self-Perception Research

Rather than just focusing on the relative strengths and weaknesses of the two theories, it is instructive to focus on their common implications. First, it is clear that in many situations attitudes "follow" behavior. People often behave in a particular way and then report attitudes that correspond to that behavior. This suggests a limitation to models such as those of "reasoned action" (Fishbein & Ajzen, 1975) and "planned behavior" (Ajzen, 1988), which assume humans are "rational individualists." In many situations, it is misguided to look at attitudes as predictors of behavior simply because attitudes "follow" behavior.

Although cognitive dissonance and self-perception theories provide different explanations as to why attitudes follow behavior, the two theories have a common implication and this concerns self-presentation. A theme arising from cognitive dissonance research is that when people appear foolish, immoral, or harmful, they feel uncomfortable. A change in reported attitudes is one strategy to make themselves appear more positive and thus feel more comfortable. Exactly the same idea is suggested by self-perception theory: People make their attitudes "fit" their behavior in order to present themselves in a more positive light.

Concepts and Issues

A vast array of research literature and everyday experiences suggests that often attitudes are shaped by behavior, rather than being the "cause" of behavior. Cognitive dissonance theory explains this by proposing that people are motivated to maintain congruence or consistency in their thoughts and actions. Self-perception theory claims that we come to know our own attitudes by observing behavior; we change our assumptions about our attitudes when our behavior changes. A theme common to both theories is that people change their attitudes and/or their behaviors in order not to appear in a negative light.

1. Briefly describe and provide an example of cognitive dissonance.
2. How does self-perception theory explain the influence of behavior on attitudes?
3. What do cognitive dissonance theory and self-perception theory have in common?

Culture and Attitudes

> I have observed that . . . almost all foreigners . . . reckon craftsmen and their descendants as lower in the social scale than people who have no connexion with manual work: only the latter, and especially those who are trained for war, do they count among the "nobility." All the Greeks have adopted this attitude.
>
> —Herodotus, *The Histories*

A very long history for attitudes is suggested by almost all of the documents that have come down to us from earlier periods, such as the description of attitudes toward manual work provided about 2,500 years ago by the Greek historian Herodotus (c. 485–425 B.C.).

Attitudes certainly are an integral part of everyday life everywhere in the world. Consider the reporting of attitudes in the modern media. One 30-minute program of world news on television contains interviews with people in different parts of the world who express their attitudes on various issues: Students on college campuses in the United States express attitudes toward abortion; shoppers in London, Paris, and Berlin manifest their attitudes toward European unification; workers in Mexico and Canada show attitudes toward the North American Free Trade Agreement (NAFTA); Protestant and Catholic representatives in Northern Ireland express attitudes toward the latest violence in Belfast; Nigerians show their attitudes toward AIDS; and villagers in India express attitudes toward birth control. However, although attitudes seem to be universal in the sense that everyone has them, expressed attitudes tend to differ in important ways.

Attitudinal Differences Across Cultures.   Researchers George Domino and Yoshitomo Takahashi (1991), for example, found that male and female medical students in Japan held attitudes more in support of an individual's right to die (commit suicide) than their counterparts in the United States. In another example, the focus was on attitudinal differences toward the training of girls and boys in rural and urban areas in India (Saraswathi & Dutta, 1990). But the urban/rural difference proved to be less powerful than differences in wealth. Common to both urban and rural poor was an attitude that those "born with a woman's fate" (Saraswathi & Dutta, 1990, p. 163) must assume the role of homemaker and obedient daughter-in-law. Among wealthier people, such as upper-caste Hindus, there were more accepting attitudes toward women gaining an education.

Attitudinal Differences Across Time.   Attitudes also differ over time, so that assessments of approval rates toward interracial marriage within the United States since 1968 show substantial increases since the early 1960s (Pettigrew, 1988; Tucker & Mitchell-Kernan, 1990). Similarly, attitudes of members of different castes in India became more liberal after the 1960s, so that individuals belonging to lower castes became more positively evaluated (Anant, 1977). Thus, attitudes tend to vary across time within any specific culture.

Attitudinal Differences Across Groups.   Surveys also reveal differences across different groups within societies. Research in the United States has shown that males hold more "tolerant" attitudes toward rapists (at least male ones) than do females and are more likely to believe in the "rape myth" that women secretly want to be raped and "ask for it" by dressing and acting in provocative ways (Malmouth, 1981). Men are also more likely than women to hold such attitudes as "sex and power are highly related" and "I would like to have sex with many partners" (Hendrick, Hendrick, Slapion-Foote, & Foote, 1985; Kilmartin, 1994). A meta-analysis by Bernard Whitley and Mary Kite (1995) showed women to have more tolerant attitudes than men toward homosexuality and the civil rights of gays and lesbians.

Another example of group differences in attitudes is provided by Peter Stringer and Gillian Robinson (1991), British researchers who edited a series of studies that reported interesting differences across gender and religious groups in Northern Ireland. While 66 percent of women reported that pornographic material should be banned altogether, only 42 percent of men thought so; and while 67 percent of Catholics expressed the attitude that the government should encourage "mixed" schools (that is, schools which both Catholic and Protestant children attend), only 57 percent of Protestants thought so. Prolife attitudes are stronger in Northern Ireland, which has more Catholics; prochoice attitudes are stronger in Britain, which has more Protestants (Montgomery & Davies, 1991).

Attitudinal Similarities Across Cultures.   Patterns of attitudes can also suggest similarities in social behavior across cultures. Evidence from research in a number of cultures suggests that individuals who enjoy a high status and have a high level of education hold more positive attitudes toward minorities. This general trend is suggested by research in Western societies, such as Germany (Wagner & Schonbach, 1984) and the United States (Ransford, 1972). It is also suggested by research in some developing societies. For example, research in India shows that high-caste Hindus (Majeed & Ghosh, 1981) and college students (Anant, 1978) tend to hold more positive attitudes toward minorities compared with the rest of Indian society.

Social psychologists have tried to progress beyond providing descriptions of attitudes to identifying relationships between attitudes and behavior that hold across cultures. In the first part of this chapter we saw that social psychologists have been preoccupied in particular with establishing the conditions under which attitudes "cause" behavior. When will an individual act according to her attitudes? When examined in cultural context, this focus on individuals "acting on their words" reveals important insights into why attitude research has taken its present path.

The Model of the Independent Individual

> Whoso would be a man, must be a nonconformist. . . . Nothing is at last sacred but the integrity of your own mind. Absolve you to yourself, and you shall have the suffrage of the world.
>
> —Ralph Waldo Emerson, *Self-Reliance*

The debate on attitudes should be considered as part of a larger discussion based on a model of people as "self-contained individuals" whose behavior is caused by dispositional characteristics. To appreciate fully the tremendous emphasis placed by social psychologists in the United States on dispositional factors, we must first consider the image of the person that is idealized in Western societies, and in the United States in particular. In this discussion, we see that attitudes, attributions, and the self are inextricably linked.

The cult of "rugged individualism" is so dominant in the United States, and has gained so much influence in Western societies generally, that it is sometimes difficult even to recognize the extent of its influence. Being immersed in the culture of the United States, we fail to recognize the ideal of individualism surrounding us. One way to unveil this ideal is to consider the portrayal and glorification of individualism in the movies.

In his important essay, Robert Warshaw (1962) defines the western movie in terms of its hero, who acts alone and by his own code of honor. The film scholar Will Wright (1975) notes that the classic plot shows a lone stranger who rides into a troubled town and cleans it up. The hero is a single male, and on those occasions when he is accompanied by family members, they tend to be killed by the forces of evil, so that he is left alone to fight as a totally independent, self-reliant person. The characters played by actors such as Gary Cooper, John Wayne, and Clint Eastwood personify the self-reliant, mobile, independent individual. They ride into town alone, fight alone, and then ride into the sunset alone.

A number of film scholars agree that *Shane* stands out as a kind of archetypical western (see Lenihan, 1980, p. 16; Wright, 1975, p. 33). Made in 1955, the film was directed by George Stevens and starred Alan Ladd; it remains one of the most popular westerns in cinema history. The story begins with the lone Shane riding down from the mountains into a valley. He befriends Joe and Marion Starret, who give him a job on their farm. The Starrets are among a group of farmers being bullied by the Riker brothers, ranch owners who are intent on driving everyone else out of the valley. The Rikers and their ranch hands cause a lot of problems for the good people of the valley, but Shane stays out of the fighting. However, when the Rikers send for a professional gunfighter, Shane's code of honor leads him to intervene. In a grand fight scene, Shane rides into town and defeats the gunfighter, as well as the Riker brothers. The final scene shows the hero alone once more, wounded and riding back into the mountains. The poignancy of this final scene is intensified by the romantic attraction that he and Marion Starret had for one another.

Attitudes and "Rugged Individualism"

Shane is the kind of character who fits the attitudinal models of social psychology, particularly the models of reasoned action (Fishbein & Ajzen, 1974) and planned behavior (Ajzen, 1991). In order to understand this "fit" better, let us look closely at two issues: first, Shane as a "man of his word," a rational being who takes action on the basis of personal attitudes and codes of honor; and second, a view of society as open and mobile, so that individuals move about freely, propelled by dispositional forces.

The story of Shane, as is true of all classic westerns, is ultimately about personal choice and courage, about individuals coming to hold certain attitudes and having the courage to act on them. Shane does not jump into the fight impulsively. He stands aloof and analyzes the situation independently, and his attitudes evolve on the basis of his own assessments. He does not talk much, but what he says *matters*, in the sense that he says what he thinks and he acts on his words. In short, his attitudes drive his actions.

In reviewing Shane's actions—his fight to protect the rights of the Starrets and the other farmers—it is clear that he did what he thought had to be done. The thrust of the film is to make us see Shane's behavior as driven by his own characteristics—the way he thought—rather than by external factors. This idealized image of the person as "thinking, then doing," so that action follows thought, is shared by social psychological models of attitudes, like the models of reasoned action and planned behavior.

This depiction of individuals requires that society be conceived as open to allow individuals to change their positions, both geographically and socially. After the gunfight through which he wins the valley back for the Starrets and the other honest farmers, Shane moves on by himself. The country is open and allows for such geographical mobility. But society is also socially open, so that the positions Shane and other

The hero in cowboy movies personifies the self-reliant, individually mobile, independent person idealized in U.S. society. Clint Eastwood, shown here in a scene from the movie *Unforgiven*, is the epitome of rugged individualism. Rather than trying to mobilize collective action, he moves from place to place and tackles each new challenge alone.

individuals achieve in the status hierarchy depend on their own attitudes and other dispositional characteristics.

Attitudes and Independent Individuals

In the rational models, such as those of reasoned action and planned
behavior, attitudes have three key characteristics. First, they are *person-
determined*; they arise through cognitive processes within individuals.
Social factors may influence attitudes, but ultimately social influences
are cognitively processed within individuals. The person, not society, is
assumed to shape attitudes and to determine their ultimate form.

Second, attitudes are assumed to be *person-contained*; they are conceived as entities that have an individual rather than a social character.
They are carried around as part of the private world of each person and
do not have a life outside the person; it is the individual who serves as
the vehicle for attitudes, not the collectivity.

The third characteristic of attitudes as conceived by the rational
models is that attitudes and behavior have a sequential relationship: *Attitudes cause behavior* (see Figure 4–6). Attitudes come first, followed by
the behavior they cause. The thinking, the cognitive process, is assumed
to come before the action. Shane, again, is an example of this—he
stood back from the action, arrived at a position, then acted according
to his attitudes. This assumed sequence—with the vast majority of social psychological research examining attitudes "causing" behavior—
underscores the idea that humans can best be understood by studying
independent minds.

Next we review research that challenges the rational account. First,
we consider the issue of consistency and culture. Then we review European research that presents attitudes as social rather than personal

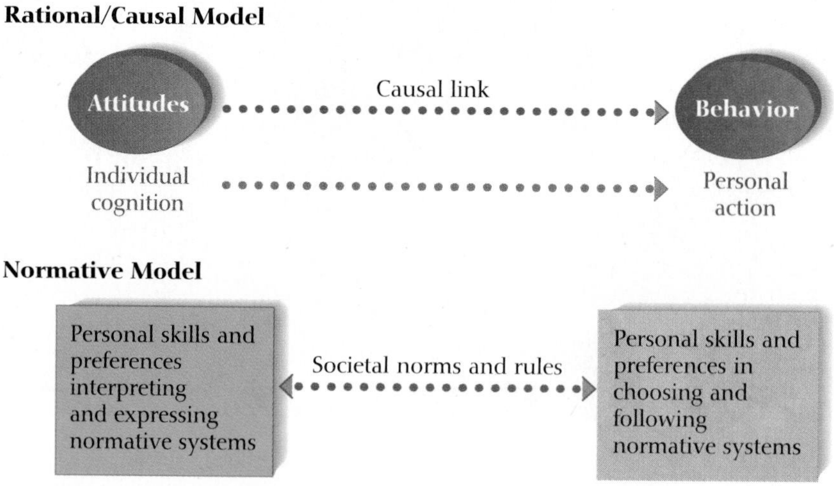

Figure 4–6 Schematic representation of the rational and normative models of
behavior.

entities, as being carried and transmitted by society rather than by the individual.

Attitudes, Consistency, and Culture

How people are required to behave in order to achieve positive evaluation depends largely on the normative system of the culture in which they live. Some researchers have argued that being able to handle inconsistency is taken to be a sign of maturity in traditional cultures such as Japan (Hong, 1992; Iwao, 1988). According to this viewpoint, cognitive dissonance theory does not explain behavior in Japan as effectively as it explains it in the United States, because consistency is valued more in American culture, and people there are more concerned with being consistent.

However, rather than simply assuming that consistency is valued in some cultures more than others, a more realistic approach would be to assume that how much importance is given to consistency *varies across domains* in different cultures. For example, in some Islamic societies considerable importance is given to consistency in following religious strictures. In such societies, "being religious" requires consistency in prayers, abstention from alcohol, paying of Islamic taxes, and following the edicts of religious leaders (who also act as political leaders). But in secular Western societies, less emphasis is placed on consistency in following religious rulings, and the mixing of politics and religion is seen as inconsistent. It is during the process of socialization that individuals learn about the importance their cultures give to consistency in various domains of social life. They learn that in their culture it is vital to be consistent in their attitudes and behavior in some domains but less so in others.

The Russian psychologist Alexander Luria (1976) conducted a series of pioneering studies in Central Asia during the 1930s that reveal fascinating features of reasoning by unschooled people in that part of the world. Luria asked participants to complete a series of incomplete syllogisms—exercises in deductive reasoning that involve two premises and a conclusion. (A famous example of a complete syllogism is "All men are mortal; Socrates is a man; therefore, Socrates is mortal.") The following is an example of the interactions that occurred during Luria's (1976, p. 108) research:

Researcher: In the Far North, where there is snow, all bears are white. Novaya Zemyla is in the Far North. . . . What color are the bears there?

Respondent: We always speak of only what we see, we don't talk about what we haven't seen.

Researcher: But what do my words imply? (repeats syllogism)

Respondent: Well, it's like this: our tsar isn't like yours, and yours isn't like ours. Your words can be answered only by someone who was there, and if a person wasn't there, he can't say anything on the basis of your words.

In another part of the research, Luria (1976, p. 58) asked participants to identify the odd item from the following four objects: a hammer, a saw, a log, and a hatchet. Again, his questions were answered in a way that schooled people would find inconsistent (and frustrating!). Rather than identifying the log as not fitting the category of "tools," a typical response was that all four items belong because, "The saw has to saw the log, the hammer has to hammer it, and the hatchet has to chop it. . . . You can't take any of these things away." Clearly, what these participants found consistent, we would find inconsistent. Patricia Murphy and Carol Miller (1997) have shown a similar kind of cross-cultural difference in consistency using American and Finnish participants.

The field research of Charles Nuckolls (1992, 1993) provides similar insights into psychological consistency and culture. During field research in South India, Nuckolls was told by Indian shamans (priests) that sometimes "false" ancestor spirits would interfere in their ceremonies and try to pass themselves off as true ones. Nuckolls suggested they should "test" the spirits to identify the true ones by asking questions only the true ancestor spirits would know (for example, "Do you remember the time we found a baby cobra in your turban?"). Although those schooled in the Western tradition would accept such a test as valid, the shamans would not.

In the course of my own travels and research, I have encountered instances of variations in psychological consistency across cultures. During a United Nations development project in the Persian Gulf region, I heard the following conversation between a Western engineer and a local supervisor:

Engineer: It is all settled then. All okay? (smiling anxiously)

Supervisor: Yes, all okay (nodding his head as he responds in broken English).

Engineer: Fine, so all the men will be ready and we shall start at seven tomorrow morning.

Supervisor: If God wills it.

Engineer: (Turning to the translator) He sounds hesitant again, what does he mean?

Translator: He said, if God wills it.

Engineer: (Addressing the supervisor) Look, let's be certain about this. I have to commit a lot of equipment out here and the men must be ready exactly at seven. Will they be ready? (turns to translator) Please ask him to confirm.

Supervisor: (Nodding his head) God willing, God willing.

Translator: He says yes, the men will be ready.

Engineer: But why does he keep saying "God willing, God willing?" If they will be ready, why does he bring God into it? Is he doubtful? (Turns to supervisor) Are you sure all okay?

Supervisor: Yes, all okay. All okay.

Engineer: (Heaving a sigh of relief) Fine, see you tomorrow morning then. (Turns to go)

Supervisor: If God wills it, yes.

Engineer: (Obviously annoyed, he throws up his hands) Oh, well, why don't we just forget about the bridge then. If God wills it, it will be built. Why should we make plans we can't keep?

Many Westerners who travel in so-called fatalistic societies experience similar frustrations. For them, the planning and execution of actions depend on individuals personally taking responsibility for events. Such an approach is inconsistent with a "fatalistic" attitude reflected in statements such as, "If God wills it, I shall start work at seven tomorrow."

Consistency in Western Cultures. But we should not assume that tolerance for psychological inconsistency is unique to traditional cultures, because it also exists in certain sectors of Western societies. Consider the domains of science and religion. The scientific method requires the testing and verification of hypotheses, whereas most major religions involve faith in phenomena that cannot be objectively tested or verified. But many tough-minded thinkers *do* believe in both science and religion, as in the case of the physicist who is also a Christian clergyman (McDonald, 1993). Charles Darwin (1809–1882), the English naturalist who (with Alfred Wallace) originated the theory of evolution by natural selection, was a scientist of genius but was also a deeply religious man. In Plato's play *Crito*, Socrates (469–399 B.C.), the "father" of critical philosophical inquiry, is shown as having both the opportunity to escape from prison to save his life and as responding in the following way to the news that he will die tomorrow if he chooses not to escape: "If the Gods will it so, so be it" (1984, p. 80).

Clearly, then, what appears as psychologically inconsistent to some individuals may be consistent to others. Also, rather than seeing ideas about consistency and inconsistency as being developed within the private world of individuals, an alternative is to see them as social and as existing before the arrival of particular individuals in society. For example, religious belief systems and ideas about science exist prior to the arrival of individuals, who then proceed to form attitudes toward God and toward science through socialization. This perspective leads us to consider shared ideas—or "social representations"—among the members of societies.

Social Representations. For some people, concepts such as "social representations" and "thinking societies" are inconsistent. Such people would argue that individuals, rather than collectivities, have "representations," and "thinking" goes on in the minds of individuals, not groups.

social representations the ideas and explanations that exist in society and are used by people to think about and interpret the world.

This leads us to ask: Is the French social psychologist Serge Moscovici (1988a, 1988b) inconsistent when he refers to a "thinking society"? No, as we shall see.

Social representations are the ideas and explanations that exist in society and are used by people to think about and interpret the world (Mugny & Carugati, 1989). Creationism and evolutionism are two sets of ideas and explanations about the world and how it came into being, and they are social representations. They exist prior to the arrival of a person into this world, but they are available to be used by him to explain the world. *Cultural* social representations, such as creationist accounts of the world, are very long-lasting and may survive many generations (Sperber, 1985). *Traditional* social representations, such as attitudes held by one group toward another, may last only a generation or two, while *fashions*, such as appropriate length of skirts or width of ties, are the most transient.

Moscovici (1984) proposes that social representations have two roles. Their first role is to *conventionalize* the world, meaning that they allow us to find a place for new phenomena in an already existing system of categories and meanings. For example, imagine you have just arrived at Istanbul International Airport and are about to step into a taxi when the driver starts gesticulating at you. Social representations guide you to recognize the hand signals as a means of communication (rather than as an automatic bodily movement, such as eye blinking, for example), and then to realize that he is telling you that he already has a passenger. The second role of social representations is *prescriptive*, in the sense that they decree what people should do in different situations. For example, social representations guide you to take another taxi or to ask the already seated passenger if it would be possible to share the ride into Istanbul.

The concept of social representations leads us to look outside the individual to study social attitudes as part of social thinking. Through the concept of social representations, we can conceptualize attitudes not as private entities within personal worlds, but as public entities that exist prior to the individual and are shared by collectivities. The more social approach of the European social psychologists Serge Moscovici, Willem Doise, and others also leads us to conceive of the person as unitary, with the self, attributions, and attitudes being inextricably linked (see Doise, 1986).

An influential example is a study by the French researcher Claudine Herzlich (1973) on the social representations of health and illness, in which she identified representations of illness as "destructive" ("I've the feeling that when an active life is hit by a serious illness, it's the end," p. 144); as a "liberator" ("I think things are certainly new, become new, because of the presence or threat or possibility of death," p. 145); as an "occupation" ("for me, it's more of an occupation when I can put up a fight against my illness," p. 150). Herzlich's research showed how the types of social representations individuals hold of illness influence their strategies for coping with their own illnesses. Lynn Payer's (1988) comparison of the United States, England, West

Germany, and France suggests that differences in social representations of health and illness are also associated with differences in medical treatments. For example, in the United States doctors are trained to view the body as a machine and all problems as technical ones with technical solutions:

> American doctors perform more diagnostic tests than doctors in France, West Germany, or England. They often eschew drug treatment in favor of more aggressive surgery, but if they do use drugs they are likely to use higher doses and more aggressive drugs. . . . The dosages in psychiatry are particularly high, sometimes as much as ten times those used elsewhere. (pp. 124–125)

British doctors view illness more as something to be tackled "keeping the upper lip stiff":

> British doctors prescribe fewer drugs (6.53 per capita) than French (10.04) or German (11.18) doctors. They are unlikely to use calcium supplements, lactobacillus, or the kinds of peripheral vasodilators used in France at all, and they use fewer heart drugs than the French and Germans, and fewer anticancer drugs than the Americans. (p. 102)

Rather than viewing the heart as a pump, as do doctors in the United States, Germans see the heart as the center of emotions:

> Germans certify fewer patients as having died of coronary artery disease (clogged arteries), but they certify more as dying of "other heart disease," undoubtedly reflecting their belief that heart disease is more complex than blocked pipes. The German way of looking at the heart and what ails it leads to fewer bypass operations and fewer artificial hearts. (p. 81)

While the Germans see the heart as the center of health, the French give that role to the liver and focus considerable attention on the liver crisis, or *crise de foie:*

> French people and their doctors attribute an extremely wide range of complaints to the liver, including painful menstruation, paleness, yellowness, and general fatigue. Both patients and dermatologists sometimes accuse the liver of causing acne or rash, dandruff, herpes, and other skin complaints. (p. 57)

The Self, Attitudes, and Culture. The concept of social representations is also creative in that it brings under one umbrella a number of topics—self, attributions, and attitudes—that are usually discussed separately. It is useful to elaborate on this with a final example.

In the chapters on the self and on attributions, we see that how the self is conceptualized in a particular culture is associated with how individuals attribute causes to events. In this section, we shall see that conceptions of the self, and particularly how the self is presented to others, are also closely associated with the attitudes individuals hold. Consider the following example.

In 1990, Harold Stevenson, Chuansheng Chen, and Shin-Ying Lee (1993) conducted a study of mathematics achievement of children in China, Japan, and the United States as a follow-up to a study first conducted in 1980. The results showed that in both 1990 and 1980 children in China and Japan scored better in mathematics than their counterparts in the United States. Of more interest to us is the attitude of mothers toward their children's performance. Although in both 1990 and 1980 only about 4 percent of Japanese and Chinese mothers reported that they were "very satisfied" with their children's academic performance, well over 40 percent of the mothers in the United States reported being "very satisfied." Despite the high media attention during the 1980s to the relative international standing of children in the United States on academic achievement tests, a slightly higher percentage of American mothers reported being "very satisfied" in 1990 compared to reports in 1980.

What explains these results? Is it that mothers in the United States were not aware of their children's standing in relation to children from competing countries? No; Stevenson and his colleagues show that the mothers in the United States had a good assessment of their children's relative standing, so it was not a lack of knowledge that led to their "very satisfied" attitudes. Rather, these findings are partly explained by the tremendous emphasis placed on positive self-presentation in the United States. The culture places high priority on "presenting a positive attitude" under all circumstances. This tendency influences all social interactions, particularly those involving the self. Thus, how the self is required by cultural norms to be presented to others influenced the mothers in the United States to portray positive attitudes toward their children's performance.

Concepts and Issues

Although present in all societies, attitudes can differ across cultures, across groups within cultures, and across time. There are also some cross-cultural similarities in attitudes. Social psychologists have attempted to establish the role of attitudes as "causes" of behavior. The cultural reason for this orientation has to do with the model of "independent individualism" dominant in the United States, its underlying assumption that individuals strive to achieve consistency, and that attitudes are located in individual minds. Cross-cultural research points to a different picture: People live with many inconsistencies. European research on social representations envisages evaluations as social, public, and an integral part of the norms, rules, and values of society, rather than personal, private, and "inside" individuals.

1. In what ways are attitudes universal and in what ways cross-culturally different?
2. What is the model of the "independent individual"?
3. How can cross-cultural research help us better understand the idea of consistency assumed in dissonance theory?

Conclusion

Researchers have discovered conditions in which attitudes predict behavior and others in which attitudes follow behavior. Individuals can be "rational individualists" and act according to their attitudes, but sometimes people manipulate their attitudes to rationalize their past behavior. Cognitive dissonance and self-perception theory accounts of why individuals change their attitudes to match their behavior have a common implication: Individuals are motivated to present themselves in a positive light. The nature of the self they are required to present in order to be evaluated positively is largely culture-dependent. The Western preoccupation with consistency and rationality led Festinger and others to propose cognitive dissonance theory. A more social approach to the explanation of thinking is Moscovici's research on social representations.

For Review

Attitudes are evaluations of people and phenomena with some degree of favor or disfavor. They seem to have always been an integral part of human social life, and they certainly are pervasive in the contemporary world.

The attitudes people hold on particular issues tend to vary across cultures, across time periods within cultures, and across minority and majority groups within cultures. But there are also important attitudinal similarities across cultures.

Attitudes have been conceived as involving one, two, or all three major elements: *affect, behavior,* and *cognition.* The relationship between attitudes and behavior has been a special focus of research.

The idea that attitudes influence behavior has a long history, and it is the focus of unprecedented research attention in modern social psychology. A number of researchers took up the challenge of using empirical research to identify the conditions in which attitudes can predict behavior. This research was in large part stimulated by the theories of "reasoned action" and "planned behavior," as well as a number of modifications, such as the MODE model.

Attitudes can better predict behavior when there is greater correspondence between attitude-behavior specificity, when multiple measures of attitudes and behavior are used, and when attitudes are derived through direct experience, are attended to, well known, and accurately measured.

Research attempting to use attitudes as predictors of behavior has followed a "causal" model of behavior, conceiving of humans as "rational individualists," independent beings whose thinking guides actions.

Cognitive dissonance theory proposes that instances of "attitudes following behavior" arise because individuals experience an unpleasant state of arousal when they become aware of two inconsistent cognitions. Self-perception theory proposes that individuals learn about their own attitudes as they come to know the attitudes of others—by observing behavior. Attitudes appear to "follow" behavior because when individuals report on their own attitudes, they infer them from their past behavior.

Although cognitive dissonance theory and self-perception theory have been used successfully to explain the same research findings, their explanatory power differs in some domains. Research supporting both theories implies that individuals are concerned about being evaluated positively by others. The requirements individuals have to meet in order to be evaluated positively vary across cultures in important ways, as does the role of psychological consistency in such evaluations.

Recent European research on social representations suggests a way of conceptualizing social thinking, including attitudes, as social and public rather than as individual and private.

A conceptualization of attitudes as "out there in society" rather than as being "created and processed" in the private minds of individuals also allows for a more integrated model of the person. It becomes possible to view the "self," "attributions," and "attitudes" as interdependent: The attitudes and attributions people hold reflect on the self they seek to present.

For Discussion

1. In what ways has research on the attitude-behavior link been influenced by a rationalist model of behavior?

2. How do cognitive dissonance theory and self-perception theory differ in their explanations of why behavior can influence attitudes?

3. How does research on automatic processes influence our picture of the attitude-behavior relationship?

Key Terms

Attitudes *100*

Cognitive dissonance *114*

Extrinsic motivation *120*

Intrinsic motivation *120*

Priming *110*

Social representations *132*

Stereotype *110*

Theory of planned behavior *106*

Theory of reasoned action *104*

Annotated Readings

A thorough review of classic and more recent attitude research is provided in R. E. Petty and J. T. Cacioppo, *Attitudes and persuasion: Classic and contemporary approaches* (Boulder, CO: Westview Press, 1996).

Leading researchers provide critical discussions of major topics in attitude research in R. E. Petty and J. A. Krosnick, eds., *Attitude strength: Antecedents and consequences* (Hillsdale, NJ: Lawrence Erlbaum, 1995).

Large numbers of social psychologists and other social scientists are engaged in attitude measurement in applied fields. A well-organized and detailed discussion of attitude measurement techniques is H. Schuman and S. Presser, *Questions and answers in attitude surveys: Experiments on question form, working, and context* (Thousand Oaks, CA: Sage, 1996).

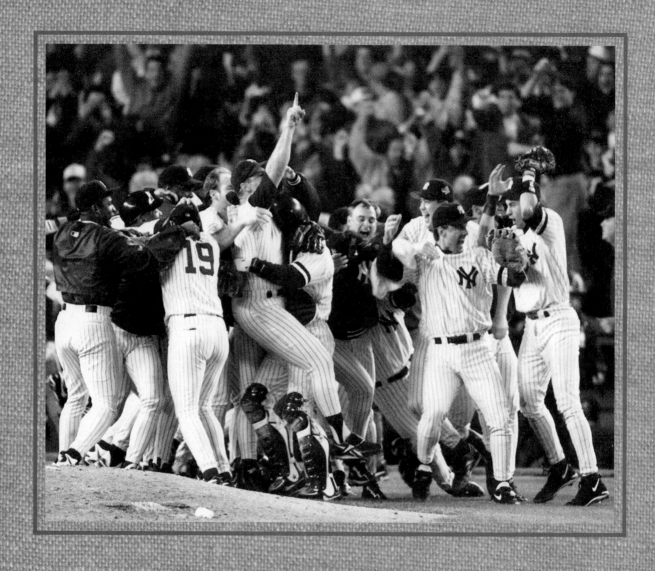

CHAPTER **5**

Attributions

◄ "We're number one! Why did we win? Well, of course, because we are the best team." This is how people typically make attributions when they achieve positive results. It is all because of factors internal to the self (drive, ambition, talent, and so on). But when they experience a negative outcome, people tend to make attributions in a different way—bad luck, terrible weather, the officials need glasses. . . .

"W hat is fate?" Nasrudin was asked by a scholar.

"An endless succession of intertwined events, each influencing the other."

"That is hardly a satisfactory answer. I believe in cause and effect."

"Very well," said Nasrudin, "look at that." He pointed to a procession passing in the street.

"That man is being taken to be hanged. Is that because someone gave him a silver piece and enabled him to buy the knife with which he committed the murder; or because someone saw him do it; or because nobody stopped him?"

Most of us, like the scholar, believe in cause and effect. Rather than seeing events as "endlessly intertwined," we explain the world around us by attributing specific causes to events. Why is John making that anti-war speech? Because he is a pacifist. Why did Carla drive her car over my bicycle? Because she is a terrible driver. Why did I fail that exam? Because the questions were unfair. For each event, we tend to identify specific factors as causes.

Why Attributions Are So Important

attribution how people identify causes.

The study of **attribution,** how people identify causes, has been central to social psychology since the 1970s (Gilbert & Malone, 1995; Weiner, 1991, 1993). Attribution was the most important topic of research in social psychology during the 1970s and early 1980s (Ross & Fletcher, 1985). Through thousands of studies, researchers have discovered that in some situations people can be systematically biased in how they attribute causes to **dispositional factors** (characteristics of a person) and **external factors** (characteristics of a situation). For example, findings suggest that we are likely to attribute John's speech to his pacifist beliefs (dispositional factors) even when we know he is playing a role in a play that calls for him to make that speech (situational factors). Similarly, I will tend to attribute Jane's driving performance to her dispositional characteristics (She is a terrible driver, she just steamrolled my bicycle!) rather than to the fact that the roads were slick. But I am likely to explain away my poor performance on an exam by attributing the cause to external factors (unfair exam) rather than to dispositional factors (lack of effort or ability on my part).

dispositional factors characteristics of a person.

external factors characteristics of a situation.

The research literature shows that attributions are both fundamentally important and extremely pervasive in social life (Hewstone, 1990). They are associated with how people orient themselves not only to themselves and to other individuals but also to the larger society (Hilton, Smith, & Kin, 1995). Consider the case of Samantha, who is unemployed. How do we explain her unemployed status? Research suggests that those who attribute the causes of unemployment to dispositional factors tend to be more politically conservative (Feather, 1985). They are more likely to explain Samantha's predicament by statements such as "She is unemployed because she is not motivated enough. Anyone can find a job if he or she really wants to."

Unemployed protester marches outside a political convention. The ways in which people make attributions tend to be associated with their political views. Those who are politically to the right tend to attribute unemployment to internal factors, such as lack of effort and ability; those politically to the left tend to attribute unemployment to external factors, such as ineffective government policy and an economy that produces too few jobs with good pay and benefits.

Those who are politically more liberal are more likely to attribute the causes of unemployment to factors external to the person. They are more likely to endorse explanations such as "The government and private industry have not created enough job opportunities for black women like Samantha." Such attributional explanations link the situation of an individual, in this case Samantha, to societal events, such as federal job–creation programs.

Social psychologists are generally in agreement about what attributions are, and most researchers agree the focus of study to be how people identify causes. However, there is less agreement about the sources of attributions. One possible source is cognitive universals. There may be cognitive mechanisms that lead people to attribute causes in particular ways, and the same cognitive mechanisms may be present in all societies. An alternative possibility is that the source of attributions is in our cultures, so that we learn to make attributions according to the norms and rules of our culture. The biases we show in making attributions happen because of the biases of our cultures.

What are the sources of attributions? How do we explain attributions? In what ways are attributions biased? These questions will guide our discussion in this chapter. First, we will examine attribution theory and consider the most influential models researchers have developed. Second, we consider two important sources of attributions: culture and personality. Third, we will chart the fascinating discoveries researchers have made through explorations of attributional biases, with a focus on attributions as associated with emotions.

Concepts and Issues

Attribution, how we make inferences about causes, is of fundamental importance in everyday social life and has been an important topic of study in social psychology since the 1970s. Social psychologists are in agreement about what attributions are, but not about the extent to which the sources of attributions are culture–based and local, and the extent to which they are based on cognitive universals.

1. Give two examples of attributions you made today.
2. Joan sends her boss, Paul, flowers for his birthday. Explain how Paul could attribute this act to internal factors, and how Joan could attribute it to external factors.

Attribution Theory: How Do We Explain Attributions?

Psychologists have developed a number of explanations that come under the general term *attribution theory*, and these explanations have three main characteristics. First, although efforts have been made to adapt models so that they compete directly with one another (e.g., Howard, 1985), the models still tend to focus on *different* aspects of attributions. They are, therefore, more accurately described as complementary rather than as competing models. Second, the models are mainly concerned with how attributions "should" take place if they proceed logically; thus, they adopt a view of human behavior as being rational. Third, not all of the influential models pay serious attention to the role of motivations and emotions.

Commonsense Psychology in Everyday Life: Heider

Fritz Heider (1944) is often described as the founder of attribution theory, and his book, *The Psychology of Interpersonal Relations* (1958), is seen as the source of many ideas that have become central to attributional research. Unlike some of the attributional theorists who followed him, Heider was concerned with motivation. He believed that people are motivated to make sense of the world, in part because knowing what causes things to happen improves our ability to predict and act on the environment. He was concerned with the "commonsense" psychology that underlies our explanations of both causality—what causes things to happen—and responsibility—what is responsible for the occurrence of an event.

In addition to distinguishing between internal causes (assumed to reside within individuals) and external causes (assumed to reside outside individuals, in the environment), Heider classified internal causes as relating to motivation and ability. John may have the ability to drive safely, but without the motivation to do so he remains a menace to everyone he drives past, or over. Heider distinguishes between levels of responsibility, the weakest being responsibility by association. If one of your friends has his license revoked and his parents accuse you of being responsible because "you failed to recognize his situation," then you are being held responsible by association. Stronger than this is *causal responsibility*, which means that you cause something to happen without intending to. If your telephone call to the police led to your friend being arrested for driving while intoxicated, you are *causally* responsible for the revocation of his license, even though this was not what you intended. Of course, you may have wanted this to occur because he was likely to kill someone, in which case you are held to be *intentionally* responsible, the highest level of responsibility.

Correspondent Inference: Jones and Davis

Imagine if, on your first meeting with Sara, she makes critical comments concerning a project about which you feel very proud. How likely are you to infer that she is an aggressive person? According to Edward Jones and Keith Davis (1965), we generally do infer that people's intentions and dispositions correspond to their actions. The theory of **correspondent inference** specifies the conditions under which we are more likely to attribute causes to the dispositional characteristics of others.

In general, actions that are "uncommon"—outside a person's social role—and entered into by choice are more likely to be seen as corresponding to dispositions. For example, if you have entered your project in a competition and Sara is the twentieth person to criticize

correspondent inference theory that specifies the conditions under which we are more likely to attribute causes to the dispositional characteristics of others.

it today, if she is one of the judges for the competition and thus her role is to comment on your project, and if she is obliged by the rules of the competition to be a severe critic, then her critical comments might tell you little about her dispositional characteristics. After all, anyone doing the job would behave in the same way. However, if Sara is the only person to comment critically on your project, if this is her first day as a new student in a class you teach, and if she volunteered the critical comments, then you are more likely to assume she is an aggressive person. After all, not many students volunteer severe criticisms of projects by their teachers during their first day in a class.

The Covariation Model: Kelley

covariation model the assumption that individuals make attributions by assessing the relationship among three types of information: distinctiveness, consistency, and consensus.

The concern with rational causal inferences divorced from emotions is to some extent evident in Jones and Davis's correspondent inference theory; but it is even more prominent in Harold Kelley's (1967, 1973) covariation model (see Figure 5–1). Kelley's model attempts to be more expansive than that of Jones and Davis. The **covariation model** considers attributions made to the physical environment, such as John inferring that Mary was late for their date because of a downpour, in addition to attributions made to other people, such as John inferring that Mary deliberately turned up an hour late for their date. If visitors from outer space were to read Kelley's model, they might imagine human beings to be rational information-processing systems, rather like computers. This is not surprising—Kelley's model was developed at a time when the cognitive revolution, with its metaphor of "humans as computers," had gained momentum.

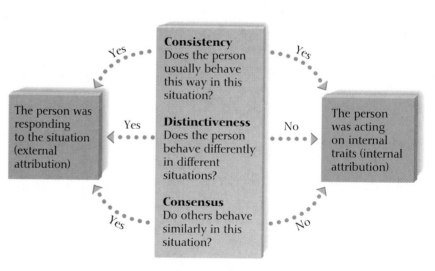

Figure 5–1   Kelley's covariation model (after Philipchalk, 1995).

Kelley assumes that individuals make attributions by assessing the relationship among three types of information:

Distinctiveness (How unique is this event?)

Consistency (How consistent is this event over time?)

Consensus (Does everyone else experience this event?)

For example, consider a case in which Jane's performance as a lawyer is at times judged to be only "barely satisfactory" but at other times evaluated as "outstanding" by a committee with rotating membership. Jane, the only female lawyer in the company, attributes her "barely satisfactory" evaluations to the law firm president's dislike of female lawyers. This is because she receives "barely satisfactory" evaluations only when the president is on the evaluation committee (distinctiveness), she receives poor evaluations every time he is on the committee (consistency), and she is the sole lawyer to receive only "barely satisfactory" evaluations (consensus).

There are also many instances when we have information about just one occurrence of an event. For example, imagine your first meeting with a person who asks detailed questions about your financial situation. What is your annual income? Do you have loans outstanding? What are your assets? Kelley accounts for how people make causal attributions when explaining such single events by reference to **causal schemas,** ideas people have about how different factors combine to produce certain kinds of effects.

causal schema   idea a person has about how different factors combine to produce certain kinds of effects.

Causal schemas are strongly influenced by cultural norms. In some non-Western cultures, such as those of India and China, the person asking such detailed questions about your finances could be a relative of a potential spouse for you, and many more detailed bits of information may be exchanged as part of preparations for an arranged marriage. In Western societies, such detailed financial questions are more likely to be asked by your bank manager when you apply for a loan. Potential in-laws would tend to acquire such information in subtle and indirect ways (of course, there are exceptions to every rule).

Toward Explanations of Emotions and Attributions

Heider's pioneering work on attributions included a concern with motivation and control: People are motivated to understand causal relations so as to have more control over events. Several subsequent theorists have attempted to make more detailed links between attributions and emotions. These attempts are important because they highlight cases in which attributions may not proceed according to the rational models put forward by Kelley and others.

Stanley Schachter (Schachter, 1971; Schachter & Singer, 1962) has argued that attributions are central to the way in which we label a given physiological arousal as a specific emotion. Adam may feel excited when walking across a rickety bridge but misattribute his excitement as

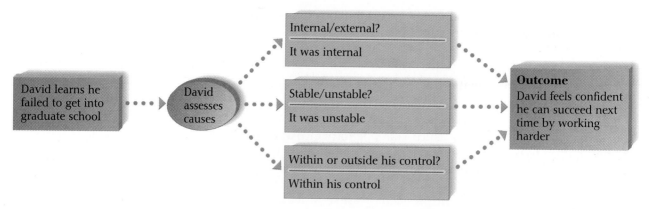

Figure 5–2   Weiner's attributional model (after Weiner, 1986).

a feeling of attraction for the girl he passed halfway across. (This topic is discussed in greater detail in Chapter 8.)

Whereas Schachter is concerned with how attributions affect the emotional labels ascribed to physiological changes, Bernard Weiner (1980, 1986) focuses on emotions associated with achievement attributions (see Figure 5–2). According to Weiner, people assess how far they have succeeded or failed in particular activities, and this leads to general positive or negative emotions. Three bases are used to make attributions for the causes of success/failure: Is the cause internal or external to the self (locus)? Is the cause stable or unstable (stability)? Is the cause within or outside your control (controllability)? The search for causes influences expectations about future success, as well as more specific emotional feelings.

For example, David experiences negative emotions after hearing he has failed to gain entrance to graduate school. He analyzes the cause of his failure and decides that it was internal (he did not work hard enough), unstable (the situation can be changed), and within his control (he *could* have worked harder and achieved much better scores). This attributional analysis leads him to feel a little ashamed that he wasted his time but also confident that he can succeed if he works hard and applies again next year. Notice, however, that a change in any one of the three bases for attribution could lead to a different outcome. For example, if David had concluded that the cause was stable rather than unstable (e.g., lack of ability, "I don't perform well on paper and pencil tests," rather than lack of effort), then he might feel satisfied with his past performance ("I did my best, that's all anyone can do") and be happy to follow a career path that does not require graduate training.

Assessing Attribution Theory

Research studies have provided some support for the explanations put forward by Jones and Davis (1965) and Kelley (1973), but it is Weiner's (1986) model that has been most extensively researched and adapted to different domains. Weiner's model has been tested in domains such as coping with AIDS (Weiner, 1988) and academic achievement (Van Over-walle, Segebarth, & Goldchstein, 1989), among others (for more detailed examples, see Graham & Folkes, 1990).

Weiner's model is also the one that has been most extensively studied cross-culturally (Bar–Tal, Goldberg, & Knaani, 1984; Betancourt & Weiner, 1982; Fletcher & Ward, 1988; Little, 1987; Louw & Louw-Potgieter, 1986; Schuster, Forsterling, & Weiner, 1989). A number of cross-cultural studies suggest that at least some aspects of Weiner's model are valid in non–Western cultures as well. Schuster, Forsterling, and Weiner (1989) conducted a study involving taxi drivers and civil servants in Belgium, Germany, India, South Korea, and England. Partici-pants were presented with the case of a person who fails to get a par-ticular job. The participants rated each of 22 possible causes for the per-son's failure to get the job (ability, attention, effort, interest, luck, mood, and so on) on the dimensions of control (To what extent controllable by the person?), stability (To what extent changeable?), locus (Does it reside internal or external to the person?), and universality (Does it in-fluence only this or also other outcomes?). Notice that universality was added to the original list of three dimensions in Weiner's model.

Schuster, Forsterling, and Weiner (1989) found fairly high consis-tency across cultures and occupational groups in how controllable, changeable, internal/external, and universal the 22 causes of failure were perceived to be. The one exception to this trend was the Indian sample, whose participants rated all causes as being more external, variable, and uncontrollable than did participants from the other four cultures. A similar trend among Indian participants is indicated by other researchers (e.g., Miller, 1984; Triandis, 1972). One interpretation is that Indians are more "fatalistic." However, if we consider only the Ger-man, Belgian, English, and South Korean participants, the results seem to provide some cross–cultural support for parts of Weiner's model, as did the earlier studies of Betancourt and Weiner (1982) involving partic-ipants from Chile and the United States, and those of Bar–Tal, Goldberg, and Knaani (1984) involving Asian–African and European–American families.

Studies that have asked participants to evaluate others following an achievement performance also show cross-cultural consistency. In these studies, participants are typically asked to assess a student according to level of ability (high or low), effort (high or low), and test outcome (pass or fail). Results from such studies conducted in Brazil (Rodriguez, 1980), England (Rogers, 1980), Germany (Rest, Nierenberg, Weiner, & Heckhausen, 1973), India (Esware, 1972), and Iran (Salili, Maehr, & Gillmore, 1976) show consistency in some areas. For example, high-ability students who fail because of lack of effort are more severely punished than low–ability students.

There is some support, then, for the proposition that participants from many different cultures see similar relations between causes of failure and the dimensions introduced by Weiner (see Bond, 1983). This is particularly true when participants are presented with a particular scenario, usually involving success or failure, and then asked to assess the outcome on the basis of a specific list of dimensions. But we also need to consider a number of broader issues that cast light on the ways in which people provide causal explanations.

Motivation for Attributions

Following Heider, attributional researchers have assumed that people are motivated to control their environment. This need leads them to try to identify the causes of events. But are different groups of people equally motivated to control their environments? An examination of different cultural groups suggests that historically some groups organize themselves toward mastering nature, whereas others are organized to live in harmony with, or be submissive to, nature (Kluckholm & Strodtbeck, 1961). This suggests that people in societies organized to dominate nature will engage in qualitatively and perhaps quantitatively different causal attributions, and some evidence exists to support this view (Miller, Bersoff, & Harwood, 1990).

People learn to make attributions "correctly," according to the normative systems of their societies. Societies organized to dominate nature, such as those of the industrialized West, encourage an attributional style that depicts humans as masters of nature. A major challenge for such societies has been to harness the power of nature, as represented by this hydroelectric dam, built by French engineers in Venezuela.

Studies show that participants in different cultures *can* make causal attributions when asked to by researchers (Bond, 1983), but this does not tell us *how often* people in different cultures actually do make causal attributions in their everyday lives. To address the issue of frequency, a more "naturalistic" research method is needed. Angela Little (1987) conducted a study along these lines with schoolchildren in Sri Lanka and England.

Little asked participants to explain the reasons for the failure or success of children engaged in different tasks, such as language tests. She found differences in the frequency with which the Sri Lankan and English participants attributed causes to particular events. She also found differences in the attributional categories used (such as ability, effort, and luck). Sri Lankan participants more frequently attributed outcome to the facilities available to the child than did English participants, perhaps because resources are more scarce in Sri Lanka. Little's results suggest that there is indeed some variation across cultures in the frequency with which people make causal attributions to explain the behavior of different groups.

Agent and Target in Attributions

Although Weiner (1985) concluded that events that are unexpected, important, and relevant to the self are more likely to be given causal explanations, attribution theorists seldom concern themselves with the characteristics of the person making the attributions or the target of attributions. For example, attribution theory does not consider whether the target of an attributional explanation is male or female or black or white, even though evidence suggests that the minority status of an attributional target tends to influence the attributions made (e.g., Romero & Garza, 1986; Stevens, 1986). For example, in the United States white teachers were shown to attribute more ability to white students than to black students with similar achievement scores (Hall, Howe, Merkel, & Lederman, 1986). Several studies have shown that performances by members of majority groups (e.g., males and whites) are attributed more to skill, whereas equivalent performances by members of minority groups (e.g., females and blacks) are attributed more to luck (Deaux & Emswiller, 1974; Yarkin, Town, & Wallston, 1982).

Related to this is a particularly interesting study by Paul Wong, Valerian Derlega, and William Colson (1988) that used a "spontaneous" method of studying causal thinking, involving two main stages. First, participants are presented with a scenario involving the successful or unsuccessful performance of a black or white target person. Then participants are asked what questions they would ask themselves given the performance of the target person and the most likely causes for such a performance.

Results showed that both black and white participants raised a higher number of attributional questions and provided more causal explanations to account for the performance of a black than a white target. Both groups of participants, it seems, were more concerned to

Attributions are made by everyone, even teachers. The biases that influence attributions are also shared by teachers. In the classroom, there has been a tendency for success by males and whites to be attributed to skill, whereas equivalent success by minority group members is more likely to be attributed to external factors, such as luck.

account for the performance of the black target group. This may be because it is assumed that a more complex set of factors (e.g., racial discrimination, environmental deprivation, cultural biases) affect the performance of blacks, and closer examination is required to make sense of such complexity. Thus, the frequency of attributions also depends on their target.

Concepts and Issues

The major attributional models have focused on the rationality of humans as independent decision makers. Research in the 1990s is returning to an examination of attribution and emotion, a topic Fritz Heider emphasized 50 years earlier. The methodology used to study attribution models may be telling us more about how people *can* make attributions in certain conditions, rather than how often and in what ways they actually *do* make attributions.

Research using the standard methodology has shown support for some aspects of the major models across cultures, but there also seem to be important cross-cultural differences both in the frequency and nature of attributions.

1. Provide an example of how two attribution models complement rather than compete with one another.
2. Do attribution models ignore emotions? Explain. Provide examples of those that do and those that do not.
3. Does cross-cultural research provide any support for major attribution models? Explain.

What Are the Sources of Attributions?

Individuals learn to make attributions as part of their socialization experiences. This learning is influenced in important ways by culture. But personal styles of making attributions also develop, leading to variations among individuals within each culture.

Culture

The vast majority of research studies on attributions have involved the assessment of how people make causal inferences about events they directly observe. In standard attributional studies, participants are presented with an event that has a successful/unsuccessful outcome and then asked to assess the causes of the outcome. Far less attention has been given to how people learn about causal relations through the "common sense" of their culture (Morris & Peng, 1994).

We saw (in Chapter 3) that the self derives many of its characteristics from culture; attribution is also closely tied to culture. Links between the self and attribution become clear when we consider these topics in cultural contexts (Fiedler, Semin, Finkenauer, & Berkel, 1995). Here we will compare individualistic and group-oriented or collectivistic cultures. In individualistic societies such as the United States, where the self is more independent, there is a greater possibility that causal attributions will be made to dispositional factors (Cousins, 1989; Markus & Kitayama, 1991). In collectivistic societies, attributions are more likely to be made to groups.

A distinction is sometimes made between culture and direct observation as sources of attributions (Wells, 1982). This distinction is somewhat artificial because socialization within a culture also influences direct observation. That is, our experiences of growing up in a culture, and as members of particular cultural groups within society, generally influence our interpretation of directly observed events. This idea is supported by research from several areas. Eyewitnesses to criminal events are often inaccurate in what they report, and their biases are in part associated with their own cultural background (Wolf & Bugaj, 1990). When the witness is of a different ethnic background from the suspect, inaccuracies tend to increase (Platz & Hosch, 1988).

Attributions in Individualistic Societies.   It is appropriate to illustrate the role of culture as a source of attributions by focusing on the United States. This is because U.S. culture has been particularly influential in social psychological studies of attributions. A stimulating point of departure for this discussion is "Letters from an American Farmer," in which Michel Guillaume Jean de Crèvecoeur (1782/1985) provided an idealized vision of life in the New World. The society he describes is a land of plenty where hard work is inevitably rewarded.

Crèvecoeur is one of the first to articulate the "American Dream," which has two key elements relevant to our discussion of attributions. First, the American Dream is an invitation to individuals rather than to groups. The individual is the important social unit, not social groups based on criteria such as gender, ethnicity, and socioeconomic status. Second, it idealizes society as a *meritocracy*, in which the position of each individual is based on personal abilities and efforts. Since it is assumed that society is open and competition is fair, individuals are depicted as enjoying the opportunity to move up or down the status hierarchy solely as a result of personal characteristics. Consequently, the American Dream is often personalized through the "rags-to-riches" stories of "great families," such as the Kennedys, the Rockefellers, the Vanderbilts, and the Fords and particularly their founders.

The American Dream implies that the root cause of people's outcomes, their successes and failures, is to be found *within themselves*. Vast opportunities are available to everyone, but progress is always conditional; there is always an *if* attached to every promise. The *if* refers to "appropriate" personal conduct: "If thou wilt work, I have bread for thee; if thou wilt be honest, sober, and industrious, I have greater rewards to confer on thee—ease and independence" (Crèvecoeur, 1782/1985, p. 402). A direct implication is that if people do not prosper, it is because of their dispositional characteristics, such as a failure to be "honest, sober, and industrious."

The focus on individuals as the primary cause of events is matched by an equally firm rejection of collectivities as being causally consequential. The American Dream idealizes a society in which the social characteristics of individuals, such as their past histories and family memberships, are irrelevant to their outcomes. This outlook is exemplified in such statements as "all men are created equal," found in the Declaration of Independence.

The United States is not the only country where the concepts of self-help and individual responsibility, and the idea that "the destiny of individuals is in their *own* hands," became popular. As described by the sociologist Max Weber (1930), these concepts and ideas were to different degrees influential in all Western societies that became industrialized (see also McClelland, 1961). However, the United States could make a special claim to being an "open" society because the ancient and often rigid social class system of European societies did not exist in the United States: There was no hereditary aristocracy or royal family.

In addition to the absence of historical class barriers, the United States also enjoyed special status as a geographically mobile society. Until well into the nineteenth century, individuals who were dissatisfied with conditions in a particular region of the country could venture into undeveloped territory and start a new community by claiming and settling virgin land. Such special historical conditions meant that concepts such as "self-help" and "open society" had far more importance in the United States than in other countries of the world (Turner, 1920).

Attributions in Traditional Societies.   It is useful to contrast the situation in the United States with that of a more traditional society, such as India. Historically, Indian society has been far more rigid, in the sense that it has had much lower mobility, both social and geographical (Silverberg, 1968). For example, the Indian caste system prescribes that an individual is born into a certain station in life and enjoys the responsibilities and rewards of only that inherited station. Caste, like gender, is something natural rather than something that people would want to escape from.

Untouchable woman sweeping the street in an Indian city. In some societies, the fate of individuals is determined by external factors, such as birth. In India, the traditional caste system puts the Untouchables in the lowest social position, and determines that their children share the same fate. The Indian federal government has tried to implement a variety of programs, including affirmative action, to reform this situation.

It has been known for individuals to move to an area where their background is unknown and then pass themselves off as a member of a higher caste (Mandelbaum, 1970), but such events are exceptions rather than the rule. The fate of the individual in Indian society is determined far more by family of birth and other external factors beyond that person's control.

Comparing Attributions in Individualistic and Collectivistic Societies. What happens if we compare attributions made by individuals in India with those made by individuals in the United States (see Figure 5–3)? First, as we saw in the discussion of the self, people in India have a greater tendency to conceive of the person in relation to social context and relationships, whereas in the United States the person is considered to be self-contained (Shweder & Bourne, 1984). Joan Miller has conducted a fascinating set of studies which show that attributions made by Indians tend to be more *contextualized* (see Miller 1984, 1986, 1987, in press; Miller, Bersoff, & Harwood, 1990; Miller & Bersoff, 1992). That is, whereas Americans tend to see an individual's actions as a matter of *personal choice*, Indians have a greater tendency to see actions as being influenced by social relationships and the responsibilities they engender.

Also, Americans are more likely to make general attributions such as "she is kind," the implication being that the kindness of this person is independent of the social context, whereas Indians tend to make contextualized attributions such as "she is a mother," implying that her kindness arises from her role as a mother. Similarly, Americans are more likely than Indians to attribute causes for promotion and demotion in the work setting to dispositional factors and less to situational factors (Smith & Whitehead, 1984).

The particular historical conditions of the United States, then, nurtured explanations of the social world that assume, first, the individual

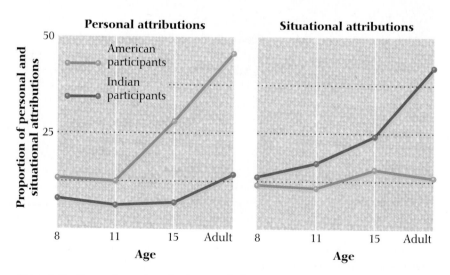

Figure 5–3 Comparison of attributions made by participants in India and the United States (after Miller, 1984).

rather than the group to be the most important social unit and, second, place particular emphasis on dispositional rather than situational factors in causal explanations.

In the contemporary world, the United States is highly individualistic, and major cross–cultural studies suggest it to be probably the most individualistic society in the world (e.g., Hofstede, 1980). This has important implications for social psychology because the United States dominates social psychological research. One implication is the focus on the individual and the neglect of situational factors in research on attributions (Moghaddam, Taylor, & Wright, 1993).

Personality: Locus of Control and Attributional Style

Just as culture influences the way attributions are made, so too does personality. Within the same culture, there tend to be wide variations in the way that people make attributions. For example, although the United States is a highly individualistic society, some Americans tend to attribute negative events, such as failure to land a particular job, to group membership rather than to other factors ("I failed to get that job because I am a member of group X, and not because I lack the necessary qualifications").

Julian Rotter (1966) introduced the term **locus of control** to distinguish between people who believe they control their own destiny (those with *internal locus of control*) and those who believe that their destiny is determined by factors external to themselves (those with *external locus of control*). In order to measure locus of control, Rotter (1971, 1973) developed a questionnaire that presents participants with pairs of statements and requires them to indicate which statement from each pair they more strongly believe. Here is an example:

locus of control   people who believe they control their own destiny versus people who believe their destiny is determined by external factors.

Do you more strongly believe statement (a) or (b) from each of the following pairs?

1. (a) In my experience, I have noticed that there is a direct connection between how hard I study and the grades I get.
   (b) Many times the reactions of my teachers seem haphazard to me.
2. (a) What happens to me is my own doing.
   (b) Sometimes I feel that I don't have enough control over the direction my life is taking.

If you select option (a) and respond similarly throughout the questionnaire, you will be classified as having an internal locus of control. The selection of option (b) and like responses will mean you are classified as having an external locus of control. The importance of locus of control is suggested by findings from studies demonstrating that in Western societies, those with an internal locus of control are better at tackling a wide range of challenges, such as school examinations, coping with illness, and problems in interpersonal relations (Phares, 1976; Strickland, 1988).

Applications: Education and Health

Researchers have been particularly intrigued by the implications of locus of control for education and health. When students become convinced that their *personal* efforts can make a difference ("Whether I get an A or not completely depends on how hard I work"), their grades improve (Peterson & Barrett, 1987). This in large part explains the success of "magic tutorial" courses that promise to make you a "straight A" student. The students who register and pay for such courses have already taken the most important step toward success—they have decided that they have to do something *personally* to change their situation. Instructors who run such tutorials invest a lot of time and effort to strengthen a person's internal locus of control, so that the student comes to believe "I can do it, it's up to me, I can do it, it's up to me." (Keep this in mind and you will never have to take one of these courses.)

The implications of locus of control are just as important for the domain of health. For example, imagine an individual who believes that all positive events are the result of external factors ("She has invited me to her party but only because most other people will be out of town that evening") and all negative events are due to internal factors ("That truck just unloaded a ton of garbage on my doorstep, but I suppose it's my fault for living in the city"). Martin Seligman and his associates have proposed that such a pessimistic **attributional style**— a tendency to make attributions in a consistent manner across different situations and times—tends to be associated with both mental and physical health disorders (Abramson, Seligman, & Teasdale, 1978; Peterson, Seligman, & Vaillant, 1988; Seligman, 1975, 1991).

Seligman has argued that with both animals (Seligman & Maier, 1967) and humans (Seligman, 1975), individuals sometimes come to believe that they are incapable of influencing the environment, so they give up trying and experience **learned helplessness.** Associated with this experience is mental depression, when individuals fail to initiate action and just sit around waiting for things to happen. More than 100 studies suggest at least a modest association between attributional style and depression (Hilsman & Garber, 1995; Sweeney, Anderson, & Bailey, 1986). A pessimistic attributional style tends to breed failure (Zullow & Seligman, 1990), just as an optimistic style tends to breed success (Seligman, 1991).

In some situations it may help us to remain more optimistic if we are less accurate in our attributions. Bettina Hannover (1995) found this in a study of East and West Berlin students, in which the West Berliners remained more self-satisfied even though they received more negative feedback on their exam performance. Hannover argued that because they were less self-serving in their attributions, the East Germans were affected more by the negative feedback they did receive.

In this domain, modern social psychological research provides empirical support for some of the intuitive insights of great thinkers. In William Shakespeare's play *Julius Caesar*, Cassius inspires Brutus to join

attributional style the tendency to make attributions in a consistent manner across different situations and times.

learned helplessness situation that occurs when individuals come to believe they are incapable of influencing the environment, so they give up trying.

A still from the 1967 film of Shakespeare's *Romeo and Juliet*. Romeo and Juliet are portrayed as characters who come to see their fate as determined by external factors. The only way they can gain control is by committing suicide. Perhaps their situation is not unlike that of individuals who see crime and drugs as the only route through which they can take control and change their own lives.

in the assassination of Caesar by persuading him that if they are "petty men" compared to the "Colossus" Caesar, it is up to *them* to change things. This is similar to athletes motivating themselves by believing that success comes from within (Si, Rethorst, & Willimczik, 1995). In essence, Cassius is saying, "We can do it, the cause of events lies within us!"

> The fault, dear Brutus, is not in our stars,
> But in ourselves, that we are underlings.
>
>   (*Julius Caesar*, act I, scene ii, line 134)

At the other extreme, in *Romeo and Juliet*, Shakespeare portrays two "star-crossed" young lovers who decide that events in their lives are determined mainly by external factors. Tragically, they come to believe that the only way they can take control is to die together.

Attributional Style Among Individuals and Societies

There is variation, then, across both individuals and societies in the way causes are attributed to events. For example, just as some individuals are more prone to attribute causes to factors internal to the self, so too are certain societies more likely than others to make such dispositional attributions. We may ask at this stage, Is there a link between explanations of events at the level of individuals and societies? Such a link is suggested by Heider's (1958) discussion of commonsense psychology and also by the concept of "social representations" arising from European research (see Chapter 4).

commonsense psychology   a set of beliefs that people share about the world which may not necessarily be true.

Commonsense Psychology.   The notion of **commonsense psychology** suggests a set of beliefs that people share about the world. These beliefs are not necessarily true. For example, in the early medieval era of Western Europe it was widely believed that bathing could be dangerous to one's health. Gradually, instead of believing that bathing can weaken the body and cause illness, people began to believe that cleanliness can be a cause of good health (Braunstein, 1988, p. 600). Moralists such as John Wesley (1703–1791) came to preach that "cleanliness is next to godliness."

Beliefs about causal links between bathing and health are examples of a society's "common sense." The French social psychologist Serge Moscovici (Farr & Moscovici, 1984; Moscovici, 1988a, 1988b) has used the term *social representations* to refer to such socially shared common sense, and earlier Émile Durkheim (1898/1974) had discussed a similar idea using the term *collective representations.* Social representations are like common sense in that they refer to ideas and explanations that exist in society and are available to individuals. An example of how certain beliefs spread and become part of a society's stock of shared common sense is provided by Moscovici's (1976a) study on psychoanalysis. He showed how psychoanalytic ideas, such as those concerning the unconscious and complexes, spread via the popular press and became part of everyday explanations for events among ordinary people. The widespread use of terms such as *Oedipus complex, ego,* and *word association* suggests that psychoanalysis has infiltrated a society's common sense.

Willem Doise and his associates at the University of Geneva have examined social representations of human rights (Clémence, Doise, de Rosa, & Gonzalez, 1995; Doise, Dell'Ambrogio, & Spini, 1991; Doise & Herrera, 1994). In a cross–cultural study involving more than 7,000 participants in 35 different countries, Doise and his colleagues showed a close match between beliefs about human rights and the Universal Declaration of Human Rights issued by the United Nations General Assembly in 1948 (Doise, Spini, & Clémence, 1997). At least in terms of expressed attitudes, advocacy of human rights was particularly strong in Christian and other monotheistic societies. Participants from all the different countries generally endorsed fundamental rights such as equal protection under the law and freedom of expression. This suggests that certain beliefs are part of an international set of social representations.

Discursive Psychology. A focus on the social construction of causal explanations has led some European researchers to develop an alternative to cognitive explanations of attributions (Harré, 1993; Sampson, 1993). Derek Edwards and Jonathan Potter (1992, 1993), British social psychologists, focus on the way people make inferences about causes in their everyday discourse. They argue that causal explanations are constructed as individuals generate their versions of events. Attributions are inseparable from memory. For example, as I talk you through my version of what happened yesterday when Carla drove over my bicycle, I am both re-creating that event (memory) and also making inferences about causes (attributions). In essence, my version of the event is presented in the form of discourse within which are embedded causal inferences.

The discursive approach leads to a focus on society rather than the individual as the source of explanations for events. **Discursive psychology** examines explanations that exist outside individuals and are often there prior to the arrival of an individual on the scene. That is, various possible explanations exist in society for the interpretation of any event. Such explanations can be adopted by individuals as they search for interpretations of the world that make sense to them and that help them to present themselves in desired ways. Imagine a black female and a white male are on the short list for a managerial position. There already exist a number of possible explanations for why each of them could succeed or fail to land the job. These explanations revolve around issues such as talent, motivation, racial prejudice, and affirmative action.

In explaining why one or the other candidate eventually got the job, people could use available explanations ("It was obvious he would not get the job, because of affirmative action," "Being black and female, she did not stand a chance"). Of course, this does not mean that individuals could not create new explanations for events. Rather, the implication is that even "new" explanations only come to life and become influential after they have been made public and shared with others.

In explaining attributional differences across gender, ethnicity, social class, and other groups (see Chandler, Shama, & Wolf, 1983; Graham & Long, 1986; Singh, Gupta, & Dalal, 1979), discursive psychology looks to variations in explanations seen as correct for different groups in society. An explanation that is correct for group A is not necessarily correct for group B. Getting drunk and singing rowdy songs in a bar may be interpreted as fun and part of the natural way of things if the intoxicated performer is a man ("Boys will be boys"), but viewed more negatively if this person is a woman (a person can be a "loose" woman, but the description is not usually applied to men). The impact of these explanations is in their adoption and use by groups who have power as well as those who lack power. Moreover, although the content of belief systems tends to vary across cultures, they serve the same function of legitimizing the social hierarchy (Pratto, Stallworth, Sidanius, & Siers, 1997; Sidanius, 1993; Sidanius, Pratto, & Brief, 1995).

discursive psychology the study of how people construct social reality, generate their version of events, and make inferences about causes in everyday life.

This approach implies that the explanations people use to account for events are to a large extent "historical," in that such accounts are specific to particular periods and tend to change over time (Gergen, 1973). Explanations of why an individual landed a job 50 years ago did not include affirmative action, because only in the last few decades has affirmative action become available as a causal explanation for events.

The discursive approach to attributions has gained support from some researchers (Edwards & Potter, 1993; Sampson, 1993), but it is still very much a fringe movement. This is partly because the approach seems to neglect the challenge of discovering universals. More specifically, the discursive approach seems to focus on context-specific behavior, rather than on looking for explanations that transcend social context. (This is related to our earlier discussions about normative and causal accounts of behavior in Chapters 1 and 2.)

Concepts and Issues

Culture and personality are two important sources of attribution. Culture influences both the way people make attributions and the way social psychologists study attributions. The independent and rational model of humans has colored attributional research, but more recent research has turned to the link between emotions and attribution, as well as the self and attribution in group-oriented cultures. Discursive research has provided an account of attributions as located in the rules of social interactions and communications. Personality has also proved to be an important source of attribution, and the concept of attributional style is very useful in health, education, and other applied domains.

1. Provide examples of two contrasting attributional styles.
2. What kind of attributional style is encouraged by the American Dream? Cite a few examples.
3. What is meant by the claim that attributions in India have been found to be more "contextualized" than those in the United States?
4. Discuss the merits of a discursive approach to understanding attributions.

Attributional Biases

One day Nasrudin was walking past a house when someone fell from the roof and landed on him, breaking several of Nasrudin's bones, while the falling man remained unhurt. Thinking back on the incident, Nasrudin said to himself, "This shows that the principle of cause and effect is not inevitable. A stranger falls off a roof and as a result it is my bones that get broken."

Research on attributions suggests that the ways in which people *actually* attribute causes to events can be biased and different from the logical processes suggested by attribution theory. As this story suggests, our thinking does not always follow logical principles. Some of the most intriguing research on attributions has focused on the nature of biases in causal explanations. Perhaps part of the reason such research has become so widely discussed is because it casts light on an "unexpected" aspect of human nature. Particularly given the computer model of human thinking that accompanied the cognitive revolution, it seems surprising to find that people can be systematically biased in making attributions.

But just as some social cognition research pushed us too far in the direction of conceiving human thinking as rational, perhaps there is now a danger that too great a focus on attributional biases will lead us to adopt a picture of humans as being totally irrational. This new fascination with humans as biased thinkers has meant that often we fail to be sufficiently critical of attributional bias research (e.g., Funder, 1987).

In the following discussion of different attributional biases, keep in mind that research suggests that human thinking *can* be biased in some situations, and not that it *necessarily is* biased in all situations. Even when bias does occur, it is often functional in the sense that it serves a purpose larger than an immediate goal of accurately estimating cause-effect relations (see Fiske & Taylor, 1991, p. 66).

The Fundamental Attribution Error

Try to predict the results of the following study, first conducted by Edward Jones and Victor Harris (1967) to test an idea proposed by Heider (1944) and called the fundamental attribution error by Lee Ross (1977). The **fundamental attribution error** (see Figure 5–4) arises because of a tendency for participants to underestimate the influence of situational factors and overestimate the influence of dispositional factors when assessing the behavior of others. Participants in the study read speeches by debaters supporting or attacking Fidel Castro, Cuba's leader. What do you think happened in the case of speeches written by debaters who freely selected to write for or against Castro? Yes,

fundamental attribution error
the tendency for observers to underestimate the influence of situational factors and overestimate the influence of dispositional factors when assessing the behavior of others.

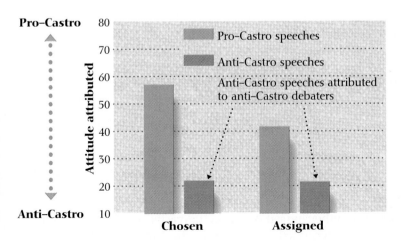

Figure 5–4 The fundamental attribution error (Jones & Harris, 1967).

participants logically assumed that the speeches reflected the person's own viewpoint.

But what do you think happened in the situation in which participants were told that the debaters were not given a choice, but were assigned pro-Castro or anti-Castro positions? The surprising finding was that participants still tended to see the speeches as reflecting the person's viewpoint. They overattributed the cause of a behavior (the speech) to internal factors. Even when participants were first required to write a pro-Castro or anti-Castro speech, they still tended to exaggerate the role of dispositional factors when considering speeches written by others (Snyder & Jones, 1974). This "error" persists even when participants dictate a position for someone else to express, because they still tend to see the other person as supporting the assigned position (Gilbert & Jones, 1986).

The fundamental attribution error may also help explain the way we interpret the behavior of people in different social roles. During everyday interactions, a great deal of behavior arises from our roles. For example, imagine your interactions with two different people, one a tourist information officer and the other a traffic officer. During the first interaction, the tourist information officer greets you with a smile, provides you with a lot of useful information, gives you free maps and coupons, and bids you farewell as if parting from a good friend. The second interaction takes place when you reach your car, which you had parked nearby, only to find that a traffic officer is writing a ticket. The officer carefully places the ticket on your windshield, politely explains your violation, and sincerely wishes you a safe and pleasant journey. The tourist information officer and traffic officer may both have pleasant personalities, but the likelihood is that you will see the traffic officer as being more unfriendly ("That monster gave me a ticket!").

A number of studies have uncovered just such a tendency for people to neglect situational factors when accounting for the behavior of others in different roles (Hui & Ip, 1989). For example, in one study participants were invited to take part in a quiz game and were randomly assigned to play the role of either questioner, contestant, or observer (Ross, Amabile, & Steinmetz, 1977). The questioners were asked to make up difficult questions and to test the general knowledge of contestants. It would seem obvious in such a situation that the questioner is in a very advantaged position to appear knowledgeable. But both the contestants and the observers concluded that the questioners actually were more knowledgeable (see Figure 5–5). Similarly, in everyday life teachers are often thought to be much more knowledgeable than they actually are, because their role puts them in the privileged position of setting the questions that students have to answer.

How Universal Is the Fundamental Attribution Error?

From a cultural perspective, the fundamental attribution error could be interpreted as another indication of the pervasive *individualism* of modern societies. Reinterpreted in this light, the fundamental attribution

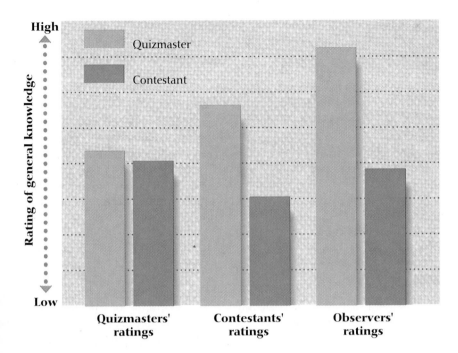

Figure 5–5 The fundamental attribution error and the quiz game (Ross et al., 1977).

error is actually not an "error" but a cultural *bias* to perceive causes as internal rather than external to individuals.

Such an interpretation receives some support from research suggesting that as children develop in Western culture, they show a greater tendency to attribute causes to dispositional rather than situational factors (Higgins & Bryant, 1982; Miller, 1984). Children growing up in India show the opposite trend, attributing causes more to situational factors (Miller, 1984). Relative to U.S. children, Indian children were also shown to absolve other people for wrongdoing more frequently when the behavior was influenced by strong emotions or immaturity (Bersoff & Miller, 1993). That is, the Indian participants gave more weight to factors outside the control of the person. Related to this is the finding that people in Japan give more importance than do people in the United States to the social role of a person when assigning responsibility for a behavior (Hamilton & Sanders, 1983).

The Actor-Observer Effect

The **actor–observer effect,** the tendency for observers to attribute others' actions to dispositional factors and for actors to attribute their actions to situational factors (Jones & Nisbett, 1972), is a natural extension of the fundamental attribution error. When Jim honks his car horn, he justifies the action by pointing to the messy traffic situation. But when Jim hears Dave honk his horn, he infers that Dave is an aggressive driver. This may be because when Jim is explaining his own behavior, he is far more aware of environmental factors. But when he is explaining the behavior of another person, he is focused on that individual rather than the environment.

actor-observer effect the tendency for observers to attribute others' actions to dispositional factors and for actors to attribute their actions to situational factors.

Although there is some experimental support for the actor-observer effect (e.g., Fiedler, Semin, Finkenauer, & Berkel, 1995; Schoeneman & Rubanowitz, 1985), the effect is not always consistent and can be reversed in some situations (Goldberg, 1981; Watson, 1982). A careful examination of such cases suggests that the actor-observer effect is influenced by the cultural norms of presenting oneself as "positive" and "autonomous." For example, in addition to seeing their own behavior as less influenced by dispositional factors, actors see their behavior as being less similar from situation to situation and also less predictable (Baxter & Goldberg, 1988). In a reversal of the effect, actors have been found to attribute their own positive behaviors to dispositional factors and their own negative behaviors to situational factors more than would observers (Chen, Yates, & McGinnies, 1988).

Self-Serving Biases

> Whether I shall turn out to be the hero of my own life, or whether that station will be held by anybody else, these pages must show.
>
> —Charles Dickens, *David Copperfield*

Most of us, it seems, have far less doubt than the central character in Charles Dickens's novel *David Copperfield*. According to Shelley Taylor (1989), we bask in the glory of our self-made *positive illusions*. One of the most often replicated social psychological findings is that people take more credit for success than for failure (Mullen & Riordan, 1988; Zuckerman, 1979). For example, when students do well on examinations, they take personal credit for the outcome and tend to see the exam as measuring what it is supposed to measure (Davis & Stephan, 1980). But those students who do poorly on an exam are more critical, raising questions about the ability of the instructor to give a fair exam.

Of course, most of us know from personal experience that the student who receives an A is far less likely to complain about the exam and to ask for a "re-read" than a student who receives a D. Similarly, athletes generally attribute victories to themselves ("The final pass I made wrapped up the game") but see external factors ("That referee needs glasses!") as the cause of defeats (Grove, Hanrahan, & McInman, 1991). Inevitably, politicians take personal credit for election successes ("My services to my constituents and my hard work led to election victory") but blame election failure on external factors ("My opponent spent much more money on the campaign") (Kingdon, 1967).

The False-Consensus Effect. We also overestimate the extent to which others agree with certain of our opinions (Mullen & Goethals, 1990). This so-called **false-consensus effect** (Ross, Greene, & House, 1977), better described as *attributional projection* (Holmes, 1968), involves

false-consensus effect
overestimating the extent to which others agree with certain of our opinions.

projecting our opinions onto others. For example, we tend to overestimate the number of others who agree with our political opinions, as well as the stand we take on politically sensitive issues, such as abortion.

The False-Uniqueness Effect.   But in some situations we tend to differentiate ourselves from others (Lemain & Kastersztein, 1971–1972) and to show a **false–uniqueness effect,** which involves an attempt to present ourselves as distinctive and uniquely good on some characteristic(s) (Goethals, Messick, & Allison, 1991). This often occurs in situations in which our abilities are being evaluated. For example, the French social psychologist Gerard Lemain asked French students to imagine they were competing for a position against students from other colleges. When the "other college" was academically superior, the students prepared their letters of application to stress their social skills and leadership abilities and generally differentiated themselves from the academically strong competitors (Lemain & Kastersztein, 1971–1972). When the "other college" was academically weak, the students prepared an application that focused on their own academic strengths.

false-uniqueness effect
overestimating the extent to which we can differentiate ourselves from others in a positive way.

Is Everyone "Better Than Average"?   We also tend to believe that we are better than the average. Studies have found that people in the United States see themselves as more intelligent and more attractive than the average (Wylie, 1979). Such beliefs seem to be intricately related to Americans maintaining a rosy vision of their future. For example, students overestimate their chances of having positive experiences in the future, such as living past the age of 80, but underestimate their chances of having negative experiences, such as being divorced (Weinstein, 1980). A survey among African–American high school athletes showed they held highly unrealistic expectations: 59 percent thought they could win college scholarships and 43 percent thought they could win contracts to play for professional teams; the comparable figures for whites were 39 percent and 16 percent, respectively, and they also showed unrealistic expectations (*Washington Post*, November 8, 1993). In reality less than 1 percent of high school athletes will win college sports scholarships, and only 1 in 10,000 will win a professional contract.

The Self-Centered Bias.   The details of research on self–serving attributions can be both instructive and amusing. Consider a study by Michael Ross and Fiore Sicoly (1977) on the **self–centered bias,** the taking of more than one's fair share of responsibility for a jointly produced outcome. Here are the steps to take in order to replicate this study. Make a list of household chores and then ask people living together the extent to which they or their partner have responsibility for each chore.

self-centered bias   the taking of more than one's fair share of responsibility for a jointly produced outcome.

If your results follow past research, you will find that in most cases the contributions of the partners add up to more than 100 percent. For example, the first partner claims to be doing 70 percent of the cleaning, and the second partner claims to be doing 80 percent of the cleaning—

The belief that "the system is open" is pervasive and often exaggerated in the United States, but the exaggerations are not in the same domains for all groups. African–American high school athletes have particularly high, and unrealistic, expectations about winning college sports scholarships and professional contracts. This may be in part because of the symbols of success advertised for each ethnic group.

resulting in 150 percent cleaning. Very interesting, is it not, that no less than 130 percent of the cooking, 165 percent of the shopping, and 140 percent of the paperwork is completed in this house, yet there always seems to be a lot of work still to be done. Similarly biased patterns are found in various relationships in which people share responsibilities for tasks (Thompson & Kelley, 1981).

Explaining Self-Serving Attributional Biases

Why do people show **self–serving biases** when making attributions, by taking credit for their successes, explaining away their failures, and generally holding positive illusions (Taylor, 1989) about

self-serving bias   basking in the glory of our self-made positive illusions; taking more credit for success than for failure.

themselves? Researchers have debated this question by contrasting cognitive explanations with motivational ones, but this may not be the most constructive way to address the issue (Tetlock & Manstead, 1985). Explanations that are either exclusively cognitive or exclusively motivational remain unconvincing, given that cognition and motivation are interconnected (Zuckerman, 1979). The debate as to which influences attributional biases more remains inconclusive (Tetlock & Levi, 1982). A more overriding explanation of attributional biases can be found in culture.

Human beings seem to be universally motivated to maintain a positive view of the self, but culture influences the ways in which individuals go about achieving this goal. According to Hazel Markus and Shinobu Kitayama (1991), persons living in the United States and other cultures that similarly foster independent selves (see Chapter 3) feel good about themselves by being unique, asserting themselves, and expressing their inner attributes. The self-serving attributional biases systematically documented in Western societies reflect an expression of such independent selves.

By contrast, people in traditional societies have selves developed to be interdependent rather than independent. Feeling good about one's interdependent self should derive from "belonging, fitting in, occupying one's proper place, engaging in appropriate action, promoting others' goals, and maintaining harmony" (Markus & Kitayama, 1991, p. 242). Most important of all, in societies that foster interdependent selves, individuals learn that they will be positively evaluated by others if they present themselves in humble, self-effacing, modest terms. For example, studies with Japanese and Chinese participants suggest that self-enhancement is evaluated negatively and self-effacement is preferred (Bond, Leung, & Wan, 1982; Yoshika, Kojo, & Kaku, 1982). Thus, a person who is modest about a superb athletic performance ("I was lucky in that all the elements worked in my favor during the race") is evaluated more positively than is someone who has an "I am number 1!" self-presentation style.

Evidence suggests that the pattern of self-serving biases found in societies more supportive of independent selves, such as the United States, is not always found in societies in which interdependent selves receive stronger encouragement, such as Japan. Japanese students estimated that about 50 percent of their peers would be intellectually more capable than themselves, and this is what we should find if a representative sample of students give unbiased evaluations of themselves (Markus & Kitayama, 1991). By contrast, U.S. students assumed only 30 percent would be more capable than themselves; thus, most of them reported themselves to be better than the average student.

Another powerful example of cross-cultural differences in attributional biases comes from studies of the explanations people give for success and failure in tasks. Studies with Western participants typically reveal outcomes, particularly success, to be attributed to dispositional factors, such as ability (Hewstone, 1990). By contrast, Japanese participants attribute success to the ease of the task and failure to lack of effort (Shikanai, 1978, 1984). Indeed, Japanese participants sometimes have a greater tendency to use ability as an explanation of failure than of success.

Attributions and Intergroup Behavior

> To them (the Yanomamo), babies die because someone sent harmful spirits . . . to steal their souls, or someone blew magical charms at them from a great distance, charms that caused them to sicken and die. Thus, in every village, the shamans spend many hours attempting to cure sick children or sick adults, driving out the malevolent forces that have caused their illnesses, and in turn, sending their own spirits and charms against the children in distant villages for revenge.
>
> —N. A. Chagnon, *Yanomamo*

> Inside the family, it's "niggers and jews"; with the neighbors, it's the same; but at parties, they suddenly become "the blacks". . . . However . . . simply changing certain terminology does not necessarily alter the basic message. In one situation, an informant said, "The niggers are all just plain lazy; they just don't want to work," but in another instance his response was: "The trouble with the blacks is that they just don't have any ambition; they just don't want to work the way the rest of us do."
>
> —E. R. Ameisen, "Exclusivity in an Ethnic Elite"

intergroup attribution   a causal inference on the part of group members about the members of their own or other groups.

An **intergroup attribution** involves a causal inference on the part of group members about the members of their own or other groups. The inclusion of groups as a unit of attribution leads to a reclassification of the traditional internal/external distinction as regards the location of attributed causes. Donald Taylor and his colleagues (Taylor, Doria, & Tyler, 1983) have proposed that intergroup attributions require four categories of attribution:

1. *Internal:* The self is the perceived cause.
2. *In-group/self-inclusion:* One's group, including oneself, is the perceived cause.
3. *In-group/self-exclusion:* One's in-group, but not oneself, is the perceived cause.
4. *External:* An agent external to oneself and one's in-group is the perceived cause.

The fourth category, external causes, could be broken down further (Moghaddam, Taylor, Lambert, & Schmidt, 1995) into causes internal to out-groups ("Group X is stopping us from improving our situation") and causes external to all individuals and groups ("We have had bad luck").

Intergroup Attributions Are Pervasive. In much of everyday social life, attributions are intergroup rather than interpersonal. Consider the Yanomamo, a group of about 20,000 village dwellers in the tropical forests bordering Venezuela and Brazil. When someone in a Yanomamo village falls sick or if crops fail or some other calamity occurs, the immediate reaction is for villagers to identity the members of an enemy village as the cause of the problem. This "They are to blame!" attributional style often leads to warfare among Yanomamo villages.

However, we need not go to South America to find examples of hostile intergroup attributions. Elizabeth Ameisen's (1990) study of white Anglo-Saxon Protestants (WASPs) in Philadelphia's Main Line shows how some Americans attribute the status of African-Americans to group characteristics, such as "lack of motivation to work."

But intergroup attributions are not made only by members of majority groups. Just as whites often provide group-based explanations for social phenomena such as unemployment, so do blacks. When West Indian (black) and white adolescents living in England assessed explanations for statistics on unemployment, educational achievement, and other social issues, they tended toward explanations that favored

Social groups often make biased attributions when accounting for success and failure. To understand such biases, we need to consider the attributions made in a wider social context and with respect to the social position of each group. Boys in English private schools, such as those in this picture, were shown to attribute failure by one of their in-group more to chance and less to lack of ability, whereas boys in state schools attributed failure more to their disadvantaged position and less to luck.

their own groups (Hewstone & Jaspers, 1982). Compared to white participants, the West Indians explained the higher rate of unemployment and lower educational achievement among blacks as due more to discrimination on the part of white authority figures and less to dispositional characteristics of blacks. The same tendency to explain social facts, such as unemployment figures, in a way that favors the in-group was demonstrated in a study involving students in Hong Kong (Hewstone, Bond, & Wan, 1983).

An interesting study involving boys in private and state schools in England also demonstrated how social groups can interpret success and failure in a biased manner (Hewstone, Jaspers, & Lalljee, 1982). The boys were presented cases in which an in-group or out-group member (boy attending private or state school) either passed or failed an examination. Private schoolboys emphasized their academic abilities and attributed failure by an in-group member more to luck and less to lack of ability. State schoolboys highlighted the advantages of private schooling and showed less of a tendency to attribute an in-group member's failure to luck. The advantages of private schooling seemed to serve as an adequate external reason for failure among the boys in state schools, so that they did not feel as strong a need to refer to luck as did the boys in the private schools.

The Ultimate Attribution Error.   A number of the self-serving attributional biases that have been identified at the level of individuals also seem to be present in intergroup attributions. The most important of such biases is the fundamental attribution error, called the ultimate attribution error when it operates at the group level (Pettigrew, 1979). The **ultimate attribution error** is perceiving desirable actions by one's own group as arising from factors internal to the group but by other groups as arising from group characteristics; similarly, seeing undesirable actions by one's own group as arising from external factors and by other groups as arising from group characteristics. It was first demonstrated in a study with Hindu and Muslim participants in India (Taylor & Jaggi, 1974). When participants were explaining socially desirable behaviors, such as helping someone, internal attributions were higher for the in-group than for the out-group ("My group member helped this person out of kindness"). In the case of explaining socially undesirable behavior, such as refusing aid to another, internal attribution was lower for in-group than for out-group ("Factors beyond a person's control prevented my group member from helping"). Similar in-group favoring biases in intergroup attributions is reported in studies of blacks, Chicanos, and Anglos in the United States (Stephan, 1977) and of Israeli and Arab students studying in the United States (Rosenberg & Wolfsfeld, 1977).

Attributions, Ethnicity, and Gender.   Social context also influences intergroup attributions, with the result that the ultimate attribution error can disappear. This is demonstrated by two studies, one

ultimate attribution error
perceiving desirable actions by one's own group as arising from factors internal to the group, but those of out-groups as arising from factors external to the group. Similarly, seeing undesirable actions by one's own group as arising from external factors, and by other groups as arising from group characteristics.

involving Malay and Chinese participants in Malaysia and the other, Malay and Chinese participants in Singapore (Hewstone & Ward, 1985). In the Malaysian context, Malays are a majority group and the Chinese are the minority group; in Singapore it is the Malays who have minority status and the Chinese who enjoy majority status. In both contexts, it was the group that enjoyed majority status that showed ethnocentric attributions, whereas the group with minority status tended to attribute causes in a way that also favored the majority group. Thus, the Chinese in Malay and the Malays in Singapore seemed to accept the negative stereotypes of themselves as minorities in their respective societies. A similar pattern of "in-group derogation" sometimes occurs when females make group attributions to men and women (Deaux & Emswiller, 1974; Feldman-Summers & Kiesler, 1974).

The attributions that men make to account for success and failure among women is associated with their general attitudes toward women (Garland & Price, 1977). Men who have a generally positive attitude toward women in managerial positions tend to attribute a woman's success more to dispositional factors ("She has the ability") and less to external factors ("She got lucky"). Similarly, the attributions made by whites for the success and failure of blacks is associated with their general attitude toward minorities (Greenberg & Rosenfield, 1979). White participants higher on ethnocentrism were more likely to attribute the success of a black person to luck than to ability.

Finally, research on intergroup attributions suggests that the explanations provided by group members for social events are closely associated with the social representations of groups. This is reflected in a study of lower- and middle-class Cubans, blacks, and whites in Miami in which participants were asked to assess reasons for their success or failure to land a job that is one step above their present position for which they are nevertheless qualified (Moghaddam, Taylor, Lambert, & Schmidt, 1995). In the case of success, the members of all groups reported the outcome to be more a result of dispositional factors than anything to do with group membership or luck. In the case of failure, the only participants who identified dispositional factors more than group or external factors as being causally determinant were the lower-class whites. This finding is in line with other research that shows a strong commitment to individualism and meritocracy among poor whites. Interestingly, middle-class blacks showed the strongest tendency to attribute failure to the treatment of their group (e.g., racial discrimination) rather than to dispositional factors. The attributional style of each group seemed to be associated with their representations about the larger society, who they are, their past history, and their present situation in relation to other groups.

These findings suggest that groups develop attributional styles in an adaptive way to help them function better in their particular social circumstances. Jennifer Crocker and Brenda Major (1989) propose that attributions may come to have a "self-protective" property, helping minorities who have traditionally been the target of prejudice to maintain positive self-esteem. This happens because when members of minority groups undergo some kind of negative experience, such as failing to get promotion at work, they may be uncertain whether the event was a result of their personal characteristics or of prejudice on the part of the evaluators. Such "attributional ambiguity" means that prejudice can often be a plausible explanation for negative outcomes.

Consistent with this proposition, female students who received a negative evaluation from a male who was prejudiced against women showed less decrease in self-esteem, compared to female students who received negative feedback from a male who was not prejudiced against females (Testa, Crocker, & Major, 1988). This suggests the counterintuitive idea that females who work in a more prejudiced environment may find it easier to maintain positive self-esteem in the face of failure. Related to this is a study showing that attractive females were less inclined than unattractive females to believe that a positive evaluation was due to the high quality of their work (Sigall & Michela, 1976). Presumably, attractive females tended to attribute the cause of their high evaluation by males to their physical features, rather than to the quality of their work.

Concepts and Issues

Studies of how people actually attribute causes to events reveal a fascinating array of biases, both when people are accounting for the behavior of individuals and when they are explaining the actions of groups. The pendulum seems to be swinging away from a picture of us as rational beings toward one of us as irrational beings. But there are two points to keep in mind. First, to demonstrate that people can show attributional biases in the context of a study does not necessarily tell us how frequently such biases actually occur in everyday life. Second, the various attributional biases are self-serving, meaning that they are intended to present the self in a more positive light. This points to a close link between attribution and the self.

1. Imagine that during the same morning a waiter serves you a delicious breakfast and a policeman gives you a ticket for speeding. How would the fundamental attribution error influence your assessment of these two people?
2. Why would we expect the fundamental attribution error not to be universal?
3. Norman sees his two sons fail to climb a tree and explains it by saying the branches are slippery because of the recent rain. When his two daughters fail to climb the same tree, he explains it by saying

they are not good climbers. Explain Norman's behavior with reference to the ultimate attribution error.

Conclusion

Attributions are important in everyday life and a major topic in modern social psychology. There are, however, a number of limitations to attribution research. First, research has focused on attributions at the individual level and neglected attributions at the group level. Second, while the available research suggests that people can make attributions in line with attribution theory, there is little "naturalistic" evidence to indicate that people actually *do* make attributions this way. Similarly, research indicates that attributions can be made in biased ways, but there is little information about how prevalent the various attributional biases are in the everyday lives of people in different cultures. The "commonsense" psychology discussed by Heider, the more recent concept of causal schemas, and the idea of social representations discussed by European researchers all have in common the assumption that there are in society shared understandings of the causes of events. This implies that such shared understandings can vary across cultures, as can the biases shown when people make attributions.

For Review

An attribution is an inference about the cause(s) of an event. Fritz Heider is often seen as the founder of modern attribution theory. A number of influential attribution models, including those of Jones and Davis and of Kelley, tend to ignore the issue of motivation. The most influential recent theory of attributions is Weiner's, which focuses on emotions associated with achievement attributions. People assess how far they have succeeded or failed in given domains, and this results in positive or negative emotions. Three bases are then used to make attributions for the causes of success/failure.

Studies show that participants, typically college students, can make attributions when asked by researchers to respond within particular limitations, but we have little indication of how and when people actually do make attributions in their everyday lives in different cultures.

A great deal of research has focused on "attributional biases," suggesting that people can show bias in the way they attribute causes to events. One such bias is the so-called fundamental attribution error, involving an overattribution of the cause of a behavior to internal factors. Other biases that have served as research focuses are the actor–observer effect and various self–serving biases, such as taking more personal credit for success than failure, overestimating the extent to which others agree with certain of our opinions, differentiating ourselves from others), believing that we are better than the average, and exaggerating our own share of the group work.

Although the vast majority of attribution research has been on attributions by individual agents on individual targets, in everyday life a large part of attribution concerns social groups. Some attributional biases studied at the individual level also seem to be present at the group level: The fundamental attribution error has been translated to the "ultimate attribution error" at the group level.

Culture is a major source of influence on how we make attributions to individuals and groups. A number of personality characteristics also seem to influence attributional style, the tendency to make attributions in a consistent manner across different situations and times.

Recent European research has focused on the "commonsense" explanations for causes of events. This research focuses on the social construction of explanations by social groups rather than mental processes within the individual.

For Discussion

1. In what ways does attribution research support the view that people can be biased in making causal inferences?
2. "Individuals as well as cultures have attributional styles." Explain and discuss this statement.
3. Apply one of the major attribution models to an episode in your own everyday life.

Key Terms

Actor–observer effect
163

Attribution 140

Attributional style
156

Causal schema 145

Commonsense
psychology 158

Correspondent
inference 143

Covariation model
144

Discursive
psychology 159

Dispositional factors
140

External factors 140

False-consensus
effect 164

False-uniqueness
effect 165

Fundamental
attribution error
161

Intergroup
attribution 168

Learned helplessness
156

Locus of control 155

Self-centered bias
165

Self-serving biases
166

Ultimate attribution
error 170

Annotated Readings

For a review of the U.S. and European literature on individual and collective attribution, see M. Hewstone, *Causal attributions: From cognitive processes to collective beliefs* (Oxford: Basil Blackwell, 1990).

A personal account of attribution research by one of the leading researchers is E. E. Jones, *Interpersonal perception* (New York: W. H. Freeman, 1990).

For the discursive approach to attribution, see D. Edwards and J. Potter, Language and causation: A discursive action model of description and attribution, *Psychological Review*, 100, 23–41 (1993).

CHAPTER **6**

Persuasion

◀   Internationalization of trade and increased efficiency in global communications have
speeded up the spread of modern advertising. This billboard in a Chinese train station
tries to persuade consumers to spend their money on particular goods, using persuasion
techniques in some ways similar to those in Western societies.

*I*t was one of those chance meetings that go against statistical odds. I was strolling down Fifth Avenue during a brief visit to New York City in the spring of 1996, when I bumped into an acquaintance from a long time back who was also just passing through the city. He was a reporter I had met in 1982, when he was covering a ferocious war between Iran and Iraq and I was part of a United Nations mission to the front. This mission was to identify civilian damage caused by military attacks on both sides. As our small team traveled through the war areas, hopping from jeep to helicopter to army plane and witnessing firsthand the misery and devastation, I had discussed with my reporter friend a question that was on our minds: What led these millions of young men to throw themselves into battle? There was so much they might achieve in their lives, yet many of them would meet an early death or be injured and suffer lifelong physical and mental disabilities. What explained their joining the "human waves" who hurled themselves against enemy fire?

We dismissed as too simplistic claims that these millions of men were forced into war by the regimes in Baghdad and Tehran, or that the two armies were made up of religious fanatics—Muslim fundamentalists who would do anything their leaders told them. Such explanations only serve to raise further questions. What makes a regime persuasive? What leads a person to join religious movements in the first place? More broadly, how do humans persuade one another?

"Well? Have you solved the puzzle yet?" asked my reporter friend years later in New York. "Why did those youngsters join the war?" Then he added in a taunting tone, "I'm just a reporter; I expect you psychologists to explain behavior in faraway places."

I proposed that such questions are actually not far removed from the life experiences of young people in Western societies: consider "born again" movements and sects, such as the Church of Scientology. In a matter of four decades, Scientology has grown from a group of several hundred devotees to nearly 7 million followers in 65 countries (*Time*, May 6, 1991), despite being dismissed as "modern magic" by some researchers (Bainbridge & Stark, 1980). What's more, some other sects have matched this phenomenal growth (Bromley & Shupe, 1979). How are people persuaded to become part of such movements? Do they join freely, or are they coerced?

We strolled on, and near Central Park we stopped to watch some con artists operating a "shell game." The game, which is thousands of years old and known in many societies, is traditionally played with three half–shells, such as walnut shells, and a dried pea (or any small spherical object about that size). The con artist places the pea underneath one of the shells, then shifts the positions of the three shells. The player, or "victim," is invited to point to the shell that has the pea underneath it, a task that seems fairly easy.

But the con artist is not working alone; he is a member of a well-rehearsed team. A second team member is a "bystander" who not only befriends and advises the victim but also serves as an example of how to win at the shell game. One of the objectives of this friendly

In all parts of the world, people can be persuaded more effectively through group pressures. After they become part of a group, they feel compelled to conform to group norms. These young Afghan men have been persuaded to risk their lives in war, and to obey orders to harm and kill others. At the ceremony below; conducted by Reverend and Mrs. Sun Myung Moon, thousands of couples are persuaded to join in a mass wedding and devote their lives to a collective cause.

bystander is to encourage victims to show their money. This serves as a "foot in the door," and is part of a technique we have already encountered in Chapter 4. A third member is the "lookout," who breaks up the game by calling out warnings about the arrival of the police—sometimes when the police are actually on their way but often simply to give the con artist an opportunity to make a clean getaway. (By the way, you should also know that skilled con artists always hide the pea in their hands, so that the victims are always wrong no matter which shell they select.)

Watching the shell game being played in New York City, the home of so many advertising and media agencies, reminded us that persuasion is also an integral part of everyday life in Western societies.

"But what makes persuasion effective?" asked my reporter friend. "Is persuasion the same as coercion? Is that man playing the shell game coerced or persuaded?"

"You are asking the right questions," I responded. "These are just the questions we psychologists have been researching."

Research on Persuasion

There is no sharp dividing line between **persuasion,** communication designed to influence another's cognition or overt behavior in which the recipient or "target of persuasion" has some measure of free choice, and **coercion,** social influence in which the recipient has no choice. Persuasion and coercion blend into one another, and there is a gray area where it seems impossible to distinguish between them (Perloff, 1993). One way in which some researchers have made a psychological distinction is to assume that if the recipients of a communication feel they do have free choice, then the process involved is persuasion rather than coercion (Smith, 1982). This element of "believing oneself to be free" or "in control" is central to persuasion because often the process begins with the introduction of tempting and seemingly harmless bait, giving us a sense of free choice even as we swallow the bait, get hooked, and are drawn in by an experienced fisherman.

The traditional approach has been for researchers to distinguish among four basic factors in the persuasion process (see Figure 6–1) (Hovland, Janis, & Kelley, 1953; McGuire, 1985):

1. The **source** of a message. *Who* is trying to persuade?
2. The **content** of a message. *What* is being said to try to persuade?

persuasion communication designed to influence another's cognition or overt behavior in which the recipient has some measure of free choice.

coercion social influence in which the recipient experiences no choice.

source who is trying to do the persuading.

content what is being said to try to persuade.

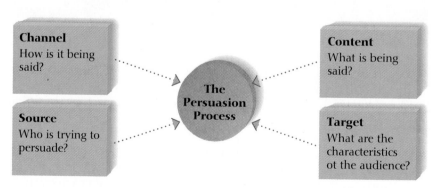

Figure 6–1 The four basic factors in the persuasion process.

3. The **channel** of communication. *How* is it being said to try to persuade?
4. The **target** of communication. *Who* is the communication trying to persuade?

channel how the message is being delivered to try to persuade.

target who the communication is trying to persuade.

The main advantage to considering these four factors separately is that researchers have been able to examine systematically the impact of each one independent of the others. For example, by sending the same message through the same channel to the same audience (target), but varying the source of the message, it has been possible to examine the effect of source characteristics independent of all other factors. This strategy allows, for example, for an assessment of how persuasive an expert is as compared to a layperson when they both communicate the same message through the same channel to the same audience.

A disadvantage of the traditional strategy of isolating each factor is that in practice all these factors are interdependent and come as a "package." The shell game serves to highlight this point. People are persuaded by a whole set of elements that combine and are part of a cultural context. For example, the con artist needs the support of the rest of his team to work the shell game successfully. (In my own observations I have noticed teams with as many as six members, coordinating their actions to work "their trade.") Researchers have recognized the limitations of examining parts of the persuasion process in isolation. Since the 1980s, researchers have focused more on the cognitive processes involved in persuasion, leading to a greater focus on the whole process, rather than its separate parts (Larson, 1995; Perloff, 1993; Petty & Cacioppo, 1986a).

The Dimensions of Persuasion

The questions "How is someone persuaded to take part in a shell game?" and "How is someone persuaded to march to war?" both concern persuasion, but at different ends of the *interpersonal-societal* dimension (see Figure 6–2).

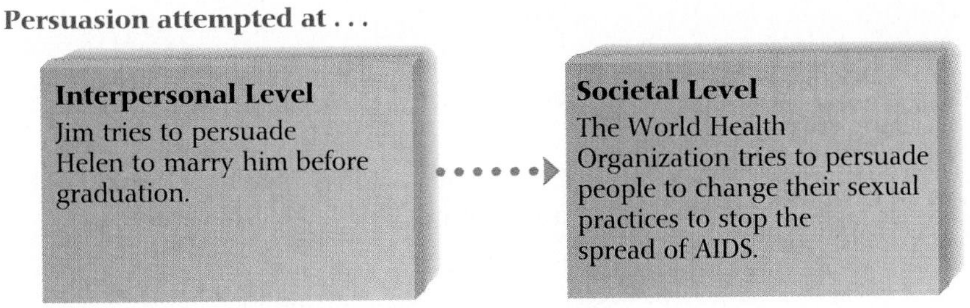
Persuasion attempted at . . .
Interpersonal Level
Jim tries to persuade Helen to marry him before graduation.
Societal Level
The World Health Organization tries to persuade people to change their sexual practices to stop the spread of AIDS.

Figure 6–2 The interpersonal–societal dimension in persuasion.

At one extreme, an individual attempts to persuade another person through face-to-face communications. For example, a young man tries to persuade his girlfriend that they should get married immediately, even though she has not yet graduated from college. At the other extreme, persuasion is attempted by very large groups of people, mostly through indirect rather than face-to-face communications channels, and targeted at mass audiences (Sraubhaar & LaRose, 1995). For example, the World Health Organization, which is part of the United Nations, uses a variety of communications channels to try to persuade sexually active people in different societies to change their practices in order to curtail the spread of AIDS.

By considering the relationship between the source, content, channel, and audience of the message, and the interpersonal-societal dimension, we can further clarify the range of behaviors that are involved in the persuasion process (Table 6–1).

Consider a case in which the source, content, channel, and audience are all at the interpersonal level. Mark has fallen madly in love with Shelley and has a plan for persuading her to marry him. He knows that she is a romantic at heart, so he has decided to play his guitar below Shelley's bedroom window and serenade her. He puts his plan into action on a moonlit autumn night. Mark sings one of Shelley's favorite love songs, she opens her window to listen, he throws her a bouquet of roses, declares his love, and offers her a diamond ring. She sighs and says yes. In this example, the source (Mark) and the audience (Shelley) are individuals, the message channel is face-to-face and verbal, and the message is adapted to the characteristics of the audience and the source.

Five years later, Mark and Shelley are happily married and have a child. They quickly realize that there are many two-career families with children in their neighborhood but no adequate child-care facilities. They help organize an activist group in their local community and start a newsletter. Their objective is to increase funding for day-care facilities. They contact local newspapers, radio talk shows, and even television stations, in an effort to influence political parties and private funding agencies, as well as the general public. Mark and Shelley are now engaged in an attempt at societal persuasion. Their activist group is the

Table 6–1	The Range of Behaviors Involved in Persuasion	
Factor	**Interpersonal Persuasion**	**Societal Persuasion**
Message source	Individual	Groups and organizations
Message content	Adapted to individual characteristics	Adapted to group characteristics
Message channel	Face-to-face and verbal	Mostly indirect and through the mass media
Message audience	Individual	Social groups and individuals

message source, the message is adapted to persuade a variety of groups, the message channel is mostly indirect and through the mass media, and the target is both groups (political parties and so on) and individuals (members of the general public).

In many cases persuasion involves both interpersonal and societal aspects. Groups and organizations, such as the activist group initiated by Mark and Shelley, communicate their messages by face-to-face and verbal channels, as well as through the media. Their audiences tend to be both individuals and other groups and organizations. Whatever the range of behaviors involved, persuasion will take place only if such behaviors are appropriate for the culture in which they take place. Mark and Shelley would have little success increasing funding for day-care centers in a culture in which the only correct way for a mother to behave is to stay at home and look after her children.

Let us consider a few more examples of the relationship between culture and persuasion before we turn to an assessment of research on the source, content, channel, and audience.

Persuasion and Culture

It is not only in New York City that passersby are persuaded to part with their money through schemes such as the shell game, nor is it only in Iran and Iraq that young people are persuaded to march to war. But the techniques of persuasion that are effective in Iran or Iraq may have little success in getting people to march to war in Western societies, and the gangs of con artists who work the shell game in New York might have little success on the streets of Tehran or Baghdad. Although persuasion is universal, the process through which it is achieved varies in some major ways across cultures. The challenge, then, is to identify how the persuasion process is likely to be similar and how it might vary across cultures. Before we consider mainstream research on the four basic factors in the persuasion process, consider a few examples of the kinds of cross-cultural variations we should keep in mind.

One of the first things Western visitors to Eastern countries such as India notice is that local people, particularly those lower in status, engage in a great deal of ingratiation—behavior, such as flattery and profuse helpfulness, that attempts to persuade others to see the individual in a positive light and as meriting rewards. American employees of multinational corporations posted to such countries find that local employees devote a great deal of effort in ingratiating themselves. Janak Pandey (1986), an Indian social psychologist, explains this high use of ingratiation by proposing that the persuasive tactics people use are influenced in important ways by the availability of resources. Because of widespread poverty in developing societies, people adopt manipulative tactics in order to gain access to scarce resources. Ingratiation helps subordinates gain some control over people who make decisions about how those scarce resources will be allocated.

Pandey's (1980) research suggests that in the Indian context ingratiation is seen as "correct" and expected behavior. Certain tactics reported as common by subjects in his research are less prevalent in Western societies, an example being self-degradation, the humbling of oneself before another. Such tactics tend to be used particularly when people find themselves in competitive situations in which a heavy price is paid if a person fails to influence those who control resources (Pandey & Rastogi, 1979).

Ingratiation is an example of a tactic that can be used in interpersonal persuasion. Culture also influences *societal persuasion.* Consider the case of advertising. Writing within the context of the United States, Anthony Pratkanis and Elliot Aronson (1991) have described this as "the Age of Propaganda," pointing out that "with 6% of the world's population, America consumes 57% of the world's advertising" (p. 4). In many

Many of the persuasion techniques used in modern Western societies are not permitted in other cultures, and would not have been permitted before the 1960s in the West. This billboard, for example, would not be allowed in most Islamic countries today.

developing countries there is very little commercial advertising as we know it in the West, in part because the market cannot support the additional expense. Another reason for the scarcity of advertising is that goods, particularly imported products, are so scarce relative to demand that as soon as they appear in the market they are snapped up. Religious factors also fundamentally influence societal persuasion. In most Islamic countries there is a ban on advertising that uses the appeal of physical attractiveness in any way. This means a ban on almost all the advertisements that we routinely see in the Western media.

A great deal of the research on persuasion in Western democracies is motivated by questions that arise from a political context, such as "How best can we persuade people to vote for our cause?" But democracy is a form of government that exists only in a minority of countries in the contemporary world. The citizens of most countries do not enjoy democratic choices, and the question "How can we persuade them to vote for us rather than the opposition?" is irrelevant because often there is no official opposition. A number of other research questions arise out of the free-market economic system. People who have little economic freedom do not get to choose among consumer goods, jobs, and many other aspects of the economy. Having no choice, they do not need to be persuaded in the same way as people in the West do. Thus, in very basic ways the persuasion research conducted in Western democracies has applicability only to Western societies, where certain types of choices are realistically available.

Concepts and Issues

Persuasion is pervasive and important in the lives of people in both Western and non-Western cultures, although the means by which people persuade can vary cross-culturally in fundamental ways. Persuasion and coercion merge into one another rather than being sharply divided. Persuasion involves a range of behaviors, from the interpersonal to the societal or intergroup.

1. Define *persuasion* and *coercion*.
2. What are the four basic factors in the persuasion process?
3. Give examples of interpersonal and societal persuasion.

The Source: Who Is Trying to Persuade?

In 1994, Marion Barry, former mayor of Washington, D.C., faced a daunting challenge: He was once more trying to persuade the residents of the District to vote for him in the mayoral elections. This seemed a particularly difficult task because 4 years earlier, on January 18, 1990, Barry had been arrested in an FBI sting operation. Millions of viewers had subsequently watched the televised tapes of how FBI agents charged into a room at the Vista Hotel to catch Barry with crack cocaine. Over the next few years, the story of Barry's tragic fall from grace was told and retold in the media, as he served time in jail. The idea that Barry would make a successful comeback seemed unlikely, particularly from the point of view of more affluent Washingtonians.

But it was not the more affluent Washingtonians Barry was trying to persuade. A major theme of his comeback campaign was *redemption*, and his target audience included the lower income, the young, the unemployed, those members of ethnic minorities who felt marginalized, and everyone who identified with Barry's message that "You can slip, but not fall; you can make mistakes, but recover!" Here was a politician who had slipped, who had personal experience of falling into hard times, who knew how difficult it was to get back on one's feet. On the night of his Democratic primary victory, Barry recited the lines of an old hymn, "Amazing grace, how sweet the sound, that saved a wretch like me" (*Washington Post Magazine*, October 23, 1994). Barry's rivals in the mayoral elections included the incumbent mayor, Sharon Pratt Kelly, but he beat them all.

Joseph Priester and Richard Petty (1995) have shown that *cognitive misers*, individuals who are particularly prone to be economical in processing information, are even less likely to scrutinize messages if the source is assumed to be honest. They use *heuristics*, or mental shortcuts such as assumptions about how good leaders behave, to make decisions more quickly. Because the amount of information available to us can be overwhelming, we all use heuristics in order to understand and evaluate the world. Thus, we all act as cognitive misers to some degree. When Clara arrives on campus as a first-year student, she is given an enormous amount of information, both inside and outside the classroom, during a few weeks. She does not have time to analyze all this information, but accepts a lot of it at face value because she has faith in the sources of the information. In evaluating Barry's messages, voters acted like cognitive misers with faith in Barry.

Rather than study complex aspects of the source as a whole, most social psychologists have adopted a "divide-and-rule" strategy. This has meant isolating factors involved in persuasion and studying them independently. Such factors include credibility, similarity, and attractiveness.

The Persuasive Individual: Leadership

charisma   exceptional personality characteristics that set a person apart from others.

Marion Barry enjoys what the German scholar Max Weber (1968) termed **charisma**, exceptional personality characteristics that set a person apart from other people. Rabindra Kanungo and Jay Conger (Conger & Kanungo, 1988), Canadian social psychologists, argue that it is charisma that sets apart really persuasive individuals, both constructive ones such as Gandhi and Martin Luther King, Jr., and destructive ones such as Stalin and Hitler. Barry is somewhere in the middle of this continuum, because he inspires political action by disenfranchised minorities but at the same time earns an infamous reputation with another segment of the electorate in the same district.

Charismatic Leadership. Kanungo and Conger are among the handful of researchers to have studied **charismatic leadership,** a style of leadership that relies on exceptional personality characteristics. Their research suggests that charismatic and noncharismatic leadership can be distinguished in three stages of the leadership process (see Figure 6–3). (Leadership is discussed further in Chapter 13, in the context of group dynamics.)

During stage 1, charismatic leaders are characterized by their higher capacity to sum up how things stand. This means they are more sensitive to existing constraints, as well as deficiencies in the present state of affairs. Consequently, charismatic leaders are more likely to identify opportunities. Two world leaders provide a historic example of this in the 1980s. Ronald Reagan called the U.S.S.R. the "Evil Empire" and articulated an opportunity to bring about changes in the world order. At the same time, the Soviet leader Mikhail Gorbachev brought about greater social and cultural freedom and paved the way for democratic reform in the former U.S.S.R.

This kind of leadership quality also makes enormous differences in the private sector. The legendary auto industry executive Lee Iacocca, the "father" of the Ford Mustang, used the almost complete collapse of Chrysler Corporation as an opportunity to rebuild the corporation (Iacocca, 1984), which has once more become an industry leader. This ability to sum up how things stand is among the most important requirements of future leaders. It leaves others believing that there is

charismatic leadership a leadership style that relies on exceptional personality characteristics.

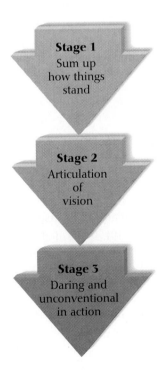

Figure 6–3 Abilities and charismatic leadership.

The "great person" theory of leadership proposes that leaders have certain characteristics, such as charisma, that set them apart from everyone else. Most would agree that Mahatma Gandhi (shown here [center] in Bombay in 1931), who led the fight for Indian independence and fought for racial justice in South Africa before that, had charisma. It has been much more difficult to establish a set of characteristics that Gandhi shares with other charismatic leaders, and that set them apart from all others.

something magical about their insight for knowing which way to turn and what to do next.

During stage 2, charismatic leaders are special because of their articulation of a vision, a dream that inspires others—Martin Luther King, Jr.'s, vision of achieving racial equality in the United States, Mahatma Gandhi's vision of an independent India, Nelson Mandela's vision of a liberated South Africa. But charismatic leaders must be able to articulate their vision in a way that can be readily adopted by their followers. The preaching style of Dr. King was particularly effective among African–Americans, and it is interesting that Marion Barry adopted such a style during the 1994 mayoral campaign.

During stage 3, charismatic leaders use innovative and daring means to achieve the articulated vision. Their unconventional strategies are seen to put them at risk. It is not uncommon for charismatic leaders to face severe physical hardships, even death, while acting outside convention (Gandhi and King were both assassinated). But their unconventionality is based on expert knowledge and special wisdom—they know their followers and they know the path they have to follow. They are daring and innovative in a way that is valued by their followers. As Kanungo and Conger (1989) noted, "Followers are more likely to attribute charisma to a leader when they perceive his or her behavior to be contextually appropriate and in congruence with their own cultural values" (p. 18).

The actions of leaders, then, will not have the same impact on different cultural groups. This idea is in agreement with the performance-maintenance (PM) model of leadership developed by the Japanese researcher Jyuji Misumi (1985). In contrast to most U.S. leadership models, which tend to assume that leadership actions will be interpreted in the same way across contexts (Smith & Peterson, 1988), Misumi's model assumes that the same leaders' action (such as checking the quality of employee work) will be interpreted differently across cultural contexts.

In a comparison of how employees in two individualistic cultures (the United States and Britain) and two collectivistic cultures (Japan and Hong Kong) interpret leader actions, the British researcher Peter Smith and his international associates demonstrated that there are some consistencies but also important differences in this domain (Smith, Peterson, Bond, & Misumi, 1990). For example, common to employees in all four countries was a concern that leaders should "sympathetically discuss" personal difficulties experienced by employees; but a concern for spending time with a leader socially was specific to employees in Hong Kong. These findings lend support to the proposition that in order to be persuasive and enjoy charisma, leaders must adapt to local cultural requirements. But charisma is only one of the factors that influence the persuasability of the source of a message (see Figure 6–4).

Credibility. Clarence Thomas or Anita Hill . . . which one seems credible to you? This question mesmerized many Americans, and even a lot of people outside the United States, in 1991. Thomas was a U.S. Supreme Court nominee accused of sexually harassing his former

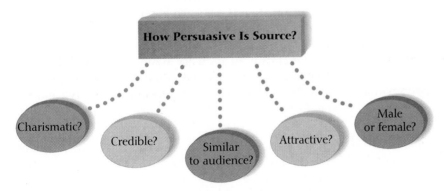

Figure 6–4   Factors influencing persuasability of source.

employee, Ms. Hill. Although Thomas won the support of the all-male Senate committee and went on to sit on the Supreme Court, many Americans continue to disbelieve his version of events.

What is it about a person that makes him or her credible? A long line of research suggests that being seen as trustworthy ("Of course I believe her, she is someone you can trust!") and as having expertise ("Well, he is someone who knows what he is talking about. I believe him!") are the key requirements (Miller, 1987).

Of these two, "expertise" seems simpler to analyze than "trustworthiness." This is because the criteria for being an expert are more clearly defined. "Experts" typically have titles, such as doctor, professor, or scientist. A message about the medical dangers of marijuana is far more likely to persuade users if it comes from scientists (Bachman, Johnston, O'Malley, & Humphrey, 1988). Experts are more persuasive when they talk about an issue that the audience has little information about and does not take a strong stand on (Petty & Cacioppo, 1986a). Rapid speech by experts can lead to greater persuasion, particularly for audience members who are moderately involved with an issue (Smith & Shaffer, 1995). For most people, experts will be more persuasive on topics such as the kind of medication one should use (note how often medical studies are cited in advertising), but less persuasive on topics such as the death penalty or abortion.

In assessing the trustworthiness of a source of a message, people tend to want to know what motivates the source. "Why is she saying that?" "What is in it for him?" (Eagly, Wood, & Chaiken, 1978). If communicators have a personal stake in a particular message, this will make them appear less trustworthy. But speakers who argue against positions that would seem to benefit them personally are seen as being more trustworthy. Howard Giles and his associates found that Anglo-accented speakers (who would generally be expected to be supportive of making English the official language of the United States, as advocated by the English-only movement) were more persuasive when they took a position against the English-only movement, whereas Hispanic-accented speakers were more persuasive when they argued for the English-only movement (Giles, Williams, Mackie, & Rosselli, 1995).

Politicians sometimes choose to speak *against* a position held by their audience, in the hope that millions of television viewers will see them as more trustworthy when the speech is reported on the national news. For example, a politician who calls for more stringent regulations to control industrial pollution will seem more trustworthy if her live audience is made up of heads of industry ("Wow, that candidate told the chiefs of industry to clean up their act!") than if it is made up of environmental activists ("Sure, she *had* to be a squeaky clean environmentalist in front of *that* group").

Similarity.   In one of his most effective speeches, the Iranian leader Ayatollah Khomeini declared that he wished he, too, was one of the soldiers in the army of Islam (referred to as *pasdars*, meaning "guardians"). The *pasdars* were for the most part poor young men, often with little formal education. They were from the families of the "Islamic masses" who provided the strongest support base for the Ayatollah during his struggle against Western governments and the spread of Western values. Part of the reason why the Ayatollah was so persuasive was because he consistently spoke of himself as being similar to the masses. He spoke the language of the common people, which tended to make his speeches seem unsophisticated to educated people.

The message that "I am really just one of you" is also used effectively by Western political leaders. By dressing casually, dropping into fast-food outlets, showing appreciation for popular music, and generally appearing more like the voting majority, leaders such as President Clinton can win popular support.

The idea that similar others should be better able to persuade us seems to fit with the similarity–attraction hypothesis (Byrne, 1971). To the strongly supported proposition that similarity leads to liking we can add that liking increases persuasion. Similar others are particularly persuasive when the issue is emotionally charged, rather than when it is factual or technical. For example, young women are more likely to be persuaded about their choice of a birth-control method, a very personal issue, if the source of the message is a same-age peer than if it is an older woman (Cantor, Alfonso, & Zillmann, 1976).

Physical Attractiveness.   Human beings are young, good-looking, fashionable, healthy, athletic, and tanned—this is the conclusion aliens would reach if they used commercial advertisements in Western societies as their source of information. Imagine if aliens got to know about us by looking at the covers of glossy magazines. They would conclude that we are all very attractive, wear sexy clothes, always smile, and have perfect skin and teeth.

The reason why attractive people stare at us from the covers of magazines, and speak to us in so many advertisements, is that, in general, physically attractive people have been found to be more persuasive. Social psychologists have demonstrated this through controlled experiments, typically involving the same message being communicated by sources of different levels of attractiveness (Chaiken, 1979, 1986). One way in which attractiveness seems to have an impact in this context is that it causes the audience to pay less attention to the content of the message and more to the source. But this can backfire if the attractiveness of the source contradicts what is prescribed by culture to be correct for a particular social role. For example, we have come to expect that a model advertising a new brand of jeans will be very attractive, but we would not expect a bank manager or accountant to dress like a swimsuit model.

Gender: Men and Women as Sources

The fact that men have enjoyed more power than women has meant that they have tended to be the sources of persuasion. Even in the political life of so-called liberated Western societies, very few women have reached the top positions. A woman president of the United States still seems unlikely, although women already occupy top political posts in a number of developing countries (including India, the Philippines, Sri Lanka, and Pakistan).

The male power monopoly is in part responsible for the nature of gender stereotypes in the media. This explains the role of women as sex symbols (the next time you are at a newsstand, look at how many magazine covers show women and how many show men, as well as how they are shown—a topic discussed further in Chapter 12). The economic purchasing power of women has increased, so there is now more investment in persuading them to be particular types of consumers, to feel that they need to have certain products in order to maintain or improve their status (Costa, 1994). Some of the messages directed at women do not blatantly endorse traditional gender stereotypes, as "You're not getting older . . . you're getting better" (see Lont, 1995).

But because traditional gender stereotypes still have influence, women will often be met by resistance when they attempt to adopt persuasive tactics used effectively by men. For example, during the 1980s, assertiveness training became popular for women in business and other areas of public life, on the assumption that if women are to succeed in the world outside the home, they must learn to be assertive like men. But Kelthia Wilson and Cynthia Gallois (1993) have shown that assertiveness does not always have the desired consequences for women, because the rules by which "assertive women" are assessed are different from those applied to "assertive men." Assertiveness on the part of women is still often seen as inappropriate ("She is too pushy and arrogant"), whereas for men the same assertive behavior is judged as appropriate ("He is a real go-getter and dynamic").

The Sleeper Effect

sleeper effect conditions under which the characteristics of the source have less influence, so that a message from a low credibility source increases in persuasiveness.

Although the characteristics of the source can play an important role in persuasion, there are certain conditions in which their effect diminishes. An example of this was identified in the 1940s and came to be known as the **sleeper effect** (Hovland, Janis, & Kelley, 1953; Hovland, Lumsdaine, & Sheffield, 1949). To appreciate this effect, recall that a source which enjoys higher credibility has been found to be more persuasive than one of less credibility. A message about the ozone layer is likely to be more persuasive if the source is "Dr. Giles, a world expert in ozone depletion" than if the source is "a bright high school student." But some time after the message has been communicated, the audience may still remember the message but forget the characteristics of the source. In this case, the persuasiveness of the message will become independent of the source, with the result that the message from the low-credibility source will increase in persuasiveness. However, more recent research suggests the sleeper effect does not have a pervasive influence in everyday life (Gillig & Greenwald, 1974; Pratkanis, Greenwald, Leippe, & Baumgardner, 1988).

Concepts and Issues

Sources of messages are likely to be more persuasive if they have charisma and if they are perceived as credible, as more similar to the audience, and as physically attractive. If performance in elections is used as an indicator, men are still more persuasive than women in politics. The persuasiveness of a message can become independent of the source, resulting in the so-called sleeper effect.

1. Describe charismatic leadership and the three stages in leadership in which charismatic leadership can be distinguished.
2. What does credibility of source involve?
3. What are some other factors that make a source persuasive?

The Content of the Message: What Is Being Said?

Betty Jo was shopping for a new pair of jeans. She had a particular brand and style in mind, one that she had seen advertised on TV recently. Betty Jo tried the jeans on in the shop; she walked around and looked at herself in the mirror from different angles. The sales staff told her she looked good, and she said the jeans felt good, and so she bought them. When she came out of the boutique, she remembered that she also needed a new calculator, one that she could use in her advanced calculus class. She had heard about a particular brand and model that had the functions she needed, but she was anxious to learn about the details of the different calculators within her price range. When she found a shop that offered a wide selection of calculators, she looked over several leading brands, read through instructions, and quizzed the sales staff about the different functions and features of each calculator. She reviewed the technical information she had gathered, then made her purchase.

Peripheral versus Central Routes

The distinction between *central* and *peripheral* routes to persuasion is part of a more recent cognitive approach to the study of persuasion (see Table 6–2). This distinction is particularly relevant to the issue of message content ("What is said?"). According to Richard Petty and John Cacioppo's (1986b) **elaboration likelihood model,** an information processing approach which proposes that central rather than peripheral

elaboration likelihood model an information-processing approach which proposes that central rather than peripheral routes to persuasion lead to more enduring change.

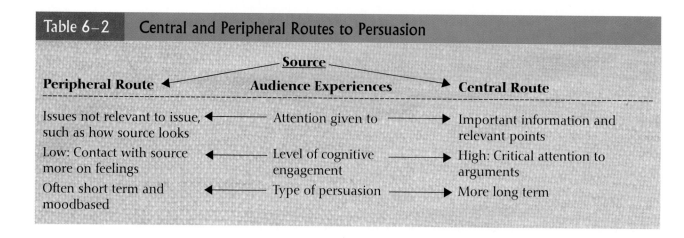

Table 6–2 Central and Peripheral Routes to Persuasion

Peripheral Route ◀	**Source** **Audience Experiences**	▶ **Central Route**
Issues not relevant to issue, such as how source looks ◀	── Attention given to ──	▶ Important information and relevant points
Low: Contact with source more on feelings ◀	── Level of cognitive engagement ──	▶ High: Critical attention to arguments
Often short term and moodbased ◀	── Type of persuasion ──	▶ More long term

peripheral route   route to persuasion taken by messages that lead to acceptance without engaging the recipient in thought.

routes to persuasion lead to more enduring change, the **peripheral route** to persuasion is taken by messages that lead to acceptance without engaging people in thought. Betty Jo was probably persuaded to buy her jeans by a message that worked through the peripheral route. The advertisement for the jeans was not designed to give information about the cloth or other technical characteristics of jeans, but to associate the jeans with a beautiful model and a fun–loving lifestyle. The outcome was that Betty Jo "felt good" about wearing the jeans, so she bought them.

The arguments that persuaded Betty Jo to buy the calculator became effective through the **central route,** because these arguments engaged her in serious thinking. She weighed the various advantages and disadvantages of the different brands of calculators rather than letting her emotions guide her. The information provided by the sales personnel gave details of the technical characteristics of calculators, as well as the various guarantees provided by manufacturers. She made her decision knowing that the particular calculator she chose had the functions she needed to complete her calculus assignments, and had a 2–year warranty as well.

central route   route to persuasion taken by messages that engage the recipient in serious thought.

In addition to which type of route, it is useful to distinguish between two aspects of message content: one, the affective versus informational features of the content (How does the message make the audience feel?), and the other, the way the content is organized (Does a message contain just one side of an argument, or does it also include counterarguments?).

Affective versus Informational Features

David wants to convince his younger brother, Sam, that the dangers of AIDS are real and that Sam should adopt safe sex practices. Should David use scare tactics and try to frighten Sam by showing him vivid pictures of young people dying of AIDS? This would be a strategy of using high–fear–inducing messages. Or would it be better to reason with his brother and provide factual evidence of the real dangers through statistical and medical information? In this case, he would be using low–fear–inducing messages.

Meta–analytic studies have shown that the fear tactic can be effective, and as a general rule high–fear–inducing messages are more successful than low–fear–inducing ones (Boster & Mongeau, 1984). High–fear–inducing messages are particularly effective when the audience has a low level of anxiety (Wheatley & Oshikawa, 1970). If Sam is not anxious about AIDS, then it would be effective for David to use high–fear–inducing messages. This is presumably because Sam has a higher tolerance for such messages.

On the other hand, an audience that is already highly anxious can be influenced more via a low–fear–inducing message. This is because such an audience is already feeling too anxious and will avoid high–fear messages that would increase their anxiety level even more. If Sam is already anxious about AIDS, it would be better not to bombard him with highly threatening information but, rather, to provide only moderately threatening material.

But fear–arousing messages will not persuade Sam unless they also suggest ways of coping with the problem at hand. Sam needs to believe that he is capable of changing his sexual practices; otherwise, his

An objective of a persuasive message is very often to get people to behave differently. Since the late 1980s, there have been attempts in many different societies to make people aware of the dangers of AIDS. It has been shown that fear–arousing messages will be more likely to persuade when they also suggest a way to cope with the problem, like this billboard, part of a government–sponsored anti–AIDS campaign in Zambia.

heightened anxiety level will not lead to the changes David hopes for (Beck & Lund, 1981). Should David also provide evidence (factual information from outside sources)? Research findings suggest he should, because evidence increases the persuasiveness of a message (Reinard, 1988). Evidence increases persuasion particularly when the person communicating the message is seen to be credible.

Petty and Cacioppo's elaboration likelihood model suggests that a lot also depends on how involved and capable Sam is in assessing the evidence. A person who has low involvement and low ability to assess evidence will rely on "surface" cues. Persuasion can then take place through the peripheral route. But if Sam happens to be highly motivated and extremely capable, he will think through the evidence and become persuaded to change his sexual practices through the central route.

Research suggests that Sam will be persuaded more by case studies than by statistics about general trends (Bell & Loftus, 1985). Case studies bring arguments to life and persuade us by personalizing messages. One good case study is often worth a thousand statistics. The best presentation will cleverly combine both, using case studies to bring to life generalizations based on statistics. Also, in practice Sam will not experience emotional and informational aspects of a message in an either/or way. He will already be experiencing a certain mood when he receives messages, and his mood will color the information he receives (Rosselli, Skelly, & Mackie, 1995), depending on what he sees to be the source of his mood (Sinclair, Mark, & Clore, 1994). When Sam sees terrible weather, rather than the information given to him by his brother, to be the reason for his bad mood, then there is a greater chance that his brother's message will be persuasive.

Organization and Style

Pedro is to represent a coalition of environmental groups in presenting their case before a government committee against the building of a new road through the local woodlands. Representatives from a major manufacturing company will be arguing for the new road on the grounds that it will allow the company to expand and, consequently, to create new jobs in the region. The environmentalists argue that the new road will bring more pollution and damage precious wildlife, and that its so-called benefits would simply be to make a few wealthy people even wealthier. Pedro wonders how he should organize the presentation (see Figure 6–5).

Research suggests that if Pedro practices his speech in front of other environmentalists, one-sided arguments will persuade them because they already agree with his position (Hovland, Lumsdaine, & Sheffield, 1949). But when he presents his case in front of an audience that disagrees with his own position, a two-sided message that gives pros and cons is better (Burgoon, 1989). The two-sided message allows the speaker to show flaws in the opposing viewpoint and to highlight the strengths of his own position.

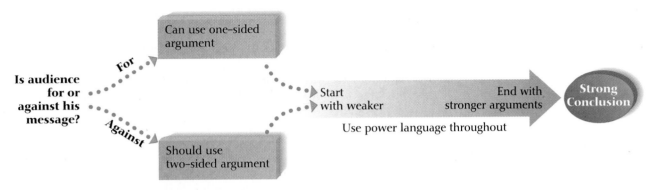

Figure 6–5 How to persuade more effectively depending on the audience.

Pedro would be advised to begin with his weaker arguments and build to a climax, so that the last argument he presents is the strongest (Walker, Thibaut, & Andreoli, 1972). Interestingly, during fieldwork in Islamic countries I noticed that this strategy of "working up to a climactic ending" is used by Muslim preachers, whose training is based mainly on a tradition of rhetoric going back to Aristotle. Their sermons can be very lengthy, sometimes lasting several hours. The first part of the sermon is typically slow in pace and simple and mundane in content. After warming up the audience, the preacher picks up the pace and brings in more powerful points, so that the best is saved for last.

With respect to how Pedro arranges his conclusion, rather than presenting his arguments and ending with words such as "And now that you have heard our arguments, I leave it up to you to reach your conclusions," he would be more persuasive if he explicitly states his conclusion (Hovland & Mandell, 1952). This is because the "open-ended" or "now reach your own conclusions" style is more effective when the audience is highly involved and follows the arguments closely (Sawyer, 1988), whereas the members of a government committee listening to lengthy debates are likely to require all the help they can get just to stay awake!

Pedro should also remember to use *power language*—a style giving an impression of confidence and authority (Bradac, Hemphill, & Tardy, 1981). For example, he should say, "It is clear that . . . ," or "Most authorities on the subject endorse the view that . . . ," or "I feel certain that. . . ." He should not say, "I'm not absolutely sure, but perhaps . . . ," or ". . . this may sound unbelievable and even silly, but we . . . ," or ". . . uh . . . I am not sure how to put this . . . uh . . . well . . . ," because such a hesitant style lowers credibility.

On the first day of committee hearings, Pedro learns he is to make his presentation after that by a representative of the "pro-road" industrialist group. He is then given a choice: to make his presentation immediately after that of the opposing group, or to allow the committee to go into recess and make his presentation after 3 days. What should he do? The opposing group will benefit from the **primacy effect,** by which information presented first has most impact.

primacy effect information presented first has greater impact.

recency effect information presented last has greater impact.

Pedro will benefit from the less common **recency effect,** whereby the information presented last has more influence. But he can increase the persuasiveness of his message by opting to present after a time gap, because the recency effect is enhanced when two messages are separated by time (Miller & Cambell, 1959). The gap allows the first message to fade, affording the second message greater opportunity to persuade.

Attitude Inoculation and Resistance

attitude inoculation exposing people to mild attacks on their attitudes on particular topics to help them build up resistance to strong attacks.

A two-sided argument may also allow Pedro to take advantage of what William McGuire (1962, 1985) has referred to as **attitude inoculation,** exposing people to mild attacks on their attitudes on particular topics so as to help them build up resistance against strong attacks. *Resistance* refers to the extent to which an attitude is able to remain unchanged in the face of attack. McGuire's research suggests that even a generally accepted idea, such as "industrial pollution is bad for the environment," is vulnerable to assault, for example, from a credible source such as an "environmental expert." (This would happen in the very likely scenario of the industrialists hiring an environmental expert to argue that industrial pollution is actually not harmful.) But if before having their belief attacked people are "immunized" by first experiencing a modest challenge, and if they then write a defense of their belief in response to the attack, they become much more resistant to such attacks.

This "vaccine for brainwash" (McGuire, 1970) plays a role in many applied domains, including political campaigns and commercial advertising (McGuire, 1989; McGuire & McGuire, 1991). Politicians now routinely incorporate into their own speeches some of the criticisms typically raised by their opponents. "Of course," they explain, "there are a few problems with the plan our party is proposing, but what plan is perfect? We all know about these kinds of problems (politician lists a few criticisms made against the party plan), but we also know that these problems are exaggerated (politician goes on to show how these problems are not serious at all)." By raising criticisms against their own positions, politicians can inoculate supporters and increase their resistance to attacks.

Another effective approach is to get the audience to take an active part in arriving at arguments in defense of their attitudes. "Think back to the last time you heard our party being attacked in this way," a politician might suggest, "and think of the steps you took to support the party." By getting people to recall supportive actions, resistance is further increased. The more people have thought about and processed a message, the more resistance they will show in the face of opposing messages (Haugtvedt & Petty, 1992). One way to get people to process a message more is to make the message more relevant to them (Haugtvedt & Wegener, 1994). If Pedro talks to people in the United States about how environmental pollution is affecting cities across their nation, this information is more likely to be processed than if he discusses how environmental pollution is affecting life in Ukraine.

Concepts and Issues

Messages that require careful scrutiny are processed through the central route, whereas emotionally laden messages persuade through the peripheral route. High–fear–inducing messages are generally effective, but only if the audience is not already anxious. An audience that is hostile to the message or is of two minds is best approached through a two–sided message, using power language and with explicit conclusions. Resistance to attitude change can be increased through several techniques, including attitude inoculation.

1. What are peripheral and central routes to persuasion?
2. In preparing a presentation, what factors should you keep in mind in order to be more persuasive?
3. What is meant by *attitude inoculation?*

The Channel of Communication: How Is It Said?

Ours is said to be the age of television, in both the national and international arenas (French & Richards, 1996). Satellites and cable have helped to internationalize television, so that it is possible to watch the

Many children in Western societies spend more time watching television than they do in school, and even when they are in school they watch television. This trend is spreading to remote parts of the world, such as this one-room school for Inuit (Eskimo) children in Canada. The trend is worrisome for many reasons, one of which is that television is a poor medium for persuasion through the central route, and a better one for persuasion through the peripheral route.

same shows and commercials in most parts of the globe. Young people are particularly influenced by this trend (Macbeth, 1996). Judith Gibbons, Maria Lynn, and Deborah Stiles (1997) found that watching television is among the most preferred free-time activities for adolescents in countries as diverse as Cyprus, India, the Netherlands, and the United States. Marie Winn (1985) has called television the "plug-in drug" for the young, pointing out that in Western societies, and probably in more and more non-Western ones, children spend more time watching television than they spend in school. The influence of television on how people think and act in the realm of politics is particularly important because it is through political power that resources are distributed among competing groups.

Television and Politics

The modern media—television in particular—have had a profound influence on politics, so much so that in the most powerful nation in the world a former movie star, Ronald Reagan, was elected president after he campaigned using a "conversational style" of speech (Jamieson, 1988). Jeffey Tulis (1987) has argued that over the last century the modern mass media have helped to change the presidency of the United States, so that it has become a "rhetorical presidency." Whereas in the nineteenth century, presidents made few speeches to the nation, modern presidents give national addresses on an almost daily basis. Television carries the messages of governing officials to the people, and there is little doubt that officials adapt messages to fit this medium. Tulis (1987, p. 190) notes that one of the factors that made Ronald Reagan "the Great Communicator" was the considerable attention he gave to television.

We should add that because television is now available in many parts of the world, the performance of leaders on television has become a crucial factor in the political life of many societies. A likely consequence of this is that the political speeches around the world will become more similar. However, audiences will still be influenced more by messages in their native tongue. In a study of Hispanics in the United States, even fully bilingual individuals (those equally competent in English and Spanish) were influenced more by Spanish-language messages inserted in Spanish TV programs than by the same messages in English inserted in English TV programs (Roslow & Nicholls, 1996).

Television is influential despite the awareness ordinary people have of its influence, an awareness that according to the research of Marian Friestad and Peter Wright (1995) is quite sophisticated and similar to that of experts. Even negative political campaign messages ("attack TV spots,") persuade audiences, despite being described by them as repulsive (Pfau and Kenski, 1990). However, not everyone is influenced by such messages in the same way. Consider the issue of gays in the military, a political hot potato in the 1990s. When Julia Zuwerink and Patricia Devine (1996) presented messages arguing against gay people serving openly in the military to an audience in favor of allowing gay people to have this right, they found that individuals who considered the attitude highly important were more resistant to the "negative" message.

In addition to influencing directly how politics is conducted, television has also helped to shape certain stereotypes, such as those about gender.

Gender and the Media

The media, and television in particular, have helped to construct gender stereotypes (Moore, 1992). A blatant bias has been the absence of women. Studies of prime-time television have shown that men appear on television far more often than women (Signorielli, 1989; VandeBerg & Streckfuss, 1992). Men often outnumber women characters 2 to 1, and the camera is more often on men.

But more subtle and probably more powerful forms of sexism also exist on television. The women who are shown tend to be younger, are more scantily dressed, have lower-status positions, and appear as less assertive (Davis, 1991; VandeBerg & Streckfuss, 1992). When men and women appear in television advertisements, the voice of authority is typically male, whereas the seller of products to do with home and family is typically female (Lovdal, 1989). The "medical doctor" telling you about the wonders of a new over-the-counter drug is male, but the sexy person expounding on the magical new kitchen cleaner is female. Even in the realm of sports, female performances are described in terms of grace and beauty, whereas male performances are portrayed in terms of "explosive power" and dominance (Sabo & Jansen, 1992). Associated with this is the tendency for women and men to use such stereotypes to advertise themselves in personal ads. As one researcher summarized the situation, men appear in personal advertisements as success objects, women as sex objects (Davis, 1990).

Gender bias in the media has been a focus of fairly extensive critical debate (Downing, Mohammadi, & Sreberny-Mohammadi, 1995). Surely this critical attention, and the wider influence of the women's movement, have ended gender bias on television. Although some changes have taken place, in showing more women working outside the home, for example, some of the old biases continue and some newer biases have emerged (Moore, 1992). Women still tend to be younger and attractive (an old bias), but there has been an exaggeration of men as family-oriented (a new bias).

The demonstration that women and men are portrayed in particular ways on television is only important if we assume that television can influence how we think and behave. A number of studies suggest that watching men and women in certain types of roles on television influences how people behave in their everyday lives, by providing them with "scripts" to follow (Geis, Brown, Jennings, & Porter, 1984). Note that this interpretation is normative rather than causal. Television does not cause people to behave in one way or another, but it does provide them with ideas about correct behavior. Such ideas can act as self-fulfilling prophesies because they can incorporate not only what women and men should do but what their limits are (Geis, 1993).

Television and Persuasion

The conclusion we might arrive at is that the most persuasive communication channel today is television. However, a more correct generalization is that the persuasiveness of a communication channel depends on the nature of the message being communicated (Taylor & Thompson, 1982).

Shelly Chaiken and Alice Eagly (1976) showed that when difficult messages are communicated to students, they are more persuasive when they are written. Easy messages, on the other hand, are more persuasive when videotaped. One explanation for this is that difficult messages require the audience to pay close attention and to have the ability to assess more complex information. Such messages will need to be processed through the central route, and this is more feasible when a message can be read, thought about, and reread. When a difficult message is presented on videotape, numerous pictorial characteristics can act as distractors, preventing the processing of information through the central route. Easy messages, on the other hand, can be processed with far less cognitive effort, and video seems to be more appropriate for the processing of such messages.

The superiority of the central route for processing complex messages will disappear if the audience is highly aroused, presumably because high arousal prevents the kind of focused attention needed for deeper cognitive processing (Pham, 1995). Ayisha is asked to summarize a French text as part of her language exam. She has time to read the text several times and digest it. However, the sexist language of the text upsets her, so that she becomes highly aroused and is unable to attend to all the points made in the text.

Concepts and Issues

Television has become the most important channel of communication in most parts of the world. The impact of television on North American politics has been profound. Easy messages are more persuasive when shown on television; difficult messages, when written.

1. Describe the role of television as a channel of communication.
2. How have women and men been portrayed on television shows?
3. Is television the most effective channel for persuasion in all circumstances? Discuss.

The Target: Who Is to Be Persuaded?

In his insightful work *The Disappearing American Voter,* Ruy Teixeira (1992) has shown that voter turnout in the United States has been declining steadily since the end of World War II. Even when we consider voting in the presidential elections, only about half of the voting-age population actually turns out to vote. This is much lower than the voting turnout used to be in the United States (it reached over 80 percent in a number of nineteen-century presidential elections) and far below that of other democratic countries (over 90 percent turnout has been achieved in recent national elections in such countries as Belgium, Austria, and Australia). Teixeira shows that low voter turnout is not peculiar to any ethnic group. Also, although lower-income groups were traditionally less likely to vote, low turnout is spreading to the middle class.

Imagine you are running for political office. What lessons does Teixeira's analysis suggest to you? A first lesson is that while the entire voting-age population is your potential target, in practice only about half of this group has actually voted and only this voting group determines who is elected to office. If you were running for political office in some other democratic countries where nonvoting levels are as low as 5 percent, you would be trying to persuade an already participatory population to cast a ballot in your favor. However, in the United States, the *highest* participation rate tends to be about half, and so the target audience can be grouped into two broad categories: those who vote, who you will try to persuade to support you; and those who do not vote, who you must persuade to participate *and* to cast a vote in your favor.

What characteristics of the audience should be taken into account by those attempting to persuade? There are two dominant approaches to this question. The first is to consider broad demographic categories, such as sex groups and age groups. This approach addresses such questions as "Are women persuaded more readily than men?" A second approach is to focus on personality characteristics of the audience, in the hope of discovering the personality profile of people who are more readily persuaded. In recent years, this second approach has led to cognitive research on relationships between message content and personality characteristics (see Figure 6-6).

Gender and Age

Are women more easily persuaded than men? The answer psychologists have given to this question has changed in the last few decades, in part as a result of critical research by women psychologists (Eagly & Carli, 1981). In the discussion of conformity in Chapter 7, we see that the traditional view of women as being more conformist than men has been successfully challenged by Alice Eagly and others through their demonstration that such differences are minimal and that they are open to various interpretations. Similarly, meta-analytic surveys show that women

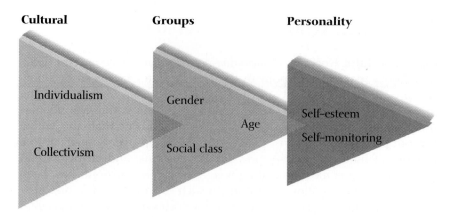

Cultural   **Groups**   **Personality**

Individualism   Gender   Self-esteem
                          Age
Collectivism   Social class   Self-monitoring

Figure 6–6   Audience characteristics and persuasion.

are slightly more influenced by persuasion attempts than are men, but it is not clear how this difference is best interpreted.

Perhaps the best interpretation rests on the different gender roles of men and women and the behaviors that the members of each category see as appropriate. One possibility is that women are trained to be more concerned about maintaining interpersonal harmony and to avoid disruptions in social relations. Consequently, there will be a greater tendency for women to go along with the suggestions of others and thus be more flexible and agreeable.

Are certain age groups more susceptible to persuasion? Research suggests that the greatest long-term impact of persuasive messages will be on young people, particularly during the late teens and early twenties when they are experiencing what is often the most dramatic transitional stage to adulthood. This is because it is during these formative years that attitudes toward social and political issues are shaped (Krosnik & Alwin, 1989). These attitudes remain fairly stable over the long term (Schuman & Scott, 1989). Religious conversions also commonly take place during these years (Brown, 1987; Hall, 1904).

What Roger Brown and James Kulik (1977) called **flashbulb memories**—vivid and essentially permanent images of events that have importance for a person—are often formed during this life stage. Each generation develops its own flashbulb memories, so that the 1960s generation carries images of the assassinations of President John F. Kennedy and Dr. Martin Luther King, Jr.; the 1990s generation may develop flashbulb memories of the fall of the Berlin Wall, the Gulf War, and the Middle East peace settlement. These memories will not necessarily be accurate pictures of events (McCloskey, Wible, & Cohen, 1988), but they will be rehearsed, revised, and reconstructed through discussions with others. Of relevance to our present discussion is the fact that these memories form part of the collective viewpoint of a generation, "persuading" people to see the world in particular ways (Fentress & Wickham, 1992). The experiences Americans have had with health-care reform in the 1990s may lead to such a memory, shaping a perception that health care in the United States is doomed to collapse (see Bogdanich, 1991).

flashbulb memory   vivid and essentially permanent image of an event that has importance for a person.

Personality Factors

During my student days, a curiosity to learn about different areas of life led me to try out a number of sales jobs. I started with the traditional encyclopedia sales and moved on to more exotic areas, such as selling works of art. One of the first things I noticed was that many salespeople believed some types of people are more easily persuaded than others. Later, as I gained more knowledge of psychological research, I realized that this assumption is too simplistic. The research literature suggests that it is useful to focus on the concepts of central and peripheral routes to persuasion, and not just on personality types. An important research question is, "What characteristics of the context or the person lead persuasion to take place through central or peripheral routes?"

For example, in sales it is often assumed that people who lack self-confidence are more easily persuaded. Psychological research shows that, indeed, self-esteem is influential in persuasion, but that individuals with low self-esteem *and* those with high self-esteem are more readily persuaded than those with moderate self-esteem (Rhodes & Wood, 1992). However, the reason for the persuadability of low- and high-self-esteem individuals is probably different: The former are persuaded because their lack of confidence leads them to be moved by just about all influence attempts; the latter, because their high confidence leads them to become engaged by sound arguments, so that they do not dismiss persuasion attempts out of hand.

Another characteristic of individuals related to persuadability is self-monitoring (discussed in Chapter 3). High self-monitors are very aware of social contexts and constantly gather information to help them adapt to their surroundings. In extreme cases they are like social chameleons, able to change and fit in, whatever the circumstances. Low self-monitors, on the other hand, are not image-conscious but look inward, to their own psychological states, as guides for action. As would be expected on the basis of these differences, high self-monitors have been found to be more influenced by image-based messages, whereas low self-monitors are more influenced by product-quality or information-based messages (Snyder & DeBono, 1985). Advertisers should regard the consumer market as segmented, so that any given product is best advertised by a number of different messages, each targeting a specific consumer group. Using the example of high and low self-monitors, for instance, car manufacturers should advertise their products using both image-based and information-based messages.

Concepts and Issues

Some studies suggest that in some cases women are more easily persuaded than men, perhaps because women are socialized to maintain interpersonal harmony. Evidence for younger people being more easily persuaded is stronger. Individuals both low and high on self-esteem and high on self-monitoring are more easily persuaded.

1. Give examples of the kinds of target characteristics social psychologists have studied in relation to persuasion.
2. Are certain sex and age groups more susceptible to persuasion?
3. How are self-esteem and self-monitoring related to persuasion?

Persuasion Through Culture

The "divide-and-rule" strategy of researchers, involving the isolation of factors such as the source, content, channel, and target of communication, has led to interesting insights, but we should also keep in mind the "big picture": Persuasion takes place in cultural contexts, and the role of culture in persuasion is fundamental.

Through the influence of culture, we are socialized to fit into society as skilled performers in schools, in families, on sports teams, and in all other contexts. Culture teaches us the persuasive tactics that are appropriate for our social roles. It also teaches us to recognize and to interpret persuasive messages in particular ways. Sang-Pil Han and Sharon Shavitt (1994) showed that college students in the United States are more persuaded by ads pitched to individualistic themes ("You, only better," "Make your way through the crowd," "The art of being unique"), whereas college students in Korea are more persuaded by ads pitched to collectivist themes ("Sharing is beautiful," "A more exhilarating way to provide for your family," "The dream of prosperity for all of us"). Do you think commercial advertisers have noticed the appeal of these different messages in the United States and in Korea? Han and Shavitt show that they have and they do pitch ads more to individualistic themes in the United States and more to collectivist themes in Korea.

Research on how men and women attempt to influence others suggests some gender differences in the use of tactics of persuasion (Buss, Gomes, Higgins, & Lauterbach, 1987; Carli, 1989; Falbo & Peplau, 1980; Howard, Blumstein, & Schwartz, 1986). For example, males seem more often to be the target of weak (plead, act helpless) rather than strong (threat, insult) persuasion tactics (Howard, Blumstein, & Schwartz, 1986). This may be because weak tactics are assumed to be safer and more effective with men, who score higher on measures of Machiavellianism, indicating that they use threat, deception, cutting corners, and other negative manipulative tactics more often than do women (Christie & Geis, 1970). Research in countries that have a high rate of immigration suggests that male members of majority groups, such as those of English descent in Australia, are more wary of assertive behavior on the part of immigrant men than immigrant women (Gallois, Barker, Jones, & Callan, 1990). This may be because, again, immigrant men are seen as the bigger threat. Such gender-associated styles of behavior are acquired through the influence of culture.

Because tactics of persuasion are acquired through culture, communication missteps can take place when people from different cultures attempt to persuade one another. Consider, for example, an exchange that took place between a U.S. student and a Korean teaching assistant

(T.A.), highlighted in the research of Andrea Tyler and Catherine Davies (1990). The exchange took place in an introductory physics laboratory course and involved a negotiation over grades. The student went to the front of the class and asked the T.A. to explain his grade. The interaction that followed was videotaped and then shown to both U.S. and Korean observers.

What for Korean observers was "correct" behavior, such as the T.A. not responding to a remark by the student, was incorrect from the perspective of U.S. observers. On the other hand, the Koreans judged certain behaviors, such as the open and public expression of emotions and disagreements, to be incorrect, although these behaviors were acceptable to U.S. observers. Clearly, the cultures of Korea and the United States had persuaded these individuals to interpret the persuasion process in different ways: "The most basic, pervasive insight gained from this analysis is that the communication broke down, in spite of the interlocutors' initial good intentions, because the participants did not share the same interpretations of many aspects of the discourse" (Tyler & Davies, 1990, p. 408).

The Business World

Such differences in interpretation lie at the heart of many problems that arise during intercultural persuasion attempts (Graham, 1985). For example, in the Japanese business context, almost all persuasion takes place in private interactions, so that by the time officials gather in a public meeting the real decisions have already been made. If disagreements seem to persist, then the public forum is abandoned once more, so that persuasion can take place in private. In this way, there is less danger of people losing face.

Unlike Americans, Japanese negotiators do not sit in public meetings to "hammer things out." As Kazuo Nishiyama (1971) pointed out: "It is not conceivable that one Japanese manager can persuade another manager or elicit attitude change in other members during the process of a meeting" (p. 152). As part of a strategy that is publicly less confrontational, Japanese make more use of indirect and private tactics, which include more use of silence (Matsumoto, 1990). In a study of experienced Japanese, American, and Brazilian businessmen, John Graham (1985) found support for the idea that Japanese make more use of a variety of indirect strategies, such as silence, for saying "no" (Ueda, 1974).

Such findings suggest that when comparing persuasion across cultures, we should include persuasion strategies that might not be used very often in our own culture but that may be used often by people in other cultures. Most of the lists of strategies used in current research are too limited because they are derived uniquely from the Western context (influential examples of such lists can be found in Falbo, 1977, and Schenck-Hamlin, Wiseman, & Georgacarakos, 1982). For example, one popular list includes 16 compliance-gaining strategies—such as *promise*: If you comply, I will reward you; *threat*: If you do not comply, I will punish you; *pregiving*: Actor rewards target before requesting compliance; *altercasting*: Only a person with "bad" qualities would not comply—but excludes indirect strategies such as *silence* and *withdrawal* (Marwell & Schmitt, 1967). However, even on this limited list cultural differences arise (Burgoon, Dillard, & Miller, 1982).

Power and Persuasion

conflict model model of social influence which assumes that both majorities and minorities are sources and targets of persuasion.

dependence model model of social influence which assumes that minorities are targets but not sources of persuasion.

Despite the cross–cultural differences that do exist, there is an important consistency with respect to power and persuasion. The French social psychologist Serge Moscovici (1980, 1985a) has developed what he calls a **conflict model** of social influence, which assumes both majorities and minorities to be sources and targets of persuasion, in contrast to the traditional **dependence model,** which assumes minorities to be targets but not sources of persuasion. Moscovici has argued that minority persuasion takes place through conversion, which involves more thinking through issues than does simply yielding to pressure, which is what majority persuasion tends to involve. When industrialists want to build a new road through a town, they can use their power and status to get their employees to support the idea. But a community group opposed to the new road would need to persuade people by the weight of their arguments because the group lacks the power needed to force people to support its plan.

Charlan Nemeth (1986, 1992; Nemeth & Staw, 1989) has extended this formulation and provided empirical support for her idea that

"Eco–Warriors" protest road construction in Great Britain. Some research suggests qualitative differences between persuasion by minorities and majorities. Lacking the power to force others to do as they want, minorities are more likely to achieve persuasion through conversion. Majority influence is more likely to come about through the use of power.

minority persuasion leads target persons to engage in more divergent thinking, which is creative and leads to a critical assessment of alternative solutions. A community group opposed to the building of a new road could offer alternative solutions to transport challenges. In contrast, majority persuasion leads to convergent thinking, which is narrow in focus. The manufacturers focus exclusively on the solution of constructing a new road, whereas critics in the community gravitate toward solutions with alternative possibilities.

Research suggesting that majority and minority persuasion lead to qualitatively different thought processes is like the distinction between central and peripheral routes to persuasion (Petty & Cacioppo, 1986b). There is some evidence to support the claim that minority persuasion does, indeed, take place through the central route (Maas, West, & Cialdini, 1987). For example, because minorities are generally seen to be low in credibility, their communications are "thought through" more diligently. As a result of such serious deliberations, the persuasion that occurs is likely to be long-lasting. This special feature of minority persuasion is probably very common in most societies.

However, we must keep in mind that the audience will not be influenced in a uniform manner by messages coming from a minority. Gordon Moskowitz (1996) has shown that audience members who hold positive views of a minority will also be more influenced by messages from that minority. If Rebecca views labor unions positively, she is more likely to be persuaded by a labor union message to vote for Jessica in the next local election.

Persuasion and Social Groups

Finally, the main focus of persuasion research has been on the individual as target and, more recently, on cognitive processes within individuals. Although this approach has led to interesting insights, a major cultural assumption in this research is that individuals act as autonomous units, able to make up their minds in isolation by receiving and processing information sent from various sources. This assumption probably has some validity in certain Western contexts, where societies tend to be more individualistic and where individuals may have more choice. But in collectivist cultures, where individuals may have fewer choices, persuasion is more likely to involve social groups "deciding." That is, individuals are persuaded more through the groups to which they belong. Consequently, whereas the process of communication from source to target may involve only one step in individualistic contexts, it is more likely to involve at least two steps (source–group–person) in collectivist contexts.

Let us consider a case in which persuasion could take place through persons deciding on their own. This case involves a message intended to persuade women to practice safe sex in order to minimize the risk of contracting AIDS. Angela receives this message while listening to the radio at her home in Santa Cruz, California. She is persuaded by the message and acts on it by insisting that her partner practice safe sex. He resists initially, but complies when she gives him an ultimatum: "If you want to have a relationship with me, it has to be this way. I have been persuaded by you on other issues, and I want you to accept my view in this instance. This has nothing to do with anyone else, it is between us, and either we agree on this or I leave and go back to New York." Such a statement is only plausible coming from individuals who see themselves as mobile and independent.

Indira hears the same message about the importance of safe sex practices on the radio while she is at her home in a village near Hyderabad, India. She too finds the message compelling, but when she subtly raises the issue with her partner this soon leads to a debate involving everyone in the village. The village elders and her parents are most directly involved, but indirectly everyone becomes involved. Indira cannot behave as a self-contained individual, she cannot act as a mobile and independent entity, because she is more directly and fundamentally tied to a collectivity. Her decisions are much more dependent on social groups than are the decisions of Angela and other people living in individualistic cultures. Persuasion in such collectivist contexts involves more of a social process and is far less a matter limited to the cognitive processes of independent persons.

In practice, persuasion in most Western contexts also depends on collective processes. Even if an individual is persuaded "in isolation" by a message, the persistence of the newly acquired belief will depend on how much it is supported by the social surroundings. Being persuaded to believe in particular religious ideas, for example, involves interacting with others on the basis of these ideas, using appropriate language, and receiving support: "Believers must learn how to use their religious beliefs properly, both generally and in specific contexts, distinguishing what may be said to family, friends, and at church from what is appropriate for funerals. Each requires a different register, which depends on the context. The beliefs themselves endure because they are socially supported." (Brown, 1987, p. 117). In practice, then, persuasion in all societies is ultimately a *social* process involving collectivities rather than individuals in isolation.

Concepts and Issues

Persuasion takes place through cultural norms and rules and is first and foremost a social and collective phenomenon. The tactics used to persuade vary across groups, such as women and men, as well as across cultures. Majority groups can persuade through power, minority groups through getting others to think through issues.

1. What does it mean to say that persuasion is a social phenomenon?
2. Give a few examples of group and cultural differences in the tactics used in persuasion.
3. How do minorities persuade?

Conclusion

The traditional approach to studying persuasion by isolating source, content, channel, and audience characteristics has yielded important insights. More recent research on central and peripheral routes to persuasion, much of it stimulated by the likelihood elaboration model, has led to a greater focus on the entire persuasion process. Persuasion is best looked at in its entirety and in cultural context. Many features of persuasion, particularly tactics, vary across cultures. But technological advances, and particularly the spread of television, have meant that persuasion now shares some characteristics in much of the Western world and increasingly in non-Western societies. These changes are not necessarily positive, because television seems to be better adapted to persuasion via the peripheral rather than the central route.

For Review

There is no sharp dividing line between persuasion, communication designed to influence another's cognition or overt behavior in which the target of persuasion has some measure of free choice, and coercion, social influence in which the target experiences no choice.

Psychologists have traditionally adopted a "divide-and-rule" strategy, isolating factors so as to identify independently the role of source, content, channel, and target in the persuasion process. More recent cognitive research has led to a highly useful distinction between two routes to persuasion: the central route and the peripheral route.

The appropriateness of persuasion strategies can vary across cultures. Many of the issues raised in persuasion research in the Western context are not appropriate outside industrialized democratic societies.

Charismatic people are more persuasive because they have a higher capacity to sum up how things stand, the ability to articulate a vision, and the ability to be innovative and daring in a culturally appropriate manner. Leaders will be more persuasive if they enjoy credibility and are seen to be attractive and similar to followers.

Women and minorities have traditionally had less experience of being the source of persuasion, and research suggests that when women use the same tactics as men they are judged differently.

The distinction between central and peripheral routes to persuasion is particularly relevant to the issue of what is said. A one-sided message is only effective with an audience that already agrees with the speaker's position; a two-sided message will better persuade an undecided audience and also help inoculate them against attacks on generally accepted ideas. When a series of competing messages is presented, the first will enjoy the primacy effect, and the last the recency effect.

Factors that can influence persuadability include gender, age, and personality.

Culture plays a pervasive role in persuasion: We are taught by culture to perform our various social roles. Culture socializes us to adopt appropriate means of persuasion, and some differences exist across cultures and across gender groups as to what is appropriate persuasion.

Although the usual research approach has involved a focus on how isolated individuals become persuaded, in everyday life persuasion takes place in social contexts and through collective experiences.

For Discussion

1. Describe the traditional research approach to studying persuasion, pointing out its strengths as well as weaknesses.
2. What implications do the concepts of central and peripheral routes to persuasion have for the impact of television in politics, education, and other areas of modern life?
3. "Minority influence strengthens democracy." Discuss this statement.

Key Terms

Attitude inoculation
198
Central route (to
persuasion) 194
Channel (of
communication)
181
Charisma 186
Charismatic
leadership 187
Coercion 180
Conflict model (of
social influence)
208

Content (of message)
180
Dependence model
(of minority
influence) 208
Elaboration
likelihood model
193
Flashbulb memory
204
Peripheral route (to
persuasion) 194

Persuasion 180
Primacy effect 197
Recency effect 198
Sleeper effect 192
Source (of message)
180
Target (of
communication)
181

Annotated Readings

For a solid overview of the social psychology of persuasion see R. M. Perloff, *The dynamics of persuasion* (Hillsdale, NJ: Lawrence Erlbaum, 1993).

For a broader discussion of issues revolving around persuasion, see C. U. Larson, *Persuasion: Reception and responsibility*, 7th ed. (Belmont, CA: Wadsworth, 1995).

More personalized discussions of persuasion in modern life are A. R. Pratkanis and E. Aronson, *The age of propaganda: The everyday use and abuse of persuasion* (New York: W. H. Freeman, 1991); and R. B. Cialdini, *Influence: Science and practice*, 3rd ed. (Glenview, IL: Scott, Foresman, 1993).

For general discussions of modern media, see J. Downing, A. Mohammadi, and A. Sreberny–Mohammadi, eds., *Questioning the media: A critical introduction* (Thousand Oaks, CA: Sage, 1995); and D. French and M. Richards, eds., *Contemporary television* (Thousand Oaks, CA: Sage, 1996).

Conformity

"Conformist, that's what you are."

"I'm not; besides, you're a conformist yourself!"

That was the beginning of a heated argument between two teenagers that I overheard during what seemed like a very long train ride along the California coast. An accident had resulted in the cancellation of earlier trains, so every seat was taken. I had no choice but to listen to what was going on right next to me.

As I looked out on the California coastline, it struck me that there was something peculiar about the accusations. The teenagers were shouting, "You're a conformist" as if it were the equivalent of "You're a liar" or "You're a thief." I could think of cultures where to be called a conformist would have positive rather than negative connotations.

Research shows that conformity in the United States is actually comparable to that in most other societies, as the teen dress code shown in these pictures illustrates.

These denim-clad youths in Caracas, Venezuela, and the three Estonian young men dressed in leather are conforming to in-group norms, but also to Western norms. Without being told, you would not know where these pictures were taken.

In many traditional cultures, powerful social mechanisms guide individuals not only to conform but also to do things as part of a group. "Doing it together" rather than "going it alone" is valued. Muslims, for example, should pray facing Mecca five times a day. But according to Islamic belief, prayers have more value when they are conducted as part of a group, rather than by an individual in isolation. It is the public nature of prayer, and the synchronized activities of a group, that give prayers special value. This contrasts sharply with the idea, prevalent in the United States, that prayers are strictly private, between the individual and God.

And despite the emphasis on individualism and nonconformity in the United States, research evidence suggests that Americans are just as conformist as people in most other cultures: The teenagers hurling accusations of "conformist" at each other were dressed almost exactly alike. But there is something unique about the United States, and that is the tremendous diversity of lifestyles available to people, in contrast to the greater homogeneity of many other societies. This diversity gives individuals more choices: They can select a lifestyle (based on sexual orientation, ethnicity, language, religion), and they can exit from one group and enter another.

These Orthodox Jewish boys in New York and Amish girls in Pennsylvania belong to minority communities that have succeeded in maintaining a lifestyle very different from that of the mainstream.

Not all groups in the United States allow easy entry or exit, in part because some groups adhere strictly to a traditional way of life, something it takes many years to learn and unlearn. For example, it would be difficult for Susan, raised as a Catholic in a Boston Irish community, to join a community of Orthodox Jews in New York or an Amish community in Pennsylvania. If she did manage to leave her group and join one of these groups, she would be a nonconformist from the standpoint of her Boston community, but her new community would expect a high level of conformity to its normative system.

Another unique feature of the United States today is its dominant position in the world: More and more people in other countries are conforming to or adopting the American way of life. When we look at young people in almost any part of the globe, the influence of American popular culture is evident. In a global context, there seems to be a decline in diversity of lifestyles, and more conformity to the Western, and particularly American, way of life.

Despite increasing conformity to Western lifestyles around the world, some societies maintain conformity to local norms. They succeed in this by teaching the young, such as these Japanese schoolboys and the saffron-clad novice Buddhist monks in Thailand, to follow tradition.

But many groups continue to resist the pressure to conform to Western ways, and preserve at least some surface features of their distinct cultures. They do this by teaching the young the correct way to behave according to their normative systems, and by enforcing conformity. In these cases, conformity serves to preserve cultural diversity. Here we see conformity serving a positive function. Conformity serves other constructive functions that are essential to social life. Most people conform to ideas about correct behavior most of the time in their societies. We do not need to have police officers looking over our shoulders: We stop our automobiles at stop signs and at red lights. We stand in line for tickets to a movie, and to get to a cash register, and in many other situations where an orderly line helps everyone get to what he or she wants. Because most of us conform most of the time, a great deal of everyday behavior is easily understood and even predicted. Scores of students come to see me in my office every week, but I know exactly which chair students sit on and they know where I sit; and the general procedure we follow is almost aoways the same, even though the content of our discussion can vary considerably. We know how to communicate with each other; we don't need to think about or decide these things each time. We can just get on with our meeting. Conformity, then, is not necessarily always bad. It also serves important positive purposes in many societies.

CHAPTER 7

Conformity and Obedience

◀ As students of social psychology, we look at this Confucian ceremony in Seoul, South Korea, in a manner influenced by our training. We notice the high level of conformity shown by group members. Although the normative system of our own society may be very different from that of Korea, we all conform to a normative system to some degree.

conformity changes in behavior that arise from real or imagined group pressure

obedience changes in behavior that arise when people follow the instructions of persons in authority.

During my student days in England, I developed a deep interest in the topics of **conformity,** changes in behavior that arise from real or imagined group pressure, and **obedience,** changes in behavior that arise when people follow the instructions of persons in authority. I used to collect interesting examples of conformity and obedience and spend hours discussing them with other students, as well as with my teachers and family members.

One of the most hotly debated issues in these discussions was how each of us would behave in situations in which other people had conformed or obeyed. Imagine if in the future you held a very promising position in a prestigious corporation but discover that top management is following policies that could harm the general public. Would you conform to company norms and keep quiet, preserving your own job and benefits, or would you blow the whistle and risk losing everything? Or perhaps you find yourself in the army. Would you obey the orders of your commanders under all conditions— even orders to harm civilians—or would you disobey and risk the consequences?

One of my friends during those students days was a microbiology major, Thomas, who maintained that he would never conform or obey in such situations. He insisted that there must be something wrong with people who do conform and obey. When I saw Thomas again a decade later he told me that he had only just realized how vulnerable individuals can be to group norms and authority pressure. He had recently moved from London to Boston and was doing research in a leading medical laboratory, where he found himself obeying instructions that he knew were unethical and would harm the careers of several other researchers. "But if I disobey now, the institute director will cut my funding," he explained in a defensive tone. "I just have to obey until I find another job." When Thomas finally did leave this research institute, he told me he had never believed it would be so difficult to disobey authority.

Thomas learned another lesson, this time in conformity, when he went back to London briefly in 1982, during the war between Britain and Argentina over the Falkland Islands (Malvinas). He had been in a London pub when TV announcers gave the news that British forces had recaptured the island. Actually, he had thought all along that the war was a terrible mistake and that Britain should never have sent troops. But everyone in the pub was cheering loudly and he felt compelled to go along with the jubilation. He dared not express his true feelings. He came out of the pub wondering how many other people felt the same way and really wanted to protest against the war. He felt so awful about what had happened that he went back to the same pub the next evening and expressed his true views, with the result that he was embroiled all night in heated arguments with supporters of the war. "They tried to make me feel like a traitor," he said, "but I was determined not to cave in and not to conform to their idea of patriotism."

Conformity and Obedience: An Overview

Conformity and obedience have been the subject of some very informative and sometimes deeply disturbing research by social psychologists. A useful start to assessing this literature is to distinguish between these two concepts, using four criteria proposed by Stanley Milgram (1974). (See Table 7–1.)

▶ *Hierarchy.* Obedience regulates relations between individuals of unequal status (manager orders subordinate to dress formally at work), conformity regulates relations between individuals of equal status (group of managers conform to group norms about correct way to dress at work).

▶ *Imitation.* Obedience does not involve imitation; rather, it involves complying with orders from authority figures. Conformity involves imitation and the adoption of similar behavior by peers.

▶ *Explicitness.* Obedience is typically in response to explicit and public commands (army officer orders soldier to shoot). Conformity often takes place in response to implicit and tacit requirements (soldier realizes that to be accepted in the group he has to conform to the norm of "treat prisoners humanely").

▶ *Voluntarism.* Those who obey explain their behavior by explicit reference to obedience ("My orders were to shoot"), while those who conform typically explain their behavior as voluntary ("I dress the way I want to, and it just happens to be in the same style as the rest of my group").

Causal versus Normative Explanations

How are we to account for conformity and obedience? According to causal explanations, factors internal (personality characteristics) and external (group norms, authority figures) to individuals cause individuals to conform and to obey. This is assumed to be a deterministic relationship, so that the presence of certain personality characteristics, authority figures, and other assumed "causes" will inevitably

Table 7–1	Ways in Which Obedience and Conformity Differ			
	Hierarchy	**Imitation**	**Explicitness**	**Voluntarism**
Obedience	Regulates people of different status	Imitation is not involved	Requirements explicit	Obedience typically admitted
Conformity	Regulates people of same status	Involves imitation	Requirements implicit	Conformity typically denied

result in conformity and obedience (effect). However, for a number of reasons, causal accounts are inadequate. It is through socialization that people learn to conform to certain norms and to obey certain authority figures, and there is continuous change in what people conform to and whom they obey.

One of the most interesting, and hopeful, aspects of these types of behaviors is that individuals can resist pressures to conform and to obey and initiate changes in entire patterns of behavior. The great spiritual and moral movements of human history, including the major religions—Christianity, Judaism, Islam, Buddhism, and Hinduism—as well as the civil rights movement and the women's movement, began with individuals intentionally refusing to conform and to obey. A normative account assumes that human beings always have some measure of choice and that they can intentionally choose to do one thing rather than another.

This does not deny the possibility that there may be universals in social behavior. A basic universal in this domain is that conformity and obedience exist to some degree in all societies, and research is leading to a more detailed picture of similarities across cultures. Lee Hamilton and Joseph Sanders (1995) examined how people in Japan, Russia, and the United States attribute responsibility for wrongdoing at the workplace. In one example, an employee dumps factory waste and causes a toxic waste spill; in another instance, an employee in a pharmaceutical company fails to carry out adequate tests for drug side effects. Participants in all three countries blamed the employee more when he or she was an authority (e.g., company manager) rather than a subordinate acting on instructions. In all known societies, some people have higher status, they enjoy greater influence, and are assigned more responsibility for their actions.

Positive and Negative Aspects

Conformity itself is normative and a positive factor in social life in most situations. Despite the arbitrary nature of most social norms, such as those pertaining to fashion, we need conformity to norms for smooth social interactions. For example, the norms of conversation, such as those stipulating that the senior person present takes the lead in initiating and ending discussions, allow meetings to be productive (Brown, 1966). Without norms, chaos would follow and very little would be achieved. However, there is also an "ugly" side of conformity, and this typically involves compliance with, and eventually acceptance of, norms that lead to harm to oneself and others. Examples are norms that lead students to participate in alcohol binges and drug taking ("*We are all going to Club Zee tonight*," the anxious first-year student is told by more senior students, the implication being that anyone under 21 years of age who wants to be part of the group has to have a fake ID to gain entrance to Club Zee, where everyone will drink) and norms that require people to derogate those considered as "outsiders" ("*We hate those people*").

Obedience also has very important positive functions, although we typically think of its negative aspects. The Holocaust, the Khmer Rouge genocide in Cambodia, mass killings in Argentina, the My Lai massacre in Vietnam, "ethnic cleansing" in Bosnia—these are some of the terrifying events made possible by obedience to authority. Social psychologists have focused almost exclusively on instances in which obedience to authority has negative consequences because of the destructive forces that can be unleashed through this process. But we must keep in mind that obedience has positive aspects and is necessary for society to survive: By obeying the instructions of a police officer, drivers avoid a traffic tie-up. If drivers disobeyed instructions, there would be more confusion and longer delays.

Despite these differences, conformity and obedience are inextricably linked: "Conformity is an overlay that makes obedience easier, quicker, and snappier because the obedience of others is evident around us" (Hamilton & Sanders, 1995, pp. 81–82). A first step in bringing about conformity and obedience is the formation of norms, the topic we turn to next.

Concepts and Issues

Conformity and obedience have both positive and negative aspects; at a basic level they are necessary for society to function. They can be distinguished using four criteria: hierarchy, imitation, explicitness, and voluntarism.

1. Describe examples of positive and negative conformity and obedience from your own experiences.
2. In what ways are conformity and obedience different?

Norm Formation

If you are out on a starry night and you look up and focus on one of those distant stars, you will most likely feel that the star is moving. This *autokinetic effect* was first reported by astronomers and later was studied by psychologists interested in perception. The researchers asked participants to look at a spot of light in a dark room. In this dark space, where participants do not know the distance between themselves and the light, a single point of light cannot be localized and may appear to be in a different place each time it is shown. The light seems to move even for people who know it does not actually move.

During the 1930s, Muzafer Sherif (1935, 1936), a Turkish psychologist who studied and later settled in the United States, used the autokinetic effect to investigate norm formation. Two features made the autokinetic effect particularly suitable. First, there tend to be individual differences in the amount of movement people perceive. Second, any report of movement is arbitrary because the light never moves. (These features continue to make the autokinetic effect a powerful tool in more recent social psychological research, as in Hogg & Hardie, 1992.)

Sherif (1935) asked participants, either individually or in groups of two or three, to sit in a lightproof and soundproof room, and gave them the following instructions:

> When the room is completely dark, I shall give you the signal *ready*, and then show you a point of light. After a short time the light will start to move. . . . Tell me the distance it moved. Try to make your estimates as accurate as possible. (p. 323)

Sherif found that when individuals are placed in the laboratory alone and asked to make repeated estimates, they establish a range of estimates that is fairly normally distributed around a median value. This median value, Sherif proposed, is a norm for the individual. Norms differed across individuals. When these individuals, who had already established "personal norms," were now put in a group and asked to make estimates, it was found that their estimates converged, resulting in a group norm. But the convergence in this condition was less than in the "groups first" condition, in which participants were first put in a group and afterward asked to make estimates in the presence of others.

Perhaps the most important of Sherif's findings is that there was a strong tendency for individuals to continue to be influenced by the group norm even when they were no longer in the group but made their estimates alone in the laboratory. Subsequent research showed that the group norm continued to influence individuals even a year later (Rohrer, Baron, Hoffman, & Swander, 1954). Thus, despite the arbitrary nature of the group norm (the group was *always* wrong in its estimates of movement because the spot of light never moved), the continued impact of this norm did not require the presence of the group (see Figure 7–1).

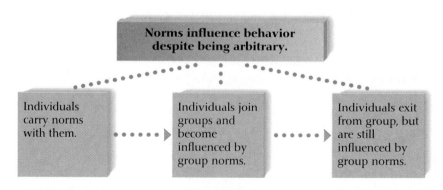

Figure 7–1 Norms influence behavior despite being arbitrary.

Spontaneous and Manipulated Norms

The norms that evolved in Sherif's (1935) early studies were **spontaneous norms,** norms that evolve naturally within groups without any effort to control norm formation. Robert Jacobs and Donald Campbell (1961) extended Sherif's basic experiment by studying **manipulated norms,** norms explicitly brought about by design. Using the autokinetic effect, Jacobs and Campbell planted confederates in the groups. By making extreme estimates, the confederates could influence the group norm to achieve a manipulated norm. Once a confederate manipulated a group norm, the confederate would be replaced by a naive subject, who became the unwitting transmitter of norms to still newer naive arrivals. The impact of the manipulated norm persisted after five generations, as in the perpetuation of a microculture.

spontaneous norm norm that evolves naturally within a group without any effort to control norm formation.

manipulated norm norm explicitly brought about by design.

Orthodox Jews celebrating a holiday in Jerusalem, 1996. An interesting aspect of social change is that although we all perceive that change takes place, we also recognize continuity across time. The United States in 1969 is in many ways different from the United States in 1999, but it is still recognizable as the same society. The Jewish community in Israel has also changed during this same time period, but it is still recognizable as the same community. This continuity comes about in large part through the transmission of normative systems from one generation to the next. This transmission sometimes takes place through formal ceremonies, but most of the time it happens through informal and tacit processes.

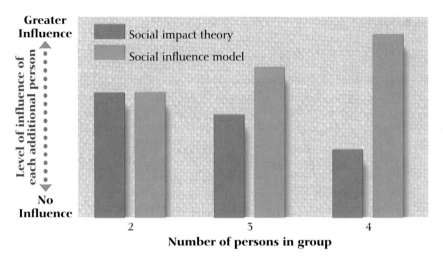

Figure 7–2 Incremental influence proposed by social impact theory and the social influence model. Social impact theory proposes that each additional confederate will have less influence than the first. The social influence model proposes that the second and third additional confederates will have more influence than the first.

Subsequent research showed that there are limits to how much norms can be manipulated and still be effectively transmitted across generations (MacNeil & Sherif, 1976). A manipulation that attempts to pull a norm extremely far away from its *spontaneous* position, the position it will have under given conditions, will be more likely to fail, in part because it makes the manipulation less plausible.

Common sense suggests that the number of people manipulating a group norm would be an important factor in creating conformity. A person is surely more likely to conform when in a group with ten confederates than with only one. Bibb Latané's (1981) **social impact theory** proposes that each additional confederate will have less influence than the first, and there is some experimental support for this theory (Campbell, Tesser, & Fairey, 1986). In contrast, the **social influence model** proposes that the second and third additional confederates should have more influence than the first (Tanford & Penrod, 1984). (See Figure 7–2.) These models may both be correct under different conditions, but the common theme they suggest is that by varying group size we can arrive at greater conformity to arbitrary norms.

But *who* is able to vary group size? Such questions raise the issue of status, because both inside and outside the laboratory some people have more influence than others in shaping group norms.

Status and Group Norms

Oh yeah, I daydream . . . I think of the head of the union the way I think of the head of my company. Living it up. I think of February in Miami. Warm weather, a place to live in. . . . You know what I'd like to do for one year? Live like a college kid. . . . Somebody has to do this work.

social impact theory theory that each additional confederate in a group will have less influence than the first.

social influence model theory that the second and third additional confederates should have more influence than the first.

If my kid ever goes to college, I just want him to . . . realize that his dad is one of those somebodies. . . . I can't really hate the colored fella that's working with me all day. The black intellectual I got no respect for. The white intellectual I got no use for. . . . I have one answer for (the black militant): go see Rockefeller. See Harriman. Don't bother me. We're in the same cotton field. (Terkel, 1985, p. 6)

Among Studs Terkel's (1985) interviews with people in different occupations is this fascinating discussion with a steelworker living on the outskirts of Chicago. The steelworker expresses himself bluntly, but his words are instructive. When we listen carefully to what he has to say, we realize that he is an example of the millions of people who are forced by their situation to conform to the norms established by others but who do not themselves enjoy much power to influence others. Melvin Kohn (1969) sees this to be a major difference between working–class and higher–class positions. The working class is associated with less power and the latter with more power to shape the normative system influencing conformity.

The contrast Kohn makes between working–class and higher–class people can be made more generally about low–status as opposed to high–status individuals. Among those who have low status because of their group memberships are members of minority groups, including women. Traditionally women have had less power than men to influence the norms and rules of society. Because men have enjoyed more power, they have shaped the norms and rules in government, education, the legal system, *and* the home. Similarly, African–Americans and other ethnic minorities have conformed to a normative system shaped by whites rather than by themselves.

Of course, it could be argued that women and other minority group members have enjoyed power in certain areas where they create their own normative systems. For example, even in traditional households there is at least one place where it is more likely that "the woman of the house" sets the rules: the kitchen. Similarly, we might argue that even during times of racial segregation in the United States, African–Americans set the rules in their own neighborhoods. Such enclaves certainly do exist and can have an important benefit, particularly when the enclave is large and can offer economic benefits to minorities. For example, sections of the economy controlled by ethnic minorities, such as Harlem in New York City or Little Havana in Miami, can be places to withdraw to in order to escape prejudice (see Chapter 10).

Although enclaves do exist and can act as shelter for minorities, in the mainstream sectors minorities conform to the normative system established by majority groups. In the law court, the school, and the workplace, among other domains, then, the norms are established by members of the majority group and minorities conform. The same trend is found in international relations, where the most powerful nations in the world have more control over the affairs of the United Nations, the World Bank, the International Monetary Fund, and other international agencies, and in this way enjoy tremendous leverage to force less powerful nations to conform to their norms.

majority influence how a majority maintains control by pressuring a minority to conform.

minority influence how a minority brings about change through the process of interactions and social conflict.

We can distinguish, then, between **majority influence**—the influence exerted by more powerful groups (such as Western nations, middle- and upper-social classes, men, whites)—and **minority influence**—the influence exerted by less powerful groups (such as developing nations, the lower classes, women, ethnic minorities). Majority influence tends to be greater, but later in this chapter we shall consider research that explores conditions in which minority influence can be increased.

The Arbitrary Nature of Norms

The painted spears were symbols of wealth and status and roughly corresponded to white tie and tails in our culture. . . . The analogy with formal dress even extended to the borrowing of ceremonial spears. An important man, caught short of them, might borrow some . . . and though everybody would know that his spears were borrowed, he at least was properly dressed for the occasion, though stark naked otherwise. . . . In pre-white times Tiwi males wore no clothing whatever. . . . Women . . . habitually carried a piece of bark that they held in front of themselves whenever they met a male. (Hart, Pilling, & Goodale, 1988, pp. 54–55)

The seceding group was nicknamed the "Nebraska Amish" or "Old Schoolers." The men wear their hair about shoulder length in the style of William Penn. They wear white shirts, brown denim trousers and gray coats, wide-rimmed hats, no suspenders, and no belts. Their trousers are laced up in back. The women wear a black kerchief tied on the head over a white covering, as bonnets are prohibited . . . of all Amish-women, these wear the longest dresses, in dark, plain colors. (Hostetler, 1980, p. 283)

The clearest features of dress that correlates with category membership in this school is the cut of jeans . . . burnouts wear wide bells, and jocks (buy) the latest fashions. The ratio of width of the bottom to the middle of the jean leg has changed over the years. . . . The width of jeans that one sees in the school spans . . . from wide bells through flares and straight legs, to pegged legs . . . in the larger context of Euro-American fashion, the continuum from bells to pegs is a continuum of fashion. (Eckert, 1982, p. 141)

The topic of clothes fashions is wonderfully suitable for exploring the various aspects of norms and social influence. One reason is because fashions in clothes are so arbitrary—there is no objective reason for preferring one style or color over another. The arbitrary nature of fashion tastes becomes particularly apparent when we look across different cultural groups. For example, among the Tiwi of North Australia the men traditionally wore nothing, apart from their ceremonial spears, and the women wore very little and then only on some occasions. In contrast, the Amish, who live primarily in Pennsylvania, Ohio, and Indiana, wear dark-colored clothing that covers all of their bodies except their faces and hands. Style of dress changes very slowly among such traditional groups, even among the young. This is obviously different from the younger generation in Western societies. But who is to say that the jeans considered "in" among Western teenagers are "better" than the clothes worn by Amish youth, or those worn (or rather, *not* worn) by Tiwi youngsters? Clearly, there are no objective criteria for making such comparative assessments.

But despite the arbitrary nature of clothing preferences, there is a general tendency for people to follow the tastes that prevail in their particular cultural group. For example, even though there is no logical reason why a Tiwi should be considered "improper" unless he is holding his painted spears, the fact is that Tiwi men *did* carry ceremonial spears. Similarly, teenagers in Western societies follow the fashion in jeans, even though what is "in" is entirely arbitrary and constantly changing.

Concepts and Issues

Despite their arbitrary nature, group norms can have an influence on the behavior of individual members even when individuals are outside the group, and such influence can be passed on to subsequent generations of group members. Majority groups have greater influence on norms and thus on the behavior of both majority and minority group members.

1. How did Sherif use the autokinetic effect in his study of norm formation?
2. Describe some examples of arbitrary norms that nevertheless have an influence on your own behavior.
3. Which groups (gender, ethnicity, social class) have the greatest influence on norms?

Conformity

We can conceptualize changes associated with conformity as being situated on a continuum ranging from complete compliance at one extreme to complete acceptance at the other (see Figure 7–3).

Compliance takes place when we change our outward behavior in order to conform, *even though we do not really believe in what we are doing.* For example, Helen wants to smoke indoors, but the other students she

compliance type of conformity in which a change in outward behavior is not accompanied by a change in beliefs.

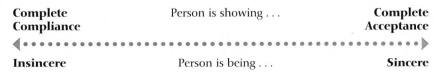

Complete Compliance	Person is showing . . .	Complete Acceptance
Insincere	Person is being . . .	**Sincere**

Figure 7–3 The compliance–acceptance continuum.

acceptance   type of conformity in which a change in outward behavior is accompanied by a change in beliefs.

wants to share a house with insist their house must be smoke-free. Even though Helen does not really agree with their decision or accept their reasoning, group pressure forces her to comply outwardly.

In many cases we have come to genuinely believe in what the group influences us to do, and this form of conformity is called **acceptance.** We may change our sexual behavior because we become convinced that the threat of AIDS is real and that the risks of contracting AIDS are very high. We may recycle because we come to believe everyone needs to do more to protect the environment. This kind of conformity is sincere, in contrast to the insincere kind involved in compliance.

It is more accurate to conceptualize compliance and acceptance as being on a continuum than as being totally independent either/or categories. This is because in many cases compliance can lead to acceptance. When individuals comply, for example, by writing an essay supporting a position against their original stand, this often leads to a shift in their own position toward acceptance (see Chapter 4). When individuals complied by writing pro-Castro essays, their attitudes became more accepting toward Castro.

Conformity to Majority-Established Norms

Our everyday experiences provide examples of how majority groups get minorities to conform to their norms. But can this kind of behavior be demonstrated experimentally? Social psychologists were excited by the discovery that such behavior can indeed be demonstrated experimentally and that laboratory research provides more detailed insights into the situation (Asch, 1951; Deutsch & Gerard, 1955). The story begins with the pioneering studies of Solomon Asch (1951, 1955, 1956), who used the laboratory technique and male undergraduate participants to explore conformity to majority-established norms. Whereas Sherif had used an ambiguous stimulus—the spot of light that seemed to move—Asch used unambiguous stimuli—lines of clearly different length.

Imagine you are a participant in one of Asch's laboratory experiments. You undergo a test designed to check your eyesight, for it was important for Asch that only participants with normal eyesight be included in the study. When you enter the laboratory for the actual experiment, you find that you are the last to arrive. The other five participants are already seated in a row of chairs. The last chair in the row is vacant, and that is where you sit. The experimenter shows you three lines of different lengths and then a standard line that is the same length as one of the three other lines. Your task is to assess which of the three comparison lines is the same length as the standard line.

Because you are the last person in the row, the other participants call out their answers first and then you have an opportunity to call out yours. Everything goes smoothly for the first few trials, because the other five participants call out what you see to be the correct answer. But then, unexpectedly, they call out what you think is the wrong answer. You find it hard to believe, for you can clearly see that, on the sixth trial, for example, line 2 is the same length as the standard, but

The norms established by groups are mostly arbitrary and sometimes wrong, but they still exert influence on the behavior of group members. Solomon Asch demonstrated the importance of arbitrarily established group norms. Participants in Asch's study could see the correct answer when they compared lengths of lines and identified a line similar in length to the standard line, and they knew that the majority of group members were reporting the wrong answer. Nevertheless, about a third of them conformed to the group norm and reported the incorrect answer.

the five participants calling out their answers before you have all said it is line 1. You rub your eyes and lean closer to get a better look at the lines. You are sure they are mistaken.

If you are similar to the participants in Asch's study, you are now feeling nervous and defensive. You do not want to look silly, to stand out from the group. You would prefer that your answers agreed with those of the rest of the group. At the same time, you feel that the group has made a mistake. The clock is ticking and everyone is waiting for your response. What are you going to do? Stick to what you think is the correct response or conform to the majority position and call out the wrong answer? This is the critical question Asch addressed through this study. The other five "participants" were actually Asch's confederates, trained to call out the wrong response on cue to assess the likelihood of your conforming to an arbitrary majority-established norm.

About a third of the participants conformed with the majority answer by calling out the wrong response. This is a very positive finding from one perspective because it means that about two-thirds of the time participants *did not* yield to group pressure. It is important to keep this in mind because there has been a tendency to discuss Asch's findings by focusing exclusively on the conformity shown by some participants some of the time rather than a resistance to group pressure on the part of most participants most of the time. Asch highlights the finding that the answers of about one-fifth of the participants remained unaffected by majority pressure.

Nevertheless, even when we do highlight the two-thirds of responses that remained unaffected by majority pressure, we still need to explain the one-third of answers that conformed. Surely this conforming behavior is more puzzling, because we know that when tested alone the participants almost never made mistakes in identifying the matching line. Perhaps Asch's findings are an outcome of the "conformist" 1950s era, when they were done? More recent studies using student samples in the United States have found lower levels of conformity (Nicholson, Cole, & Rocklin, 1985). A second possibility is that the "Asch effect" is peculiar to Americans. Studies involving groups of participants outside the United States (such as Brazilians, Lebanese, and Chinese) have demonstrated similar levels of conformity, while studies involving participants from some other groups (for example, the Bantu of Rhodesia and Fijians) suggest higher conformity (Chandra, 1973; Matsuda, 1985; Milgram, 1961; Whittaker & Meade, 1967).

This relates to our earlier proposition that Americans are not necessarily less conformist than people from other cultures when tested in the same experimental situation. However, because their society provides individuals with a wider array of normative systems, individuals in the United States can conform and yet demonstrate a greater range of behaviors as a population.

Particularly interesting are findings from studies using Asch-type situations that show lower levels of conformity among some groups. For example, in a British study the Asch effect was found for samples of West Indian youth and probation officers but *not* for students (Perrin & Spencer, 1981). Even more surprising are findings that German and Japanese participants were less conformist than Americans (Frager, 1970; Timaeus, 1968). People in these cultures seem to conform more within in-groups with which they have strong allegiances but conform less to norms established by strangers. Thus, conformity among Japanese seems to be higher compared to conformity among Americans in the context of the family, the school, the work organization, and other important in-groups, but perhaps the same or even less during interactions with strangers such as fellow participants in a social psychological experiment.

Conformity and Socialization

We have seen that one way to consider the relationship between culture and conformity is to place participants from different cultural backgrounds in the same experimental situation and examine possible differences in their responses. A number of theorists have speculated that any differences in conformity can be traced to socialization practices. A useful point of departure for such research is societies with relatively simple economic systems.

Researchers have discovered an intriguing relationship between socialization practices and different types of subsistence economies (Barry, Child, & Bacon, 1959; Poggie, 1995). Subsistence economies are typically classified with respect to how much food they can accumulate. In general, hunting and fishing economies are low on food accumulation, whereas pastoral and agricultural economies are high. Hunting and fishing often depend on independent effort and personal initiative. In contrast, most important farming activities, such as bringing in the harvest, rely on collective effort and group cooperation. Low–food-accumulation societies have been found to nurture independence and high–food–accumulation societies tend to strengthen dependence.

These different socialization practices are highly functional. Those who live by hunting and fishing often find themselves alone in unfamiliar terrain and need to be self-reliant. Farmers, on the other hand, need to work the same land year after year. It would be impractical if hunters and fishermen stayed in the same spot but farmers wandered off away from home.

The Canadian researcher John Berry (1966, 1967) postulated that socialization practices should lead to less conformity among participants from low–food–accumulation societies in an Asch-type situation. He tested this proposition by studying the Temne of Sierra Leone in Africa, characterized by a high–food–accumulation economy, and the Eskimo of Baffin Island in Canada, who have a low–food–accumulation economy. In support of his hypothesis, the Eskimo conformed less than the Temne. This suggests that environmental characteristics create a need for certain types of behavior, the society recognizes this need by encouraging certain levels of independence, and as a consequence individuals conform to different degrees.

An alternative to examining the conformity behavior of different groups in the same experimental context is to assess qualitative differences in conformity behavior across cultures. Interviews with participants in Asch-type conformity situations strongly suggest that "feelings of control" are central to the conformity experience. Participants typically report feeling a lack of control and a sense that they are pressured by the situation to come under majority control. John Weisz and his associates proposed that the key to understanding conformity behavior internationally is the distinction between *primary control*, by which individuals improve their own rewards by changing the present situation (Jeannine attempts to change the organization she works for in a way that will result in a higher status and more income for herself), and *secondary control*, which involves individuals improving their own rewards by accommodating to things as they exist (Jeannine changes her own behavior in order to fit in better where she works and in this way achieve higher status and rewards) (Weisz, Rothbaum, & Blackburn, 1984).

There is considerable evidence to support the view that primary control is valued in the United States, whereas secondary control is more highly valued in Japan (Weisz, Rothbaum, & Blackburn, 1984). For example, Japanese give higher priority to aligning themselves to others, whereas Americans give higher priority to autonomous pursuits (Morris, 1956). In this connection, research shows that Japanese participants have more external and Americans more internal locus of control (see, for example, Evans, 1981). This is related to the discussions in Chapter 5, which suggest that people in the United States have an internal attributional style directed at changing the world through personal effort and depending on dispositional characteristics.

Gender and Conformity

Are females more susceptible to majority pressure than males? Research on this question represents a classic example of how the culture of the times influences social psychology. The way the issue of gender and conformity has been tackled has changed dramatically over time, particularly through the influence of female social psychologists.

Until the 1970s, it was generally accepted among social psychologists that females are more susceptible to majority influence than males (Cooper, 1979; Nord, 1969). However, starting in the late 1960s, researchers began to report *not* finding the typical trend (e.g., Allen & Levine, 1969), and by the early 1970s, they were reinterpreting previous findings on gender differences and conformity, pointing to factors such as biases in experimental tasks as being the sources of such differences (e.g., Sistrunk & McDavid, 1971).

The dramatic shift in discussions about gender and conformity was introduced through the critical research of Alice Eagly and a number of other female social psychologists, including Linda Carli, Wendy Wood, and Lisa Fishbaugh (Carli, 1989; Eagly, 1978, 1983, 1987; Eagly & Carli, 1981; Eagly & Wood, 1991; Eagly, Wood, & Fishbaugh, 1981). These researchers elevated the whole discussion by pointing out how various, often subtle, factors could be involved in gender and conformity behavior. For example, Eagly and Carli (1981) found that female participants conform more than do males mainly in studies reported by men. But in studies reported by women, there is more likelihood of females and males conforming to the same extent. This may well be because male experimenters set up studies and select stimuli that will lead male participants to feel more confident and females less confident.

Also, female researchers may be more inclined to report the absence of gender differences in conformity behavior because it disconfirms traditional gender stereotypes. Certainly the starting assumptions of reviewers such as Alice Eagly seem to be fundamentally different, as may be their motivations for conducting research reviews. At the very least, Eagly and her colleagues begin by questioning traditional stereotypes.

Another insightful interpretation arising from Eagly's research is that under certain conditions women conform more to majority pressure than do men because women are more concerned than men about the larger group of which they are a part and less about independence. This interpretation would seem to be in line with cross-cultural research showing that boys tend to engage in more *egoistic dominance*, a self-serving behavioral strategy, and girls in more *prosocial dominance*, a group-serving behavioral strategy (Whiting & Edwards, 1973). It also agrees with research among adults in the United States showing compatible trends (Buss, 1981). In line with the idea that men value independence and being seen as nonconformist, Eagly, Wood, & Fishbaugh (1981) found that men increased their nonconformity when they believed they were under surveillance by other group members.

We have, then, moved away from such stereotypic generalizations as "Females supply greater amounts of conformity under almost all conditions than males" (Nord, 1969, p. 198) to reinterpreting patterns of male and female conformity in more subtle ways. The writings of Eagly and others have explicitly brought to the forefront ideas on gender and status. Males and females do not enter groups as "status-less"; sex functions as a vital status cue. This is because in almost all societies males are generally in positions of higher status than females (see Chapter 12). This status difference may be the most important factor in explaining any gender differences found in patterns of conformity.

In a sense, social psychological research has changed with changing gender stereotypes. At a time when traditional stereotypes were more firmly entrenched, research reported females to be more conformist than males; when gender stereotypes began to change, researchers reported either no significant gender differences or a more complex picture of conformity patterns and gender. This trend is similar to that found in research on prejudice, where studies from the 1930s onward reported African–American children as showing a preference for the white out–group, but from the late 1960s researchers reported less or no significant level of "in–group derogation" (see Chapter 10). In research on both conformity and prejudice, changing results may be partly explained by research findings reflecting changing normative behavior.

The research spearheaded by Alice Eagly has not only changed our views about gender and conformity but is also a classic example of a minority influencing a majority, the topic we turn to next.

When the Few Change the Many

A minority is powerless while it conforms to the majority; it is not even a minority then; but it is irresistible when it clogs by its whole weight.

—Henry David Thoreau, *Civil Disobedience*

There is a tradition of minority dissent in the United States, which was stronger in the early history of the nation. The American Revolution began with a dramatic act of civil disobedience: the colonists throwing tea into Boston Harbor. The concern for minority rights, as opposed to the authority of a central government, is reflected in the ideas of Thomas Jefferson and Thomas Paine and documents such as the Bill of Rights. Perhaps the ultimate voice of dissent was that of Henry David Thoreau and other American transcendentalists, who endorsed adherence to moral rather than just governmental rules.

The tradition of dissent is perhaps best symbolized in recent times by Martin Luther King, Jr. (1929–1968), who wrote his "Letter from a Birmingham City Jail" (1963) after being arrested for refusing to prevent a civil disobedience march. King followed the motto "Freedom is never voluntarily given by the oppressor; it must be demanded by the oppressed." In terms of strategy, he adopted the nonviolent path of passive resistance used years earlier by Mahatma Gandhi (1869–1948) in South Africa and in India.

Rosa Parks on a bus after the U.S. Supreme Court ruling that banned segregation on public vehicles. The power of a minority to influence social change has been demonstrated many times in history, but in few cases in as dramatic a manner as when Mrs. Parks challenged the Jim Crow system on December 1, 1955. Her refusal to give up her bus seat to a white passenger led to her arrest, and sparked an African-American boycott of bus lines in Montgomery, Alabama. The eventual success of the desegregation movement is reflected in many legal and social reforms since the 1960s.

But social psychology in the United States has been concerned more with control than with rebellion and has approached issues from the perspective of the majority rather than the minority. True, from the 1950s on, researchers in the United States did explore the impact of the relative size of a minority on conformity behavior (Asch, 1951). There was consistency in findings showing that increasing the size of a minority to more than one dramatically increases resistance to majority influence, so there is less conformity (Allen, 1975). Research findings also suggest that when an individual is opposed by a unanimous majority, conformity will increase with the size of the majority only if the majority members are seen as having arrived at their positions independently (Wilder, 1977, 1978). However, this line of research still treats the minority as a *target* rather than as a *source* of influence.

It has been European researchers, and particularly the French social psychologist Serge Moscovici (Moscovici 1974, 1976b, 1980, 1985a, 1985b; Moscovici, Mucchi-Faina, & Maas, 1994), who have turned Asch's question on its head. Instead of asking, "How does a majority influence a minority?" they have asked, "How does a minority influence a majority?" The contrast between the approaches of Solomon Asch and Serge Moscovici represents a classic example of how social psychological research can be so dramatically different across societies. Despite the historic roots of dissent in American society, modern social psychology in the United States adopts the perspective of the majority and is concerned with control. Thus, the key research question has been "How can a majority influence a minority?"

A tradition of conflict, nurtured by the writings of Niccolò Machiavelli (1469–1527), Karl Marx (1818–1883), Sigmund Freud (1856–1939), and Vilfredo Pareto (1848–1923), among others, influenced Moscovici and some other European researchers in their focus on how the *minority can bring about change* through the process of social conflict. As we discuss in Chapter 14, in the domain of intergroup relations also, there are fundamental differences between American and European research in that European researchers have focused more on conflict and social change.

From the perspective of reform seekers, Moscovici has probably asked the more important question, because he has focused on social change and the forces that lead to progress. Every great religious and political reform movement began as a minority movement and only succeeded by confronting authority and forcing change. From Jesus Christ and his small band of followers 2,000 years ago to twentieth-century movements that finally gave legal recognition to women, African-Americans, and other minorities—all began with a handful of

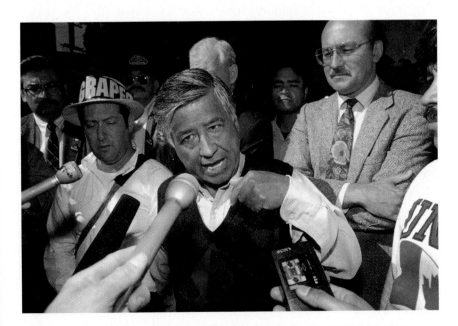

Cesar Chavez at a United Farm Workers Protest meeting. The best strategy for a minority attempting to gain influence is to be persistent and consistent in its stand, but not be seen as unreasonable and stubborn. This is sometimes a daunting task, because minorities typically have little influence on how they are presented in the media. Too often, minorities are dismissed as "radical" and "disruptive" by those intent on maintaining the status quo.

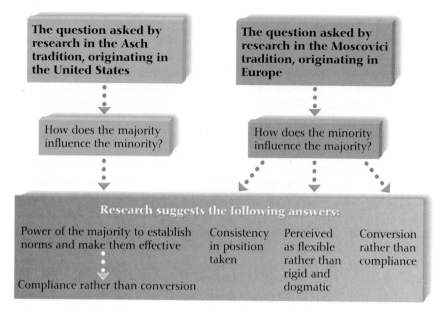

Figure 7–4 Two traditions of research on social influence.

disorganized and resourceless people, often ridiculed and disdained by the majority in their own time.

Starting in the 1960s, Moscovici and his associates explored the conditions in which a minority can influence a majority (Moscovici, Lage, & Naffrechoux, 1969). Moscovici's ideas have stimulated an impressive body of experimental studies, the results of which allow us to make three general points (see Figure 7–4). First, there is strong support for the proposition that minority *consistency* is a necessary (but not sufficient) condition for minority influence (Maas & Clark, 1984). This implies, for example, that an environmental group with a consistent position on industrial pollution is more likely to have influence than if it shifts its position. But there are certain conditions under which inconsistency leads to influence. For example, a person who shifts from a majority position to a minority position is even more influential than a person consistently espousing the minority position. (Imagine the effect if the former chief executive officer of a major logging company joins a "save our forests" movement!)

A second factor that can affect minority influence is *rigidity*. A minority that is perceived as rigid and dogmatic, as opposed to committed and confident, will enjoy less influence. A minority may be even more influential if it is able to adopt two different styles: rigid with authorities, but flexible and willing to negotiate with the public (Mugny, 1982, 1984).

Finally, Moscovici's research has led to the bold proposition that minority influence leads to conversion rather than compliance, whereas majority influence is more likely to lead to compliance rather than conversion (Maas & Clark, 1984). This implies that a consistent minority that succeeds in being viewed as committed rather than dogmatic will lead people to rethink their position, and result in a genuine change of perspective. This is qualitatively different from majority influence, which can often involve compliance without conversion.

Culture and Conformity

Society in the United States has a strong tradition of regarding conformity as "bad." This is reflected, for example, in the way parents socialize their children. The Turkish social psychologist Çiğdem Kağitçibaşi (1984, 1996) reported a number of studies on values that demonstrate this point. One study included interviews with over 20,000 adults in nine countries (Indonesia, South Korea, Philippines, Singapore, Taiwan, Thailand, Turkey, United States, and West Germany). As part of this study, parents were asked about the qualities they considered most desirable in children, among them "to obey their parents" and "to be independent and self-reliant." Whereas U.S. parents thought it desirable for children to be independent and self-reliant but not necessarily to obey their parents, parents from countries such as Indonesia and Turkey thought it much more desirable for children to obey their parents but showed less enthusiasm for independence and self-reliance.

Interestingly, the pattern of responses among parents from the newly industrialized society of South Korea (and, to a lesser extent, Singapore, Taiwan, and Thailand) was quite similar to that of the United States. This may be because industrialization is associated with a number of changes in social life, changes that tend to place more emphasis on the individual and personal independence than on the collectivity and group dependence. Among such changes are the breakup of the extended family; weakening of ties to local communities, tribes, and church; and greater social and geographical mobility. One outcome is that independence rather than dependence becomes desirable.

The most extreme example of this view is found in the United States, where "dependence" and "conformity" are seen as negative. The implication is that conformity somehow takes away from people as independent beings. Certainly at one level the American hero, as depicted in film by Clint Eastwood, Tom Cruise, and the like, is the epitome of rugged, self-contained individualism and nonconformity.

In a sense, the acceptance of nonconformity as an ideal has become conformity in the United States. "Doing your own thing," "Going my own way," and "Being an original" have become slogans to which people are supposed to conform. Advertisers take advantage of this cultural characteristic by telling people to "Be an original! Buy brand X." The slogan "Be an original" is so powerful that it sells products even when the purchase of brand X makes a person just like the multitudes of others who own the same product (How can brand X jeans make someone an original when 10 million other people are wearing the same jeans?). In everyday life it is also very clear that "conformist" is a negative label in the United States. To call someone a conformist is to suggest a lack of certain essential characteristics, such as independence and courage.

This generally negative attitude toward conformity may lead us to assume that U.S. society requires less conformity than do other societies, particularly more traditional ones. There is a tendency to view non–Western societies as "tight," meaning that they are more formal and orderly, and Western societies, particularly the United States, as "loose," implying that they are more informal and expressive (Pelto, 1968). But this classification is too simplistic to be useful, as is the assumption that there is less conformity in the United States.

During my first summer in the United States, I was invited by some friends to visit a ranch they owned. This was to be my first experience staying at a ranch, and my hosts had promised me that I would meet some real cowboys, and if I plucked up the courage I could help round up some cattle. I was very excited about this trip and did my best to prepare myself appropriately.

But what exactly is "appropriate" for life on a ranch? I had wonderful images of the West in my mind, a mixture of *Tombstone, Unforgiven,* and *Lonesome Dove.* Obviously a ranch is not a "formal" place, but does that mean that on a ranch "anything goes" and I could dress and act as I liked? Certainly not! The more I asked around, the more it became clear that elaborate norms and rules have to be followed by people staying at a ranch. I could not wear a city suit, but had to conform to the local dress norms, which required me to wear blue jeans, boots, and cowboy hat and shirt. But much more complex than this were norms concerning things like campfires, water tanks, and cattle crossing over from other ranches to our side of the fence and from our side of the fence to neighboring farms.

Robert Ellickson (1991) conducted a fascinating study of how neighbors settle disputes, such as those involving cattle going astray, in rural Shasta County, California. He selected this area because it "offers a saga replete with cowboys, scoundrels, barbed wire, citizen petitions, and other details that connect to venerable traditions in the United States" (pp. 1–2). What he discovered was that in the majority of cases, ranchers and farmers maintained law and order *not* by resorting to legal action involving the state but by bringing to effect the norms of neighborliness that everyone in the community was aware of and most people followed. Interestingly, in some cases the local norms contradicted state laws, but everyone ignored "the law" and conformed to local norms.

Of course we do not need to go off campus to find classic examples of conformity to local norms rather than state or federal law. Consider an example that we as students and professors know well: the "lawlessness" of academic photocopying. The legal guidelines for classroom copying are designed to prevent the copying of published material, such as research papers in social psychology journals, year after year without prior consent. But very few of us actually have a good knowledge of photocopying law, and "most professors, certainly most law professors, would flunk if quizzed on the details of legal restrictions on copying for classroom use" (Ellickson, 1991, p. 261). But although academic photocopying is "lawless," in the sense that it does not abide by federal law, it does conform to local academic norms. For example, such norms allow the photocopying of papers published in journals, but not the copying of sections from a commercial text for distribution in class.

Thus, the fact that a group of people is not following one set of norms does *not* mean that they are behaving with disregard for all norms. Cowboys on a ranch do not follow the norms of city slickers; they conform to the normative system of a ranch. Students and professors do not follow the federal law pertaining to photocopying, but they do act according to local campus norms for photocopying. In each case, differences in behavior can in large part be explained with reference to different normative systems.

Societies tend to differ with respect to the variety of normative systems that flourish within them. Some societies, such as that of the United States, allow considerable diversity. Multitudes of **subcultures,** with distinct norms, rules, values, and other human–made characteristics used to distinguish a group from the dominant culture, exist in such heterogeneous societies, based on ethnicity, religion, language, sexual orientation, economic status, and the like. A ride through urban centers of New York City, Los Angeles, Miami, or Chicago very quickly reveals a vast array of thriving normative systems and diverse lifestyles. In more homogeneous societies, such as that of Japan, there is less variety in subcultures. The dominance of a single uniform culture is felt to a greater extent, so that there is less diversity in lifestyles and greater agreement about what constitutes correct and incorrect behavior.

But the availability of a greater variety of normative systems in the United States should not lead us to assume that Americans are less conformist that other people. Later in this chapter, we review evidence

subculture   distinct norms, rules, values, and other human–made characteristics used to distinguish a group from the dominant culture.

Gay men relaxing in New York's Greenwich Village. Although conformity and obedience are present in all societies, there is considerable cross–cultural variation in the diversity of subcultures in each society. The United States is a highly heterogeneous society, with many different subcultures. This allows people in the United States a greater choice with respect to the subculture they wish to live in. However, once individuals join subcultures, conformity and obedience are often just as high, or even higher, than in other societies. These gay men, for example, conform to their own local norms and rules, even though they are nonconformists in the context of heterosexual society.

demonstrating that people in the United States are as conformist as people from most other societies. However, in the United States *the possibility exists for selecting from a greater variety of normative systems.*

Concepts and Issues

Conformity in some domains is essential to the survival of society, but in some situations conformity is a threat to democratic life. Alongside a research tradition of examining conformity of minorities to majority–established norms, there has emerged a tradition of exploring conformity of a majority to minority norms. Those with lower status have tended to be more conformist, and this status difference may explain slight differences in conformity among women and men. In the United States and some other Western societies a greater diversity of lifestyles exists, but the level of conformity among people living each lifestyle is probably as high as among people in non–Western societies.

1. What is the difference between compliance and acceptance?
2. In what ways do Asch and Moscovici differ in their approaches to studying conformity?
3. Describe some cross–cultural similarities and differences in conformity behavior.

Obedience to Authority

The following discussion is organized around four main questions: Whom do we obey? How much do we obey? Who obeys? Why do we obey? Our discussion will show that there is considerable cross–cultural variation with respect to whom we obey and how much we obey, but the possibility of universals increases with respect to who obeys and why we obey.

Whom Do We Obey?

To obey God we must obey the Prophet;
to obey the Prophet we must obey Imam Ali;
to obey Imam Ali we must obey the clergy,
especially Imam Khomeini;
and to obey Imam Khomeini we must obey his successor,
His Eminence Ayatollah Khamenei, the leader of the Islamic Revolution.

—Ayatollah Azari–Qomi (cited in Abrahamian, 1993)

This statement comes from one of the leading mullahs in the Islamic Republic of Iran. A Western equivalent of this statement might be something like:

To obey God we must obey his son Jesus;
to obey Jesus we must obey his disciples;

to obey his disciples we must obey the clergy,
especially the Pope;
and to obey the Pope we must obey his successor, . . .

A religious leader who made such a statement would carry little authority among the general population in Western societies, for various historical reasons. For example, the directives of successive popes banning contraceptives and divorce have not been put into practice, even in traditional Roman Catholic societies such as those of Italy and Spain. In the United States there has historically been a separation of church and state. However, in the Islamic Republic of Iran church and state have been inseparable since the revolution of 1978, and the word of religious authorities is now backed by the authority of government. This points to an important cross-cultural variation we need to keep in mind when considering the issue of obedience: whom we obey varies considerably across cultures. It is the belief of the individual, as learned through culture, that determines who is obeyed.

There are usually historical reasons why an authority figure commands obedience in some cultures but not in others. The diminished authority of church leaders in Western societies can be traced at least as far back as the Renaissance, when a new view of human beings and our place in the universe began to evolve. This new view has been associated with modern science and the important breakthroughs that successfully challenged traditional church views of our place in the universe. Galileo's (1564–1642) proof of the Copernican theory exploded the myth that the earth is at the center of the universe. Charles Darwin's (1809–1882) evolutionary theory replaced the idea that humans were created separate from the rest of the biological universe with the idea that we are on a continuum with all other life-forms. Such developments diminished the authority of the church and increased that of scientists, but not in all societies.

Science is sometimes referred to as a "new religion," but the authority of scientists is far from universal. This is in part because many people, in both Western and non-Western societies, have little idea of what scientific research entails. For example, consider entering a village in Ghana, Africa, and asking people to take part in an experiment on obedience. Villagers would probably respond by asking, "You say you are a scientist, but what exactly is that?" "Why are you here asking questions—are you working for the government?" "What is an experiment and what do you want with us?" But it is not only in remote villages that one might be asked such questions. In my research in various Western societies I have sometimes been asked similar questions.

There is also another reason why the authority of scientists is not universal, and this has to do with the *explicit rejection of what scientists are sometimes seen to represent*. For example, during research in Iran after the revolution of 1978, I found that Western-trained scientists were regarded with suspicion by Islamic fundamentalists. A "cultural revolution" was proclaimed in 1981, leading to the closing of universities and an attempt to "reeducate" professors and "Islamicize" the universities—just as the cultural revolution led by the Chinese revolutionary leader

Mao Tse–tung during the late 1960s led to the closing of universities in China and an attempt to "reeducate" professors there. These are cases in which scientists, far from being figures of authority, become marginalized because they are seen as "tools" of foreign influence.

How Much Do We Obey?

It is with respect to *how much* we obey that the greatest surprises, and disappointments, about human behavior arise. In the most penetrating social psychological explorations of obedience, such as Ervin Staub's (1989) *The Roots of Evil* and Herbert Kelman and Lee Hamilton's (1989) *Crimes of Obedience*, a major puzzle revolves around the issue of how far people are willing to obey authority figures. Actions in Nazi Germany, as well as countless other more recent examples of extreme human-rights abuses, show that even the most pessimistic estimates may be too optimistic. It seems that some people at least are often much more willing to obey orders to harm others than is generally assumed.

This tendency to underestimate the extent to which people will obey instructions from authority figures to harm others was brilliantly demonstrated in a series of laboratory studies at Yale University by Stanley Milgram (1974). In order to set the stage, Milgram used the cover story that he was conducting research on the effects of punishment on learning. He advertised for volunteers aged 20–50 who would be paid $4 an hour (plus 50¢ carfare). People with a broad range of occupations and ages volunteered, and Milgram was able to include participants with varied backgrounds in each of his studies.

Nazi troops marching in the 1930s and Serb commandos in Bosnia in the 1990s. Research on obedience to authority raises a number of questions that are of historical as well as contemporary importance. If a dictator comes to power, will ordinary people obey orders to harm minorities? The answer seems to be that some people, those high on authoritarianism, will be more likely to obey, but others will resist. A major challenge is how we can arrange social life so that the numbers and influence of authoritarians will be less in the future, and the numbers of people who resist orders to harm others will be more.

Upon arrival at a social psychology laboratory at Yale University, the participant would be introduced to a person who was supposedly also a participant but was actually a confederate of the experimenter. This confederate was a mild-mannered 47-year-old accountant, trained for the role of learner. It was explained that as this was a learning experiment, there needed to be a teacher and a learner. The two participants drew lots to decide which role each would play. In fact, the outcome of the draw was predetermined, so that the real participant would always be assigned the role of teacher.

Learning Task.   The lesson conducted by the teacher (participant) involved a word-association task. The teacher read a series of word pairs to the learner, then read the first word of each pair followed by four terms. The learner's task was to identify which of the four terms had originally been paired with the first word of each pair. For example, the teacher would read the pair *blue-box*. Later, at the testing stage, the word *blue* would be followed by four terms: *sky, ink, box, lamp*. The learner had to press one of four switches, which would light up one of the numbered quadrants in an answer box in front of the teacher (in this case number 3, representing *box*, was correct).

Administering Punishment.   Since the study was purportedly about the effects of punishment on learning, it was not difficult for Milgram to justify the introduction of an instrument for administering punishment. This was a "shock generator," consisting of 30 switches set in a horizontal line, labeled SHOCK GENERATOR, TYPE ZLB, DYSON INSTRUMENT COMPANY, WALTHAM, MASS., OUTPUT 15 VOLTS–450 VOLTS. The switches were marked, increasing from 0 to 450 volts in 15-volt increments. Each group of four switches was also clearly marked, going from lowest to highest voltage: "slight shock," "moderate shock," "strong shock," "very strong shock," "intense shock," "extreme intense shock," "danger: severe shock," with the last two switches ominously marked "XXX."

To ensure that the participants realized what the punishment involved in practice, a shock of 45 volts was administered to the wrist of every participant. This level of shock is just painful enough to support the authenticity of the punishment instrument.

Instructions to Participants.   Participants were instructed to punish the learner for every mistake made, and *to increase the voltage level each time the learner gave a wrong response.* To ensure that the participants were fully aware of the shock levels they administered, they also had to call out the voltage level before administering a shock. If participants reached the maximum level of 450 volts, they were to continue to give shocks at this level.

Directives from the Authority Figure.   Imagine you are a participant in Milgram's study and you have already given shocks as high as 120 volts, in response to which the learner shouted that the shocks were becoming painful. You feel uncomfortable about increasing the shock level and you look over to the scientist for guidance. The scientist is

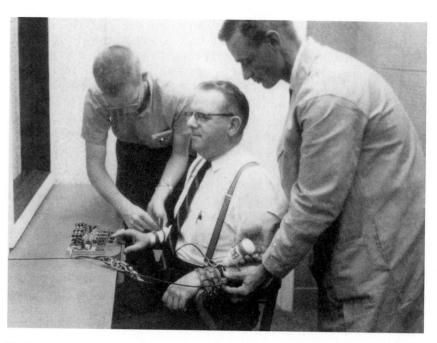

The "learner" is attached to the apparatus in a Milgram study. Stanley Milgram's studies on obedience to authority raise timeless questions about the nature of human beings. They force us to reconsider such assumptions as "atrocities are the work of a crazy or psychologically abnormal minority." In Milgram's studies, repeated in many different cultures, participants screened to represent a psychologically normal population were ordered by an authority figure, a scientist, to administer electric shocks to a "learner" (actually an accomplice of the experimenter). More than 60 percent of the participants obeyed and administered what they believed to be harmful, sometimes deadly, shocks.

trained to respond to you with a sequence of "prods," starting with a gentle one ("Please continue") but moving to a much stronger prod if required ("You have no other choice, you *must* go on"). The scientist also responds to your inquiries by telling you that although the shocks are painful, they do not lead to permanent tissue damage, and that you must go on until the learner has learned all the word pairs, whether he likes it or not.

Reaction from the Learner.   The learner was trained to give a predetermined set of responses at each level of shock, ranging from no response at all below 75 volts to much more violent responses at higher shock levels. Between 75 and 105 volts the victim grunted, but at 120 volts he shouted that the shocks were becoming painful. When the voltage was increased to 150, the victim cried out, "Experimenter, get me out of here! I won't be in the experiment any more! I refuse to go on!" The cries of desperation became more agonized as the voltage was increased, until at 300 volts the learner let it be known that he could no longer provide answers to the memory test. After this point all that was heard from the learner were cries of agony, until 330 volts was reached and the learner did not respond in any way to the questions or to any further shocks given.

Predictions About the Outcomes.   One of the reactions psychologists often get to their research is the response "I could have told you those results before you did the experiment. It was so predictable!" Well, Milgram ensured this would not apply to his studies by describing his experimental procedures to groups of laypeople and experts and asking them to predict the outcomes. Their almost unanimous prediction was that participants would refuse to administer shocks of more than minimal voltage to the learners. After all, the participants in Milgram's studies were screened so that his final sample was a "normal" cross section of adults. These were not the sadists, psychopaths, and generally assumed abnormal types we think of as being responsible for harming helpless victims. These assumed abnormal types, the individuals who took part in the Holocaust and other atrocities, invariably defended themselves by pleading, "I was following orders." But this is just an excuse they use—or is it?

"I Was Following Orders," Revisited.   The startling result of Milgram's studies was that about 65 percent of participants were fully obedient. Cross-cultural replications of this study in places as different as Australia (Kilham & Mann, 1974), East Africa (Munroe, Munroe, & Whiting, 1981), Italy (Ancona & Pareyson, 1968), Jordan (Shanab & Yahya, 1977), Germany (Mantell, 1971), and the Netherlands (Meeus & Raaijmakers, 1986) have demonstrated considerable cross-cultural variation in the percentage of participants who show full obedience, from 40 percent in Australia to 90 percent among a Dutch sample. However, these studies also demonstrate that *in all cultures a substantial percentage of participants, certainly above 40 percent, are fully obedient.* These results highlight the powerful influence of the situation, because taken together they show that large percentages among "normal cross sections" of people in different cultures are fully obedient in the Milgram experimental situation.

Research showed that obedience would be *decreased* under certain conditions: if the authority figure is in a different room from the participant (teacher) and communicates by telephone; if the participant is physically closer to the learner when shock is administered; if a fellow participant (actually a confederate) refuses to administer shock; and if there are two authority figures and they disagree as to whether shock should continue to be given. (See Figure 7–5.) But even under these conditions, some participants continued to be obedient.

This outcome raises certain moral dilemmas: To what extent should we hold individuals responsible for showing obedience to authority? This is a particularly pertinent question when the case involves individuals trained to follow orders. Consider Lieutenant William Calley, who was the only person convicted for misconduct in the My Lai massacre in which hundreds of Vietnamese civilians, including many women and children, were executed. Calley claimed that he was only doing his job, following orders as a good soldier should (Hammer, 1971). A soldier who questions orders could be court-martialed and even executed. When he was asked in court what he was trained to do if he had doubts about an order, Calley responded that he was supposed to carry out the order and then make his complaint.

Figure 7–5 Factors that have an influence on level of obedience.

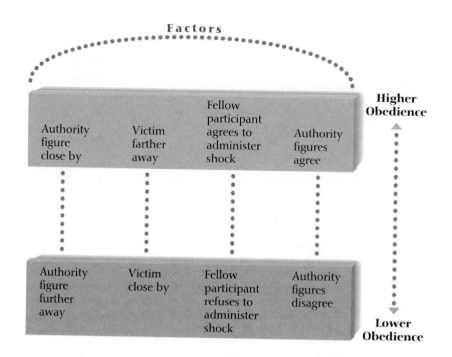

But we need not go to such extreme cases for examples of obedience leading to wrongdoing. During the final examination for one of my psychology classes recently, two students were caught cheating. In his "defense," one of the students explained that he was a first-year student and as such had been obliged to obey the fourth-year student who had "instructed him" to take part in the collusion. As the newcomer saw it, first-year students have a duty to obey and pay their dues. This kind of explanation is often associated with a claim that "anyone would have done the same in this situation; it was not me, it was the circumstances." But this begs the question: Is there not something special about the people who obey in such circumstances? Surely not all first-year students would "obey" a fourth-year student. Similarly, in much more extreme cases, in which authority figures instruct a person to harm others, it seems likely that some people are more prone than others to obey such instructions.

Who Obeys?

A very important finding from the Milgram (1974) studies is that *not everyone is obedient to authority*. A significant percentage of participants, from about 60 to 10 percent, depending on their culture, *refused to be fully obedient*. A parallel to this can be found in the real world, where individuals often refuse to obey authority orders to harm others. For example, during the years of Nazi rule in Germany there emerged a number of "heroic rescuers" such as Oskar Schindler (whose story was told in the book and film *Schindler's List*) who tried to help Jews escape. Also, there are various accounts of German soldiers carrying out altruistic acts to help Jews in labor camps (Staub, 1989). But what is special about those who *did* obey?

Gender.   A very striking theme emerges when we examine the characteristics of those who order acts harmful to others, as well as those who actually torture others psychologically or physically (Stover & Nightingale, 1985). Throughout history both those who have ordered destructive acts and those who carried out such acts against others have invariably been men. Related to this is the near–universal finding that women are less aggressive than men and that they score higher on empathy than do men (see Chapter 11). These differences may lead us to expect women to be less obedient in the Milgram situation because to obey would mean to harm the learner.

But research on conformity has traditionally supported the view that women are more likely to "fall in line." Also, given that women have generally been in lower–status positions, in which one is expected to be obedient to authority (the traditional Christian marriage vows included the promise from the bride that she would "honor and obey" her husband–to–be), we may expect women to be more obedient. Thus, there are reasons to expect both higher and lower levels of obedience on the part of women in the Milgram obedience experiment.

Milgram (1974) did use a sample of females in his research but found no gender difference in levels of obedience. A study by the Australian researchers Wesley Kilham and Leon Mann (1974), using a laboratory procedure similar to Milgram's, found that females were *less* obedient. This Australian study is particularly interesting because it used two teachers (one of whom was a confederate) and a learner (who was also a confederate). One of the teachers acted as the "transmitter," the person who recorded the learner's responses and announced if the responses were correct or incorrect. If a response was incorrect, the transmitter said, "Incorrect response, administer —— volts." The second teacher was the "executant," the person who actually administered the shocks. The naive participant was the transmitter or the executant, depending on the condition. The results showed that females were far less likely to obey than males, particularly when they were in the executant position.

Personality Characteristics.   Intuition tells us that those who are more obedient probably have personality characteristics that are in some ways different. This assumption led a group of social psychologists to explore the personality characteristics of what became known as the authoritarian personality (Adorno, Frenkel–Brunswik, Levinson, & Sanford, 1950). Theodor Adorno and his colleagues were moved by the horrors of World War II and the threat posed by fascism. If technologically advanced nations such as Germany could be taken over by fascists, how could the world be defended against future would–be Hitlers? They reasoned that certain types of personalities had a potential for supporting fascism and thus posed a threat to democracies. In order to better identify these authoritarian personality types, they studied a sample of 2,000 middle–class, white, non–Jewish, native–born residents of California, and from this research developed the *Potentiality for Fascism,* or *F-Scale.*

Research using the F–Scale suggests that the **authoritarian personality** is submissive and obedient to authority but repressive and vindictive toward minorities and those who violate conventional

authoritarian personality   a personality type that is submissive and obedient to authority, but repressive and vindictive toward those who violate conventional values.

values. Predictably, authoritarians have been found to be more obedient in the Milgram obedience experiment (Elms & Milgram, 1966).

The Canadian researcher Bob Altemeyer (1981, 1988a, 1988b) has taken the position that authoritarians are necessarily supporters of right-wing ideology. Consequently, Altemeyer's measure of authoritarianism is termed the *Right-Wing Authoritarianism Scale*. But this perspective seems to reflect the liberal bias of Western academia, where "left-wing" has traditionally been associated with "antiauthority." This association would not have made much sense in the struggle of freedom fighters to topple the communist ("left-wing") regimes that were part of the Soviet empire. In Poland during the 1980s the Solidarity movement, which enjoyed the active support of the Roman Catholic Church, fought to overpower a "left-wing" government that was by any standard dictatorial.

Rather than labeling authoritarians as right-wing or left-wing, then, it is more accurate to describe them as enemies of freedom everywhere. The authoritarian type may be described as universal, insofar as in all cultures some individuals are more likely than others to be submissive to authority and prejudiced against those deemed deviant by authority figures. According to such a viewpoint, authoritarians are submissive to authority rather than followers of any particular ideology (Taylor & Moghaddam, 1994, pp. 30–31). In theory, authoritarians could be used to limit freedom by cracking down on right-wing or left-wing political groups, depending on who is seen as "the enemy."

But there are severe limitations to explanations of obedience based on personality characteristics. This is in part because the behavior of individuals tends to be highly dependent on cultural context rather than any supposed consistency in personality characteristics (Mischel, 1968). Adorno et al.'s F-scale is referred to as the *potential* for fascism scale, implying that authoritarian behavior would manifest itself only under certain conditions. We need to consider the larger cultural factors influencing obedience.

Culture. A very powerful answer to the question "Who obeys?" is "Those who are brought up to obey." This response places the emphasis on the characteristics of cultures that nurture obedience. For example, Alice Miller (1983) has examined child-rearing practices prevalent in Germany from the seventeenth to the twentieth centuries and found obedience enjoyed the highest value. The challenge facing parents was seen to be to break the will of the child and to force obedience, almost through any means and at any price. Such restrictive child-rearing practices appear to have been particularly resistant to change in Germany (see Staub, 1989).

But there are also fundamental differences in the way the members of different groups are socialized to obey. For example, culture often specifies different types of obedience to be "correct" for boys and girls. But this does not mean that there is a universal pattern to the level of obedience shown by males and females. In an analysis of factors important in child rearing across 110 societies, David Zern (1984) found that obedience was to some extent emphasized more for girls than boys, although not very consistently. There are societies in which females show no more obedience than males. This suggests that obedience depends on how society defines gender roles rather than on being a member of the sex category male or female. The different kinds of education available to males and females seem to be particularly crucial in this regard.

There seem to be cross-cultural similarities in certain differences across social classes in obedience training. Melvin Kohn's (1977) cross-cultural research suggests that parents from low socioeconomic status (SES) groups value and emphasize obedience more than do middle-class parents. One interpretation of this cross-cultural consistency is that for lower SES parents, correct behavior revolves around obedience. It is normative for them to obey others, and they teach their own children to behave correctly as they understand correct behavior. A domestic laborer, an office cleaner, or a factory worker is expected to follow directives rather than to show innovation and creativity, irrespective of whether he or she lives in Brazil, Nigeria, China, or the United States. People in middle-class positions, such as lawyers, doctors, engineers, researchers, and so on, are expected to show more innovation and creativity rather than just to obey authority figures. This is because they *are* authority figures themselves. They educate their own children for filling authority roles in the future.

The research of Herbert Kelman and Lee Hamilton (1989) underscores the role of education in attitudes toward crimes of obedience, the consequences that sometimes ensue when authority gives orders exceeding the bounds of morality or law (as in the My Lai massacre). These researchers found that their participants, consisting of samples from the U.S. adult population, had a more supportive attitude toward crimes of obedience if they had a lower level of education. They suggest that citizens should be empowered through being socialized to become active participants in both the formulation and implementation of government policies. Formal education is not sufficient to protect society from crimes of obedience. A broadly based civic culture, one that will lead individuals to disobey authority when they are ordered to carry out acts that they believe to be illegal or immoral, is essential.

We often think of this type of citizenry to be peculiar to Western democracies. But upon close examination, a number of "simpler" non-Western cultures prove to provide the conditions necessary for citizens to disobey authority when they believe they must. For example, it is sometimes assumed that village life must involve rigid conformity and obedience and harsh punishments for those who rebel against authority. But for people of south central Africa, village life traditionally has involved shifting membership and open groups. Ian Cunnison (1960) studied village life in the Luapula Valley of this part of Africa and found that people "move from one headman to another until they find a village which, in their own experience, is healthy, harmonious, free from sorcery and premature death, and where they prosper" (p. 285).

In 1971 Lt. William Calley was brought to trial and convicted of the premeditated murder of at least 22 Vietnamese civilians in March 1968 at what became known as the My Lai massacre. In his defense, Calley declared that he was acting as a good soldier and following orders. Should his interpretation of his orders have led to a court-martial of his superiors? Would you and I have acted differently if we were in his position? Is it something about Lt. Calley or about the situation that led to the killings?

Why Do We Obey?

We have seen that whom we obey, how much we obey, and who obeys are all to a large extent dependent on culture. At one level we can claim that the overriding reason why we obey is also cultural, because culture teaches us that it is correct to obey authority. Western culture teaches us to have a high regard for science, and under certain conditions to be obedient to the authority of scientists, as were participants in Milgram's studies.

The power of culture to influence obedience is demonstrated in a series of simple but fascinating field studies on the influence of a uniform (Bickman, 1974; Bushman, 1984). In one such study, Leonard Bickman (1974) had a confederate dressed as either a guard (rather like a policeman, but without a gun), a milkman, or a civilian approach participants on a street and ask them to pick up a paper bag, or to give a dime to a stranger, or to move away from a bus stop. Participants were shown to obey the guard more than the milkman or civilian. In a variation on this theme, Brad Bushman (1984) showed that a person in a firefighter's uniform will be obeyed more often than a civilian, even though the request being made ("Give him a dime!") has nothing to do with the authority role in question.

The relevant point here is that culture teaches us to be more obedient to people in certain roles. Conversely, culture also teaches people in certain roles to expect people to obey them. Moreover, we learn from culture how to play authority roles, as well as roles submissive to authority. This dominant–subordinate relationship was brilliantly demonstrated by one of the most well-known simulations in social psychology, the prison study of Philip Zimbardo (1972, 1973). The initial purpose of the study was to explore the roles of guards and prisoners in a prison situation. The stereotypes we have of guards and prisoners are that certain authoritarian, perhaps even sadistic, types of personalities will be attracted to the position of prison guard, and the prisoners ("criminals") will tend to be aggressive and socially deviant. When we hear about violence in prisons, we tend to assume the source to be the personality characteristics of guards and prisoners.

In order to discount the "personality-based" explanation for prison conditions, Zimbardo carefully screened the participants in his study. From among 100 or so applicants to a newspaper announcement ("Wanted: Volunteers for an experiment on prison life—$15 a day. The experiment will last two weeks"), Zimbardo selected 24 participants. On the basis of extensive psychological testing, this group was judged to be "normal" and representative of intelligent, middle-class male youth. Participants were randomly assigned to play the role of guard or prisoner.

To make the simulation as realistic as possible, the Palo Alto Police Department intervened to arrest half of the participants. To their embarrassment, these participants were picked up at their homes, placed in a police car, and taken to a police station, to be handcuffed and booked. The other half of the participants, the guards, were placed in charge of the prison, where there were bars on the doors, prison uniforms, clubs for the guards, and strict visiting hours for anyone wanting to meet with the prisoners. The guards were simply instructed to keep order, and once the simulation started, the experimenters did not intervene.

The surprising outcome of this simulation was that it had to be abandoned after only 6 days, well short of the planned 2 weeks, because the treatment of the prisoners by the guards was far more aggressive and dehumanizing than had been expected. The prisoners broke down and became passive acceptors of brutal treatment, and the guards seemed to enjoy thinking up new ways to degrade prisoners. Of course, this was not an exact replication of prison life but a simulation of how these bright, middle-class young men imagined they should play the roles of guards and prisoners. But in "playing" these roles, there came a point when it was difficult to distinguish between the self and the role.

The results of Zimbardo's simulation seem shocking because they challenge Western assumptions about individual freedom and responsibility. Surely normal, bright, young, middle-class men would not act in this way. An even more extreme example of such a phenomenon is provided by Colin Turnbull's (1972) study of the Ik, a traditional hunting-and-gathering group of people now situated in northern Uganda, near the border with Kenya. Turnbull begins the account of his research by pointing out, "In what follows, there will be much to shock, and the reader will be tempted to say, 'how primitive . . . how savage . . . how disgusting' and, above all, 'how inhuman'. In living the experience I said all these things over and over again" (p. 11). His research showed that social life among the Ik involves extreme selfishness and a total concern with personal survival, to such an extent that parents deprive children of food and children even refuse water to aged parents. How did the Ik become like this? Why is it that cheating and stealing food is common among them?

The explanation seems to be in the terrible conditions in which the Ik live. Formerly a hunting-and-gathering tribe that roamed freely in pursuit of game, the Ik were forced by modernization and nation-state boundaries to live in a confined territory with very limited natural resources. Life for the Ik became a fierce struggle for survival, so much so that they seemed to have completely abandoned the values we associate with human social life.

> The lack of any sense of moral responsibility toward each other, the lack of any sense of belonging to, needing or wanting each other, showed up daily and most clearly in what otherwise would have passed for familial relationships. The Ik still recognized them as such, verbally, but the recognition was not matched by any corresponding action. When Bila was suffering most from her infected breast, which dripped pus over her nursing child or the food she was eating . . . she was amazed—amazed not that illness could be spread like this but amazed that anyone should think she should worry about spreading it. When, at its height, Bila was in great pain and was sitting outside . . . crying, holding her breast under which a little puddle of pus and blood had formed, Atum, her father, took notice of her only to ask if she had to sit there—she was blocking the entrance and her crying gave him a headache. (Turnbull, 1972, p. 218)

Such extreme conditions, similar to those found in Nazi concentration camps, where many of the values we normally associate with "human nature" disappear, underline the power of the situation to shape behavior. Reports on economically poor groups in northeastern Brazil tell of mothers who let some of their own children starve, explaining that "they don't want to live" (Scheper–Hughes, 1990). Our behavior, it seems, is much more dependent on the social context than the dominant Western model of "self–contained individualism" assumes.

Of course, by emphasizing the importance of context in shaping behavior I am not suggesting that individuals are not responsible for their own actions. Normative accounts of behavior assume individuals have an important measure of freedom in choosing how they behave. The same is assumed by people of different cultures, as is clear in the legal arena. Cheryl Drout and Yumiko Kataoka (1997) found some basic similarities among Americans and Japanese in their blame of the three U.S. servicemen who raped a 12-year-old Okinawan girl in 1995.

Concepts and Issues

The study of obedience is of fundamental importance because we must better understand the "crimes of obedience" that have persisted in modern times. Social psychological studies have demonstrated how even ordinary people can follow orders from an authority figure to do harm to others. Studies in the tradition of Milgram and Zimbardo underline the power of the situation to shape behavior in all cultures. But we must keep in mind that not everyone obeys orders to do harm to others, and that those who do harm to others are blamed by most people in all cultures.

1. Describe the basic design of the Milgram studies of obedience to authority.
2. Why is it important that Milgram selected "ordinary people" as participants in his studies?
3. What have we learned from studies on the authoritarian personality?

Conclusion

The classic studies of Sherif, Asch, and Milgram on norm formation, conformity to group–established norms, and obedience to authority have helped to demonstrate certain conditions in which conformity and obedience occur. Norms are arbitrary but they have a powerful influence on the behavior of individuals. Because majority groups enjoy greater power to influence norms, they can influence the behavior of both majority and minority group members. Those in positions of authority can both shape norms and more directly influence behavior by issuing orders.

Conformity and obedience are best explained through normative accounts, particularly the thorny question of *why* people conform and obey. Those researchers who have focused more directly on the why question (e.g., Adorno, Frenkel-Brunswik, Levinson, & Sanford, 1950; Staub, 1989) have tended to assume that conformity and obedience to authority are due to some form of "weakness" or "defect" in personality. This assumption underlies the tradition set in *The Authoritarian Personality* (Adorno, Frenkel-Brunswik, Levinson, & Sanford, 1950), which was heavily influenced by Freudian psychology. A normative account depicts some level of conformity and obedience as essential for the survival of society. Harm arises when societal norms lead people to assume that the correct way to behave in their situation is to give the incorrect answer (as in Asch's studies) or to obey an order to inflict pain (as in Milgram's studies).

For Discussion

1. Why is it important that a substantial number of participants did not conform in Asch's study and did not obey in Milgram's study?
2. "Minority influence can be even more important than majority influence." Discuss this statement, with reference to the research of Asch and Moscovici.

3. "Those with power shape norms, and norms influence everyone." Discuss this statement, giving examples to clarify your views.

For Review

Conformity involves being influenced by real or imagined group pressure. Such group pressure is routinely exerted in society by the rules and norms people are expected to follow. Conformity can be conceptualized as being on a continuum from compliance to acceptance.

Sherif demonstrated experimentally the process of norm formation and showed how individuals can be influenced by arbitrary group-established norms even after they have left a group. Asch demonstrated how arbitrary majority-established norms that are wrong can still influence a minority. Cross-cultural research has shown that the "Asch effect" can be replicated with other cultural groups and that Americans are less conformist than some other groups but more conformist than certain others.

Cross-cultural research suggests a direct link between conformity behavior and the socialization practices of a culture, so that cultures that value self-reliance and independence in children will develop adults who conform less in the Asch-type situation. The key distinction is the variety of normative systems that exist in a society rather than the level of conformity among individuals. In many situations people in Western societies are as conformist as people in other societies, but they tend to have a wider selection of normative systems from which to choose. The variety of normative systems is particularly extensive in the United States.

The traditional view that females are more conformist than males has been challenged successfully by Eagly and others, leading to a more complex and subtle understanding of the relationship between gender and conformity. European research has turned the traditional question of conformity on its head by asking, "Under what conditions can a *minority* influence a majority?"

Research on obedience to authority suggests that while there is considerable cross-cultural variation with respect to *whom we obey* and *how much we obey*, there is greater similarity across cultures with respect to *why we obey* and *who obeys*.

The Milgram research suggests that under certain conditions even normal people will obey authority figures to do harm to others. Cross-cultural research supports the view that under certain conditions what we generally consider to be "humane social interactions" break down. But people do not obey all of the time and some individuals routinely refuse to behave in a negative manner.

Modern institutions have tremendous power to bring about conformity and obedience, as is demonstrated by Zimbardo's prison simulation. The power of such institutions derives from their total control over the roles, rules, and norms that people are obliged to follow.

Key Terms

Acceptance *230*
Authoritarian
  personality *249*
Compliance *229*
Conformity *220*
Majority influence
  228

Manipulated norm
  225
Minority influence *228*
Obedience *220*
Social impact theory
  226

Social influence
  model *226*
Spontaneous norm
  225
Subculture *241*

Annotated Readings

For a firsthand account of the classic studies in this area, see S. Milgram, *Obedience to authority: An experimental view* (New York: Harper & Row, 1974).

For a discussion of controversies surrounding the Milgram studies on obedience, see A. G. Miller, *The obedience experiments: A case study of controversy in social science* (New York: Praeger, 1986).

An enlightening consideration of Milgram's obedience studies in relation to the trials of Nazi leaders after World War II can be found in J. Persico, *Nuremberg: Infamy on trial* (New York: Viking Press, 1994).

A broader discussion of the psychology of crimes of humanity is presented in E. Staub, *The roots of evil: The origins of genocide and other group violence* (Cambridge: Cambridge University Press, 1989).

The research on the authoritarian personality is discussed in its wider context in B. Altemeyer, *Enemies of freedom: Understanding right-wing authoritarianism* (San Francisco: Jossey–Bass, 1988).

A good representation of minority research is S. Moscovici, A. Mucchi-Faini, and A. Maas, eds., *Minority influence* (Chicago: Nelson–Hall, 1994).

A masterful account of how people keep order by adhering to local norms, which are informal and tacit, rather than resorting to formal law, can be found in R. C. Ellickson, *Law without order: How neighbors settle disputes* (Cambridge, MA: Harvard University Press, 1991).

Disturbing examples of conformity and obedience associated with torture are found in E. Stover and E. O. Nightingale, eds., *The breaking of bodies and minds: Torture, psychiatric abuse, and the health professions* (New York: W. H. Freeman, 1985).

A fascinating set of historical cases involving conformity and social influence is found in the nineteenth–century publication C. MacKay, *Extraordinary popular delusions and the madness of crowds* (New York: Harmony Books, 1841/1980).

CHAPTER *8*

Liking and Loving

◀ Romantic love and friendship remain one of the most fascinating and complex topics
researched by social psychologists. There seems nothing as natural as two people
becoming lovers or friends, yet the way in which this "simple" behavior takes place
varies considerably across cultures. Are there any universals in this domain? There are
some strong contenders, such as the tendency for people to be attracted to similar
others.

P erhaps it was because we were in Paris and it was spring, or perhaps the sight of lovers strolling along the city sidewalks had something to do with it, but we were all shocked when our new friend Zahra announced that next month she would be marrying a man she had never met. The four of us were sitting in a sidewalk café. We were part of a language-immersion program, and we had gotten to know each other fairly well during the previous two weeks. The first among us to react to the unexpected announcement was Hannah, an Australian student about the same age as Zahra. "But how do you know it will work out?" she asked.

"How does anyone know if a marriage will work out?" came the reply. "Besides, love will grow. We will be friends at first, and then love will come when we have a family."

"What about the magic of romance?" asked Ryan, the fourth person in our group. This sparked a debate about liking and loving. Things became more heated when I tried to explain about scientific studies of friendship and romantic love. "You can't study such things scientifically!" declared the three others in one voice. Sitting in that café on that beautiful spring day, it was hard not to sympathize with them.

Like most people, students of social psychology prefer to think that intimate relationships are based on deep feelings, shared emotions, and higher human values, not scientific theories and calculation. After all, this is friendship and love we are talking about, not stocks or the bottom line.

Then we read the scientific explanations. Confronted by the cold language of exchange theory and other social psychological theories, we ask ourselves: Do such terms as "minimizing costs" and "maximizing rewards" really explain intimate relationships? Do we enter friendship and love relationships while all the time calculating ratios between "inputs" and "outcomes," as some major theories suggest?

We generally imagine intimate relationships as spontaneous, as mysterious but wonderful experiences that happen only if "the chemistry is right." They cannot be planned or forced; they involve experiences that sweep us away. In D. H. Lawrence's controversial novel *Lady Chatterley's Lover*, the heroine's feelings for her lover, a gamekeeper on her family estate, are so strong that she is willing to abandon everything to be with him. During an intimate moment early in their affair, the gamekeeper tries to warn Lady Chatterley about the scandal that would follow discovery:

> "But what when folks finds out?" he asked at last, "Think about it! Think how lowered you'll feel, one of your husband's servants."
>
> She looked up at his averted face.
>
> "Is it," she stammered, "is it that you don't want me?"
>
> "Think!" he said. "Think what if folks finds out—Sir Clifford an'a'—an'everybody talkin'—"
>
> "Well, I can go away."
>
> "Where to?"
>
> "Anyware! . . ."
>
> "But 'appen you don't want to go away."
>
> "Yes, yes! I don't care what happens to me." (1928/1959, p. 172)

Lady Chatterley is willing to give up everything—her aristocratic life, her high status, her family—for the sake of love for one of her own servants. In contrast to depictions of such euphoric "madness," the scientific theories explain intimate relationships as analogous to the give-and-take found in the economic marketplace, as involving calculations of costs and benefits. No wonder we feel uneasy about scientific research in this area.

In the next section, we take a closer look at the major scientific theories that try to explain friendship and romantic love. These are important examples of intimate relationships (Brehm, 1992), although there are other types, such as broken marriages, that we do not consider. Throughout, we keep in mind that in these domains there can be a complex relationship between culture and gender. For example, in a study of friendship patterns among college students in India and in the United States, John Berman and his associates (Berman, Murphy-Burman, & Pachauri, 1988) found that in the United States, female same-sex friendships were more intense than male ones. Typically, about two-thirds of females and only one-third of males report having a friend to whom they revealed absolutely everything (Bell, 1981). This difference was not found among Indian participants. Friendships between Indian males proved to be as intense as those between Indian females.

Theories of Attraction

In all human societies, people prefer certain others and have likes and dislikes, sometimes very strong ones, toward other individuals. Your own experiences will tell you that after meeting a new set of people, such as other students during orientation week at college, you fairly quickly develop preferences. Why is it that you prefer to be friends with John rather than with David or with Jane rather than with Sara? Social psychologists have provided various theoretical explanations (Brehm, 1992; Dion & Dion, 1996; Hatfield & Rapson, 1993; Hendrick & Hendrick, 1992).

Exchange Theories

Jane is a straight-A student in her final year of law school. She already has very attractive job offers from three prestigious law firms. Jane is an excellent swimmer and dancer, and most men find her very attractive. What do you think her future spouse should be like? A wet blanket who failed to graduate from high school, is unattractive, and does not have the motivation to hold down any job for more than a few months? Surely if she did marry such a man, you might think it is an "unfair bargain." Similarly, you would think it an unfair exchange if someone you had thought of as a friend did nothing for you, borrowed money from you but never paid you back, threw a party at your home

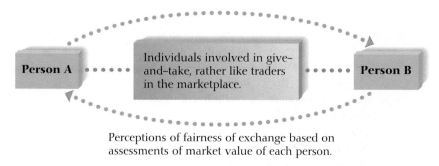

Perceptions of fairness of exchange based on
assessments of market value of each person.

Figure 8–1 Social exchange theory presents individuals in intimate relationships as
engaged in give–and–take.

social exchange theory
proposition that we assess the
contributions of each person in
intimate friendship and love
relations.

and left without cleaning up, and then lost your class notes two weeks
before finals.

Such cases of extreme inequality in social relations are instructive,
for several reasons. First, the fact that we recognize them as unfair
endorses the **social exchange theory,** which proposes that people
expect their behavior, including in intimate friendship and love
relations, to lead to some sort of commensurate return (Homans, 1961;
Kelley, 1979; Thibaut & Kelley, 1959). This suggests that at least when
the contributions appear to be very unequal, the notion of give–and–
take becomes applicable to a relationship. Social exchange theorists
have generally assumed that individuals are motivated to give and take
in such a way that they themselves get the best deal possible. Second,
the fact that some people are happy in relationships that seem to out–
siders as being unfair suggests that how people judge fairness in such
situations is at least partly subjective. Although Jane's family and
friends may think she is in an unfair relationship, she may insist that
she has a wonderful husband and remain devoted to him for the rest of
her life (see Figure 8–1).

The idea of "fair exchange" may influence our choices in mate se–
lection. Each of us seems to have a fairly good idea about our own
popularity rating, and we also develop a good idea of which others
match us (Murstein, 1986). Think back to when you were applying to
colleges and you knew what your academic standing was (on the basis
of SAT score, school record, and the like). A student with an average
academic record would most likely not apply to the schools that re–
quire the highest grades. If such a student did so, even after being ad–
vised against it by family and teachers, then rejections would arrive by
mail. Of course, an academically average student who happens to be a
champion athlete may gain entrance to academically first–rate colleges
because of her total profile. The same kind of compensation can take
place in interpersonal relations. A handsome young man may marry an
older woman and live happily ever after with her money, or a beautiful
young woman may marry a famous older writer (the actress Marilyn
Monroe and the playwright Arthur Miller, for example). This idea of
fairness being based on subjective perceptions is further elaborated by
equity theory.

Equity Theory

Imagine you have a new friend who takes every opportunity to make enormous sacrifices for you. With each passing day, you feel that your new friend does more favors and buys more gifts for you without your being able to do as much in return. One of the predictions of equity theory is that you will feel uncomfortable about such a one-sided relationship. But why?

A starting assumption of equity theory is that people strive to achieve fairness in their relationships and that they feel distressed if they perceive unfairness (Messick & Cook, 1983; Walster, Walster, & Berscheid, 1978). But distress will be experienced both by those who put into a relationship (input) more than they get out of it (outcome), as well by those who get out of a relationship more than they put into it. This ability to explain why those who get an unfairly high outcome from a relationship feel uncomfortable is one of the strengths of equity theory (Taylor & Moghaddam, 1994). A second key assumption is that fairness is subjectively defined by individuals as the *ratio of inputs and outcomes* for those involved in a relationship (see Figure 8–2).

Thus, for Jane to see a relationship as just, it is not necessary that she perceive herself and her boyfriend as having the same outcome, because their perceived inputs may be very different. If she sees herself putting little into the relationship relative to how much he puts in, then she will still see the relationship as fair if she gets little out of the relationship relative to him.

Consequently, although equity follows the social exchange theory tradition of depicting people as selfish agents in an economic marketplace, it is primarily a psychological theory because it focuses exclusively on subjective perceptions of what makes a fair exchange. The very subjectivity of inputs and outcomes means that relationships

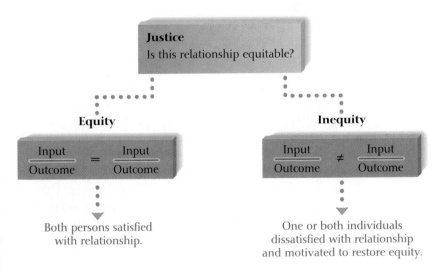

Justice
Is this relationship equitable?

Equity

$$\frac{Input}{Outcome} = \frac{Input}{Outcome}$$

Both persons satisfied with relationship.

Inequity

$$\frac{Input}{Outcome} \neq \frac{Input}{Outcome}$$

One or both individuals dissatisfied with relationship and motivated to restore equity.

Figure 8–2 Schematic representation of equity theory (after Taylor & Moghaddam, 1994).

which are objectively very unfair can be subjectively manipulated to seem fair. For example, although John actually puts very little into his relationship with Jane and gets a great deal of benefit from it, he persuades her that this is not the case.

Balance Theory

Social exchange theory also assumes that how fair an exchange is seen to be will determine how satisfied a person is in a relationship. In contrast, balance theory typically focuses on sets of relationships, such as those among three or four people. Rather than dealing with perceptions of fairness, **balance theory** is concerned with how our relationships with several others match, or balance, one another.

Let us suppose you invite home a friend you like a lot, but your family reacts very negatively. They make critical comments about this new friend, and even demand that in the future you not bring this person home. You will probably feel distress. Balance theory was originally developed to explain such experiences of inconsistency in a person's beliefs (Heider, 1958). In this case there is inconsistency between "I really like my new friend," "I love my family," and "My family dislikes my new friend." An assumption in balance theory is that people find inconsistency distressing and will change some aspect of a situation to achieve balance.

For example, imagine John brings Jane home to meet his parents, and both his mother and father like Jane. This is an example of a balanced relationship. But if it should turn out that his parents dislike Jane, then the relationship would be unbalanced: John likes his parents and he also likes Jane, but his parents dislike Jane (see Figure 8–3). In

balance theory proposition that people find inconsistency in relationships distressing and will change some aspect of a situation to achieve balance.

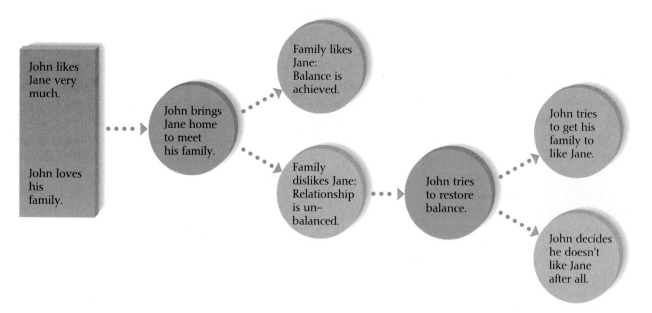

Figure 8–3 Schematic representation of the balance theory account of intimate relationships.

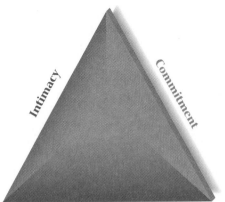

Figure 8–4 Schematic representation of the triangular theory of love (Sternberg, 1986, 1988).

such a situation, John will attempt to regain balance, perhaps by trying to persuade his parents that Jane is actually a wonderful person and they have misunderstood her. John may also restore balance by changing his own mind about Jane ("My parents were right after all, she is wrong for me"). Balance theory is an example of psychological explanations that assume people strive to maintain consistency in their thinking and in their social relations, and become distressed by inconsistency. (Another example of this kind of explanation is cognitive dissonance theory, which we discuss in Chapter 4.)

A more recent addition to theories in the balance tradition is Robert Sternberg's (1986, 1988) triangular model of love. The **triangular model of love** assumes three basic components to love relationships: intimacy, passion, and decision/commitment. An ideal balanced situation exists when each side of the love triangle is sufficiently present and love is experienced with high intensity—that is, when two people share an intense level of friendship, passion, and commitment (see Figure 8–4). However, according to Sternberg, this ideal is difficult to achieve, and many relationships lack either both or one component. Examples would be a love based on passion alone, without intimacy or commitment (such as the infatuation associated with "love at first sight"), or one based on intimacy and commitment but without passion (such as a marriage in which passion has faded), or one based on intimacy and passion but without commitment (as in a holiday romance).

The triangular model, then, is really a *typology* of intimate relationships, with the assumption that the ideal is a balanced relationship involving intensely experienced passion, intimacy, and commitment. Of course, real-life relationships are constantly changing, and their excitement stems from the shift from one type to another, so that a relationship based on intimacy could change to include passion and commitment. A major difference between modern Western-style marriage and non-Western arranged marriages is that in romantic marriages typically passion is the most important side of the triangle during the initial stage of the marriage, but in arranged marriages commitment is the most important. The priority given to commitment stems from the fact that entire families and communities invest in the

triangular model of love   model that assumes three components to love relationships: intimacy, passion, and decision/commitment.

future of a marriage (see discussions in Barnett, 1993). In the West, marriage has come to be a personal relationship between two independent individuals, often with little real investment on the part of the larger family and community.

The unease we feel about arranged marriages, and about theories that portray intimate relationships as involving an economic give-and-take, perhaps arises because we prefer to see love and friendship as determined by our personal feelings. We want to believe in being swept away rather than seeing ourselves as amateur accountants and bankers, counting up costs and returns. But an even greater challenge to a romantic picture of intimate relationships is posed by an evolutionary perspective that has become particularly influential since the 1980s.

Sociobiological Explanations

sociobiology   the scientific study of the biological basis of behavior.

Sociobiology, the scientific study of the biological basis of behavior, explains intimate relationships using ideas from evolutionary theory and places social behavior in the context of our very long evolutionary past (see Buss 1994a, 1994b). It is assumed that humans act "selfishly" to maximize the possibility of perpetuating their own genes. This has different implications for men and women because their different physiological characteristics lead them to use different strategies for reproduction and gene perpetuation. Women can have fewer offspring than men: Women can have children over a maximum of about a 25-year period and require 9 months for each pregnancy, but in theory men can father thousands of children, from puberty until they die (see Figure 8–5).

Sociobiologists have achieved mixed results from their attempts to predict behavior in intimate human relationships. For example, consider attitudes toward chastity. Women are always absolutely certain that they are the mothers of their children. Men, on the other hand, can never be completely certain that they are the fathers. One way in which men could be more certain is if they show a preference for mates who have sex with them exclusively. Thus, if a key factor influencing behavior is the evolutionary goal of perpetuating our

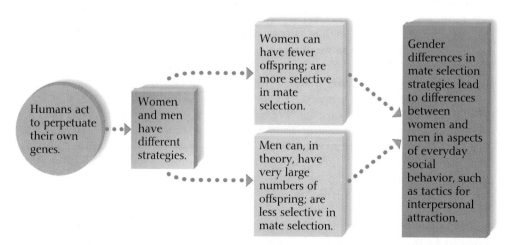

Figure 8–5   A sociobiological view of intimate relationships.

Young wife, older husband. A general trend across most societies is that women are younger than their husbands. But there is variation across cultures as to how many years' difference there is between the ages of wife and husband—a year or so in some cultures, a decade or so in others. According to exchange theory, the marriage of a younger woman and an older man typically involves an exchange: youth exchanged for higher earning power. From another perspective, sociobiologists see this age difference as associated with differences in reproductive strategies. Females, who can have fewer offspring, maximize their investment by ensuring that their partners are good providers for their young. Men maximize their investment by selecting younger, healthier partners.

genes, then men everywhere should value chastity. But research shows that how men view chastity is influenced by culture: Surveys of attitudes toward chastity reveal that some men, particularly in Scandinavian countries, see chastity as unimportant when seeking a prospective mate (Buss, 1994a).

Sex differences in reproduction suggest that women, who can have far fewer offspring than men, need to be more selective and to maximize each investment by ensuring that their partners can provide resources needed for the survival of the young. Men can afford to be less selective, but they can maximize their investments by selecting partners who have the health and youth required to reproduce. These factors lead sociobiologists to expect that in selecting spouses, men will give more importance to physical attractiveness and women will give more importance to resources. These expectations have in general matched the research evidence (Buss, 1994a, 1994b), even in some details of everyday behavior. For example, men show a preference for women who show themselves available as short-term mates (Schmitt & Buss, 1996).

However, for the most part, sociobiological accounts of mate selection have not been tested against other theoretical accounts. Rather, it has been shown that sociobiological accounts can explain certain trends, but that these same trends could also be explained by other theories. For example, consider the highly important issue of the age difference typical in male–female marriages. Cross-cultural studies reveal that in most cultures, males prefer younger wives and females prefer older husbands. The size of the difference varies across cultures, but this variation is greater for men than it is for women. That is, in most societies women prefer their husbands to be about 2 to 5 years older than themselves, but male preferences range more widely, from wishing for a wife 2 years younger to one about 7 years younger (Buss, 1994a, 1994b). This age difference ensures that men generally are more experienced and resourceful than their wives and can thus better maintain their dominant status. Thus, the age difference between husbands and wives can also be explained by reference to power and resources: Men are the majority (or more powerful) group and they try to ensure their superiority by selecting wives who are less experienced and thus easier to influence. As we would expect on the basis of this interpretation, in societies where women have achieved greater political and economic power (for example, Scandinavian societies), there is less of an age gap in male–female marriages. (It is interesting to speculate what would happen if women always married younger men.)

Concepts and Issues

Theories in social psychology have provided an interesting picture of individuals in intimate relationships as being concerned about achieving fairness and balance or as guided by evolutionary forces.

1. In what ways are social exchange theory and equity theory similar?
2. What makes the triangular model of love an example of balance theory?
3. Describe, from a sociobiological approach, gender differences in romantic relations.

The Theories in Cultural Context

It is useful to consider theories of attraction in cultural context, and in this way to highlight the role of local rules and norms in intimate relationships. Underlying these theories are four major assumptions:

That we want to maximize our personal rewards

That we work out our gains and losses rationally

That we try to maintain equilibrium in our relationships

That human behavior is causally determined

The first assumption is that we are egocentric; we are primarily concerned with our own welfare. Exchange theories see this egocentrism in our motivation to maximize our enjoyment or "rewards" and minimize our suffering or "losses," as we "give and take" in the social marketplace. Sociobiological theories see us as trying to maximize the chances of survival for our genetic kind. From the sociobiological viewpoint, we are "rewarded" when our genes survive.

A second assumption is that we make rational calculations, that we solve problems consciously and logically. This assumption is particularly influential in give-and-take scenarios depicted by exchange theories and equity theories. A third assumption central to a number of the theories, such as balance theory and the more recent triangular theory of love, is that we are motivated to maintain psychological balance in our intimate relationships.

Another theme common to these approaches is that human behavior is causally determined, either by evolutionary forces or motivations to achieve balance, equity, or the like. A closer look reveals some shortcomings with this approach. For example, sociobiologists argue that the male preference for younger females is intended to maximize reproductive success—younger women can have more children. But is this account convincing in our present situation, when the number of children in most middle-class families is so low?

An alternative to the sociobiological perspectives is a *cultural perspective*. For example, normative systems guide individuals to the "correct" way to select a spouse. One such norm could be "It is more correct for a 30-year-old man to marry a 22-year-old woman than for a 30-year-old woman to marry a 22-year-old man." Notice that in both age combinations, the woman is young enough to have at least three children—more than the average for college-educated women in the United States. Thus, the explanation that one combination is seen as more correct than the other because of a need to have children is not a good one in the present cultural context.

Evaluating the Theories

Critics have pointed out that the very language of the theories we have discussed—"inputs," "outcomes," "rewards," "costs," "profits, "balance"—arise out of a culture in which economic values are fundamentally important in intimate relationships (Deutsch, 1975; Sampson, 1975). In addition to their being "local" and reflecting the cultural characteristics of Western societies, a more specific limitation of these theories is that even in the Western context they are only relevant to some types of short-term relationships among individuals with high mobility.

One group of people who fit this description are students in Western societies. Such individuals are typically very mobile; for example, they generally move from home to college and then from their college town to another city or even another country thousands of miles away to start their professional careers. Also, students typically experience a variety of friendship and love relationships, most of which prove to be short term. So it is not surprising that the major theories of intimate relationships fit the characteristics of student life since they evolved out of research on student populations.

When people are used to moving about and to having short-term relationships, it makes more sense that they should be concerned with equitable exchanges, that they should keep track of "inputs" and "outcomes." When there is little time to develop long-term commitment, loyalty, and all the other characteristics we consider important in stable, intimate relationships, it makes sense to be concerned with give-and-take and not to make significant sacrifices. However, not all relationships follow the pattern typically experienced by college students.

Research among people involved in intimate long-term relationships in Western societies suggests that they take pains to avoid "keeping score," and that this seems to be essential for achieving happy friendships and marriages (Buunk & Van Yperen, 1991; Clark, Mills, & Corcoran, 1989). Indeed, if one of the partners in a long-term relationship did keep score, it would probably cause pain to the other partner. Why is this?

Perhaps the answer lies in the security that comes with long-term relationships. Couples marry intending to remain together for life and are optimistic about avoiding divorce (despite a divorce rate of 50 percent for first marriages and 60 percent for second marriages in the United States). Feelings of security may allow people in such relationships to contribute without keeping score. Feelings of security would be even stronger in traditional societies, such as those found in Asia and Africa, where the divorce rate is typically much lower than in the West.

However, the results of research on long-term relationships could also be used to support exchange theories generally and equity theory specifically. It could be argued that couples in secure relationships are prepared to invest in a relationship without regard for short-term outcomes because, first, an "investment" in the group benefits them personally in the long term ("My partner and I are together for life, and anything good for the family will be good for me"). Second, security is itself a sort of outcome or return on investment. All of this leads us to a potential shortcoming of equity theory: the lack of precise definitions for what constitutes inputs and outcomes. For example, is security an outcome?

The Pervasiveness of Romantic Love

Imagine if I jumped out from this page and asked you the following question: "If someone had all the other qualities you desired in a marriage partner, would you marry this person if you were not in love?" In the late 1960s, well over twice as many American men replied "no" to this question as did women (Kephart, 1967). By the late 1980s, however, more than 80 percent of both men and women said "no" (Simpson, Campbell, & Berscheid, 1986). The majority of both men and women in the United States now consider love to be a prerequisite to marriage. One explanation for this is that economic independence has allowed women to choose a marriage partner on the basis of love rather than material needs. However, this does not explain why romantic love has become so central to the lives of *both* men and women.

If anyone for a moment doubts the central place of romantic love in the modern Western world, he or she need only look through a list of successful films or television shows, or review the best-selling novels, or turn on the radio and listen to popular songs. There is no avoiding the conclusion that the boy–meets–girl theme dominates the modern media. Together with some students, I recently took part in a day-long contest to find the longest unbroken string of songs with a "love" theme played by any radio station. Several of us found stations that played nothing but such songs all day. A more challenging task would have been to find radio stations that play songs about anything else.

Of course, romantic love is not exclusive to Western societies. The notion of people falling in love is found in one form or another in most human societies, even in those in which marriages are traditionally arranged by families or friends. An analysis of songs and folklore in 166 societies suggested that what we recognize as romantic love is already present in 88.5 percent of them (Jankowiak & Fischer, 1992). But what is unique about romantic love in late twentieth-century Western societies is its pervasiveness: the idea that everyone should marry only when they are in love. Such an idea is fairly new historically and is still limited to Western societies.

"It Happened Just Like in a Fairy Tale"

Bob and I met in a training course in Chicago. At the time I was living in L.A. and Bob was living in New York, and completely by accident we were suddenly thrown together for five days. We found we had a lot in common . . . we even like the same kind of Chinese food. By the time the training course ended we were madly in love! We kept up a long-distance relationship for 9 months, spending all our money on telephone calls and plane tickets, and then we got really lucky. A new company in Miami offered me a job, and then offered Bob a job too after I told them this was my condition for accepting. Things happened very quickly after that. I remember calling early on a Sunday morning to tell my mother about our plan to get married, and both of us getting so excited on the phone. We had a fairly big wedding in Vermont, where my mother and some other members of my family still live. A lot of people flew in—my dad from New York, Bob's father and stepmother from Arizona, his mother from Philadelphia, his sister from Ohio where she is going to college—it was a wonderful family gathering. Amazing as it sounds, for me love and marriage have gone together like a horse and carriage, but not because I planned it. It all just happened like in a fairy tale." [Sara, 32-year-old public relations manager]

The case of Sara is a good illustration of a modern romantic love marriage in Western societies. Before the women's movement and the large-scale entering of the professions by women during the second half of the twentieth century, it was rare for women to experience the level of geographical mobility and freedom of choice enjoyed by Sara. Sara was already financially independent and living apart from her family before her marriage. She met and fell in love with her future husband while attending a training course in a city other than where she worked. She then entered a long-distance romance, and finally married when she and Bob could find jobs in the same city. It was Sara who telephoned her parents to let them know she was getting married, rather than her parents arranging a marriage and informing her about her future spouse. Family members did come together for her wedding ceremony, but after the wedding they went back to their separate lives.

More and more people are sharing Sara's experience. Look around your class. Within another 10 years, most of the students you see sitting around you will be in other cities and some will have moved to other countries. Industrialization and the internationalization of trade have led to a more mobile labor force, so that people change cities and even countries and continents more often. Industrialization has also created opportunities for women to enter the labor force and to become financially independent.

These societal changes mean that traditional systems of arranged marriage are no longer viable. The community and the family support systems that made arranged marriages possible are often not available anymore, even if we wanted to use them. People are forced to rely on their own talents and connections, or on those they can hire to help them—such as professional dating services. Even in cases in which the community and the family are available, the financial independence of women and their newly won legal rights mean that they have more freedom to act on their own choices.

Will Hollywood Love Become Universal?

Perhaps no other feature of Western culture is being exported and internationalized more than romantic love "Hollywood style." Over the last century in Western societies we have seen increasing acceptance of the idea that one should marry for love, and that when love (defined as a passionate, euphoric feeling) dies it is only right to break up a relationship and start over again. This idea is spreading to non–Western societies, such as that in China (*Beijing Review*, 1988). As societies become industrialized and more individualistic, the percentage of people who believe that love must precede marriage increases. Differences still remain, however. A study of young people in 11 countries (Australia, Brazil, England, Hong Kong, India, Japan, Mexico, Pakistan, the Philippines, Thailand, and the United States) revealed that the most collectivistic societies had the highest percentage of "yes" responses (India 49 percent and Pakistan 50.4 percent, compared to the United States 3.5 percent and England 7.3 percent) to the question "If a man (woman) had all the other qualities you desired, would you marry this person if you were not in love with him (her)?" (LeVine, Sato, Hashimoto, & Verma, 1995).

But we should be careful about equating modern views on romantic love with particular patterns of sexual behavior. A detailed national

In many societies marriages still take place according to ancient traditions, as is the case for this Russian Orthodox couple. Traditional marriages typically involve a joining of families rather than just two independent individuals. In contrast is "Hollywood–style love," based on two individuals acting independently on the basis of personal feelings rather than communal obligations. Hollywood-style love is not unique to Western societies: The Saigon couple below is heading off into the sunset on a motorcycle, looking for adventure and romance in their new lives together.

survey by John Gagnon and his associates found that Americans are actually conservative in their sex lives (Gagnon, Laumann, Michael, & Michaels, 1994). About 85 percent of married women and 75 percent of married men report being faithful to their spouses. On the other hand, it may be that many men and even some women in Islamic societies are more "liberated" in sexual practices than we assume. For example, Shahla Haeri (1989) has conducted a detailed study of "temporary marriages" among Shi'i Muslim men, who are permitted to have four permanent wives (allowed to all Muslim men), as well as an infinite number of temporary wives. Women are allowed only one husband of any kind. A temporary marriage can last a very short time (15 minutes) or much longer (50 years). Haeri shows that temporary marriages are used by men for indulging in extramarital affairs. It may be that the percentage of men who have had sexual relations with more than one woman at a time is higher among Shi'i Muslim men than the 25 percent reported by Gagnon, Laumann, Michael, and Michaels (1994) in the United States. Such cases highlight the importance of local norms and rules in intimate relationships.

Within culturally diverse societies such as those of Canada and the United States, there are also important variations in intimate relationships. A study of Indians in Canada showed that the idea that marriage precedes love tends to be endorsed more by first-generation immigrants, those who were born abroad and moved to the adopted land, than by second-generation immigrants, whose parents came from abroad but who were themselves born in the adopted land (Vaidyanathan & Naidoo, 1991). Another study showed that Asian Canadians tend to interpret love more as based on friendship and caring rather than something "mysterious," compared to European Canadians (Dion & Dion, 1993). Each wave of new immigrants to North America will probably serve to increase such variations.

Further Similarities Across Cultures

Evolutionary processes (Buss, 1985, 1994a) and physiological processes (Walsh, 1991) help to establish certain boundaries in human mate selection and the experience of romantic love. In order to understand better the role of culture in this context, it is useful to consider the experience of emotions in romantic love from a social psychological perspective. We have seen that the idea of falling in love is found in many cultures (Jankowiak & Fischer, 1992). Of course, in some cultures falling in love is an enchanting experience that generally does not influence the choice of spouse. For people in Western societies it is now considered a democratic right for each person to marry for love. Despite these major differences, there seem to be certain important similarities in the experience of romantic love as reported in many societies. This is suggested by Stanley Schachter's (1964) **two-component model of emotion,** which proposes that common to most experiences of romantic love are at least two steps: physiological changes in the person and an interpretation of such physiological changes according to the norms and rules of the culture. A number of fascinating studies support this idea (Hatfield & Walster, 1981).

Imagine you are a tourist in western Canada, and you reach the Capilano Suspension Bridge, which spans 450 feet across the Capilano River. During the 6 years I lived in Canada, one of my most thrilling experiences was to walk across this bridge and admire the natural beauty of the landscape. One thinks twice about walking across the bridge, because it is only about 5 feet wide, and below it is a drop of several hundred feet to white-water rapids. Donald Dutton and Arthur Aron (1974) arranged for

two-component model of emotion theory which proposes that common to most emotional experiences, such as romantic love, are at least two steps: physiological changes in the person and interpreting such physiological changes according to the norms and rules of the culture.

an attractive female research assistant to interview men either while they were crossing this bridge or after they had crossed. Do you think there would be any differences between these two groups of male participants about how attractive they found the female interviewer?

Dutton and Aron predicted that those men who were interviewed while on the bridge would be physiologically aroused because of the thrill of being on the bridge, whereas those who had gotten across the bridge and had time to calm down would be less aroused. They reasoned that because of higher arousal, the male participants interviewed on the bridge would misattribute the causes of their arousal and assume that the female interviewer was the cause (see the discussion of attributions in Chapter 5). The results confirmed this prediction. To check their results, Dutton and Aron also did the same study using a male interviewer and found no differences. They also used a much smaller, less exciting bridge and found no differences.

The idea that physiological arousal from some peripheral source (e.g., being on an exciting bridge) can be misattributed and result in increased attraction to another source (e.g., an attractive interviewer) has been supported by a number of other studies (e.g., White, Fishbein, & Rutstein, 1981). But there are also studies that fail to show this trend (Kendrick, Cialdini, & Linder, 1979). It may be that physiological arousal can lead us both to more strongly like those we already find attractive and more strongly dislike those we already find unattractive (Allen, Kendrick, Linder, & McCall, 1989). Thus, for example, if Carole finds Adam attractive, then he should risk taking her to an exciting place for a date. However, if she is generally turned off by him, then being in an exciting place with her may make him even less appealing from Carole's viewpoint. But such a process takes place within a normative system, and whether Carole comes to feel that she has fallen in love with Adam depends on cultural norms.

Similarly, the influence of chemical processes involved in experiences of love should be considered in cultural context. Anthony Walsh (1991) has described how the first "head-over-heels" period of falling in love is typically associated with a rush of chemicals, such as dopamine, norepinephrine, and phenylethylamine (PEA), which give people a "high." Secret love affairs may also be pleasurable in part because of the high that comes from doing something that involves danger (Wegner, Lane, & Dimitri, 1994). But this high does not last, perhaps because the body builds up a tolerance to these chemicals. It may be that such chemical processes are common to most or even all people who report falling in love. However, the critically important question is, How has culture socialized people to interpret such chemical changes?

Some people have been socialized to interpret the end of this high feeling as the end of one love affair and as the right time to move on. The increased rate of divorce in Western societies is in part due to contemporary interpretations of what the experience of love is, as well as the role of love in marriage. If romantic love continues to be interpreted as necessarily involving a "natural high," and marriage is seen to be a failure without such a love binding a couple together, then it seems likely that divorce rates will remain high or perhaps even increase rather than decrease—unless a pharmaceutical company manages to develop drugs that prevent the body building up tolerance to PEA and other chemicals that allow lovers to get a "kick" out of each other.

Varieties of Love

In many non–Western societies, love associated with marriage is not a euphoric high, but a more mundane yet long–lasting type of companionship. But we need not go to non–Western societies to discover that there are many different ways of loving. Following earlier work (Lee, 1976) on the typology of love, since the 1980s researchers have explored the many different types of love relationships (Hendrick & Hendrick, 1992, 1993). For example, some relationships are based more on friendship ("We are each other's best friend"), whereas others are more passionate ("It was love at first sight") or based on game playing ("I like to tease my lover and maintain an air of uncertainty") or are pragmatic ("I made a list of the qualities my future spouse should have, and then found a person to fit the picture"). There are many different types of love relationships, indicating that in the future love could evolve along different paths.

Concepts and Issues

The increasing influence of Western societies has been associated with the spread of what we have termed Hollywood–style romantic love: a euphoric, mysterious experience that leads one person to feel passionate toward, and make sacrifices for, the other. The major social psychological theories contradict this popular view of romantic love since they depict people as rational, self-centered, balance-seeking, and concerned with survival. A cultural explanation of friendship and love relies on local rules and norms, and sees individuals as maintaining friendships and love relationships according to what they see to be correct behavior in their given context.

1. What are some of the assumptions underlying social exchange theory, equity theory, balance theory, and sociobiology?
2. Is Hollywood–style romantic love universal? Discuss why or why not.
3. What is the two–component model of love?

Attraction: Why We Like and Love Others

We are now in an era when finding friends and marriage partners is primarily our own responsibility. This can be a wonderfully exciting and fulfilling experience. However, although friendship and love are popularly thought of as being in the realm of fairy tales, even these mysterious experiences turn out to proceed in certain regular patterns. For example, we may assume it to be a part of the magic of romance that Sara fell in love while on a trip to a faraway city, but the scientific research points to *proximity, similarity,* and *attraction* as having played crucial roles in her romance: Sara fell in love with a person who was located close to her (she and her future husband attended same training course), it turned out that they had a great deal in common and that they found each other attractive. These three factors play a central part in both friendship and love.

Proximity

We can only get to like and to love people with whom we have contact. This means that out of the nearly 6 billion people in the world, our pool of potential friends and lovers is actually very limited. We come into contact with only a small fraction of the people who share our country, our city, and even our college or university. Thus, if there really is one "special person" just for us, our chances of actually meeting that person among the billions of other humans are very limited. Social psychologists have shown that, in practice, our friendships and romantic loves are strongly associated with proximity, the physical distance between people.

Research in the 1930s showed that marriage takes place on a higher than chance basis between men and women who live in the same

A group of college students spend time together. For people to get to like and love one another, they first have to meet. Proximity is a critical factor, because those who are often near one another have more opportunities to interact and develop relationships. The more people interact, the more likely they will like one another. So people tend to become friends with those who live nearby. This general trend has many exceptions: You probably know people who dislike (or even hate) their roommates.

neighborhood (Bossard, 1932). A series of follow–up studies showed that marriage is more likely to take place between people who have been students in the same class or worked together on a job (Katz & Hill, 1958). But there was an important limitation to these studies because it was difficult to isolate the unique influence of proximity. People who live in the same neighborhood, take the same class or work at the same company may have chosen to be where they are in order to be in the company of others whom they already know and who share their own ethnic, religious, educational, or other characteristics.

Also, our choices about where we live, go to school, and work are made within certain limitations, such as income (Wheeler, 1971). For example, on an average student budget it would be impossible to rent an apartment in the most expensive part of most cities. Discrimination has also been an important factor in determining where people live (Rose, 1971). Despite legal reforms, ethnic segregation patterns have persisted in the United States and Canada (Moghaddam, 1994; Tobin, 1987). Visible minorities tend to be segregated more than minorities whose phenotypical features allow them to blend into the mainstream more easily. Consequently, the fact that people tend to marry others from the same parts of the city, or even the same school or job, may be because of similarity on the basis of ethnicity and income, for example, rather than proximity.

In order to tease out the influence of proximity itself, researchers needed a context in which strangers are thrown together more or less randomly. Where can we find such a "natural experiment"? You are right, the university campus and the dormitories provide just such a setting. Every year, hundreds of thousands of students, particularly those in their first year, find themselves living in the same dormitories with people they have never met before. Does proximity play a role in which students become friends and which ones become romantically attached?

Studies of both single and married students more or less randomly brought together through campus housing showed that proximity is highly important in friendship formation (Evans & Wilson, 1949; Festinger, Schachter, & Back, 1950; Newcomb, 1961). Students who share rooms or live on the same dormitory floor are more likely to have frequent interactions and show a higher than chance tendency to become friends. In the social psychology class I am teaching as I write this chapter, about 20 percent of the students report they had both a very good same–sex friend, and a person whom they dated for a while, live on the same floor, or on the floor below or above, where they lived during their first year. One female student had her best female friend live in the room directly above her, and her boyfriend live directly below her during her first year.

But a more careful look at how proximity influences attachment shows that *location*, where one is situated (in a room at the end as opposed to in the middle of a corridor) also plays a critical role. This is because location influences interaction patterns. A location that is central and close to the main traffic routes (e.g., next to the staircase used by people on different floors) allows people to interact more with others. Similarly, sitting in a place that allows direct interaction with another leads to more intimacy (Insko & Wilson, 1977). If you want to interact a lot with others, it is best to sit in the middle of a row rather than at either of the ends. The place traditionally reserved at the head of the table for the person with the highest status also allows the greatest possibility for interacting with others.

Contact and Liking

The idea that greater contact will lead people to like one another is central both to interpersonal and intergroup attraction. This idea underlies the **contact hypothesis** (Amir, 1976), which proposes that under certain conditions, the more the members of different groups, such as ethnic minorities and majorities, interact with one another, the more they will grow to have favorable attitudes toward one another. Think back to the historic legislation on desegregation, the integration of schools, and the policy of busing. All of these were influenced by the idea that if whites, blacks, and other ethnic minorities interact more, they will become more favorable toward one another. In Chapter 14 we discuss the subtleties of the contact hypothesis, but for now we should recognize the pervasive influence of the assumption that contact leads to liking.

contact hypothesis   under certain conditions, the more the members of different groups interact, the more they will grow to have favorable attitudes toward one another.

The power of contact is sometimes acknowledged in a very different way. In many non–Western societies, particularly those in which the population is predominantly Muslim, strict limitations are imposed on the contact that women can have with people outside their immediate family. In most Islamic societies, women have to cover all of their body except their hands and part of their face when they go out in public. When they are speaking with a man other than their husband or a member of their immediate family, they should not make eye contact, nor should they laugh loudly or behave in any way that might be interpreted as "attractive" from the point of view of the opposite sex. Implicit in these restrictions is the idea that if women are allowed to interact freely with men, then intimate relationships are more likely to develop between women and men who are not immediate family members.

Exposure, Familiarity, and Liking

A rational explanation of why contact leads to liking could be that given the chance to get to know other people, we will tend to like most of them and only dislike a few. Thus, in the majority of cases, increased social interaction with others leads to attraction rather than repulsion. For sure, we *dislike* a few people we get to know, but in the vast majority of cases our propensity to find appealing features in others means that the more we get to know them, the more we get to like them.

Two Spelman College students. A strong contender for a universal in the domain of liking and loving is similarity–attraction. Research in many different cultures lends support to the idea that people are attracted to others who are similar to themselves. In contrast, dissimilarity–attraction works in a minority of cases.

Our "liking" disposition is functional, in the sense that it allows us to cooperate with a greater number of others and to cope better with environmental challenges. If we generally disliked most other people, we would find it much more difficult to get tasks done. (I am sure you know a few individuals who *do* seem to dislike almost everyone, but they are not going to be contributing much to group life.)

A functional approach also leads to the idea that we should like those things that are more familiar. As human beings evolved, they continually struggled to make more efficient use of the natural environment. They had to learn to discriminate among fruits, herbs, animals, and even other people—some would help them survive and others would more likely harm or even kill them. Although some level of risk taking helped people make new discoveries, the general survival strategy for everyday life has been to prefer the known and the familiar rather than the unknown and unfamiliar. This may explain why there is a general tendency for human infants and young animals to prefer the familiar and show anxiety when confronted by the unfamiliar (Eibl-Eibesfeldt, 1989, p. 170). And although anxiety shown by human infants toward strangers seems to be universal, sex and ethnicity have some role in this process. For example, girls tend to show anxiety toward strangers earlier than boys (Lewis & Michalson, 1983), and white infants have been found to show more fear toward black strangers than toward white strangers (Feinman, 1980).

If we have evolved to prefer the familiar, then we should have greater liking for things to which we have had more exposure. Through meta-analysis of the hundreds of studies on the **mere exposure effect,** the positive association found between liking for and repeated exposure to novel stimuli, it was shown that simply being more familiar with something does lead to greater liking (Bornstein, 1989). The research of Robert Zajonc (1970, 1980) and others shows that merely being exposed to something, such as a face, or a foreign word, or a piece of music, leads us to like it more, even if we are not aware that we are being exposed (Kunst-Wilson & Zajonc, 1980).

The powerful effect of exposure on liking has been put to use in advertising and political campaigns (Suedfeld, Rank, & Borrie, 1975). By repeatedly exposing us to "brand X" and to "political candidate Y," advertisers and political campaign managers have found they can influence our preferences. In this sense, "selling consumer goods" and "selling political candidates" have something in common. Anthony Pratkanis and Elliot Aronson (1991) have labeled this "the Age of Propaganda," and even asserted that now voting for a presidential candidate is "the same kind of decision as choosing a laundry detergent or a breakfast cereal or evaluating nonsense words and Chinese ideographs" (p. 136).

"Wait a minute!" You may be thinking, "I can remember times when a repeated advertisement or tune got to be really annoying. What about the familiarity breeds contempt idea?" Advertisers are certainly aware of a *wear-out effect,* which means that an advertisement seems to have a limited life. Both research and practical experience suggest that even successful advertisements have less impact over time, and so variations are needed to make them effective again (see Mitchell 1993; Schumann, Petty, & Clemons, 1990). A strategy of "repetition with variation" seems to be most effective. However, although variations are necessary, rather like minor themes in a piece of music, the main theme must be exposure. Frederick Allen (1994) showed in his study of Coca-Cola that although over the twentieth century there have been many changes in Coca-Cola ads, the "relentless" exposure has never let up. As if to underline the role of consistency, consumers rejected the New Coke during the 1980s, forcing the company to rethink marketing strategies and once again launch the Old Coke.

mere exposure effect the positive association found between liking for and repeated exposure to novel stimuli.

Similarity

I knew a lot about my husband before I met him. I was already 22, and my family was trying to find a suitable match for me. My oldest great-aunt, who is very experienced in these things, told my mother about Krishno and said he would make a good choice. She knew his grand-mother very well, and so one day it was arranged that my mother and his mother would meet at my great-aunt's. After the families got to know each other a little better and explained their financial situation and ex-pectations, it was arranged for me and Krishno to meet. Of course, we are of the same caste and our families have been living in the same town for a long time, so we already had a lot in common. I was very nervous the day I first met him, but my mother told me a lot of good things about him and said if I did not like him I could say no. But I already felt posi-tive about the match, because from what my family and friends told me, I knew we had a lot in common. He wanted to have three or four chil-dren, he liked to stay at home a lot rather than go to parties and restau-rants. I was told that he had liked my picture a lot, and I also found him attractive when we finally met, so I decided it would be a good match. We have been married for 11 years and have three children. I love my children and my husband and I am happy about the way things were arranged. [Chandana, 33-year-old Indian computer-software engineer]

I was getting tired of the singles bar scene, and fairly desperate to try something different. I was 30-something and I had tried it all, even blind dates set up by friends of friends. Then one day, I received one of those computer dating ads and I thought, why not? Surely it can't get worse? I filled out a form and sent it in, then had an interview, and then filled out more forms. They asked me about all the details of my life, from my edu-cation and income to all the stuff about how much I love and hate cer-tain things. Then, they set me up with dates. The first two were not fan-tastic, but they were not bad either. At least it turned out that I had a lot in common with the men I had been matched with. Charlie was the third date, and it went like magic from the start. We were living together after 3 months, and we got married on the anniversary of our first date. [Angela, 35-year-old high school teacher]

When students in Western universities hear about arranged mar-riages involving educated young people in non-Western countries, their immediate reaction is a mixture of puzzlement and disbelief. When stu-dents in non-Western societies learn about computer dating, they often react equally negatively. But it is interesting to step back and recognize that arranged marriages and computer dating have something funda-mental in common: Both involve matching a man and a woman on the basis of similarities.

In the case of arranged marriages, the families of the man and woman try to match the couple; in computer dating, information about each person is fed into a computer and the machine compiles a list of the best matches. Even the information that is used to match people is very similar. Next time you receive a mailing from a computer dating

The powerful influence of similarity–attraction in liking and loving relations is reflected in seemingly very different ways of selecting spouses—for example, computer dating, being tried out by this man in Japan, and more traditional marriages involving community influence if not arrangement, as represented by this Cambodian couple. Computer dating programs work by gathering information about individuals, then matching couples on preferences and characteristics. The basic assumption of computer dating is that those who are more similar are more likely to make a successful match. Arranged matches also involve a search for partners with similar backgrounds and tastes, on the assumption that similarity leads to attraction.

service, read the questionnaire. You will typically find they ask a set of questions under the title "Tell us about yourself" (What is your age? What is your educational background? What is your current income? What are your relationship goals?), and another set of questions under the title "Tell us about the person you would like to meet" (Which age group do you prefer dating? What minimum educational background do you prefer? What areas of interest would you like to share with someone?). People in the West may be surprised to learn that these are exactly the sorts of questions that guide families in arranging marriages. Moreover, the general assumption in both computer dating and arranged marriages is that similarity and attraction are associated.

The preference people show for similar others was noted more than 2,500 years ago by Aristotle (1932) with respect to friendship formation, and it has been extensively tested by Donn Byrne (1971) and other modern social psychologists (e.g., Neimeyer & Mitchell, 1988) in the Western context. The **similarity–attraction hypothesis,** which asserts a positive association between similarity and attraction, is supported by research in an impressive array of domains, including similarity on attitudes; on smoking, drinking, and premarital sex; on economic characteristics; on being a morning rather than evening

similarity-attraction hypothesis hypothesis that asserts a positive association between similarity and attraction.

dissimilarity-repulsion hypothesis
hypothesis which asserts that people
are repulsed by dissimilarity.

opposites-attract hypothesis the
hypothesis that we are attracted to
people who are different from us.

person; and on race (see Byrne, 1961, 1971; Byrne, Clore, & Worchel, 1966; Olsak, Perreault, & Moghaddam, 1997; Rodgers, Billy, & Udry, 1984; Watts, 1982).

This relationship seems to be true cross-culturally as well. Don Byrne and his associates (see Byrne, 1971, pp. 208–211) found that this relationship holds in a study involving college students from Hawaii, India, Japan, Mexico, and the mainland United States. The opposite of this has also been proposed and tested: The **dissimilarity–repulsion hypothesis** predicts that people are repulsed by dissimilarity. In a test of the idea that attitude similarity does not lead to liking but that attitude dissimilarity leads to repulsion (Rosenbaum, 1986a, 1986b), Ramadhar Singh and Lynne Tan (1992), using student participants at the National University of Singapore, and Stephen Drigotas (1993), using student participants at the University of North Carolina at Chapel Hill, found support for the similarity–attraction hypothesis. Their findings show that similarity–attraction comes into effect first; dissimilarity-repulsion can come into effect at a later stage in the social interaction process.

There is also cross-cultural support for similarity-attraction from a long line of studies showing that people prefer others who share their own lifestyle and group membership (Sumner, 1906; Taylor & Moghaddam, 1994). For example, Robert LeVine and Donald Campbell (1972) have shown that in a vast range of world cultures there is a strong and consistent tendency for people to prefer their own kind, those who are similar rather than dissimilar to them. In a recent study of English-Canadians, French-Canadians, Jews, Chinese, Greeks, and Indians in Canada, my students and I found the similarity-attraction link to be strong: All groups showed a preference for similar others (Olsak, Perreault, & Moghaddam, 1997).

The similarity–attraction hypothesis would seem to have a natural rival in the **opposites–attract hypothesis,** that we are attracted to people who are different from us. In our everyday lives, we often assume that friendship and love relationships are based on complementarity. For example, we may assume that a person who feels a need to dominate would "match" the needs of a person who is submissive (Leary, 1957). But empirical tests of such hypothetical complementary relationships have produced mixed results (Byrne, 1971, p. 184; Nowicki & Manheim, 1991). The research evidence suggests that people marry those whose personalities are similar rather than dissimilar to their own (Berscheid, 1985; Buss, 1985).

Perhaps in an ideal world, complementarity would play a bigger role in social relations. Both our everyday experiences and the ideas of psychodynamic theorists such as Alfred Adler (1956) suggest that by compensating for each other's weaknesses, we can all become more complete. For example, if Jim is very shy and finds it difficult to make friends, then by marrying Samantha, who is very outgoing, he can become more sociable. Unfortunately, in practice it seems that Jim and Samantha will not be attracted to one another: Jim will probably marry someone who is reserved like himself and Samantha will very likely marry another outgoing person.

However, complementarity does have some role in interpersonal attraction. In the next section, we see how individuals sometimes compensate for some weakness or shortcoming they may have (e.g., compensating for a lack of money by being very creative or physically attractive) in order to match the strengths of a partner.

Physical Attractiveness

> The North American beauty ideal is becoming an international one, part of a global culture machine, where each woman is encouraged to aim to be whiter, more Western, more upper class. Women factory workers in Malaysia are provided with make-up classes by their employers, and Asian women undergo eyelid surgery to Westernize their eyes. (Unger & Crawford, 1992, p. 335)

Rhoda Unger and Mary Crawford are among the critics who have pointed out that women, more than men, are judged on the basis of criteria for physical beauty. And these criteria tend more and more to be white and Western—even in non-Western societies. One interpretation of these trends could be based on power differences between men and women and between Western and non-Western societies. Men have more power than women and are thus able to define the criteria by which both men and women will be assessed. By ensuring that women are assessed on how they look, rather than first on their intellectual or other abilities, men maintain their advantaged position. Similarly, Western nations enjoy greater power than non-Western societies, and so Western criteria for beauty become international.

The spread of Western ideals of physical attractiveness seems to endorse the idea that "beauty is in the eye of the beholder," implying that society constructs notions of beauty, and that we could come to see many different human features as beautiful. Also, we could change the role of attractiveness in gender relations so that men are assessed on the basis of how attractive they are more than women. These interesting possibilities raise a number of questions for social psychologists. First, how important is physical attractiveness in social relations? Second, are women assessed on the basis of physical attractiveness more than men? Third, is physical attractiveness completely culture-bound and "in the eye of the beholder"?

The Pervasive Influence of Physical Attractiveness

> Fair tresses man's imperial race insnare,
> And beauty draws us with a single hair.
>
> —Alexander Pope, *The Rape of the Lock*

It is an unfair world we live in! This is the typical response of students to the results of social psychological research on the pervasive influence of physical attractiveness. Physically attractive people receive more favorable treatment in just about every way that has been tested, across different age, sex, and cultural groups (Eagly, Ashmore, Makhijani, & Longo, 1991). Attractive people generally receive more help from others (Besons, Karabenick, & Lerner, 1976), are more favorably evaluated at work (Cash, Gillen, & Burns, 1977), and are more popular as dates (Green, Buchanan, & Heuer, 1984). Presumably, less attractive people are more likely to be lonely, which means they are more likely to be stigmatized (Lau & Gruen, 1992). The bottom line is that attractive people, both men and women, are paid more for the work they do (Frieze, Olson, & Russell, 1991).

halo effect tendency for a few outstanding characteristics to influence the overall assessment of a person.

As if this were not enough to make us think it is an unfair world, the research evidence also suggests the existence of a **halo effect,** a tendency for a few outstanding characteristics to influence the overall assessment of a person. Those who are more attractive are assumed to have various other positive qualities (Calvert, 1988; Dion, Berscheid, & Walster, 1972; Dion & Dion, 1987; Eagly, Ashmore, Makhijani, & Longo, 1991). In addition to being thought more exciting and sexy (which we might expect), attractive people are also thought to be better adjusted, more honest, and to have more fulfilling lives and more successful marriages.

This preference for attractiveness extends to the very young, so that we generally favor more attractive infants (Corter, Trehub, Boukydis, Ford, Clehoffer, & Minde, 1978), and attractive children are more popular in the nursery (Dion & Berscheid, 1974). More attractive newborns even receive more attention from their mothers while still in hospital (Langlois, Ritter, Casey, & Sawin, 1995). It seems that being born attractive brings all kinds of advantages.

But even more intriguing is research evidence suggesting that infants show preferences for a more attractive face (Langlois, Roggman, Casey, Ritter, Rieser–Danner, & Jenkins, 1987; Langlois, Roggman, & Rieser–Danner, 1990). Infants as young as 2 months old have been found to look longer at female faces that have been rated as more attractive by adults. Presumably, the infants look at a particular face longer because they find it to be more pleasing. These results suggest some basic inborn aesthetic preferences (Langlois, Roggman, Casey, Ritter, Rieser–Danner, & Jenkins, 1987, p. 367). We shall say more about possible universals of beauty later, but for now we have to add two points to this seemingly unfair story of attractive people getting all the breaks.

First, probably because they are treated more favorably and sought out, attractive people tend to become more confident and to have better social skills (Goldman & Lewis, 1977; Hatfield & Sprecher, 1986). Thus, the self–fulfilling prophecy comes true. But there is no evidence that our higher expectations lead attractive people to become more intelligent or honest! A second point is that there may be a few negative aspects to being very attractive. For example, an attractive person who is told "Your report was wonderful" may wonder, "Am I being complimented for my report, or because of my looks?" (Hatfield & Sprecher, 1986). These kinds of attributional ambiguities may lead attractive persons to see their attractiveness, rather than their intellectual or other talents, as the source of their success (recall the discussion on attributional ambiguity in Chapter 5). Of course, attractiveness is not a firm basis for success, because it inevitably fades:

> For never-ending Time leads summer on
> To hideous winter and confounds him there,
> Sap checked with frost, and lusty leaves quite gone,
> Beauty o'ersnowed and bareness everywhere.
>
> —Shakespeare, *Sonnet 5*

Attractiveness and Gender

> Snow White was so beautiful, even in death, that the dwarfs could not find it in their hearts to bury her. . . . Far away, Snow White's Prince heard of the maiden who slept in the glass coffin. He had searched far and wide to find Snow White. Finally, one day, riding through the trees, he saw her . . . and gazed upon her beauty once more. Slowly, the Prince knelt down and gently kissed Snow White. . . . Suddenly, Snow White began to stir. She . . . was alive! Snow White kissed each dwarf goodbye. Then the Prince lifted her up onto his horse and led her away to his castle on the hill. And they lived happily ever after. (Walt Disney's *Snow White and the Seven Dwarfs*, n.d., pp. 88–96)

In many different societies, physical attractiveness is considered a more appropriate criterion for assessing women than men. In the Western context, fairy tales stress the central importance of beauty for women, and bravery and intelligence for men. In the best-known fairy tales, such as *Snow White* and *Cinderella*, the female heroine is rescued by a prince because of the impact of her beauty. If Snow White had not been beautiful, it is safe to assume the prince would not have taken much notice of her.

In major reviews of research studies on the role of attractiveness, the consensus is that physical attractiveness is of greater importance for women than for men (see Feingold, 1990). Given that this research started in the 1930s, and so much has changed in gender roles since then, surely we should find that more recent studies would show a different trend? Now that women are more economically independent, surely they will also be free to choose their partners on the basis of attractiveness?

There is some evidence that modern women do give importance to physical attractiveness, and that the male-female difference traditionally reported is not always consistent (Reis, Nezlek, & Wheeler, 1980). Some evidence suggests that androgynous characteristics may be attractive in both men and women (Green & Kendrick, 1994). Interestingly, in his meta-analyses of the major studies in this field, Alan Feingold (1990, 1992) found that male-female differences are greater in self-reports than in actual behavior. That is, women *say* they give less importance to looks than men, but in their behavior they are less different than their verbal reports suggest. Perhaps the reported difference arises because women

Courtship on horseback, China. Non-Western societies sometimes allow women considerable influence in the choice of a spouse, but often in subtle ways. This young Kazakh woman on the plains of Xinjiang, China, will be chased by suitors, who will try to steal a kiss from her. She may keep out of reach of some suitors, but slow down just enough for a preferred suitor to catch her.

feel it would be incorrect for them to admit that they give importance to looks, whereas men see it as correct.

A related finding is that American women are influenced more by their peers when making judgments of beauty. William Graziano and his associates showed that among students at Texas A&M University, women were particularly influenced by negative assessments made by their peers (Graziano, Jensen-Campbell, Shebilske, & Lundgren, 1993). If they learned their peers had rated a male or a female face as physically unattractive, they were less likely to rate the face as attractive. This may be because in the context of the United States, men are socialized to be more independent than women and to rely less on peers.

On the basis of research with participants in the United States, Graziano, Jensen-Campbell, Shebilske, and Lundgren (1993) speculated that "for women, male beauty may be better regarded as a dependent effect variable that is a consequence of interpersonal processes" (p. 530). This kind of gender difference may arise from the minority status of women (women have less power and are more easily influenced), but it could also be used to support an evolutionary view that the processes that underlie judgments of beauty are different in men and women (Kendrick & Keefe, 1992).

Similarly, the greater importance of physical attractiveness for women can be interpreted to support two dramatically different explanations. The sociobiological account is challenged by many different research orientations that we might pool under the label *cultural*. These include feminist critiques of contemporary culture and psychology (see Callaghan, 1994; Jackson, 1992; Unger & Crawford, 1992), which emphasize that gender roles are socially constructed and that traditional gender roles reflect the subordinate status of females. From this perspective, the fact that women give more importance to makeup and cosmetic surgery than men arises from changeable power relations rather than stable genetic differences. In some contexts, such as the traditional society of Haiti, both women and men are free in sexual relations, and both sexes give importance to "looks."

Who Is Attractive?

> Lese men are extremely attracted to their stereotypical characterization of Efe women, specifically Efe women's body hair. . . . Lese men speak among themselves of how exciting *torumbaka* (or public hair) is to them. *Torumbaka* is used specifically to refer to hair around the navel, or between the breasts; it is said to be unique to the Efe and is also said to have the power to produce instant erections among men. (Grinker, 1994, p. 81)

Roy Richard Grinker's detailed study of relationships between the Lese, a farming community, and the Efe, their Pygmy hunting partners, in eastern Zaire, seems to suggest that, indeed, beauty is in the eye of the beholder. Efe women are seen to be sexy because of hair on their chests, but in Western societies women are constantly bombarded with advertising telling them how they can more effectively get rid of body hair. Perhaps then, as Naomi Wolf (1991) argues in *The Beauty Myth*, there is no such thing as universal beauty. Women depicted as beautiful in the paintings of Rubens in the seventeenth century would be considered too fat by contemporary standards, as would even Marilyn Monroe and other glamour queens of the 1960s. Both male and female fashion models today, who are tall and thin, would have been considered ugly in some other eras.

However, although there is considerable cultural variation in notions of beauty, we can also discover some consistencies, particularly in judgments of facial features. One proposition, pioneered by the creative genius Francis Galton (1878), is that "averageness" is beautiful. Galton created composite faces by superimposing photographs one on top of another. He found that the result was a more attractive face than any of the originals. Modern researchers using computer–generated composite faces have found supporting evidence (Langlois & Roggman, 1990). But further research has shown that at least for English and Japanese college students, a composite of very attractive faces is judged to be more appealing than a composite of moderately attractive faces (Perrett, May, & Yoshikana, 1994).

Studies of attractiveness using international faces (Cunningham, 1986) suggest that "baby-face" features—a small nose, small chin, large and widely separated eyes—are thought to be attractive in both men and women. One could argue that these preferred features are all indicators of good health and thus good potential as a mate. This idea seems to be supported by an intriguing study by Devendra Singh (1993) on waist-to-hip ratios of women and their perceived attractiveness to men. Earlier studies had reported a gradual trend toward the idealization of thinness among American women since the 1960s (Garner, Garfinkel, Schwartz, & Thompson, 1980). But Singh (1993) argued that despite changes over time in American ideals of beauty in women, a lower waist-to-hip ratio has consistently been seen as more attractive, and this is because a low ratio indicates health, youth, and higher reproductive potential in women. Singh studied data for body measurements of Miss America contest winners from 1923 to 1987 and for *Playboy* centerfolds between 1955 and 1965 and 1976 and 1990. He found that in spite of the reduction in body weight over the years, the waist-to-hip ratio of these women remained low and within a narrow range. Singh also showed that men ranging in age from 25 to 85 years old perceive women with lower waist-to-hip ratios as more attractive, suggesting that this preference goes across several generations.

Singh and other sociobiologists may be correct in proposing that indicators of reproductive potential are associated with ideals of beauty. It may even be that some indicators of health are used in many different cultures. But beyond these very basic similarities, there are enormous cross-cultural variations in particulars. For example, small feet were so admired at one time in China that foot binding was practiced (Curtin, 1975). The young girl's feet were so tightly bound as to prevent normal growth. By adulthood, the woman would have "dainty" but useless feet, and would need to be moved from place to place by servants. The dainty-footed Chinese beauty would be considered a cripple by most people today. Female circumcision, still practiced in about 40 countries, is another example of a custom that is supposed to enhance the appeal and worth of women (Slack, 1988). Naomi Wolf (1991) and other feminist critics have argued that more subtle but nevertheless powerful biases are also inherent in Western societies, with the result that images of "beauty" continue to be used to control and limit women.

Even among young people in one culture, there are variations in what turns people on (Baldwin et al., 1996). John Bargh and his associates showed an extreme example of this in their study of men who sexually harass women (Bargh, Raymond, Pryor, & Strack, 1995). They showed that for men who are more likely to harass, there is a stronger association between attraction to a female and exercising power over her. Other research suggests that these "bad guys" are not winners with women (Jensen-Campbell, Graziano, & West, 1995). Men who showed themselves to be more prosocial were rated as more attractive and sexy (Jensen-Campbell, Graziano, & West, 1995), and men who communicate well are also seen as more attractive (Sprecher & Duck, 1994). Good news: Nice guys do not finish last in attracting women.

Concepts and Issues

Interpersonal attraction is facilitated by three key factors: physical proximity, similarity, and attractiveness. The influence of proximity seems to be common to many cultures. The influence of similarity and attractiveness is more varied across cultures, first, because the criteria used for assessing similarity and attractiveness vary considerably across cultures, and second, because traditionally it has been males who enjoy the power to choose women using such criteria as attractiveness. The influence of these three factors extends to both friendship and romantic love.

1. What is the role of proximity in intimate relationships?
2. What is the contact hypothesis?
3. Describe the mere exposure effect.
4. Does the evidence support similarity–attraction, opposites–attract, or dissimilarity–repulsion? Discuss.
5. Does being physically attractive bring advantages or disadvantages? Explain.

Conclusion

Intimate relationships, including friendships and romantic love, are found in all human societies. However, local norms and rules influence such relationships so they are in important ways different across cultures. In accounting for intimate relationships, social exchange theory, equity theory, and sociobiology have depicted people as self-centered, rational, and attempting to maximize the survival of their own genes. These explanations are appealing in limited ways but do not seem viable for explaining many human experiences of friendship and love, both within and across cultures. However, some aspects of intimate relationships do seem to be universal. All such relationships involve changes in physiological state and an interpretation of such changes according to local rules and norms. Similarity–attraction seems to be universal, and some gender differences in mate selection are common to many cultures.

For Review

The major theories of interpersonal attraction tend to assume we are self-centered and rational in our behavior. Exchange theories assume that we try to maximize our profits during the give and take of social relations; equity theories adopt a similar orientation; and the various balance theories assume that people are motivated to maintain balance in their relationships with others. Sociobiological theories seem particularly useful for outlining the very broad framework in which cultural practices and social behavior evolve.

The nature of friendship and love is ultimately best understood in a cultural context. Although the idea of romantic love is found in most societies, the belief that for everyone marriage should follow romantic love is pervasive only in modern Western societies.

The role of culture can be further identified by considering two major stages in the experience of love: an increase in physiological arousal and a labeling of that arousal according to the normative system of a culture. A number of studies suggest that physiological arousal due to one source can be misattributed to another source, and this evidence underlines the plasticity of the experience we call love.

A close examination of mate selection in Western and non-Western societies suggests that three factors play a key role: proximity, similarity, and attraction. Although they probably play a similar role in all cultures, how these three factors are defined varies considerably across cultures.

For Discussion

1. How does sociobiology explain gender differences in intimate relationships?
2. Discuss the relationship between individualism and modern romantic love.
3. What is the role of culture in the two-component model of emotion?
4. What seem to be some universal and local aspects of physical beauty?

Key Terms

Balance theory *264*

Contact hypothesis *279*

Dissimilarity-repulsion hypothesis *284*

Halo effect *286*

Mere exposure effect *281*

Opposites-attract hypothesis *284*

Similarity-attraction hypothesis *283*

Social exchange theory *262*

Sociobiology *266*

Triangular model of love *265*

Two-component model of emotion *274*

Annotated Readings

For general overviews of research on intimate relationships, see S. Brehm, *Intimate relationships*, 2nd ed. (New York: McGraw–Hill, 1992); and S. S. Hendrick and C. Hendrick, *Liking, loving, and relating* (Pacific Grove, CA: Brooks/Cole, 1992).

More focused discussions on romantic love are E. Hatfield and R. L. Rapson, *Love, sex, and intimacy: Their psychology, biology, and history* (New York: HarperCollins, 1993); C. Hendrick and S. S. Hendrick, *Romantic love* (Newbury Park, CA: Sage, 1993); R. J. Sternberg and M. L. Barnes, eds., *The psychology of love* (New Haven, CT: Yale University Press, 1988); and A. Walsh, *The science of love: Understanding love and its effects on mind and body* (Buffalo, NY: Prometheus Books, 1991).

Related to romantic love are the discussions on concepts of beauty in K. A. Callaghan, ed., *Ideals in feminine beauty* (Westport, CT: Greenwood Press, 1994).

For examples of research studies on intimate relationships, see the *Journal of Social and Personal Relationships* and *Personal Relationships*.

CHAPTER **9**

Altruism

◀ A member of the famous French group, Doctors Without Borders, at work in Somalia in 1992. Human beings show an enormous range of social behavior, with altruism being at the extreme positive end. Some people make tremendous sacrifices to help others in need, sometimes traveling thousands of miles to places that are foreign to them to assist people they have never met before and who they will never see again. Such behavior is particularly striking when, as is very often the case, the help provider is from a Western capitalist society, where competitiveness and materialism are emphasized and where looking out for "number one" is supposed to be the norm.

During the early 1980s, I worked on several United Nations projects designed to get food and supplies to refugees in the Near East. The Soviet invasion of Afghanistan caused millions of Afghan men, women, and children to flee across the southern Afghan border into Pakistan and Iran. It was clear that the refugees pouring in from the north faced very difficult conditions in the harsh environment of that region. They were far from home, without food or shelter, and lacked even the most basic equipment needed to make a new start. However, there was help at hand. Through the World Food Programme and other international organizations, refugee camps were established, food and medical supplies were made available, and support was provided for millions of people.

As I stood on the Afghan border during a particularly bad sandstorm, watching thousands of refugees struggling toward the emergency camps, I found myself asking, "Why do people from the other side of the world send help to other people—people they will never meet?" "Why do people in New York, London, or Paris, for example, contribute to organizations that provide help to people in the developing world?" One of the merits of raising this question is that it highlights the fact that even in the context of competitive and individualistic Western societies, people do help one another in many circumstances.

The traditional approach in discussions of *altruism*, behavior intended to help others, is to ask, "Why do people *not* act altruistically?" Perhaps this bias is inevitable, given the contemporary emphasis in North America on individual rights rather than obligations and duties (Moghaddam, 1997a, Chapter 7). The political scientist Robert Putnam (1995) has pointed out that in the United States people are participating less in community and voluntary organizations, a trend that is associated with a decline in voluntarism and trust generally.

Between 1965 and 1995, the proportion of people in the United States saying that most people can be trusted fell from 54 to 35 percent, and those who believed the government can be trusted to do the right thing most of the time fell from 76 to 25 percent (Morain & Balz, 1996). At the same time, the gap between the top money earners and the rest of the population has been increasing in the United States (Frank & Cook, 1995), even more so than in Europe (Burtless & Smeeding, 1995). White-collar crime and dirty business have become common in both public and private organizations (Punch, 1996). Such cultural changes in the United States are associated with a skepticism toward prosocial behavior among researchers. Many doubt if altruism exists.

I adopt a more positive approach, because people still *do* continue to help others. It is insightful to ask, "Why *do* people show altruism toward others?" After all, modern Western societies are typically described as competitive and individualistic. From this perspective, it should surprise us that people do help others.

The Many Faces of Altruism

Altruism is behavior intended to help another, without regard for benefit to oneself. One of the challenges inherent in this definition is how we should define "benefit." In some cases, it is easy. If Charlan climbs up a tree to rescue a neighbor's cat in order to get the $100 reward offered by the owner, then a monetary benefit has been received for help given. But suppose Charlan climbs up the tree, rescues the cat, and then refuses to take the reward. Would this be true altruism? Not necessarily, because she may intend to benefit from the good opinion the neighbor now has of her. "What a wonderful person Charlan is," the neighbor will tell everyone. Now, what if Charlan does take the $100 reward but gives it as an anonymous donation to charity? Surely this will count as true altruism? No—again, an objection can be raised, for Charlan may intend to "benefit" from the self-satisfaction she feels at having made a charitable donation. "What a wonderful person I am," she may say to herself, as she glows in self-praise.

The question of whether true altruism does exist can lead to philosophical and theological issues far beyond the scope of this text. For our purposes, it is sufficient to note that helping others is often associated with benefits for the self. The key difference between opposing camps of researchers is the issue of whether there is more to helping behavior than just these benefits:

> Advocates of *universal egoism* claim that everything we do, no matter how noble and beneficial to others, is really directed toward the ultimate goal of self-benefit. Advocates of *altruism* do not deny that the motivation of much of what we do, including much of what we do for others is egoistic. But they claim there is more. They claim that, at least under some circumstances, we are capable of a qualitatively different form of motivation, motivation with an ultimate goal of benefitting someone else. (Batson & Oleson, 1991)

One of the themes of this chapter is that despite the intensely competitive climate of contemporary Western societies, people do help others in many situations. Indeed, as we shall see, researchers have generally neglected the vast range of voluntary helping behaviors.

Heroic and Nurturant Altruism

Human beings help one another in many different ways. Consider some of the aspects of altruism illustrated in Figure 9–1. Altruism can be shown by a person toward a stranger, or a group of strangers, or toward family and friends, or by one group toward another. Help is sometimes provided for a short time, as when an injured passenger is pulled out of a derailed train, and in other situations for a much longer time, as when an AIDS sufferer is helped through the last years of life.

altruism   behavior intended to help another, without regard for benefit to oneself.

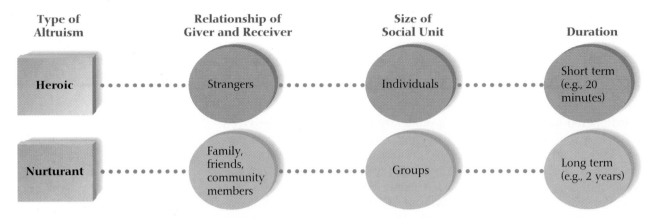

Type of Altruism	Relationship of Giver and Receiver	Size of Social Unit	Duration
Heroic	Strangers	Individuals	Short term (e.g., 20 minutes)
Nurturant	Family, friends, community members	Groups	Long term (e.g., 2 years)

Figure 9–1 Two types of altruism.

Rescuers pulling a passenger from a derailed train may be putting their own lives at risk and engaging in *heroic* intervention, whereas those people who provide support to AIDS sufferers are engaged in *nurturant* intervention.

These variations by no means exhaust the many different ways in which humans show altruism, but social psychological research has focused a great deal on why individuals do *not* help. The question is obviously important in the context of modern Western urban centers, where people routinely find themselves in situations in which others who are strangers to them seem to be in crisis. The emergencies often involve sudden illness, fire, robbery or mugging, automobile accidents, or rape or other violent attacks. Typically, these emergencies require what I'll refer to as heroic altruism (coming to the assistance of a mugging victim) rather than nurturant altruism (providing sympathetic help for someone who has lost a close family member).

Heroic altruism is often short term, requires physical action, and is public, or "visible." Most important, heroic altruism does not commit the helper to a long-term relationship. A person who runs into a smoke-filled house to save some strangers is not committed to stay and develop long-term relationships with the fire victims. **Nurturant altruism,** on the other hand, requires a longer involvement, tends to be private rather than public, and is passive in the sense that the help-giver may spend more time listening and sympathizing than taking decisive action.

In the context of traditional values, heroic altruism tends to fit a more masculine gender role, whereas nuturant altruism is a closer fit for a traditional feminine gender role. Classic Hollywood movies show a male hero crashing through burning doors, disarming villains, chasing runaway horses, and even flying "faster than a speeding bullet." The vast majority of research so far has focused on this kind of altruism. Not surprisingly, this has meant that men have been found to show more altruism than women (Eagly & Crowley, 1986).

heroic altruism altruism that is often short term, requires physical action, and is public, or "visible."

nurturant altruism altruism that requires long-term involvement, tends to be private rather than public, and is passive rather than active.

This American woman taking part in a Habitat for Humanity house-building project in Atlanta, Georgia, and this Indian woman ladling food for the poor are both helping needy people in their communities. Do the similarities in their behavior suggest that true altruism exists and is present in both Western and non–Western cultures? I believe it does, but most researchers disagree. True altruism requires that the helper assist others without expecting anything in return. Perhaps the American woman is taking part in the Habitat for Humanity project in order to put it on her résumé and increase her chances of getting into graduate school. Perhaps the Indian woman is giving food to the poor in the hope of being reincarnated into a better life. One of the challenges for experimental social psychologists has been to design studies that enable us to test such questions.

The Kitty Genovese Murder: Prototype for Altruism Research

To appreciate the focus on heroic altruism, it is useful to review briefly the seminal contributions of Bib Latané and John Darley (1970) and an event that more than any other stimulated research in this area—the murder of Kitty Genovese in 1963 (we discuss aspects of this research in Chapter 2). Kitty Genovese, on the way home from work, was attacked while walking the short distance from her car to her apartment in

Queens, New York. The time was the early hours of the morning. Her attacker stabbed her, but ran off when her screams brought a response from neighbors.

What kind of a response? Some residents did turn on their lights, and someone seems to have shouted from a window, but little else happened. After things quieted down, the attacker came back and resumed his assault. Again the victim, too weak to get away, called for help, and again the attacker became frightened and ran off. But help did not come. The attacker returned, and this time killed the young woman.

Why had the neighbors not helped Kitty Genovese? Almost 40 of them had been aware of the attack, which lasted about the same number of minutes. Yet not one person had taken the trouble to call the police until after the victim was dead. The story was carried in most major newspapers and discussed at length by experts. Latané and Darley were dissatisfied with the available explanations and proposed a novel way of interpreting such tragic events. Their interpretation was centered on two related concepts: **pluralistic ignorance,** whereby bystanders assume nothing is wrong because other people present seem to see nothing wrong, and **diffusion of responsibility,** a decrease in the sense of responsibility felt by each person in association with the number of people present.

pluralistic ignorance when bystanders assume nothing is wrong because other people present seem to see nothing wrong.

diffusion of responsibility a decrease in the sense of responsibility felt by each person in association with the number of people present in a situation.

Pluralistic Ignorance.   To understand the concept of pluralistic ignorance, it is useful to ask: "How do we know what the right thing to do is in any given social situation?" Imagine you are invited for dinner to the family home of a person you have recently met. You like your new friend a great deal and want to make a positive impression on the family. When you arrive as a guest at your new friend's home, do you

1. Say hello and march straight into the kitchen?
2. Tell your host you have had a tiring day and need to use the master bedroom for a snooze?
3. Take off your clothes and take a shower?
4. Follow the cues given by your host as to where you should sit to socialize while waiting for dinner?

If you do 1, 2, or 3, you are very unlikely to be invited to that house again. There are clear rules for the behavior of guests (e.g., guests should not enter bedrooms uninvited), and when guests are unsure about what they are supposed to do, they look to the host to provide cues. Throughout the process of becoming socialized in a particular culture, we acquire the skills to "read" social situations and to recognize the appropriate behavior. For example, if you are invited to a home in Japan or in many other "traditional" societies (including most Islamic societies), the first thing you do as you enter is take off your shoes. Becoming a social being involves becoming socially skilled in such practices.

But a special feature of many emergencies is that, by definition, they involve unexpected and unusual situations that we have never or rarely personally experienced before. Very few of us have witnessed an

In modern societies, specialists are expected to help solve problems: Police tackle crime, firefighters fight fires and sometimes unexpected natural disasters, social workers provide assistance to the economically and socially deprived, medical professionals help save lives. The prevalence of specialization and specialists may be one reason why people tend not to offer help to others, like this Mexico City woman begging on the street. This firefighter is expected to save the little girl, as he has done, because it is "his job." Research suggests that the presence of others inhibits the likelihood of anyone offering help if the cues for action are ambiguous, and everyone looks to everyone else for guidelines as to what to do.

attack by a knife–wielding killer. When we do suddenly find ourselves in such a situation, we often do not know how to interpret what is hap–pening (Is this really an emergency, or kids playing a game, or some drunks play–acting?) or what course of action to take (Should I ignore them? Call the police? Try to intervene?). Consequently, we look to other people, and use their behavior as a guide. Of course, while we are looking at them, they are also watching us for clues. This suggests that in ambiguous situations, there is a greater likelihood of the **bystander effect.** That is, the presence of others can actually decrease the likeli–hood of anyone taking action, because each person is looking to the other people in the situation for guidance.

bystander effect   the fact that the presence of others can actually decrease the likelihood of one person acting, because each person is looking to the others in the situation for guidance.

Research results have confirmed the bystander effect. In a situation in which one person in an elevator "accidentally" dropped something on the floor, the half–dozen other passengers would look around but were less likely to offer help than if there was only one other passenger (Latané & Dabbs, 1975). Similarly, when people engaged in completing a questionnaire heard a female researcher apparently have an accident and call for help, they offered help 70 percent of the time if they were alone but only 40 percent of the time if they were in the company of another participant (Latané & Rodin, 1969). In each of these cases, those who were in the company of others looked to these others for guidance on how to interpret the situation, and consequently became less helpful, because the other participants were also looking to them for cues.

If the ambiguity of a situation influences helping behavior in this way, then people should be more likely to provide help in situations in which others provide unambiguous guidance for action. This idea is supported by a number of studies in which, for example, people are found to be more likely to donate blood if they have just observed another person volunteer to donate blood (Rushton & Campbell, 1977), and more likely to stop to help a stranded motorist if they have just witnessed another person stop to help (Bryan & Test, 1967). Evidence also suggests that when the call for help is unambiguous, and when we can clearly see that others present also recognize the call for help, we are more likely to offer help (Solomon, Solomon, & Stone, 1978). Thus, the presence of others only inhibits the likelihood of our offering help if the cues for action are ambiguous and everyone in the situation looks to everyone else for guidelines as to what to do.

The concept of pluralistic ignorance highlights the *social and shared* basis of our behavior. What we come to see as appropriate behavior is derived from the behavior of others, and we come to share ideas about what we should do in particular situations. One consequence of such perceptions is a diffusion of responsibility.

Diffusion of Responsibility. Imagine you are a participant in a psychology experiment purportedly designed to find out about your views on personal issues. In order for you to be able to speak in confidence, you are seated in a cubicle. As you interact with other participants via an intercom system, one of them seems to experience a seizure. He gasps and calls for help. What would you do? Would you rush out of the cubicle and try to help him?

Darley and Latané (1968) found that participants were far more likely to help if they thought they were the only other person in the experiment. When a person was led to believe there were more than two participants, and thus other people who could hear the call for help, the likelihood of help being provided decreased. Why was this? One possibility is that when participants thought that other people were also aware of the call for help, they felt less personal responsibility because the responsibility was shared by others and thus diffused. Another possibility is that when participants thought that others were also aware of the call for help, they looked to these others as guides and would not offer help if nobody else seemed to see it as appropriate in such a situation.

Reassessing Bystander Research. The research of Latané and Darley (1970) stimulated a great deal of interest in helping behavior and influenced hundreds of social psychological studies in this area (for a review, see Schroeder, Penner, Dovidio, & Piliavin, 1995). The prototypic bystander–intervention study, inspired by the Kitty Genovese killing, involved heroic altruism. That is, strangers would find themselves in a situation in which someone seemed to need the help of the other(s), and such help typically involved short-term heroic intervention. In many of the studies the participants were male and the person needing help was female (experiment titles such as "lady in distress" reflect this trend; see Latané & Rodin, 1969). Of course, the fact that heroic altruism entails strangers and short–term duration means that the laboratory seems to be an ideal study setting. After all, the typical laboratory study involves strangers coming together for brief interactions. Although naturalistic field studies were conducted in the 1960s (see Bryan & Test, 1967), it was not until decades later that a sufficient number of such studies showed that helping behavior in the laboratory is often very different from that in the field (Spacapan & Oskamp, 1992). We discuss such differences later in this chapter.

Concepts and Issues

Research has focused on heroic altruism, using bystander intervention as the research prototype. A bystander effect has been found, presumably because there is a diffusion of responsibility when other people are also present. The neglect of nurturant altruism reflects a cultural bias in the research.

1. What are some of the difficulties in defining altruism?
2. What is heroic altruism? Nurturant altruism?
3. Describe the prototype procedure for studies on altruism.

Explaining Altruism: A Pessimistic Bias

From the outset, the attention of researchers was riveted on dramatic cases in which strangers failed to show heroic altruism toward someone in distress. Given this orientation, perhaps it is not surprising that the model developed by Latané and Darley (1970) focused on factors that would lead a bystander *not* to help.

As Figure 9–2 illustrates, in order for help to be offered, the bystander has to

1. Notice that something is wrong (hear someone cry out).
2. Interpret the situation as one requiring intervention (decide that "that was a cry for help, and someone should intervene").
3. Take personal responsibility (decide that "I had better do something").
4. Know the appropriate action to take ("The correct thing to do here is to call the police").
5. Take appropriate helping action (make the call to the police).

Having the social skills to read the situation correctly and take appropriate action is the key to Latané and Darley's model, which is really a descriptive model of how and when social rules are appropriately followed.

Subsequent models of helping behavior can be divided into two very broad categories: social/cultural models and sociobiological

Figure 9–2 The process of bystander intervention (after Latané & Darley, 1970).

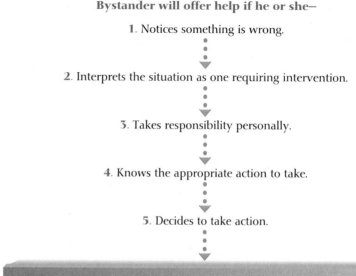

Bystander will offer help if he or she—

1. Notices something is wrong.

2. Interprets the situation as one requiring intervention.

3. Takes responsibility personally.

4. Knows the appropriate action to take.

5. Decides to take action.

All of these steps must be completed in order for help to be provided.

models. Among these, only a few can be described as "optimistic," in the sense that they assume people help others primarily because they want to improve the situations of those they help. The majority of the models have a pessimistic bias, and assume we offer help for basically selfish reasons.

Social / Cultural Explanations

The majority of explanations of altruism favored by social psychologists have a social and/or cultural basis (Figure 9–3) (see e.g., Batson, 1991; Clark, 1991). We begin by considering these social/cultural explanations, moving from those that assume people to be self-centered to those that assume people to be genuinely concerned about improving the lot of others.

social exchange theory theory of social behavior based on the assumption that during social interactions people keep track of inputs and outcomes and attempt to maximize their profits.

Social exchange theory is based on the assumption that during social interactions people maintain an account of their inputs and outcomes and attempt to maximize their profits (Homans, 1961, 1974; Thibaut & Kelley, 1959). A useful way to remember the basic proposition of the theory is through the phrase *mini-max*: Individuals attempt to *minimize* their inputs and *maximize* their outcomes. People are assumed to be selfish even when they offer help to others, because they provide help only when they expect an adequate return. Social psychologists offer a variety of social exchange explanations to account for altruistic behavior.

arousal cost-reward model theory that people are aroused by the suffering and distress of others and will try to relieve that arousal by helping the distressed person using the least costly and most rewarding means.

Do We Help Others in Order to Make Ourselves Feel Better? According to the **arousal cost–reward model** (Piliavin, Dovidio, Gaertner, & Clark, 1981), people are aroused by the suffering and distress of

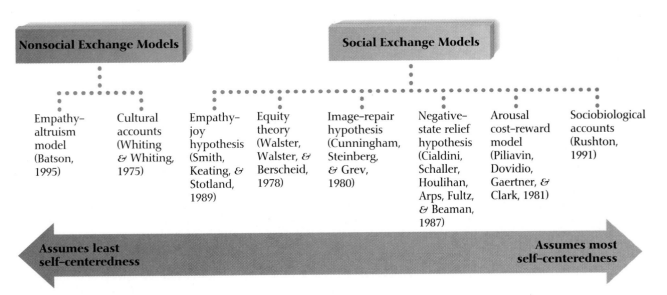

Figure 9–3 The major social/cultural explanations of altruism, on a continuum of least to most self-centeredness.

others (see Figure 9–4). *When attributed to the other person's needs,* such arousal can be unpleasant, and in such cases people will try to alleviate the unpleasantness by helping the person in distress. But in trying to lessen their own discomfort, people will choose the least costly and most rewarding means. For example, a passerby who hears cries for help and notices a house on fire will be aroused by the distress of those trapped inside the house. The method adopted by the passerby to relieve his arousal, whether he tries to pull the victims from the fire himself or whether he summons the fire department, will depend on his assessment of what the costs ("I may get hurt myself") and rewards ("People will see me as a hero") would be.

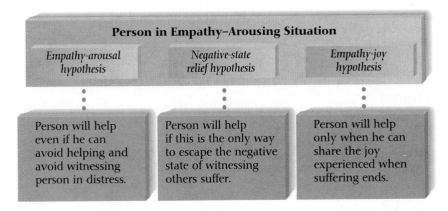

Figure 9–4 Conditions for helping under various models.

There is some empirical evidence to suggest that under some conditions empathic arousal is associated with increased help offered to a person in distress, and the likelihood of help being offered does increase if the costs to the helper are lower (Dovidio, Piliavin, Gaertner, Schroeder, & Clark, 1991). A series of experiments has been conducted to test the arousal cost–reward model and to compare it with the most important optimistic altruism model, the empathy–altruism hypothesis (Batson, 1990, 1991).

empathy-altruism hypothesis
hypothesis that when people feel empathy, they become motivated to act, with the ultimate goal of helping the person for whom empathy is felt.

The **empathy–altruism hypothesis** proposes that when people feel empathy, they become motivated to act, *with the ultimate goal of benefiting the person for whom empathy is felt.* Daniel Batson (1991, 1995), perhaps the leading champion of an optimistic view of human nature in social psychology, has pointed out that the empathy–altruism hypothesis is proposing something of fundamental importance because

> not only does it contradict the common assumption in psychology that all motivation is ultimately directed toward the egoistic goal of increasing our own welfare, but it also contradicts the underlying assumption that human nature is fundamentally self-serving. (p. 63)

To test this optimistic view against the more pessimistic arousal cost–reward model, a series of studies employ the tactic of varying the ease of escape for those witnessing a person in distress (Batson, 1987). If the motivation of participants is simply to avoid arousal at the lowest cost to themselves, they should opt to escape without helping the person in distress. In the typical experiment, participants witness a "worker" (actually a confederate of the experimenter) engaged in a task and receiving electric shocks. The worker is described as having values that are similar (high empathy) or dissimilar (low empathy) to those of the participant. It quickly becomes obvious that the worker is under considerable stress. Participants are given the opportunity to help the worker by taking the shocks themselves.

To manipulate the ease of escape from this empathy-arousing situation, some participants are told that if they do not help, they will not observe the worker take shocks any longer (escape possible); others are told they will continue to observe (no escape). Thus, participants have either high or low empathy with a worker receiving electric shocks in a situation in which they can or cannot avoid watching the person in distress. As expected by the empathy–altruism hypothesis, those in the high-empathy situation tend to help the victim, *even when the escape option is open to them and they could have not helped and also avoid watching the person in distress.* This finding suggests there is more to helping others than just self-interest.

negative-state relief hypothesis
hypothesis that feeling empathy for someone in distress involves a temporary feeling of sadness and that people are motivated to relieve that sadness by mood-enhancing experiences, like helping others and feeling good about doing it.

The "Good Mood" Motive.   Another influential egoistical account of helping behavior, the negative-state relief hypothesis, is proposed by Robert Cialdini and his associates (Cialdini, Schaller, Houlihan, Arps, Fultz, & Beaman, 1987; Schaller & Cialdini, 1988). The **negative-state relief hypothesis** states that feeling empathy for a person in distress involves a temporary feeling of sadness and that people are motivated to relieve such sadness by mood–enhancing experiences. One way to enhance one's mood is through the positive social and self–evaluations that follow helping other people. Mariam sees Joe struggling to make a few dollars by panhandling. She feels sad about this, particularly because she knows Joe has AIDS. She gives Joe $5 and feels happier.

However, since according to the negative–state relief hypothesis people's foremost objective is to enhance their own mood, when they are offered the opportunity to improve their mood through means other than helping, they should take the less costly route. In one study participants who had the option to be entertained by a comedy show did not tend to offer help to a person in distress. In another manipulation, participants were told that because they had taken a mood–fixing drug, helping would not enhance their mood. In this condition, those experiencing high empathy for the person in distress tended not to offer help. Although these results suggest that participants offered help only when they thought it was the only way to improve their own mood, other studies have obtained quite different results, and tend to support Batson's more optimistic view of altruism (Schroeder, Dovidio, Sibicky, Mathews, & Allen, 1988).

It is not surprising that it has proved challenging to test competing predictions from the empathy–altruism hypothesis and the negative–state relief hypothesis. Both hypotheses agree that individuals feeling empathy for someone in need are likely to feel sad, and that following helping, these individuals are likely to feel happier. The subtle point of dispute is the motivation underlying helping: The empathy–altruism model proposes that people are motivated *to improve the situation of others*, whereas the negative–state relief hypothesis proposes that individuals help others *in order to get in a more positive mood themselves*.

The "Good Image" Motive.   The negative–state relief hypothesis, then, proposes that the negative effect of witnessing someone in distress can be overcome by various methods of mood enhancement. A similar idea is put forward by the **image–repair hypothesis,** which assumes that people want to have a positive social image, and their social image is "damaged" when they harm another person (Cunningham, Shaffer, Barbee, & Kelley, 1990; Cunningham, Steinberg, & Grev, 1980). In order to repair such damage, a person will do good deeds; but the target of such favors need not be the person who was harmed in the first place. For example, Joe accidentally kicks over a box of carefully organized class notes Bill was using to study for tomorrow's exam. Following this incident, Joe tries to repair his damaged image by offering to do the shopping for the week for everyone else in his house. This good deed does not help Bill specifically, but it does present Joe as a "good guy" again.

> image-repair hypothesis
> hypothesis that people want to have a positive self-image, that their social image is damaged when they harm someone, and that they will do good deeds to repair their image.

The Justice Motive.   The image of the person as self-centered and exchange-oriented is also presented by a number of theories centered on the theme of equity or fairness (see Taylor & Moghaddam, 1994,

equity theory   theory that conceptualizes human relationships as a form of economic exchange and assumes that people are motivated to achieve equitable relationships and will be unhappy with inequity even when they benefit from the situation.

just-world hypothesis   the hypothesis that people are motivated to see the world as just, and that this can lead to a lack of helping, as when a victim is seen as not deserving help.

Chapter 5). But according to **equity theory,** self-centeredness manifests itself in subtle ways (Walster, Walster, & Berscheid, 1978). It is proposed that people are motivated to achieve equitable relationships and will be unhappy when there is inequity, *even if they personally benefit from the situation.* However, by psychologically manipulating the value of how much they put into a relationship and how much they get out of it, even an objectively inequitable relationship can be perceived as just. For example, even though Pete has not received a pay increase for years, his millionaire boss refuses to help him, arguing that middle managers like Pete make very little contribution to the success of the company.

Justice theories generally assume that people are motivated to see the world as just, and a counterintuitive prediction is that this can lead to a lack of helping. Mel Lerner's (1977, 1980, 1991) **just-world hypothesis** proposes that rape victims are often blamed for the violent attack they have experienced ("She should not have been out that time of night." "What does she expect when she goes into a bar wearing a dress like that?"), because people are motivated to see the victim as the "problem." Blaming the victim implies that the individual does not deserve help and that the world is actually just.

In the 1990s, there has been more focus on cultural aspects of the justice motive. Justice is seen to be served when people get what they are entitled to, and entitlements are based on ideas about rights and obligations of people in different roles (Lerner, 1991). Of course, such ideas vary across cultures, as well as over time in any one culture. When I attended boarding school in London in the 1960s, it was generally accepted that boys who misbehaved deserved to be physically beaten (yes, I did misbehave). Teachers applying the same physical punishment today would probably be arrested and charged with assault.

Albert Pepitone and Kathleen L'Armand (1997) have argued that justice is seen to be served when bad things happen to bad people and good things to good people. When scenarios of life events involving good/bad people and outcomes were presented to students in the United States, they did see justice as predicted (Pepitone & L'Armand, 1996). Studies with Korean (Hong, 1997) and African-American (Starr, Sloan, & Kudrick, 1997) participants support this general finding, although they also indicate some cross-cultural differences.

An example of such differences is found in a study that also incorporated the distinction between the outcome people *should* receive and the outcome people *will* receive (Lee, Pepitone, & Albright, 1997). Both Chinese and U.S. participants believed that good people should receive better outcomes than they will receive. However, whereas the Chinese participants believed bad people should receive worse outcomes than they will receive, the U.S. participants believed bad people should receive better outcomes than they will receive. One interpretation of this is that Americans were more tolerant of bad behavior; another is that they believe bad behavior has been punished too severely in the past.

Although equity theory and the just-world hypothesis are concerned with justice, at the same time they assume that people pursue self-interest. It is exactly in order to better serve their self-interest that people are seen to need an agreed-upon set of justice rules. Because exactly what is a just outcome is defined subjectively, helping behavior can be shaped to maximize self-interest.

But the distortion of justice need not always be motivated by self-interest; experimental studies suggest it can also arise from empathy for others (Batson, Klein, Highberger, & Shaw, 1995). For example, in one study, female student participants showed an "unjust" preference in reward allocation for another female student who reported that she was suffering because of the breakup of a romantic relationship. In another study, male and female students showed preferential treatment for a child suffering from a muscle-paralyzing disease, even though this meant less favorable treatment for other ill children. Clearly, in a situation in which resources are scarce, helping another person gain access to resources is both altruistic and unjust; it both helps another person and gives that person an "unfair" advantage. Research findings also suggest that people in collectivistic cultures give more priority to equality when distributing rewards than do the members of individualistic societies (Leung & Bond, 1984).

Of course, a justice motive can also lead people to enormous self-sacrifice. A sense of duty and a strong belief in justice were partly what moved those who helped protect Jews from Nazi persecution during World War II, at the risk of their own lives (Oliner & Oliner, 1988).

Empathy-Altruism Model. The most influential social model that does not assume we are guided primarily by calculation and self-centered motives is Batson's (1991, 1995) empathy-altruism model. What makes this model different from all others is that it proposes that there *is* true altruism. Batson (1994) differentiates among four motives for prosocial behavior:

Egoism—behavior ultimately intended to benefit the self (Liam does charity work in order to win votes)

Collectivism—behavior intended to benefit the group (Liam does charity work in order to benefit the community)

Altruism—behavior intended to benefit others without regard for benefit to oneself (Liam does charity work in order to help others)

Principlism—behavior intended to uphold a principle (Liam does charity work because he believes the rich have a duty to help the poor)

These motives can sometimes conflict: Participants in studies provided help to those in need, even when this meant a violation of fairness (Batson, Batson, Todd, & Brummett, 1995; Batson, Klein, Highberger, & Shaw, 1995). Parents sometimes allocate family resources to a child in need of extra help, even though this means their other children receive an "unfairly" smaller piece of the pie.

Although seeing others in distress can put us in a bad mood, and attempts at helping others can improve our mood, beyond such self-centered consideration we help others for the sake of bettering *their* situation (Batson, 1991; Batson & Weeks, 1996). Batson and his associates have shown experimental support for this optimistic model by demonstrating that empathically aroused participants will help a person in distress, even when they could improve their own moods by other means without bearing the cost of providing help (see Batson, 1995, for a review). Indeed, people help others even when unsuccessful help makes them feel worse.

Sharing Others' Joy.   But what if people help others in order to share the *joy* of the needy person's relief? Emma helps Charles to prepare for his final examination at law school because she is motivated to share the joy when Charles learns he has passed. This is just the interpretation proposed by the **empathy–joy hypothesis** (Smith, Keating, & Stotland, 1989): People are less likely to offer help when they will not receive feedback on the effect of their helping, or when the likelihood of the needy person's improvement is low. This is because when there is no feedback, the helper cannot share the joy of the needy person's relief. Also, it is only possible to share the joy if the needy person's situation actually does improve.

Some experimental evidence does support this position (Smith, Keating, & Stotland, 1989), although a number of other studies suggest it is wrong. They demonstrate that empathically aroused participants select to get feedback from a person in distress irrespective of the likelihood that the distressed person's situation is improved (Batson, Batson, Slingsby, Harrell, Peekna, & Todd, 1991). Once again, the more optimistic view of Batson's empathy–altruism model seems truer to life. When volunteers are concerned about the plight of a town struck by a hurricane, they typically do not stop helping if communications break down and they get no feedback, or even if they learn that the chance of the victims surviving has decreased and a human tragedy has become unavoidable.

Do We Help Others Because of Genetics?

Imagine you are on a cruise and suddenly hear warning sirens, followed by an announcement from the ship's captain that everyone must abandon ship. You rush to the deck and find very few spaces left on the remaining lifeboats. With you are your only child, your cousin, a more distant and older relative, a friend, and a recent acquaintance. Whom would you select as having priority to get on the lifeboat? If you are like most of the other people I have presented this scenario to, you will give first priority to your child. Sociobiologists propose that you will show this bias because your child is genetically most similar to you than are the others (Rushton, 1988, 1989, 1991). Sociobiological accounts of altruism have gained considerable influence, just as they have influenced the

---

empathy–joy hypothesis
hypothesis that people are less likely to offer help when they will not be able to share the joy of the needy person's relief, or when the likelihood of improvement is low.

way social psychologists view other major domains of behavior, such as liking and loving (Chapter 8) and aggression (Chapter 11).

At first glance, helping behavior might seem to contradict basic evolutionary ideas. After all, the concept of survival of the fittest might be taken to imply that all individuals are in a state of continual competition and that there is no role for helping behavior in evolution. This puzzle was clearly recognized by Charles Darwin (1859/1993) in his analysis of social insects. Building on Darwin's ideas, Herbert Spencer (1893/1978) pointed out that through reciprocal altruism those who are connected by birth can improve the chances of their own kind surviving. This idea was developed more fully by modern sociobiologists (Dawkins, 1976; Hamilton, 1964; Wilson, 1975). Using the example of the sinking ship, sociobiologists argue that through **kin selection** (choosing your own child to go on the lifeboat first), one increases the chances of one's own genes being passed on. The unit of interest becomes the gene rather than the individual person, and it is in this sense that we should understand the idea of **selfish gene,** a term used by some researchers to depict helping behavior as part of a complex pattern of competition for survival between genes rather than between the persons who act as vehicles or carriers for the genes (Dawkins, 1976).

Kin selection has been shown to be strong in areas that are biologically significant. Eugene Burnstein, Christian Crandall, and Shinobu Kitayama (1994) presented participants with scenarios in which another person required their help. When help was needed on an everyday matter ("Can you help me cross the road?"), participants helped those in greater need (sick and poor before the healthy and the wealthy, irrespective of blood relationships). But when help was needed in a life-and-death situation, then kin were given preference over nonkin.

But now we arrive at an interesting puzzle. On the one hand, sociobiologists claim that we help those who are genetically similar to us, and on the other hand almost all of the social psychological research focuses on helping between strangers. Given that in individualistic Western societies, at least, helping between strangers is important, how do sociobiologists claim we recognize genetically similar others? If I am driving along in my car and see a vehicle with a flat tire by the side of the road, how can I judge the amount of genes the help-seeking driver and I share so that I can decide to offer or not offer help?

For sure, we share on average about 50 percent of our *rare* genes with our offspring and siblings and about 25 percent with the next-in-line relatives (grandchildren, nieces, nephews), and so on, but how do we know what amount of genes we share with strangers? Phillip Rushton (1989) argues that we know how genetically similar we are to strangers we meet because genetic similarity is the source of behavioral and attitudinal similarity. We are more helpful toward others who look, act, and hold attitudes similar to those of our genetic relatives. However, the evidence for this view and for "genes for altruistic behavior" is not convincing (Buck & Ginsburg, 1991). Family members typically share a social history, and the ties that develop during their shared lives

kin selection   choosing to help or save one's own child or a close relative to increase the chances of one's own genes being passed on.

selfish gene   term used to describe helping behavior as part of a complex pattern of competition for survival between genes rather than between individuals.

could just as well explain preferential helping toward others who are genetically part of the same family.

Assessing the Theories in a Cultural Context

> In the United States, and perhaps in all advanced capitalist societies, it is generally accepted that the true and basic motive for human action is self-interest. It is the primary motivation, and it is the one from which other motives derive. . . . This cultural presupposition has shaped the approach of psychologists to the topic of "prosocial behavior."
>
> —John Darley, "Altruism and Prosocial Behavior Research"

With the sole exception of Batson's (1991) empathy–altruism hypothesis, all the major explanations of helping behavior assume that individuals are ultimately guided by self-centered motives. Unless there is "something in it for them," they will not help others. This "something" or "self-centered motive" could be shown in several ways: to help oneself overcome empathic arousal (Piliavin, Dovidio, Gaertner, & Clark, 1981) or a bad mood (Cialdini, Schaller, Houlihan, Arps, Fultz, & Beaman, 1987) suffered as a result of witnessing someone in distress; to repair an image that was damaged as a result of being seen to do harm to another (Cunningham, Steinberg, & Grev, 1980), or to share the joy a needy person experiences upon being relieved (Smith, Keating, & Stotland, 1989); to maintain one's perception of the world as just (Walster, Walster, & Berscheid, 1978); or to improve the survival chances of one's own genetic kind (Rushton, 1988). Only the empathy–altruism hypothesis proposes that in addition to all other factors, people have a genuine desire to help others. How are we to explain this mostly pessimistic outlook?

Cross-cultural research demonstrates that the pessimistic explanation does *not* fit what we know about human behavior. As Alan Fiske (1991), a psychological anthropologist, pointed out:

> The axiom of the primacy of selfish individualism is contradicted by numerous cross-cultural studies and historical analyses and by examination of ethnographic evidence from a wide variety of cultures. (p. 176)

A fascinating example is provided by Fiske's (1990) own field research among the Moose (pronounced MOH–say), who live in West Africa. Moose villages are located in areas where there is a severe lack of arable land and water. Despite being one of the poorest people in the world, the Moose are extremely generous with their resources. They freely give land that is not currently in use to anyone who makes a request, even if the person is a stranger. They never collect rent or sell land, but give it without regard to compensation. Similarly, they freely share water with the needy, even though it does not rain at all for 6 months of the year.

The Moose also freely provide labor to help others when it is requested. They work together without keeping track of how much work was completed by each person. When Moose men are forced by land shortage to travel to the Ivory Coast and sell their labor outside their own communities, upon their return they share much of what they have earned with other Moose people. Even though they are aware of the market-economy exchange system in which individuals sell their labor and accumulate personal wealth, they prefer to maintain their own altruistic community-based system.

But we need not go to West Africa to find examples of genuine altruism and cases that do not match the egoistic market-driven social exchange accounts of prosocial behavior. In an insightful report of field studies appropriately entitled *In Sickness and in Health*, Suzanne Thompson and Jennifer Pitts (1992) examined long-term spousal relationships in situations in which one of the couple has become chronically ill. Actually, this is a situation that many of us in Western societies will face, because most individuals who live to early old age are likely to suffer from coronary heart disease, cancer, or stroke. What will be the reaction of our spouse if we are among the millions who do suffer such long-term chronic illness? Dominant social exchange types of explanations propose that individuals seek maximum rewards at minimum costs—implying that marital satisfaction will plummet when one spouse becomes totally dependent on the other. But Thompson and Pitts (1992) have revealed a much more positive picture: Marital satisfaction is not adversely affected, and the problems that do arise are often associated with the caregiving spouse being *overprotective*.

What are we to make of cases such as the Moose in West Africa and couples in Western societies who care for each other "in sickness and in health, for better and for worse"? From the perspective of the social psychological theories, which with one exception propose that people are basically self-centered, altruism among the Moose and spousal caregivers is of enormous significance. *Humankind* in fact shows a great variety of prosocial behaviors, from absolute egoism to true altruism. The major source of such variations is culture: "If we want to know how and when people will be altruistic or otherwise prosocial, we have to understand the culture of the people in question" (Fiske, 1991, p. 178).

Concepts and Issues

The various social exchange explanations of altruism, as well as the sociobiological accounts, assume people to be self-centered and only helpful to others if it serves their own purposes. The biases in these explanations arise from the model of human behavior dominant in North American social psychology, which depicts humans as self-contained, self-centered individuals. But strong evidence has been gathered in support of the empathy-altruism model, the only one that assumes altruism to exist.

1. What do the various exchange models have in common, and in what ways are they different?
2. Are you convinced by the empathy-altruism model? Why?

3. How does sociobiology account for altruism?
4. How do justice theories explain the "blame the victim" phenomenon?

Toward a Cultural View of Prosocial Behavior

The powerful influence of culture lends support to the social learning view that, like other important aspects of human behavior, prosocial behavior is learned through socialization (Bandura, 1986; Bandura & Walters, 1963). An enormous range and variety of prosocial behaviors is shown by people in different cultures (Feldman, 1968; Graves & Graves, 1983; Innes, 1974; L'Armand & Pepitone, 1975; Mussen, 1977).

The field research of Beatrice and John Whiting among 3- to 11-year-old children in six countries (India, Japan, Kenya, Mexico, the Philippines, and the United States) demonstrated two important points (Whiting & Edwards, 1988; Whiting & Whiting, 1975). First, the children from different countries showed considerable variation in prosocial behavior. Those from Kenya, Mexico, and the Philippines exhibited the highest levels of prosocial behavior, and those from Japan and India the next highest. Children from the United States were the least prosocial.

Second, the pattern of prosocial behavior shown by the children was strongly associated with socialization practices, such as involvement in the responsibilities of family life. More prosocial behavior was shown by those socialized from an early age to take on responsibilities in the family and in the larger community *not* for material rewards but because it is considered as the correct thing to do. The early family- and community-oriented socialization of children in the more traditional societies contrasts with the training of children in the United States, where young people typically do jobs around the house (clean the windows, baby-sit a younger sibling, wash the car) only for material rewards. In the language of social learning theory, these studies suggest a greater tendency for children in the United States to be trained to show prosocial behavior only when they are positively reinforced through material rewards.

But it would be too simplistic to generalize that people in the United States show less prosocial behavior than people in other cultures. Such a quantitative difference is not always found. For example, comparisons across the United States and the more socialist society of the Netherlands actually show a higher percentage of Americans as "altruistic" (Liebrand & van Run, 1985, Table 1). In another study comparing subjects in India and the United States, it was found that Indians showed a lower level of helping, although Indians belonging to the Brahmin caste (a high-status group) showed more helping toward other Brahmins (L'Armand & Pepitone, 1975). These findings suggest that particularly when making cross-cultural

Research strongly suggests that altruistic behavior can be learned by children. These little girls live in the Yunnan Province of China, where it is normative for older children, particularly girls, to look after their younger siblings (they are busy feeding their young brother). The two American boys are also helping their family; but in the United States, children are often materially rewarded for doing chores around the house. Such rewards tend to decrease prosocial behavior, because people learn to provide help only when it is rewarded.

comparisons, it is essential that we distinguish between help given to in-group and out-group members.

Cross-cultural comparisons suggest that under some conditions people in the United States tend to be more helpful than people in traditional societies toward out-group members. This may be because the higher mobility and individualism of U.S. society lead Americans to interact more with out-group members and be both dependent on and helpful toward strangers generally. In less mobile and more collectivistic societies, interactions with outsiders are less frequent, and less help is offered to them.

The Meaning of Prosocial Behavior

To explain prosocial behavior, we must ultimately explain the *meaning* of help in a cultural context. That is, what meaning do providers and receivers of help attribute to help seeking and help receiving? For example, giving help might be interpreted as charitable and an indication of kindness ("He did a kind act, helping Sally to start the car") or it might be seen as a display of power and status ("He only helped to show how much she needs him"). Receiving help might be interpreted as a way for the receiver to strengthen ties with the help-giver ("She asked for his help so that they would communicate more in the future"), but it might also be taken as a sign of the receiver's weakness ("She asked for help because she really is incompetent").

The crucial importance of meaning is highlighted by research on help-seeking behavior. Although from a strictly material point of view people who need help would be better off if they sought outside help, from a psychological point of view seeking outside help may threaten a person's or group's independence and status (Nadler, 1991). Such a perceived threat to one's competence seems to explain why in many situations people do not seek needed help (Dew, Dunn, Bromet, & Shulberg, 1988). It also helps explain why individuals are more likely to seek help when they can remain anonymous, as the increasingly popular radio counseling programs (Raviv, Raviv, & Yunovitz, 1989) and computer communications systems allow (Karabenick & Knapp, 1988).

Cultural rules governing gender relations lead women to seek help more often than men. Such rules allow women to present themselves as "in need," whereas men should be tougher and more independent, particularly on emotional and personal issues. For example, more women seek medical help (Stomberg, 1981), and on college campuses more women seek the help of counseling centers (Robertson, 1988). Arie Nadler and his colleagues have found that young women are more likely to present themselves as in need to more attractive males, perhaps because this will lead them to be appreciated as more feminine by the attractive male helper (Nadler, Shapira, & Ben-Itzhak, 1982). This gender-related pattern of help-seeking behavior seems to be socialized from an early age, so that girls seek more help than do boys in classes (Nelson-LeGall & Glor-Scheib, 1985). Thus, the meaning of help is in part dependent on the gender of the seeker and the provider.

The fundamental importance of the meaning of help is also underlined by the research of Mary Gergen and Kenneth Gergen (1974) on attitudes toward international aid. The Gergens examined public opinion toward aid in a diverse group of aid-receiving nations, including Brazil, India, Iran, and Uruguay. Even when the quantity of the aid was about the same, the perceived value tended to vary, depending on what the motive of the donor was seen to be. Aid from a donor perceived to be well-meaning was valued much more highly. Aid from a poorer donor nation was valued more than that from a richer one, presumably because it implied a bigger sacrifice on the part of the donor. Also, response to aid was less positive when minorities in the donor country, such as Native Americans and African-Americans, were seen to be mistreated.

Help and Social Relationships

A cultural perspective leads us to view helping behavior as part of a larger moral system binding individuals together in social relationships (Miller & Bersoff, 1994). Reciprocity becomes more than just give–and–take between individuals, because the help exchanged has to be appropriate for a given context. The goal of exchange becomes much more than just maximizing material rewards because the value of help is not just material. This is clearly shown by research in Sweden, Japan, and the United States demonstrating that people appreciate help more when there is an opportunity or obligation for them to reciprocate (Castro, 1974; Clark, Gotay, & Mills, 1974; Gergen, Morse, & Bode, 1974). If the goal of such exchange was to maximize material rewards, it should not matter if reciprocity is impossible or if the donor is a rival— but it does (Searcy & Eisenberg, 1992).

The extensive role that helping plays in establishing social relationships is demonstrated in a lengthy field study of *guanxixue* (pronounced guan-shee-shwe), meaning "doing favors for people," in China by Mayfair Mei–hui Yang (1994). *Guanxixue* involves

> the exchange of gifts, favors, and banquets; the cultivation of personal relationships and networks of mutual dependence; and the manufacturing of obligations and indebtedness. What informs these practices and their native descriptions is the conception of the primacy and binding power of personal relationships and their importance in meeting the needs and desires of everyday life. (Yang, 1994, p. 6)

Through in–depth interviews and observational research, Yang was able to reveal the pervasiveness of *guanxixue* in the everyday social life of the Chinese, both before and after the Cultural Revolution launched by Mao Zedong in the late 1960s. Through *guanxixue*, individuals in China create a social network involving many others who become morally obligated to them. An important feature of these seemingly mundane social practices is that they have survived the large–scale political and economic changes (Moghaddam & Crystal, 1997). Despite official opposition, *guanxixue* continues to thrive in China and seems destined to outlive communism.

Something akin to *guanxixue* is evident in certain aspects of Western social life, particularly in the political domain. Political interest groups often work on the assumption that if they can provide "favors" (for example, by mobilizing voter support or by less direct methods, such as providing subtle but supportive publicity) to politicians in different political parties, this will widen their networks of influence. At critical times they may support a politician who has been neutral, or even opposed to, the interests they represent, with the intention of creating indebtedness and obligation.

In everyday life also, the creation of such obligations plays a subtle but pervasive role, even in intimate relations. For example, George provides moral support for his girlfriend when she plays soccer in order to make her more obligated to him and make it easier to persuade her to attend his upcoming family reunion.

A cultural account of prosocial behavior leads us to view helping and being helped as involving much more than just instrumental benefits. People do not provide help in order to give material benefits; help is often given as a means of creating indebtedness and manufacturing obligations. Also, help is accepted or rejected not only on the basis of need but on the basis of social concerns and expectations about relationships: "Do I want to have a closer relationship with this potential donor? Is being indebted to this person likely to bring positive or negative consequences in terms of social relationships with people other than the donor?"

Being indebted to a local millionaire has very different implications from being indebted to an unemployed neighbor. In business circles, the prestige of an individual or company is often established by the "class" of others who act as lenders. Statements such as "I had to borrow money from Bill Gates last week" and "I feel indebted to Ross Perot now because he let me hitch a ride to California with him on his jet" have implications for the nature of one's social relationships, and are not just a matter of instrumental gain or benefit.

Culture provides the rules and norms by which people go about using prosocial behavior as part of a larger system for managing social relationships. Such rules and norms tell us when and how it is appropriate to seek and to offer help. Again, if the objective were merely to maximize material benefits, then people should take help whenever it is offered, irrespective of the characteristics of the donor. But this is not the case, since the meaning of help is critical for those involved. Older people in the United States tend to be particularly sensitive about independence and being able to cope on their own. This is probably why people over the age of 60 tend to be more reluctant to seek help, even when they are in need (Lieberman & Tobin, 1983).

Factors That Influence Helping

Culture establishes the rules and norms that give meaning to prosocial behavior and guide both help-seekers and help-providers. In the United States, competitiveness is highly valued and people think well of themselves when they behave competitively, whereas in Mexico, cooperation and altruism are more highly valued and people think well of themselves when they show these characteristics (Kagan & Knight, 1979). It is in the context of social rules and norms that we can better understand the influence of the various factors, such as the characteristics of help-seekers and help-providers, that researchers have found to be influential in prosocial behavior.

Characteristics of Seekers and Providers. In interpreting evidence that women both seek more help than men (Nadler, 1991) and receive more offers of help (Pomazal & Clore, 1973), we must keep in mind that such findings are likely to be context-specific. That is, whether women receive more or less help than men or are more or less helpful than men depends on the rules appropriate to a given situation (Zarbatany, Hartmann, Gelfand, & Vinciguerra, 1985). Most of the studies that show women receive more help focus on heroic altruism rather than nurturant altruism (Eagly & Crowley, 1986; Otten, Penner, & Waugh 1988). In long-term relationships requiring emotional help, women are likely to be more prosocial, in line with the cultural rules that socialize girls to become "caring women."

A number of other characteristics of help-seekers and help-providers have been found to be influential. For example, help tends to be offered more often to similar than to dissimilar others (Dovidio, 1984). In line with this, help is more likely to be offered to people of one's ethnic in-group, perhaps in part because we assume in-group members to be more similar to us generally (Frey & Gaertner, 1986). We are also more likely to offer help to those who already have established a social relationship with us, no matter how slight, as compared to complete strangers (Howard & Crano, 1974). Once again, these findings point to the important role of prosocial behavior in the larger context of social relationships.

Characteristics of the Context. The original surge in social psychological research on prosocial behavior came as a result of the Kitty Genovese murder and other terrible events involving nonhelping among bystanders in large urban centers. Research by Stanley Milgram (1977) has demonstrated that people who live in small towns are more likely to offer help than are residents of large urban centers. Part of the process of learning to live in a modern urban environment involves becoming skilled in *avoiding* help-seeking others while being able to get the right kind of help to achieve one's personal goals. In a related study

These Israelis are harvesting eggplant on a kibbutz, a form of community, typically small and agrarian, where the collectivity is responsible for providing food and shelter for all the members. People who live in communities such as these are more likely to seek help to achieve communal goals, whereas people in large urban centers are more likely to seek help to achieve personal goals.

comparing people in kibbutzim (small communities organized along egalitarian lines) and city societies in Israel, Arie Nadler (1986) found that kibbutz dwellers were more likely to seek help from others to achieve communal goals, whereas city dwellers were more likely to seek help to achieve personal goals. Of course, city dwellers everywhere are likely to face greater time constraints and to have a lot of other people around them. Both time constraints and the presence of others tend to diminish prosocial behavior (Latané & Darley, 1970).

In the context of collectivistic societies, altruism also becomes more collectivistic, involving groups rather than individuals. In a study entitled *Getting Ahead Collectively*, the noted economist Albert Hirschman (1984) described grassroots development projects involving very poor people in six Latin America countries (Dominican Republic, Colombia, Peru, Chile, Argentina, and Uruguay). Perhaps the most important benefit of people helping one another was the dispelling of isolation and mutual distrust and the emergence of stronger and healthier social networks. The same kinds of patterns emerge in some aspects of Western life, such as among grassroots organizations that have grown in response to the AIDS epidemic. This indicates that changes in circumstances are associated with different patterns of altruism.

The importance of the context is underlined by research demonstrating that some findings from laboratory studies conflict with those from field studies. Laboratory research suggests that people go out of their way to avoid seeking help, whereas field research suggests that people often go out of their way to seek help (Wills, 1992). One plausible explanation for this paradox is that in the laboratory, participants (who are very often undergraduates) see themselves as being in a "testing" situation, being observed by their professors. They try to prove themselves by doing what they have been trained to do: go it alone. Also, in the laboratory the *social* function of help seeking, that of creating relationships, is missing. People are there for about an hour, and often with anonymous others. Consequently, there seems little point in trying to extend one's social relations in such a context. In contrast, in the real world, people seek out the help of others *in order to extend their social relationships*, in addition to the instrumental reason of fulfilling a need.

Concepts and Issues

A cultural view proposes that altruism is socialized behavior, which changes across cultures according to local norms and rules. Altruism plays an important part in creating and extending social relationships. The meaning of an altruistic act depends on the context, the provider, the receiver, and other characteristics of the culture. An offer of help may be taken as an insult, a sign of goodwill, a debt paid, or a favor given—all depending on cultural interpretations.

1. Cite evidence that altruism is socialized.
2. Why is it important to consider the *meaning* of help-giving behavior?

3. In what ways do gender differences in altruism suggest a role for culture?
4. Give some examples from your own experiences of people using altruism to create obligations and to extend their social networks.

Conclusion

Social psychologists have displayed considerable ingenuity in using field and laboratory procedures to examine the motivations underlying prosocial behavior. Such studies have typically focused on brief interactions between strangers, in which help of a "heroic" kind has been called for. Although such helping behavior does have a place in everyday life, perhaps even more important are long-term helping relationships, which are now receiving more research attention (Spacapan & Oskamp, 1992). Research in diverse cultures suggests that prosocial behavior is invaluable in creating and extending social networks, and that the meaning of an act of altruism has to be understood within the rules and norms of a given culture.

For Review

Altruism is defined as behavior intended to help another, without regard for a benefit to oneself. The major social psychological research on altruism was a response to the Kitty Genovese murder, a particularly horrifying example of bystander nonintervention.

The main focus of experimental laboratory research has been on heroic altruism, involving short-term intervention by a person taking physical action to help a stranger, rather than nurturant altruism, involving long-term emotional support.

The main question addressed by researchers has been "Why does the bystander not help?" The first explanations, provided by Latané and Darley, revolved around the ideas of "diffusion of responsibility" and "pluralistic ignorance." Explanations of prosocial behavior have tended to be pessimistic, perhaps reflecting the "self-centered individualism" of Western societies.

Latané and Darley's initial theory proposed that people will help only if they overcome a number of obstacles. Subsequent theoretical models focused more on the question of whether or not there is true altruism. Only one of the influential theories, Daniel Batson's empathy-altruism model, proposes that people help out of a genuine desire to do good for others. The other major theories assume behavior to be egoistic.

One set of theories—the arousal cost-reward model, the negative-state relief hypothesis, and the image-repair hypothesis—sees helping others as a way of improving the helper's own mood or image. The social/cultural theories see helping as a means by which a person overcomes the negative impact of either witnessing someone in need or being seen as harming (and thus creating a need in) another. It is assumed that help will be offered if it is the least costly, or only, alternative to serve one's own interests.

Another set of theories sees us being motivated by more indirectly selfish motives: We help others in order to share the joy of the needy person's relief; we do, or do not, offer help in order to maintain our perception of the world as a just place. Sociobiological theories hypothesize that we are more likely to help others who share more of our genes, a helping strategy for maximizing the likelihood that our own genes will survive.

Although experimenters have devised ingenious laboratory procedures for testing some features of the pessimistic theories, it is still premature to make positive judgments about their validity. Field research and cross-cultural research provide clear evidence that under certain conditions behavior in everyday life is best described by the more optimistic empathy–altruism model.

A cultural perspective leads to us to highlight the meaning of helping in a social context and the function of prosocial behavior in creating and managing social relationships.

For Discussion

1. "With one exception, the major social psychological accounts of altruism assume people to be self-centered." Discuss this statement.

2. Why has research focused on heroic altruism rather than nurturant altruism?

3. What are some of the generalizations we can make about the conditions in which people provide help?

Key Terms

Altruism 297

Arousal cost–reward model 304

Bystander effect 301

Diffusion of responsibility 300

Empathy–altruism hypothesis 306

Empathy–joy hypothesis 310

Equity theory 308

Heroic altruism 298

Image-repair hypothesis 307

Just-world hypothesis 308

Kin selection 311

Negative–state relief hypothesis 306

Nurturant altruism 298

Pluralistic ignorance 300

Selfish gene 311

Social exchange theory 304

Annotated Readings

A general overview of research on altruism is provided in D. A. Schroeder, L. A. Penner, J. F. Dovidio, and J. F. Piliavin, *The social psychology of helping and altruism: Problems and puzzles* (New York: McGraw–Hill, 1995).

An optimistic view of altruism as proposed in the empathy–altruism model is outlined in C. D. Batson, *The altruism question: Toward a social psychological answer* (Hillsdale, NJ: Lawrence Erlbaum, 1991).

S. Spacapan and S. Oskamp report on interesting field studies of altruism in *Helping and being helped: Naturalistic studies* (Newbury Park, CA: Sage, 1992).

For an example of the meaning of helping in social relationships in a non–Western culture, see M. M. Yang, *Gifts, favors, and banquets: The art of social relationships in China* (Ithaca, NY: Cornell University Press, 1994).

Accounts of altruistic behavior in real–life settings are found in S. P. Oliner and P. M. Oliner, *The altruistic personality: Rescuers of Jews in Nazi Europe* (New York: Free Press, 1988).

Altruism

A s I sipped coffee in a small café and revised my lecture notes for my next class, I overheard two students debating.

"Human beings are basically good when they come into this world," the first one said. "If they behave badly later as adults, it's because society corrupts them."

"No, you've got it backward," the second student replied. "We are born self-centered and society tries to improve us. Left to ourselves, we would never do anything altruistic."

Altruism, doing something for others without expecting a reward, is central to debates about what humans are *really* like. While the topic of whether or not there is true altruism has received considerable research attention from social psychologists, far less attention has been given to the changing nature of altruism across time and across cultures. In Western industrial societies, altruism is becoming less and less personal and increasingly professional. Instead of intervening directly to provide help, people are more likely to give money or other support to professionals who intervene on society's behalf.

Helicopter rescue of a skier in difficult winter conditions.

A rescue team working quickly to get an injured person out of a wrecked car.

Red Cross worker assessing damage in a building, New York City.

Neighborhood people helping put out fires during the Los Angeles riots, 1992.

The professionalization of altruism in Western societies has happened in part in order to improve the effectiveness with which help can be provided in emergencies. A person stranded in the middle of rough, snowy terrain can be saved by a helicopter rescue team, but such a team has to be made up of highly skilled, trained professionals. When a serious automobile accident occurs, emergency medical staff, firefighters, and others must reach the spot quickly to save lives and look after the injured. After a major fire, knowledgeable specialists need to examine the structures that are left and make estimates of safety measures needed, costs, and so on.

Police, firefighters, social workers, lawyers, marriage counselors . . . there seems no end to the list of experts who are trained to take over "helping" responsibilities. People are willing to step over a man lying unconscious on the pavement in the belief that "it is the job of the city authorities to help him. That's why we pay taxes, so the government can hire professionals to help those in need." If the man is hurt, then the authorities have to deal with it; if he has been attacked and robbed, it is a job for the police. In short, the responsibility for helping lies squarely on the shoulders of professionals.

Crosby, Stills & Nash concert for hurricane relief, Miami, 1992.

This distancing of ourselves from those needing help is paralleled by our distancing ourselves from family and community, once a rich source of wisdom and support. We seek help from marriage counselors, rather than our parents; we tell our intimate secrets to therapists and lawyers, rather than confide in family. In seeking as well as providing help, we use professionals as intermediaries rather than get involved with others directly.

But it would be simplistic to characterize altruism in the West as professionalized and that in non–Western societies as personal. When buildings were burning during the Los Angeles riots of 1992, some individuals personally intervened to help others. After Florida and other parts of the Southeast were badly hit by hurricane Andrew in 1992, artists took part in concerts and thousands came in support to give to a relief fund. Just as altruism can be personalized in Western societies, it can be professionalized in developing societies. Organizations such as World Vision Relief helped to feed and shelter victims after the 1988 floods in Bangladesh and the earthquake in El Salvador.

World Vision staff bagging red lentils (dal) for distribution in Bangladesh during a flood in 1988.

Food line after an earthquake, El Salvador.

Perhaps the most important aspect of helping behavior, irrespective of whether it is personal or professional, is its meaning. Consider a situation where a woman offers food to a man in a street. There are many ways in which such an offering could be interpreted. It may be seen as a sign of her power and his weakness; she could feel powerful and he powerless. He may even feel insulted or ashamed, depending on the meaning of the behavior in a cultural context. Such an offering has a very different meaning in Thailand: Look at the photograph of the woman offering food to Buddhist monks. She has knelt down; the giver is privileged to have her offering accepted. She is doing her duty, but giving help is also something that has religious value for her.

Woman offering food to monks, Thailand.

Prejudice

◄ A "White Power" march in Georgia. The persistence of prejudice in modern societies represents a clear challenge to the optimistic view that educational, scientific, and legal progress will put an end to this problem. The spread of literacy and formal education has not resulted in an end to prejudice. Almost everyone in the United States receives at least basic schooling, but such opportunities have not led to enlightenment for everyone. Neither has the reform of the legal system ended prejudice. Discrimination on the basis of race, sex, religion, age, and national origin continues, but in much more subtle form.

"**W**hy don't they go back where they came from? We don't want their kind here!"

The thickset man who snarled these words was English, and the targets of his remark were a dozen or so Pakistanis who had just stepped off a plane at London's Heathrow Airport. It was the early 1970s: Hundreds of thousands of South Asians were pouring into England and, perhaps for the first time, were experiencing prejudice.

A decade later, I heard almost the same statement, but this time it was expressed by a Pakistani man, and the unfortunate targets were Afghani refugees. I was surveying the situation of Afghani refugees flooding into Pakistan and Iran. The influx angered some local residents, including an irate Pakistani, who shouted at the newcomers: "We do not want these robbers here!"

Another decade later, during a research trip to the Los Angeles area, I was confronted by a man who needed no prodding at all to express his views about what needs to be done to "save" American society: "Get these damned Mexicans out of here," he snapped. "We don't want them here. I don't want to live near them, I don't want them working with me, I don't want them in school with my kids. They are the cause of a lot of the crime and drugs and everything else that's going wrong with our country."

These three incidents are separated by more than 20 years and three continents, but they are all too similar. Each reflects intolerance toward particular outsiders, or out-group members. About a century ago, Mark Twain applied his critical wit to enlighten us about an experiment he conducted to explore such intolerance among humans, whom he called "Reasoning Animals," and animals, referred to by him as "Higher Animals":

> Among my experiments was this. In an hour I taught a cat and a dog to be friends. I put them in a cage. In another hour I taught them to be friends with a rabbit. In the course of two days I was able to add a fox, a goose, a squirrel and some doves. Finally a monkey. They lived together in peace; even affectionately. Next, in another cage I confined an Irish Catholic from Tipperary, and as soon as he seemed tame I added a Scottish Presbyterian from Aberdeen. Next a Turk from Constantinople; a Greek Christian from Crete; an Armenian; a Methodist from the wilds of Arkansas; a Buddhist from China; a Brahman from Benares. Finally, a Salvation Army Colonel from Wapping. Then I stayed away two whole days. When I came back to note results, the cage of Higher Animals was all right, but in the other (filled with humans) there was such chaos of gory odds and ends of turbans and fezzes and plaids and bones and flesh—not a specimen left alive. These Reasoning Animals had disagreed on a theological detail and carried the matter to a Higher Court. (Twain, 1974 pp. 180–181)

Twain's sharp wit points to a question we social psychologists need to address systematically: Is **prejudice**—an attitude toward others based solely on group membership—an example of a universal social behavior? That is, do people in all or almost all societies show prejudice

prejudice an attitude toward others solely on the basis of group membership.

toward others? Rupert Brown (1995), an English social psychologist, put forward what is probably the consensus among modern researchers: Prejudice is a common, everyday phenomenon found among ordinary people, rather than something unusual and restricted to a deviant group.

Then a second, related question arises: Even if prejudice is universal, does this suggest that it is inevitable and something we just have to learn to live with, or can it be reduced? This second question is just as important as the first because it leads us to explore not just the kind of beings we are but what we could become. There is little doubt that we can find examples of prejudice in many different societies throughout the world (see Bowser, 1995). But perhaps in our becoming, our growing as human societies, we can reduce prejudice to a level where it no longer poses a problem.

This chapter is organized into three main parts. The first clarifies the main concepts and examines the complexities associated with the measurement of prejudice. The second reviews the major psychological processes associated with prejudice. A puzzle to be solved here concerns this question: To what extent is prejudice inevitable, something that just occurs naturally? One viewpoint is that universal cognitive processes independent of culture make prejudice inevitable. Another perspective is that cognitive processes, such as categorization and stereotyping, are themselves cultural and can be influenced through changes in culture.

The final section discusses a cultural explanation of prejudice. Our review will bring us to a puzzling issue: On the one hand, self-reported attitudes, as well as actual changes in the legal system, suggest that prejudice has declined markedly; on the other hand, measures of actual behavior and a variety of everyday experiences reported by targets of prejudice such as women and ethnic minorities suggest that prejudice has not declined. How do we explain this situation? Our review of some possible solutions to this puzzle prepares the way for the discussion of intergroup discrimination in Chapter 14, where we also consider the broader challenge of managing cultural diversity.

Defining and Measuring Prejudice

Imagine if you were told that next semester you will be sharing a room with a student from England, or France, or Saudi Arabia, or Israel. The mere knowledge that your new roommate will be from a particular country is likely to trigger certain attitudes based on beliefs about what he or she is like (English people are reserved, French people have artistic flair, and so on; see Fiske & Neuberg, 1990). Some of these attitudes or prejudices will be positive, others negative. It is the negative prejudices that have been the particular focus of social psychological research, in large part because these have been seen as social problems.

Prejudice and Discrimination

In a classic scholarly work on prejudice, Gordon Allport (1954) wrote: "Prejudice in the simple psychological sense of negative, overgeneralized judgement exists just as surely in caste societies, slave societies, or countries believing in witchcraft as in ethnically more sensitive societies" (p. 11).

Two points need to be added here. First, although prejudice seems to be universal, it also varies in some ways across cultures, so that, for example, prejudice toward French people changes as we move from Canada to Algiers. A second point is that from one perspective it does not matter if prejudice *is* prevalent and even universal, because prejudice is an attitude, which may not translate into behavior. Even if the attitude is expressed verbally, this does not necessarily mean that a person will carry out an act.

discrimination　actual behavior directed at others on the basis of category membership.

Discrimination involves actual behavior directed at other people on the basis of their category memberships. Sara refuses to allow her teenage daughter to invite any nonwhite children to her fourteenth birthday party; Clara does not rent out her apartment to qualified Hispanic applicants; and Jim votes against the hiring and promotion of qualified women candidates. These behaviors directly impoverish the lives of members of minority groups, but, as Benjamin Bowser and others have argued, they also have a negative impact on the lives of members of majority groups (Bowser & Hunt, 1996). A democratic system is necessarily impaired when discrimination takes place, in part because discrimination denies society the talents of those who are discriminated against.

The relationship between prejudice and discrimination is a topic of some debate, like the relationship between attitudes and behavior. Just because Simon holds prejudiced attitudes about women does not mean he will discriminate against women, or even express his views openly. Today most people are aware of the norms for political correctness, as well as legal restrictions on prejudice and discrimination. These new norms reflect what Irwin Katz and Glen Hass (1988) referred to as a *humanitarian-egalitarian* sentiment in U.S. culture, which dampens at least overt prejudice. Consequently, prejudice is now more complex and tends to be expressed in more subtle ways (Sears, 1988).

Sources and Targets of Prejudice

racism　prejudice toward ethnic minorities.

sexism　prejudice toward women.

power minority　group that has little control over the distribution of important resources; may be the numerical majority.

The terms **racism** and **sexism** denote prejudice toward ethnic minorities and women, respectively. Although women as a group outnumber men, they still have less political and economic power. Similarly, ethnic minorities are numerically in the majority in some areas of the United States (in parts of California and Florida) and in some areas of the world (blacks in South Africa), but they tend to have less power. For this reason, the tradition is to refer to women and ethnic minorities as **power minorities,** groups that have less control over the distribution of important resources (such as funding for various social and economic programs and top posts in government, industry, and education). Sometimes a group can be both a numerical and a power minority, as is the case for the Burakumin in Japan and the Kurds in Turkey. In the United States the most important **power majority,** the group that has most control over how important resources are distributed, is made up of white males, mainly of Western European descent.

When we look at the global scene, the ethnic compositions of the power majority and power minority groups tend to vary across societies (DeVos, 1992), but the position of the gender power minority is more stable. For example, in the United States, it is people of white European descent who are the power majority; others (including Asians) are part of a power minority (Shinagawa, 1997). In Japan, those of "pure Japanese" descent are the power majority and all others (including Europeans) are "outsiders," and part of a power minority. But consistent across the United States and Japan is the minority power status of women: White women in the United States hold less power than do white men, and women in Japan hold less power than men (Giele & Smock, 1977).

The power minority position of women has traditionally been justified by shared beliefs. It is often easier to identify such biased beliefs by looking at other cultures. Gui-Young Hong (1997) has described the case of M, a woman in Korea: "The death of her husband and two sons brought M unbearable maltreatment and abuse from her in-laws. They held her responsible for breaking the first son's family line and

power majority group that has most control over how important resources are distributed; may be the numerical minority.

There is cross-cultural consistency in the relationship between group status and prejudice in that minority groups are typically the target of prejudice. Women tend to suffer prejudice more than men, even in industrialized societies. In Japan, women work, but often in low-status positions, such as that of this elevator operator in a Tokyo department store. In the United States and much of Europe, heated debates about government policy have often been associated with stereotypes about "welfare queens," women who are supposed to be living in luxury at taxpayer expense. These young mothers at a Los Angeles center are typical of poor women who suffer such prejudice and discrimination.

'justified' their maltreatment under the Confucian ideology on virtuous women" (p. 10). In Western societies, women now escape such explicit discrimination, but some other groups do not. For example, Christian Crandall's (1994) research suggests that prejudice and discrimination against obese people are still blatant in the United States.

Irrespective of their particular characteristics, the targets of prejudice are stigmatized and have what Erving Goffman (1963) refers to as a **spoiled identity** (Figure 10–1): The identity they derive through their group membership puts them at a disadvantage that cannot be overcome, even by enormous effort. They suffer either (1) tribal stigmas, being members of ostracized racial, ethnic, or religious groups; (2) abominations of the body, including being handicapped or being disfigured; and (3) blemishes of individual character, including being addicted to drugs or alcohol. A fourth category, gender stigma, is needed, because in most societies half of the population has suffered spoiled identity on the basis of their sex group membership (see Chapter 12). The common feature of these target groups is their lack of power to create their own identities. One implication, perhaps, is that only when women have the power to create and make effective an equally positive image of themselves, and only when blacks have the power to put "Black is beautiful" into practice, can they escape prejudice.

Is it the case that power majorities are always the source of discrimination and power minorities always the target? The way we generally use terms such as *racism* and *sexism* seems to suggest that this is so. Consider the following scenario:

> My friend came back from work in a very unhappy mood today, complaining about sexism at the office. The manager had directed several sexist comments at my friend and everybody else at work just laughed about it.

If you are like the vast majority of my students, you imagine the friend to be a female, a member of a power minority, and the manager to be a male, a member of the power majority.

spoiled identity   identity derived from group membership that puts a person at a disadvantage.

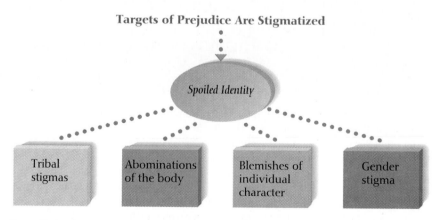

Figure 10–1   Elements of spoiled identity (after Goffman, 1963).

Ethnic minorities certainly seem to see themselves as targets of discrimination, which often leads them to attribute their failures to racism. In a study I conducted with colleagues at McGill University and Georgetown University, white, black, and Cuban mothers in Miami, Florida, were interviewed to find out how they would explain the outcome if they applied for a job for which they were qualified but were not selected (Moghaddam, Taylor, Lambert, & Schmidt, 1995). It was the black participants, particularly those who were middle class, who attributed their failure to racism against their ethnic group. Perhaps this is because black middle-class participants were most directly in competition with whites for better jobs, housing, and other resources and had greater opportunity to experience prejudice and discrimination.

But members of minority groups also run the risk of exaggerating the prejudice majority group members feel toward them. A research project in a multiethnic community college in Montreal brought me face-to-face with an intriguing example of this phenomenon (Moghaddam, Taylor, Pelletier, & Shepanek, 1994). We were asked to collaborate in this research as a way of trying to better understand relations between groups of students in the college. Our participants were French-Canadians, the majority group in this context, and four immigrant groups who constituted the minority groups: European Francophones (from France and Belgium), Jews, Latin Americans, and Haitians. Through a variety of measures, we first asked immigrant participants to rate how much they thought of themselves as being Canadian and how much they still saw themselves as being outsiders (e.g., foreigners). Next we asked them to rate how much they thought French-Canadians (the majority group in this context) saw them as being Canadian and how much they saw them as being outsiders. We then asked French-Canadians to rate how much they actually saw each immigrant group as being Canadian and how much as being outsiders.

We discovered that several minority groups, particularly the Haitians, who are considered black, overestimated how much they were seen as outsiders and underestimated how much they were seen by the French-Canadians as Canadians. The reverse was true for the European Francophones, who underestimated how much they were seen as outsiders and overestimated how much they were seen by French-Canadians as Canadians. A possible consequence has been that Haitian immigrants generally expect to be rejected when they interact with members of the majority group, whereas European Francophone immigrants are generally confident (even overconfident) of being received favorably.

Another factor complicating the situation is that prejudice not only involves majority versus minority groups but also at times minority versus minority. Such prejudice can be in the shape of "blacks versus browns" (Miles, 1992), or blacks versus Jews (Clark, 1992). The results of a national survey in the United States revealed that 42 percent of blacks and 46 percent of Hispanics believed Asians to be "unscrupulous, crafty and devious in business" (Holmes, 1994). The idea that "blacks want to live on welfare" was endorsed by 31 percent of Asians and 26 percent of Hispanics, while 68 percent of Asians and 49 percent of blacks believed that Hispanics "tend to have bigger families than they are able to support."

Kathy Russell, Midge Wilson, and Ronald Hall (1992) have discussed an array of evidence showing black-on-black bias, with lighter-colored individuals being preferred by other African-Americans (see also Cross, 1991). Their book was inspired by an experience Russell had when she was dumped by an African-American date because he thought her too dark to have children with! Such incidents are examples of minority group members' adopting prejudiced views that originate from some parts of the larger society. They show that prejudice against out-groups is by no means unique to white males (Bowser, 1995), but because in many parts of the Western world white males enjoy greater power than any other group, they have more opportunities to discriminate or act on the basis of their prejudiced attitudes.

But bias against minorities is less likely to be recognized if the perpetrator is also a member of a minority group. When Robert Baron and his associates presented participants with scenarios in which men or women were biased against a woman, both female and male participants judged the sexism as more extreme when the perpetrator was male (Baron, Burgess, & Kao, 1991). In another study, Baron and his team found differences in how likely members of minority and majority groups are to perceive prejudice: Women were more likely than men to perceive sexism against men and racism against ethnic minorities, and African-Americans were more likely than Caucasians to perceive racism against members of both majority and minority groups (Inman & Baron, 1996). These results suggest that the perception of prejudice depends on the characteristics of the perpetrator and the perceiver.

How Should We Measure Discrimination?

An important practical question confronting culturally diverse societies is: How much intergroup discrimination actually takes place? Getting an answer to this seemingly simple question has proved to be a complex matter. A simple and direct way to measure discrimination would seem to be to ask potential sources and victims of discrimination. But majority group members might distort the actual level of discrimination they show through impression management and the use of symbolic racism, for example. What about asking the potential victims? As we shall see, this has also proved to be a complex but nevertheless enlightening exercise.

Recent research on the experience of minority group members with discrimination has provided several major surprises. The first is that minority group members do *not* have low self-esteem. The assumption that they do arose out of a long research tradition going back to the pioneering work of the African-American couple Kenneth Clark and Mamie Clark (1947) which showed a preference for white rather than black dolls among black children (also see Taylor & Moghaddam, 1994, p. 172). By the 1950s, the notion of "self-hate" was invoked to describe low self-esteem among ethnic minorities (Allport, 1954). Jennifer

Crocker and Brenda Major (1989) have critically assessed the literature to discover that ethnic minorities, women, gays, the physically disabled, and a number of other minority groups do not have low self-esteem (this links up to our earlier discussion on self-protective attributional strategies among minorities, Chapter 5).

The Personal/Group Discrimination Discrepancy.   Major and Crocker (1989) argued that members of minority groups can maintain high self-esteem by attributing failures to discrimination. When Jim, an African-American, fails to get a job, he blames this on racism rather than on his own performance. This explanation leads us to expect that members of minority groups report high levels of discrimination leveled at themselves personally. But this expectation is contradicted by a series of studies reporting that minority group members perceived a higher level of discrimination directed at their group as a whole than at themselves as individual members of that group (Taylor & Moghaddam, 1994). That is, they give higher ratings to the question "To what extent has your group been discriminated against?" than they do to the question "To what extent have you personally been discriminated against?" Taylor and his associates referred to this phenomenon as the **personal/group discrimination discrepancy** (Taylor, Wright, Moghaddam, & Lalonde, 1990), and noted that it was first encountered by Fay Crosby (1982, 1984a, 1984b) in a study of working women in Boston. A closer study of the literature revealed that other researchers had also encountered this phenomenon, though all reported it was not an intended outcome of their research (Guimond & Dube–Simard, 1983; Taylor, Wong–Rieger, McKirnan, & Bercusson, 1982).

Donald Taylor and his associates conducted the first experiment designed specifically to test the personal/group discrimination discrepancy (Taylor, Wright, Moghaddam, & Lalonde, 1990). These researchers asked two groups of Canadian immigrants, Haitian and Indian women, about their perceptions of both personal and group discrimination within Canadian society. The findings showed that participants did perceive higher levels of discrimination being directed at their group as a whole than at themselves personally (see Figure 10–2).

personal/group discrimination discrepancy   tendency for minority group members to perceive a higher level of discrimination directed at their group as a whole than at themselves as individual members of that group.

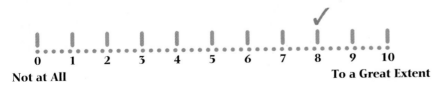

To what extent has your group been discriminated against?

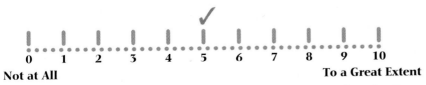

To what extent have you personally been discriminated against?

Figure 10–2   Typical pattern of responses of participants in research showing the personal/group discrimination discrepancy (after Taylor, Wright, Moghaddam, & Lalonde, 1990).

This initial confirmation was followed by a series of experimental attempts to identify the best explanations for this discrepancy (Ruggiero & Taylor, 1994, 1995, 1997; Taylor, Ruggiero, & Louis, 1996; Taylor, Wright, & Porter, 1994). A number of wording variations were tried (e.g., asking about discrimination experienced by the *average* person in the group), but no significant difference in response patterns was found. In a laboratory study, participants were able to identify correctly the actual level of personal and group discrimination present in a situation, and so the personal/group discrimination discrepancy does not necessarily occur because of lack of ability to make reality-based assessments of discrimination (Taylor, Wright, & Ruggiero, 1991).

Two plausible explanations are, first, a denial of personal discrimination and, second, an exaggeration of group discrimination (Crosby, 1984a, 1984b; Taylor, Ruggiero, & Louis, 1996; Taylor, Wright, & Porter, 1994; Zanna, Crosby, & Loewenstein, 1986). The psychological literature suggests a number of compelling reasons why individuals may be motivated to deny discrimination against themselves, such as a desire to avoid the shame associated with being victimized; and so *denial* has gained favor. But this interpretation directly contradicts the proposition of Crocker and Major (1989) to the effect that members of minority groups use discrimination as a way of protecting their self-esteem.

Recent studies by Karen Ruggiero and Donald Taylor (1997) suggest that denial is used only when there is uncertainty as to whether discrimination is or is not present. They propose that each task-related activity has four elements: performance self-esteem (how I did on the task), social self-esteem (how others evaluate me), performance control (success/failure on a task), and social control (how others treat me). (See Figure 10–3). A minority group member who performs poorly on a task

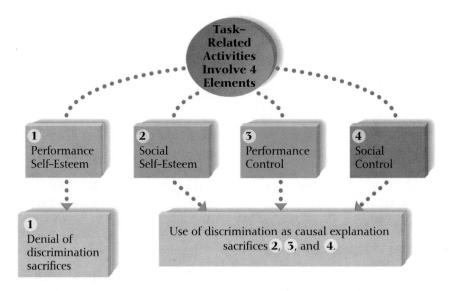

Figure 10–3 Denial of discrimination is often the most psychologically beneficial strategy for minority group members (after Ruggiero & Taylor, 1997).

but denies discrimination as a cause is sacrificing performance self-esteem. However, this individual is not sacrificing the other three elements: He or she can enjoy high social self-esteem and can also assume that he or she has high control in performance and social domains. An individual who believes "I did badly because of discrimination" can protect performance self-esteem but sacrifices social self-esteem, as well as a sense of control in performance and social domains. Ruggiero and Taylor (1977) argue that minority group members deny personal discrimination because the benefits of doing so outweigh the costs.

The Generalized Personal/Group Discrepancy. An intriguing new twist developed in this research after a central assumption—that the personal/group discrimination discrepancy is specific to the domain of discrimination—was questioned. An alternative possibility is that there exists a **generalized personal/group discrepancy,** involving a tendency for individuals to rate the effect of a phenomenon as less on themselves than on their group, irrespective of the domain (Moghaddam & Studer, 1997). Some evidence does support such an interpretation. For example, a national survey among school superintendents and principals showed participants perceived a 39 percent increase in school violence in their own districts but a 63 percent increase in neighboring districts and a 97 percent increase in the nation's schools as a whole (Boothe, Bradley, Keough, & Kirk, 1993). A survey of perceptions of the economic recession conducted in Germany showed that while only 39 percent reported their personal situation to be "not so good" or "bad," 87 percent reported the situation for the general population to be in a poor state (*Die Zeit*, September 30, 1994).

generalized personal/group discrepancy a tendency for individuals to rate the effect of a phenomenon as less on themselves than on their group.

A generalized personal/group discrepancy was tested by asking participants about their personal and group experiences in a variety of different negative and positive domains, including improvements in technology, the economy, computers, the threat of AIDS, and discrimination (Moghaddam, Stolkin, & Hutcheson, 1997). In order to achieve a more sensitive differentiation between "personal" and "group," three levels of group were included: close friends, gender group, and the population in general. Results confirmed that people perceive the impact of events on their groups as greater than on themselves, with the size of the effect increasing with the size of the group.

The original personal/group discrepancy had been identified in studies involving minority group participants, such as women in the United States or visible minority immigrant women in Canada (Taylor, Wright, & Porter, 1994). But in our research a generalized discrepancy appeared for members of both the minority (women) and the majority (men) groups. The generalized personal/group discrepancy may be another example of an **availability heuristic,** a rule of thumb leading to estimates of the likelihood of an event on the basis of how readily instances come to mind (Tversky & Kahneman, 1974). Participants rate the impact of events as higher on larger groups because they find it easier to bring to mind examples of such an impact when there are larger numbers of people from which to draw.

availability heuristic a rule of thumb leading to estimates of the likelihood of an event on the basis of how readily instances come to mind.

Spectators at a Puerto Rican Day parade in New York City. Received wisdom suggests that minorities who are the target of prejudice should have low self-esteem. However, reviews of the literature suggest that this is not the case, that, in fact, they enjoy surprisingly high self-esteem. A possible explanation lies in the isolation of ethnic minorities, who often live in ethnic neighborhoods, shop in ethnic stores, and socialize within their communities. This kind of social and economic base allows minorities to look within their in-group when making evaluations and social comparisons, rather than only to the white mainstream. They may suffer discrimination in the white mainstream, but within the in-group they are protected and proud.

This research highlights the difficulties of measuring subjective perceptions of discrimination. The next time you read a headline reporting that "80 percent of X people say they have been discriminated against," ask yourself, "How exactly did they measure discrimination?"

Concepts and Issues

Prejudice against minorities is a major societal problem, even if it is not expressed openly or directly, because inherent in attitudes are inclinations to act in particular ways. The prejudiced person is more likely to discriminate against particular groups when opportunities arise. People tend to report higher levels of discrimination against their group(s) than against themselves, and one interpretation is that this is because of denial, perhaps motivated by a need to maintain a sense of control in both task–related and social arenas. Evidence demonstrating a generalized discrepancy suggests that people perceive the effect of events as greater on groups than on themselves because of an availability heuristic.

1. Define *prejudice* and *discrimination.* In what ways are they different?
2. What is meant by *spoiled identity?*
3. Give examples of minority and majority groups, as well as power minorities/majorities and numerical minorities/majorities.
4. What is the personal–group discrimination discrepancy, and how does it differ from the generalized personal/group discrepancy?

The Cognitive Basis of Prejudice

Is human cognition a source of prejudice? Does the way human beings process information about the world mean that prejudice is inevitable? Does the way we categorize and store information about the social world lead to prejudice? Such questions evolve from a cognitive approach to understanding prejudice, an approach that emphasizes universal aspects of information processing (Devine, 1995). The implication is that prejudice may arise automatically as a result of the way we humans think rather than as a consequence of social contexts or particular personal motivations. In assessing this cognitive approach, we begin by first looking at what happens when people categorize the social world into "them" and "us." Prejudice and discrimination can come about only if there is a group that can serve as a target for negative beliefs, feelings, and actions. Next, we review the concept of stereotypes and consider the subtle ways in which they have an effect.

Social Categorization

Think back to the last time you went shopping in a crowded mall. There was so much hustle and bustle, so many goods on sale, such an assortment of colors, shapes, and noises as shoppers made their way through the crowds, while the music and announcements from the loudspeakers added to the general hubbub. Did you see and hear all this as a blur? No, you managed to scan the scenery, pick out the shops and goods you wanted, and home in on particular items. Our ability to deal with such vast amounts of information is enhanced through **categorization:** the grouping of phenomena. For example, while looking through the mall, we can quickly categorize shops into groups, such as "shops with clothes that I tend to like" vs. "shops with clothes that are not for me," or "shops that are too expensive" vs. "shops that are more in my price range."

categorization the grouping of phenomena.

It is generally agreed that all human beings categorize both nonsocial (e.g., colors) and social (e.g., people) phenomena. But there does tend to be some cross–cultural variation in the way categorization is carried out. For example, participants representing 98 different language groups used an exhaustive color chart to reveal how color is depicted in their particular language (Berlin & Kay, 1969). The results show that the number of color categories used varies considerably across languages. Some languages use only two categories, dark and light; others use hundreds. However, there are some consistencies across most groups, as in the case of the order in which basic color terms enter languages. The general trend (although there are some exceptions) is that if a language only has two color categories, the basic colors will be black and white; if a third is added, it will be red; a fourth will be either green or yellow (see Brown, 1991).

With respect to the social world, also, there seem to be some minimal consistencies in the way individuals from different cultures categorize people. Perhaps the only universal categorization of the social world is based on us versus them, or in–group versus out–group (LeVine & Campbell, 1972). A gender–based categorization, grouping people as either male or female, is fairly common across cultures, but there are variations on this theme. Among several Native American tribes, for example, the *berdache*, a morphological male who behaves in a female manner, forms a third gender (Williams, 1992).

Consistencies Across Nonsocial and Social Categorization

As an Eastern European Jew who found refuge in England after World War II, Henri Tajfel had firsthand experience of prejudice and discrimination, and as a social psychologist he tackled these problems with a particular passion. Perhaps his most important contribution as a researcher is his demonstration of certain consequences of categorization that are common to both social and nonsocial arenas. Among such consequences are, first, the exaggeration of the similarity of items placed in the same category and, second, the exaggeration of differences between items placed in different categories (Tajfel, 1957, 1959; Tajfel & Wilkes, 1963).

In an experiment that serves as a prototype, participants were asked to estimate the lengths of eight lines that actually differed in length by a constant ratio. For participants in Condition 1, the four shortest lines were labeled A and the four longest B. For participants in Condition 2, the eight lines were randomly assigned to groups A and B. Participants in Condition 3 were shown the lines without labels. After a series of presentations, participants in Condition 1 showed a systematic tendency to exaggerate the differences between lines in groups A and B and also to see lines within each category as more similar in length than they really were. This *between-group differentiation* and *within-group homogeneity* was not present in estimates made by participants in the other two conditions.

But what has the estimation of lines got to do with prejudice against other people? A lot, Tajfel would respond, because the same basic

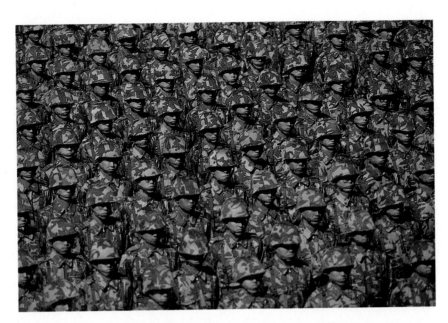

"They all look alike to me! I have a hard time telling them apart." People sometimes have this experience when they visit a foreign country where the people are culturally and phenotypically very different from themselves. People from Asia and Africa sometimes feel this way when they visit the Scandinavian countries and see crowds of white, blond people. Westerners experience this out–group homogeneity effect when they travel in Asia or Africa and are confronted by scenes such as this group of Japanese self-defense troops. The significance of this effect is that it can lead to other people being seen, and even treated, as an unindividuated mass. This can make it more difficult for personal relationships to develop and more likely for prejudice and out–group hostility to occur.

consequence of categorization could be present in people categorization. Subsequent research on how individuals perceive members of in–groups in contrast to members of out–groups provides evidence to support this view (Judd & Park, 1988; Park & Rothbart, 1982; Rothbart, Dawes, & Park, 1984), although some exceptions have been reported (Judd, Park, Ryan, Brauer, & Kraus, 1995). It seems that most individuals perceive more variability within their own group ("We are different individuals with our own special personalities") than they do within outgroups ("They all look the same to me, I really can't tell them apart"). I was struck by the power of this phenomenon when a senior scientist at a major university confessed to me that the Southeast Asian women who apply for doctoral program and medical school places "all look like clones" to him. Clearly, it is not just people with little education who think along these lines and need to be better informed.

One of the practical consequences of this perceptual bias is that in legal proceedings witnesses are more accurate in identifying members of their own race than they are members of other races (Anthony, Copper, & Mullen, 1992). This is true for both blacks and whites (Bothwell, Bringham, & Malpass, 1989). The applied implications of this bias are discussed further in Chapter 15.

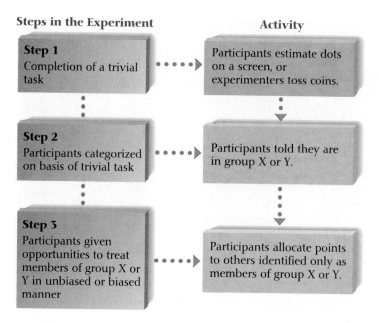

Steps in the Experiment

Activity

Step 1
Completion of a trivial task

Participants estimate dots on a screen, or experimenters toss coins.

Step 2
Participants categorized on basis of trivial task

Participants told they are in group X or Y.

Step 3
Participants given opportunities to treat members of group X or Y in unbiased or biased manner

Participants allocate points to others identified only as members of group X or Y.

Figure 10–4   Steps and activities in the minimal group paradigm (after Tajfel, Flament, Billig, & Bundy, 1971).

minimal group paradigm   an experimental demonstration of intergroup bias using arbitrary and apparently trivial criteria for group formation.

Tajfel's most important research on categorization actually involved social phenomena and had implications of even more direct importance for the topic of prejudice. Together with Michael Billig, Howard Giles, John Turner, and other associates, Tajfel developed a procedure called the **minimal group paradigm,** an experimental demonstration of intergroup bias using arbitrary and apparently trivial criteria for group formation (see Taylor & Moghaddam, 1994, chapter 4). (See Figure 10–4.) First, participants carried out a trivial task, such as estimating how many dots are flashed on a screen. Second, they are given feedback informing them simply that they have been placed in either group X or group Y on the basis of their responses on the trivial task. Participants are then asked to allocate points to other members of groups X and Y, without knowing their identities. Research has shown that even placing people in such minimal groups can lead to in-group favoritism. However, people from less competitive cultures may not show the same bias, as demonstrated by Margaret Wetherell's (1982) research using Samoan and Maori participants. (Tajfel's research is discussed further in Chapter 14.)

Culture and Categorization

Some evidence supports the idea that there are continuities from nonsocial to social stimuli in the way we perceive categories, and that we perceive in-group members as more dissimilar ("We are individual persons") and out-group members as more homogeneous ("They are an undifferentiated mass, all alike"). This evidence (e.g., see Messick &

Mackie, 1989; Quattrone & Jones, 1980), to a large extent, ignores two issues. One is that studying *social* perception by using nonsocial stimuli (such as lines) can be misleading because certain exaggerations may occur that are not present in everyday life (Markus & Zajonc, 1985). A second, more fundamental, point is that contextual factors influence social perception, and these may influence people to see the in-group as more homogeneous than the out-group, thus negating the out-group homogeneity effect.

Evidence for the important role of contextual factors is provided by Yueh-Ting Lee and his associates, who have explored the relation between culture and intergroup perceptions (Lee, 1993, 1995; Lee, Albright, & Malloy, in press; Lee, Jussim, & McCauley, 1995; Lee & Ottati, 1993, 1995). Research among a number of samples outside the United States has shown the opposite of the out-group homogeneity effect. Chinese participants saw themselves as more homogeneous when faced with the threat of what they saw to be an inaccurate negative stereotype (e.g., "Chinese are dishonest"). In another study, a small group of female British professors saw themselves as more homogeneous than they did male British professors (Brown & Smith, 1989). Perhaps this is because the female professors have the common experience of being members of a power minority.

Related to this evidence are the results of a number of studies on the objective reality, or the "kernel-of-truth," theory, which suggest that how we perceive other people *does* reflect their actual characteristics (Lee, Albright, & Malloy, in press; Lee & Ottati, 1993). If people in culture X are more alike than are people in culture Y (in terms of clothing style, material possessions, customs, and the like, for example), then people in both cultures will most likely recognize this difference. Chinese participants saw themselves as more similar to each other than they saw Americans. This is exactly the opposite of the traditional finding "We are all different, they are all alike." On the other hand, American participants in the same study saw themselves as more heterogeneous than they saw Chinese (here, we are back to the traditional finding "We are all different individuals, they are all the same"; see Lee & Ottati, 1993).

Of course, whether the real characteristics of groups influence social perception or not depends on what is perceived to be a real characteristic in the first place. The "kernel-of-truth" idea is itself context-dependent (see Crystal & Watanabe, 1997, for a related discussion). It may be that in some cultures homogeneity is preferred to heterogeneity, and people *prefer* to see the in-group as more similar. This is exactly what the Chinese participants said (Lee & Ottati, 1993). Americans value "being different," and it may be this preference that leads them to see the in-group as different people, as "independent individuals."

Stereotypes

Do you know what my idea of hell is?" asks the first woman. "What?" responds the second. "A place where Italians run the government, the English do the cooking, and the Swiss are the lovers!

stereotype   culturally based but
often unfounded generalization
about groups.

Most of us are familiar with such jokes, which incorporate stereotypes, a hot topic for social psychological research (Mackie & Hamilton,
1993; Macrae, Stangor, & Hewstone, 1995; Oakes, Haslam, & Turner,
1994; Spears, Oakes, Ellemers, & Haslem, 1996). A **stereotype** is a
culturally based but often unfounded generalization about groups
(Hamilton & Sherman, 1994). Research has highlighted the often inaccurate expectations stereotypes raise (Judd & Park, 1993). For example,
it is obviously wrong to expect that all the English people one meets
are lousy cooks. (I lived in England for 19 years and can vouch that
some English people are first-rate cooks.)

Mood and Prejudice.   When are people more likely to use stereotypes? Some research suggests an association between mood and prejudice (Dovidio, Gaertner, Isen, & Lowrance, 1995; Esses & Zanna, 1995;
Stephan, Ageyev, Coates-Shrider, Stephan, & Abalakina, 1994). One reason for the importance of this topic is that the relationship between
bad mood and prejudice may be universal: People everywhere may be
more likely to be prejudiced when they are in bad moods. The research
of Gerrod Parrott suggests that people can regulate their own moods
(Parrott, 1993, 1994; Parrott & Sabini, 1990), and there are various reasons why one may want to be in a bad mood: in order to behave in a
prejudiced manner toward others, for example. Through getting oneself
to become envious of particular others, one may come to resent them
(Parrott & Smith, 1993). By extension, a powerful leader could regulate
the emotional climate of a society so that people come to resent target
groups, as Hitler influenced many Germans to resent Jews.

Stereotypes and Intergroup Perceptions.   Research on stereotypes has
also helped us to understand how the members of different groups
view one another. For example, ethnic stereotypes such as "Turks are
treacherous," "Jews are shrewd," "Blacks are happy-go-lucky" are reported among U.S. college students (see Taylor & Moghaddam, 1994).
Most such descriptive studies have reported negative out-group stereotypes. However, negative in-group stereotypes were indirectly revealed
in a study conducted in France. Native French people were asked to
rate actual ("what they are actually like") and ideal ("how they should
be in the ideal") French people, as well as actual and ideal immigrants
from North Africa and Southeast Asia on a number of traits, such as
hardworking, clean, and trustworthy (Lambert, Moghaddam, Sorin, &
Sorin, 1990). Interestingly, when the stereotypes of actual and ideal
groups were mapped onto one another, it was found that the group
stereotype closest to the French ideal was not that of the French themselves but that of the Southeast Asian immigrants.

By reporting the French actual as farther away from the French
ideal than the Southeast Asian actual, French participants in this study
were being critical of the in-group, at least indirectly. They were saying,
for example, that the French are not as hardworking as they should be,
and that the Southeast Asians are closer to the ideal to which French
people should aspire.

One way to conceptualize stereotypes is as socially acceptable or normative ways of viewing different groups. Research suggests that stereotypes exist in all cultures (Leyens, Yzerbyt, & Schadron, 1994). A stereotype is not an inevitable consequence of social categorization but an outcome that fits in with prevailing social norms. As social norms pertaining to groups change, stereotypes of groups also change. Thus, for example, as social norms about women and ethnic minorities have changed since the 1960s, stereotypes have shifted to some extent in the direction of the new politically correct views.

The interpretation of stereotypes as culturally based generalizations about groups still leaves the question open: Are stereotypes generally correct or incorrect? The traditional view has been to describe stereotypes as incorrect and generally bad (see Taylor & Moghaddam, 1994, Chapter 8). From the 1930s, at least, social psychological research has emphasized the inaccuracy of stereotypes. For example, LaPiere (1936), whose research on attitudes we touch on in Chapter 4, found that stereotypes about Armenians in California often being in trouble with the law were wrong. The evidence showed they tended to have fewer brushes with the law compared to national averages. This tradition of viewing stereotypes as inaccurate has been strengthened since the 1970s by social cognitive research, which has continued to emphasize biases in making judgments about the world (Fiske, 1993b; Jussim, 1993). A succinct summary of the social cognitive view of the way people make judgments about the world would be: "Their judgments are generally inaccurate, and systematically biased."

Stereotypes and System Justification. A cultural perspective leads us to focus more on the meaning of a stereotype in a given context rather than trying to establish how wrong or right it might be irrespective of context. There certainly *is* some truth to some stereotypes, such as those held by Greeks and Americans with firsthand knowledge of Greeks and Americans (Triandis & Vassiliou, 1967; see Triandis, 1994, for a broader discussion). A generally more important issue, however, is the *meaning* of the stereotype of blacks as "too pushy" and "undemocratic" in the current context of life in the United States. To appreciate the significance of such stereotypes, we need to consider the larger culture: the struggle over affirmative action, the historical emphasis on individualism in U.S. society, and the renewed focus on self-help in American politics (see Moghaddam, 1997a, Chapters 6 and 7).

John Jost and Mahzarin Banaji (1994) have taken us some way toward understanding the wider function of stereotypes. They propose that in addition to serving as *ego justification* (i.e., serving to protect the status of the self) and *group justification* (i.e., serving to protect the status of in-groups), stereotypes also serve as *system justification*. That is, stereotypes legitimize existing status hierarchies so that those with high status are presented as superior and those with low status are presented in a negative light—corresponding to their social positions.

Stereotype Threat.   Imagine a gang of violent criminals has been identified in your neighborhood, and their specialty is robbing people who use ATMs. A photograph of the criminal gang appears in the local paper, and several of the gang members look a lot like you. Family members, friends, neighbors—it seems everyone has noticed the similarity. You try to forget this issue, but when you are standing in line at an ATM you notice that the woman in front of you has a copy of the newspaper in her hand and seems a little nervous. Does she imagine you are going to mug her? You wonder whether you should say something to ease her mind, but would this only make

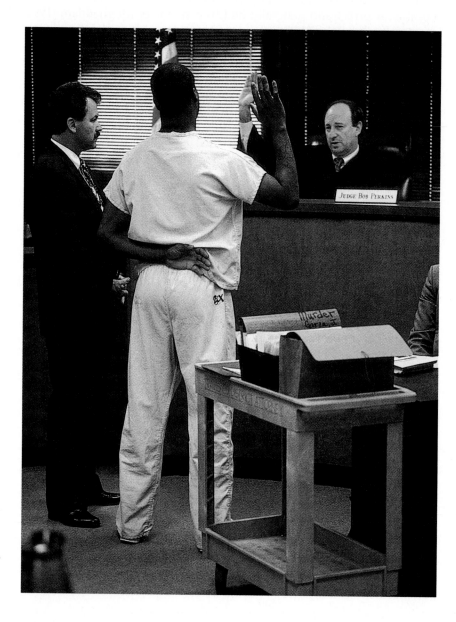

Black defendant before a white judge. A goal of democratic societies is for the legal system to operate objectively, independent of whatever biases might exist in society. Social psychological research shows that this ideal has not been fully achieved, even in the more developed Western democracies. In the United States, ethnic minorities are more likely to receive harsher punishments than whites who commit the same offense.

matters worse? As she gets her money and rushes away, you wonder if she is hurrying because she is afraid of you, or maybe she has not even noticed you and is rushing because she is late for an appointment.

This "threat in the air," of being stereotyped (as a violent criminal), has a powerful impact on you. Fortunately, it goes away after a few days, when the police catch the real criminals. You feel relieved. But for some people, such as women and ethnic minorities, argues the African-American social psychologist Claude Steele (1992, 1997), the barrier of stereotype threat is always present. A *stereotype threat* is "the event of a negative stereotype about a group to which one belongs becoming self-relevant, usually as a plausible interpretation for something one is doing, for an experience one is having, or for a situation one is in, that has relevance to one's self definition" (Steele, 1997, p. 616). When Mariam makes mistakes in some mathematical calculations in her thermodynamics class, she is anxious because she is aware of the negative stereotype women still suffer in engineering school ("Women are not much good at math"), whereas her classmate John makes the same mistakes but suffers no such anxiety.

Evidence in support of this idea comes from a series of studies in which women and men were tested in advanced math and advanced literature, under various conditions (Spencer, Steele, & Quinn, 1997). Female and male participants were matched on math and literature abilities. In conditions where the test was particularly difficult, women underperformed relative to men on the math test but not the literature test. Spencer et al. (1997) argue this happened because of the stereotype threat in the domain of math. In another study, participants taking an advanced math test were told either that the test generally showed gender differences or no gender differences (Spencer et al., 1997). The "gender differences" condition suggests that the stereotype of women's lesser ability in math is correct. Thus, a stereotype threat is present for women participants in this condition. The results showed a dramatic difference in the performance of women students; they performed similarly to the men in the "no stereotype threat" condition, but far worse than men in the "stereotype threat" condition.

Steele's (1992, 1997) account of stereotypes is powerful, because it effectively links micro, or individual, level processes to the macro, or cultural level, processes. A stereotype threat or a "threat in the air" (Steele, 1997, p. 613) is not something inside a person's mind; it is something "out there" as a feature of a culture. At the same time, whether or not one is influenced by a stereotype threat depends to some extent on personal intentions and interpretations. If Mariam identifies herself as a math major and cares about doing well in math, then she is more likely to be influenced by a stereotype threat in the context of a difficult math test. On the other hand, some individuals, such as those high on authoritarianism (Altemeyer, 1988a), are more likely than others to use negative stereotypes and thus put into effect a stereotype threat. But Steele's account implies that it is extremely difficult to solve the problem of stereotypes at the level of individuals; cultural reform is needed to ensure that stereotype threats are not pervasive.

Concepts and Issues

Categorization of both nonsocial and social phenomena is a universal: In all known societies, there is, at least, a division of people into "us" and "them." One consequence in many instances is between-group differentiation and within-group homogeneity, but these categorizations are not common to all cultures. Shared ideas about groups form the basis of stereotypes in society. Stereotypes about minorities tend to be negative.

1. Give examples of social categorization in your life.
2. Have you come across between-group differentiation and within-group homogeneity in interactions with others? Discuss.
3. What is the basic procedure for the minimal group paradigm?
4. Give some examples of how culture can influence categorization and stereotypes.

Toward a Cultural Explanation of Prejudice

Biases against minorities have proven to be resilient, and some evidence suggests that prejudice continues to exist but manifests itself in a more subtle fashion: modern or symbolic sexism and racism in contrast to old-fashioned or traditional sexism and racism.

Is Prejudice Against Minorities Declining in the United States?

Research on prejudice raises this puzzling question: Is prejudice against minorities declining in the United States? Attitudinal surveys show that in the 1960s only about 45 percent of whites would vote for well-qualified black candidates, a figure that went up to 81 percent in the 1980s; in the same period the percentage who agreed that white and black children should attend the same schools went up from 65 percent to 90 percent, and those opposed to laws against intermarriage went up from 39 percent to 66 percent (Schuman, Steeh, & Bobo, 1985). Fewer people now endorse negative stereotypes of blacks (Dovidio & Gaertner, 1986), and self-reported prejudice against minorities, including women, seems to have declined (Hochschild & Herk, 1990).

But do self-reported attitudes tell the whole story? A number of researchers have looked closely at subtle measures of prejudice and concluded that the situation is not as rosy as may appear from reports of attitude surveys. Patricia Devine and Andrew Elliot (1995) have shown that what may be changing is knowledge about, rather than endorsement of, stereotypes. Their evidence suggests a stable negative stereotype of African–Americans.

A study conducted by an African–American male and a white female (Whittler & DiMeo, 1991) focused on the reactions of white members of the general population in the southeastern United States to black and white actors in advertising. Unlike several other studies that had used student participants and found that the race of actors did not influence viewer reactions (see Whittler & DiMeo, 1991), it was found that these members of the general population were more likely to purchase the products when the actors were white. This was regardless of the positive or negative self–reported attitudes of the participants toward blacks. One interpretation of this finding is that even participants who explicitly expressed more positive attitudes toward blacks implicitly use negative stereotypes (Greenwald & Banaji, 1995).

But what about in the courts? Surely everyone is now equal in the eyes of the law and receives equal treatment in the judicial system. Once again, detailed examination of research findings shows that actual behavior is in some ways different from explicitly expressed attitudes and is discriminatory toward blacks and probably toward other minorities as well. Studies of archival evidence show that for similar offenses in similar circumstances, black offenders in the United States tend to receive stiffer sentences than whites (Baldus, Woodworth, & Pulaski, 1985, 1994), are less likely to be allowed bail or receive probation, and in general receive less just treatment (Ayres & Waldfogel, 1994; Brown & Hullin, 1993; Burnett, 1994; Meyer & Jesilow, 1996). Despite the mounting evidence showing discrimination against African–Americans, the judicial system is slow to reform (Bright, 1995).

A fairly extensive meta–analysis of the literature showed that in experimental juror studies, in which participants act as a jury in a mock trial, racial bias persists in both the southern and northern parts of the United States (Sweeney & Haney, 1992). A similar racial bias exists in legal decisions in Canada and perhaps other societies (Rector & Bagby, 1995). These results indicate a continuing challenge for intergroup relations, particularly because many experimental studies use students as participants, and this younger, better educated group is assumed to be less prejudiced than the general population.

Perhaps science is the final bastion against injustice? But the traditional view of science as an objective enterprise conducted by politically neutral specialists has been shown to be flawed (see Moghaddam, 1997a). Even research in areas such as chemistry can be influenced in important ways by social psychological factors, such as subjective perceptions and biases (Latour & Woolgar, 1979). In the domain of the social sciences, including social psychology, Anthony Greenwald and Eric Schuh (1994) studied almost 30,000 citations in the psychology literature and found a pattern of in–group favoritism among non–Jewish–named and Jewish–named authors, even among researchers who study prejudice! Citations are important in research because authors gain status when they are cited often. Greenwald and Schuh discovered that non–Jewish–named and Jewish–named authors cited more others whose names fell into the same ethnic category as themselves. Given that researchers who study prejudice have the avowed goal of solving this problem, we must assume that they are not aware of the biased way in which they are citing the work of other authors.

Explanations for the Puzzle

How, then, are we to explain this situation? On the one hand, there are a number of indications that intergroup relations have improved. Self-reported prejudice has declined, and legal reform has been implemented so that everyone is now equal in the eyes of the law. On the other hand, there are still numerous indications that prejudice is prevalent (Katz & Taylor, 1988). For example, during the mid–1990s there was a rash of fires in predominantly black churches in the southern parts of the United States. This kind of intolerance seems out of place at the turn of the twenty–first century, when tolerance is supposed to be the norm. Let us consider some possible explanations.

Change as Impression Management/Self-Presentation.
One possibility is that since the civil rights movement of the 1960s, after which legislation made racial, gender, and most other group–based discrimination illegal, people learned to *present themselves* according to the new norms and rules regulating correct behavior. (This will remind you, I hope, of Erving Goffman's [1956] emphasis on self-presentation in everyday life, discussed in Chapter 2.) Fay Crosby and her colleagues have argued that antiblack sentiments persist much more than the survey results would suggest because the surveys only reveal successful impression management by whites (Crosby, Bromley, & Saxe, 1980). Direct measures of prejudice and discrimination do not necessarily reveal internalized values but, rather, compliance with newly prevalent ideas about correct behavior (Dovidio & Fazio, 1992).

Given that impression management is to some extent involved, how should researchers study prejudice and discrimination? One answer is through indirect measures that do not give participants the opportunity to think through issues and consciously manage self-presentations. Imagine you are a research participant and your task is to say if a number of word pairings could "ever be true" or are "always false." The word pairings always include either black or white, presented with either positive (e.g., efficient) or negative (e.g., lazy) traits. If you are like most white participants, you will respond faster to positive traits paired with white and negative traits paired with black (Dovidio, Evans, & Tyler, 1986). A number of other studies using indirect measures (e.g., Gilbert & Hixon, 1991) have shown that merely activating a racial stereotype, by including words or images associated with ethnic minorities, influences the behavior of research participants. Most interesting is that this research has revealed similar implicit biases for participants who on direct or explicit measures had significantly different scores on racial prejudice.

Once again, what this research seems to be telling us is that if we ask white participants about their racial attitudes directly, they are likely to manage their impressions and express positive intergroup attitudes. But if we use implicit, indirect measures, we are more likely to unearth negative racial prejudices against minorities.

From Traditional to Symbolic Racism. Imagine you were a researcher in South Africa in the 1950s, well before the collapse of apartheid, the official policy through which the Afrikaaner–dominated South African government used to keep races separate and unequal. Afrikaaners at that time described themselves as racially superior. If you, as a researcher, asked Afrikaaners about their attitudes toward blacks, they would express their prejudices directly (although you used both direct and indirect methods of studying such prejudices; Pettigrew, Allport, & Barnett, 1958). In some parts of the United States and other Western societies as well, whites would have expressed antiblack prejudices without much compunction during the 1950s. This kind of "old–fashioned" racism was based on ideas such as "Blacks are not as smart as whites." But since the 1970s, there has been increasing pressure for people to conform to a new set of democratic norms, based on the idea that group–based differences are not important. It is not group membership that counts, according to the new norms, but individual characteristics.

This has influenced the way people talk about all power minorities, including women and blacks. The public discourse tends to be supportive of meritocracy now, so that fewer people explicitly express attitudes such as "Women are too emotional to be good managers" or "Blacks are lazy." However, according to some researchers this does not mean that prejudice has declined; it only means that old–fashioned racism and sexism are out and so-called symbolic racism and sexism are in (McConahay, 1986; Sears, 1988). Thus, as we approach the twenty–first century, we have "modern" racism and sexism, which reject traditional racist and sexist beliefs (e.g., "Women and blacks are not as smart as white men"), but camouflage prejudices within more sophisticated principles of meritocracy and justice (Swim, Aikin, Hall, & Hunter, 1995). See Figure 10–5 for a comparison of old–fashioned and modern racism and sexism.

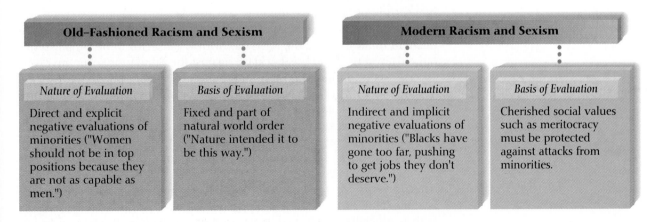

Old–Fashioned Racism and Sexism		Modern Racism and Sexism	
Nature of Evaluation	*Basis of Evaluation*	*Nature of Evaluation*	*Basis of Evaluation*
Direct and explicit negative evaluations of minorities ("Women should not be in top positions because they are not as capable as men.")	Fixed and part of natural world order ("Nature intended it to be this way.")	Indirect and implicit negative evaluations of minorities ("Blacks have gone too far, pushing to get jobs they don't deserve.")	Cherished social values such as meritocracy must be protected against attacks from minorities.

Figure 10–5   A comparison of old–fashioned and modern racism and sexism.

Modern prejudice is sometimes expressed in terms of blacks, women, and other minorities "going too far" and threatening cherished values. Prejudiced individuals sometimes qualify such statements by asserting that "of course women should be treated as equals, but these feminists have just gone too far, they are over the top" or "blacks have made the mistake of pushing for too much and so a lot of reverse discrimination is going on and honest white people are suffering as a result." In this kind of discourse, racism and sexism are indirect, and meritocracy and fair play are cited as the underlying reasons for opposition to the minority group in question.

Modern prejudice, then, involves positioning minority groups as a force that is working against cherished social values. This means that the story lines prejudiced people adopt have to be convincing for themselves personally and also at the group level (see Tan & Moghaddam, 1995, in press). Just what kinds of story lines are convincing depends a great deal on the cultural context in which the discourse is taking place. In the U.S. context, individualism and meritocracy are readily available and generally endorsed, so they can be used to create a strong story line (Gaertner & Dovidio, 1986). That is, a statement that begins with the view that "the American way is for everyone to have equal opportunities" or "we all have to compete on level ground" taps into traditionally valued sentiments associated with democracy.

But also found in the United States and other Western societies are strong historical racist tendencies, rooted in colonialism and the era of slavery. These racist feelings can be tapped through other culturally appropriate story lines, through phrases such as "Women and blacks are pushing to get an unfair advantage."

Symbolic Racism in Non-Western Societies. Does symbolic prejudice also exist outside Western societies? In a number of non–Western societies, we can find people discussing the issue of democracy, minority rights, and specific policies such as affirmative action in some ways similar to what is going on in the United States. For example, in India, where affirmative action programs have been put into place to try to improve the situation of the Untouchables, there is also what seems to be a recognizable voice of symbolic racism using meritocratic arguments to try to prevent minorities from gaining power (see Singh, 1988, for a review). Attempts to improve the situation of the Burakumin, a supposedly racially different minority in Japan, have met with what seems to be similar resistance (Hawkins, 1986). This backlash against the Burakumin even involved special lists of Burakumin names and addresses being purchased by major corporations, such as Nissan and Mitsubishi, to safeguard against hiring them "by mistake" (DeVos & Wetherall, 1983).

But the basis on which minorities become the target for prejudice can vary considerably, depending on the most compelling story lines in any given culture. In societies in which religion and politics are explicitly and directly connected, religious affiliation can more readily become a basis for targeting particular out-groups. An example is the Islamic Republic of Iran, where prejudice against members of the Baha'i faith is officially sanctioned, because they are seen as enemies of Islam.

In the former U.S.S.R., for a time those with any religious affiliation suffered officially sanctioned prejudice, following the Marxist idea that "religion . . . is the opium of the people," meaning that it drugs them into accepting the status quo and not mobilizing for collective action.

Hidden Prejudices in Western Societies. Such cross-cultural examples lead to this question: "What kinds of prejudices remain prevalent in Western societies but, for the most part, are hidden from us because we live and breathe them?" One example that strikes me whenever I return to the United States after travel abroad is prejudice against overweight people, who constitute a stigmatized group in U.S. society (Allon, 1982).

Over a period of a week in 1997, I kept a record of how many times I was exposed to advertising, information, and discussions on the topic of weight as I went through my daily routine in Maryland, U.S.A. In addition to television, radio, and newspapers, I included magazine and book covers, food and other product labels, pamphlets through the mail, and discussions with other people. The total was an astounding 114 times. Modern societies are becoming more and more concerned with the issue of weight, just as they increasingly idealize slimness. This process is so accepted and pervasive that we seldom acknowledge its many negative aspects, such as size discrimination. For these women demonstrating for their rights, discrimination based on size is a serious issue.

Next time you are passing a stand showing American magazines, stop and spend a few minutes looking over the magazine covers. Two things will immediately be apparent. First, the vast majority of covers show young, slim, attractive females, and sometimes males. Second, advertised on the covers will be articles and guides about weight loss, such as the following, which I found when I recently browsed through magazines on display: "How to lose 20 lb without stress," "Ten tips for a trim figure," "Is your body ready for show at the beach this summer?" "A rock hard stomach in just two weeks."

This "weight watch" industry thrives on the idea that people can and do control their own weight and that *those who are overweight are to blame* (Crandall, 1994). People perceived as overweight are routinely stigmatized and blamed for their condition (Weiner, Perry, & Magnusson, 1988), so they try to compensate for the prejudice of others and present themselves in a more positive light (Miller, Rothblum, Felicio, & Brand, 1995).

The "problem of weight" does not affect men and women equally: From adolescence onward, and perhaps even earlier, women are scrutinized much more than men on this issue. This results in women being more concerned about their appearance generally and their weight specifically (Pliner, Chaiken, & Flett, 1990). In some studies, over half the adolescent females surveyed in the United States reported themselves to be overweight (Fallon & Rozin, 1985). Jennifer Crocker, Beth Cronwell, and Brenda Major (1993) showed that when overweight and normal-weight college women received either positive or negative feedback from a male evaluator, the overweight women tended to blame their weight rather than the evaluator for the outcome.

Social Change: A Multilayered Process

The challenge of reducing prejudice and discrimination is part of the broader challenge of how to bring about social change (Moghaddam & Crystal, 1997; Moghaddam & Harré, 1995). It has proved to be very difficult to manage social change, as successive Western and non-Western governments everywhere have discovered. It is not necessarily that politicians do not want to bring about the changes they promise us (increase the numbers of jobs, decrease crime, improve health care, provide better education, lower inflation, achieve better race relations, end sexism, and so on), but their ability to do so has been very limited. Problems such as racism and poverty seem resistant to change. There seems to be some truth to the saying "The more things change, the more they stay the same."

One way to conceptualize change is as multilayered. At the macro level there is political and economic change (changes in governments and economic policies). These can come about fairly quickly and involve power suddenly moving from the hands of one group to another, as occurred during the French Revolution, which toppled the monarchy and created a republic in 1792, and the bloodless revolution that toppled communism in Eastern Europe and the former U.S.S.R. in 1989. In contrast to such rapid change at the macro level, at the micro level there are slower social psychological changes in the everyday behaviors of individuals in interaction—for example, how two lovers behave toward one another, how parents socialize their children, and how two people who have just met get to know one another better.

In considering change, then, we need to consider the possibility that the speed of change at the macro level is often different from the speed of change at the micro level (Moghaddam & Crystal, 1997). For example, a government can in one day vote into place new legislation making discrimination against women and minorities illegal. However, it is not possible to achieve an overnight change in the way people behave toward in-group and out-group members in their everyday interactions. This is in part because each bit of behavior involves socially acquired skills and requires time and effort to learn. Just think about how many years parents have to train a child to get to the stage of being able to converse properly with strangers, friends, and family.

Some observers argue that at the deepest levels, fundamental change in social relationships, such as those involving race and gender relations, can only come about slowly over generations, both among the general public and among experts and politicians. The historian Kenneth O'Reilly (1995) has analyzed racial politics and concluded that in many ways the policies followed by U.S. presidents, from George Washington to Bill Clinton, have remained very similar and generally antiblack. Attempts to bring about change at the more micro, everyday life, level through affirmative programs have also failed to shift prejudice against minorities (e.g., Tougas, Brown, Beaton, & Joly, 1995).

From a cultural perspective, change in social relationships is inevitably slow because the norms and rules that regulate the details of everyday life are difficult to shift (Moghaddam & Crystal, 1997; Moghaddam & Harré, 1995). It is sometimes easier to learn to express new attitudes verbally than it is to change actual behavior. One may express politically correct attitudes about race relations, but yet not change how one behaves toward the members of out-groups, particularly in the subtle and detailed aspects of social interactions such as eye contact, body posture, voice tone, and so on. The implicit and subtle nature of these persistent behavior patterns might explain why blacks, women, and other minorities continue to report discrimination against themselves, when on the surface discrimination would seem to have ended (also, see Greenwald & Banaji, 1995).

Historical Change and Prejudice

"I never met with so many pleasant girls in my life, as I have this evening; and there are several of them you see uncommonly pretty."

"*You* are dancing with the only handsome girl in the room," said Darcy, looking at the eldest Miss Bennet.

"Oh! she is the most beautiful creature I ever beheld! But there is one of her sisters sitting down just behind you, who is very pretty, and I dare say, very agreeable. Do let me ask my partner to introduce you."

"Which do you mean?" and turning round, he looked for a moment at Elizabeth, till catching her eye, he withdrew his own and coldly said, "She is tolerable; but not handsome enough to tempt *me*; and I am in no humour at present to give consequence to young ladies who are slighted by other men"

—Jane Austen, *Pride and Prejudice*

This conversation between the proud Mr. Darcy and his more amiable friend Mr. Bingley takes place at a ball in the early part of Jane Austen's classic novel *Pride and Prejudice*. Darcy is from an aristocratic family, and he looks down in haughty pride at the members of the "lowly" Bennet family, going so far as to try to stop his friend Bingley from marrying one of the Bennet sisters. Darcy's pride, and the prejudices he bears against those he considers "unworthy," are not lost on Elizabeth Bennet. She develops her own prejudices against him, and refuses to marry him when he unexpectedly falls in love and proposes to her. Even during his proposal, Darcy manages to insult Elizabeth by telling her frankly how he has struggled to overcome his feeling of love for her because he knows that in terms of social standing her family is far below his own.

But Jane Austen brings this story to a happy ending. Elizabeth realizes how Darcy has overcome his pride, and toward the end of the novel we learn that, "gradually all her former prejudices had been removed," and they do marry. In reading a novel such as *Pride and Prejudice*, we are very aware that in order to understand the characters and their prejudices we must first appreciate the culture in which they live. This is an intuitively obvious point, reinforced by teachers of English literature. It is all too easy to neglect this lesson when we come to try to understand prejudices in the contemporary world and to imagine that "cognitive mechanisms," such as stereotyping, can exist outside culture and independent of the norms of a particular era, and even independent from feelings (Stangor, Sullivan, & Ford, 1991).

Prejudice is a cultural phenomenon and it changes over time, both in its level and in how it is expressed. For example, earlier we saw that prejudice as measured by expressed attitudes has declined, in part because of new rules for political correctness. Another example is provided by findings suggesting that although black children were ambivalent about identifying with their ethnic in-group in the 1940s, in the 1950s, 1960s, and 1970s they showed a stronger commitment to identifying with the black in-group (Fine & Bowers, 1984). However, by the 1980s there seemed to be a change again, with black male children distancing themselves from the ethnic in-group. Such shifts reflect historical changes in perceived prejudice.

Male Bashing?   There is a continuous struggle between competing groups to define prejudice and to verify its sources and targets. As I looked through a newspaper recently, I found no less than three articles on controversies surrounding so-called reverse discrimination and the avowed negative impact of affirmative action. There is now a growing literature that depicts the white male as "victim" and discusses the psychological pressures placed on the members of this "new victimized group." Christopher Kilmartin (1994) has provided examples of male bashing, such as a lapel button "Men are living proof that women can

Tiger Woods in the final round of the Western Open, July 6, 1997. Legal and political reforms have helped to decrease blatant discrimination. Antidiscrimination legislation has meant that champion golfer Tiger Woods could not be excluded from major golf tournaments or from previously "whites only" golf courses, but he has been a victim of racial slurs. More subtle forms of discrimination continue. The courage and outstanding talent shown by individuals like Tiger Woods open up new territories and set new standards of achievement for other minorities.

take a joke" and a greeting card with "Men are scum" on the front, and on the back "Excuse me. For a second there, I was feeling generous" (p. 25). As further evidence, Kilmartin cites the best-selling book, *Men: An Owner's Manual. A Comprehensive Guide to Having a Man Underfoot* (Brush, 1984), and suggests we try to imagine the cultural reaction of equivalent messages directed against women or ethnic minorities.

Some commentators have claimed that in the United States specifically and Western societies generally, the focus has been on the rights of victims and that we need to place greater emphasis on self-help, personal responsibility, and what Terry Eastland (1996) has called "color-blind justice," which treats everyone as equal. If we really want to achieve a meritocracy, the argument goes, then people must be judged only on individual merit and not on group membership. The attempt to use race and gender to redress past grievances is doomed because the past cannot be undone and new grievances will be created.

In a vigorous defense of affirmative action, Barbara Bergmann (1996) has argued that race and gender are not needed in order to redress past grievances or to increase diversity, but to combat ongoing and entrenched discrimination against women and ethnic minorities. Social psychological research supports the view that prejudice and discrimination against women and ethnic minorities, and also the economically poor, continue—but in a more subtle and implicit manner (Cyrus, 1993; Devine, 1995; Duckitt, 1992; Feagin, 1991; Gaines & Reed, 1995; Greenwald & Banaji, 1995; Lott & Maluso, 1995).

Normative Systems and Prejudice. A cultural explanation of prejudice emphasizes the role of the normative system in society generally, as well as the family and peers more specifically. It has long been known that prejudice begins in childhood (Horowitz, 1936). Attitudes toward out-groups are internalized as individuals grow up in their families, peer groups, and the larger community, and are expressed in a way designed to win approval (Glock, Wuthnow, Pilavin, & Spencer, 1975). As we would expect from this line of argument, there is a high association between the intergroup prejudices of children and their parents (Ehrlich, 1973) and peers (Glock, Wuthnow, Pilavin, & Spencer, 1975). Parents and peers help to define correct behavior; they apply the standards by which individuals are evaluated. For some individuals, being a successful person means being a person who dislikes group X and likes group Y.

Prejudice is understood best in the broader context of how individuals present themselves. Nicholas Emler and Stephen Reicher (1995) have argued that much of the delinquency shown by adolescents is a concern to uphold and "manage" personal and group reputations. Prejudice against certain groups can be one of the strategies used to manage reputations ("Jim sure is one of us. Did you see the way he roughed up those X guys?").

Research on the authoritarian personality (Adorno et al., 1951; Forbes, 1985) and related research on fascism (Billig, 1978) suggest that prejudice is part of a larger ideological orientation acquired by individuals through socialization. However, although the roots of prejudice are found in the larger society, some individuals are more likely than others to find themselves among families and peers who endorse hostile intergroup attitudes and behaviors. Thus, although it would be a fundamental mistake to see prejudice as limited to a small number of bigots (Taylor & Moghaddam, 1994, p. 172), the *ecological niche* in which some individuals develop leads them to be more prejudiced. Research on authoritarianism has identified these people as being rigid, conventional, and more likely to see the world in categorical, right/wrong terms (i.e., they do not see shades of gray on issues). The Canadian social psychologist Bob Altemeyer (1981, 1988a, 1988b), who has spearheaded research on authoritarianism since the 1980s, emphasizes the role of social learning in prejudice, arguing that

> highly submissive, conventional people easily come to feel gravely threatened by social change or disorder. This fear seems to originate with their parents' warnings that the world is a dangerous and hostile place, though it may be reinforced by the mass media's emphasis on crime and violence in our society. Other emotions, such as envy, may feed the authoritarian's hostility, but not to nearly as great an extent. (1988b, p. 38)

An implication is that prejudice can be eliminated only through large-scale educational programs designed to affect society generally, rather than a selected group of "prejudiced" people.

Concepts and Issues

Despite legal reforms that make sexism, racism, and other forms of discrimination against minorities illegal, research suggests that discrimination continues. Modern forms of discrimination are more subtle but just as detrimental for their targets and for the larger society. It has proved very difficult to bring about behavior change in this area, perhaps because change at the macro level, involving the economic, political, and legal systems, can come about faster than change at the micro, personal, level of everyday behavior.

1. What evidence is there that prejudice against minorities is declining? What evidence suggests it is persisting?
2. Explain what is meant by impression management/self-presentation, and how this is related to reported decline in prejudice.
3. In what ways is symbolic sexism/racism different from traditional sexism/racism?
4. What is meant by social change as a "multilayered process"?

Conclusion

Social categorization seems to be a universal phenomenon, so that the grouping of people, "us" and "others" at the simplest level, takes place in all societies. In many societies a consequence of such categorization is perceptual biases: *We* are different individuals; *they* are more homogeneous. Groups tend to vary in terms of power and status, and minority groups tend to be the target of negative biases. Legal and political reforms have made discrimination on the basis of sex, race, religion, national origin, and the like illegal. This has been associated with a change in the ways in which biases against minorities manifest themselves. Traditional, or "old-fashioned," sexism and racism have been replaced by more subtle "symbolic" forms of sexism and racism. In order to understand better the complexities of this situation, we should conceptualize change as multilayered. The maximum speed of change at the macro political, economic, and legal levels is faster than that at the micro everyday social behavior level. Laws can be changed overnight; social behavior generally takes longer.

For Review

Prejudice is an attitude toward others solely on the basis of group membership. Prejudice can be expressed in the form of a negative attitude toward out-groups. The terms *racism* and *sexism* denote prejudice toward ethnic minorities and women, respectively. The terms *minority* and *majority* are used in reference to groups who have less and more power, respectively, even though numerically minorities may be the larger group.

Discrimination involves actual behavior directed at other people on the basis of group membership. The targets of prejudice are stigmatized and have what Goffman refers to as "spoiled identity."

Members of minority groups often see themselves as the target of prejudice, although in some cases they may exaggerate negative attitudes toward themselves. They may also adopt the prejudices prevalent in some parts of the larger society, which has led to minority versus minority prejudices.

Possible explanations of the personal/group discrimination discrepancy were thought to be denial of personal discrimination and/or exaggeration of group discrimination. However, subsequent research has shown this phenomenon to be generalized to many other domains, so that people generally see events as affecting their group more than themselves.

Measures of expressed attitudes suggest that prejudice in the United States has declined since the 1970s. However, measures of actual discrimination portray a more pessimistic picture. Three possible explanations for the gap between expressed attitudes and actual measures of discrimination are change as impression management, change from traditional to symbolic racism, and change as multilayered.

Since the 1970s, research has focused on the cognitive basis of prejudice, particularly social categorization and stereotyping (making generalizations about groups). All human beings seem to categorize the social world using the basic categories "us" (in-group) and "them" (out-group). In the Western context, members of the in-group tend to see themselves more as different individuals and members of the out-group as more homogeneous. However, cross-cultural research suggests that in other societies and in some conditions people may minimize within-group differences.

Stereotypes tend to vary across cultures, but their larger legitimization function may be common to many cultures. In all societies that have status inequalities and hierarchies, stereotypes serve to justify the existing social structure.

Cognitive explanations of prejudice are not sufficient because cognition is itself fundamentally influenced by culture. Prejudice arises through socialization processes, which explains the high association between the prejudices of young people and those of their parents and peers. Prejudice is a social phenomenon rooted in the normative system of the larger society, rather than a problem caused only by a fringe group of fanatics.

For Discussion

1. How does the relationship between prejudice and discrimination parallel the relationship between attitudes and behavior as discussed in Chapter 4?
2. Does the evidence suggest that cognitive processes (categorization, out-group homogeneity, and the like) make prejudice inevitable and universal?
3. How has prejudice changed during the last few decades of the twentieth century?
4. What kinds of challenges do we face when we try to measure prejudice? Discuss.

Key Terms

Availability heuristic   *339*

Categorization   *341*

Discrimination   *332*

Generalized personal/group discrepancy   *339*

Minimal group paradigm   *344*

Personal/group discrimination discrepancy   *337*

Power majority   *333*

Power minority   *332*

Prejudice   *330*

Racism   *332*

Sexism   *332*

Spoiled identity   *334*

Stereotype   *346*

Annotated Readings

Overviews of the social psychological literature on prejudice can be found in R. J. Brown, *Prejudice: Its social psychology* (Oxford: Blackwell, 1995); and B. Lott and D. Maluso, eds., *The social psychology of interpersonal discrimination* (New York: Guilford Press, 1995).

Gordon Allport's classic discussion of prejudice is very much worth reading: *The nature of prejudice* (Garden City, NY: Doubleday/Anchor, 1954).

Reviews of research on stereotyping are presented in Y. T. Lee, L. Jussim, and C. McCauley, *Stereotype accuracy: Toward appreciating group differences* (Washington, DC: American Psychological Association, 1995); and J. P. Leyens, V. Yzerbyt, and G. Schadron, *Stereotypes and social cognition* (Thousand Oaks, CA: Sage, 1994).

Bob Altemeyer discusses attempts to identify the roots of authoritarianism in *Enemies of freedom: Understanding right-wing authoritarianism* (San Francisco: Jossey-Bass, 1988).

CHAPTER *11*

Aggression

◄ Hockey players battle it out, January 1996. During the six years I lived in Canada, I saw many ice hockey games and many violent fights involving players. During my years in England and other countries where soccer is king, I witnessed many violent fights, and even deaths, involving spectators. When humans, and particularly men, show such high levels of aggression even in "friendly" sporting events, can we really hope to control aggression in the larger world? By examining the roots of aggression, social psychologists are helping to address this enormous challenge.

When Joseph Paul Franklin was interviewed by the news media after his appearance in court in Clayton, Missouri, on November 18, 1996, the self-confessed multiple murderer answered every question, and then added, "The only thing I'm sorry about is that it's not legal." When asked, "What's not legal?" he responded, "killing Jews" (Gladwell, 1997). I was reading Franklin's case history, involving shootings in Georgia, Utah, Indiana, Tennessee, Illinois, and possibly many other states, when I became distracted by a disturbance outside. From my window, I saw a delivery truck blocking the road, holding up a line of cars and a school bus. One of the car drivers sounded his horn several times, then ran over to the truck and started yelling. When the truck driver failed to move the truck quickly enough, the angry motorist banged his fist several times on the side of the huge vehicle and yelled even louder.

aggression behavior intended to harm another human being.

We encounter acts of **aggression,** behavior intended to harm another being, in our everyday lives, but very seldom the extreme aggression shown by killers such as Joseph Franklin. Why is it that normally calm and polite people, such as you and I, sometimes blast our car horns, slam doors, and shout at others? And why do the Joseph Franklins of this world murder other people? Are such different types of aggression explained by the same factors?

Defining and Explaining Aggression

Increasingly, humans are seeing aggression as a challenge to survival. Modern societies seem to be moving away from "underdeveloped" people who have normative systems that enable them to live fairly peaceful lives involving little aggression. For example, the Tasaday of the Philippine rain forest were found living a Stone Age existence in the late 1960s. Outsiders who researched this "primitive" group were surprised to find that aggression had little part in their daily lives (Nance, 1975). At least some bands of our own Stone Age ancestors were probably similarly nonaggressive.

angry aggression emotional behavior intended to harm, such as murder in the heat of passion.

instrumental aggression a calculated, premeditated attack designed to gain material benefit for the aggressor.

Social psychologists study aggression in order to try to understand its origins and, it is hoped, to contribute toward a more peaceful world (Baenninger, 1991; Baron & Richardson, 1994; Berkowitz, 1989, 1993; Felson & Tedeschi, 1993; Geen, 1990; Geen & Donnerstein, 1983; Groebel & Hinde, 1988; Huesmann, 1986; Mummendey, 1984; Potegal & Knutson, 1994; Tedeschi & Felson, 1994). In this literature, a distinction is commonly made between emotional or **angry aggression,** such as a murderous act arising from intense momentary passion, and **instrumental aggression,** a calculated, premeditated attack designed to gain material benefit for the aggressor (see Figure 11–1). Angry aggression is "hot" action, instantaneous and impulsive; instrumental aggression is "cold" action, planned in advance. In angry aggression, the main objective is to cause pain to the other; in instrumental aggression, the main goal is to gain a desired object.

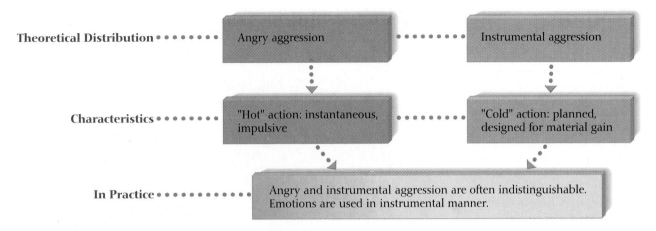

Figure 11–1 Major types of aggression.

A number of social psychologists have tried to focus exclusively on angry aggression (e.g., Berkowitz, 1994; Geen, 1990). However, although the distinction between "angry" and "instrumental" aggression is useful conceptually, and although we can find instances that seem to involve only angry aggression or only instrumental aggression, in practice the two are often inseparable. This is because the emotion of anger can be used in an instrumental manner. Jim Averill (1982, 1983) has argued that in some cases people "make themselves angry" as a means of achieving a goal. How anger is used instrumentally depends on the subtleties of cultural norms and rules. People using anger and "throwing fits" must be aware of just how angry they can become in any given context. For example, David throws a temper tantrum when his sister refuses to let him use her car. His anger is used to indicate just how badly treated he is and to make the rest of the family pay more attention to his needs. But he is aware that if he throws a fit too often, his anger may lose its effect.

Jerry Parrott's (1993) research also shows that people can manipulate their moods by recalling good and bad memories. The implication is that David could make himself even more angry by recalling all the other times he badly needed a car and was not allowed to use his sister's. This line of reasoning suggests that in practice angry and instrumental aggression are often inseparable.

The Effect of Cultural Norms

Another challenge faced by researchers, although it is seldom acknowledged, is that what is seen as aggression in one culture may not be seen that way in another. For example, among groups of people who believe that sorcery is effective, a person casting a charm intended to harm others is acting aggressively. In Sri Lanka, sorcery has been described as "a technique of killing or harming someone," using spells, charms, and

Voodoo temple in Haiti. Although aggression is found in all societies, there are wide variations in both degree and kind. In some societies, it is normative to show high levels of physical aggression. Verbal aggression is more normative among middle-class people in the West, physical aggression among the lower classes. In Haiti, aggression can take the form of casting a spell against someone. Whereas for most outsiders the objects in a Voodoo temple would not be meaningful and the spells cast would not seem dangerous or aggressive, for believers these are potential "weapons" against enemies. This underlines a general point: The recognition of aggression often requires shared systems of meanings.

incantations (Obeyesekere, 1975). Similarly, the Indian psychologist Agehananda Bharati (1983) discusses sorcery as a form of violence that is believed to be effective in many countries, including India, Bangladesh, Nepal, and Pakistan.

The fact that aggression can be defined differently by different cultural groups can lead to major problems in multicultural societies. Consider the case of Salman Rushdie, the author of *The Satanic Verses*, who was condemned to death by the Iranian revolutionary leader Ayatollah Khomeini. Most Westerners saw the death sentence as an act of aggression, whereas to the followers of the Ayatollah, the aggressor was Salman Rushdie, because he had intended to harm Islam and Muslims. This incident took on international dimensions because Rushdie was an

Indian living in England, and the book was published and sold in the West, where freedom of expression is a democratic right. But millions of Muslims also live in Western societies and some of them took part in demonstrations at which copies of *The Satanic Verses* were burned and shouts of "Death to Rushdie" rang out. Such incidents dramatically make the point that in defining aggression we must be careful to keep in mind subjective interpretations.

The search for a causal model of aggression has led researchers to lump an enormous variety of behaviors—including horn honking, wife beating, rape, homicide, riots, political rebellions, and revolution—in one category. This strategy is problematic from a cultural standpoint because it neglects the *meaning* of particular actions. The meaning of horn honking is very different from a political revolution, and both of these are very different from rape. It is very unlikely that people honk their horns, commit rape, and participate in political revolutions for the same reasons.

In many cases, meaning is associated with power differences between groups in society. A political uprising is a "crime of violence" from the standpoint of those in power, but it could be a humanitarian attempt at liberation and an end to rule by violence from the perspective of the revolutionaries. As the saying goes, "One person's revolutionary hero is another person's terrorist." From the perspective of those in power, it makes strategic sense to define any act of political rebellion as "aggressive," in order to weaken the opposition. Psychologists have been criticized for acting in favor of those in power (Billig, 1976), and in the domain of aggression research, psychologists once again seem to be lining up with the politically powerful when they, too, label political rebellion as aggression.

Normative and Causal Explanations of Aggression

It is useful to make a broad distinction between two types of theoretical explanations of aggression, causal and normative (see Figure 11–2). Some explanations are *causal* because they view aggression as being determined by particular factors. For example, they see aggression as caused by genetic and physiological factors, such as the stimulation of particular parts of the brain, or by environmental factors, such as heat

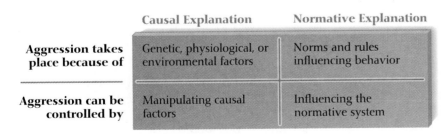

	Causal Explanation	**Normative Explanation**
Aggression takes place because of	Genetic, physiological, or environmental factors	Norms and rules influencing behavior
Aggression can be controlled by	Manipulating causal factors	Influencing the normative system

Figure 11–2 Causal and normative explanations of aggression.

and overcrowding. Causal explanations follow the logic of "If *X*, then *Y*," as in "If temperature rises, then aggression will increase."

The other, *normative* explanation depicts aggression as behavior that is influenced by the norms and rules of particular cultures. From a normative perspective, we can best understand aggression by reference to the cultural norms and rules that define correct behavior in a given setting. In adopting this perspective, we must keep in mind three points.

First, different sets of norms and rules may be applied to different groups in a given society. For example, in most societies the norms and rules regulating aggressive behavior are different for men and women. Typically, men are socialized to use more direct aggression, overt behavior explicitly intended to harm another being (Bjorkqvist, Lagerspetz, & Kaukiainen, 1993; Bjorkqvist, Osterman, & Lagerspetz, 1994; Hines & Fry, 1994). In a meta-analysis of the literature, Alice Eagly found that sex differences in aggression are greater in the realm of physical than verbal aggression (Eagly & Steffen, 1986) (see Figure 11–3). In line with this, a study conducted in Argentina showed that women use more indirect aggression, covert behavior implicitly intended to harm another being, such as gossip, rumor, and insulting someone behind his or her back (Hines & Fry, 1994).

The preference women seem to show for indirect and verbal forms of aggression may originate in their having less physical strength. "Strong" and "aggressive" are stereotypically male descriptors. The different standards applied to men and women also mean that when women commit violent acts such as homicide, they suffer from double stigmatization: once for going against the formal legal code and a second time for behaving contrary to their gender role (Heidensohn, 1991).

Second, this diversity in normative systems provides a range of opportunities, at least for some people, to select from a variety of lifestyles. Some individuals can and do select to move from one normative system to another. Whether it is the goods they buy, the politicians they vote for, or the general lifestyle they adopt, individuals can and do use what the economist Albert Hirschman (1970) refers to as the *exit option*—just opting out of one way of doing things and taking up another. But they can also choose a *voice option*, which involves trying to change things without opting out, and this leads to our next point.

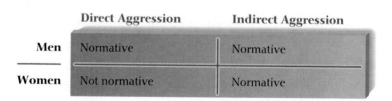

Figure 11–3 Gender and forms of aggression.

Third, even within the confines of a given normative system, individuals behave intentionally and with some measure of autonomy. People can follow the norms and rules of their cultural group, but they can also choose to try to change the accepted ways of doing things. Each generation of young people seems to discover rebellion afresh, so that at least some aspects of how mom and dad did things are automatically rejected and alternative lifestyles arise. Societal changes reflect the intentional choices people make with regard to the normative system (see Chapters 12 and 14, on gender and intergroup relations).

In our review of the various explanations for aggression, we will see that the most generally convincing account is a normative one—that is, an account that views individuals as having some measure of freedom to select intentionally between normative systems and to pattern their behavior to conform to accepted views about "correct" behavior in a given culture.

Concepts and Issues

It is often difficult in practice to distinguish between angry and instrumental aggression because people regulate their emotions to achieve instrumental goals. The greatest emphasis has been on causal explanations of aggression, but the meaning of aggression can only be understood through a normative approach.

1. Distinguish between angry aggression and instrumental aggression and between direct aggression and indirect aggression. Give examples.
2. Give an example of how the same behavior can be interpreted as aggression by some people but not by others.

Physiological Explanations

Some causal models of aggression focus on physiological characteristics. These explanations see genes or hormones or some other physiological feature of the person as "causing" aggressivity. Another explanation sees the causal factors in the environment. For example, a large body of literature exists on the association between temperature and aggression. A more complex causal explanation emerges from the evolutionary perspective, specifically ethology and sociobiology.

Research on the physiological basis of aggression has captured the imagination of the public and is given wide coverage in the media (e.g., Gladwell, 1997). As we review this research, keep in mind a key question: Do physiological explanations tell us why aggressive persons such as Joseph Paul Franklin choose particular targets? In other words, do they tell us about the fundamentally important issue of the meaning of aggression?

The "Aggressive Gene"

"Some people have aggressive genes." "You can make a person aggressive by stimulating the right spot in the brain." These are examples of explanations people give on the assumption that aggression is best explained by physiological characteristics. At least since the nineteenth century, researchers have attempted to discover distinct physiological features that would identify highly aggressive people, perhaps because it would make the task of coping with aggression a lot easier. Just imagine: Such research could lead to the development of a drug or a medical procedure to help prevent individual and collective aggression—perhaps put an end to murder and war. Such fantastic prospects seemed to open up when researchers first identified what seemed to be a link between chromosomes and aggression.

Human beings generally have 46 chromosomes, arranged in 23 pairs. For the normal male, sex is determined by an XY chromosome pair. However, there are a number of chromosomal abnormalities among the general population. One example is the XYY combination, which occurs in about 1 in every 3,000 males. When it was discovered that over 3 percent of the men in a sample from a prison population were XYY, this overrepresentation led some researchers to believe that the additional Y chromosome is a source of aggressivity (see Witkin et al., 1976). Subsequent research revealed a more complex picture.

There does seem to be a tendency for XYY men to be overrepresented in the prison population (Radcliffe, Masera, Pan, & McKie, 1994; Schroder, De La Chapelle, Hakola, & Virkkunen, 1981; Witkin et al., 1976). However, being in prison does not necessarily make one a more aggressive person. People serve time in prison for many different offenses, most of which do not involve violence. Also, XYY men tend to be bigger, and in those cases in which they are more aggressive, it may well be because they were always bigger than others in their age group and learned that aggression pays. XYY men tend to score lower on standardized intelligence tests. Their overrepresentation in prison may simply mean that they are not smart enough to get away with crimes. Finally, XYY men make up only about 3 to 4 percent of prison populations. How do we explain the other roughly 96 percent who are chromosomal "normals"?

The Brain and Aggression

Charles Whitman had seemed like an agreeable young man, before he set off on a shooting rampage. He killed his wife, his mother, and a receptionist at the University of Texas at Austin. He then took a rifle and many rounds of ammunition to the tower of the university administration building, and randomly shot and killed another 14 people before a police marksman ended his life. An autopsy showed that Charles Whitman suffered from a malignant tumor that had caused extensive damage to his brain. Would his rampage have been prevented if the brain tumor had been identified and removed earlier? Perhaps yes, because there are a number of cases in which aggressivity decreases following the removal of a brain tumor (Moyer, 1976).

Researchers have used a number of different techniques to examine the relationship between aggression and brain function. In addition to case studies such as that of Charles Whitman, researchers have used lesioning and ablation of neural tissue, as well as direct electrical stimulation of brain sites, particularly the hypothalamus, which is assumed to be associated with aggressivity. Jose Delgado (1969) has provided extraordinary demonstrations of how aggressivity can be turned on and off in monkeys and other animals by implanting radio receivers in their brains and providing electrical stimulation by remote control.

The technology for applying electrical stimulation to human brains—and perhaps controlling human aggressivity—has been demonstrated, albeit in a primitive manner (Heath, 1963). Does this imply that as we develop more advanced technology for electrically stimulating the human brain, we will have a way to end aggressivity and war? Or, frighteningly, will we be able to manipulate people so that they attack the targets we choose, when we choose? Fortunately for everyone, human aggression is not "caused" by electrical stimulation of the brain, or brain chemistry more generally, and could not be controlled in such a way.

First, even research with monkeys and other animals shows that electrical stimulation of "aggression centers" does not always lead to aggressivity without the presence of an appropriate target (Delgado, 1969). To take a dramatic example, if the aggression center in the brain of a mongoose is electrically stimulated, it will very likely attack another nearby animal if that animal happens to be a rat, but not if it happens to be a tiger.

More important, demonstrations that show electrical stimulation of aggression centers neglect the fundamentally important question of *what it is in the real world that leads the aggression center to become stimulated.* The answer that biochemical processes, or even specific neurotransmitters, lead to the stimulation of aggression centers does not answer this fundamental question, but simply raises additional questions—for example, What is it in the world outside that influences body chemistry to change and to affect aggression centers in particular ways?

To use a sports analogy, to explain human aggression through reference to physiological changes is rather like explaining a game of tennis by discussing changes in the skeletal musculature as the player moves around the court and hits the ball. We may arrive at a thorough understanding of the physiological changes going on in a tennis player throughout a game, but we still do not have even a basic understanding of what the game is about. Certain parts of the brain may become activated when the player is about to hit the ball, but such activation does not explain anything about why the player tries to hit the ball (or why a player would not hit a ball she or he estimates is going "out") and where the player is directing the ball. To understand tennis, we have to know the rules of the game and the skills players develop to win within the rule system. Similarly, aggression can be understood only when we understand the normative system of the social world in which it takes place.

Tennis player intent on the game. Aggression by human beings can only be fully understood and explained within a cultural context. To try to explain human aggression through reference to physiological changes is rather like explaining a game of tennis by describing changes in the skeletal musculature as the players position themselves and return the ball. To appreciate the meaning of what the players are doing, we need to know the rules of the game. It is the rule system of tennis that guides the behavior of players, and the meaning of their actions is lost if we neglect the rules. But we could describe in perfect detail all of the physiological changes players experience during a game and still know nothing about what they were doing and why.

Hormones and Aggression

The mass media continue to be enthralled by reports about the apparent links between chemicals in the body and aggressivity. When researchers at Johns Hopkins University reported that male mice lacking the neurotransmitter nitric oxide fight more against other males and are more sexually aggressive against females (Nelson et al., 1995), this made international news. In discussions about human violence in the media, there are routine references to studies apparently showing a link between the sex hormone testosterone and aggression, typically among men but also in some cases among women (Archer, 1991; Moyer, 1976). In the case of women specifically, the idea has been discussed that a rise in the ratio between estrogen and progesterone during menstruation leads to greater hostility (Hoyenga & Hoyenga, 1993). But, again, we must question the extent to which such possible relationships can explain social behavior and aggression against particular targets.

This point becomes even clearer when we consider the issue of **hate crimes,** crimes that are motivated by racial, religious, ethnic, or sexual orientation hatred or bias. In the early 1990s, the Federal Bureau of Investigation (FBI) developed a uniform system of collecting and reporting hate crimes in the United States. Some of these crimes involve extreme aggression against a member of a minority group—killing, maiming, setting a person's house on fire, and the like. There were 7,466 hate crimes reported to the FBI in 1992, and 7,587 reported in 1993 (U.S. Department of Justice, 1992, 1993). When we look at the details of who was targeted, it becomes immediately clear that the targets are not randomly selected. For example, during 1992 and 1993, almost 59 percent of hate crimes motivated by race were against African–Americans and almost 88 percent of hate crimes motivated by religion were against Jews. To point to testosterone levels as a cause of this type of aggression is misguided because the target of aggression is not in any way associated with hormones.

hate crimes crimes motivated by racial, religious, ethnic, or sexual orientation hatred or bias.

Concepts and Issues

Research on a genetic basis for aggression, on an "aggression center" in the brain, and on the relationship between hormones and aggression has found some interesting trends but has not identified causes. Aggression takes place in a cultural context and can only be understood in relation to the *meaning* of events. There are particular cultural reasons why African–Americans and Jews are the targets of hate crimes in the United States.

1. Why have researchers been interested in studying aggression among XYY males?
2. What can research on the brain and aggression, and hormones and aggression, tell us about aggression?

Other Causal Explanations

Apart from physiological explanations, a wide range of other causal explanations has stimulated research. We shall discuss four of these: the physical environment and aggression, evolution and aggression, frustration and aggression, and a realistic conflict approach to aggression.

The Physical Environment and Aggression

I pray thee, good Mercutio, let's retire;
The day is hot, the Capulets abroad,
And, if we meet, we shall not 'scape a brawl;
For now, these hot days, is the mad blood stirring.

—*Romeo and Juliet*, act III, scene 1

These words are spoken by Benvolio, a member of the house of Montague, who cautions his friend Mercutio that if they meet anyone from the enemy Capulet household on such a hot day, there will surely be bloodshed. The idea that high temperatures make it more likely for people to behave aggressively was not new in Shakespeare's era, and it has continued to be influential. Today newspaper headlines repeat dire warnings about riots, such as those in Los Angeles, in the "long, hot summers," and security forces throughout the world are well aware that "summer madness" can bring collective violence and looting.

The idea that environmental stressors, such as heat, noise, over-crowding, and pollution, can lead people to behave aggressively gained a lot of influence in modern psychology. This is partly because of the lingering influence of the behaviorist school, which proposes that aggression is a response to external stimuli. The notion that high temperatures and other environmental factors lead to aggression also fits a causal model of behavior and is therefore in line with the search for cause–effect relationships in psychology more generally.

Extensive field research has been conducted to examine the temperature–aggression relationship, with almost exclusive focus on "angry" or "hot" aggression. Researchers have followed our everyday language, which suggests that we fight when "tempers flare" and we get "hot under the collar." If this is true, then people living in regions with hot climates should be more aggressive than those living in cooler climates. And there should be more aggression during hotter times of the year.

Regional Differences. The Italian criminologist Cesare Lombroso (1899/1911), a pioneer in this research area, showed that homicide rates are higher in southern Italy and in the south of England, where temperatures are higher, than in the northern parts of each country. Similar results were reported for the United States (Brearley, 1932). However, we must take care not to jump to premature conclusions on the basis of such studies, because the northern and southern parts of countries such as the United States, England, and Italy differ in so many other ways. This is suggested by the research of Richard Nisbett and his colleagues on cultural differences between the north and the south of the United States (Cohen & Nisbett, 1994; Nisbett, 1993; Nisbett & Cohen, 1996).

Nisbett argues that the most compelling explanation for this difference in the rate of violent crime is the culture of honor that characterizes the southern United States. The central feature of a *culture of honor* is that any threat to property or reputation is dealt with by violence. Cultures of honor have evolved in many different parts of the world where the economy has historically been based on herding. Herdsmen live precarious lives, in that their entire wealth (the herd) is on display for all to see and thus is vulnerable to attack.

Such cultures base honor on strength and endorse the use of violence to gain and protect honor. They arise in situations in which individuals are vulnerable to attack (for example, when they have to protect cattle in vast open spaces) and where government authorities representing law and order are weak or nonexistent (for example, the nearest sheriff is a three–day ride away). In such contexts, the man who fails to protect his honor stands to lose everything. When the stakes are so high, even a verbal insult can lead to a deadly reaction.

The higher rates of homicide for white males in the herding (hills and dry plains) regions as compared to farming regions, irrespective of temperature, seem to support the culture of honor explanation. Contrary to the temperature–aggression explanation, Nisbett's research shows that it is in the cooler regions of the southern United States that homicide rates are higher. These are the more rural and traditionally herding regions.

Nisbett and his associates devised a number of creative ways of experimentally testing the culture of honor explanation (Nisbett & Cohen, 1996). They reasoned that if southerners take insults more seriously than do northerners, this should be reflected by their reactions to insults under controlled laboratory conditions. The participants were students studying at the University of Michigan. In one experimental situation, a confederate of the experimenter bumps into the unsuspecting participant and then calls the participant an "asshole." The results reveal that northerners were more likely to be amused than angry at this incident, whereas southerners were more likely to be angry.

In another experimental situation, a group of participants who had earlier been insulted and a second group who had not been insulted were presented with the following scenario:

> It had only been about 20 minutes since they had arrived at the party when Jill pulled Steve aside, obviously bothered about something.
>
> "What's wrong?" asked Steve.
>
> "It's Larry. I mean, he knows that you and I are engaged, but he's already made two passes at me tonight."
>
> Jill walked back into the crowd, and Steve decided to keep his eye on Larry. Sure enough, within 5 minutes Larry was reaching over and trying to kiss Jill.

Participants had the task of completing this story. More than 75 percent of southerners who had earlier been insulted completed this story with Steve injuring or threatening to injure his challenger, but only 20 percent of noninsulted southerners did so. The insult manipulation worked in a different way for northerners. A smaller group of them ended the scenario with violence if they had earlier been insulted (41 percent) than not (55 percent). In other studies Nisbett and his associates showed that southerners, but not northerners, showed a marked physiological reaction to an insult, as reflected by a rise in their cortisol and testosterone levels (Nisbett & Cohen, 1996).

This research on the culture of honor indicates a number of cultural differences between southerners and northerners, and shows that such differences can influence aggression and other behaviors in complex ways. The presence of such differences, which are often subtle, may account for why only one (Anderson, 1987, study 2) among a number of field studies (deFronzo, 1984; Robbins, DeWalt, & Pelto, 1972; Rotton, 1986; Schwartz, 1968) has demonstrated the temperature–aggression relationship in a clear-cut manner. But it may be that the social role of all men in most societies is influenced by a culture of honor, which leads men to be more aggressive than women, particularly when they are in the public eye and their manhood is seemingly being tested (Lightdale & Prentice, 1994).

Seasonal Temperature Variations and Aggression: Field Studies. A number of field studies in the United States suggest a tendency for violent crimes to increase with the hotness of the year (Anderson, 1987, study 1), the season (Rotton & Frey, 1985), the month (Lester, 1979), and the day (Cotton, 1986). Field studies in Korea, Germany, France, England, Italy, and other societies outside the United States have been interpreted by Craig Anderson (1989) as revealing a similar trend. Once again, however, we must keep in mind that a number of studies have failed to find a relationship between seasonal temperature variations and violent crime, political violence, and the like (e.g., Brearley, 1932; Cerbus, 1970; Michael & Zumpe, 1983; Schwartz, 1968).

Also, even if in some cases seasonal temperature variations do seem to coincide with violent crime, such a finding is open to many different interpretations. For example, the fact that incidents of rape reach their highest rate during the hot summer months could be associated with the tendency for people to be out more, and to wear less. This "social contact" explanation is sometimes rejected on the grounds that domestic violence is also highest during the hottest months, even though it is during the winter that families are indoors together the most and presumably have more opportunities to behave aggressively toward one another. If social contact is the explanation, then domestic violence should be highest during the winter months—but this is not the case. A counterargument to this point is that the temperature indoors does not vary a great deal over the year, suggesting that temperature changes are not the cause of seasonal variations in domestic violence.

In addition, the social contact explanation seems to fit the seasonal pattern of another major type of aggression—homicide. There are two peaks in homicide rates over the year, in late summer, during the hottest days, and also in December, during some of the coldest days of the year (and some of the most socially active, because of the Christmas celebrations). A possible explanation is that these are periods during which people interact a lot and find themselves in "killing" situations.

Clearly, then, field studies on the relationship between temperature and aggression do not give us a clear picture. Typically, when social psychologists have been faced with conflicting evidence from field studies, they have turned to laboratory experiments to try to clarify the relationship between variables.

Street scene during the most recent Los Angeles riots. "The long, hot summer!" Few people who have been in riot–stricken urban centers such as Los Angeles, Detroit, or Miami can hear this phrase and not feel dread. Riots involving thousands of people have cost lives, ruined businesses, and destroyed entire neighborhoods. Why do such riots usually take place during the summer? On the surface, at least, this question seems to be explained by the relationship between temperature and aggression: Surely heat causes aggression. On closer examination, the relationship between temperature and aggression turns out to be more complex, and not a causal one.

Laboratory Studies. A series of laboratory studies has been conducted since the early 1970s to investigate the temperature–aggression relationship (Baron, 1972; Baron & Bell, 1975, 1976; Bell, 1980; Bell & Baron, 1977; Boyanowsky, Calvert, Young, & Brideau, 1981–1982; Palamarek & Rule, 1979). The basic method has been to create a situation in which a participant has an opportunity and a reason to act aggressively toward another participant (actually a confederate of the experimenter). For example, the person is placed in a learning situation in which another supposed participant has to learn new material. Aggression is typically expressed by allowing participants, placed in a setting that is either hot or cold, the opportunity to administer electric shocks each time the "learner" makes a mistake. The temperature of the laboratory is the key independent variable, with the "shocks administered to the learner" as the dependent measure.

Most of the laboratory studies testing the temperature–aggression relationship have been conducted by a small number of researchers following very similar procedures. Thus, from the perspective of traditional experimental social psychology, which relies heavily on laboratory procedures, if there is a relationship between temperature and aggression, it should have been uncovered by this body of laboratory research. But hotter temperatures sometimes led to more aggression and at other times to less aggression (Anderson, 1989). The picture has not been cleared up by laboratory studies that incorporate emotions such as anger, because participants who were cold but angry showed more aggression than those who were hot and angry (e.g., Baron & Bell, 1975, 1976).

Craig Anderson and his associates have attempted to clarify this situation by proposing that high temperatures can influence aggressivity through different routes: *hostile affect*, feeling aggressively toward a target ("I felt so angry I wanted to kick him out of the door"); *hostile cognition*, having aggressive thoughts toward a target ("All the time she was talking, I kept thinking I would like to push the cake right in her face"); *perceived arousal*, how "worked up" I perceive myself to be ("I felt so mad at him"); and *physiological arousal*, how aroused a person actually is (Anderson, Anderson, & Deuser, 1996; Anderson, Deuser, & DeNeve, 1995). The most important general conclusion from research on these routes is that high temperatures can influence aggressivity by changing how people interpret ambiguous social situations. When the bus arrives half an hour late on a hot day, John is more likely to interpret the situation as appropriate for him to abuse the bus driver.

Evolutionary Views on Aggression

A number of thinkers have argued that since humans share a long evolutionary history with other organisms, we can learn a great deal about human aggression by taking an evolutionary viewpoint. We shall consider two varieties of this line of thinking, the ethological line associated with Konrad Lorenz (1966) and others (e.g., Eibl–Eibesfeldt, 1989) and the sociobiological viewpoint associated with E. O. Wilson (1975), Richard Dawkins (1976, 1982), and others (e.g., Daly & Wilson, 1988a, 1988b). A common theme among these writers is their emphasis on the function of behavior in the long–term adaptation of organisms to environmental conditions. They focus on the question "What purpose does aggression serve in survival?" A major difference between the ethological and sociobiological viewpoints is that the latter focuses more on the gene as the unit of analysis.

The Ethological Perspective.   Imagine you are sitting in your favorite restaurant, being served your favorite meal. Do you look at the food in front of you with hate in your eyes and angrily say to yourself, "I am going to destroy this food! I shall cut it up, tear it apart, chew it, and devour it!" Well, according to Lorenz (1966), in the vast majority of cases killing in the animal world is rather similar to your sitting down to eat your favorite meal. It does not involve hate, anger, or killing for the sake of anything else except getting a meal. When a lion chases a gazelle across the African plain, it is just chasing its next meal. In effect, this is a case of instrumental aggression. This kind of interspecies killing is also *functionally* very different from intraspecies aggression.

Lorenz and other ethologists have argued that intraspecies aggression, such as that between two lions, rarely results in one of the combatants being killed. When death does occur, it is usually by accident. For example, two antelopes fighting may get their antlers locked, be unable to pull them apart, and simply starve to death as a result. But such an outcome is unexpected and fairly rare relative to the total number of fights each antelope gets into throughout its life. The reason why intraspecies fighting does not usually result in death, or even serious injury, is because animals have evolved inhibitory mechanisms that limit aggression by both animals and allow the defeated animal to escape relatively unharmed.

For example, when two wolves fight and one of them gains the upper hand, the defeated wolf signals that he accepts defeat by moving back, lowering his head, and baring a vulnerable part of his body. The victor generally accepts this signal of surrender and the fight comes to an end. The function of such fighting is to establish a pecking order among males so that the strongest males have more access to females, and so their genes are more likely to be passed on.

However, a male who proves to be the strongest this season may in a season or two be surpassed by a competitor who is too young and inexperienced to win the fight this time around. Thus, it is functional that each round of fighting simply serve to identify winners without resulting in the death or serious injury of losers. By gathering information about each other during the escalation stages—transition points in the type of aggression shown leading to the actual physical fighting—animals can make more accurate estimations of their relative strengths and in this way clarify the winner with minimum physical damage to either party (e.g., see Archer & Huntingford, 1994).

But to what extent is this ethological model applicable to humans? Lorenz and others argue that it is applicable in important ways because during their long evolutionary history humans did develop mechanisms to cope with the very limited killing capacities of other humans. To appreciate how difficult it would be for us to kill one another without the use of weapons, imagine that another student decides to kill you. Now, like our ancestors hundreds of thousands of years ago, this student has only his bare hands to use. He can punch, kick, bite, scratch, and so on, but he has no weapons. How would you react? Perhaps you could outrun him. If not, you could call for help. As a last resort, you could look into his eyes and plead for mercy.

Killing you with his bare hands would not be so easy because he would hear your cries, smell you, sense your breath, feel your body. It turns out that very few people are "natural" killers, and that even soldiers in war feel revulsion when they have to kill at close quarters (Grossman, 1995). Lorenz argues that evolutionary acquired inhibitory mechanisms make it difficult for humans to kill one another with their bare hands. When the potential victim gives signals of defeat, we react by showing compassion.

But what if your classmate could kill you using a high-powered rifle . . . or could aim at you with an intercontinental ballistic missile? You would be nothing but a dot on the radar screen. In such situations there would be no possibility for inhibitory mechanisms to come into play. You would have no opportunity to plead, and the attacker would not see or hear you. The weapons available to us today mean that the inhibitory mechanisms that helped prevent killing are no longer effective. Recall from our discussion in Chapter 7 that in Milgram's (1974) studies on obedience to authority, it was also found that a greater distance between the "source" and the "target" of aggression meant a greater likelihood for higher levels of aggressivity to occur. Because of the distance technology places between aggressor and target, modern science has allowed us to bypass the evolutionary safety valves that work for other organisms (Figure 11–4).

But modern technology does provide possible solutions to this problem. We could use television and other mass media to bring us closer to the reality of aggression. One reason why there was so much opposition to the Vietnam War among the general public in the United States may have been because television brought the war into our living rooms. Governments have become very aware of the potential influence of television on public support for war. Before the main bombardment of Iraqi forces by Allied troops during the Gulf War in 1990–1991, the Bush administration negotiated with the media and established limits on what could be shown and when.

The Sociobiological Perspective.   The sociobiological perspective on aggression also emphasizes the function of aggression in the long-term adaptation of humans to their environmental conditions, but it focuses on the gene rather than the individual as the unit of analysis (Dawkins, 1976, 1982; Wilson, 1975). As suggested by the title of Richard Dawkins's book, *The Selfish Gene*, a main thesis is that aggression is a strategy that allows some genes to compete and survive at the expense of others. In this scenario, we are convenient vehicles, or "carriers," for genes.

As carriers, we act aggressively against those who are genetically dissimilar to us, because out-group members are the carriers of competing genes. Van den Berghe (1987) argues that aggression against ethnic out-groups (as reflected in hostility between blacks and whites, for example)

	Weapons of Destruction	Distance Between Attacker and Target	Effectiveness of Inhibitory Mechanisms
Early human history	Primitive tools and weapons	Not more than 20 feet or so, often within arm's length	Maximum effectiveness
Twenty-first century	Advanced computer-guided technology	Could be continents apart	No chance to become effective, unless target can be seen

Figure 11–4   Inhibitory mechanisms in ancient and modern times.

can be explained by this genetic strategy. Reports in the mass media seem to suggest this explanation is plausible. On January 4, 1993, a *Newsweek* cover story reported a pattern of rape and "ethnic cleansing" in Bosnia: Males killed competing out-group males and raped women. In the scientific literature, there are reports of seemingly similar patterns of aggressive behavior across species. Richard Connor and his associates have reported alliance formation among male bottlenose dolphins to fight off other males and to "herd" females (Connor, Smolker, & Richards, 1992). Joseph Manson and Richard Wrangham (1991) report what they describe as similarities between humans and chimpanzees in patterns of intermale aggression for the purpose of gaining access to females.

But how convincing is genetic similarity as an explanation for human aggression? Let us look at two examples of how the sociobiological explanation has been applied to interactions between people who live in smaller communities and tend to know one another. First, consider Napoleon Chagnon's (1992) research among the Yanomamo on the border between Venezuela and Brazil. The Yanomamo live in small villages of between 40 and 300 inhabitants and are among the most aggressive people ever documented. The men fight to establish their status within the village, and Chagnon argues that most of the fighting

The Yanomamo of the Amazon jungle, seen here in a ritual display of strength to guests arriving for a feast, are among the most physically aggressive people in the world. Sociobiologists have used the case of the Yanomamo to argue that aggression is best explained by genetic similarity. Among these violent people, blood relatives are less likely to be targets of aggression, and more likely to be allies in fighting. But the sociobiological account proves to be too simplistic in the larger picture: During World War II, Germans allied with Japanese and Italians to fight the British, the French, and the Americans, among others. Genetic similarity does not explain such alliances.

is about resources and women. Warriors from each village raid other villages to kill men, steal resources, and kidnap women. About a quarter of the men die violent deaths. Blood relatives are less likely to be the target of aggression and more likely to be allies. This targeted aggression is possible because the communities are small enough so that the members of each village personally know people in their own and surrounding villages.

Another example of sociobiology applied to small groups is the research of Martin Daly and Margo Wilson (1988a, 1988b, 1990), who have studied homicide within families. Daly and Wilson show that the murder of blood relatives is rare compared to the murder of nonrelatives. Adopted children are far more likely to be killed or mistreated than blood-related children. When people kill their own children, argue Daly and Wilson, it is usually because the parentage is less well established, or there is phenotypic deformity, or because scarcity of resources makes survival of the infant unlikely anyhow.

Critics argue that Daly and Wilson's account of homicide is not valid (George, 1989). When parents kill a stepchild, it is because of genetic dissimilarity. When parents do not kill a stepchild, it is because parents need to maintain "networks of social reciprocity" (establish social support systems). Thus, even in the case of interactions in families and other small groups, the sociobiological account is not very convincing because it is not testable.

phenotype physical features.

genotype genetic makeup.

At the societal level, conflicts involving nations and large groups are explained even less satisfactorily through reference to genetic similarity. Even if we take the view that **phenotype** (physical features) is an indication of **genotype** (genetic makeup), in most wars the armies are brought together on the basis of political allegiance, not phenotypic similarity. During World War II, the Germans had the Japanese as allies, and they fought against the English, the Russians, and the Americans. Surely if genetic similarity was the criterion, the battle lines would have been drawn very differently (the Germans would be allied with the English rather than the Japanese, for example).

The sociobiological account is even less convincing when the focus shifts to homicide at the societal level. For instance, in the United States over 80 percent of homicides involving white perpetrators involve white victims, and over 90 percent involving black perpetrators involve black victims. That is, crime statistics reveal that *most homicides are within the ethnic group*—exactly the opposite of the prediction made by sociobiologists (Uniform Crime Reports, 1993; Williams–Meyers, 1995). This trend is not the scenario typically portrayed in the mass media, where the stereotypic picture is of a black perpetrator and white victim.

The Frustration-Aggression Hypothesis

Most of us seem to be familiar with some version of the following story in three acts:

Act One: Joe has a terrible day at work because his boss picks on him. He leaves work feeling totally frustrated.

Act Two: Joe arrives home, slams the door, and immediately starts shouting at his wife and children.

Act Three: Joe's wife screams at their son, who gets angry and chases the cat out of the house.

In our everyday lives we often assume that frustration leads to aggression. By assuming this association, we are agreeing with an idea that is central to Sigmund Freud's explanation of aggression (see Freud, 1921/1953–1964; 1930). But whereas Freud saw aggression as one possible outcome of frustration, other researchers postulated a much more specific link in the form of the **frustration–aggression hypothesis.** This hypothesis represents one of the major causal explanations of aggression (see Figure 11–5). It states that frustration, the blocking of goal–directed behavior, evokes a state of instigation to act aggressively and that aggression is always preceded by some kind of frustration (Dollard, Doob, Miller, Mowrer, & Sears, 1939).

Even though this hypothesis in its original form was found to have overstated the case for a causal link between frustration and aggression, it has remained the most important idea in social psychological research on aggression (Geen, 1995). One way in which the frustration-aggression hypothesis overstated the case is the claim, not supported by subsequent research, that aggression is always preceded by frustration. In actuality, people act aggressively for all kinds of reasons. Jim may hit Joe because he wants to grab Joe's money, rather than because he is experiencing frustration.

Research has also shown that aggression is just one possible outcome of frustration (Geen, 1990). An important determinant of what arises from frustration is the person's understanding of the kinds of responses that are available (Geen, 1990). The key question is, "What has the individual *learned* to do when experiencing frustration?" Slogans

frustration-aggression hypothesis
idea that frustration evokes a state of instigation to act aggressively and that aggression is always preceded by some kind of frustration.

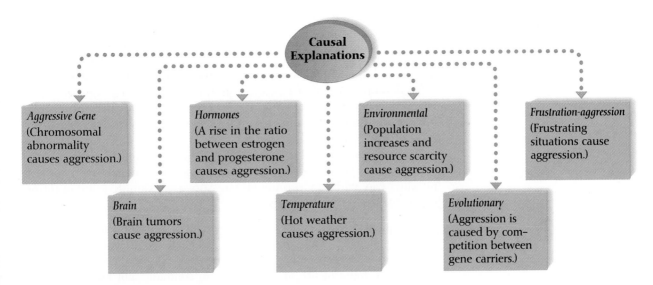

Figure 11–5 Causal explanations for aggression.

such as "When the going gets tough, the tough get going" and "No pain, no gain" suggest that some individuals are socialized to try even harder when facing frustrating situations.

A major shortcoming of the frustration–aggression hypothesis, then, is that it fails to consider variations in how people cope with frustration. Leonard Berkowitz (1962, 1989, 1993) reformulated the frustration-aggression hypothesis and proposed that the power of frustration to cause aggression depends on the level of arousal induced by the frustration. In one of the studies interpreted as supporting this reformulation, adult participants came to believe they had the task of teaching children some new material (Vasta & Copitch, 1981). In actuality there were no children, and a preprogrammed set of responses was designed to make the participants think that the children's performance was deteriorating over the course of the session. In a control condition, the children easily learned the task. Each time a child "responded," the participant had to throw a switch. It was hypothesized that those in the experimental condition would find the poor performance of the children frustrating and that the subsequent arousal would cause aggression. The fact that these participants used more force on the switch is interpreted as supporting this hypothesis.

cognitive neoassociationist model model of aggression which proposes that cognitive associations are learned through rewards and punishments.

Berkowitz's model of aggression is usually referred to as **cognitive neoassociationist** because it proposes that cognitive associations are learned through rewards and punishments. Through socialization, individuals develop aggressive cognitive–associative networks. When people experience arousal, such networks are more likely to become active; they are more likely to have aggressive thoughts. Brad Bushman (1996) found that people more prone to aggression also were more likely to make word associations with aggressive words. For these people, presumably frustrating situations lead to both aggressive thoughts and actions.

The view that aggression is one possible consequence of frustration is also supported by studies looking at the relationship between social and economic stress indicators, such as unemployment, and various measures of aggression, such as homicide and suicide (Messner, 1980). In a major cross–cultural study that included data from Austria, Finland, Germany, India, Israel, Japan, New Zealand, Norway, Sweden, Switzerland, the United Kingdom, and the United States, Simha Landau (1984) demonstrated that poorer economic conditions can be associated with higher levels of violent crime. It could be argued that poorer economic conditions represent frustrating experiences and that such frustration "causes" greater aggression.

However, we must be very careful about jumping to such conclusions, because people in different societies are not socialized to cope in the same way with environmental stressors. For example, Landau found that, contrary to the hypothesis,

> in spite of growing inflation, the weakening of the family as a social support system . . . most measures of aggression and violence in Japan showed a decrease rather than an increase . . . the data regarding aggression and violence in Japan seem to contradict not only our model but also some commonly accepted explanations according to which

modernization "causes" or "produces" an increase in violent and other crimes. . . . Any attempt to understand the surprising findings for Japan must take into account some of the basic characteristics of Japanese society. (p. 154)

Landau speculates that there has evolved in Japan an elaborate network of informal social control, which is used effectively by the Japanese police force. Police officers' personal knowledge of their neighborhoods and citizen participation in crime prevention form part of this picture. Other important elements are the core of morality or ethics of the Japanese, centered on feelings of shame, duty–loyalty, and respect. Such cultural characteristics mean that the impact of economic stressors is not the same in Japan as in the United States, for example.

The same point could be made using other indicators. Consider the issue of population density, which is about 120,299 people per square mile (the highest in the world) in Bombay, India, as compared to "only" 11,473 in New York City (U.S. Bureau of the Census, 1990). The cultural practices of Indians in Bombay allow them to cope with such relatively extreme population densities while displaying levels of violent crime that are still low compared with those found in New York City.

The Realistic Conflict Approach

Saddam Husseins of the future will have more, not fewer opportunities. In addition to engendering tribal strife, scarcer resources will place greater strain on many peoples who never had much of a democratic or institutional tradition to begin with.

—Robert Kaplan (1994, p. 66)

A number of influential social psychologists, such as Muzafer Sherif, adopt a **realistic conflict model:** Competition for scarce resources is the root cause of conflict (see Taylor & Moghaddam, 1994). Given that even more severe resource scarcity will probably arise in the twenty-first century, humankind faces a challenging future. Within the next 50 years, the human population is likely to exceed 9 billion, and global economic output may quintuple. These two trends will result in a sharp scarcity of renewable resources and an increased likelihood of violence (Homer–Dixon, Boutwell, & Rathjens, 1993). The realistic conflict approach is in some ways similar to the evolutionary account of aggression, but it also shares some similarities with frustration–aggression theory.

Both the realistic conflict and the evolutionary approach view aggression as arising from competition for scarce resources. If John and Dave both want the same piece of property, they will compete for it: 100,000 years ago they may have used clubs, 100 years ago guns, more recently lawyers. The evolutionary model goes a step farther by proposing that the resources are just a means to an end, the end being to be more attractive to females so as to have a better chance of passing on one's genes.

realistic conflict model idea that competition for scarce resources is the root cause of conflict.

The realistic conflict view and the frustration–aggression explanation both assume resource scarcity will lead to increased aggression. However, the way the theories explain the link is different. Realistic conflict theory assumes the process to be rational and direct, in the sense that the competing parties know what they are after and use aggression as an instrumental means to the goal, access to resources. The frustration–aggression view, on the other hand, is that resource scarcity leads to aggression indirectly and perhaps irrationally, because stressful environmental conditions create frustration, which may then lead to destructive aggression without the parties involved actually realizing what is going on.

Concepts and Issues

Researchers seeking causal explanations have cited aspects of the physical environment (such as temperature, resource scarcity, frustrating circumstances), competition for survival at the levels of individuals and genes, cognitive associations learned through rewards and punishments, and hormones as possible causes of aggression. A shortcoming shared by all these explanations is their inability to explain the meaning of aggression and why particular others are selected as targets of aggression.

1. Is aggression explained by temperature changes? Why or why not?
2. What does the "selfish gene" refer to?
3. Give examples of frustration–aggression from your daily life.
4. Give examples of how aggression could arise from increasing population and competition for resources.

A Cultural View of Aggression

The last few decades of the twentieth century have witnessed a dramatic increase in violent crime among young gang members in major urban centers in the United States (Baron & Kennedy, 1993; Bell & Jenkins, 1993; Friedlander, 1993; Martinez & Richters, 1993a, 1993b). When a 17–year–old member of a street gang was charged with murder, his response was to say gleefully, "Hey great! We've hit the big time!" (*Newsweek*, 1993). In another gang–related incident, an 11–year–old boy committed a revenge killing, and was himself killed by two teenage brothers from a competing gang (*Time*, 1994). How can we explain this terrifying pattern of gang warfare among children?

The view advocated in this text is that aggression, like all other social behaviors, involves individuals acting according to rules and norms they see to be appropriate for a given context. This account of aggression places primary emphasis on the acquisition of skills to identify and use normative systems. In the case of the young street gang members, their aggression must be understood in the context of rules and norms they see to be appropriate guides to behavior. Again and again,

Members of the Crips gang. A normative account of aggression gives importance to the cultural characteristics of people, particularly the norms and rules they share. Among some youth gangs, such as the Crips ("Gangstas who fear no cops") in California, it is normative to be violent. Conformity to gang norms is strictly enforced and violations of gang culture are severely punished. The normal thing to do is to have and to use guns.

the research shows that gang members commit aggressive acts when they see this to be "the right thing to do" in a given situation.

A Social Learning View

Social psychologists who take a **social learning theory** approach, which assumes our behavior is learned through observation and imitation and by our being rewarded and punished, also emphasize the learned characteristic of aggressive behavior. This orientation owes a great deal to Albert Bandura's (1973) research; he established the classic paradigm for social learning experiments.

In a typical study, nursery children in the experimental group observe an adult "role model" enter a room in which there are several toys, including a large, inflated, plastic clown. The model plays with the toys for a little while, then proceeds to hit the plastic clown. Other children, who were in the control condition, saw the same model play with the clown, but in a nonaggressive manner. In both conditions, the children were merely passive observers. When children from both groups were allowed to play freely with the toys, those who had observed the aggressive acts tended to imitate them.

Subsequent research has shown that the tendency for children to imitate observed aggressive behavior is increased if (1) the model is seen to be rewarded after acting aggressively, (2) if other adults present

social learning theory theory that behavior is learned through observation and imitation and by being rewarded and punished.

Figure 11–6 Social learning view of aggression in children.

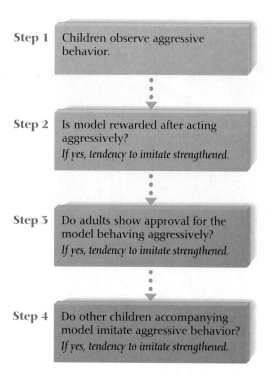

Step 1	Children observe aggressive behavior.
Step 2	Is model rewarded after acting aggressively? *If yes, tendency to imitate strengthened.*
Step 3	Do adults show approval for the model behaving aggressively? *If yes, tendency to imitate strengthened.*
Step 4	Do other children accompanying model imitate aggressive behavior? *If yes, tendency to imitate strengthened.*

show approval for the model behaving aggressively, and (3) if the model is accompanied by a child who also imitates the aggressive behavior (see Figure 11–6) (Bandura, 1965; Eisenberg, 1980; Leyens, Herman, & Dunand, 1982).

Social learning theory inevitably leads us to look to the mass media, and television particularly, as a source of "models" for children to imitate. One line of research suggests that children learn scripts from the episodes they see depicted in the media (Huesmann, 1986). For example, children watch how a movie hero beats up and kills a gang of people who threaten him, then they use that script as a guide for their own behavior in a situation for which they see the script as appropriate. This explanation links up with Erving Goffman's (1956) dramaturgical model, which assumes that people acquire skills to present themselves in particular ways in different contexts (recall our discussions of Goffman's ideas in Chapter 10). Thus, for example, Jim acquires scripts from movies about his favorite tough guy hero and uses such scripts to present himself as a tough guy in his own everyday interactions.

The concepts of **learned scripts** (information learned about a normative sequence of events for given social situations) and **dramaturgical roles** (expectations about how people in a specific social position will behave) also help explain differences between violent crime across ethnic groups and across sex groups. Homicide is the leading cause of death among young black men in the United States, and it occurs at almost 10 times the rate for young white men (Cadenhead, Durant, Pendergrast, & Salvens, 1994; Gibbs, 1984). This dramatic difference is

learned script information learned about a normative sequence of events for given social situations.

dramaturgical role expectation about how people in a specific social situation will behave.

due in part to the role models available to black and white youths, with black youths being particularly exposed to violent role models (see the discussions in Majors & Gordon, 1994). Similarly, at least part of the higher physical aggressivity of males compared to females is due to differences in available role models (Galdue, 1991; Lightdale & Prentice, 1994). Both men and women expect men to be more aggressive and are more likely to approve of men behaving aggressively.

According to a cultural account of aggression, the relationship between the media and viewer behavior is not causal or direct, because of the effect of cultural norms and rules. In light of this, we can better appreciate why cross-cultural studies of the effects of televised violence show the effect to vary across societies. For example, in studies of television viewing and aggressivity among boys and girls in Austria, Finland, Israel, Poland, and the United States, among boys early television viewing was found to be associated with aggressivity in Finland, urban Israel, Poland, and the United States, but not in Austria (see Huesmann & Eron, 1986). Among girls, early television viewing was found to be associated with aggressivity in urban Israel and the United States, but not in Austria, Finland, or Poland. We are starting to understand better how cultural systems mediate the influence of television violence at different stages of human development (Levine, 1996), as well as for individuals with different personality characteristics (Bushman, 1996).

Historical Comparisons

One way to understand better the relationship between culture and aggression is to make historical comparisons. We begin by comparing two very different societies located in the same geographical region at roughly the same time: a group of native Australians and a group of European colonists in Australia.

Life Among the Tiwi in Australia. Before the 1980s, the Tiwi people of north Australia lived an isolated existence on Melville and Bathurst islands, having little contact with outsiders, including mainland Aborigines (Hart, Pilling, & Goodale, 1988). Many fascinating social practices evolved among the Tiwi, including very effective norms and rules for handling disputes that could potentially lead to interpersonal or intergroup fighting. The vast majority of disputes involved older men accusing younger men of having adulterous intentions, fulfilled or otherwise. Typically, the accusation (something like, "You young scoundrel! You have been hanging around my camp in order to seduce my youngest wife!") would quickly evolve into a "legal trial," with the older man publicly haranguing the younger, and a crowd gathering to witness the proceedings. After 20 minutes or so of verbal accusations and abuse against the young man, the older man would cast aside his ceremonial spear and take aim at the accused with his hunting spears. The younger man was obliged by custom to stand more or less on the same spot, rather like a batter waiting for the pitcher to throw, but he could maneuver out of the way of the spears as they sped by.

Being much more agile than his typically ancient adversary, the younger man could avoid the spears and make the old accuser look incompetent and silly. However, this would not be prudent, because Tiwi society does not approve of such disrespectful conduct toward elders. Thus, it was best if the younger man took the diplomatic route of allowing himself to be hit and wounded, usually after showing his agility and doing crowd–pleasing, spear–dodging stunts for a while. But he needed to be skilled in bringing about the wounding incident, because he did not want too serious a wound—just enough for blood to flow, so that everyone would agree justice has been served. This would please the crowd, satisfy the older man, and get the younger man off the hook with an injury that would heal quickly. One important element of the procedure was that the rules of Tiwi culture would not allow family, friends, or supporters of the young accused to come to his aid. In this way, collective fighting was avoided and disputes were generally settled with minimal social disruption.

Life Among White Settlers in Australia.   The Tiwi of north Australia were still practicing their traditional forms of conflict resolution several centuries after the technologically more advanced Europeans had landed in Australia following the pioneering voyage of Captain James Cook in 1770. The British brought with them their own systems of justice, which turned out to be in some ways far more aggressive than those of the Tiwi. Australia at this time was a penal colony, a place to which convicts were exiled.

Typical of the convicts sent to Australia was Laurence Frayne, an Irishman convicted of theft in Dublin and eventually transported in 1830 to Norfolk Island, situated to the east of Australia in the Pacific Ocean. During his years of labor, he was beaten, starved, and cruelly treated in just about every way imaginable. After a flogging, he would try to relieve his bloody and torn–up back by pouring his ration of water on the floor, urinating to enlarge the puddle, then lying down:

> with my sore shoulders on the exact spot where the water lay. . . . I was literally alive with Maggots and Vermin, nor could I keep them down; to such a wretched and truly miserable state was I reduced, that I even hated the look . . . of myself. . . . The trifle of soap allowed me to wash . . . was stopped from me. . . . (Hughes, 1986, p. 465)

A quick way out of the misery was suicide, but this path was often denied convicts by their religious upbringing. They did not want to replace the temporary hell of their prison on earth with what they believed would be eternal damnation in the next world. So they adopted another solution: A group of them would draw lots to choose one person to die, the other to kill. The rest of the group would act as witnesses. This kind of "Roman death" involves premeditated, planned aggression. The person killed would escape prison life, while the killer and the witnesses would gain temporary relief because they had to be taken from Norfolk Island to Sydney, where they would receive better treatment, to stand trial.

The Dilemma of Modern Weapons.   As these examples suggest, cross-cultural comparisons reveal considerable variations in aggressive behavior (Goldstein & Segall, 1983). For example, the Tiwi are a relatively nonaggressive group who seldom engage in homicide; in this they are different from many other societies. They are very different from Europeans, but they are also very different from other non–Western groups, such as the Yanomamo, a South American tribe who routinely engage in fierce and lethal fighting (Chagnon, 1992). Differences in aggressivity are also evident across modern societies. The United States is a society high in aggressivity, as indicated by homicide rates, compared to Norway, for example (Landau, 1984).

But even though there is variation in aggressivity across societies, modern weapons have created a common dilemma for all humankind. This dilemma has arisen from, on the one hand, the established tradition of bestowing honor on the soldier, the "strong man," the "macho hero," and on the other hand, an abhorrence of aggressive acts and violence generally. In his influential book *A History of Warfare*, the military historian John Keegan (1993) argues that soldierly virtues have been given high status in a wide variety of different cultures throughout history. After all, a civilization that could not defend itself militarily was likely to be overpowered by its neighbors. Military might allowed Europeans to establish colonies all over the world. But this same tendency to honor the "strong man" becomes a problem when city streets become war zones. How can the army be honored, but aggression be kept out of our everyday lives?

A plausible explanation for how this dilemma arose is provided by the ethologist Konrad Lorenz (1966), who pointed out that in a period of time that is infinitesimal in evolutionary terms, we have jumped from being about to throw sticks and stones to being capable of precisely pinpointing and annihilating entire cities on the other side of the globe. This newly found capacity to do harm has strengthened our doubts about the tradition of honoring the aggressive "hero." The destructive potential of the weapons of modern warfare gives us cause to rethink and to seriously reconsider our own future. What are we doing to ourselves? In Leo Tolstoy's great masterpiece, *War and Peace*, written about events during the Napoleonic wars, we find early expression of this modern dilemma:

> Some tens of thousands of men lay sacrificed in various postures and uniforms on the fields and meadows . . . where for hundreds of years the peasants . . . had harvested their crops and grazed their cattle. At the ambulance stations the grass and earth were soaked with blood for two acres round. . . . Over all the plain, at first so bright and gay with its glittering bayonets and puffs of smoke in the morning sunshine, there hung now a dark cloud of damp mist and smoke, and a strange sour smell of saltpetre and blood. Storm clouds had gathered, and a drizzling rain began to fall on the dead, on the wounded, on the panic-stricken, exhausted and hesitating soldiers. It seemed to say: "Enough, enough; cease. . . . Consider. What are you doing?" (Tolstoy, 1955, pp. 366–367).

Comparing the Same Society Across Time

Another approach to exploring the relationship between culture and aggression is to compare the same society across historical periods. One of the clearest indicators suggesting that aggression is influenced by normative systems is historical data on violent crime. In a major cross-national study of violent crime, Dane Archer and Rosemary Gartner (1984) analyzed data from 110 nations. They demonstrated a strong tendency for violent crime to increase after major wars, in both defeated and victorious nations. Why is this? The explanation they proposed is that as a consequence of war there is a general acceptance or legitimization of violence. The social acceptance, and even adulation, of violence leads to a fall in the threshold for resorting to violence. The normative system endorses aggression as "the correct way to behave," and now people behave violently following even the slightest provocation.

A disturbing aspect of this "legitimization of violence" is that both veterans and nonveterans show an increase in violence. This suggests a generalized behavioral shift across society. A similar shift seems to be evident when we review historical evidence for a given country. For example, consider homicide rates in England, where detailed criminal records allow us to go back 700 years. Compared to his medieval ancestors, the modern Englishman faces only about 5 percent risk of being murdered (Gurr, 1981). Obviously, such shifts need to be understood in the context of changing normative systems.

Sexual Aggression in the Modern Era

"Men are animals," said the first woman, a middle-aged lady waiting on the checkout line.

"At least they can't get away with it anymore," responded her friend.

I was standing behind these two women and I could see they were looking at a newspaper headline that told of a priest who had been sexually abusing orphan boys for over 30 years. Everywhere we turn these days, sexual aggression by men is being highlighted: sexual abuse of boys (Friedrich, 1995), wife rape (Bergen, 1996), acquaintance rape (Wiehe & Richards, 1995), sexual harassment at work (Rutter, 1996), and sexual assault on college campuses (Schwartz & DeKeseredy, 1997). It is almost always men who are the perpetrators of sexual aggression, and women and children who are the victims (Allison & Wrightsman, 1993; Hall, 1996). As suggested by the title of one of the discussions of this topic, women seem to have "no safe haven" against sexual assault (Koss, Goodman, Browne, Fitzgerald, Keita, & Russo, 1994).

Incidence of Sexual Aggression.   But is sexual aggression being reported and highlighted more in the United States because of the newfound freedom enjoyed by women and other minorities, or because, indeed, there now is a higher level of sexual aggression than in other societies? There are at least two sources of data relevant to this question. One source is surveys of potential victims. A comparison of college students in Hong Kong and the United States did show higher sexual aggression among students in the United States (Tang, Critelli, & Porter, 1995). On the other hand, cross-national surveys in countries as different as South Korea, New Zealand, and the United States show that very similar numbers of women, around one in four, in all these societies have experienced completed or attempted rape (Koss, Heise, & Russo, 1994). This is far higher than officially reported levels in the United States (FBI, 1994) or in other countries (Rozee, 1993).

A second source of information is official crime statistics, which are probably far less reliable in most countries. These figures indicate almost no sexual aggression in some societies, but this is at least in part because of the stigma associated with being the victim of such aggression (Rozee, 1993). A girl who reports being a rape victim would bring shame on herself and her family in traditional Muslim societies.

Within the United States, official crime statistics suggest that African-Americans are overrepresented among those arrested for crimes involving sexual aggression (FBI, 1994). A national survey focusing on rape revealed the same trend (National Victims Center, 1992). However, this trend might be explained by the overreprentation of African-Americans among the poor. Rape is more prevalent among the poor in the United States, irrespective of ethnic background (Koss, Gidycz, & Wisniewski, 1987).

Both self-report surveys and official statistics indicate lower rates of sexual aggression among Asian-Americans (FBI, 1994; Koss, Gidycz, & Wisniewski, 1987). This might be explained by social desirability. Collectivistic Asian cultures may lead women and men to avoid reporting sexual aggression, both officially and unofficially. Another possible explanation is that the more collectivistic culture of Asian-Americans results in less sexual aggression, perhaps because of the closer ties between individuals and communities and because of the deterrent power of shame. The same complexity arises when we try to explain the lower incidence of sexual aggression among Latin Americans (Sorenson & Siegel, 1992): Is there really less sexual aggression in Latin America, perhaps because of Roman Catholic traditions, or is it that victims often refrain from reporting sexual aggression because they do not want to be stigmatized?

Rape Myths.   Although it is difficult to determine changes in the incidence of sexual aggression, a number of other important issues can be clarified, helping us to identify possible universals in this domain. First, although the perpetrators of sexual aggression are almost always men, not all men are sexual aggressors (Allison & Wrightsman, 1993). Even if men could commit rape without the possibility of ever getting caught, over two-thirds of them report there is not even a slim chance of their doing so. But some men seem to be more prone to committing rape, and their inclination may be explained by several factors.

Research suggests that some men derive as much, or more, pleasure from witnessing scenes of rape and other forms of sexual aggression than they do from witnessing consensual sexual relations (Barbaree & Marshall, 1991). These men may prefer sexual aggression because it is more pleasurable for them. Related to this are findings suggesting that for some men having power over a woman is associated with sexual pleasure (Bargh, Raymond, Pryor, & Strack, 1995).

Another characteristic of men more prone to sexual aggression is their belief in **rape myths,** false but pervasive beliefs about the sexual desires of women that excuse sexual aggression against them. Rape myths revolve around the idea that women "really" want to be over-powered by men, to be controlled and "persuaded" to have sex. Women will resist and protest openly, but beneath the surface, the "rejection" is not really a rejection, the "no" is not really a no, and even though they often do not even realize it themselves, women actually "want" to have sex with a man who dominates them. Rape myths are present in mild forms even in many "family entertainment" stories: The male hero grabs the girl, she resists, he kisses her and she struggles, pounding her fists on his chest. Gradually, her resistance fades, and she embraces him.

rape myth   false but pervasive beliefs about the sexual desires of women that excuse sexual aggression against them.

Military training today involves the use of smart weapons and guided missiles that can hit targets hundreds of miles away. Such "hits" do not require the attackers to see the targets; only dots on a screen are visible, as the targets are hit and the lighted dots fade away (left). Killing becomes an impersonal, technical task. Research suggests that increased distance between attacker and target makes it more likely that higher levels of aggression will be shown. There is an alarming similarity between modern military training and the "virtual reality" games in which youngsters hit moving targets (right). There is the same impersonal, technical aspect to the violence, so that victims are just targets, not individuals.

The story ends with her smiling contentedly and walking off into the sunset with her arms around her man.

The power of the rape myth is its socially shared nature: When a group of people accept rape myths, then rape becomes a correct way to behave among this group. Martin Schwartz and Walter DeKeseredy (1997) have shown that sexual assault continues on campuses in large part because of the peer support perpetrators receive. The male student accused of raping a classmate who came to his party and enjoyed a few drinks often receives sympathy and support from other students, who also endorse his view that "she wanted it." Even some women endorse rape myths, perhaps because blaming the victim enables them to maintain the belief in a just world (recall our discussion of the just-world hypothesis in Chapter 9).

Related to rape myths, Neil Malamuth and his associates followed up a group of men for 10 years and found support for their proposal that sexual aggressors have two key characteristics: They prefer to have sex without emotional ties, and they play a masculine role that shows hostility and suspicion toward women (Malamuth, Linz, Heavey, Barnes, & Acker, 1995). At the root of sexual aggression seems to be socialization processes that teach some men to be aloof, distant, and controlling toward women and to view them only as sexual objects.

Toward Solutions

The modern world seems to be preoccupied with violence. Our attention is riveted to this problem through the constant reminders we get from the media, politicians, church leaders, educators, and other opinion leaders. In this chapter I have argued that aggressive behavior can best be understood in its cultural context, because it is through cultural norms and rules that we learn when and how to be aggressive. An implication of this argument is that we can socialize individuals to be aggressive, to attack and to kill particular targets, or not to be aggressive (Hall & Barongan, 1997).

In practice, there are some limits on how aggressive we can train most people to become. Throughout human history, certain institutions have specialized in training people, men in particular, to attack and destroy targeted "enemies." The most important example of such institutions in modern societies is the military. A major goal of military institutions is to train individuals to kill. They are given years of intensive training in how to use destructive weapons in order to become effective "killing machines." But how effective is this socialization?

Dave Grossman (1995), a professor of military science, argues that despite thousands of years of refinement, military training is still unable to do a very effective job of molding individuals into killers. Most people experience serious psychological traumas after killing, so that they are more likely to be sick rather than to feel elated when they do kill. Societies offer "absolution" to their soldiers by cheering them in parades, honoring them, awarding them medals, and making them feel like heroes. Despite all this, records of the way soldiers behave during combat show that they often try very hard to avoid killing the enemy. During World War II, for example, it was not unusual for up to 80 percent of riflemen to fail to fire their weapons at an exposed enemy. Some of them would "freeze" or fire into the air or into the ground—do almost anything to avoid killing. The firing rate was much higher among U.S. soldiers in Vietnam, who went through more intensive and sophisticated desensitization programs. But perhaps this was at a greater psychological cost, since Vietnam veterans as a group suffered unusually high rates of social and psychological problems, including mental illness, suicide, and homelessness.

If most humans are loath to kill, and suffer psychological distress when they do kill, why is it that homicide rates among young, urban-dwelling males have been rising so dramatically? One reason could be that young males are being desensitized to the evils of killing by the games they play (e.g., shooting at moving human targets in video games; see Zuckerman, 1987), by the glorification of violence in the media and in contemporary culture generally. Grossman (1995) argues that this socialization is very similar to the experiences of soldiers being trained to kill in battle. At least a few recipients of this training come to perceive city streets as the killing fields. It may be that these few are physiologically disposed to behave more aggressively.

The most effective programs for decreasing aggressivity have been those that target the young and influence behavior by changing the norms and rules of everyday life. One such program is described by David Johnson and his colleagues, who provided 30 minutes of negotiation and mediation training every day over 6 weeks for elementary school children (Johnson, Johnson, Dudley, & Acikgoz, 1994). The children became skilled in identifying potential conflict situations, as well as the correct way to interact with others so as to decrease the likelihood of aggression. Longitudinal studies will tell us the extent to which the participants retain these skills in later life.

Concepts and Issues

Historical comparisons of societies demonstrate enormous variation in types and levels of aggressivity. In some societies aggression is at a minimum and expressed in ritualized situations, whereas in others it is normative and at a high level. Modern media provide roles and scripts for aggressive behavior and teach the young that aggression is appropriate behavior in many situations. Rape myths have a powerful and detrimental impact and in part explain sexual aggression against women.

1. How does social learning theory explain aggressive behavior?
2. Give examples of variations in aggressivity in different societies.
3. Does experience suggest it is easy to train humans to kill one another? Discuss with examples.

Conclusion

Social psychologists have studied aggression extensively and from a variety of theoretical viewpoints, particularly looking for cause–effect relationships. The physiological characteristics of some individuals, and the physical characteristics of the environment, may in some cases lead to a higher predisposition to aggression, but the meaning of aggression is only explained through a cultural perspective. Crimes of hate, sexual assaults, and other types of aggression are directed at selected targets, usually women and other minorities. Aggression is seldom random and involving strangers; most sexual assault involves acquaintances. Rape is often an attempt to dominate and humiliate another person, and derives its meaning from the roles of men and women in the larger society.

For Review

Aggression is behavior intended to harm another human being. There are enormous variations in the levels of aggression across cultures. In developing explanations for aggression, social psychologists have distinguished between "emotional" or "hot" aggression and "instrumental" or "cool" aggression. However, in practice this distinction is not plausible because people can and do use emotions instrumentally in order to achieve their goals.

We can also distinguish between causal and normative accounts of aggression. The former views aggression as caused by factors internal or external to the person, whereas the latter sees aggression as involving individuals identifying and following what they see to be appropriate social rules and norms in given situations.

Among the causal models of aggression, those that see aggression as caused by genetic factors continue to receive serious attention. Other causal explanations have been based on the idea of "aggression centers" in the brain, on hormonal imbalances or biochemical abnormalities, and on a temperature–aggression link (the focus of extensive study).

The ethological perspective holds that the inhibitory mechanisms developed by humans to cope with their very limited "natural" killing abilities are overridden by technologically advanced weapons, which distance the source from the target of aggression. The sociobiological perspective is that people are more likely to show aggression against genetically dissimilar others.

The frustration–aggression hypothesis is the most influential causal explanation and is derived from Freud's work. In its original form, the hypothesis states that frustration evokes a state of instigation to aggress, and aggression is always preceded by some form of frustration. The hypothesis was later reformulated to predict that the power of frustration to cause aggression depends on the level of arousal induced by the frustration.

Research evidence suggests that these causal models are not plausible because social behavior is patterned by cultural rules and norms rather than "caused" by factors internal or external to people. Aggressivity can be explained to a large extent by the rules and norms that prescribe "correct" behavior in given contexts. Individuals look to the media, the family, the school, the peer group, and other sources to find out how they should behave in the social world.

For Discussion

1. "Physiological factors explain why aggression takes place, but not why it takes place against particular targets." Discuss this statement.
2. Compare realistic conflict theory and frustration–aggression theory explanations of aggression.
3. What evidence do we have that aggression is influenced by culture?

Key Terms

Aggression *366*

Angry aggression *366*

Cognitive neoassociationist
  model *386*

Dramaturgical role *390*

Frustration–aggression
  hypothesis *385*

Genotype *384*

Hate crimes *375*

Instrumental aggression *366*

Learned script *390*

Phenotype *384*

Rape myth *396*

Realistic conflict model *387*

Social learning theory *389*

Annotated Readings

General overviews of aggression are R. A. Baron and D. R. Richardson, *Human aggression*, 2nd ed. (New York: Plenum Press, 1994); L. Berkowitz, *Aggression: Its causes, consequences, and control* (New York: McGraw-Hill, 1993); J. T. Tedeschi and R. B. Felson, *Violence, aggression, and coercive actions* (Washington, DC: American Psychological Association, 1994); and M. Potegal and J. F. Knutson, eds., *The dynamics of aggression: Biological and social processes in dyads and groups* (Hillsdale, NJ: Lawrence Erlbaum, 1994).

The influence of the media on aggression is discussed in M. Levine, *Viewing violence: How media violence affects your child's and adolescent's development* (New York: Doubleday, 1996); L. R. Huesmann and L. D. Eron, eds., *Television and the aggressive child: A cross-national comparison* (Mahwah, NJ: Lawrence Erlbaum, 1986).

For more on culture and aggression, see R. E. Nisbett and D. Cohen, *Culture of honor: Violence and the U.S. South* (Boulder, CO: Westview Press, 1996).

Sexual aggression is discussed in J. A. Allison and L. S. Wrightsman, *Rape: The misunderstood crime* (Newbury Park, CA: Sage, 1993).

Gender

◀ Mother and infant: The image is immediately recognizable by people everywhere. It suggests the traditional role of women as homemakers, wives, and mothers. In modern industrialized societies, in addition to their responsibilities in the home, most women also work outside the home. Increased economic power has been accompanied by higher political and social influence. But fundamental questions remain about gender roles and relationships between women and men: Are there gender differences in social behavior? If so, what are the sources of such differences? To what extent can they be altered?

I hardly recognized my former student, Cindy, when I walked into her office. She had changed from an undergraduate in jeans and bright casual shirts, with an overstuffed backpack, to a medical specialist in a white lab coat. It was her office I had entered now, as a patient. After giving me some ointments for a case of poison ivy and assuring me that I "would live," she took her old professor to lunch and talked about a dilemma she faced. "Almost every day my mother finds a new way of reminding me about my biological clock and how little time I have left to have children. But I really don't see how I will be able to balance family and career responsibilities. Of course, I am one of the fortunate women who actually have a choice."

The next day I traveled to Miami to interview a group of women who do not have a choice: working–class mothers from an ethnic minority who have little education or money and who are forced to work outside the home because of financial necessity. These individuals suffer multiple discrimination: as members of an ethnic minority, as economically poor, and as women.

Women in the United States and some other countries are now equal in the eyes of the law, and they have made a great deal of progress in many professions formerly closed to them, such as medicine, law, and engineering. The special challenges faced by women of different social classes and ethnicities are receiving more and more attention in social psychological research (Burn, 1996). But enormous challenges still lie ahead in Western and non–Western societies.

Consider, for example, the following trends in the global context (United Nations, 1991):

▶ According to studies conducted in Asia and Africa, women work an average of 13 hours more a week than do men in these regions. For women everywhere the number of hours of work is generally higher than it is for men.

▶ Of 8,000 abortions in Bombay performed after parents learned the sex of the fetus through amniocentesis, only one fetus was male.

▶ The number of illiterate women in the world rose by more than 50 million between 1970 and 1980, while the number of illiterate men rose by only about 4 million.

▶ Even when women do the same work as men, they typically receive between 30 and 40 percent less pay on average worldwide.

▶ Although women make up almost 50 percent of the world population (in the industrialized world, the ratio of women to men is 106 to 100, but in Asia and the Pacific there are only 95 women for every 100 men; United Nations, 1991, p. 11), less than 5 percent of the world's heads of state, heads of major corporations, and holders of top positions in international organizations are women.

But, we might ask, are these global trends not contradicted by the situation in the United States and other Western societies? In some areas, at least, the answer is no. For example, after a long and bitter struggle women in the United States gained the right to vote in 1920, but by

1981 only 105 women had been elected to the U.S. Senate (see Ornstein, Mann, & Malbin, 1994; Wormser, 1982). The media made much of the "year of the woman" in the House of Representatives election of 1992 (see Cook, Thomas, & Wilcox, 1994), but, still, women made up a mere *11 percent* of the House. The same elections brought the number of women in the Senate up to a grand total of six. These are hardly major breakthroughs, particularly when one considers that the United States has not even once had a woman president or vice president. Keep in mind that a number of traditional societies, including Sri Lanka, India, and Pakistan, have had women as successful national leaders.

In both the United States and in more traditional societies, women tend to achieve power through a "widow's mandate" or by having some close blood relationship with male leaders. It was not until 1979 that a woman, Nancy L. Kassebaum, was elected to the U.S. Senate without being preceded in office by her husband. Classic examples in traditional societies are that of Indira Gandhi, who became the prime minister of India, following in the footsteps of her father (Jawaharlal Nehru), and Benazir Bhutto, who became prime minister of Pakistan, as was her father (Z. A. Bhutto).

It is surprising perhaps that the most influential woman to have emerged as a strong national leader in a Western society is England's Margaret Thatcher, whose account of her years as prime minister makes it clear that she was "tougher" than most of the male politicians (Thatcher, 1993). In one sense Thatcher was going against the stereotype of women in politics since she is an archconservative, whereas research by Shirley Ogletree and her associates suggests that voters tend to perceive women candidates as more liberal, and concerned with minority rights, peace initiatives, and social and environmental programs (Ogletree, Coffee, & May, 1992). Sue Thomas (1991, 1997) has shown that this perception of women officeholders as giving more priority to moral and cultural issues is largely correct: Gender of political officeholders does make a difference in policies adopted. Children and families receive more support from women officeholders (see also Jelen, Thomas, & Wilcox, 1994).

Gender and Sex: An Overview

Sex is the biological category people belong to, whereas **gender** is the social role ascribed to people who fall in either the male or female sex category. Throughout most of the world and in many major areas of life, including politics, business, and education, gender is still fundamentally important. That is, how one behaves and how others behave toward one is in important ways dependent on one's gender. But we need to progress beyond generalities and to identify more precisely the social psychological profiles of females and males. Toward this goal, we begin by considering theoretical explanations in the psychology of gender. These range from explanations that emphasize inherited differences between females and males, to those that highlight the role of socialization processes (Beall & Sternberg, 1995).

sex   biological category to which a person belongs.

gender   the social role ascribed to people who fall into either the male or female sex category.

Men of the Wodaabe tribe dressed for the *geerewol*. The plasticity of gender roles is demonstrated by societies in which men and women behave very differently from what in the West is considered appropriate. Consider the Wodaabe tribe of Nigeria, for example. During the *geerewol*, a seven-day celebration, the most handsome males compete in dances. They are judged and admired by women, who select winners on the basis of charm, personality, endurance, and other criteria. Men dress to be beautiful. They decorate themselves and behave in ways we might consider feminine, showing off the whiteness of their eyes and teeth (an important criterion for beauty in their culture).

In a critical review of the empirical research on gender differences, we discover that this issue is not just a matter of academic research but of politics as well. Florence Denmark (1994), Jeanne Marecek (1995), and others are educating us toward a better understanding of how the science and politics of research on gender have become inseparable. There are two main research questions here. First, to what extent are there gender differences in social psychological characteristics of males and females? Second, which of these characteristics are attributable to sex (biological makeup)?

Research evidence suggests that gender roles are extremely malleable and that differences between men and women could be made much smaller or larger through selective socialization processes. In other words, I believe that culture is to a very large extent responsible for gender roles. This view is supported by cross-cultural research, which demonstrates enormous variability in the gender roles. However, sex differences (the distinct biological characteristics of men and women) also influence gender roles. Specifically, sex differences influence how easy or difficult it is to change gender roles in any given domain. Because women are capable of bearing children and men are not, for example, social behavior related to this sex difference may prove more difficult to change.

In the final section, the focus of our discussion shifts to the cultural factors that influence change. Cultural practices are extremely powerful and subtle in the way they maintain traditional gender roles. Even when by law women should enjoy equal opportunities, many aspects of the normative system serve to hold them back, as we see in a detailed examination of women in science.

Concepts and Issues

Sex is a biological category, and gender is the social role ascribed to the members of the different sexes. There are some biological differences between the sexes and these are universal, but gender differences are socially constructed and vary considerably across cultures.

1. Define the terms *gender* and *sex*.
2. What are some of the indicators suggesting that women and men have not yet reached parity in the global context?

Explaining Gender Differences

Two broad categories of explanations for gender differences exist. One is derived from evolutionary theory and gives importance to inherited characteristics. The other category is cultural and emphasizes the role of environmental factors in shaping gender roles and thus gender differences. We can find in both camps at least some theorists who also discuss the interaction between inherited and environmental factors, but typically researchers have paid only lip service to an interactionist perspective.

Evolutionary Accounts

> With animals having separated sexes, there will be in most cases a struggle between the males for the possession of the females. The most vigorous males, or those which have most successfully struggled with their conditions of life, will generally leave most progeny.
>
> —Charles Darwin, *Origin of Species*, p. 623

According to Darwin's epoch-making theory of evolution, the struggle for survival is won by those who leave behind the highest number of

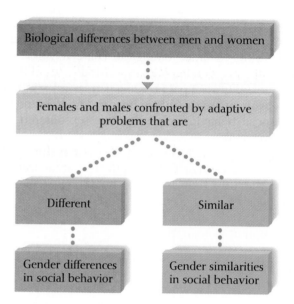

Figure 12–1 Evolutionary psychology view of gender differences and similarities.

offspring. Success in breeding depends on meeting and solving adaptive problems. Using Darwin's theory as a launching pad for their research, evolutionary psychologists have postulated that females and males will be different in those areas in which the sexes are confronted by different adaptive problems, and similar where they face the same or similar problems (see Figure 12–1). For example, women have been confronted by the problems of childbirth, men have not. This has meant that women have developed adaptations that men have not, such as a physiology for producing labor contractions and a cervix that dilates to allow the birth of the infant. But both men and women have faced the problem of regulating body temperature and have developed the same mechanisms, such as sweat glands, to deal with it.

In those areas in which they face different adaptive problems, men and women have developed specialized survival strategies. Women can conceive a limited number of children over approximately a quarter of a century, but men can sire an almost limitless number of children over the course of their adult lives. An example of the assumed behavioral consequences of these differences is that, as a general rule, males compete in order to gain access to females, so as to increase their chances of leaving behind a higher number of offspring. Females are more selective in mate preference, and they face the different problem of finding a reliable and resourceful partner to protect their offspring. (See also the discussion of evolutionary accounts of attraction and romantic love in Chapter 8.)

Evolutionary psychologists have gathered a wide variety of evidence in support of the proposition that gender differences in social behavior and cognitive functioning are predicted by the different adaptive problems faced by men and women. Studies show that, for example, at least in Western societies, men are more likely to desire and to give consent to casual sex (Buss & Schmitt, 1993; Oliver & Hyde, 1993).

An international study involving samples from 37 nations showed that women give more importance to sound financial prospects in a mate than do men (Buss, 1989).

Evolutionary psychologists have also attempted to link emotional experiences with adaptive problems. To see how they did this, answer the following question:

> What would upset or distress you more: (a) imagining your partner forming a deep emotional attachment to someone else or (b) imagining your partner enjoying passionate sexual intercourse with that other person? (Buss, Larsen, Westen, & Semmelroth, 1992, p. 252)

A number of different studies in several cultures have found that women showed more distress about emotional than about sexual infidelity, whereas the opposite pattern was true for men (Buss, 1994a; Buss, Larsen, Westen, & Semmelroth, 1992; Wiederman & Allgeier, 1993). This result is in line with predictions that men would be more concerned about maintaining control over the sexual activities of their partners because they are assumed to be less than 100 percent certain of being the father of their putative children. Of course, evolutionary psychologists do not claim that all men consciously suffer this doubt, only that unconsciously it plays a role in their behavior.

But the sociobiological claim that everywhere men dislike sexual infidelity and women dislike emotional infidelity is contradicted by cross-cultural evidence (Ortner & Whitehead, 1981). Husbands among the Semai of central Malaysia, for example, share their wives with others of their age group (Llewelyn-Davies, 1981). The supposed universality of emotional jealousy among women is disputed by societies in which women and men have sexual relations with no implications for love or marriage and women have enjoyed freedom to select their sexual partners (see the examples in Marshall & Suggs, 1971).

The sociobiological claim about gender differences in attitudes toward infidelity is also disputed by evidence gathered in the United States. Ralph Hupka and Adam Bank (1996) found that both men and women in the United States were more distressed over sexual than emotional infidelity if they preferred traditional gender norms and made sharp distinctions between men and women ("men are strong; women are emotional" and so on). This suggests that internalized norms and rules, rather than sex, explain attitudes toward infidelity.

One of the few cognitive tasks on which men and women seem to differ is tests of spatial rotation, such as tests involving the mental rotation of three-dimensional figures (Masters & Sanders, 1993). The tendency for men to score higher than women on such tests is interpreted by evolutionary psychologists as originating from the adaptive challenges men faced in hunting tasks (see Ashmore, 1990). (Of course, this assumes that men did all the hunting, which could well be an invalid assumption.) In their efforts to hunt animals, people had to search in territories far away from their main groups, they had to track and find prey, then accurately throw spears, stones, and other objects to bring the hunt to a successful conclusion, before finding their way back to camp again. Such tasks, it is assumed, nurtured visual-spatial ability. If we accept the assumption that men were the hunters and women stayed at home, presumably men's visual–spatial ability would benefit. However, this kind of explanation, which on the face of it is conceivable, is difficult to test. This points to a more general shortcoming of sociobiological explanations of social behavior: They are almost always post hoc, meaning they assume causal links between events after the events have taken place.

In the few other domains in which gender differences could be argued to be consistent and consequential, it seems even more difficult to argue a link between such differences and possible differences in the adaptive problems faced by men and women. For example, there are also reported differences between men and women on various tests of verbal ability, with women scoring higher (Halpern, 1992). From an evolutionary psychology perspective, one might have expected the opposite. Surely on hunting trips men would spend a lot of time talking and relating tales to one another (around campfires and so on), as well as sharpening their communications skills because their very lives depended on effective communications. Should not these adaptive problems have led men to develop stronger verbal skills than women?

Men do score slightly higher on average than women on some tests of quantitative problem-solving ability (Benbow & Lubinski, 1993). But, once again, we might have plausibly postulated the exact opposite from an evolutionary psychology perspective. Even if we accept the assumption that in their early history men and women specialized in tasks along traditional lines, women could have engaged in many tasks (keeping track of supplies and people, gathering, dividing up, and distributing food and water) that would nurture quantitative skills.

But perhaps the evolutionary and cultural accounts of sex differences in behavior are compatible. John Archer (1996) has argued that, first, evolutionary theory does a better job of explaining sex differences but that socialization processes themselves arise from the different adaptive challenges faced by women and men during the course of evolution. This suggests that as women and men face new challenges, socialization processes should change. Missing from this explanation, of course, is any discussion of power, status, and the politics of gender relations.

Women and men do not passively accept just any socialization processes that evolution might produce; they *actively* shape these processes to attain particular goals—such as maintaining or extending their own power positions. Socialization processes are the products of intentional and politically motivated humans, not of a "neutral" evolutionary process. The recognition that evolutionary approaches do not provide a satisfactory explanation of gender differences has led to greater emphasis on cultural explanations.

The Influence of Culture

There is disagreement about the psychological domains in which men and women differ, as well as disagreement concerning the stability and origins of such differences (Eagly, 1995). A number of theorists have

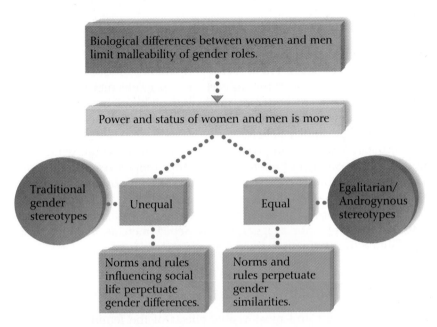

Figure 12–2   Cultural view of gender differences and similarities.

challenged the idea that gender differences are fundamentally genetic in origin (Jacklin, 1989). They postulate that culture is the main source of such differences. In important ways, the behavior of individuals is shaped through socialization processes to match gender–role expectations. Gender differences are explained by the different experiences of men and women in the course of their own lives rather than by differences in the adaptive problems faced by women and men in the course of evolution (Figure 12–2).

The political implications of these orientations are enormous (Wilkinson, 1997). If we take the view that women and men differ in psychological functioning and social behavior because of different socialization experiences that take place in the course of their own lifetimes, then it is assumed that we can intervene to alter gender differences by manipulating socialization processes. But if we assume that gender differences arise as a result of different adaptive problems over the course of evolution, then change can only be possible over a relatively long period of time. Moreover, gender differences become a part of the "natural" order of things rather than a feature of intended power inequalities that characterizes male–female relations. Feminist psychologists have favored an interpretation of gender differences that postulates socialization processes as the most valid explanation, and this perspective has had a profound impact on modern research (see Eagly, 1987; Haug, Whalen, Aron, & Olsen, 1993; Howard & Hollander, 1996; Miller, 1993; Unger & Crawford, 1996; Wilkinson & Kitzinger, 1996).

For example, a number of researchers have reported that sex differences in mathematical ability are associated with higher math anxiety among girls, the perceived value of math to the student, and the gender–role beliefs of parents (see Eccles & Jacobs, 1986). What is perhaps surprising is that the expectations of parents about the math performance of girls and boys influences math anxiety at a very young age, so that a gender difference is detectable in the primary school years (Entwisle & Baker, 1983). A study of children in China, Japan, and the United States revealed that as early as first grade, mothers tended to believe that boys are better at math and girls are better at reading (Lummis & Stevenson, 1990). Perhaps as a result of these expectations, the children had similar beliefs.

Perhaps even more important than research on actual gender differences is research on beliefs about gender differences. Rhoda Unger and Mary Crawford (1996) have highlighted the important finding that people believe gender differences are greater than they actually are. Very small and probably culturally created gender differences on math tests, for example, are exaggerated to depict men as mathematically more gifted than women.

Androgyny: Culture and Gender Categories

One of the earliest and most visible effects of the feminist movement on psychological research was in the area of sex roles. Prior to the 1970s, masculinity and femininity had been conceptualized as being on opposite poles of a single continuum: A person had to be either masculine or feminine. This viewpoint was prevalent in both the discipline of psychology and in the larger society. Furthermore, it was assumed that individuals who achieved a good fit with their sex type would be better adjusted psychologically. Thus, a masculine male and a feminine female were assumed to be psychologically healthier (see Lenney, 1991).

By the early 1970s, a number of researchers had challenged this view (Constantinople, 1973). They put forward the idea that a person could be high on both masculinity and femininity, or low on both, or indeed medium on both, since they are independent of one another. This shift in perspective owed a great deal to the feminist movement and the attack on rigid demarcations of sex roles (Friedan, 1963).

The next step was for Sandra Bem (1974) and Janet Spence and her associates (Spence, Helmreich, & Stapp, 1974) to develop tests that provided independent measures of masculinity and femininity. The first and the most influential of these, the **Bem Sex–Role Inventory (BSRI),** included both a masculinity scale and a femininity scale and set the pattern for many scales that were developed subsequently (the terms *sex role* and *gender role* are used synonymously in this literature). Table 12–1 shows the 40 items that made up the masculine and feminine scales. Individuals would be judged feminine if they scored high on the feminine traits and low on the masculine ones; judged masculine if they scored low on the feminine traits and high on the masculine ones; and judged **androgynous** if there was little difference between their scores on the feminine and masculine items.

This new approach to measuring sex roles inspired a large body of research to reassess the relationship between femininity, masculinity, and androgyny and psychological health. Findings showed that masculinity, but not femininity or androgyny, is related to mental health

Bem Sex-Role Inventory   a test that provides independent measures of masculinity and femininity.

androgynous   an individual who shows little difference between his or her scores on feminine and masculine items in a test designed to measure masculinity and femininity.

Table 12–1	Bem Sex-Role Inventory: Masculine and Feminine Items

Masculine Items	**Feminine Items**
Acts as a leader	Affectionate
Aggressive	Cheerful
Ambitious	Childlike
Analytical	Compassionate
Assertive	Does not use harsh language
Athletic	Eager to soothe hurt feelings
Competitive	Feminine
Defends own beliefs	Flatterable
Dominant	Gentle
Forceful	Gullible
Has leadership abilities	Loves children
Independent	Loyal
Individualistic	Sensitive to the needs of others
Makes decisions easily	Shy
Masculine	Soft-spoken
Self-reliant	Sympathetic
Strong personality	Tender
Willing to take a stand	Understanding
Willing to take risks	Warm
	Yielding

(Whitley, 1983, 1985). This may be because masculine traits are seen as positive by the larger society and feminine traits are seen as less so (i.e., society values someone who "acts as a leader," is "aggressive," "ambitious," and so on, more than someone who is "affectionate," "yielding," "loves children," and so on; see Broverman, Vogel, Broverman, Clarkson, & Rosenkrantz, 1972).

Culture and the Malleability of Gender

Judith Lorber (1994) is among a growing number of researchers who argue that gender is socially constructed and can be changed through appropriate socialization. Lorber points to a whole variety of sexual relationships, such as those involving **hermaphrodites** (individuals born with some organs of both sexes), **transsexuals** (those anatomically born of one sex and socialized as such but who feel they belong to the other sex), and **transvestites** (those who take on the dress and appearance of the opposite sex), that fall outside the categories of male and female.

In the Western context, at least, individuals whose sex at birth is ambiguous are not allowed to remain ambiguous for long (Money & Ehrhardt, 1975). The general belief, among both the medical community

hermaphrodite   an individual born with some organs of both sexes.

transsexuals   those born anatomically of one sex and socialized as such, but who feel they belong to the other sex.

transvestites   those who take on the dress and appearance of the opposite sex.

In South Africa's Kalahari Desert, a man teaches his son to hunt with bow and arrow. Evolutionary accounts of gender differences highlight the assumed differences in adaptive challenges faced by women and men. The role of men as hunters is supposed to have led to the strengthening of certain abilities, such as visual-spatial abilities (for example, rotating a three-dimensional figure in your mind and describing what it would look like from a different angle). But such conjectures are difficult to test. A simpler and more accurate explanation may be that differences in how they are treated and taught while they are growing up, rather than genetically acquired factors, explain the gender differences still found in some psychological domains.

and the lay public, is that it is important to determine the sex of an individual as soon as possible after birth. When a child is born with ambiguous physiology, physicians routinely inform parents that the infant is "really" a boy or a girl, but needs some treatment in order to meet all the criteria of his or her "true" sex (Kessler, 1990). Interestingly, the decision to declare a sex-ambiguous child a girl or a boy is often determined by cultural beliefs more than it is by medical criteria. For example, because of the reluctance that modern physicians and parents have for removing the penis, an individual born with what seems to be a normal penis will be declared a male, even though the internal organs of such as individual match those of females (Kessler, 1990).

In a number of other cultures, sex-ambiguous individuals are permitted to remain in a third category outside the traditional male and female groups (Money, 1986). Individuals in this third category retain more freedom to change category membership, and this may happen as an individual moves from one life stage to another. For example, in the Dominican Republic, hermaphroditic males who seem to be biological females at birth are often assigned the gender role female during early childhood but are reassigned as male as they reach puberty (Wierda, 1992).

The case of the hermaphrodites in the Dominican Republic is instructive because in the United States the same individuals may have been given surgical and hormonal treatment to remain female all their lives. These so-called pseudohermaphrodites obviously suffer a hormonal disorder and thus their situation could at one level be explained by biological processes, but the key issue is how such individuals are treated by the culture (Herdt, 1990). The categorization of all people as either male or female is the prevalent style in the industrialized Western world, but more numerous and more flexible categories are also possible, as shown by the experiences in other cultures (Money, 1986).

Gender in a Global Context

Shawn is a liberated woman and very interested in travel and in learning about different cultures. After several trips to Europe, she decides that before she finishes college she would like to do something really exciting and different. She applies for and gets a two-month summer job as an assistant to two reporters who will be visiting the Islamic Republic of Iran. When she arrives in Iran, she eagerly seeks out Iranian women who can speak English, and wants to know about their lives. But in order to be allowed to go out in public, she has to conform to local dress codes. Women have to wear dark clothes, and all of the head and body must be covered except for the face and hands.

Shawn learns that marriage involves very different arrangements in Iran, where the population is predominantly Shi'ite Muslim. In Shi'i Islam, men are allowed to have four wives, as is customary for all Muslim men, but they can also have "temporary" wives (Haeri, 1989). A man can be married or unmarried when he takes on a temporary wife, but women must be single to take on a temporary husband, because women can only have one husband. A temporary marriage can last from a few minutes to several decades.

As Shawn gathers more information about Iranian society, it seems to her that women are treated very unfairly. Women inherit almost nothing from their husbands, and their inheritance from their parents is far less than that of men. Women are seen as unfit to fill certain important positions; for example, they cannot be judges. After two months, Shawn returns to the United States and recounts her experiences. Compared to the treatment of women and men in Iranian society, she concludes that Western societies seem to treat women and men very similarly.

Cultural accounts of gender are faced with the challenge of demonstrating that, actually, women and men continue to be socialized and treated differently in the United States and other Western societies. It is this difference in socialization, the argument goes, that accounts for differences we find in the social behavior of women and men. The greater gender equality found among African–Americans relative to white Americans (see Filardo, 1996), for example, is a result of socialization differences.

What makes it easy to recognize differences in the treatment of men and woman in some developing societies is that they are public and explicit. In the United States and other Western societies, the differential treatment of the sexes is often camouflaged, implicit, and far more subtle (Moghaddam & Crystal, 1997). But research shows that from the moment parents see ultrasound pictures of their baby in the womb, they describe girls as softer, weaker, cuddlier, calmer, more delicate, and so on, than boys (Sweeny & Bradbard, 1988).

This subtlety of differential gender treatment means that it is often overlooked. This is in part because we can be misled by changes in the law that have made discrimination on the basis of sex illegal and by the rhetoric of equal rights; misled, that is, into thinking that what is in the law and what is expressed in rhetoric *is* the case in reality. Also, because people are now socialized to act in a politically correct manner, they learn to camouflage discrimination more effectively. For example, the business section of a national U.S. newspaper offers readers the opportunity to "take the sexual harassment test" (Grimsley, 1996) and find out what behavior could and could not be used to take them to court for sexual harassment.

Implicit in this discussion is the idea that the target of harassment is female and the source is male. At the same time, many males in supervisory positions now routinely ensure themselves against sexual harassment lawsuits, and perhaps as a result act with less fear. These trends suggest that formal, legal events are not always accurate indicators of what is actually taking place in everyday life. Equality has been achieved by law, but not necessarily in practice.

I am reminded here of several cases I have come across in which a woman is very liberated in her speech and very active in work and political and social activities outside the home, but a close look at her actual behavior at home, with her husband, her children, in the kitchen, and so on, reveals her to be behaving very traditionally in private contexts. She and her family look liberated from the outside, but in numerous subtle ways she actually is responsible for the home—the kitchen, the laundry, the cleaning, and really has a second job at home—whereas her husband has only his job outside the home.

This may be why changes in marital quality (how well husband and wife get on and so on) are associated with distress for women but not necessarily for men (Barnett, Raudenbush, Brennan, Pleck, & Marshall, 1995). When things do not go well at home, women suffer more because they are seen as more responsible for family life. Arlie Hochschild (1990) conducted a field study of women who come home from work to face what she calls "the second shift." Through detailed case studies, she showed that such women often suffer serious problems, including exhaustion and extreme anxiety. Surveys in the United States suggest that married and cohabiting women who work outside the home do about twice as much housework as their male partners (Blair & Lichter, 1991). Interestingly, African–American men do about 40 percent of the housework, compared to 36 percent for Hispanic men and 34 percent for white men (Shelton & John, 1993).

Cross-cultural research reveals that women do most of the housework and child care in most societies (Engle & Breaux, 1994; United Nations, 1991). There are some cross-cultural variations: Meals are prepared by women almost all of the time (94–98 percent) in some societies (such as Venezuela and Peru), but "only" most of the time (74–81 percent) in some other societies (United States, United Kingdom, Canada). When work is organized so that fathers can be physically present in the home more of the time, their participation in child care and housework tends to increase. But the corporate culture experienced by middle-class parents in the United States, and probably other Western societies, pushes fathers and mothers to spend more and more time

A familiar image in today's world: A working mother rushes along as her child tries to keep up. Many women work a second shift at home when they return from their day jobs. In many subtle ways, gender relations in the privacy of the home have remained static, so that women still have more responsibility than men for caring for the children, cooking, shopping, and managing home life.

working outside the home (Hochschild, 1997), while the larger culture puts pressure on women to take on the greater share of responsibilities in the home.

Related to this are findings from cross–cultural research which show that women in industrialized societies are even more likely than women in developing countries to experience depression (Culbertson, 1997). Research shows a female–male ratio of about 2:1 for depression in industrialized societies, but a 1:1 ratio in developing countries. One reason for this difference may be that the "two–shift" treadmill is more common in the industrialized world. In a study colleagues and I conducted with immigrant women, we discovered that women who worked outside the home suffered higher levels of psychological distress (Moghaddam, Ditto, & Taylor, 1990). This was unexpected, because in line with traditional research findings we had predicted that immigrant women homemakers would feel isolated and more distressed. The higher levels of distress among immigrant women working outside the home may be because of the discrimination they experience in the work setting, combined with the "second shift" they endure at home.

Hochschild (1990) also highlights the feelings of guilt and distress experienced both by mothers who do and those who do not work outside the home. Those who follow a career face criticism, often subtly expressed, from relatives and friends for leaving their children in the care of others. Such criticism persists even if it is obvious that the mother has no choice and must work outside the home because the family bills could not be paid otherwise. But homemakers also face criticism, as explained by one of Hochschild's (1990) participants, "If you want to know what shunning feels like, go to a cocktail party, and when they ask you what you do, say, 'I'm a housewife'" (p. 244).

Cultural accounts of gender, then, propose that despite the progress toward legal equal rights and equal treatment, women and men are still socialized to conform to different stereotypes and to adopt different ideals. Let us take a closer look at their case.

Culture, Gender Stereotypes, and Gender Ideals

Imagine you enter a playground where 20 or so girls and boys aged 3 to 5 are playing, looked after by two adult teachers. What kinds of social behaviors are you likely to witness as you watch the little children at play? First, most of the children will be playing in sex-segregated groups, girls playing with girls and boys playing with boys. If the teachers attempt to break down the sex segregation, the children show strong resistance and tend to go back to play with members of their own sex group. You notice that this sex-segregated pattern is the same for a group of 6- to 11-year-olds playing nearby.

When the teachers insist that the children form mixed-sex groups to play a new game, you notice that the boys get more than an equal share of resources during the game. The girls try to move the group closer to the teachers, as if to get protection, and when they succeed the girls in the game get a more equal share. You also notice that whereas the girls influence one another fairly effectively when they are in all-girl groups, they have far less influence on the male group members in mixed-sex groups. Girls in all-girl groups pause, listen to one another, and attend to social relations and "being nice," whereas boys in all-boy groups have more conflicts and care less about listening to and offending others. It is not that girls are not assertive, but you notice they simply try harder to tone down violence and conflict.

Eleanor Maccoby (1988, 1990) has argued that these kinds of early gender differences are primarily *social*, in the sense that they manifest themselves in social interactions and depend on the characteristics of the participants. She points out that "interactive behavior is not just situationally specific, but . . . it depends on the gender category membership of the participants" (1990, p. 514). It is only when girls and boys are brought together to interact socially that their behavior patterns become apparent. Such patterns would remain hidden if the participants in such studies were studied as isolated individuals in a laboratory. For example, a little girl who is active when playing with other girls is more likely to become passive and stand on the sidelines when put in a game with a group of boys. Her "passivity" can be properly understood only in relation to the characteristics of her partners and the *social relations* in which she is engaged (for more detailed examples, see Jacklin & Maccoby, 1978; Maccoby & Jacklin, 1987).

Such gender differences in part reflect the power of socialization to influence behavior, particularly through stereotypes and conceptions of correct behavior. Over a quarter of a century ago, Jeanne Block (1973) demonstrated through cross-cultural research that even by the age of 3 to 4 years, little girls and boys have already acquired some basic notions of how members of their gender group are supposed to behave. Of course, notions of "correct behavior" do vary across cultures and over time in any one culture, but there is consistency in the finding that the influence of socialization for gender roles becomes effective very early in life. The cross-cultural research of John Williams and Deborah Best (1990a) also demonstrates that basic elements of gender stereotypes are acquired by children very early, certainly by the age of 5 and perhaps as early as two years of age (for example, see Perry, White, & Perry, 1984).

What happens to gender stereotypes and gender ideals as children grow to become adolescents has been explored cross-culturally by Judith Gibbons, Deborah Stiles, and others (e.g., Gibbons, Stiles, Perez-Prada, Shkodriani, & Medina, 1996; Gibbons, Stiles, & Shkodriani, 1991; Stiles, Gibbons, & De La Garza Schnellmann, 1990; Stiles, Gibbons, & Peters, 1993). This research has shown support for the finding that girls across a diverse array of cultures hold fewer traditional attitudes toward gender roles than do boys. More interesting, Gibbons and her associates showed that the adolescent sons and daughters of mothers who work outside the home hold less conservative gender-role attitudes, and this finding holds across samples from societies as diverse as Iceland, Mexico, Spain, and the United States. Once again, the importance of available role models is

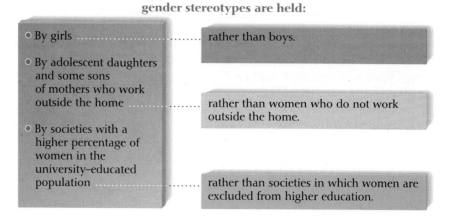

Cross-cultural research shows that less traditional gender stereotypes are held:

- By girls .... rather than boys.

- By adolescent daughters and some sons of mothers who work outside the home .... rather than women who do not work outside the home.

- By societies with a higher percentage of women in the university-educated population .... rather than societies in which women are excluded from higher education.

Figure 12-3 Factors associated with less traditional gender stereotypes.

underlined by this finding; if a nontraditional mother is available to set standards, then adolescents of both sexes move in a more liberal direction. Related to this, John Williams and Deborah Best (1990b), in a 14-country study, found that in societies with a higher percentage of women working outside the home and in the university-educated population, gender roles were less differentiated (see Figure 12-3).

These findings are in line with new approaches to child development, emphasizing the active role of individuals in trying to make better sense of the world, and the powerful influence of cultural surroundings on individual thinking and behavior (Meltzoff & Gopnik, 1997). People are not born with the characteristics of men or women, intelligence or lack thereof, high or low self-esteem, and so on. Rather, they become adults with certain characteristics through being taught and trained in particular cultures.

Concepts and Issues

Evolutionary psychologists argue that gender differences arise from the different adaptive problems faced by males and females. A cultural explanation proposes that biological differences set some limits to the malleability of gender, but this still leaves room for an enormous amount of variation in gender roles. Gender is to a large extent socially constructed, with individuals being socialized to conform to gender stereotypes from the first day of life. Differences in the socialization of girls and boys are mostly very subtle, and often unnoticed.

1. Why do evolutionary psychologists give importance to differences in the adaptive problems faced by women and men?
2. What is meant by the term *androgynous*?
3. Give examples that suggest gender is malleable.
4. How do gender roles differ for girls and boys and for women and men? Give examples.

Gender Differences: Now You See It, Now You Don't

Roughly a quarter of a century ago, Eleanor Maccoby and Carol Jacklin coauthored an influential book that reviewed the available literature on gender differences (Maccoby & Jacklin, 1974). Their argument, which was in line with the thinking of many feminists at the time and since then, was that there are few attributes on which the sexes differ consistently. In those few cases in which there is consistency across studies, the amount of difference across sex groups is negligible. Since the publication of Maccoby and Jacklin's review, scores of literature reviews on gender differences have been conducted using the new technique of meta-analysis (see Eagly, 1995). But despite the attempt to make such reviews more objective by using meta-analysis, politics still influences how gender differences are reported. The tendency has been to show an alpha bias and exaggerate differences or a beta bias and minimize differences (Hare-Mustin & Marecek, 1988).

The main tendency among feminists seems to have been to argue that there are minimal differences. As Alice Eagly (1995) has observed

> Much feminist research on sex differences was (and still is) intended to shatter stereotypes about women's characteristics and change people's attitudes by proving that women and men are essentially equivalent in their personalities, behavioral tendencies, and intellectual abilities. (p. 149)

By demonstrating the sameness of men and women in psychological domains, the intention of these researchers was to move closer to equality of opportunity and parity in social status for men and women. If, in fact, women are not different from men on important traits, then this is yet another reason why they should enjoy the same opportunities to become the boss, hold the office of university president, be the CEO, the head of government, and so on.

But some feminists have adopted the alternative strategy of arguing that there *are* gender differences on important traits, and it is a good strategy for women to emphasize certain differences. Carol Gilligan (1977, 1982) has argued that moral reasoning in men and women *is* different. Gilligan was attacking a point of view we discuss in Chapter 14, best represented by the research of Lawrence Kohlberg, who argued that the development of moral reasoning takes place according to stages that are universal across cultures and sex groups. Gilligan's argument that on moral issues women speak "in a different voice" has proved to be very influential. She has proposed that in making moral decisions men pay more attention to adhering to rules and laws, taking a justice perspective, whereas women give primary attention to caring for people rather than sticking to abstract rules and laws. A few studies have found support for this perspective (Ford & Lowery, 1986; Smetana, Killen, & Turiel, 1991), although meta-analytic reviews of gender differences on traditional moral reasoning tasks do not reveal a clear-cut picture (e.g., Thoma, 1986).

Tansu Ciller (pronounced "chiller") became Turkey's first woman prime minister in 1994, after becoming the youngest university professor of her generation. This is an extraordinary feat, because she came to power in an Islamic country at a time when religious fundamentalism was on the rise. Although reforms have given women in the United States, Canada, and other Western societies equality in the eyes of the law, in practice political leadership in Western societies is still in the hands of men.

But the idea that women adopt a more "caring" moral perspective is supported, at least indirectly, by the finding that women score higher on empathy and are more nurturant—a trend that makes a lot of sense given the traditional role as mother and caretaker (Eagly, 1987). Also in line with this is the finding that women typically are lower on physical aggression, although they may be as aggressive as men in indirect, verbal ways. Again, this trend matches the traditional social role of women as homemakers; physical aggression is traditionally perceived as masculine rather than feminine.

United Nations surveys of crime in countries around the world show that fewer women than men are imprisoned for crime generally, but women are far less likely to be convicted of violent crimes. For example, the international surveys show that for every woman convicted for assault, about 15 men were convicted (Harvey, Burnham, Kendall, & Pease, 1992). Some research suggests that in the United States black Americans do not associate masculinity with aggressivity and competitiveness as much as do white Americans (Smith & Midlarsky, 1985).

Of course, there is little doubt that socialization plays a fundamentally important part in bringing about this kind of difference. For example, boys take more math courses than girls, no doubt because they are *expected* to do so by their parents, teachers, and others around them, and this accounts for some of the gender differences found on the math section of tests such as the SAT (Wilder & Powell, 1989). Also, the content and style of tests are more "male–friendly" than "female–friendly" and this may be working against females on a number of cognitive ability tests (Hyde, Fennema, & Lamon, 1990).

The Power of Gender Stereotypes

In their 30–nation study of sex stereotypes, John Williams and Deborah Best (1982) formulated a functional explanation for the nature of such stereotypes. According to their argument, there are two aspects to gender stereotypes: a differentiation aspect and a legitimization aspect. *Differentiated* gender roles and division of labor along sex lines is found to be an effective way of coping with life's challenges (e.g., humans found it efficient to divide up tasks, so men hunted for food and women looked after children). At the same time, it becomes adaptive for society to *legitimize* this differentiation.

> If females are to have principal responsibility for the care of the young, it is reassuring to believe that they are—or can become—affectionate, gentle, patient, sympathetic, and so on. If males are to serve as hunters and warriors, it is comforting to believe that they are—or can become—adventurous, aggressive, courageous, energetic, independent, self–confident, and the like. (Williams & Best, 1982, p. 237)

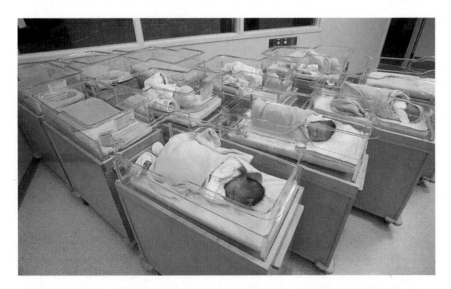

Newborns in a hospital nursery, Portland, Oregon. What are the sources of gender differences? Those who believe that women and men are taught to be different point out the subtle and early nature of such teaching. To check this for yourself, go to a hospital maternity ward and visit the nursery. Notice how adults talk about and interact with the babies. Research shows that from the first hours of their lives, infant girls are described as "cute," "delicate," and "fragile," whereas infant boys are referred to as "tough," "big," and "strong." These comments are made even when on the basis of objective criteria there are no clear gender differences.

But this "justification" explanation assumes, sometimes explicitly, that there is a real and significant rift between what men and women are really like and what gender stereotypes tell us they are like. Is there evidence to show this assumption is valid? The answer is yes (Hoffman & Hurst, 1990). For example, gender stereotypes are often used to describe infants and children who have not yet developed gender stereotypic behavior (Condry & Condry, 1976). If you want evidence of this yourself, just go to the maternity ward of a hospital and take note of how adults talk about newly born females ("She is beautiful . . . so graceful . . . sweet natured") and newly born males ("Look at that tough little guy . . . waving his fist around . . . a go-getter already"). Even when the behavior and role of men and women is scripted, just the fact that it is a man or it is a woman in a particular role and doing particular things can invoke gender stereotypes (Taylor, Fiske, Etcoff, & Ruderman, 1978).

Actual differences in the behavior of women and men in everyday life are very subtle and small in many domains, although as we have already noted, such differences do exist (Eagly, 1995). But in general, the differences assumed in gender stereotypes do not match the differences found in empirical research. As Curt Hoffman and Nancy Hurst have noted

> There would seem to be little correlation between the size of a sex difference and the degree to which it is emphasized in the stereotypes. The stereotypes feature prominently a number of dimensions on which men and women differ only slightly (e.g., influenceability) or on which, as far as we now know, they do not differ at all (kindness, patience, ability to make decisions, ability to think clearly, and many others). (1990, p. 198)

Susan Fiske (1993a) has elaborated on the justification function of stereotypes, describing how stereotyping "operates in service of control" (p. 623). By this she means that those who enjoy power also come to exert control over the less powerful through stereotypes, as well as other means. Stereotypes have a descriptive function, which is to say they incorporate generally held beliefs about a group of people (e.g., "women are sentimental," "men are analytical," "women are moody," "men hate to wash clothes," and so on). The members of a culture are aware of such beliefs, whether they themselves are biased or not. But stereotypes also have a prescriptive function, which is to say they provide guidelines for what members of particular groups should be like (e.g., "women *should* be soft-spoken," "men *should* take command"). Through their descriptive and prescriptive aspects, stereotypes can be used to exert control over people. Men tend to be in positions of power more often, and thus have greater opportunities to use stereotyping as a control mechanism.

Women can suffer **false gender consciousness,** which comes about when people misperceive the characteristics and interests of their gender. This tendency may still be pervasive in the United States, despite outward signs of progress. Women in both the United States and India were found to base their self-descriptions more on gender stereotypes than did men (Dhawan, Roseman, Naidu, & Rettek, 1995). A study involving participants from Japan and the United States showed gender differences based on traditional stereotypes to be present in both societies (Hatfield & Sprecher,

false gender consciousness
tendency for some individuals to misperceive the characteristics and interests of their gender.

1995). In some ways, women in the United States may even suffer a greater degree of false gender consciousness. Jeanine Cogan and her associates (Cogan, Bhalla, Sefa-Dedeh, & Rothblum, 1996) found that compared to Ghanaian women, U.S. women showed greater concern about thinness, were more likely to have suffered eating disorders, and also had more experience of weight as an interference in social life ("I would love to go to the beach, but how can I put on a swimsuit with a body like this?").

The higher status of men in society is associated with intriguing patterns of stereotyping. For example, one line of research shows that the stereotype of a mature, healthy, socially competent person is closer to the stereotype of a mature, healthy, socially competent male than it is to the stereotype of a mature, healthy, socially competent female (Broverman, Vogel, Broverman, Clarkson, & Rosenkrantz, 1972). But the outcome is not always so positive for men. For example, Alice Eagly and Mary Kite (1987) studied stereotypes held by a sample of U.S. students of men and women of 28 different nationalities and found that the stereotypes of men were more similar to the stereotypes of nationalities, particularly in *unfavorably* evaluated countries. Thus, although the participants held negative stereotypes of Iranians and Cubans, women in these countries escaped the effect of these negative stereotypes, perhaps because they are seen as powerless and not responsible for events.

The Subtleties of Modern Sexism

Imagine the following scene. A woman enters a clothing store and tries on several pairs of pants and skirts. She chooses a pair of pants and says to the salesperson, "This is great, I still take the same size as I did when I was in college 20 years ago." According to a report by Margaret Pressler (1997), this could well be because of size inflation—designers' altering size measurements in order to make buyers feel better. Pressler cites industry experts as saying that this "feel-good trend" is more noticeable with women's clothes than men's. Such subtle differences in the treatment of women and men often go unnoticed, and can be better assessed in contrast to more blatant differences.

Two Examples of Blatant Injustice.   In what is perhaps the first great American novel, *The Scarlet Letter*, Nathaniel Hawthorne (1850/1961) describes the ordeal of Hester Prynne, a young woman who is convicted of adultery in a late seventeenth-century New England Puritan community. Our modern values lead us to sympathize with Hester as she courageously refuses to name her lover and is forced to endure imprisonment and, even worse, to wear the letter "A" (for "adulterer") as a mark of shame.

The unjust treatment of women seems so blatant when we look back to former times in Western societies, or to other traditional societies today. Consider female circumcision, more accurately described as female genital mutilation, which is still practiced in more than 40 countries around the world (Slack, 1988). Raqiya Abdalla (1982) has described her own experience when she was circumcised as a young girl:

> Women . . . held me tight and the midwife parted my legs. . . . I was full of fear . . . when she started the cutting, I screamed loudly and fought to free myself. One of the women filled my mouth with cloth, another one closed my eyes and they kept me tight and suffocated with their bosoms until I nearly ran out of air. By the time the operation was over, I was exhausted and hardly breathing. My mother told me that the operator used six thorns to sew up my wound, three on each side. I did not know what was happening to me except that I was feeling severe pain. (p. 108)

From a modern Western perspective, two aspects of this situation are immediately striking: first, the unjust and shameful treatment of women, and second, the active participation of women in perpetuating the injustices they themselves suffer. This also becomes apparent in Hawthorne's *The Scarlet Letter*. When Hester Prynne's punishment is being discussed, one of the women present suggests they brand the "A" on Hester's forehead, but is outdone by another with an even more cruel plan:

> What do you talk of marks and brands, whether on the bodice of her gown, or the flesh of her forehead?" cried another female, the ugliest as well as the most pitiless of these self-constituted judges. "This woman has brought shame upon us all, and ought to die. Is there not law for it? Truly, there is, both in the Scripture and the statute-book. Then let the magistrates, who have made it of no effect, thank themselves if their own wives and daughters go astray! (p. 48)

Such blatant injustice seems distant and foreign to us in the context of our everyday lives in modern Western societies. But although blatant discrimination and injustices have declined in the modern Western context, more subtle forms of sexism remain. Consider the findings of Ian Ayres (1991), who investigated the way car salespeople interact with men and women during sales negotiations. Ayres used female and male collaborators who negotiated to purchase cars. The collaborators were trained to follow identical scripts and to record events as they made their offers and proceeded with negotiations. The findings showed that white males received much better prices than white women and black men. Such "price discrimination" is unexpected, because it is generally assumed that free-market conditions will establish a fair price for everyone, irrespective of gender and race.

A similar trend of discrimination against women in the marketplace has been reported with respect to how brokers treat women investors (Cummins, 1993). In two separate studies, potential investors with identical profiles, except that they were either women or men, were sent to brokers. The results show that potential women investors were short-changed, in that brokers offered them less information and guided them toward less lucrative deals. Let us look at some other examples of this kind of seldom-noticed discrimination.

Aminata Diop, 22, who escaped circumcision by running away from her home country, Mali. One of the ways in which men have maintained their superiority is by imposing limiting, or even crippling, forms of dress and bodily presentation for women. Extreme forms of this are foot-binding as once practiced in China, and female circumcision as still practiced in some Islamic societies. Less extreme but similarly crippling limitations involve dress codes that require women to cover themselves from head to toe and that prevent them from participating in many activities.

"Face-ism": Modern Sexism. The faces stare at us from magazine covers, from the pages of newspapers, from posters on buildings, and from hundreds of other places as we go about our daily lives. They smile at us, those young, healthy, beautiful faces. Most of them are trying to sell us something, and we know it, but we look at them anyway. In the majority of cases they are female, and when they are male they tend to be shown differently. Erving Goffman was one of the first researchers to notice differences in the ways in which men and women are presented in advertising, and he conducted a detailed study of how social messages are communicated in advertising.

face-ism   a tendency for public
photographs of men to focus on their
faces and for those of women to
focus on their bodies.

For example, Goffman (1976) pointed out how men in advertisements are placed in administrative or "managerial" roles, both in work and nonwork settings. Men are more likely to be shown as the doctor and women as the nurse. More revealing is that in nonwork situations also men are "in charge"—such as when a man is shown supervising his family's making a sandcastle on the beach. Penny Belknap and Wilbert Leonard II (1991) demonstrated the usefulness of Goffman's concepts in an analysis of advertisements in both traditional (e.g., *Good Housekeeping*) and modern (e.g., *Ms.*) magazines. Other research confirmed that women in advertising are typically depicted as sexual objects, beautiful, and dependent on men (Venkatesan & Losco, 1975). Perhaps the most intriguing finding to have emerged from this line of research concerns the phenomenon of **"face-ism"**—a tendency for public photographs of men to focus on their faces and of women to focus on their bodies.

The face and head are the centers of mental life, personality, and identity, while the rest of the body is symbolically less important. When a photograph focuses more on the face, the person depicted is perceived as more intelligent and ambitious (Archer, Iritani, Kimes, & Barrios, 1983, study 5). In a study of five American periodicals, including *Time*, *Newsweek*, and *Ms.*, a strong tendency was found for women to be represented by their bodies and men by their faces. This trend was true even for *Ms.* magazine (Archer, Iritani, Kimes, & Barrios, 1983, study 1).

But perhaps face-ism is an American phenomenon? To test this possibility, a study was conducted of 13 publications from 11 other nations (Archer, Iritani, Kimes, & Barrios, 1983, study 2). The results showed the same trend as found in the United States, suggesting that face-ism is pervasive. Is it possible that face-ism is a feature of modern times? To test this possibility, artwork across six centuries was examined—920 portraits and self-portraits (Archer, Iritani, Kimes, & Barrios, 1983, study 3). The result was a demonstration that face-ism is centuries old.

Women in Science: A Case Study

In 1984, women made up 19 percent of the Ph.D. graduates in chemistry in the United States. These women should have been making their mark as faculty members at major universities by the mid-1990s, but this promise was not realized (see Brennan, 1996). In 1976–1977, there was a total of two tenured and tenure-track women on chemistry faculties at the Massachusetts Institute of Technology, one at Stanford University, and one at Columbia University. In 1994–1995, the situation had not changed, so despite the enormous increase in the number of women with doctorates in chemistry (from 10 percent of the total in 1974 to 30 percent of the total in 1994; Brennan, 1996, p. 13), these three prestigious institutions still had only four female tenured and tenure-track chemistry faculty members among them.

Studies of the situation of women in science as we approach the twenty-first century have clearly shown that the "pipeline" is leaking badly. That is, although there is very little, if any, real difference between men and women in science at the primary school level (before the teenage years), women gradually drop out of the science track as they move through the education system (Astin & Astin, 1993). By the time the doctoral level is reached, women have moved out of the sciences in large numbers (Alper, 1993). For example, in 1993 only 8 percent of the doctorates awarded in engineering, 11 percent in physics, and 16 percent in computer science went to women (Alper, 1993, p. 409). Women make up 45 percent of the U.S. work force, but only 16 percent of employed scientists and engineers (Alper, 1993, p. 409). On the other hand, 58 percent of doctorates awarded in psychology and 62 percent in health professions went to women. How are these trends best explained?

First, let us deal with the simplest explanations, the first being based on innate ability. One line of argument is that women move out of the sciences because they have less mathematical ability than men. This view seems to be supported by the results of SAT scores, for example, which show men scoring on average higher than women on mathematical ability. However, test scores show that many women do score higher than many men on mathematical ability. These are clearly women who *have* the ability to do well in science. If ability is the key factor explaining the very high dropout rate, then we should find no difference between women and men who are in the top 1 percent of the math talent pool. But even when we look only at the most mathematically gifted students, far fewer women than men finally earn doctorates in science (Alper, 1993). Obviously, something more than just ability is causing leaks in the pipeline.

In some contexts women have had to perform much better than men to make comparable progress. For example, when a 14-year-old South Korean girl scored only 136 points on the high school entrance exam, it seemed she had missed her chance of getting into college. But then her family found out that while girls need 138 points to gain entrance, boys need only 117! Protests from women and activist groups so far have led to very little actual reform in South Korean education (Kristof, 1996).

Another of the more mundane explanations is that women do not progress as far as men in the science hierarchy because of marriage and family obligations. This, too, turns out to be too simplistic. Jonathan Cole and Harriet Zuckerman (1987; see also Zuckerman, Cole, & Bruer, 1991) have shown that married women with children publish as much as their single female colleagues. Thus, the lower publication rate of women than men in the sciences is not explained by marriage and motherhood.

One possible explanation is that a critical mass is needed before a minority group can make a breakthrough. Given that it is only recently that large numbers of women have begun to attain higher levels of education both nationally and internationally (Finn, Dulberg, & Reis, 1979), perhaps they still do not have an organized critical mass to enable them to break through in science. But a more detailed look at the situation suggests that more must be done than just increasing the numbers of women in key positions. In a study of 30 academic science departments in five disciplines (biology, chemistry, physics, computer science, and electrical engineering), it was found that some women faculty members "felt they had to be tougher on women students than men, to prepare them to meet the higher standards they would be held to as women" (Etzkowitz, Kemelgor, Neuschatz, Uzzi, & Alonzo, 1994, p. 53).

Like members of other minorities, women have learned that when one of their group breaks through and gets a key position, that "new elite" member is not necessarily going to help the collective cause. Not all African-American entrepreneurs who succeed in business turn around and pour money back into the black community. In some situations, members of minority groups may use their minority status to attain a position, but then become "individualists" as soon as their own personal success is assured (these successful women want to play "queen bee," as one female colleague put it to me). Part of the controversy surrounding the confirmation of U.S. Supreme Court Justice Clarence Thomas arose because of the perception among some parts of the population that he has himself benefited from the fruits of the civil rights movement (e.g., affirmative action), but having "made it" is now an individualist espousing a self-help, anti-collective-action philosophy.

But apart from the issue of critical mass, there may be more subtle reasons for the underrepresentation of women in the higher echelons of science. Two such reasons have to do with the relationship between science and traditional gender roles, and the culture of the scientific community. On the one hand, in the culture of the larger society science is still viewed more as a masculine than a feminine activity (National Research Council, 1991; Zuckerman, Cole, & Bruer, 1991). Associated with this are traditional gender roles, which nurture gender differences in career aspirations as well as cognitive functioning in some domains (see Figure 12–4). This explains in part why fewer women study science and choose science as a career. On the other hand, the culture of science, as an activity and community, is itself more masculine than feminine (Keller, 1986). Let us look at these ideas in more detail.

Gender and the Culture of Science.   In the last decades of the twentieth century, a number of efforts have been made to make the culture of science more "gender-free" (Barinaga, 1993; Bleier, 1986). The contention has been that even in domains such as medical research, male domina-

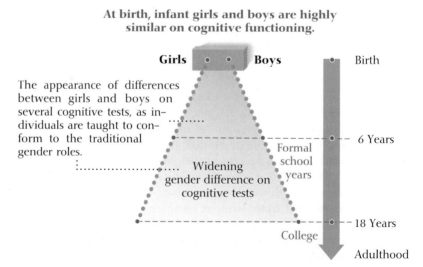

Figure 12–4 A cultural view of gender differences on cognitive tests.

tion has led to biases in research. Here are some of the more visible ways in which this occurs: The National Institutes of Health (NIH) had a very long tradition of including only men in clinical trials for new drug development (see Healy, 1995). This meant that in at least some cases the drugs developed had unexpected side effects for women, but not for the group for which they had been developed. The practice of excluding women from clinical trials finally changed in the 1980s, in part because a woman, Dr. Bernadine Healy, became the director of the NIH.

Another example of gender bias is found in research on birth control. First, contraceptives have almost exclusively been meant for use by women, so it is women who have to put up with side effects, both medical and psychological. Second, since the contraceptive revolution of the 1960s, very little has been invested to develop more effective contraceptives with fewer side effects (*Chemical & Engineering News*, 1996). If men were the ones taking "the pill," some have argued, then research on contraceptives would have progressed a great deal faster.

Male domination of the science culture has also biased results in more subtle ways. Consider the young science of primatology, the study of the higher mammals, including monkeys, apes, and humans. A major assumption underlying the entire field was that primate social activity is basically centered on what males do. The "fathers" of this new science focused particularly on male pecking order, as well as competition between males to reproduce. It was only when women researchers entered the field and focused more on females and the young that a very different picture emerged (Morell, 1993).

Jane Goodall, Dian Fossey, and Birute Galdikas were the vanguard, and by the early 1990s women made up over 50 percent of the American Primatology Society (Morell, 1993, p. 428). These women showed that females have a lot more influence than was first assumed, that they also are involved in competition, and that there is a great deal of diversity in the female/male hierarchies (Miller, 1993). The assumption that social life is centered on the activities of males, particularly the competition for access to females, proved to be too simple and just wrong (see Morgan, 1989). Unfortunately, some social psychologists who follow a sociobiological approach are still using this outdated model.

Women Scientists: What Happens to the Best of the Best?   We saw that even when the mathematically brightest women and men are considered, far more women than men end up in nonscience careers. This suggests that even when women have the ability, they are more likely to be part of the "leak in the science pipeline." The leak was enormous in the years before affirmative action, as Margaret Rossiter (1995) tells the story of women scientists in the years 1940–1972. Some have suggested that the culture of science is still highly sexist, but in more subtle ways. As Barbara Kantrowitz wrote in a 1994 *Newsweek* article about computing, "Cyberspace, it turns out [is] . . . marred by just as many sexist ruts and gender conflicts as the Real World." The research of Gerhard Sonnert and Gerald Holton (1995) suggests the same is true for all of science.

These researchers studied the experiences of women scientists who had been the recipients of prestigious postdoctoral fellowships from the National Research Council, the National Science Foundation, or the Bunting Institute at Radcliffe College. Through questionnaires and in–depth interviews, they tracked the careers of these extremely bright women and found that the barriers against them were often extremely subtle. Male colleagues would neglect to pass them key information about meetings or neglect to introduce them to visiting scientists.

The fundamentally important role of the details of everyday activity is highlighted by such research. Sexism now is very seldom blatant, but far more discreet and often implicit, unnoticed, and often unintended. A consequence is that women scientists, even the very best, achieve less in their careers, a trend also shown by research in Europe (Talapessy, 1993).

Finally, evidence in support of a cultural explanation of performance in science comes from research on academic achievement among different ethnic groups, such as Indochinese refugee families that moved to the United States in the 1970s and 1980s. The children of these refugee families have performed better in science subjects, and particularly in math, than other ethnic groups, including white males. Are we to believe that ethnic differences in math scores are a result of evolutionary processes?

A far more valid explanation has been offered by Nathan Caplan, Marcella Choy, and John Whitmore (1992), who, in a detailed study of 1,400 refugee households, found that the family's commitment to academic accomplishment, and the culture of achievement created in the home, is a much more plausible explanation. During the high school years, refugee children spent over twice as much time as other American children on homework. But doing homework was not a lonely, individual activity for these children. Caplan, Choy, and Whitmore (1992) describe a typical after–school scene in a refugee family home:

> After dinner, the table is cleared, and homework begins. The older children, both male and female, help their younger siblings. . . . The younger children, in particular, are taught not only subject matter but how to learn. Such sibling involvement demonstrates how a large family can encourage and enhance academic success. The familial setting appears to make the children feel at home in school and consequently, perform well there. (p. 40)

Just as the home setting and parental attitudes in part explain ethnic differences in science performance, they also explain gender differences.

The Challenge of Change.   Research on the experiences of women scientists underlines the complexities and subtleties of culture and the enormous challenges we face when attempting to steer culture toward particular goals. Experience shows that it is very difficult to change human behavior by adopting a "top–down" approach. Despite legal and political reforms, women in the late 1960s through the late 1970s became more aware of the external constraints in their ability to meet "equality" goals, as shown by their tendency to point to external factors as more responsible for their situation (Doherty & Baldwin, 1985).

In addition to reforms at the top, involving the formal laws and regulations at the governmental and institutional levels, we need to attend to the subtleties of everyday interactions, to the rules and norms that pattern everyday behavior. Just as African-Americans find that changes in the formal laws of the land do not necessarily put a stop to racism, women have discovered that being equal in the eyes of the law is not enough to bring about equality in their everyday lives. Everyday social relations, the informal world of women and men, must also change.

At the international level, it is critical that women gain equality in education and employment. Alice Schlegel and Herbert Barry III (1986) have demonstrated in a study of 186 nonindustrialized societies that the more women contribute to the material wealth of a family, the greater their range of choices in marriage partners, the more they are valued, and the lower the incidence of rape.

Concepts and Issues

The issue of gender differences remains controversial. Some researchers have argued that women differ from men in several areas, such as moral thinking. Others have argued that gender differences are for the most part artifacts, in that they arise from biases in research and testing methods. The focus has now turned to the subtleties of modern sexism and particularly the powerful influence of gender stereotypes. Studies on highly talented women in science highlight the role of informal rules and norms in perpetuating discriminatory practices against women. These studies also suggest that changes at the societal level can often come about faster than changes at the level of everyday social behavior.

1. What are some of the functions of gender stereotypes?
2. Compare an evolutionary and a cultural explanation of gender differences in verbal and math scores (when/if they are found).
3. Give examples of modern sexism.
4. What lessons can we learn from the experiences of talented women in science?

Conclusion

Sex differences set some limitations on the malleability of gender roles, but these limitations still allow for enormous variations in the behavior of women and men across cultures. In many Western and non–Western societies, men continue to enjoy higher status and more power. During the last few decades of the twentieth century sex discrimination has been declared illegal, at least in Western societies, but women still suffer subtle forms of sexism. Modern sexism is more difficult to combat because in many instances it is an integral part of socialization for both women and men, and because some women also help to perpetuate the problem by using and passing on traditional gender stereotypes.

For Review

Sex refers to a biological distinction between male and female; gender refers to the social role ascribed by society to individuals in each sex category.

In most Western societies men and women enjoy equal rights under the law, but in political representation, economic power, and other areas, women still have lower status throughout the world.

Men and women differ on a number of cognitive abilities, with women scoring higher on verbal tests and men scoring higher on mathematical tests. These results have been replicated in a number of different cultures. In the social domain, men tend to be more aggressive than women, and women more empathic and nurturant than men. Again, this trend holds true across a number of different cultures.

The sources of these differences, however, are debatable. One group of researchers, sociobiologists among them, believes that gender differences are rooted in evolutionary processes. The implication is that gender roles can only be changed over the very long term. This viewpoint is challenged by a second group, feminists among them, which argues that gender roles are socially constructed and have environmental roots. The implication is that gender roles can be changed within decades rather than over hundreds of years or even much longer time periods.

The measurement of masculinity and femininity as the opposites on a bipolar scale has been criticized by researchers who believe that a person could be high, or low, or medium on both masculinity and femininity.

The malleability of gender roles is demonstrated by enormous cross-cultural variations and by the existence of more than two sex categories in some non-Western societies.

Cross-cultural research on social development has shown that children learn gender roles from a very early age, certainly as early as 3, but that those whose mothers are more educated and who work outside the home hold less differentiated gender stereotypes. Gender stereotypes both describe the social role of men and women and prescribe how they should behave.

Unlike traditional, or blatant, sexism, modern sexism is more subtle and covert. An example is "face-ism," the tendency for men to be represented in paintings and photographs by their faces, and women by their bodies. Studies of modern women also reveal the subtleties of modern sexism. Professional women often work a "second shift" when they get home from their work outside the home, since they are the ones who have more responsibility for the home and family life. Even women who are among the elite in mathematical ability do not do as well as men in science careers. They are disadvantaged, some have argued, by the masculine culture of science.

For Discussion

1. Compare evolutionary and cultural explanations of gender differences and discuss their compatibility.
2. Why is the issue of gender controversial?
3. Discuss modern sexism using examples from research and from your everyday experiences.

Key Terms

Androgynous 412

Bem Sex–Role Inventory 412

Face–ism 428

False gender consciousness 424

Gender 405

Hermaphrodite 413

Sex 405

Transsexuals 413

Transvestites 413

Annotated Readings

Discussions by leading researchers in the field of gender and sex are presented in A. E. Beall and R. J. Sternberg, eds., *The psychology of gender* (New York: Guilford, 1995).

A review of sex differences by probably the leading expert in the field is A. H. Eagly, *Sex differences in social behavior: A social role interpretation* (Hillsdale, NJ: Lawrence Erlbaum, 1987).

Researchers discuss the development of sex differences in M. Haug, R. E. Whalen, C. Aron, and K. L. Olsen, eds., *The development of sex differences and similarities in behaviour* (London: Kluwer Academic, 1993).

J. E. Williams and D. L. Best consider gender from a cross–cultural perspective in *Sex and psyche: Gender and self viewed cross-culturally* (Newbury Park, CA: Sage, 1990).

A discussion of evolutionary views of gender relations can be found in D. M. Buss, *The evolution of desire: Strategies of human mating* (New York: Basic Books, 1994).

S. Wilkinson and C. Kitzinger have edited a collection of different feminist views on gender and sex in *Representing the other: A feminist & psychology reader* (Thousand Oaks, CA: Sage, 1996).

A more cohesive and focused feminist view is presented in R. Unger and M. Crawford, *Women and gender: A feminist psychology*, 2nd ed. (New York: McGraw-Hill, 1996).

Gender

When my first child was born, she was a fairly large baby, 8 pounds and 10 ounces. A visitor to the maternity ward assumed she was a boy and remarked, "What a big, tough boy. He's going to be a go-getter." After being alerted to the "It's a girl!" balloon floating above the baby, the visitor added, "Oh, I should have known, those dainty fingers have to belong to a girl. She's adorable. Look at those cute dimples."

Step by step, and mostly in subtle and implicit ways, those around us treat girls and boys differently and teach children how to become women and men according to the normative systems of our cultures. Is it really surprising that some studies have found women and men to differ in some aspects of social behavior, such as aggressivity, moral thinking, and empathy? Surely not; it is perhaps even more surprising that they do not differ in more fundamental ways.

Hidden behind a screen, a male professor lectures to female students in Iran.

Rajasthani women draw water from a village well, India.

Woman working in the fields in China.

Perhaps the most important source of gender differences is power disparity: In both developed and developing societies women still have less power than men—in the case of some societies, a lot less power. Gender power disparity is most easily recognizable when we examine societies that are distant from Western ideals (of course, this means that Western societies are distant from *their* ideals). In the Islamic Republic of Iran, for example, men have control over women in ways that most outsiders see as unacceptable: A woman's testimony in court has half the weight of a man's; fathers and not mothers retain custody of children after divorce; women are not permitted to become judges, or to travel abroad without the written permission of their husbands, or to shake hands with a man unless he is a close blood relative, or to show any part of their body except the face and hands in public. These and other restrictions obviously make public life difficult, as when women attend classes taught by male professors.

437

Protest against rape, a crime often justified through blaming the victim, who is invariably female, Austin, Texas.

But we should not jump to the conclusion that women in developing societies are in every way worse off than women in developed societies. When we brush aside surface differences, some deeper similarities concerning the situation of women as members of a power minority in all societies are revealed. Here are just two examples.

Research among professional women in the United States shows that they often work a "second shift." Tracy gets up before anyone else in the family to prepare breakfast and the kids' lunches. She rushes the kids to school, then races to the office to start her day. After finishing a long day at the office, she speeds back home to do the bulk of the work in preparing dinner and getting the children to bed. She runs the home in addition to her office. This "second shift" is a common experience for most women in developing societies, whether they work in the fields in China or in India, or have gone through college to become professionals.

A second example of experiences common to women in both developing and developed societies arises out of a tendency for people to "blame the victim." Social psychological research suggests that we blame victims in part because we are motivated to see the world as a just place: "Jill was raped after she left the party. What does she expect when she comes dressed like that and drinks and dances all night? She was asking for it." In Western societies the social climate and legal system at least allow Jill to report the crime against her to the police and to publicly protest. In many parts of the world, the tendency to blame the victim is strong enough to prevent such crimes from even being reported.

Welfare hotel resident and health worker, San Francisco.

438

The late Indira Gandhi as prime minister of India.

Eight of the nine current women U.S. senators, 1997.

U.S. Supreme Court judges, 1997.

The "blame the victim" phenomenon is pervasive, but often in subtle ways. Women are overrepresented among the economically poor, a group that tends to be seen as "deserving what they get." Particularly in individualistic societies, where self-help and individual responsibility is given priority, lower-class women often experience hostile social climates and difficult living conditions.

In both developing and developed societies, one way in which women can try to improve their position is to gain access to power. Women have progressed particularly well along this path in some Asian societies, an example being Indira Gandhi of India. By comparison, women have made little headway in getting to the White House in the United States, and the numbers of women who hold important political office, such as U.S. senator, are still very few. Some consider it a success that two women now sit on the U.S. Supreme Court, but just imagine what the reaction would be if out of nine justices, seven were women and only two were men.

CHAPTER *13*

Group Dynamics

◄   A group of executives at work. After I had assigned group tasks for students in a social psychology class, one of them asked me, "Why can't we work by ourselves, or at least be in groups with our friends, rather than be assigned to groups?" One of the goals of education is to train students to collaborate with others, because as working adults much of their time will be spent in groups composed of individuals who are brought together to complete certain tasks. Such groups are typically diverse in terms of ethnicity, gender, and cultural background, and disband after completing their given tasks. In many non–Western societies, in contrast, people stay in groups composed of family and community members: These groups are based on personal rather than functional relationships and last for a lifetime.

The bodies of the mostly young soccer fans were lined up across the playing field of the National Stadium in Guatemala City. On October 16, 1996, at least 83 people died and hundreds were seriously injured when people were trampled and suffocated during a stampede as fans tried to force their way through a narrow concrete passageway leading into the stadium. At least 15 children were among the dead. Three days of national mourning were observed in Guatemala (Carrasco, 1996).

I was at an airport when I read about this tragedy. When an elderly man who was sitting next to me saw the headline of the newspaper I was reading, he sighed and said,

"Why do people put themselves in such danger? Humans are just dangerous when they get into groups!"

"What do you mean?" I asked, always interested to hear more about what people have to say about such issues.

"What do I mean? You can have a perfectly normal, healthy human being turn into a total savage just by joining a group. Look at these people killed in the soccer stadium stampede. I bet if we met them on their own, they would be as normal and decent as you or I, but look what happened to them when they became part of a group. Their minds were taken over."

"But what about all the news about groups doing good?" I responded, pointing to some other headlines in the same newspaper. "Here is a story about a group of citizens helping homeless people, and here is another one about firefighters saving lives, and. . . ."

But he stopped me in midsentence and said,

"All of those types of good deeds put together do not undo the terrible things people do when they are in groups. I know the nicest individuals who turn violent and unpredictable when in a group. Don't you realize that people are willing to do terrible things in groups, things they would never do alone?"

The stranger got up and walked away.

Are Groups Good or Evil?

It is true that there are many examples of individuals in groups behaving in highly destructive ways. There is the infamous case of Rodney King being beaten by a group of Los Angeles police officers in 1991. Then there are the riots that followed the acquittal of the police officers who beat Rodney King and the devastation of parts of Los Angeles as crowds destroyed property and fought with the police. The traditional interpretation of such events is that when part of a group individuals are more likely to disregard the social norms and rules that restrain behavior and to lose a sense of personal responsibility. Some researchers have attempted to explain this behavior by introducing the concept of **deindividuation,** referring to a lower self-awareness and decreased personal responsibility in group settings (Festinger, Pepitone, & Newcomb, 1952).

deindividuation the loss of one's sense of identity as an individual person, associated with lower self-awareness and decreased personality in group settings.

A related explanatory concept is that of **diffusion of responsibility** (see Chapter 9), which has been used to explain the apathy shown by bystanders toward people in need of help. In research on altruism, bystanders were found to be more likely to ignore requests for assistance if other bystanders were also present. This is another example of people doing things in groups that they would not do alone.

diffusion of responsibility the tendency for bystanders to ignore requests for assistance if other bystanders are also present.

A Normative View

But instead of the traditional picture of individuals in groups suggested by deindividuation and diffusion of responsibility, I want to propose an alternative view based on group norms. People in groups do not behave differently because they "lose" themselves or feel a diffusion of responsibility. Rather, they behave differently when they recognize and adopt group norms that are different (see Figure 13–1). The "antisocial" behavior of individuals in groups does not arise from a disregard for all norms or a loss of the self, but from an adherence to a different set of norms and an identification of the self with a group that upholds these different norms. As Stephen Reicher (1984a, 1984b) has argued, individuals do not lose their identities when they join groups, they take on different identities. The police officers who beat Rodney King were acting according to the norms of their own group.

Evidence for this alternative interpretation comes from research on street gangs. William Sanders (1994) conducted field studies of juvenile gangs involved in drive-by shootings and "gangbangs" (a generic term

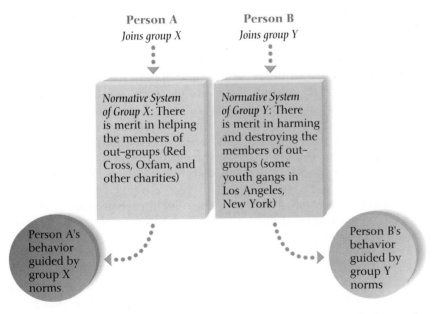

Figure 13–1 The members of different groups behave differently when they recognize and follow norms and rules that are different.

for gang violence, such as knifings and beatings). His research demonstrates that when engaging in violent acts, such as blowing off the heads of rivals with high-powered automatic weapons, gang members are behaving correctly, according to the norms and rules of their own group. Other studies confirm this picture and show that gangs such as the Bloods and Crips in Los Angeles and the Vice Lords in Chicago influence the behavior of their members through a powerful normative system that is in important ways different from that of the larger society (Sheldon, Tracy, & Brown, 1997; Vigil, 1988; Walsh, 1993). Thus, group membership can be more accurately described as involving "individuation" to develop a new self and behave differently, rather than "deindividuation" as in "losing" the self and self-awareness. Each act of violence commits gang members more strongly to the norms endorsed by the gang, and moves them farther away from the norms of the larger society (Sanders, 1994).

Evidence for a normative account of why people behave differently in groups also comes from a long line of laboratory research arising from the ideas of Kurt Lewin (1948, 1952). Lewin proposed that a group comes into being when a set of individuals become interdependent: They recognize that they have to carry out a task together and that they share the same fate in terms of success or failure. Using the idea of interdependence, Morton Deutsch (1949) created groups with either cooperative norms (individual group members would be assessed on how well the group performs, so everyone would receive the same rewards) or competitive norms (individual members would be assessed on how well they performed in the group, higher rewards going to better-performing individuals). The results, confirmed by later studies (Rosenbaum et al., 1980), showed that the different norms prevailing in the groups led to very different behaviors: Participants in groups with cooperative norms liked one another more and performed better.

Reicher (1984b) used student participants from science and social science disciplines in the United Kingdom to demonstrate a similar point. Social science students are known to be more pro animal rights than science students. When participants were placed in contexts in which their group affiliations were more salient (they were addressed as "science group" and "social science group" and seated separately), their attitudes toward animal rights became more different than when there was no reference to their group memberships. This is probably because the group condition brought group norms to the forefront and led to normative behavior for the members of each group.

A major theme of this chapter, then, is that when individuals join groups they become influenced by the norms and rules of those groups. Of course, group members do not need to be consciously aware of norms or rules to be influenced by them. In many cases, norms and rules are informal rather than formal and implicit rather than explicit. Gang members may not be able to articulate the norms for how they are supposed to behave toward out-group members, even though in practice they do behave in the expected manner.

The Rodney King beating, Los Angeles. Do people, and particularly men, behave differently when they are in groups? Some researchers believe they do. Each of these Los Angeles police officers, caught on video beating a man named Rodney King, may have treated his African–American victim courteously if they had met one-to-one. As a group, they behaved destructively. But there are many positive aspects of groups: In some very important contexts, they allow individuals to be more creative, and to reach much higher goals. Think of the superior performance achieved by individuals on sports teams and by corporations in competitive markets. Groups are not necessarily positive or negative in themselves; it is the normative system of the group that guides positive and negative behavior.

The Consequences of Group Membership

Two different ideas about the consequences of group membership have existed side by side. On the one hand, there is a history of people viewing groups in negative terms. A strong hint of this is found in Jean Jacques Rousseau's opening statement in *The Social Contract*: "Man is born free, and yet we see him everywhere in chains" (1947, p. 5). By implication, it is through group life that otherwise free individuals become shackled. Other examples of scholars with a negative view of group life in more recent times include the French researcher Gustave LeBon (1897), the U.S. social psychologist William McDougall (1920), and Sigmund Freud (1921/1953–1964).

On the other hand, there is also a tradition of viewing groups as positive, as a means through which individuals come to achieve higher performance and experiences. Consider support groups, such as Alcoholics Anonymous, and therapy groups (Sadock, 1975), such as those popularized by Carl Rogers (1971). And what about the numerous community and grassroots groups that serve important social functions (Bertcher & Maple, 1996)? Of course, an invaluable and generally positive role is played in the lives of young children by the most important group of all, the family (Bronfenbrener, 1986).

So should we regard groups as having a liberating and enriching influence on individuals, or should we see their impact as restricting and detrimental? Our discussion in this chapter will show that groups have both positive and negative aspects, but in general they are a highly valuable and, in many ways, indispensable feature of human societies.

Just look at these people: Don't they look silly? Would we let ourselves get involved in such a situation? Yes, the truth is we would. The power of groups lies partly in their ability to set norms and rules for behavior ("Of course the correct way to behave is to have everyone put their feet on the shoulders of the people in front, then walk on their hands"). The norms and rules that define correct behavior can be arbitrary, yet still have a powerful impact on individuals.

What Is a Group?

A useful way of sorting through the numerous definitions of a group is to separate definitions that give primacy to *objective* factors from those that give primacy to *subjective* factors. An example of the first is to consider a group as a number of people who share a common fate (Lewin, 1948), such as all those who are born in the same era, like the members of Generation X, or the baby boomers who were born in the years immediately after World War II. An example of a subjective definition, on the other hand, is to consider people to be a group when they perceive or self-categorize themselves as a group (Tajfel, 1978; Turner, Hogg, Oakes, Reicher, & Wetherell, 1987).

You can probably see shortcomings in both the objective and subjective approaches to defining a group. For example, people who seem to be part of a group on objective criteria may reject being labeled as such (as in the case of a person saying, "Yes, I was born in 1945, but I do not feel I am part of the baby-boomers group, and I resent being referred to by this label. In fact, in terms of tastes and values I have more in common with the members of Generation X than I do with baby boomers"). Also, what if a person categorizes himself as a member of a group, but his subjective perception does not match the objective situation? An example is when ethnic minority children misidentify with the white group (Clark & Clark, 1947), or when people who on economic criteria are working class think of themselves as middle class.

This dilemma led the British social psychologist Rupert Brown to adopt a definition of a **group** that combines both subjective and objective criteria: "A group exists when two or more people define themselves as members of it and when its existence is recognized by at least one other" (Brown, 1988, pp. 2–3). According to this definition, a group exists when it is seen to exist by its members as well as by at least one outsider. But this definition is not a perfect solution. It does not cover, for example, secret societies that see themselves as groups but are not recognized as such by outsiders.

group   an entity that exists when two or more people define themselves as members of it and when its existence is recognized by at least one other person.

Types of Groups

There are many different ways of classifying social groups. Most or perhaps all cultures have **in-groups,** groups to which people belong, and **out-groups,** those to which they do not belong. Even during periods in their histories when groups lived in total or near isolation, there were concepts of "us" or "our people" and "others" or "outsiders" beyond their borders (Figure 13–2).

in-group   group to which a person belongs.

out-group   group to which a person does not belong.

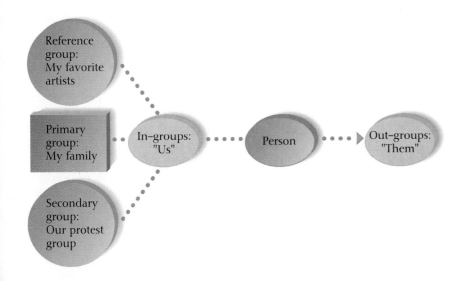

Figure 13–2 Schematic representation of types of groups.

primary group   group that has a small membership and frequent face-to-face interaction, is marked by strong ties of affection, and exists for a long time.

Another useful distinction is among *primary groups, secondary groups,* and *reference groups*. **Primary groups** have a small membership and were described by Charles Cooley (1902) as having the following five basic characteristics:

1. Frequent face-to-face interactions
2. Strong personal identification with the group
3. Strong ties of affection among group members
4. Multifaceted relationships
5. Existing over a long period

The most important example of the primary group is still the nuclear family, consisting of husband, wife, and their children. Family members typically interact with one another on a daily basis, identify strongly with the family, and have strong ties of affection. Relationships within the family are multifaceted (including providing each other with material, moral, and emotional support and services) and long term (a parent is a parent for life).

secondary group   group with opposite characteristics of primary group: little face-to-face interaction, weak group identification, weak ties of affection, and short-term existence.

Secondary groups have the opposite characteristics of primary groups. Their main features are

1. Few or no face-to-face interactions
2. Weak identification with the group
3. Weak ties of affection among group members
4. Limited, often functional relationships
5. Short-term existence

An example of a secondary group is a number of people who get together to protest the closing of a bridge. If their protest is effective, the bridge may be opened quickly and the group will disband. If the goal is not reached, the protest group may gradually grow into a strong, enduring organization, forging new relationships in a neighborhood. In this case, a secondary group may develop into a primary group, with strong ties of loyalty and affection.

But people are not always members of the groups that influence them. For example, Chris is a college student who continuously follows the fortunes of his favorite basketball team. He reads about the latest fitness and training ideas they use, and he even follows their diets. He goes to great lengths to learn what they eat every day, and what vitamin supplements they take. He buys training equipment endorsed by them and tries to watch every game. He will never be a member of the basketball team he cherishes, but they influence him in his everyday life, from the way he talks, walks, and dresses to what he eats and drinks. They are for him a **reference group**—that is, a group to which he does not belong but with which he identifies.

reference group   a group to which a person does not belong but with which she or he identifies.

Sharp lines do not exist between these types of groups in practice. For example, anthropologists have described numerous communities that are organized into bands of small, unstable, and mobile groupings of 50 or so people, whose members regularly leave to join other bands

A Pakistani family works as a team in their apricot orchard, preparing the harvest for sale and for storage. Modern Western societies are characterized by groups that are temporary, composed of individuals who are initially strangers, and who are often diverse in terms of ethnicity, religion, gender, and place of origin. In many non–Western societies, groups tend to be more lasting: They are composed of family or community members who know one another intimately, and are of the same ethnicity, gender, religion, and geographical region. These differences mean that issues important in Western contexts where groups are constantly forming and re-forming, such as team-building and loyalty, are not always relevant in non–Western contexts.

and later return (Murdock, 1949). In such communities, it is not at all clear that a distinction could be made among primary, secondary, or reference groups.

The Universality of Groups

Groups are a universal feature of human social life. Anthropologists have pointed out that in all the societies we know, there are groups of one kind or another (Coon, 1946). This is true even in the most individualistic societies, such as the United States. But although groups are found in all human societies, there are cross-cultural variations in the types of groups that have prominence.

A more accurate generalization is that primary groups exist in most societies, but secondary and reference groups have a more limited role, or may not exist at all, in some societies. In most collectivist societies people tend to belong to fewer groups, but such groups tend to be more stable and long term. For example, in the major societies of Asia and Africa, the extended family is a stable and enduring group of tremendous importance. People tend to live and work with other members of the extended family, and their friendships also tend to be made within or at least through the extended family. Most important, they will generally marry through the intervention of the family, sometimes through traditional arranged marriages. And they will not belong to many groups outside the extended family.

This situation tends to be different in Western societies, in which people often belong to numerous groups, most of which are temporary. Students tend to belong to a number of groups at college (study groups, music groups, sports groups, social groups, fraternities, political groups), but most such groups end after senior year, and many of them change from year to year or even semester to semester. Having graduated, students typically move on to graduate school, jobs, and other activities, often in different cities, and join other groups in their new locations. This is not to suggest that stable and extended families and relationships are not valued in the United States, simply that they tend to be less prevalent.

Concepts and Issues

A group exists when it is recognized by its members. Groups exist in all societies; the simplest classification involves "us" (in-group) and "them" (out-group).

1. Define the following terms: group, deindividuation, diffusion of responsibility, primary group, secondary group, reference group.
2. Give examples from your own experiences of how groups can have both positive and negative influences on individual behavior.

How Do Groups Influence Behavior?

A wide range of explanations has been offered as to how groups influence the behavior of individual members (Brown, 1988; Paulus, 1989). These range from explanations that the mere presence of other group members leads to arousal and change in behavior (cyclists achieve better times when racing in groups than when racing on their own) to explanations that assume more complex cognitive processes are involved in group influence (Jill compares her own views on capital punishment with those of her friends and shifts her position to become more like them). Underlying most of these explanations is the fundamental process of social comparison.

In his seminal elaboration of **social comparison theory,** Leon Festinger (1954) concerned himself only with comparisons of opinions and abilities. He argued that people compare themselves to others on opinions and abilities as a means of reducing uncertainty and achieving accurate self-evaluations. Festinger assumed that if "objective"

social comparison theory theory that when no objective measures are available, we compare ourselves with others in order to make more accurate self-evaluations.

Students check their SAT scores at St. Ignatius High School in Chicago. How do we assess our own status? One way is through social comparison. An initial view was that where available, we prefer to use objective criteria like test scores for evaluating ourselves. But such "objective" measures are seldom sufficient: Students typically want to know how well they did compared to others in the class. A B+ means one thing if everyone else in the class got a grade of B or below, but quite another thing if everyone else got A's. This suggests that ranking within a group often matters more than performance according to objective criteria.

criteria are available, rather than social markers such as "the opinions of others," objective criteria would be preferred. However, subsequent research has shown that, first, people use social comparisons to assess their own situation on much more than just opinions and abilities; and second, that "objective" criteria are not always preferred (Miller, 1977; Wood, 1989).

For example, when students learn their grades, they typically want to know how well they did in comparison with other students. Similarly, track athletes are not just interested in their own times for a race, they want to know how fast their competitors ran. Course grades and race times are examples of objective measures, but people generally consider them to be insufficient. They want to know how they did in comparison with their competitors.

Social comparisons play a fundamentally important role in shaping norms, rules, and more generally, the culture of a group. By comparing themselves to other in-group members, individuals find support for certain views about correct behavior; they also are influenced by other in-group members as to what is correct behavior. For example, Fred expresses the view that the justice system is biased against minority groups. When he compares his views to those of the ethnic minority in-group, he finds a lot of support for his views and feels encouraged to take more extreme positions. As Brenda Major (1994) has pointed out, social comparisons help to *legitimize* the way things are done. They serve both as a check on social reality and as a support for the in-group's view of social reality. Therefore, they play a key role in the group influence process.

But the power of group influence is not necessarily always beneficial. As we have noted throughout this text, tremendous emphasis is placed on *individual mobility* and personal freedom in Western societies. A subtle implication of this tendency has been a negative view of groups and collective behavior generally (Taylor & Moghaddam, 1994). We shall see that this pessimistic view is also present in modern social psychology, reflected by concepts such as *social loafing* (people work less in groups), *groupthink* (people in groups often converge on unwise courses of action they would have avoided if making decisions individually), and *risky shift* (people make riskier decisions in groups).

Working in Groups: Social Loafing

Imagine you have agreed to participate in a social psychological experiment, and you have just stepped into a large psychology laboratory. Feeling anxious, you look around to see if you can find clues as to what kind of a study it is. What exactly will you be expected to do? As a research assistant greets you, you notice a number of strange-looking machines at the end of the room. Attached to them is a long rope. The research assistant explains that you will be one of a group of people who will pull on this rope, as in tug-of-war. You are blindfolded (to avoid being distracted) and placed in the front position, so that the rest of the group will be lined up and pulling the rope behind you. In addition to pulling the rope as part of a group, you are also given opportunities to pull on your own.

Although participants in this study believed they were sometimes pulling as part of a group and sometimes on their own, they were actually always pulling on their own. Being blindfolded and in the front position, they never realized that the "rest of the group" never pulled with them. The findings showed that individuals pulled harder on the rope when they believed they were pulling on their own than when they thought they were pulling as part of a group. This procedure experimentally established what a number of writers had speculated, that individuals working in groups exert less effort than when working on their own (Ingham, Levinger, Graves, & Peckham, 1974). In the 20 years since this initial study, a variety of different procedures have been used by scores of researchers to demonstrate the pervasiveness of social loafing (see the meta-analysis on this literature by Karau & Williams, 1993).

social loafing a tendency for people to exert more effort when working on a task individually than as part of a group.

Social loafing refers to a tendency for people to exert more effort when working on a task individually than as part of a group (Latané, Williams, & Harkins, 1979). When a number of individuals are working in a group, social loafing or "free riding" is less likely to happen if the performance of group members is individually identified (Williams, Harkins, & Latané, 1981). A closer examination of the research on social loafing will act as a useful introduction to the topic of group behavior and culture.

Social Loafing and Individualism.   From one perspective, social loafing seems to make perfect sense. After all, are human beings not creatures who strive to maximize their personal gains? By allowing individuals to compete freely and be rewarded for their personal efforts, we encourage entrepreneurship and enterprise. At the same time, as each person strives to maximize personal gains, the creative potential of individuals is released, leading to the growth of new organizations, new industries, and of course new jobs and wealth opportunities. You probably recognize this line of argument as being associated with free market thinking in politics.

On the other hand, we have plenty of examples of the negative consequences of not rewarding individuals for their personal efforts. The most notorious example, repeatedly cited since the late 1980s, is the collapse of the U.S.S.R. and the Eastern bloc. The inability of communist societies to compete with the capitalist world seems to be explained by the differences in reward systems. Why should people work hard in communist countries, when individual rewards are not dependent on personal effort? Social loafing seems to be inevitable in such settings; each person puts in less effort, and group productivity declines.

But studies with participants from collectivist cultures, such as China, have shown that social loafing is less evident in these cultures and that the opposite is also possible (see Gabrenya, Latané, & Wang, 1983; Gabrenya, Wang, & Latané, 1985; Karau & Williams, 1993). That is, under some conditions people exert more effort when working as part of a group than when working on their own. Aspects of such conditions include a greater emphasis on loyalty and responsibility to groups and on getting ahead collectively. Thus, it seems that social loafing is not an inevitable part of human behavior but a phenomenon that depends on cultural circumstances.

Reassessing Social Loafing.   Studies of social life in other societies can act as a mirror, illuminating neglected aspects of our own societies. The differences in social loafing across cultures lead us to reassess social loafing in Western societies, where the phenomenon was first reported. According to received wisdom, Western societies are individualistic and it makes sense that people in such societies should be motivated when their individual efforts are recognized, and thus to show social loafing in group situations when only group performance is recognized.

But just as people in collectivist societies sometimes show less or no social loafing, are there situations in which social loafing decreases or even disappears in Western contexts? For example, consider a team of four in a bobsled race, or an eight-person rowing crew in competition, or a crew on a sailboat . . . or an entire nation during wartime, when countless personal sacrifices go unnoticed (this discussion on whether or not social loafing is inevitable is related to the debate on altruism in Chapter 9). Surely these and many other examples can be cited to show that social loafing is not inevitable, even in individualistic Western societies.

Think back to your own experiences of working in teams. Imagine if members of your team were aware of a weak link in your group, that

Construction workers pave a street in Chapel Hill, North Carolina. How often have you seen this kind of scene: The majority of the group stands around watching as one or two people work hard. Experimental studies have demonstrated this phenomenon, called social loafing, in laboratories. In individualistic societies people sometimes put less effort into their work when they are in a group and have shared responsibility for a task, compared to when they work on their own and are personally responsible. The reverse has been found in some collectivistic cultures, where participants worked harder as part of a group than on their own.

one of you was not particularly strong in a certain area. Might not the other team members work even harder to compensate? Research suggests that under some conditions this is exactly what happens, so that increased effort by some group members can compensate for the lesser efforts of others (Williams & Karau, 1991). More specifically, group members will try to compensate for the lower performance of others in their group when they are challenged by what they are doing, and when they find the task appealing and involving. This suggests that all group members are potentially social loafers or compensators, depending on how engaging the task is for them. This point underlines the importance of social context and factors such as the kinds of challenges a group faces as influences on whether or not social loafing will occur.

Laboratory research may not provide an accurate picture of social loafing in everyday life. This is because laboratory studies typically involve groups of strangers who in most studies never actually get to know one another or have an opportunity to develop group allegiances. The research participant who is blindfolded and told, "You are pulling on this rope as part of a team" does not necessarily feel she belongs to a team. Such laboratory "groups" lack cohesion, solidarity, leadership, and other features that can lead people to work harder in groups than on their own in the world outside the laboratory. But groups in the world outside the laboratory also have other characteristics that we need to consider.

Leadership

The 39 bodies were laid out on their backs on beds, dressed in black pants, black shirts, and black shoes. Their faces were covered by purple cloths. Each body had identification on or near it. The spacious California mansion that had been their home was spotless, and everything indicated that the suicides had been conducted in an orderly manner. Sometime during late March 1997, the first group of Heaven's Gate cult members had been helped to die by a second group, then the second group had received help from two individuals, who then completed the plan by killing themselves. Cult members had earned a living designing Web sites, so they were intelligent enough to acquire valuable technical skills. Why did their intelligence let them down? One reason was the persuasive power of their leader, a charismatic man who dominated the group. Their leader seemed to be terminally ill, and cult members were persuaded that they should leave this world with him. "Once he is gone," one of them wrote, "there is nothing left here on the face of the earth for me" (Gleick, 1997, p. 32).

One way in which groups influence their members is through **leadership,** a process by which a leader directs group members toward the attainment of specific goals. Most researchers have assumed that leaders are of central importance in human societies (Hogan, Curphy, & Hogan, 1994; Northouse, 1997). Freud (1921/1953–1964) believed that only groups with leaders can be effective (see Chapter 14). The Italian social theorist Vilfredo Pareto (1848–1923) proposed that all human societies are characterized by inequalities, and in all political systems elites rule over nonelites (Pareto, 1935). Buzzwords such as "communism," "capitalism," and "equality" are simply smoke screens used by elites to camouflage their control of resources and the perpetuation of inequalities (see Taylor & Moghaddam, 1987, Chapter 7). Pareto, whose ideas influenced fascist movements in Europe and elsewhere, argued that the Marxist ideal of a classless society, as depicted in the *Communist Manifesto* (Marx & Engels, 1848/1967), is an unrealistic dream.

Some societies strive toward equality. Perhaps the most successful have been the smaller ones. The !Kung bushmen of the Kalahari (Botswana and Southwest Africa) are hunter–gatherers who live in groups of about 25 persons (Lee, 1979). They have developed norms that prevent the accumulation of possessions or an excessive rise in status by individuals. If a member of the group does accumulate private possessions and refuses to share with others, it becomes legitimate for everyone to ridicule, raid, and ostracize this person. Those who are seen to show off about their abilities or looks are mocked and put back in their places by the majority.

Attempts by larger societies to achieve equality and function without an elite or leader class have been less successful. Revolutions to

leadership process by which one person directs group members toward the attainment of specific goals.

bring about greater equality have tended to have a paradoxical effect, so that new leaders emerge to perpetuate inequalities (Middlebrook, 1995). Thus, the communist revolution in Russia led to dictatorial leadership in the former U.S.S.R. In China, Chairman Mao Tse–tung continued the opulent traditions of prerevolution rulers and became one of the "new emperors" (Salisbury, 1992). Modern societies have found it very challenging to develop the kinds of skills required to function without leaders.

Explanations of Leadership. A wide variety of explanations have been offered for leadership (Northouse, 1997). The trait approach, or the **great person** explanation, proposes that leaders have certain personality traits in common that make them suitable for authority positions. Trait approaches attempt to explain leadership independent of context. They suggest that a person with the "right stuff" would become a leader in any culture. **Charisma,** a mysterious quality that some leaders have, is sometimes cited to explain leadership. Leadership qualities are supposed to be universal. Although plausible on the surface, this explanation does not receive strong research support (Hogan, Curphy, & Hogan, 1994). Most researchers have concluded that leaders in politics, business, education, and other sectors do not necessarily have special, shared characteristics.

Some researchers have argued that, at least in the business setting, leaders do have special characteristics (Kirkpatrick & Locke, 1991). Among their characteristics are supposed to be drive, desire to lead and influence others, trustworthiness and honesty, creativity, flexibility, intelligence, and expert knowledge. This is a rosy and perhaps simplistic picture of business leaders. A critical look at how and why business leaders reach the top reveals some of their less positive characteristics, such as ruthlessness and willingness to sacrifice others.

A rather harsh picture is presented by Carl Raushenbush (1937) in his classic book on the American automobile manufacturer and engineer Henry Ford, perhaps the most influential and successful business leader in modern times. Ford introduced assembly–line production, and "Fordism" became for many synonymous with capitalism. In fighting and controlling labor unions, Ford showed enormous cunning and a cutthroat mentality that few could match. Of course, this is not to say that business leaders have only negative characteristics. The Ford Foundation is a symbol of their positive influence. But a realistic picture of leaders should highlight both their positive and negative characteristics.

Some researchers have supported an interactionist explanation of leadership, one incorporating both the characteristics of the person and of the situation. An influential example is **contingency theory,** which proposes that the effectiveness of a leader in achieving group goals depends on the characteristics of the leader and of the situation (Fiedler & Garcia, 1987). But little progress has been made in showing what characteristics of the leader and the situation are important, and how they interact in practical situations outside the laboratory (Peters, Hartke, & Pohlman, 1985). One important reason for this may be that leadership is dynamic and constantly changing: Leadership is not dependent on

---

great person theory proposition that leaders have certain personality traits that set them apart and make them uniquely suitable for positions of authority.

charisma exceptional personality characteristics that set a person apart from others.

contingency theory proposition that the effectiveness of a leader in achieving group goals depends on the characteristics of the leader and of the situation.

fixed features of persons and situations but on fluid social relationships guided by norms.

Leadership as Relationships in Culture.   The focus of much of the research on leadership has been on the characteristics of the leader, or the situation, or both. Very little attention has been given to the nature of relationships between leaders and followers and the normative systems in which they evolve. Rather than focusing on the characteristics of Martin Luther King, Jr., and the characteristics of the situation, we should focus more on the norms of his era and the relationships that evolved between him and his followers. Research in China (Ling, 1989), India (Sinha, 1980), and Japan (Misumi, 1985) shows that leader–follower relationships that are positive in terms of both personal relationships and productivity are the most successful. The nurturant and moral aspects of leader–follower relationships have been highlighted in these collectivistic cultures.

What would it mean to focus more on leader–follower relationships? One implication is that we give more attention to communications between them (Conger, 1991). It is through language specifically and discourse more generally that leaders and followers are able to reconstruct how the world is seen. A new vision of reality is constructed through this relationship. The "dream" of Martin Luther King, Jr., was not a private dream, it was already present in the relationship he had with his followers. When he gave his historic "I Have a Dream" speech, he was articulating a dream that was already embedded in the relationships of many Americans in the late 1960s. These people had rejected the norms of the past and adopted new norms about how the members of different ethnic groups should behave.

Concepts and Issues

The mere presence of others influences human behavior. In Western cultures, social loafing sometimes arises in group settings. Leaders emerge in groups in almost all cultures. Rather than viewing leadership as something arising from the characteristics of the person or the situation, we should conceive of it as a kind of relationship within a cultural context.

1. Give examples of how social comparisons serve to legitimize the in-group's view of the world.
2. Recount your experiences with social loafing.
3. Does evidence support the great person theory of leaders? Discuss reasons for your answer.

Group Decision Making

There are all kinds of reasons why groups should make better decisions than individuals and why the old saying "two heads are better than one" should be correct. After all, by communicating with one another and sharing ideas and information, by pooling know-how and experience, group members can take advantage of resources superior to those available to individuals making decisions on their own. Furthermore, group discussion should identify any biases individuals may harbor, so that prejudices arising from personal preferences can be put aside.

However, studies of group decision making reveal that groups often fail to use their potential advantages. For example, they fail to make use of the information available to individual members but not shared by all group members (Stasser, 1992). Also, groups often seem to be just as biased, and perhaps even more biased, than individuals. In practice, collective decisions are very seldom the result of purely rational and objective processes. Let us take a closer look at some of the ways in which such biases come about. We begin by considering what happens through the mere presence of other people, who may or may not be part of a group.

Social Facilitation

The mere presence of others has been found to influence the way people (and animals) behave (Guerin, 1993), and this seems to be common to most societies. The pervasiveness and power of social facilitation is reflected by the fact that people have to undergo lengthy training in order to overcome it. Meditation, for example, usually involves intense concentration and learning to be oblivious to the presence of other people and external distractions. By chanting mantras and repeating formulas such as "Ave Maria," spiritual discipline is developed. But novices find themselves easily distracted by other people, and for most of us it is extremely difficult not to be influenced by other humans.

Very early in the history of social psychology, researchers became intrigued by how the presence of others influences task performance (Triplett, 1898). After a century of research, this domain is still fascinating because research findings suggest that performance on a task sometimes improves and sometimes deteriorates in the presence of others. An influential idea for explaining these apparently contradictory findings was put forward by Bob Zajonc (1965), in his *drive theory of social facilitation*. The main idea behind this theory is that the presence of others is arousing (for example, imagine you are on your own and learning to serve on a tennis court when some passersby stop to watch; you will probably feel excited and nervous). As arousal increases, the tendency increases for the occurrence of dominant responses, these being the responses most likely to be made in a given situation.

If a task is well learned, the dominant response will be correct, but if a task is poorly learned, the response will be incorrect. For example, if a tennis professional is serving, the presence of a crowd will more likely bring out the best in her play; but if I am serving, the presence of a crowd will certainly result in even more double faults! However, even professional players will perform poorly in high-pressure situations, as in the case of major league baseball players who have lower batting averages when they are in critical situations (Davis & Harvey, 1992).

But Zajonc's (1965) account of social facilitation comes out of a research tradition that emphasizes stimulus–response associations and

Young Vietnamese monks at prayer. Human beings are influenced by the mere presence of others, often in positive ways. Individuals perform better on many types of tasks when they are in the company of others. The powerful influence that the mere presence of others can have on us becomes clear when we try to avoid being influenced. It is often only through years of intense training and meditation that people can focus on their inner selves and remain unaffected by their surroundings. But to achieve such focused attention, individuals find it useful to train in settings where everyone else is also striving toward similar goals, as in this Vietnamese Buddhist monastery. Thus, even in training designed to help us focus inward, we find it useful to be influenced by others.

neglects human thinking and higher mental faculties, such as comprehension. This research tradition is associated with the behaviorist school, which dominated psychology from the second to the sixth decade of the twentieth century. Although the mere presence of others is still seen by some researchers to be a compelling explanation of social facilitation (Schmitt, Gilovich, Goore, & Joseph, 1986), other researchers have pointed to the role of the distractions caused by other people (Baron, 1986) and the apprehension associated with being evaluated when one presents oneself in public (Carver & Scheier, 1981). The latter explanations are reminiscent of Erving Goffman's ideas on self-presentation (see Chapter 3).

Using Goffman's (1959) ideas, one could argue that the presence of others leads a person to be more concerned with presenting a particular image of the self. How much effort is put into presenting a successful self will depend to a large extent on the audience. If the audience is more important to a person and demands to see a successful self being presented (as in the case of sports fans cheering for their team), then more effort will be put toward a winning performance. If a professional sports team is playing in front of the home crowd, then in order to save face and present a successful self, it is more important that the team win. This may help explain the home advantage enjoyed by sports teams, an advantage found in many different arenas (Brown, 1987; Courneya & Carron, 1992).

Animals also enjoy a "home advantage" when they compete with other animals, in the sense that they tend to win more fights in their own territories (Lorenz, 1966). But it is a mistake to assume that because there is a similarity in the way animals and humans behave, the reason for their behavior must also be the same. The home advantage may come about for animals for very different reasons than it comes about for humans. For example, for animals a home advantage might come about through instincts associated with territoriality, whereas for humans it much more likely to come about through learning (see Bell, Fisher, Baum, & Greene, 1990, Chapter 8).

Groupthink

> The more amiability and esprit de corps among members of an in-group of policy-makers, the greater is the danger that independent critical thinking will be replaced by groupthink, which is likely to result in irrational and dehumanizing actions directed at out-groups.
>
> —Irving Janis, *Victims of Groupthink*, p. 198

groupthink the tendency for people in groups to converge on unwise courses of action they would have avoided if they were making the decision individually.

Irving Janis (1971, 1972, 1982; Janis & Mann, 1977) has highlighted a fundamental paradox in group behavior: Greater cohesion and attraction among in-group members is often associated with terrible mistakes in group decision making. Other factors that increase the likelihood of **groupthink** are threatening situations (leading people to feel "We are in danger") and directive leadership, in which the leader seeks endorsement of his views rather than an honest assessment. More recent studies have also highlighted the key role of leadership style in bringing about groupthink (Schafer & Crichlow, 1996). Among the most important symptoms of groupthink are an illusion of invulnerability ("We are number one!"), a strong belief in the group's morality ("Of course we are right!"), negative stereotypes of enemy leaders (weak, stupid, and so on), self-censorship, and a false sense of unanimity within the group. All these factors can result in even very smart and successful people making very unwise decisions.

Janis's research arose out of the particular dilemmas experienced by the United States during the 1960s, but in some ways his findings have broad value for all human societies in which decision making is conducted through group activities. Let us first consider a few cases of groupthink identified by Janis.

On April 17, 1961, the U.S. Navy and Air Force and the Central Intelligence Agency provided support for an army of Cuban exiles as they invaded Cuba at the Bay of Pigs. The invasion, which got the go-ahead from the newly elected President John F. Kennedy and his group of advisers, was a fiasco. By the third day all the invading forces had been captured, or killed, or had fled. But the military defeat was nothing compared to the symbolism of the event. The United States lost much credibility throughout the world for having attacked its tiny neighbor. Even traditional allies of the United States criticized the government for having undertaken such an "obviously" disastrous project. The attempt may have played into the hands of the U.S.S.R., pushing Cuba into the open arms of the Soviets. Very soon after the Bay of Pigs, the Cubans allowed a buildup of Soviet troops and missiles on their island, just 90 miles from the U.S. mainland.

John F. Kennedy meeting with his cabinet and advisers, October 1962. Kennedy, reputed to have been very intelligent, probably one of the most intelligent of all U.S. presidents, also made some of the most unintelligent decisions in the history of U.S. foreign policy. One such decision led to the disastrous Bay of Pigs invasion of Cuba during which thousands of lives and U.S. prestige on the world stage were jeopardized. How can we explain such a contradiction? One plausible explanation lies in *groupthink*, a process that can lead even very bright people to make wrong decisions.

Now consider another example of disastrous group decision making, this time involving the war in Vietnam. Between 1964 and 1967, President Lyndon Johnson met on a weekly basis with a small group of advisers, all of whom were known for their devotion to humanitarian ideals. Yet this same group endorsed a policy of increased aerial bombardment, population displacement, search-and-destroy missions, and "whatever violence is necessary" to destroy the enemy, to win over the population in North Vietnam, and to win the war. Evidence suggests that Johnson and his advisers did not even do a good job of seeking military advice from outside their circle about how to achieve objectives in Vietnam (McMaster, 1997). The actual outcome of the policy of escalation was the alienation of more and more people, both in Vietnam and in the United States.

We could continue adding to the list of group decision disasters in foreign policy. For example, we should add the Carter administration's mistaken decision to send in helicopters to try to free the hostages held in Iran in 1980. This mission ended very badly when the rescue crew got stuck in a remote part of Iran, and the images of burnt-out helicopters and dead personnel were flashed around the world. But perhaps the greatest blunder of the twentieth century was made by the British Prime Minister Neville Chamberlain and his inner circle when they made an agreement with Germany's Adolf Hitler in September 1938. Despite all the evidence showing that Hitler was following an expansionist policy, Chamberlain and his group accepted Hitler's word that he would not continue to invade other countries. Events soon showed that Chamberlain and his trusted advisers were fundamentally misguided about Hitler's intentions and plans.

Is such bad decision making unique to Western democracies? A long list of incidents suggests not: the invasion of Kuwait by Iraq's Saddam Hussein and his army leading to international embargoes on Iraq in the early 1990s; the continuation of the Iran–Iraq war for eight long and futile years in the 1980s; the invasion of Afghanistan by the U.S.S.R. and the attempt to prop up a puppet communist regime there in the 1970s; the attempt to achieve and to export a cultural revolution in the Maoist China of the late 1960s. The list of enormous blunders made in dictatorships seems endless. However, one difference is that when such blunders occur in dictatorships we cannot be sure to what extent they are the result of a demagogic leader taking another wrong turn, and to what extent they involve a group decision.

But because groupthink effectively weakens democratic processes, it may well be that groupthink acts to narrow the gap between dictatorships and democracies. Most important, even in democratic societies groupthink stifles dissenting voices and prevents open and critical discussion of a group's assumptions. The censorship that arises is very similar to that found in dictatorships.

Groupthink is by definition antidemocratic because it involves a group becoming isolated from the rest of society and making decisions in a vacuum. How can such isolation be prevented? Two answers are at hand. First, the work of the French researcher Serge Moscovici and his colleagues (Moscovici, Mucchi-Faina, & Maass, 1994) suggests that the role of minority or dissenting voices is critical (see Chapter 6). Dissenters who stick to their positions and are persistent in their efforts can persuade the majority. As John F. Kennedy (1956), who later became the president of the United States, showed in his award–winning book *Profiles in Courage*, it is sometimes the lone voice of a courageous person that turns the tide of events.

But research also shows a vital second way in which groupthink can be prevented. The research of Philip Tetlock and his colleagues (1992) suggests that factors such as group procedures and situational threats are not as important in bringing about groupthink as Janis had assumed. However, a factor that may have been underestimated by Janis is that of leadership and accessibility to *accurate* information. For example, when President Jimmy Carter endorsed a catastrophic plan to rescue the hostages in Iran, he and his advisers tried to be open to different views and ideas. The fact is that they failed to gather accurate information about the situation inside Iran.

Janis may have oversimplified the causes of groupthink (see McCauley, 1989; Tetlock, Peterson, McGuire, & Feld, 1992), but he has made a lasting contribution by highlighting the power and pervasiveness of this phenomenon. This issue is of the highest importance for democracy: When individuals cannot put forward ideas or facts that run contrary to the assumptions of the group, when the group fails to look outside and recognize the legitimacy of alternative viewpoints, there is a real danger of groupthink.

A Group Is Different from the Sum of Its Parts

Imagine if each member of President Johnson's inner circle had been interviewed individually about the decisions he would make on Vietnam. The sum of such individually taken decisions would very likely be different from the actual decisions made by the group together. Something different and new emerges when individuals get together to make decisions in groups. The phenomenon of groupthink demonstrates a principle put forward by **Gestalt** psychologists early in the twentieth century: The *whole is more than the sum of its parts*, implying that we should study individuals in cultural context.

Gestalt idea that the whole is more than the sum of its parts.

But what explains the influence people have on one another in group decision making? The mere presence of others seems too simplistic an explanation for most types of social influence among humans because it does not give enough importance to argumentation and norms. We invest tremendous resources in trying to influence one another through argument. In particular, we try to influence the norms and rules that regulate social interactions in our group.

The phenomenon of groupthink shows that irrational group decisions can arise when individual group members fail to communicate openly and express what they really believe, at the same time neglecting different viewpoints internal and external to the group (see Figure 13–3). Charles Dickens (1854/1977) brilliantly portrays examples of this in *A Tale of Two Cities*, a story set at the time of the French Revolution of

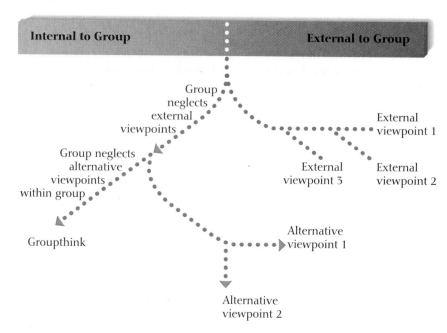

Figure 13–3   The context of groupthink.

1789. Monsieur Defarge and other moderates among the revolutionaries keep their real opinions to themselves, so that the group decision becomes more and more extreme. Defarge tries to put the brakes on by suggesting that the killing of the French aristocrats and their associates must stop somewhere,

> "Well, well," reasoned Defarge, "but one must stop somewhere. After all, the question is still where?"
> "At extermination," said madame.
> "Magnificent!" croaked Jacques Three. The Vengeance, also, highly approved.

In response, Defarge is forced to lend some support by saying, "Extermination is good doctrine . . . in general, I say nothing against it. But. . . ."

Unfortunately, as is the case with so many other moderate voices in so many other similar situations, Defarge fails to be forceful enough in elaborating on his "but," and the group keeps going along extremist lines.

The Puzzle of Risky Shifts

But group decision making can also go astray when people speak out and *do* try to persuade one another. An example of such skewed group decision making is the phenomenon of the so-called **risky shift,** which also provides a picture of how research findings can be interpreted in many different ways.

risky shift   the proposition that people in groups make riskier decisions.

Do people take greater risks when they are on their own or when they are acting as part of a group? Implicit in the work of various writers has been the idea that people in groups can become "unruly crowds," "mobs," and "gangs" with a strong tendency to behave irrationally and to take larger risks (Taylor & Moghaddam, 1994). At the same time, it has been assumed that people with more education and training can work in organized groups to achieve more rational decision making and behavior. Thus, the kinds of groups one finds in politics, business, and education (groups such as the members of a government cabinet, a chief executive officer and her advisers, the deans of a university) should make less risky decisions.

But in the early 1960s a surprising finding on group decision making reversed the traditional view that intelligent people in decision-making groups become more cautious. It was unexpectedly reported that groups are more inclined to make risky decisions (Kogan & Wallach, 1967). Imagine you were given an opportunity to invest time in a research project that may or may not prove to be a success and earn you extra credits. Would you be willing to commit to such a project if the chance of success were 1 in 10? Probably not! How about a 9 in 10 chance of success? Probably yes. But what is the greatest risk you would accept? A 5 in 10 chance of success, or perhaps even a 3 in 10? The surprising findings of a preliminary group of studies suggested that if you made the choice on your own you would be more cautious than if you made the choice as part of a group of students.

The risky-shift finding was originally reported in the United States (Stoner, 1961) but was replicated in other Western countries, such as Canada, England, and France (Fraser, Gouge, & Billig, 1970; Kogan & Doise, 1969, Vidmar, 1970), as well as in countries geographically distant from the West, such as Israel and New Zealand (Bell & Jamieson, 1970; Rim, 1963).

The excitement caused by the risky-shift phenomenon was in part because it went against conventional wisdom, but also because it seemed to have widespread implications. For example, did this finding mean that the boards of governors of banks, the trustees of universities, and the countless other decision-making groups that we assume to be conservative and cautious are actually inclined to take risks that bankers, university administrators, and other decision makers would not take as individuals? Is our future in the right hands? Should we rely more on individuals to make decisions, such as when to declare war? But an even more fundamental question remained. Part of the appeal of the risky-shift phenomenon was the puzzle of how it could be explained. Why would people in groups take greater risks?

Risky Shifts or Cautious Shifts: The Importance of Norms

Serge Moscovici and Marisa Zavalloni (1969) brought a new perspective to the risky-shift phenomenon by demonstrating that shifts in group decisions do not occur in just one direction. Rather, group interaction

group polarization   the finding that group interaction tends to lead to a more extreme position on an already existing orientation.

tends to lead to a more extreme position on an already existing orientation. In some cases, the existing orientation is to endorse risk taking, but in other cases it is to endorse caution. This **group polarization** was demonstrated by David Myers and George Bishop (1970) by having groups of more and less racially prejudiced persons discuss racial issues. The two groups shifted positions so that they were further apart after discussions than they had been before, with the prejudiced group becoming more so and the less prejudiced group becoming less so (for more detailed discussion of group polarization, see Myers & Lamm, 1976).

The most convincing explanation for this phenomenon involves the role of social comparison, information exchange, and argumentation in influencing group norms, and group culture more broadly. When individuals are placed in a group and participate in group discussions, they can gain new information from others and also be influenced by the views and arguments of others. Moreover, through social comparisons they come to realize their own position on an issue relative to the rest of the group. Most important, they recognize the orientation of the group on the issues at hand, and they identify the views that are positively supported by the group. For example, they come to realize that in-group members have positive attitudes toward group X and negative ones toward group Y. They identify this as a group norm and also presume that one way to be more positively evaluated is to move further in the same direction. In this way, a less prejudiced group moves toward becoming even less prejudiced, and a more prejudiced group shifts to being even more prejudiced.

If such an explanation of group polarization were valid, then the same decision-making task should elicit risky or cautious shifts depending on the already existing tendency of the group to value risk or caution. If according to group norms risk taking is highly valued, then group discussion should lead to greater risk taking. But if, on the other hand, group norms endorse cautious behavior, then group discussion should lead to a cautious shift. This explanation is supported by studies in Uganda (Carlson & Davis, 1971) and Liberia (Gologor, 1977), both countries where risk taking is valued less than typically found in the United States. It was found that Ugandan and Liberian participants initially made less risky choices than U.S. participants, and their decisions shifted to a more cautious position after group discussions.

A similar process may explain the shifts that take place in fashion. A slight tendency toward shorter skirts, or wider trouser bottoms, or narrower ties, or the color red may lead more and more people to identify these as fashionable and positively valued, the "in" things to wear. Such recognition may lead people to wear shorter skirts, trousers with wider bottoms, narrower ties, and more red. On the other hand, if there arises a slight trend toward longer skirts, narrower trousers, and so on, these trends will become accentuated. In the domain of fashion, such trends often begin by chance and tend to be arbitrary: "arbitrary" in the sense that there is no objective reason why long skirts are better than short ones or wide ties are better than narrow ones, for example. In the case of other norms, also, at least some of them may be arbitrary and begin by chance.

Concepts and Issues

Individuals are influenced by the mere presence of others. Decision making in groups sometimes becomes biased, resulting in groupthink, risky shift, and cautious shift.

1. Does social facilitation adequately explain biases in group decision making? Explain.
2. How does groupthink come about?
3. Do groups always make riskier decisions? Give reasons for your answer.

"Bowling Alone"

No man is an Island, entire of it self; every man is a piece of the Continent, a part of the main.

John Donne, *Devotions XVII*

Humans are social beings, and throughout this text I have argued that it is our cultural surroundings that shape the central features of our social behavior. We have also seen that there are important cross-cultural variations in the degree to which the individual is treated as an independent entity rather than as dependent on the group. In societies such as the United States, individuals are socialized to behave as independent units. For example, in Chapter 8 we noted that marriage in the United States and in other Western societies is being seen more and more as a union of two independent persons who meet (by chance rather than by "arrangement"), fall in love, decide as independent adults to get married, and then inform their relatives and friends. In a sense, then, persons in individualistic societies tend to have looser ties with groups, even the most important primary group, the family.

One of the concerns increasing individualism is raising is that traditional groups, such as the family and the community, are now being undermined (Avineri & de-Shalit, 1992; Warren & Lyon, 1988). In an intriguing analysis of individualism in the United States, Robert Putnam (1995) showed that from 1980 to 1993 league bowling decreased by 40 percent at the same time that there was a 10 percent increase in the total numbers of bowlers. This **bowling–alone** trend, which involves a weakening of community ties and responsibilities, is indicative, Putnam has argued, of a decline in group life in the United States (Figure 13–4). In line with this thesis, Putnam has identified a similar trend of decreased participation in group and community activities in a wide variety of other areas, such as membership in voluntary organizations (e.g.,

"bowling alone" decline in league bowling as indicative of a decline in community ties and responsibilities in the United States.

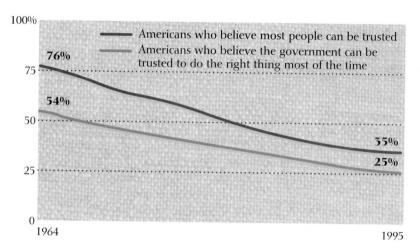

Figure 13–4   Indications of a decline in social capital, 1964–1995 (after Morain & Balz, 1996).

social capital   societal resource composed of informal networks, organizations, and norms.

Boy Scouts, Red Cross), labor union membership, and voter turnout in local and national elections. This trend is, according to Putnam, associated with a decline in **social capital,** which is composed of informal social networks, organizations, and norms.

One of the reasons social capital is important is that it helps to broaden the sense of self, so that people think more in terms of "we" and less in terms of "me" (see the discussion in Chapter 3 on the sense of self in individualistic and collective cultures). The decline in social capital has involved a decline in the trust people have in each other and in basic institutions. The percentage of people in the United States who believed that most people can be trusted declined from 76 percent in 1964 to 35 percent in 1995, whereas the percentage who responded that government can be trusted to do the right thing most of the time declined from 54 to 25 percent in the same period (Putnam, 1995).

This "bowling-alone" tendency may actually be a relatively recent feature of U.S. society. Barry Shain (1994) has argued that in its earlier history, at least before the eighteenth century, American culture was community-based. The French writer Alexis de Tocqueville (1845), who traveled and wrote about American society during the 1830s, noted the strong community-based nature of the culture. Indeed, he claimed that belonging to associations was a stronger theme in the United States than anywhere else in the world. In the twentieth century, however, there has been a gradual decline in communal participation.

But the communitarian call for a greater sense of responsibility and less emphasis on personal rights (see Etzioni, 1993) is not just an attempt to return to a past ideal. We face new challenges in a very new kind of social world, and the solutions of the past are not likely to be effective. We now look to specialists in different domains, such as clinical psychologists, psychiatrists, social workers, applied social psychologists, and so on, for solutions to our social problems. Armed with modern research methods and technologies, such specialists have stepped in to try to fill some of the gaps left by the demise of community.

But our relationship with specialists is in some ways paradoxical. Increasing individualism has led people in Western societies to become more independent from traditional groups and communities (such as the family and the local church), but it has made us more dependent on specialists (see Moghaddam, 1997a). In the United States, particularly, people fight fiercely against government intervention, and young women and men are keen to break away from family ties and "interference." However, the same individualists are willing to be dependent on specialists. They will tell their intimate secrets to psychologists and other specialists but be much more reluctant to share the same experiences with family and friends. Perhaps, then, people in the United States and other individualistic cultures are not experiencing more or less independence than people in collectivistic societies but simply a different type of dependency in relationships.

Concepts and Issues

Increased individualism in the United States and other Western societies has been associated with a fragmentation of communities. This trend is accentuated by increasing specialization.

1. What does Putnam mean by "bowling alone"?
2. Why are social capital and community important?

Conclusion

Groups are a universal aspect of human social life. Individual behavior changes when people join groups, but the nature of this change varies considerably across cultures. In some situations, groups make riskier decisions, but in others they are more cautious. Groupthink can arise if group leaders isolate themselves from outside influence. An important aspect of group life is the relationship between leader and followers and the norms that evolve from that relationship.

For Review

A group exists when two or more people define themselves as its members and when its existence is recognized by at least one other person. Groups are universal features of human life, although there are fundamental variations in the nature of group life across societies.

Among the different types of groups are in-groups, groups to which persons belong, and out-groups, groups to which they do not belong.

Primary groups (such as the family) are small and allow for face-to-face interactions between members; secondary groups (such as work organizations) are large and often have functional relationships; reference groups are those with which individuals identify and are influenced by, but to which they do not actually belong (as in the case of a professional sports team influencing a team supporter).

Groups influence individuals through the social norms and rules they establish and support. Such norms and rules regulate the lives of group members by providing guidelines as to how group members should behave. Individuals assess their own situation through making social comparisons. Although influence can come about through the mere presence of others (social facilitation), the nature and direction of such influence largely depend on group norms.

Group norms and rules are particularly influenced by leaders. Leadership is common to almost all societies; those that function without leaders tend to be small and simpler in forms of production and work. The great person theory of leadership has not received much research support. The contingency theory explanation of leadership has gained influence, but it too lacks consistent research support. An alternative view is to see leadership as residing in social relationships, rather than in individuals or situations.

Social psychological research has focused a great deal on the negative aspects of group influence, and this perhaps reflects the value placed on individualism and personal rights in the United States.

In social loafing, individuals exert less effort on a task when they are in a group than when on their own; in groupthink, individuals converge on unwise courses of action they would have avoided if making decisions on their own; in group polarization, individuals in groups make both riskier and more cautious decisions than they would make on their own.

A number of movements outside traditional social psychology, but very powerful in the larger society, place a great deal of importance on the benefits of group life. This is reflected in various approaches to therapy (such as group therapy and support groups) as well as more recent attempts to revive grassroots communities. The communitarian movement and similar movements attempt to use social groups to solve some of the enormous social problems that are associated with increasing individualism.

For Discussion

1. "Groups are found in all societies, but group life differs in many ways across cultures." Explain this statement.

2. Imagine that a CEO asked you for advice about the kinds of biases that can creep into group decision making. What would you tell her?

Key Terms

"Bowling alone" 467
Charisma *456*
Contingency theory
 456
Deindividuation
 442
Diffusion of
 responsibility *443*
Gestalt *463*

Great person theory
 456
Group 447
Group polarization
 466
Groupthink *460*
In-group *447*
Leadership *455*
Out-group *447*
Primary group *448*

Reference group
 448
Risky shift *464*
Secondary group
 448
Social capital *468*
Social comparison
 theory *450*
Social loafing *452*

Annotated Readings

Leading researchers discuss different aspects of behavior in groups in P. B. Paulus, ed., *The psychology of group influence*, 2nd ed. (Hillsdale, NJ: Lawrence Erlbaum, 1989); and in S. Worchel, W. Wood, and J. A. Simpson, eds., *Group process and productivity* (Newbury Park, CA: Sage, 1992).

Group behavior with specific focus on cultural diversity is discussed by leading researchers in C. Granose and S. Oskamp, eds., *Cross-cultural work groups* (Thousand Oaks, CA: Sage, 1997).

I. L. Janis, the innovator of groupthink, presents his ideas in *Groupthink*, 2nd ed. (Boston: Houghton Mifflin, 1982).

J. Misumi presents an outline of a Japanese research program on leadership in *The behavioral science of leadership: An interdisciplinary Japanese research program* (Ann Arbor: University of Michigan Press, 1985).

The relationship between individuals and larger group processes is discussed in F. M. Moghaddam, *The specialized society: The plight of the individual in an age of individualism* (Westport, CT: Praeger, 1997).

CHAPTER *14*

Intergroup Relations and Multiculturalism

◄ What is Michael Jordan doing in downtown Barcelona? The answer seems obvious to people in the late 1990s, because we assume that his image will have the same effect in Barcelona as it does in Chicago, or anywhere else for that matter. Nike has made the same assumption and invested enormous amounts of money in worldwide advertising using Michael Jordan's image. But this cultural "coming together" has not meant an end to hostile clashes and wars. Intergroup conflicts, ethnic genocide, and mass destruction continue to be challenges for all humankind.

The Nigerian driver did a great job of weaving in and out of the New York City traffic to get me to my dinner meeting on time. On the way, she explained that the colorful decorations in the taxi were the handicraft of her Jordanian partner, who drives the night shift. When she dropped me off at my destination, a Polish restaurant close to Central Park, the hostess led me to the table where I found the others in my group already seated: four women—a white Catholic American, a Jewish-American, an African-American, and a Chinese-American—and five men—two WASPs, an Italian-American, a Mexican-American, and a Korean-American. The Polish waiter took our orders, and as we enjoyed our meal a heated debate on the question of the global village ensued.

Two very different points of view emerged within our little party. The first group, perhaps in the majority, were of the opinion that the world really is becoming like one big village, with everyone becoming more similar and having more and more contact with other villagers. A second group disagreed, arguing that it is only on the surface that people are becoming more similar and the village more integrated. At a deeper level, they proposed, the world is actually becoming more fragmented, and intergroup differences, rather than intergroup similarities, characterize modern life.

Both viewpoints had merit, and pointed to a puzzling paradox. On the one hand, lifestyles around the world do seem to be getting more similar as modernization spreads (Yang, 1988). The same goods and services can now be found in many different countries—the same or very similar hotel chains, restaurants, and shopping malls; the same fast-food outlets; and, of course, the same films, music, and other forms of popular entertainment, created or at least strongly influenced by Hollywood.

The homogeneity of lifestyles is perhaps most clearly apparent in the popular culture of the youth around the world. The music, clothes, and tastes of young people have become very similar, so that students who study for a year abroad fit in fairly quickly. Much of this homogeneity is associated with the internationalization of trade (Adler, 1986). International corporations are sending their goods and employees to what were once thought to be impregnable and distant places, such as China. There is a renewed emphasis on free trade, with the European Union, the North American Free Trade Agreement, and other major trading blocs seemingly washing away national and local differences.

Improved communications have made the village even smaller. We receive news instantly about events in distant places: war in Burundi, an earthquake in Turkey, a bomb attack at the Olympics, riots in Los Angeles, a terrorist attack in Saudi Arabia. As soon as it happens, we know about it. The same television programs are watched by billions of people in over 100 different countries, and new technologies such as satellite dishes and electronic mail are allowing people living under dictatorships to overcome censorship. In short, national, regional, ethnic, religious, and cultural differences seem to be fading away.

But this rosy picture of global unity was rejected by the group in our party that argued that, at a deeper level, the world is actually becoming more fragmented. Separatist movements seem to be growing in strength in every part of the globe: Quebec separatists in Canada; Irish, Welsh, and

Scottish nationalists in the United Kingdom; Basques in Spain; Moros in the Philippines; Aceh and Timor rebels in Indonesia; Flemish nationalists in Belgium; Kurds in Turkey, Iran, and Iraq; Sikhs and Kashmiris in India; Tamils fighting for an independent state in Sri Lanka; Tibetan nationalists in China; Chechnians and numerous other would–be breakaway groups in Russia and the former Eastern bloc countries; Hutus in Burundi; the Western Sahara independence movement . . . the list seems endless. Add to this radical antigovernment groups such as the Freemen in the United States, and the picture becomes even murkier.

The image of cohesion and homogeneity is deceiving, this group argued, because just as some parts of the world are integrating (e.g., East and West Germany), other parts are fragmenting (e.g., the former Czechoslovakia). The separatist aspirations of these hundreds of groups are associated with regional and local conflicts, so that as we move into the twenty–first century numerous local wars are being fought around the world (Gurr, 1994).

The revival of ethnicity has also strengthened fragmentation and intergroup differences (Lambert & Taylor, 1990). Since the 1960s, there has been an ethnic revival; larger numbers of people now identify with their ethnic groups in the United States and Canada and in many other societies (Boucher, Landis & Clark, 1987; Gurr, 1994). The revival of in-digenous or heritage cultures among African–Americans and Native Americans in those two nations is just one manifestation.

Two parallel and apparently contradictory movements are evident throughout the world. On the one hand the internationalization of trade, improved communications, and increases in the movement of people have helped to make the global village a reality. Parts of the United States, such as this street in Brooklyn (left), are small–scale representations of cultural diversity in the global village. We are, it seems, becoming one united world, a sort of giant Brooklyn. On the other hand, separatist movements strive toward a very different goal: These Quebec separatists are saying yes to independence from the rest of Canada.

Similarly, this second group argued that fundamental differences in lifestyles persist. Consider differences in the pace of life as an example. Using indicators such as walking and talking speed, the time it takes to buy stamps in a post office and to get change in a bank, and the accuracy of bank clocks, research has shown differences in the pace of life across societies (from fastest to slowest: Japan, United States, England, Taiwan, Italy, Indonesia) and within the United States (fastest, northeastern cities; slowest, West Coast cities) (see LeVine, 1990). From this second viewpoint, then, continued differences in lifestyles and the renewed emphasis on intergroup differences and on separatism indicate that the world is only superficially a global village.

Theories of Intergroup Relations

"Conflicts occur when people fight over money, power, and resources," explained one of the people at our table that evening in New York. "It's purely a matter of economics. Like Saddam Hussein—he wanted to grab more oil for himself, so he attacked Kuwait. The United States needed to defend its own oil interests, so we attacked Iraq. When economic interests clash, then people become enemies and get to hate one another."

"No, no, it's the other way around. Subjective understandings and feelings come first, then economics," objected another person in our party. "It does not matter if people do or don't have conflicting economic interests in reality, it only matters how they perceive their own situation. Conflicts arise out of irrational psychological states, and then people justify the fighting by rational economic interests. They fight each other often for reasons they don't understand themselves, then they make up rational reasons for fighting."

Is there a solution to this puzzle? How can we explain a situation in which peace and harmony should be within our grasp, yet conflict and violence actually seem to be increasing? As social psychologists, we can draw on a rich research literature on intergroup relations and multiculturalism to help us tackle these questions (Abrams & Hogg, 1990; Brewer & Miller, 1997; Brown, 1988; Taylor & Moghaddam, 1994; Worchel & Austin, 1986).

We shall begin by considering the major social psychological theories of intergroup relations, as well as examples of empirical research used to test the major theories. Then we critically assess two contrasting policies for managing culturally diverse societies: namely, assimilation and multiculturalism.

The two viewpoints expressed at dinner that night help us to organize the major social psychological theories of intergroup relations. It is useful to conceptualize these theories as lying on a continuum, at one extreme of which is "psychological state" as the main factor behind intergroup conflict, and at the other, "material conditions" (see Figure 14–1). If we think of this continuum in terms of traditional research designs (see Chapter 2), at one extreme are the theories that propose the

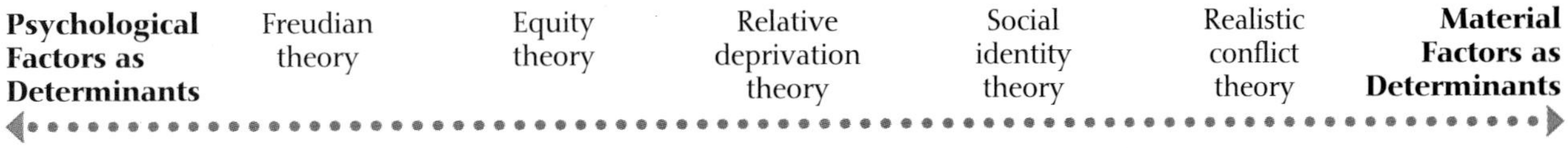

Psychological Factors as Determinants	Freudian theory	Equity theory	Relative deprivation theory	Social identity theory	Realistic conflict theory	Material Factors as Determinants

◀• •▶

Figure 14–1 Social psychological theories of intergroup relations.

independent variable to be psychological state, and at the other are theories that propose the independent variable to be economic conditions. In both cases the dependent variable is the type of intergroup relationship.

Theories Based on Psychological States

Three major theories give particular importance to psychological states: Freudian theory, equity theory, and relative deprivation theory.

Freud and the Irrational Basis of Intergroup Conflict

Sigmund Freud lived during a turbulent period in human history, and as a Jew in Austria had firsthand experience of intergroup persecution. He lived through World War I and fled Vienna as a refugee to England at the beginning of World War II, when the Nazis invaded his home city. Freud thought long and hard on the question of war, and although many of his ideas about individual human behavior lack credibility in light of research evidence, some of his insights pertaining to intergroup relations are simply brilliant (Freud, 1921/1953–1964).

Freud adopted an *irrationalist* view of behavior, meaning that he assumed people are often unaware of why they behave as they do. This viewpoint highlights the role of unconscious factors, a perspective that is once more gaining influence among experimental researchers (Greenwald & Banaji, 1995). He began by describing a group as a set of people emotionally tied to one another through identification with a leader. For Freud, the only groups worth considering were those with leaders, because leaderless groups are unable to achieve cohesion and effective action. Movements such as civil rights and women's liberation only make headway, he would argue, during periods when they enjoy strong and effective leadership.

Leadership and Libido. How do groups achieve cohesion and conformity among their members? This question is answered in part by the role of the leader and also in part by the concept of **libido,** the energy of those instincts that have to do with all that may be included under the term *love*. Each individual is linked by libidinal ties to the leader, as well as to the other members of the group (see Figure 14–2). For example, in the Roman Catholic Church, each church member is tied to the leader (Christ), as well as to other Catholics, and these two-way libidinal

libido the energy of those instincts that have to do with all that may be included under the term *love*.

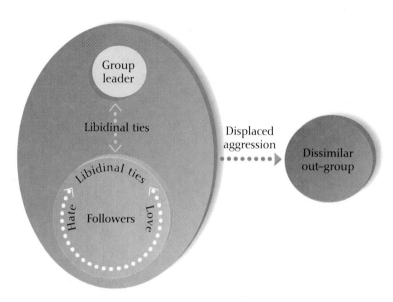

Figure 14–2   A Freudian model of intergroup relations.

ties ensure effective group cohesion. Similarly, in an army, the troops have libidinal ties to the commander in chief, as well as to each other.

But libidinal ties involve hatred as well as love, conflict as well as harmony. In Freud's psychology, love and hate are fused, so that the presence of one means the other is also there (Freud, 1921/1953–1964). This is one reason, Freud would argue, that a couple can show deep love one day but intense hatred the next; be in a perfect marriage for years, then become embroiled in a no-holds-barred divorce proceeding. The presence of both love and hate in libidinal relationships means that some level of psychological ambivalence exists in groups.

How do groups deal with the mixed feelings of their members? The answer to this question is provided by a brilliant but pessimistic insight: One can always "bind together a considerable number of people in love so long as there are other people left over to receive the manifestations of their aggressiveness" (Freud, 1930, p. 114). Freud argued that negative feelings within groups will be redirected or displaced, through the influence of the leadership, toward nonmembers. The targets of such displaced aggression are not selected randomly. Rather, they are selected systematically on the basis of similarity: The more dissimilar the out-group, the more likely its members will become a target. Thus, for example, an ethnic group will displace aggression onto more dissimilar ethnic out-groups.

Freud's model is "hydraulic" in the sense that he believed the energies motivating group behavior do not dissipate if they do not attain their original goal, but become redirected onto an alternative target. This idea was taken up in frustration-aggression theory, which asserts that frustration always leads to some form of aggression and aggression always stems from frustration (Dollard, Doob, Miller,

Mowrer, & Sears, 1939). Subsequent research has shown that frustration, being an unpleasant experience, leads to aggression only under some conditions (see Chapter 11), but the original frustration–aggression hypothesis, inspired by Freud, proved to be highly stimulating to researchers.

Freud's Theory: An Evaluation.

Freud explained intergroup conflict in terms of psychological ambivalence and displaced aggression. Rather than seeing material interests as the cause of war, he argued that nations put forward their interests in order to justify their irrational actions ("passions"). Freud's group psychology is of contemporary and perhaps universal importance because of three central themes he introduced: first, the idea that psychological states, such as unconscious feelings of resentment and frustration, serve as the original source of intergroup aggression; second, the view that through displaced aggression a group can increase internal cohesion and rally more effectively behind a leader; third, the view that similarity plays an important role in intergroup attraction.

Although Freud wrote with great insight, not all of his propositions about intergroup relations are precise and focused enough to be testable. But in several important instances they have been tested, and subsequent research has supported his views. For example, the role he envisaged for similarity in intergroup relations has been supported by modern research (Byrne, 1971; Osbeck, Moghaddam, & Perreault, 1997; Pilkington & Lydon, 1997). It seems that in everyday life the notion that "opposites attract" is seldom true and that similarity does lead to attraction in the vast majority of cases.

But each of the main contributions made by Freud to an understanding of intergroup relations has severe cultural limitations. First, his notion that psychological energies act as the original source of intergroup conflict takes on a different meaning when we consider that some groups have managed to live in peaceful conditions for long periods of their known history (these include groups in the United States, such as the Amish, as well as the Tiwi and other non-Western groups; see Eibl-Eibesfeldt, 1989, and his discussion of an innate inhibition against killing). If what Freud discovered was truly a universal process, then we should not find such wide variations in intergroup aggression. Second, displaced aggression may under certain conditions strengthen group cohesion and group leadership, but this prediction makes more sense in hierarchical societies in which leadership is more formalized. Third, culture prescribes the kind of similarity that influences intergroup relations. In traditional cultures, for example, by far the most important basis for similarity is often family ties. If a person is a member of the family group, then he could be completely dissimilar on all other criteria but still be treated preferentially. Finally, Freud's emphasis on irrationality and the inevitability of conflict is peculiarly European, and comes from a long tradition of viewing society as composed of groups with clashing interests (see Taylor & Moghaddam, 1994).

Equity Theory

"A global village has to be open in order to be fair," insisted one of the participants in our discussion that night in New York. Whenever people discuss intergroup relations and multiculturalism, justice and fairness become central concerns. Equity theory is primarily concerned with what people think is fair, and how they behave when they believe they are not being treated justly (Messick & Cook, 1983; Walster, Walster, & Berscheid, 1978). Like Freud's approach to intergroup relations, equity theory gives primary importance to subjective perceptions of the world. Also, just as in the case of Freud, equity theory is heavily influenced by the culture in which it has been developed, in this case the United States.

Equity theory follows the U.S. tradition of conceptualizing human relationships as being a form of economic exchange (Blau, 1964; Homans, 1961, 1974). The terminology of equity theory—"inputs," "outcomes," "investments," "profits," "costs," "rewards"—portrays a marketplace. A major goal of each individual is to maximize personal outcomes by manipulating inputs and outcomes. Inputs are the contributions (such as skills, efforts) a person or group makes in a transaction, and outcomes are the rewards or punishments they receive (such as monetary or status benefits or losses). But at the heart of the theory is perceived justice: **Equity theory** proposes that individuals try to achieve justice in their relationships and feel distress when they perceive injustice. A situation is perceived to be just when the ratio of inputs to outcomes for one party in an exchange is equal to the input/outcome ratio of the other party (see Figure 14–3).

equity theory theory that conceptualizes human relationships as a form of economic exchange, and assumes that people are motivated to achieve equitable relationships and will be unhappy with inequity even when they benefit from the situation.

Maintaining Psychological Balance. Equity theory assumes that if people perceive this ratio to be unequal, they will experience psychological discomfort. For example, if the top managers in a corporation feel that the ratio of their inputs to outcomes is far less than the input/outcome ratio for workers, they will feel uncomfortable about this situation. In this sense, equity theory is in the tradition of U.S. psychological theories that give central place to the idea of psychological balance (see the discussion on psychological balance and cognitive dissonance theory in Chapter 4). But the theory proposes that balance can be restored through psychological manipulation of inputs and outcomes

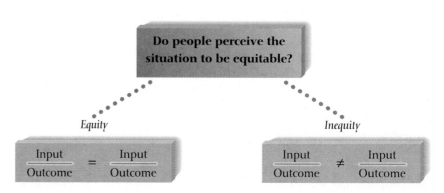

Figure 14–3 Schematic representation of equity theory (after Taylor & Moghaddam, 1994).

as well as an actual change in inputs and outcomes. That is, rather than actually changing how much they and the workers put in (for example, changing hours of work) and how much they get out (changing hourly wages), top managers can simply change their psychological assessments of inputs and outcomes (a CEO may reason that "the value of my work as CEO is much higher during these days of corporate downsizing, so it is only fair that I receive a million–dollar bonus this year. If it were not for me, a lot of the workers would have been laid off.").

A very effective and often used way of restoring psychological equity is to blame the victim. About 2,500 years ago, the Greek historian Herodotus described the abduction of Greek women by Persian raiders and commented that according to the Persians "it is obvious that no young woman allows herself to be abducted if she did not wish to be" (1954, p. 14). The views of people toward rape victims in our own era reflect a similar attitude (Thornton, 1992). The *just-world hypothesis* proposes that people blame the victim because they are motivated to see the world as just, and so anything that happens to other people is the fault of individuals rather than society (Lerner, 1977, 1980). Presumably, we feel safer conceiving of the world as a place where bad things happen only to people who deserve them.

Equity Theory: An Evaluation.   The equity theory view that humans are in exchange relationships may be valid for middle–class North America, where economic values seem to pervade so much of life, even intimate relationships of liking and loving (Billig, 1976; Deutsch, 1975; Sampson, 1975). But there is evidence that even in this context, equity becomes less important than equality for some groups (Watson, 1985). For example, evidence suggests that compared with males, females are more likely to be concerned with equality (rewards should be allocated equally, independent of inputs) than equity (greatest rewards should go to those with highest inputs) when allocating rewards (Leventhal & Lane, 1970).

A number of important social psychological theories, such as equity theory, are based on the idea of social exchange. They assume that social relationships involve give and take. People make investments and expect appropriate outcomes, just like these traders on the French stock market in Paris. When group members do not receive adequate returns, they become dissatisfied and try to change the situation. Research suggests that although such descriptions may be appropriate for some temporary relationships, long–term relationships often involve commitment and an explicit rejection of the whole idea of exchange.

Ultimately, equity theory is a reflection of a cognitive approach that reigned supreme in the 1970s and 1980s, in which people were conceptualized as self-serving, calculating decision makers. The French social psychologist Serge Moscovici (1972) said he found it difficult to understand this view of social life until he visited the United States and appreciated the culture that gave rise to this perspective. But a deeper analysis of American society as we near the twenty–first century suggests that the social exchange approach misses the mark in the United States itself. Issues of justice are not resolved by isolated minds, they are based on social relationships and the norms and rules that evolve from relationships. When Charlotte remains loyal to her partner even though he has AIDS, this is not because of her mental calculations of inputs and outcomes, but probably in spite of them. Her relationships with her partner, their families, and their community and the norms and rules she sees as appropriate tell her what is correct behavior for her in this situation. Like most people most of the time, she behaves correctly according to local norms and rules.

Relative Deprivation Theory

"One thing the global village and the communications revolution have done is to help me appreciate how fortunate we are in the West," explained one of my dinner companions that evening. "All those television images of famine, war, thousands of refugees on the move . . . we really are relatively fortunate."

Any time a group of people assess their own situation, they tend to do so by making comparisons with people in other groups (see Olson & Hafer, 1996; Olson, Herman, & Zanna, 1986). Leon Festinger's (1954) original formulation of social comparison theory proposed that people make social comparisons in order to arrive at an accurate assessment of their own abilities and opinions. More recent research shows that social comparisons play a wider role in decisions about entitlements (Kruglanski & Mayseless, 1990). For example, how employees feel about the salaries they receive ("Am I paid enough?") will depend a great deal on how they compare with similar others ("No, my salary is too low compared to others with similar qualifications and experience"). These judgments have more to do with arriving at a subjective picture of relative standing than achieving an objective assessment of worth.

relative deprivation a belief that one is worse off than others with whom one compares oneself.

The main challenge facing relative deprivation theorists has been to specify the conditions under which people feel deprived. **Relative deprivation** is a belief that one is worse off than others with whom one compares oneself. Typically, researchers have presented participants with a scenario about an individual who lacked a desired characteristic, X, and have incorporated as independent variables in the scenario the factors assumed to be important in bringing about relative deprivation (dependent variable). Different versions of the scenario present the person as (1) seeing or not seeing another person who possesses X, (2) feeling that he is or is not entitled to X, (3) having or not having attained X in the past, or (4) assumed or did not assume responsibility for currently lacking X (see Figure 14–4). Participants are asked to study the

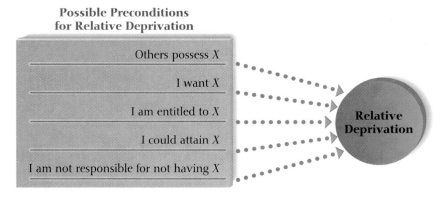

**Possible Preconditions
for Relative Deprivation**

Others possess *X*

I want *X*

I am entitled to *X*

I could attain *X*

I am not responsible for not having *X*

**Relative
Deprivation**

Figure 14–4 Relative deprivation theory.

scenario and assess the extent to which the main character would experience feelings of deprivation (see Bernstein & Crosby, 1980; Crosby, 1982). This line of research has not led to a clear picture of any systematic relationships between preconditions or causes and feelings of relative deprivation.

Some effort has been made to distinguish between feelings of deprivation at the personal or "egoistical" level ("I am badly off compared to other people in my group") and the intergroup or "fraternal" level ("My group is badly off compared to other groups") (Runciman, 1966). Of particular interest here is the possibility that fraternal deprivation will help predict collective action. Suppose Dick feels fraternal deprivation and Sam does not; presumably Dick is the potential activist, the one who is more likely to join in collective action to improve the lot of his group. Surely feelings of group deprivation should be linked to collective action?

Paper-and-pencil assessments that have asked research participants what they would do under certain conditions have shown fraternal deprivation to be a better predictor of discontent than egoistical (individualistic/personal) deprivation for a number of groups, including white Americans, African-Americans, Chinese immigrants, French-Canadians, and Muslims in India (Abeles, 1976; Dibble, 1981; Dion, 1986; Guimond & Dube-Simard, 1983; Tripathi & Srivastava, 1981; Vanneman & Pettigrew, 1972). However, the relationship between feelings of relative deprivation and actual behavior has been demonstrated in only a small number of studies (Birt & Dion, 1987).

One reason for the complexity of the relationship between reported feelings of deprivation and actual behavior may be that people often manage self-presentations according to social goals, rather than private feelings. Janet feels relatively deprived and believes her salary should be higher, but presents herself as cheerful and contented when meeting with the company president. The Canadian researcher Jim Olson and his associates have explored this issue (Olson & Hafer, 1996), which originates from Erving Goffman's (1956) account of self-presentation in everyday life (see also Jones & Pittman, 1982). They found that under some conditions research participants altered their self-presentations to match that of their partners. If the partners were angry about a situation, for example, they, too, would show anger. Presumably, participants behaved in this way so as to be better liked by their partners.

Relative Deprivation Theory: An Evaluation. Perhaps the greatest challenge to researchers who give primacy to psychological factors is to establish concrete links between the subjective experiences of people and their actual behaviors. Little headway has been made toward this goal, opening up this line of research to the criticism that psychological factors are irrelevant to the study of collective action (McCarthy & Zald, 1977). Some researchers have argued that material factors determine psychological experiences (realistic conflict theory, on the right of the continuum in Fig. 14–1). Researchers who believe in the primacy of psychological factors would have a much stronger case if they took into consideration the role of culture rather than attempting to manufacture causal relations between psychological factors (such as feelings of deprivation) and behavior (such as aggressivity) independent of culture.

This becomes clear when we consider cultural differences in how people are trained to cope with feelings of frustration, deprivation, and general dissatisfaction with unfair treatment. Cultural norms prescribe what is just and unjust in the first place, as well as correct responses to different conditions, a topic we discuss further at the end of this chapter. For example, Western visitors to Bombay and other major Indian cities often express astonishment at the passive manner in which millions of people accept their life conditions. Literally entire families live on the streets, in intensely crowded and impoverished environments. Why are there not riots, as sometimes happens in major cities in the United States, when minorities experience injustices? One explanation for such passivity could be a religion that socializes individuals to accept their fate in the present life and patiently await changed conditions in the next.

But we need not go as far as India to find such examples. Consider the situation of racial minorities and indigenous people in North America. One of the major reasons for the lack of effective collective action by minorities against exploitation by Western European settlers is that they often lacked a clear idea of when and how they were being treated unjustly (see Bolaria & Li, 1988). For example, Native Americans, who did not believe that land could be personal property, did not appreciate the injustice of trading land for trinkets.

Related to this is cross-cultural research showing that men have a higher preference for hierarchical relationships between social groups and a "winner take all" attitude in competitive intergroup situations (Sidanius, Pratto, & Bobo, 1994; Sidanius, Pratto, & Rabinowitz, 1994). An implication is that men are more tolerant of inequalities between groups.

Concepts and Issues

Primacy is given to psychological factors by Freudian theory, relative deprivation theory, and equity theory accounts of intergroup relations. These theories emphasize the irrational nature of human behavior and the fact that conflicts often lead to fewer material resources for all groups.

1. Give examples of the ethnic revival from your observations and everyday experiences.
2. What is an irrationalist view of behavior?
3. Have you witnessed displaced aggression? Give examples.
4. What influence does culture have on how people experience and cope with frustration, deprivation, and fairness?

Theories Based on Material Conditions

Two major theories give particular importance to material conditions and resources: social identity theory and realistic conflict theory. A number of newer and less influential theories also share this orientation, including the five-stage model and resource mobilization theory.

Social Identity Theory

"I do not believe the global village will work out," protested one of my dinner companions, "because people do not want to become like everyone else. We all want to be different, but of course in a positive way. Think about what would happen if you went to a party in a new outfit, and a longtime friend came up and complimented you on how great you looked, but added that right in the next room at the same party there is a person in exactly the same outfit. In fact, you two look the same, almost like twins. Despite the fact that your friend said you look wonderful, the idea of there being at the same party a person who looks just like you and is wearing the same outfit would not be at all pleasant. You would probably feel unhappy about this situation."

The idea that people want identities that are both positive and distinct is central to social identity theory. **Social identity theory** proposes that people strive to achieve a positive social identity and will take individualistic or collective steps to remedy the situation if they feel they have an inadequate social identity. This is the most influential intergroup theory since the 1980s (Abrams & Hogg, 1990; Tajfel, 1982; Tajfel & Turner, 1979).

social identity theory
proposition that people strive to achieve a positive social identity and will take steps to remedy the situation if they feel they have an inadequate social identity.

The Minimal Group Paradigm. Imagine you are asked to participate in a laboratory study. At the laboratory, you are asked to estimate the number of dots flashed onto a screen. In a second and apparently unrelated part of the research, you are told you will be allocating points to unidentified members of groups X and Y. For the sake of convenience, the criterion for membership in these groups is how many dots a person estimated on the first task. You have just taken part in the minimal group paradigm, a laboratory procedure through which participants are placed in groups labeled X and Y on a trivial basis, then found to show in-group favoritism.

The findings of the minimal group paradigm were a surprise when they were first reported in the early 1970s, because they seemed to demonstrate intergroup bias in a situation involving "minimal" or even meaningless groups. This seemed to suggest that factors such as common goals, common fate, similarity, and attraction are not necessary for groups to form and intergroup bias to occur. As soon as people are categorized into two groups, even with labels such as X and Y, they could show intergroup bias (of course, this does not negate the possibility that in some situations people show favoritism toward out-groups rather than in-groups, as found in the case of some ethnic minority members; see Taylor & Moghaddam, 1994). Social identity theory evolved out of attempts to explain this puzzling finding.

Social identity is that part of a person's self-concept which is derived from membership in social groups. For example, Kelly spends a lot of time playing basketball, and her social identity is in large part derived from the value and emotional significance attached to her being on the basketball team. A number of different theoretical orientations have developed from the original theory (Taylor & Moghaddam, 1994, Chapter 4), but their central element remains social identity.

How do people react when they feel they have an inadequate social identity (i.e., one that is not distinct and/or positive)? This is the most important question addressed by social identity theory. When their social identity is inadequate, the theory postulates, people will try to change the situation (see Figure 14–5). Which strategy they select will depend on a number of conditions. If they perceive the present intergroup situation as unstable ("We *can* change our group position compared to other groups") and illegitimate ("The present intergroup situation is *not* right"), they will use one or several of these strategies: absorption, redefining characteristics, creativity, and direct challenge.

Absorption involves attempting to merge into a majority group so as to share their rewards. An example is immigrants to the United States assimilating into mainstream culture, learning English, and changing their cultures and even their names. A classic illustration of *redefining characteristics* is the slogan "Black is beautiful." A more recent example is

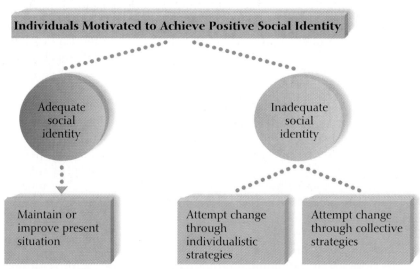

Figure 14–5   Schematic representation of social identity theory (after Taylor & Moghaddam, 1994).

Vietnamese–American teenagers raise money for a Boy Scout troop. Perhaps the most important feature of any culture is its dynamism; cultures constantly evolve. In immigrant–receiving societies, such as the United States and Canada, this dynamism is evident and generally accepted: Each new group of immigrants brings with it different ways of life, and influences the main body of society. The mainstream in such societies is constantly changing and being rejuvenated by fresh ideas and lifestyles. A similar process is now underway in many European societies, even those which on the surface might have seemed impervious to outside influences. The impact of South Asians in the United Kingdom, North Africans in France, and Turks in Germany makes this clear.

the redefinition of feminine management styles as positive, so that empathy and other "feminine" qualities become desirable. A group may use *creativity*, for example, by introducing new dimensions for intergroup comparison and evaluation, such as Native Americans introducing their ancient cultural traditions as a basis for comparison with those of settlers from Western Europe. Finally, a minority group may *directly challenge* majority groups and attempt to change the intergroup situation through direct and explicit competition. Direct challenge is the strategy that is most likely to lead to **social change**—change in the relative power and status of minority and majority groups.

social change   change in the relative power and status of majority and minority groups.

social mobility attempt to exit from the minority group and gain entrance to a higher-status group.

When people feel they have inadequate social identities but do not see alternatives to the present situation ("There is no way the situation will ever change") and view the present situation as legitimate ("Things are right as they are"), two main individualistic strategies are available. One is **social mobility:** A person attempts to exit from the minority group and gain entrance to a higher-status group. For example, Daphne tries to move from her present losing baseball team and get a place on a winning team. Of course, social mobility is not possible if a group is closed and exit from it is impossible. Daphne could not exit from her sex group and become a male (although in rare cases people do have sex-change operations). The other strategy, intragroup comparison, involves people comparing themselves to other in-group members to arrive at a more favorable social identity ("My salary and treatment are not good compared to those of the male lawyers in the company, but compared to those of the other women I am very well off").

Social Identity Theory: An Evaluation.

Social identity theory provides a highly stimulating and useful account of intergroup relations as far as it goes, but the theory actually stops short just when group life gets most interesting. Among the issues neglected by social identity theory that research shows to be culturally dependent, four are of particular importance. The first concerns the extent to which people want to belong to groups rather than remaining outside as independent individuals. Marilyn Brewer and her associates (Brewer, 1991; Brewer, Manzi, & Shaw, 1993) have proposed in **optimal distinctiveness theory** that individuals are motivated to achieve an equilibrium between opposing needs for assimilation (belonging to groups) and differentiation (remaining independent from groups). Evidence suggests that such needs are culturally dependent, so that in collectivistic cultures people feel a greater need to have very strong ties with a few groups, whereas in individualistic cultures people feel a need to have a more casual membership in a larger number of groups, but remain more independent of any one group (Triandis, 1995).

optimal distinctiveness theory proposition that individuals are motivated to achieve equilibrium between opposing needs for assimilation and differentiation.

A second issue that needs more attention concerns the relationship between self-esteem and intergroup discrimination (Hogg & Abrams, 1990). Social identity theory evolved out of laboratory research on minimal groups (Taylor & Moghaddam, 1994, pp. 70–73). Tajfel and his associates discovered that even when participants were categorized arbitrarily into groups X and Y on the basis of a trivial criterion, without direct contact with other group members and without knowledge of their identities, participants would still show favoritism toward the in-group. This finding raises questions about the relationship between self-esteem and discrimination. Does discrimination lead to a higher self-esteem for the source of discrimination? Does Sandy's self-esteem increase as a result of her not selling her house to a member of an ethnic minority? Or is it that low self-esteem leads to discrimination against out-groups (Hogg & Sunderland, 1991)? (Sandy suffers low self-esteem, and as a result discriminates against ethnic minorities.)

Finally, social identity theory outlines a series of strategies people could adopt when they feel their social identities are inadequate, but it neglects the vitally important issue of the *preferences people show*. Will they, for example, give priority to absorption, redefining characteristics, or social mobility? If Sandy has the option of absorption or social mobility as a means of improving her social identity, which will she prefer? This shortcoming is to some extent addressed by the five-stage model of intergroup relations (Taylor & McKirnan, 1984).

The Five-Stage Model

The **five-stage model** proposes that all intergroup relations pass through the same five stages in the same order, and that the most capable members of a disadvantaged group will first attempt to move into the advantaged group individually. Only if they find their path to progress unfairly blocked will they resort to collective action. This was demonstrated in studies by Donald Taylor and his associates (Taylor, Moghaddam, Gamble, & Zellerer, 1987; Wright, Taylor, & Moghaddam, 1990). Participants in these studies started by being members of an "unsophisticated decision making group," with the task of assessing the case of a pizza delivery man who is stabbed by one of his clients. Participants were told that they could move up to become a member of the "sophisticated decision making group" if their assessment was judged to be good enough. In the second part of the study, participants were provided with feedback about their performance.

In one condition, participants were given blatantly unfair assessments and were discriminated against ("We do not want you in the sophisticated group because of your sex"). Next, participants selected from a range of alternative courses of action, including acceptance of the decision, individual protest, retaking the test individually, or collective action. Results show that participants far preferred individual courses of action. Even when the possibility of success through personal action was as low as 2 percent, they still selected individual rather than collective action. This preference for individualistic responses to perceived discrimination has also been reported by Richard Lalonde and his colleagues (Lalonde & Cameron, 1994; Lalonde, Majumder, & Parris, 1995; Lalonde & Silverman, 1994). Even when ethnic minority participants faced overt discrimination in important domains such as housing and employment, they still preferred individual action.

The research of Carolyn Hafer and Jim Olson (1993; in press) suggests that individuals who have a stronger belief in a just world are less likely to take action in situations in which they are treated negatively. They are more likely to attribute the negative outcome to some aspect of themselves that they cannot do anything about, or to bad luck ("I just do not have the ability," "It is my fate," and so on). Of course, this kind of self-defeating orientation to negative experiences is more likely for people who are socialized to believe they have less talent and should expect fewer successes, as is still the case for minorities in many parts of the world.

This brings us to an important negative implication from research related to the five-stage model concerning **tokenism,** the practice of

five-stage model proposition that all intergroup relations pass through the same five stages in the same order, and that the most capable disadvantaged group members will first attempt to move into the advantaged group individually.

tokenism the practice of appearing to implement equality of opportunity by including or hiring a representative of a minority group.

some organizations of appearing to implement equality of opportunity by hiring a representative of a minority group. Research suggests that tokens do work to safeguard the existing power structure because the presence of even a token diminishes the probability of collective action (Wright, Taylor, & Moghaddam, 1990). Minorities seem to say to themselves, "Well, that black woman made it to the top, so it must mean the way is open for us all." This leads them to try to get ahead individually rather than to try to mobilize their group to reform the system. Second, tokenism gives minorities a sense that they are expected to do poorly and this further handicaps them (Saenz & Lord, 1989). Laurie Cohen and Janet Swim's (1995) research suggests that being a token handicaps women more than men.

However, there are several reasons to be more hopeful about the possibility of collective action by minorities experiencing discrimination. Field research among ethnic minorities demonstrates that individual mobility was preferred by the less talented rather than the more talented, as predicted by the five-stage model (Moghaddam & Perreault, 1992). This research suggests that the preferences shown by disadvantaged group members for different strategies for improving their position will be highly associated with cultural values. Also, there needs to be a refinement of the measures used to assess preferences for different types of behavior in response to discrimination. More refined measures reveal a picture of members of minority groups as highly resentful of their predicament and supportive of group responses (Louis & Taylor, 1997). Taken together, these factors suggest solid potential for collective action among minorities.

Realistic Conflict Theory

"I once read a science fiction novel about aliens attacking the earth, and in order to defend themselves all humans had to put aside national and other differences and cooperate," explained one of our dinner companions during that evening in New York. "A world government was formed and slowly but surely everyone realized how petty ethnic, religious, and other differences are, and how very similar all human beings are. I think if we had a common goal, such as having to defend earth against aliens, then we would quickly make the global village a reality. But without a common goal, we compete with each other for a bigger piece of the global pie, and inevitably get into fights with competitor groups."

The idea that common goals bring people together, or that group conflicts arise out of real clashes of interests, is not new or surprising. In our everyday lives we often assume that if two persons or groups both want a resource that is scarce, such as two nations wanting control of the same oil fields, conflict between them is likely to arise. Moreover, conflicts over material resources will lead the two groups to hold negative attitudes toward each other. On the other hand, when the material interests of two groups coincide, they will think well of one another and the members of each group will be positively disposed to the

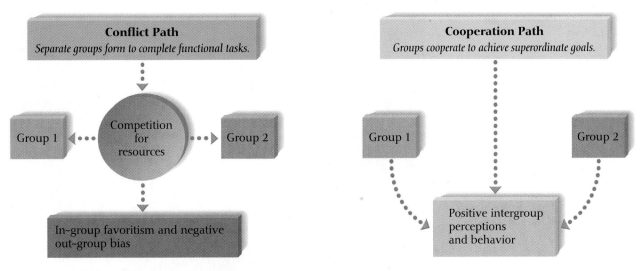

Figure 14–6 Realistic conflict theory.

members of the other. This "materialist" explanation of intergroup relations is the basis of realistic conflict theory, which proposes that intergroup conflict arises from conflicts over material resources (Sherif, 1966) (see Figure 14–6). What is surprising about this theory, which gives primacy to economic factors and is in this sense similar to Marxist theory, is that it was developed in the United States, a capitalist society.

Realistic conflict theory is closely connected to a specific series of field studies (Sherif, 1951, 1966; Sherif, Harvey, White, Hood, & Sherif, 1961; Sherif & Sherif, 1953). These studies were conducted in summer camps, with the experimenters acting as camp staff. Participants were all white middle–class boys aged 11 to 12 years, purposely selected to form a homogeneous population so that sex, ethnicity, and other factors could not act as a basis for group formation and discrimination.

There were four stages to the studies. During *friendship formation*, the boys arrived at the camp and got to know each other. The researchers studied and recorded friendship patterns. During *group formation*, the boys were divided into two groups in a way that ensured that best friends were always separated. This was done in order to discount interpersonal attraction as an explanation for later group cohesion and intergroup aggression. During *intergroup conflict*, the two groups competed in a series of tasks, such as tug–of–war and bean toss. During the fierce competitions that ensued, the groups of boys developed very negative attitudes toward one another. Out–group members, who included former best friends, now became hated enemies, and their projects and belongings were attacked and damaged. More aggressive individuals emerged to take over leadership positions in each group.

Having arrived at a situation of intergroup conflict, the challenge now was to once again achieve peaceful relations. How was this to be

Greenpeace activists hang a banner on the Arc de Triomphe in Paris in 1992. A powerful idea for achieving intergroup harmony is *superordinate goals,* and perhaps the best example of such goals is environmental protection. All of us desire this goal, but none of us can achieve it without the cooperation of others. But even such an obviously important goal is associated with intergroup conflict. The French secret police blew up one of the Greenpeace vessels near New Zealand, in an effort to stifle protests against French nuclear testing in the Pacific.

superordinate goals   goals that both conflicting groups desire, but that neither can achieve without the cooperation of the other.

done? The solution researchers arrived at was to use **superordinate goals,** goals that both groups desire to achieve but that neither can achieve without the cooperation of the other. In one situation, a truck bringing food to the camp apparently broke down and the boys had to cooperate in order to achieve the superordinate goal of bringing in their food. After several such incidents, during which the material interests of the boys coincided, their attitudes toward one another gradually changed to being positive. The fundamental idea was that material conditions determine psychological processes in intergroup relations.

Resource Mobilization Theory

Another influential theory that adopts a materialist view of intergroup relations is **resource mobilization theory,** which proposes that conflicts arise when those with resources mobilize people to take collective action (McCarthy & Zald, 1977) (see Figure 14–7). In answer to the question "What gives rise to riots and other forms of collective action?" relative deprivation theory and other psychologically based accounts of intergroup relations respond that it takes psychological factors, such as feelings of frustration and anger. Nonsense, say the resource mobilization theorists; feelings and frustrations do not account for collective action. What makes collective action possible is resources (defined very broadly to include money, status, intellectual abilities, skills, and the like). If one has the resources, one can manufacture and manipulate feelings of discontent. This explains why collective movements arise in certain historical eras and not others.

For example, why did the civil rights movement and the women's liberation movement gain momentum in the United States in the 1960s and 1970s? Was it because African-Americans and women were treated particularly badly and came to feel higher levels of deprivation? Not at all; they had always been mistreated, and the potential for their feeling intense relative deprivation was always present. However, the new element in the 1960s and 1970s was that people with resources decided it was in their own interests to change the situation. The media and the education system were used to mobilize these collective movements. Resource mobilization theory, then, claims that with adequate resources it is possible to influence collective movements in important ways.

But resources and culture are both involved in the process of conflict, according to an intriguing new approach to the topic. In exploring the roots of violence, Ervin Staub (1989, 1996) has provided an expansive account that begins with material conditions, in the realistic conflict

resource mobilization theory theory that conflicts arise when those with resources mobilize people to take collective action.

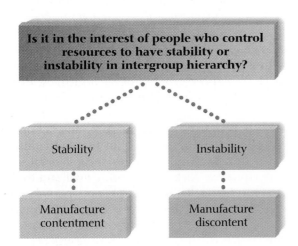

Figure 14–7 Resource mobilization theory.

tradition, but also incorporates culture. Staub's account is basically materialist, in that he views difficult life conditions as creating the potential for intergroup violence. The extent to which this potential is realized, however, depends on cultural rules and norms.

Staub (1989, 1996) begins with the proposition that humans have certain fundamental needs, such as for material necessities and a positive identity. Under difficult life conditions, it becomes extremely challenging to meet these needs. People can organize and solve life problems, but events might also take a more destructive turn. For example, people might elevate their own group in order to appear superior to others. They might target particular minorities as scapegoats. The cultural characteristics that increase the potential for a group experiencing difficulties to turn against others include: a history of devaluation, when it is normative for group members to devalue out-groups; authority orientation, when it is normative to obey authority figures; and orientation on pluralism, when minority cultures are marginalized and minority voices are ignored.

Justice and Culture

Central to all of the major intergroup theories is the issue of justice (Deutsch, 1973, 1985). Are women receiving fair treatment in society? Is this a just society for ethnic minorities? These are fundamentally important questions, but as social psychologists we must take a further step and ask: Do people apply principles of justice in the same manner across contexts?

That principles of justice will be consistent across situations is advocated by Lawrence Kohlberg's (1963, 1976) model of moral reasoning. Three broad sequences of moral reasoning are proposed: *preconventional* (behavior guided by reward and punishment—"I will not drink and drive because I would get caught and punished"); *conventional* (behavior guided by social convention—"I will not drink and drive because it is against the law"); and *postconventional* or *principled* (behavior guided by general moral principles—"I will not drink and drive because I might hurt someone, and it is wrong to put lives in danger"). According to Kohlberg, only those who reach the stage of postconventional reasoning can be expected to apply general moral principles. He argued that these individuals apply principles of justice in a similar manner across contexts.

An alternative perspective is to argue that most adults are capable of applying postconventional reasoning, but that individuals will do so only when such a strategy would support their general viewpoint. In support of this perspective, Nick Emler and his colleagues (Emler, 1983; Emler & Hogan, 1981; Emler, Renwick, & Malone, 1983) found that individuals of left-wing, moderate, and right-wing persuasions shifted their ground on moral principles, depending on circumstances (see also Sparks & Durkin, 1987). This may remind you of the actions of certain politicians who tend to staunchly uphold and then completely lose sight of key principles as they go in and out of office.

In another series of studies, participants were presented with moral dilemmas and asked to evaluate the behavior of a central character (Moghaddam & Vuksanovic, 1990). For example, one scenario was about a mother who was caught shoplifting, and in her defense argued that she stole food for her children. Another scenario involved a television anchorwoman who refused to change her hairstyle and clothing to suit the demands of her employers. Participants were found to change their judgment of such actions, depending on whether the mother was described as "Mrs. Singh in New Delhi" or "Mrs. Lambert in Montreal" or "Mrs. Borzov in Moscow." The Canadian participants in these studies showed stronger support for human rights in New Delhi and Moscow than they did in the Montreal context, perhaps because they saw a greater need in the first two settings.

Thus, it seems that people uphold principles of justice to different degrees across contexts. Other research suggests that there are important cross-cultural variations in ideas about justice. For example, comparisons involving Japanese and Australians (Kashima, Siegel, Tanaka, & Isaka, 1988), Indians and Americans (Berman & Singh, 1985), Chinese and Americans (Leung & Bond, 1984; Leung & Lind, 1986), Japanese and Americans (Mahler, Greenberg, & Hayashi, 1981), Colombians and Americans (Marin, 1981), Koreans, Japanese, and Americans (Kim, Park, & Suzuki, 1990), and Turks and Americans (Aral & Sunar, 1977) strongly suggest that the principles of justice people use often vary in important ways, as do preferences for how conflicts over justice issues should be resolved. For example, a common finding is that a system of reward allocation based on needs rather than merit is seen as less just by participants in the United States and other individualistic cultures than by participants in India and other more collectivistic cultures.

Some Practical Applications

Although the materialist approach to intergroup relations may appear to be harsh (or even cynical), it has led to some highly interesting practical applications, particularly through the concept of superordinate goals. In industrial relations, for example, dispute negotiators have used superordinate goals to resolve conflicts between management and labor unions (Blake & Mouton, 1962). In education, a "jigsaw" procedure has been introduced, placing students in project groups and giving each member of the group information that is vital for the successful completion of the entire project. In this way, students become interdependent, and the cooperation of everyone is required in order for the group to succeed in its assigned task (Aronson, Stephen, Sikes, Blaney, & Snapp, 1978). Results of repeated experimental trials with the jigsaw classroom show that it improves cooperation and liking across ethnic lines, leads to a more positive attitude toward schooling, and even improves self-esteem and exam performance.

The jigsaw classroom, however, seems to go against the self-help ethic of U.S. culture. But we must be careful to consider both the

prisoner's dilemma game gaming research situation in which two accomplices in crime confront a dilemma: If one betrays the other, the betrayer gets off free and the other gets a heavy sentence; but if both keep quiet, both get light sentences.

positive and negative consequences of this ethic. On the negative side, the focus is on personal interests and progress, so that psychologists can be forgiven for concluding that humans in the U.S. model are basically self–centered and intent on maximizing profits. This assumption pervades gaming research, which uses paradigms such as the **prisoner's dilemma game (PDG)** to study behavior in conflict situations.

The PDG owes its name to an imaginary situation in which two accomplices in crime awaiting trial are confronted by a serious dilemma. Each prisoner has the choice of keeping quiet or informing the authorities about the crime. If both keep quiet, both get off with light sentences. If one keeps quiet and the other informs, then the one who kept quiet receives a heavy sentence and the informer is set free. If both inform, both receive a moderately severe sentence. Neither prisoner knows what the other is going to do, so each must take the risk of choosing blindly. The assumption in PDG research, as in all gaming studies, is that people will try to maximize personal rewards. (PDG research is discussed further in Chapter 15.)

But the self–centered style of behavior assumed to be the norm for the United States also has some positive consequences. The assumption, explicit in the rhetoric of right–wing political movements, is that the unburdened enterprising spirit of people pursuing personal interests leads to great productivity and wealth, and consequently brings benefits to everyone. For example, the entrepreneur who is left free to build an empire and amass a fortune will also build corporations and create thousands of jobs, leading to increased wealth for all. The American automobile engineer and manufacturer Henry Ford comes to mind, with the computer entrepreneur Bill Gates being a more recent example.

Concepts and Issues

Realistic conflict theory and resource mobilization theory give the highest importance to the role of material conditions in intergroup relations, while social identity theory and the five–stage model also give importance to this role. A central theme in all intergroup theories is justice. Perceptions of fairness in the allocation of resources is influenced by context.

1. What is the difference between personal and social identity, according to Tajfel?
2. What does social identity theory propose are the main strategies people adopt when they have an inadequate social identity?
3. "Realistic conflict theory and resource mobilization theory both propose that psychological experiences are determined by material conditions." Explain.
4. "The preferences for strategies outlined by social identity theory and the five–stage model are influenced by culture." Give examples of how preferences might vary across cultures.

From Theory to Practice: Managing Cultural Diversity

The major social psychological theories of intergroup relations have been associated with experimental studies that attempt to meet scientific criteria. For example, realistic conflict theory was developed in association with the boys' camp studies (Sherif, 1966) and social identity theory with the minimal group paradigm (Tajfel, 1982). The vast majority of social psychological research on intergroup relations has been conducted in laboratories using artificially created groups made up of students who are brought together briefly for the purposes of a study. But now we turn to a different literature, involving field studies with participants of different ethnicities, and focusing on assimilation and multiculturalism.

The Challenge of Cultural Diversity

Cultural diversity presents both challenges and opportunities (see Berry, 1984, 1991). In a highly influential book titled *Managing Cultural Differences*, Philip Harris and Robert Moran (1991) discuss how business managers can be more effective when doing business with Latin Americans, Asians, Europeans, Middle Easterners, and Africans. For example, they point out that in East Asian societies, "the group is the most important part of society and is emphasized for motivation," but in the United States the "individual is the most important part of society and the person is emphasized for motivation, although team emphasis is growing" (p. 394). Harris and Moran's discussion is part of a growing movement in the U.S. business community to become better prepared for work in the culturally diverse global market, although American managers still lag behind East Asians and Europeans in this regard (Harris & Moran, p. 8). The business world is investing in new ways of managing cultural diversity because this strategy makes sound financial sense. The global market demands that we be able to do business with people from many different cultures.

At the national level as well, governments and businesses are faced with the challenge of how best to manage cultural diversity. This challenge pervades every domain of decision making (Moghaddam, 1992a, 1994). Should city planners attempt to develop urban areas in the form of "ethnic mosaics," with identifiable ethnic neighborhoods? Or should they attempt to achieve a city in which people from different ethnic backgrounds are mixed together? Should educational, cultural, and other services be developed to strengthen ethnic cultures and the distinct features of each group, or in a way that minimizes differences and increases similarities? Today these fundamentally important questions confront all societies around the globe.

The two main approaches to managing cultural diversity have been assimilation and multiculturalism. **Assimilation** involves an attempt to achieve a more homogeneous society through the abandonment of

assimilation the abandonment of heritage cultures by minorities in an attempt to "melt into" mainstream society.

multiculturalism the retention and further development of heritage cultures, with the goal of achieving a cultural mosaic.

heritage cultures (the traditional culture of their groups) by minorities. **Multiculturalism** involves the retention and further development of heritage cultures, with the goal of achieving a cultural mosaic.

In the North American context, assimilation and multiculturalism are historically associated with the American melting pot and the Canadian celebration of diversity traditions (Lambert & Taylor, 1990). But since the 1980s, there has been a reassessment of the merits of assimilation and multiculturalism throughout North America, as well as in Australia and in other immigrant-receiving societies (National Advisory and Co-ordinating Committee on Multicultural Education, 1987; Poole, De Lacy, & Randhawa, 1985).

Assimilation in a Global Context

"Melting-pot assimilation" is a deeply entrenched theme in the United States, where the mixing of different peoples was expected to create, in the words of Ralph Waldo Emerson, "a new race, a new religion, a new state, a new literature" (see Sherman, 1921, p. xxxvi). In Israel Zangwill's play *The Melting Pot*, which became a hit at the turn of the century, America is described as "God's crucible, the great Melting Pot where all the races of Europe are melting and re-forming!" (1909, p. 37). Such "melting away" of differences was ensured in part by the pressure-cooker conditions of the American West, where settlers had to mix, co-operate, and assimilate in order to survive (Turner, 1920). By the 1920s, empirical research showed that assimilation was taking place among immigrants, and that by the second and third generations immigrant families typically lost their heritage languages, acquired English, became better educated, and moved from inner cities to suburbs as they came to enjoy the benefits of middle-class life (Park, 1950).

Assimilation has also been dominant in the former communist bloc countries, both before and after the collapse of communism. According to Marxist ideology, the focus should be on social class differences and not on ethnic, religious, gender, and other such "peripheral" group differences (Marx, 1852/1979; Marx & Engels, 1848/1967). Such reasoning led to the suppression of local, national, and ethnic movements by successive Soviet leaders, most notoriously Joseph Stalin. But a more practical reason for the suppression of cultural minorities in many countries, including Russia, has been the determination of central governments to maintain strong control. In the 1990s, for example, the attempt by Chechnya to break away from Russian control led to a long and bitter war with the central government in Moscow. The suppression of cultural and political rights in Singapore in deference to Chinese government priorities is another example.

This "practical" reason is also relevant in developing nations, where the establishment of a strong central government and a uniform national identity is seen as a prerequisite for modernization. Ethnicity and tribalism are viewed as primitive and as a threat to progress. For this reason, efforts are made to create a uniform national culture. An essential feature of such a modern culture is ideas and attitudes that promote savings, investment, and economic innovation on a *national* scale (Inkeles, 1983).

Social Psychological Assumptions Underlying Assimilation

While assimilation has been the main policy for managing cultural diversity in the United States, two different kinds of assimilation have been advocated. Robert Park (1950) assumed that **minority assimilation** takes place; that is, minorities abandon their heritage cultures and languages and take on the majority way of life. An alternative view is that **melting-pot assimilation** is taking place; that is, both minority and majority groups contribute to the formation of a new and common culture (Lieberson & Waters, 1987). Both forms of assimilation assume that intergroup differences will be washed away, and both make a number of social psychological assumptions.

A first set of arguments in favor of assimilation revolves around the assumption that similarity leads to attraction. An impressive literature exists to support the similarity–attraction hypothesis (see Chapter 8). The idea that people are positively disposed toward more similar others is supported by research at both the interpersonal level (Byrne, 1971) and the intergroup level (Brown, 1984; Osbeck, Moghaddam, & Perreault, 1997). A second set of arguments in favor of assimilation is based on the notion that differences serve as a potential basis for conflict. Earlier in this chapter, we discussed the Freudian view that dissimilar outgroups will be the target of displaced aggression. Cross–cultural evidence suggests that a vast array of societies around the world are negatively disposed toward dissimilar others (LeVine & Campbell, 1972). Presumably, if the in-group is more homogeneous there will be fewer ready-made targets within society, and displaced aggression will have to find external targets. The general thrust of these arguments is that a homogeneous society, in which people are more similar to one another, is more harmonious and cohesive.

But the significance of a homogeneous society goes far beyond the benefits reaped through similarity attraction. Central to this issue is the ideal of meritocracy, a social system whereby individuals advance and are rewarded according to personal merit. The United States wholeheartedly adopted the ideal of meritocracy, at least in theory. The New World was to have an aristocracy of talent, rather than one based on birth and descent, as in Europe. But if personal rewards and status were to be dependent on self-help and individual responsibility, it was only fair that everyone have the same opportunities. Immigrants who were not equipped with the mainstream culture and language would be at a huge disadvantage. In order for meritocracy to work, newcomers would need to assimilate into the mainstream. Those who insisted on remaining different ran the risk of becoming marginalized.

According to this proassimilation, promeritocracy view, then, the education system and other social services should be used to merge minorities into the mainstream. We next consider the assumption that by bringing people into contact under certain conditions, we create more positive intergroup relations.

The concern with intergroup contact grew out of the particular conditions of social life in the United States. The United States has been

minority assimilation abandonment of their heritage cultures by minorities and adoption of the majority way of life.

melting-pot assimilation situation in which both majority and minority groups contribute to the formation of a new and common culture.

Two U.S. firefighters on the job. Many important reforms in the United States, such as desegregation, were based on the idea that increased contact between the members of different groups leads to more positive intergroup attitudes. This assumption is shown to be valid, but only under certain conditions. Most important is that individuals from different groups must have opportunities to get to know one another well, enjoy equal status, be in cooperative rather than competitive relationships, and be in an environment that values intergroup contact and equal rights. Fortunately, at least some work environments now meet such criteria.

described as a land of immigrants, but it is also a land marked by the experience of slavery. Given the past experiences of intergroup tensions in the United States, a major concern of researchers has been: Under what conditions can we bring people together to enjoy peaceful relationships? A solution that has appealed to both researchers and practitioners is to increase contact: Desegregation in schools is an important example.

Research has led to the identification of a number of conditions that must be met in order for contact to improve intergroup relations (Amir, 1969, 1976; Pettigrew, 1986). According to the contact hypothesis, certain conditions are necessary in order to make possible reductions of stereotypes and improvements in relations: (1) social interactions are intimate so that people get to know one another, (2) the parties enjoy equal status, (3) the surrounding social climate is supportive, and (4) the purpose of the interaction is cooperation rather than competition. A major assumption is that prejudice arises out of ignorance, and the solution is to create conditions in which people get to know one another (Kalin, 1996).

Donald Taylor and I have argued that the issues of contact and conflict should be approached differently (Taylor & Moghaddam, 1994). Received wisdom tells us that relations between individuals follow relations between groups: If blacks and whites are in conflict, then individuals from these groups will also experience conflict. But evidence suggests that often relations at the interpersonal level are surprisingly amicable and do not follow relations at the intergroup level. Individuals can have amicable relationships even when their countries are at war; Romeo and Juliet love one another even though their families are enemies. How is this possible?

Evidence suggests that the following strategies are used by individuals to make this possible (Taylor & Moghaddam, 1994). Where intergroup contact is frequent and necessary, individuals can bias their interactions so that both in terms of quality and quantity, their relations with out-group members are more superficial. Their conversations with out-group members, for example, will tend to be on topics like the weather and good restaurants, rather than on justice, inequality, and other substantial issues. People can also perceive the situation and the interaction in other than intergroup terms and deny the existence of intergroup tensions. Individuals dissociate themselves from group conflict and focus on personal rather than group relationships, as did Romeo and Juliet:

> O Romeo, Romeo! wherefore art thou Romeo?
> Deny thy father, and refuse thy name:
> Or, if thou wilt not, be but sworn my love,
> And I'll no longer be a Capulet.
>
> —*Romeo and Juliet*, act II, scene 2

A Critical Assessment of Assimilation

The assimilation model faces a major challenge from research suggesting that even the most trivial of intergroup differences can be used as a basis for intergroup prejudice. This research uses the minimal group paradigm, described earlier in this chapter. Moreover, research using the minimal group paradigm shows that even a very trivial basis for social categorization can be reinterpreted as important, in order to justify in-group favoritism (Moghaddam & Stringer, 1986). To take a real-world example, even something as trivial as a very slight intergroup difference in height was used to justify intergroup differentiation and discrimination in Rwanda (Maquet, 1961), where Hutu and Tutsi groups continue to slaughter each other in the 1990s.

Given the potentially important role of even trivial differences as a basis for discrimination, the role of phenotypic characteristics (what group members look like) becomes particularly important. African-Americans, Asian-Americans, and other minorities may assimilate into the mainstream as far as attitudes, values, and lifestyle generally are concerned, but phenotypic differences between these groups and whites are likely to remain. Research using the minimal group paradigm suggests that even a slight phenotypic difference, such as skin color or facial features, can be used to differentiate and discriminate. Similarity can never be achieved to such an extent that all intergroup differences are eradicated. All of this suggests a limit to the potential of assimilation.

Multiculturalism

Multiculturalism as a policy for managing cultural diversity has been adopted officially in immigrant–receiving countries, such as Canada and Australia, which face the challenge of integrating large numbers of new arrivals annually (Moghaddam & Solliday, 1991). As a "social–intellectual movement that promotes the value of diversity as a core principle and insists that all cultural groups be treated with respect and as equals" (Flowers & Richardson, 1996, p. 609), multiculturalism is influential in many Western and non–Western societies. This newfound influence has come about mainly through the increased political power of ethnic minorities.

Within psychology, Blaine Flowers and Frank Richardson (1996) put forward four main reasons why we should attend to cultural differences. First, psychology claims to be a science of *human* behavior, and this implies that human behavior in all parts of the world, and with all its differences, must be investigated. Second, a colorblind approach to the study of human behavior is flawed because it neglects genuine differences, and it overlooks the discrimination that *does* exist. Third, a critical tradition in psychology urges the discipline to act against the exploitation and oppression of minorities. Finally, by attending to cultural differences, psychologists help to achieve a blossoming and sharing of cultures. But in order to further assess multiculturalism as a policy for managing cultural diversity, we need to clarify the varieties of multiculturalism.

Laissez-Faire versus Active Multiculturalism. Most societies include some minorities that are different in terms of ethnicity, religion, or other criteria relevant to the culture. In some cases, majority groups have a *laissez-faire* attitude in that they neither promote nor suppress cultural differences. In such situations, multiculturalism in the sense of cultural diversity persists, but not as a result of intentional supportive action on the part of majority groups. An example of this phenomenon is the persistence of Chinatowns in large urban centers in the United States and Canada. In *active multiculturalism*, majority groups

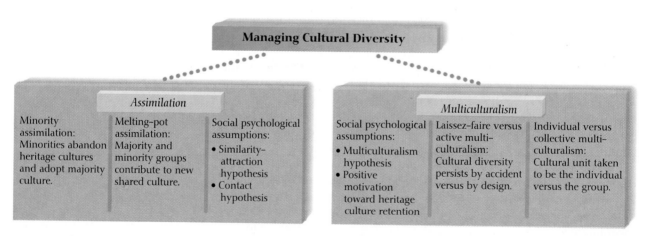

Figure 14–8 Types of assimilation and multiculturalism.

The art gallery at Wanuskewin. The new Canadian heritage park just outside the city of Saskatoon represents both the hopes and the challenges of cultural diversity. The park is called Wanuskewin, meaning "seeking peace of mind." It is devoted to the Plains Cree Indian, and within its boundaries are wildlife, prairie grasses, archaeology dig sites, and a visitors center that includes an art gallery. Such efforts raise hopes about the preservation of minority cultures, but they also raise challenges: In the future, will minority cultures be found only in heritage parks and museums?

intentionally support the cultural heritage of minorities. This is true in Canada, for example, where the federal government provides financial and legal support for minority associations, schools, and various social services. It is also true in Australia, where since the 1970s the federal government has supported the heritage culture of the Aborigines.

During the last few decades of the twentieth century, there has been a shift of emphasis from laissez-faire to active multiculturalism. This is associated with the strengthening of ethnic collective movements around the world (Belanger & Pinard, 1991). As ethnic minorities mobilize and gain political and economic influence, they are able to put pressure on public and private agencies to respond to their needs. As a consequence, these agencies offer their services in more than one language, hire more members of ethnic minorities, and offer some programs specifically directed at ethnic minorities. In Canada, for example, French, the language of a minority, now also enjoys the status of "official language."

Individual versus Collective Multiculturalism. Multiculturalism is typically associated with collectivities and group cultural characteristics. In this sense, then, the unit of analysis is exclusively the group, and the term *collective multiculturalism* is accurate, referring to the equal and respectful treatment of the heritage cultures of groups. However, such an emphasis on the group seems to contradict basic tenets of meritocracy, where the characteristics of *individuals* are supposed to be the focus. Ali is supposed to be evaluated on the basis of his individual characteristics and not his family background, ethnicity, and so on.

In order to avoid possible contradictions between collective multiculturalism and meritocracy, an alternative is to conceive of each individual as the carrier of a unique culture. Just as Maiga has special cultural characteristics, so does Zipporah. Each of them is in this sense a carrier of culture. Such *individual multiculturalism* would endorse the responsibilities and rights of each person as a cultural unit, independent of group memberships (Moghaddam, 1993). Rather than being influenced by group affiliations, people would be influenced by individual characteristics. The achievement of such an ideal would be associated with an end to prejudice and discrimination.

Linguistic Diversity. A central aspect of multicultural policy has been support for minority languages. The seminal research of the Canadian social psychologist Wallace Lambert has demonstrated the viability of additive bilingualism, meaning that learning additional languages enriches rather than detracts from scholastic performance and overall success in life (Lambert, 1969, 1978; Lambert & Taylor, 1996). In addition, educating minority children in their heritage language, the language of their own ethnic group, strengthens their self-esteem and their pride in the ethnic group (Wright & Taylor, 1995). This is a benefit not provided by learning a second language. This suggests that newcomers to North America and other immigrant-receiving societies should be encouraged to maintain their heritage languages, as well as to become proficient in the majority language.

What kinds of factors will determine whether a group retains its heritage language? According to Howard Giles and his colleagues, language retention is associated with ethnolinguistic vitality, "that which makes a group likely to behave as a distinctive and active collective entity in intergroup situations" (Giles, Bourhis, & Taylor, 1977, p. 308). A group has greater vitality when it has more members, enjoys higher status, and also has more control over resources (Giles & Coupland, 1991). The members of such a group will be proud to identify with the ethnic in-group and pass their heritage culture on to the next generation.

Of course, group identities are not static, they continually change. The French Canadian researcher Richard Clement has emphasized the fluid nature of identity; multiple identities exist and become more or less salient depending on the context (Clement & Noels, 1992; Noels & Clement, 1996). George does not present himself to Mr. Clark, his prospective father-in-law who works for the tobacco industry, in the same way as to his boss at work, who is taking legal action against the tobacco industry.

Social Psychological Assumptions Underlying Multiculturalism

At least two major social psychological assumptions underlie multiculturalism. The first is that people have positive attitudes toward the retention of minority heritage cultures and languages. Research reveals that majority group members do have such positive attitudes (Berry, 1997; Berry, Kalin, & Taylor, 1977). So do some "nonvisible" ethnic minorities (those who are phenotypically more similar to the majority; Lambert, Mermegis, & Taylor, 1986; Taylor & Lambert, 1996).

However, research shows that "visible" minority group members (those who are phenotypically more dissimilar) are ambivalent on this question. This may be because by retaining heritage cultures they will tend to be perceived as even more different and thus become more likely targets for discrimination (Moghaddam & Taylor, 1987; Moghaddam, Taylor, & Lalonde, 1987, 1989). Retaining and celebrating differences can be costly in societies in which discrimination against minorities persists, even though such discrimination may now be more subtle.

A second assumption underlying multiculturalism concerns the so-called multiculturalism hypothesis (Lambert & Taylor, 1990). This is at the heart of Canada's policy of multiculturalism and, as articulated by the former Canadian Prime Minister Pierre Elliot Trudeau, proposes that an internal sense of ethnic security would result in more open and accepting attitudes toward other groups (Government of Canada, 1971). The multiculturalism hypothesis represents an important bridge between field research on ethnic minorities and laboratory research. The common link between these two literatures is the association between social identity and behavior toward out-groups.

A Critical Assessment of Multiculturalism

The multiculturalism hypothesis and social identity theory can both be interpreted to predict that an in-group with a more positive social identity will be favorably disposed toward out-groups, but field research has not shown strong support for this idea (Berry, Kalin, & Taylor, 1977; Lambert, Mermegis, & Taylor, 1986). One problem may be that there are important exceptions to the predicted association. There are numerous historical examples of groups that outwardly seemed to have a positive social identity, but at the same time behaved extremely badly toward out-groups, such as the Nazis in 1930s Germany.

Rather than positive social identity leading to positive behavior toward out-groups, it may be that inadequate social identity leads to discrimination against out-groups. For example, in assessing the social identity of people such as Hitler, it seems reasonable to assume that underneath the outward show of confidence, they actually lack confidence: "Hitler was high-strung and habitually anxious about everything. He was a rigid and infantile character who felt deeply unworthy and was afflicted by neurotic fears and obsessions" (Fischer, 1995, p. 301).

Research on authoritarianism also suggests that extremist religious and political groups are characterized by a similar lack of confidence (Adorno et al., 1950; Altemeyer, 1981, 1988a, 1988b). Fascist movements seem to feed on fears and weaknesses in the face of perceived uncertainty and unknown threats, rather than arising out of feelings of security and confidence (Billig, 1978; Gregor, 1974). Finally, laboratory research does support the view that depressed self-esteem is associated with discrimination (Hogg & Sunderland, 1991). Consequently, although the research literature does not as yet clarify the relationship between positive social identity and positive behavior toward out-groups, a stronger case seems to exist for the idea that inadequate social identity is associated with discrimination against out-groups.

cultural relativism the viewpoint that all phenomena can be assessed only from the perspective of the culture in which they exist.

A second critical point concerns the apparent association between multiculturalism and **cultural relativism,** the viewpoint that all phenomena can be assessed only from the perspective of the culture in which they exist. This viewpoint would propose, for example, that foot binding as practiced in China or female circumcision as practiced in some Islamic countries can be judged as right or wrong only within the value system of the particular societies in which they occur. The direct implication (which is obviously flawed) is that there are no valid universal rules for assessing behavior, and that each group must judge its own people according to its own standards (Moghaddam, 1992b). According to this logic, universal human rights are not valid, and organizations such as Amnesty International have no right to interfere in the internal affairs of independent states. A similar position is taken by some hip-hop and rock groups whose music is obviously sexist and supportive of violence against women, but who claim that the majority has no right to judge their "minority culture" music.

It is a mistake to assume that multiculturalism necessarily condones cultural relativism (Moghaddam, 1992b). Indeed, in order for multiculturalism to work, there must be certain universal rules to allow communication and understanding to take place. For example, without mutual respect and orderly turn-taking, there can be no meaningful dialogue. Furthermore, in a situation in which universal rules of justice are not accepted, the weak will necessarily suffer because they cannot use the law to protect their interests.

Concepts and Issues

The concept of superordinate goals has proven useful in organizing group cooperation. One strategy for managing cultural diversity is for minority groups to assimilate into a majority culture, to make society as homogeneous as possible. But differences can be manufactured and used as a basis for differentiation and discrimination, even in seemingly homogeneous societies. Multiculturalism is a policy for managing cultural diversity. Support for heritage languages and bilingualism is a major component of this policy. The multiculturalism hypothesis receives only weak support from research evidence. Much stronger evidence is available for the concept of additive bilingualism.

1. Explain the terms *assimilation, multiculturalism,* and *heritage culture.*
2. Explain some social psychological assumptions underlying assimilation.
3. What is the multiculturalism hypothesis?

Conclusion

Intergroup relations and multiculturalism are emerging as important topics in social psychology, in part because of the increased presence of women and ethnic minorities in debates, both in social psychology and in the larger society. Many of the research leaders are either women (Jennifer Crocker, Fay Crosby, Marlyn Brewer, Charlene Nemeth, Brenda Major) or members of ethnic minorities (Muzafer Sherif, Turkish-American; Henri Tajfel, Jewish refugee from Eastern Europe). Also, as social psychology becomes more international, intergroup relations and multiculturalism become more important topics through the influence of scholars from Europe (Mick Billig, Rupert Brown, Willem Doise, Serge Moscovici), Canada (John Berry, Ken Dion, Don Taylor), and other regions outside the United States (John Turner and Mike Hogg in Australia). These developments enrich social psychology and make it an even more exciting discipline, one that can better explain social behavior in contemporary societies, characterized as they are by cultural and linguistic diversity.

For Review

Group behavior in a changing world seems in some ways paradoxical. On the one hand, the internationalization of trade and communications systems is moving us toward a global village (more unity and greater homogeneity). On the other hand, separatist regional and nationalist movements, together with a global ethnic revival, seem to be leading to greater fragmentation.

The major social psychological theories can be conceptualized as lying on a continuum. At the one extreme is psychological state as the main factor behind intergroup conflict and at the other are material conditions.

The psychological state theories include Freud's irrationalist account, equity theory, and relative deprivation theory. Freud's idea of displaced aggression inspired the highly influential frustration–aggression theory. Equity theory conceptualizes human relationships as a form of economic exchange. Relative deprivation theory tries to specify the conditions in which people feel deprived. The greatest challenge for researchers has been to demonstrate a relationship between feelings of deprivation and participation in collective action. This challenge is made more complex by the many cross-cultural variations in how people are socialized to cope with life challenges and potentially frustrating experiences.

Theories that give importance to material conditions include social identity theory, realistic conflict theory, the five-stage model, and resource mobilization theory, the first two being the most influential. Social identity theory assumes that people desire to achieve a positive and distinct social identity. Conflicts arise when those with inadequate social identity take action to change the status relationships of the in-group and out-group(s). Realistic conflict theory assumes that conflicts arise out of conflicting material interests but can be resolved through superordinate goals (goals desired by both groups but not attainable without the cooperation of both).

At the heart of intergroup relations is the issue of justice. Research suggests that people do not always apply justice principles in the same manner across contexts but, rather, vary their applications to suit their viewpoints in each context. Conceptions of justice itself tend to vary across cultures, with allocation of reward according to merit as opposed to need being endorsed more in individualistic than in some more collectivistic cultures.

The main policies for managing cultural diversity have been assimilation and multiculturalism. Assimilation relies on intergroup contact to increase similarities and thus gradually increase attraction and cohesion. But no matter how homogeneous society becomes, there will always exist some differences that could serve as the basis for intergroup biases and conflict.

Multiculturalism rests on the notion that a sense of security and positive in-group identity will lead to open and accepting attitudes toward out-groups. Research has not provided clear support for this hypothesis, although there seems to be more support for the view that inadequate social identity leads to prejudice against out-groups.

For Discussion

1. "The major intergroup theories assume that people are self-centered and primarily concerned with improving their own personal situations. This reflects the individualism of Western society and social psychology." Discuss this statement.

2. "If Freud is correct and humans are irrational, then we can dismiss the theories that assume material resources to be the main issue in intergroup relations." Discuss this statement.

3. "Similarity-attraction persists across cultures, but the multiculturalism hypothesis only works under some conditions." Discuss this statement.

Key Terms

Assimilation *497*

Cultural relativism
506

Equity theory *480*

Five-stage model
489

Libido *477*

Melting-pot
assimilation *499*

Minority
assimilation *499*

Multiculturalism
498

Optimal
distinctiveness
theory *488*

Prisoner's dilemma
game *496*

Relative deprivation
482

Resource
mobilization theory
493

Social change *487*

Social identity
theory *485*

Social mobility *488*

Superordinate goals
492

Tokenism *489*

Annotated Readings

An overview of the literature by two leading U.S. researchers is M. B. Brewer and N. Miller, *Intergroup relations* (Pacific Grove, CA: Brooks/Cole, 1997).

D. M. Taylor and F. M. Moghaddam present an overview of the international literature with heavy emphasis on major theories in *Theories of intergroup relations: International social psychological perspectives,* 2nd ed. (Westport, CT: Praeger, 1994).

R. J. Brown, a leading British researcher, discusses group and intergroup dynamics in *Group processes: Dynamics within and between groups* (Oxford: Blackwell, 1988).

A variety of perspectives is presented by leading researchers in S. Worchel and W. G. Austin, eds., *Psychology of intergroup relations* (Monterey, CA: Brooks/Cole, 1986).

Discussions on social identity theory, the most influential theory since the 1980s, appear in D. Abrams and M. A. Hogg, eds., *Social identity theory: Constructive and critical advances* (London: Harvester Wheatsheaf, 1990).

Discussions of links between the self and social identities are found in M. B. Breakwell, ed., *Social psychology of identity and the self concept* (London: Academic/Surrey University Press, 1991).

Two classic works that are very much worth reading are M. G. Billig, *Social psychology and intergroup relations* (London: Academic Press, 1976); and M. Sherif, *Group conflict and cooperation: Their social psychology* (London: Routledge & Kegan Paul, 1966).

The role of language in intergroup relations is discussed by two world leaders in H. Giles and N. Coupland, *Language: Contexts and consequences* (Pacific Grove, CA: Brooks/Cole, 1991).

CHAPTER 15

Applying Social Psychology:
Conflict Resolution, the Law, and the Developing World

◀   South Korean troops patrol the 38th parallel, the dividing line between North and South Korea. The twentieth century has witnessed two world wars and countless regional and local conflicts. The twentieth century has witnessed legal reforms that guarantee human rights for all humankind, but in practice prejudice on the basis of race, religion, sex, and other group memberships continues. The twentieth century has witnessed tremendous advances in technology, enabling the richest countries to move further ahead, but widening the gap between developed and developing societies. Social psychologists have had some success in applying their knowledge and skills to solve practical problems, but major challenges await them in the twenty–first century.

o many problems in the world," sighed a very elderly African woman seated next to me in a hotel lobby. From the newspaper she was reading, *Kenya Times*, I guessed her to be Kenyan.

"Look at all these troubles," she added, inviting me to look over the headlines of her newspaper. They told of ethnic conflicts, food shortages, violent crimes, and a host of other social issues. It struck me that the stories in the Kenyan newspaper were very similar to ones in the newspaper I was reading, the *Washington Post*.

"Who is going to solve these problems? There are hundreds of psychologists attending a conference right here in this hotel. I would like to ask them what they intend to do about these problems."

"Well," I said sheepishly, "I am one of those psychologists."

"I thought you might be," she responded triumphantly. "What can you do to solve these problems?" she asked, pointing to the newspaper headlines.

I took a deep breath and plunged into a description of **applied social psychology,** the application of social psychological knowledge to solve practical problems in domains such as conflict resolution, national development, and the law. The reaction of my elderly listener was similar to the reaction of many of my young students: surprise and admiration for what has been achieved, but also a sense of awe in the face of the complexity of the problems plaguing human societies. Perhaps because of this complexity, social psychologists have tried to make the task of finding solutions more manageable by isolating and simplifying aspects of the world.

applied social psychology the application of social psychological knowledge to the solution of practical problems.

The scenes being shown on the television news broadcast were terrifying yet familiar, heart-wrenching yet by now routine. Weary, hungry, and helpless children, women, and men . . . thousands of exhausted refugees trying to return to their homes after having been driven out by fighting.

This time it was Hutus in Zaire returning to their country, Rwanda, in Central Africa. The haunting image of a seemingly endless trail of humanity moving slowly but steadily toward an uncertain future remained with me well after the program had ended. The extent of the tragedy was underlined by the inability of authorities to give even roughly accurate estimates of just how many refugees there were.

The Central Africa refugee crisis that gained international attention in late 1996 is part of a continuing conflict with a long and complex history. The Hutus make up about 85 percent of the population in the neighboring countries of Rwanda (total population 6 million) and Burundi (total population 7 million); the Tutsis make up about 14 percent in both countries. Despite being numerically outnumbered by about 6 to 1, and despite migrating to the region about 1,500 years after the arrival of the Hutus, the Tutsis have been the majority power group. The dominant position is in large part explained by the support they received from Germany and then Belgium, the colonial powers that controlled the region from the nineteenth century until independence in 1962.

Since the late 1950s the Hutus have fought to topple their Tutsi rulers, and conflicts between the two groups have been bloody and often ruthless. Fighting became even more intense when Hutus blamed Tutsis for the death of Rwanda's Hutu president in a mysterious air crash in 1994. This event triggered the slaughter of about 500,000 Tutsis and moderate Hutus by Hutu forces. Tutsi forces fought back, resulting in well over a million Hutus taking refuge in neighboring Zaire.

The news program was followed by a special report on the Hutu refugees, and as I watched the images of starving and helpless children, I thought of the gap that seems to exist between such complex and entangled real-world conflicts and the conflict situations studied by social psychologists. For the most part, social psychologists have contributed to conflict resolution by studying simulated conflicts in *experimental games*, which place individuals and groups in competition with one another under varying conditions controlled by the experimenter. Lester Zeager and Jonathan Bascom (1996), for example, used a game-theory approach to try to understand better a key aspect of conflict situations involving refugees. In the study, participants played the part of government officials and United Nations representatives negotiating the control of resources to be used to assist refugees.

The simulated conflict situation used in gaming research is, on the surface at least, very different from the kind of real-life conflict situation of the Hutus and Tutsis. But despite the surface differences, as well as some deeper ones, social psychologists have made important practical contributions to conflict resolution.

Social Psychological Research on Conflict Resolution

Most studies of human values highlight the importance people give to peace and security (Rokeach, 1973; Schwartz, 1992). Social psychologists have also regarded **conflict,** a perceived incompatibility of interests, as negative, and worked toward the goal of achieving peace.

The topic of **conflict resolution,** the application of psychological knowledge to achieve peaceful relations between individuals and groups, has received a great deal of attention from social psychologists, with the vital practical aim of achieving a more peaceful world (Deutsch, 1993, 1994; Kelman, 1997; Rubin, Pruitt, & Kim, 1994; Sandole & van der Merwe, 1993; Worchel & Austin, 1986). The major conflict resolution strategies developed by social psychologists have grown out of a rationalist tradition which assumes that conflicts arise out of misunderstandings, misperceptions, and misattributions. Each side loses trust in the other and develops exaggerated fears of being threatened and attacked by the other. Such an escalating spiral of destructive conflict can lead to total war.

conflict   a perceived incompatibility of interests.

conflict resolution   the application of psychological knowledge to achieve peaceful relations between individuals and groups.

The best way out of this dilemma, it is proposed, is to facilitate communications, to help each side see the point of view of the other more accurately, and to avoid stalemate by achieving gradual movement of the sides toward a mutually acceptable settlement. In practice, this is similar to Secretary of State Henry Kissinger's "shuttle diplomacy" in the Middle East, through which Kissinger dominated U.S. foreign policy from the late 1960s to 1974 during the Nixon and Ford administrations.

The Rationalist View

But what motivates people to develop biased perceptions of their competitors? What will motivate them to put aside misunderstandings and work toward peace? Social psychologists working in the rationalist tradition do not believe that peace will come about because people are motivated toward peaceful ends. Rather, they assume that people are self-centered and will work toward peaceful ends if they recognize that this is in their interest. People are assumed to be self-serving and motivated to maximize personal gains.

The rationalist tradition in conflict resolution is often represented by Muzafer Sherif's realistic conflict theory, which assumes that conflicts arise out of real conflicts of interest, and can best be resolved

This is a sight that seemed unthinkable just a few years ago: A U.S. secretary of state in Hanoi, shaking hands with a Vietnamese foreign minister (June 27, 1997). How is it that these "bitter enemies" have signed agreements for the establishment of consulates in each other's countries? One explanation lies in superordinate goals: Both parties want to reach a goal that they are unable to attain without the cooperation of the other. This example suggests that, under certain conditions, conflict resolution can be achieved using a rational model. However, the decades-long war that preceded this agreement does not fit such a model.

when the two conflicting parties see it as being in their own interests to work toward a superordinate goal (a goal both parties desire, but neither can attain without the cooperation of the other). The challenge for peacemakers, then, is to help the two sides identify and adopt superordinate goals.

Another way in which social psychologists have approached this problem is to use the metaphor of "the tragedy of the commons" (Hardin, 1968). The term *commons* is derived from a tradition in England for there to be open grazing grounds near or in the middle of villages and towns. Because the commons could be used by all to graze their cattle, it would obviously be profitable for any one person to graze as many of his cattle as possible. However, if everyone used the commons, then very soon the grass would disappear and no one would be able to graze cattle. The solution is for everyone to recognize that the personal interest of each is best served by safeguarding the general interest of the collective. Research in both Western and non-Western societies using a game simulation of the "tragedy of the commons" shows that when participants act on short-term self-interest, the common resource (such as pastureland, or forests, or clean water, or the like) is quickly depleted (Sato, 1987).

Implicit in the rationalist approach is the ideal of an independent thinker who pursues self-interest within a social system in which the maximizing of personal profits leads to greater riches for all. Using the commons metaphor, ideal persons are those who use the commons in such a way as to maximize their gain but ensure the survival of the resource for all. Of course, this ideal can easily be translated to the business context. For example, factory owners should recognize that by being satisfied with more modest profits they can ensure the better survival of the environment, and thus themselves.

Gaming Research: The Prisoner's Dilemma

Gaming research examines decision making that takes into account the actions of other(s) whose interests may conflict with the participant (Bennett, 1955; Fudenberg & Tirole, 1991); it is the most important strategy used to explore conflict resolution in social psychology (Fisher, 1989), as well as in other related disciplines such as political science (Morrow, 1994) and economics (Gibbons, 1992). We can better appreciate the appeal of the gaming approach by looking more closely at the prisoner's dilemma game, a classic example of a gaming experiment extensively used in social psychology since the 1960s (Dawes, 1991; Nemeth, 1972).

The prisoner's dilemma game (PDG) derives its name from an imaginary situation involving two partners in crime who have been apprehended and are awaiting trial. The prisoners are not allowed to communicate with one another, but the fate of each depends in a vital way on decisions made by the other. Each has the option of informing on the other or keeping quiet. If both keep quiet, both receive a light sentence. But if one informs and the other keeps quiet, the informer is set

gaming research   research that examines decision making, which takes into account the actions of others whose interests may conflict with those of the participant.

free and the one who refused to talk receives a very heavy sentence. If both inform, they each receive a light sentence.

Each prisoner may hope to win by informing on the other, but counting on the other to keep quiet. However, neither can be sure that the other will not also inform and get both of them at least a light sentence. Even more risky is the option to keep quiet in the hope that the other will also keep quiet, because the other may talk and result in the partner getting a very heavy sentence. These various options and risks are represented in a payoff matrix, which is either zero–sum or non–zero–sum. In a **zero–sum** payoff matrix, each player necessarily wins at the expense of the other, who suffers an equivalent loss (if Charlotte wins an extra $100, then Emily necessarily loses $100). The total gains and losses of both players add up to zero. But wins and losses of the two players in a **non–zero–sum game** depend on their own personal choices, and the sum of choices does not have to add up to zero (if Charlotte wins $100, Emily does not lose $100).

> **zero-sum game** game in which each player necessarily wins at the expense of the other.

> **non-zero-sum game** game in which both players can win if they act cooperatively.

The prisoner's dilemma game is typically designed to be *mixed motive*, in the sense that players have the option of behaving competitively or cooperatively. Such games are typically designed to have a solution that achieves maximum outcomes for both players (in the example above, this was achieved by both players keeping quiet). The prisoner's dilemma game, then, is mixed motive (the two players can either act competitively or cooperatively), non–zero–sum (the sum of their outcomes is not necessarily zero) with a best rational strategy (see Figure 15–1).

In order to get the best mutual outcome for both, the two participants in Figure 15–1 should choose strategy *C*, as this would give them 6 points each. But by selecting strategy *C*, both participants leave themselves open to opportunistic moves by the other. If person *B* chooses strategy *C*, but person *A* chooses strategy *D*, then person *B* receives −1 and person *A* receives +9. Similarly, if person *A* chooses strategy *C* and person *B* chooses strategy *D*, then person *A* receives −1 and person *B* is rewarded +9. In terms of the fable of the two prisoners, this situation would be equivalent to one prisoner keeping quiet and the other "spilling the beans," so the prisoner who refuses to talk gets a heavy sentence and the one who talks is set free.

The prisoner's dilemma game has strong appeal to social psychologists interested in conflict resolution because the dilemma it presents seems to be like the dilemmas confronting national leaders at the global level. Consider, for example, the situation of the United States

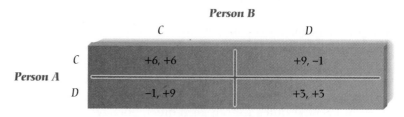

Figure 15–1   Matrix of rewards in a typical prisoner's dilemma game.

and communist China as we approach the year 2000. Each is under pressure to maintain or increase arms expenditure or else risk losing influence on the world stage. If both decreased their expenditure on vast armies, then in both countries more resources could be allocated to education, health, and the environment. But if one unilaterally decreases arms expenditure, the risk is that the other will keep increasing and gain greater influence on the world stage through military strength.

Gaming Research: The Trucking Game

A fundamental assumption underlying the prisoner's dilemma game is that we can learn about real-life conflict at the intergroup level (such as that involving the Hutus and the Tutsis, or the United States and China) by studying conflict at the interpersonal level in the laboratory. This assumption underlies most of the simulations used in gaming research.

Morton Deutsch (1962, 1973, 1985, 1993), a leading researcher in this domain since the 1960s, has declared that "nations as well as individuals acquire information, make decisions, and take actions, and that they will act in similar ways under similar conditions" (1969, p. 1091). Although Deutsch is correct to assert that both nations and individuals acquire information, make decisions, and take action, the contention that they will "act in similar ways under similar conditions" has been rejected by other scholars (see Billig, 1976; Taylor & Moghaddam, 1994).

A second important assumption underlying the work of Deutsch and other researchers in the gaming tradition is that human behavior is causally determined (Deutsch, 1973, 1985). Just as astronomers predict the movements of bodies in space through the causal laws of physics, so psychologists can predict the behavior of people through causal laws of psychology. The implication is, of course, that people and planets are both pushed around by external factors.

Deutsch himself developed an influential experimental game through which to study conflict, a game that reflects the two assumptions of (1) conflict being essentially the same at the interpersonal and intergroup levels, and (2) human behavior being causally determined. This is the *trucking game*, which typically involves two individuals who are asked to imagine they are operating two competing trucking companies (see Deutsch, 1985). The companies earn income by transporting merchandise from location *A* to location *B*, but they also have operating costs calculated at a fixed rate per unit of time. For example, if a company receives 1,000 points for each trip made, but takes 900 seconds to complete each trip, and if a point is equivalent to a second, then only 100 points profit remain. Obviously, the shorter the route, the more profitable the venture.

In a typical trucking game, a short and a long route are available. The shorter route only has one lane, and so cannot be used by both companies at once. The players are forced to come to an agreement, particularly if neither is powerful enough to dictate terms. Experimenters can create power disparity by giving one of the players control of gates that allow access to the short route. Not surprisingly, the player with more power has been found to make more profit. But players in such a situation of power disparity have been found to make less profit than players who are on a more equal footing with one another. One reason may be that unequal power is more likely to be associated with the use of threat by one party to get what it wants, as well as attempts at retaliation by the other party. This could result in both parties wasting resources and becoming entangled in spiraling destructive conflict.

Experimental Gaming Research and Real-World Conflict

The prisoner's dilemma game and the trucking game both seem far removed from the kind of "hot" real-life conflict exemplified by the Hutus and Tutsis in Central Africa. Typical studies in gaming research involve one-to-one conflicts, and we know that individuals often behave differently in groups than when they are alone. In support of this, studies that have compared how participants behave in gaming situations (such as those involving the prisoner's dilemma game) on their own, compared to when they are in a group, show important differences in behavior. When negotiators were single individuals, they could come to a compromise more readily than when there was a two-person group negotiating on either side (Stephenson & Brotherton, 1975).

A similar trend was found by researchers specifically using the prisoner's dilemma game. Two teams of two participants each play against each other for rewards, and then the two members of each team play again to settle how their winnings will be divided. In this way, each intergroup trial was followed by an intragroup trial. Comparisons of participants' behavior when they were part of a team and when they were on their own showed higher competitiveness in the intergroup situation (Wilson & Katayani, 1968; Wilson & Wong, 1968).

Of course, the behavior of participants in a gaming situation will depend a great deal on how they believe they *should* behave. From the normative perspective described in Chapters 1 and 2, we would expect that participants who enter a gaming situation behave in a way they see as appropriate for the context. This implies that we can influence their levels of competitiveness by changing their ideas about the experimental situation, and the literature supports this idea (see Fisher, 1989; Pruitt & Rubin, 1986).

An example is provided by a study in which the prisoner's dilemma game was run in the standard manner in condition 1, but participants in the three other conditions were told that behavior in such studies is usually interpreted in the context of international negotiations (condition 2), or economic bargaining (condition 3), or interpersonal interactions (condition 4) (Eiser & Bhavnani, 1974). Results showed that behavior was most competitive when participants believed they were to be assessed in the context of economic bargaining. One interpretation of this result is that participants saw competitive behavior as most appropriate when economic self-interest was at stake.

Culture and Gaming Research

From the early years of gaming research, cross-cultural studies have been conducted to examine how participants from different cultures would behave in the same situation. Versions of the prisoner's dilemma game have been particularly popular among cross-cultural researchers. One series of studies found Belgian children to overtake American children in competitiveness as they got older, so that as college students Belgians were more competitive than Americans (McClintock & McNeel, 1966; McClintock & Nuttin, 1969; McNeel, McClintock, & Nuttin, 1972).

Some studies go beyond mere comparisons and suggest reasons for cross-cultural differences. Studies using a gaming procedure with participants in Zambia (Bethlehem, 1975) and Liberia (Meeker, 1970) suggest that as people become more Westernized, their level of competitiveness in such contexts increases. Another situational factor influencing competitiveness is the amount of resources available in a society. Studies involving Indian participants suggest that the scarcity of resources in Indian society leads them to be comparatively more competitive (Druckman, Benton, Ali, & Bager, 1976; L'Armand & Pepitone, 1975).

But a broader assessment of gaming research from a cross-cultural perspective suggests that the prisoner's dilemma and other, similar games are too restrictive to allow for cross-cultural differences to emerge (see Leung & Wu, 1990). They typically reduce social interactions to two-person situations, a case that does not fit important types of social conflict. Many conflict situations involve large social groups or categories, such as gender, ethnicity, political or professional organizations, and even cultural groups and social classes.

Third-Party Intervention

Herbert Kelman (1997) is among a number of social psychologists who work in a rationalist tradition but do so in the international arena (see Sandole & van der Merwe, 1993). They often act as a third party, facilitating communications and negotiating between two parties in a dispute. Kelman (1997) has been particularly active in Israeli-Palestinian negotiations, trying to influence macro-level politics through micro-level interventions. At the micro level, problem-solving workshops involve politically active but unofficial representatives of different interest groups. Discussions are private and confidential. Small groups are composed of three to six representatives of the two sides and two to four third-party mediators. After the norms for discussion are clarified, the parties explain their views and concerns. When these have been clarified and understood, the parties are encouraged to engage in joint problem solving.

The purpose of the workshops is to bring about change in the individual participants. Kelman (1997) sees these individual level changes as a means of bringing about macro changes. He proposes five ways in which the workshop group influences change at the macro level.

▶ *The group as a microcosm.* The group serves as an arena in which the forces and trends in the larger society can appear. Participants are aware of the various concerns and interests of the larger society and explore ways of jointly solving problems.

▶ *The group as a laboratory.* The workshop is a separated space in which new ideas are developed and tested. Some of these ideas may be promising and can be introduced into the larger society.

▶ *The group as a setting for direct interaction.* Some aspects of international conflict take place at the individual level. These include empathy and taking the perspective of the other. The workshop provides a context in which individuals can develop these skills.

▶ *The group as a coalition across conflict lines.* Participants in workshops have an opportunity to unite across traditional conflict lines. They can become symbols of how intergroup differences can be addressed through joint problem solving.

▶ *The group as a nucleus for a new relationship.* The workshop provides participants with the experience of new relationships across group lines. Individuals learn to understand and trust members of the "opposition."

Reassessing Conflict Resolution and Rationality

One important characteristic of the conflict resolution strategies adopted by social psychologists is their optimistic faith in human rationality. In both laboratory and field research studies, and in direct intervention in applied projects, social psychologists have assumed that once people recognize the best strategy for maximizing personal profits, this is the strategy they will prefer. But world history provides many examples of far more destructive approaches to intergroup relations.

In some conflict situations, at least one of the combatants seems intent on causing as much destruction as possible, irrespective of the ultimate costs to the self and the in-group. Hitler is at the top of the list in the twentieth century, but there are countless lesser characters: Saddam Hussein and the Ba'athist party leaders in Iraq, Pol Pot and Khmer Rouge party leaders in Cambodia, Gustav Husák in Czechoslovakia, and Todor Zhirkov in Albania are a few examples. During the Gulf War in 1991, Saddam Hussein directed that oil be released into the Caspian Sea, causing severe environmental pollution. The Nazis destroyed Warsaw, even its trees, seemingly out of pure rage. Such acts of destruction do not fit neatly with a rationalist view of conflict.

But we students of social psychology do not have to go very far to find examples that illustrate the irrational and destructive aspects of human behavior. Such negative characteristics are found even in the traditional bastions of intellect and rationality: universities. I have witnessed university faculty members form factions and become so antagonistic toward one another, so overpowered by hatred, that it seemed they would pay any price to destroy their opposition. A number of important psychology departments have experienced this type of factionalism in their recent past. If people trained to be rational behave in such a destructive manner, then perhaps Freud did not exaggerate the irrational tendencies in humankind.

This rationalist account of conflict is part of a larger "social psychology of the nice person" that had its beginning in the United States. The French social psychologist Serge Moscovici (1972) described the grave difficulties he has with certain maxims implicit in social psychological research:

> "We like those who support us"; "the leader is a person who understands the needs of the members of his group"; "we help those who help us;" "understanding the point of view of another person promoted cooperation." (pp. 18–19)

Particularly from the point of view of minority groups, these ideas gloss over and simplify the problems they face. Think of a situation in which those with more power intentionally attempt to exploit those with less. Managers in private corporations or officers in the army may intentionally put pressure on those under their command to provide sexual favors. This situation has not arisen from any "misunderstanding"; both perpetrators and victims know that exploitation is going on. Similarly, when a corporation provides poor working conditions and low wages, and fires any employee attempting to form a union, both employee and employer can understand the situation: The group with power is intentionally exploiting those with less power.

Studies of exploitation in developing countries, such as June Nash's (1979) detailed cultural account of the lives of miners in Bolivia, show the plight of minorities there to be even more difficult because they often face severe reprisals when they rebel. When in the 1960s students and teachers joined miners to protest about conditions in the mines, the army attacked mining communities, pulling miners out of their houses and shooting them in front of their families to set an example.

Traditional conflict resolution approaches assume that those in conflict can be brought to understand one another better, to adopt superordinate goals, and to live side by side in peace. But in practice there are many situations in which this is not possible, and a "fight to the death" becomes inevitable. Consider the forces of democracy within the former Eastern bloc. Could they live side by side with the communist regimes? The situation in Romania was typical. Nicolae Ceauşescu ruled the country with an iron fist from 1965 to 1989, when he and his wife were executed. The Ceauşescu dictatorship and the brutal suppression of human rights in Romania did not arise from "misunderstandings," but from an intentional effort by those in power to maintain their monopoly for as long as possible. Such cases of exploitation, which can also exist in a different way in Western societies, highlight the shortcomings in what Moscovici has described as the "social psychology of the nice person" and underline the need for more attention to be given to anger, rage, and evil as sources of violence and conflict (Diamond, 1996).

Finally, we must question the assumption that conflict is inevitably bad and something that should always be avoided. In situations in which injustice continues, and those benefiting from injustice insist on defending the status quo, there may be no way of avoiding conflict for change to happen. Opponents of slavery in the nineteenth century and opponents of apartheid in the twentieth, were forced to enter into conflict as a way of changing the world. Similarly, if a person is attacked by a knife-wielding maniac, the only way to stay alive may be to "enter into conflict" and fight the attacker. In such circumstances, it would be impractical (and unsafe) to rely on improved communications, superordinate goals, or any similar tactic.

Concepts and Issues

Social psychologists have contributed constructive concepts and methods, such as superordinate goals and the prisoner's dilemma game, toward more effective conflict resolution. But their practical contributions have been limited by several assumptions: that conflict at the interpersonal level is essentially the same as that at the intergroup level and that one can best explain conflicts through rational accounts of behavior.

1. Describe the rationalist tradition in conflict resolution research.
2. Design a payoff matrix for a prisoner's dilemma game, using Figure 15–1 as an example.
3. Identify two assumptions that underlie gaming research methods, such as the prisoner's dilemma game and the trucking game.

Social Psychology and the Developing World

From its beginnings in the mid–nineteenth century, modern psychology evolved in Western societies and in large part took shape in response to the practical needs of those societies. Most of these needs were new and emerged as a result of rapid and widespread changes, such as industrialization and urban growth, enormous movements of populations from rural to urban areas, and the fragmentation of church, family, and other traditional institutions.

modulative psychology
psychology that has evolved by psychologists reacting to problems created by rapid change and attempting to modulate their consequences.

What has emerged in this rapidly changing context has been described as **modulative psychology,** meaning that it has evolved by psychologists reacting to problems created by rapid change and attempting to modulate their consequences (Moghaddam, 1990). For example, researchers have focused on how people can best cope with the stress of life in modern urban environments (Lazarus & Folkman, 1984), and how the physical environment of modern workplaces (factories, offices) can be organized to allow people to feel some measure of control over the physical spaces they occupy (Sundstrom, 1986). In short, a major practical question confronting Western psychology has been: How can we best cope with rapid change?

In contrast, the major question confronting psychologists in the developing world has been: How best can we bring about faster change? This is because the pace of change in most of the developing nations is judged to be inadequate, and sometimes even moving in the wrong direction. As an authoritative report summed up the situation:

> Since the rate of growth of population was well above rates of growth in GDP [gross domestic product] in Africa, Latin America and West Asia, per capita income fell in these three regions. Economic conditions were worse in 1992 than in 1971 in much of Africa. In Latin America, gross domestic product per capita was lower in 1992 than in 1981. (United Nations, 1994, p. 3)

Surveys of living conditions in much of the developing world reveal little improvement since the 1970s, and in some cases even a worsening situation (International Development Research Centre, 1992; United Nations, 1994). Despite some progress brought about by technological breakthroughs in agriculture, and despite efforts to control population levels, population increases still threaten to outstrip food supply. Between 1950 and 1990, as many people as populate a city the size of New York were added to the human race *each month* (Brown, Kane, & Ayres, 1993). On almost every measure, the gap between the richest and the poorest societies in the world has been increasing rather than decreasing. For example, it is estimated that the number of illiterate people in the developed world will decline from 47.8 million in 1970 to 15.7 million in the year 2000, but in the same time period the number of illiterate

A street in Bangalore, India. One of the most influential social psychological approaches to conflict resolution is realistic conflict theory, which proposes that conflicts arise out of differences in material interests between groups competing for scarce resources. Resources become more scarce when there is overcrowding. In today's interconnected world, overcrowding in one part of the globe is sure to have an impact on other parts. Poverty and overcrowding in the developing world are not "their" problem; they are everyone's problem.

people in the developing countries will increase from 842.3 million to 919.7 million (United Nations, 1994, p. 172).

Generative Psychology

generative psychology
psychology intended to generate positive social change through direct intervention.

Given conditions in much of the world, there is an urgent need for a psychology that will generate positive change, referred to as a **generative psychology** (Moghaddam, 1990). Examples of such generative approaches can be found in the community social psychology projects of Latin America (Sanchez, 1996; Sloan, 1990). Many such projects involve social psychologists intervening with the explicit goal of empowering a local community group. In one project, for example, a group of very poor women living in a Brazilian shantytown received help to overcome stereotypes of themselves as lazy and passive (Lane & Sawaia, 1991). Researchers guided the women to organize themselves and then to successfully produce and distribute handicrafts.

Another example is the work of the Turkish social psychologist Çigdem Kağitçibaşi (1996). Through the Turkish Early Enrichment Project, Kağitçibaşi focused on the home and attempted to influence the family context as a means of providing a richer and more nurturing environment for the growing child. Researchers attempted to bring about changes in mother–child interactions, such as more effective communications, increased verbalization of experiences, and better acceptance of the child's autonomy. A major challenge for Kağitçibaşi and her team was to achieve a balance between the needs of a child growing up in an urban setting and attending modern schools and the needs of a family life that is emotionally interdependent and is traditional in important respects. While the child needs greater independence to learn and to explore the outside world, the traditional family emphasizes dependence and obedience.

community social psychology
the application of social psychological knowledge to strengthen and mobilize communities.

At a more basic level, **community social psychology** (the application of social psychological knowledge to strengthen and mobilize communities) in the non–Western world has involved the intervention of social psychologists in order to alter perceptions so that certain "normal" situations will be reassessed (Freire, 1985). Social psychologists have intervened to change perceptions of very high population increases and high population densities so that instead of being seen as natural, such situations are seen as problems in need of remedies. As a consequence, for the first time people involved in the projects perceived the problem of "crowding" and felt the need for more **personal space,** a portable, invisible boundary that surrounds each person, into which others may not trespass (Aiello, 1987).

personal space a portable, invisible boundary that surrounds each person, into which others may not trespass.

A similar kind of "reconstruction" has been going on in Western societies through the intervention of psychologists. For example, social psychologists have helped to change public perceptions about energy sources, so that more people now see it as a problem that we are so reliant on nonrenewable energy sources and still use so few renewable energy sources. In short, social psychologists have helped to make the conservation of energy a public issue (Stern & Aronson, 1984).

Social Psychology and National Development

Particularly since the early 1980s, social psychologists have increased their efforts to contribute directly to the modernization efforts of developing societies (Blackler, 1983; Carr & Schumaker, 1996; Sloan, 1990; Triandis, 1984). There is a greater readiness to incorporate the contributions of social psychology because both researchers and practitioners now recognize the central importance of psychological issues in development (United Nations Development Programme, 1990, 1993).

Early attempts by psychologists to contribute to national development efforts in developing societies involved simplistic models of change and uncritical approaches to the issue of development. These models assumed that by motivating individuals to become entrepreneurial, an entire economy and society could be modernized. They also accepted without question that the path to progress lies in following the footsteps of Western societies. But in trying to modernize peoples such as this Pygmy family in Central Africa, Western influences have all too often led to the collapse of traditional communities. Even more visible than the collapse of social systems is the collapse of ecologies, as is clear in this mining area in Brazil.

Until the 1970s, national development tended to be assessed almost exclusively on the basis of economic criteria, such as the gross national product, and material wealth generally (Moghaddam, 1997a, Chapter 5). However, we now recognize that material wealth does not necessarily equal development. For example, the oil-producing Arab countries have enjoyed very high incomes since the sharp rise in oil prices in 1973, but this material wealth has yet to translate into development in human areas. These countries still import the vast majority of their skilled labor force from abroad. They have built modern hospitals and educational institutions, but their populations have not acquired the characteristics to match. These experiences have led to the realization that national development does not involve just more roads and bridges; it also involves changes in attitudes, values, gender roles, and social relations.

The fact that people are seen to be at the center of national development has created a golden opportunity for social psychologists. Let us consider the experiences of social psychologists in one area in which they have a relatively long history of research and practice in the context of developing countries.

A fundamentally important psychological concept central to national development is that of motivation, defined as directed action. Think back to research on social loafing (Chapter 12), which showed that when the personal effort of individuals working in groups is not identified, individuals exert less effort in a group than when working on their own. In other words, individuals seem to lose motivation when they work in groups where their personal efforts are not recognized. In the context of developing societies, a logical next step toward faster national development would seem to be to design programs that get people to think in individualistic terms, in order to increase their *personal* motivation.

One of the most influential and innovative social psychologists to enter this arena has been David McClelland (McClelland, 1961; McClelland, Atkinson, Clark, & Lowell, 1953). He has conducted extensive studies of motivation and national development and continues to influence research (see McInerney, 1995). McClelland created programs to alter the motivation of individuals toward economic growth (McClelland & Winter, 1969). These training programs were used to strengthen a "need for achievement" in Indian businessmen, focusing particularly on personal goals and individual work skills. The idea was to make motivated entrepreneurs out of the Indians, on the assumption that economic growth is based on individual enterprise. From this perspective, national development is driven by a "bottom-up" process, with the personal characteristics of individuals shaping the economy (Singh, 1977). But when follow-up studies were conducted after the training sessions, it was found that the participants went back to their former behavior patterns.

Of course, McClelland was not the only Western expert to discover that it is very difficult to change behavior patterns in other societies. More recent assessments of attempts to influence work motivation in developing nation contexts reveal a similar lack of success (Blunt &

T'Boli people of the Philippines. Social psychologists working in the domain of national development have recognized the complexity of change and the need for the active participation of individuals in directing change. People are not passive bystanders, waiting for factors to "cause" them to behave in one way or another; they actively try to influence events in directions that match their values and ideals. The T'Boli people of Mindanao island, in the southern Philippines, have consciously turned their backs on the modern world. They continue to farm, fish, dress, and behave much in the ways of their ancestors—shunning development and "progress" on the Western model.

Jones, 1992) While McClelland's approach focused on motivation at the intrapersonal level, others have attempted to speed up changes at the societal level. This is a "top–down" approach, in the sense that it is assumed political and economic changes at the macro level will inevitably shape the behavior of individuals at the micro level. However, this approach does not seem to be any more successful at achieving rapid change in behavior patterns. Richard Critchfield (1983) has described village life in different parts of the world and noted that attempts to bring about rapid modernization through top–down approaches have often ended in disaster. For example, in the 1970s enormous amounts of money, modern technology, and know–how were poured into rural areas of Iran to modernize agriculture. By the end of the decade, most of the major large-scale modern farms that had been established had failed.

Perhaps part of the difficulty of trying to bring about change using ideas and technologies imported from the West is that the social behavior of people in non-Western societies is at least in some ways very different. Studies with participants from collectivistic cultures, such as that of China, have shown that there is less social loafing in these cultures, and in fact in some conditions people exert more effort when working as part of a group than when working on their own (see Gabrenya, Latané, & Wang, 1983; Gabrenya, Wang, & Latané, 1985; Karau & Williams, 1993).

Another difficulty in exporting motivation programs from Western countries is that what motivates people can vary considerably across cultures. Colonial powers found that in Africa the work practices of locals were very different from those of people in Europe (Wober, 1975). The idea that one should work to earn money, acquire savings, and purchase additional goods was not part of the African lifestyle. Instead, people in Africa worked long enough to ensure adequate food and shelter, without displaying an insatiable desire to accumulate money. In fact, the idea of working for money was alien to most African economies. In order to transform local work practices, colonists imposed taxes on Africans that could only be paid in money. Of course, in order to earn money, Africans were forced to work in colonial programs.

Reassessing Change from a Cultural Perspective

During the 1970s I made several overland trips from England to the Middle East, traveling through what were then communist Eastern European countries. Although I experienced a great deal of change across countries such as Bulgaria, Turkey, and Iran, I was always struck by the high level of similarity in details of government bureaucracy. For example, my fellow travelers and I came to refer to one recurring behavior pattern as "was at desk . . . will return." This was the phenomenon of government bureaucrats leaving some signs on their desks, such as a pair of glasses or even a jacket, to indicate that they had arrived at work, are doing something somewhere, and will be back sometime in the future. I later discovered that the same phenomenon exists in many other societies. For example, the behavior is referred to as "not-on-seat" in Nigeria (Munene, 1995).

From the perspective of those who want to speed up development, a phenomenon such as "was at desk . . . will return" may seem irritating but hardly of monumental importance. Certainly, it is annoying and inefficient to find that a public servant is missing when one wants to conduct official business, but this is an event at the micro or everyday level of social interaction. Surely behavior at this everyday level does not play an important role in something as important and large scale as national development. Well, according to a new way of conceptualizing social change (Moghaddam & Crystal, 1997) social behavior at the everyday level *does* play a vitally important role in national development.

This new approach to cultural change takes the middle ground between two extreme positions. The first extreme is to see cultural change as involving a top-down process, whereby large-scale economic and political changes cause changes at the micro level of personal characteristics, such as how people think and feel. The second extreme involves the view that cultural change is a bottom-up process, whereby micro-level changes in feelings, beliefs, motivation, and so on cause large-scale economic and political changes. Both extreme views neglect the interaction between changes at the micro and macro levels, between what goes on inside individuals and what takes place at the national level.

There is often a difference between the speed of change at the macro and micro levels. In some cases, change at the micro level is faster than at the macro level. For example, when micro-level changes associated with the sexual revolution and the gay rights movement took place, national government and religious authorities attempted to preserve traditional sexual practices and the traditional family (by outlawing gay marriages, for example). But in the majority of cases, changes take place at the large-scale level faster than at the small-scale level. For example, at the national level the legal code of the United States and of many other Western countries makes it illegal to discriminate on the basis of gender and race. But in everyday social life at the micro level, such discrimination continues in many areas.

This distinction between micro and macro changes is highlighted through Stephen Weigert's (1996) study of traditions in Madagascar, Kenya, Cameroon, Congo/Zaire, and Mozambique. Weigert found that on the surface politics and war are conducted in a modern way, involving what Westerners would recognize as political parties and military forces. But at a deeper level, political and military activities in these regions are guided by traditions that precede the arrival of colonial powers, traditions interwoven in everyday social life. For example, although the rebel leaders in the Congo were trained in modern fighting tactics, their actual tactics were often more influenced by traditional religious views. The rebel leader Pierre Mulele acquired a reputation for having supernatural powers, enabling him to walk invisible through government lines, to be bulletproof, and so on.

It has been proposed that a major reason why it is so difficult to achieve cultural change is because the maximum speed of change possible in everyday social behavior is slower than the maximum speed of change possible at the macro level (Moghaddam & Crystal, 1997). Political elections, changes in legal codes, shifts in economic policy, and declarations of war and peace can happen very quickly. In contrast, everyday social practices are much more difficult to change. A government can in one day vote into law new ways in which members of different sexes and races are supposed to interact, but actually changing everyday practices to fit the law can take a great deal more time. This discrepancy between the maximum speed of change at the macro and the micro levels explains some of the perplexing failures to bring about reform in both Western and non–Western societies.

Concepts and Issues

Social psychologists have made constructive contributions toward national development, particularly through their work on motivation. National development is now viewed not just as economic change but more broadly as human development, involving changes in everyday behavior. Motivation is recognized as something residing in social relationships and the normative systems of societies rather than something inside individual persons. Researchers have also given closer attention to the nature of cultural change and differences in the speed with which change can be brought about at the societal (macro) level and the interpersonal (micro) level.

1. Give two examples to illustrate generative psychology in the developing world.
2. What is motivation, and why have social psychologists interested in national development focused on it?

Social Psychology and the Law

The central question of the Simpson trial is: Did he do it? How you answer the question is virtually an identification of the type of person you are.

As I was reading these lines from an article by Joel Achenbach (1995, p. 28), two middle-aged white men sitting in front of me on the train were having a heated discussion about the Simpson trial. Both men were convinced that O.J. Simpson, a legendary black athlete, was guilty of the murder of his white ex–wife and a male friend. Each was outdoing the other in expressing outrage at the not guilty verdict. As the train stopped at another station, four young African-American men stepped on board, and the two white men in front of me began to talk in whispers.

"He got away with murder . . . murder, . . ." said the first white man.

"What has happened to the justice system? It seems we can't trust in the system anymore," said the second, in a lower voice.

"No, it's not the system that's gone wrong. It's the people who sit on the juries. . . ."

The two white men got up and left the train at the next station. After this, the four African-American men started talking in louder voices, and it immediately became apparent that they too had the O.J. Simpson trial on their minds, and that they too had not wanted to be overheard by people on the other side of the racial divide. Before the four African-American men also left the train, I had heard enough to realize they saw the police as the real culprits in the O.J. case. The police had planted evidence to "fix" O.J. Simpson, they were certain of that (such conspiracy ideas are discussed in Gibbs, 1996).

This incident took only about 10 minutes, but it captured much of what is essential about psychology and the law. In theory, the law should be implemented in an impartial manner, and the decisions juries make should be based solely on the merits of a case. But social psychologists have discovered that in practice our conceptions of justice are intricately associated with cultural values (Hamilton, 1992), and the judgments made in a case can be influenced by who is being judged and who are the judges. For example, the majority of white people in the United States came to believe O.J. Simpson to be guilty, while the majority of black people became convinced that he is innocent (Gibbs, 1996).

How could there be such fundamental differences of opinion about the same case? Why should people who have heard the same case being argued by the same lawyers, with the same evidence being presented, come to such different decisions? We can better solve this puzzle if we think of the task of lawyers representing each side as storytellers. The objective of the lawyers on a case such as that of O.J. Simpson is to use the available evidence to construct a story that will convince the audience of their version of the truth. And the most important members of the audience are the judge and the jury. In a broader context, judge and jury are members of a larger community and can be influenced by what happens outside the courtroom: "Judges, who decide law, have no immunity from community" (Finkel, 1995, p. 95).

A lawyer in a trial is only one of many people who construct a story, and whose story may ultimately influence the verdict. During the trial, there are other characters, with minor and major roles, whose constructed stories can influence the final verdict. Among these characters are eyewitnesses to the crime and members of the jury.

Eyewitness Testimony: Two Views

"I saw what happened, I was there!" This is surely what every criminal dreads hearing and what every prosecuting attorney regards as a blessing. A witness to a crime: Can there be a more reliable source of evidence? This is the attitude in many Western and non–Western countries. Lawrence Rosen (1989) has described the central importance of eyewitnesses and oral testimony in Islamic law. In my own experience of living in Islamic societies, I found that eyewitness testimony is given even more importance in Islamic courts than it is in Western courts. However, more discrimination is made in Islamic courts between the value of testimony given by different eyewitnesses. The testimony of a woman carries less weight than that of a man, and "it is generally assumed that neighbors are more reliable than witnesses living at a great distance, that relatives are more likely to lie on behalf of kinsmen than strangers are" (Rosen, 1989, p. 310).

But is having an eyewitness like having a video camera recording the scene of the crime? Social psychological evidence suggests not. An eyewitness is far more like a storyteller who will give a particular version of a tale, change parts of it to fit the listener, and even be influenced by what the listener asks.

reconstructive memory   the biased re-creation of an earlier experience.

In an influential study, Elizabeth Loftus (1979) demonstrated some intriguing aspects of the **reconstructive memory** (the biased re-creation of an earlier experience) involved in eyewitness testimony. Participants were shown a film of a traffic accident and then asked to estimate how fast the vehicles had been traveling when they "collided" with one another. Other participants were asked the same question, except that the word "collided" was replaced by "smashed," "bumped," "hit," or "contacted." This simple manipulation of the question led to eyewitnesses making different estimates of speed, from about 40 miles per hour among those asked how fast the cars were going when they "smashed" into one another, to about 30 miles per hour among those asked the question using the word "contacted." When the eyewitnesses were asked about what they had seen a week later, those in the "smashed" group were more likely to have "seen" broken glass, which had not been in the original scene.

Perhaps the critical factor is how confident eyewitnesses are of the reports they are giving. If Mary reports that she is absolutely sure she saw the defendant pull out a knife, does her high confidence mean we should believe her testimony? Both legal experts and people on the jury tend to think so, but evidence suggests that confidence is not a good indication of accuracy (Luus & Wells, 1994). But surely the jurors will be able to tell which eyewitnesses are accurate in their accounts and which are not? Unfortunately, evidence suggests that jurors are not very good at distinguishing between accurate and less accurate eyewitness accounts (Lindsay, Wells, & Rumpel, 1981).

You are correct if you conclude that social psychological research does not leave us with much faith in eyewitness testimony. When over 60 leading experts were asked to identify findings about eyewitness testimony that would be strong enough to report in a law court, the list they arrived at included these items:

▶   The confidence with which eyewitnesses give testimony is not a good indication of information accuracy.

▶   Eyewitness testimony about events can be influenced by the wording of questions they are asked.

▶   Eyewitness testimony about an event is often influenced by their experiences after the event.

▶   Eyewitnesses make more mistakes identifying the members of other races than members of their own race.

▶   Eyewitnesses sometimes identify as a wrongdoer someone they have actually seen in a different context (Kassin, Ellsworth, & Smith, 1989).

Rethinking Eyewitness Testimony

The vast literature on eyewitness testimony has focused on errors made by eyewitnesses, and the evidence paints a grim picture. Received wisdom suggests that we should regard eyewitness testimony with suspicion, particularly if the witnesses are children (Ceci, Ross, & Toglia, 1989) and if they are identifying people who belong to a race other than their own (Anthony, Copper, & Mullen, 1992). A whole host of factors, including the instructions given by judges and questions asked by the police, can influence the testimony given by eyewitnesses (Kassin, Ellsworth, & Smith, 1989).

This emphasis on errors made by eyewitnesses has served a useful purpose: It has alerted those in the justice system, as well as the general public, to the biases that can arise. However, it may be that there has been too great an emphasis on errors in eyewitness testimony, just as research on causal inferences has focused too much on attributional biases (Chapter 5). It is useful to realize that almost all of the eyewitness testimony studies have been conducted using experimental simulations, with a focus on what *can* happen. We have very little information about the accuracy of actual eyewitnesses in real court cases, except for the small number of cases in which people have been found to be wrongly convicted (Brandon & Davies, 1973). Such cases typically become notorious and find their way into the popular media, whereas the thousands of cases involving eyewitness testimony that lead to correct convictions do not.

Perhaps the best way to assess the literature on eyewitness testimony is at two levels. As citizens supportive of human rights, we should be concerned with *every* case of error in eyewitness testimony. From this perspective, the focus on errors is justified. But as researchers concerned with achieving an accurate understanding of social behavior, we should be wary of the possibility that the research focus on biases has led to an exaggerated view of errors in human judgment.

Jury Decision Making

Whereas eyewitnesses are supposed to act as isolated individuals, reporting what they saw without being influenced by others, juries are expected to act as a group and come to a collective decision. Jury members collectively listen to different stories being constructed by lawyers, eyewitnesses, expert witnesses, judges, and others, then exchange stories until they have arrived at a commonly agreed-upon version of events. The story negotiated by a jury is rather like a **social memory,** an agreed-upon version of the past (Fentress & Wickham, 1992).

social memory an agreed-upon version of the past.

Nancy Pennington and Reid Hastie (1992) propose that juries construct stories about events by inferring causes and intentions—in other words, by making attributions. Not surprisingly, a great deal of attention has been given to the kinds of biases that creep into this story construction (Hastie, Penrod, & Pennington, 1983; Pennington & Hastie, 1986; Stalans, 1993). Juries do not do a good job, for example, of discounting coerced confessions when giving their verdicts (Kassin, 1997). There is a

Student reactions to the O.J. Simpson verdict, October 3, 1995. Look closely at the people in this picture. Do you see any patterns in their behavior? Do you notice that one group of people seems overjoyed, and the other group looks glum? What divides these people, and why are they reacting so differently? One group are African–Americans, the other white Americans. Both are reacting to the not guilty verdict at the end of the O.J. Simpson trial for the murder of his ex–wife and her friend. At the very least, the different reactions suggest differences in perceptions of the justice system. African–Americans seem to have less faith in the objectivity of the system, and seem more willing to believe that white police officers may try to frame black defendants.

long history of researchers identifying a racial bias in the U.S. legal system (Johnson, 1941; LaFree, 1980; Pfeifer & Ogloff, 1991). Such biases are more likely on issues that are ambiguous. In a case in which a defendant pleads not guilty by reason of insanity, there is no doubt who committed the crime; the defendant has admitted being the killer. But the issue of whether or not the defendant was insane, even temporarily, when he committed the crime is typically far more complicated and unclear.

In some rape cases questions arise not only as to who committed the crime, but also as to whether or not the victim consented (Borgida & Brekke, 1985). Research suggests that in rape cases the harshest punishments are given by white jurors when the defendant is black and the rape victim is white (Pfeifer & Ogloff, 1991). Some evidence suggests that both white and black jurors are biased in favor of defendants from their own race (Hymes, Leinart, Rowe, & Rogers, 1993). This supports what became generally believed in the O.J. Simpson case: The race of the jury does matter.

A word of caution is required at this stage, however. It would be misleading to assume that all jury decision making is flawed. In his thoughtful analysis of jurors' notions of the law, Norman Finkel (1995) has assessed *commonsense law,* what ordinary people think is just and fair. In some instances, commonsense law does differ from *black-letter law,* the formal law that law school students study, judges interpret, and researchers analyze. But Finkel concludes that when jurors' decisions are critically examined, they are, for the most part, sound.

Sexual Harassment and Culture

Sexual harassment, uninvited sexually oriented behavior, is another domain involving considerable ambiguity (Tata, 1993). The Equal Employment Opportunity Commission (EEOC, 1990) has published some general guidelines as to what constitutes sexual harassment, but in practice their interpretation depends on subjective perceptions of specific cases. In recent research, sexual harassment scenarios of the following type have been used (Gowan & Zimmermann, 1996):

▶ Female police officer is subjected to numerous sexual comments and is recipient of sexually insulting graffiti, posters, and has sexual items placed in her mailbox by co-workers.

▶ Unmarried, tenured, female professor pays unwanted attention to male, unmarried, junior faculty member. He complains to department chair.

Some evidence suggests subtle but important gender differences in perceptions and reactions to these kinds of harassment, and to sexually oriented behavior at work more generally. Women have a generally more negative attitude toward these behaviors in the workplace (Tangri, Burt, & Johnson, 1982), probably because they are more likely to be victims of sexual harassment (DeAngelis, 1996; Jones & Remland, 1992). Men have been found to identify fewer behaviors as sexual harassment than do women (Tata, 1993). Women are shown to react more adversely to environments involving subtle sexual behaviors, where it is more difficult to pinpoint the harassment (Popovich, Gehlauf, Jolton, Somers, & Godinho, 1992).

Irrespective of gender, people who have been the victims of sexual harassment show more awareness and concern for sexually oriented behavior at work (Gowan & Zimmermann, 1996). This is in line with the research of Mary Inman and Bob Baron (1996) showing that women are more likely than men to perceive racism directed at African-Americans and sexism directed at men; African-Americans are more likely than whites to perceive racism against both whites and other African-Americans. Thus, the kinds of decisions reached by juries on sexual harassment cases depend to some extent on the composition and previous experiences of the jury. This is part of a broader issue of the relationship between sexual harassment and culture.

Sexual harassment is interpreted according to the norms of a culture at a particular historical period. What we understand to be sexual harassment in the United States at the approach of the twenty-first century would not necessarily have been recognized as such at the beginning of the twentieth century. When we look across cultures, sexual

sexual harassment uninvited sexually oriented behavior.

There is almost always a rift between formal law, that which defines what is legal, and the informal norms and rules that prescribe correct behavior in a culture. During the 1990s, this disparity was highlighted by a number of much-publicized court cases involving accusations against the U.S. military, and particularly the navy and a number of military training schools. The Citadel, a military college that was until recently all-male, came under attack when female first-year students alleged sexual harassment. One such student, Jeanie Mentavlos, is seen here arriving at the Charleston, South Carolina, federal courthouse with her lawyer to attend a hearing. At the heart of the conflict is a struggle to change cultural norms and rules so that correct behavior for group members (in this case, men in the military) comes closer to formal law.

harassment can change shape even more dramatically. In the Islamic Republic of Iran, a woman who wears sexy clothes, or even laughs out loud or sings in public, could be prosecuted, because such behavior could be interpreted as sexual harassment against men. In some instances, societies can have diametrically opposite views about what constitutes sexual harassment. Consider the following scenarios:

The United States: An important male visitor arrives to inspect a government office. He shakes hands with all the male employees, but makes a point of not shaking hands with the female employees.

Saudi Arabia: An important male visitor arrives to inspect a government office. He shakes hands with male employees and also makes a point of shaking hands with female employees.

In Saudi Arabia unmarried men and women are not supposed to touch, not even during greeting ceremonies. A man who insists on shaking the hands of women who are not his close relatives is not behaving correctly. In most Western societies, a man would be seen as acting incorrectly if he refused to greet women in the same way as he greets men. These kinds of cross-cultural variations in the international arena remind us that we should be sensitive to cultural variations in how jurors interpret behavior within our own multicultural societies.

Psychology, the Law, and Culture

Studies of legal systems across cultures show that what is seen to be just and how justice is assessed vary considerably around the world (Starr & Collier, 1989). In Morocco, Islamic law courts are presided over by a single judge who decides cases (Rosen, 1989). Juries do not have a role in this system. Oral rather than written evidence is given more importance. Another major difference from courts in the United States is that "the defendant is whichever party the court believes is most likely to possess knowledge of the issue at hand and thus most able to swear to the matter" (Rosen, 1989, pp. 310–311). In the Moroccan legal system, the party who takes the oath first wins.

Dennis Fox (1993) is among a number of social psychologists who have argued that there is a more fundamental bias in the relationship between psychology and the law (Prilleltensky, 1989). Rather than focus on biases in eyewitness testimony, jury decision making, or some other detail of the legal system, these critics have challenged the neutrality of the law. They have pointed out that the idea of law as above and beyond politics is a myth, and that psychologists should be far more critical of the legal system as an instrument in the hands of the powerful. Fox (1993) has called for social psychological research in relation to the law to "support the powerless rather than the powerful" (p. 239).

Here we can see a link between social psychological research on the law and social psychological research on conflict resolution and national development. In all three areas, critics have pointed out a need for a more generative psychology, one that instigates social change (Fox & Prilleltensky, 1997). In conflict resolution research, the change would be toward resolving conflicts to the greater benefit of the less powerful parties. In research on national development, intervention would be toward changing society to improve the lives of the deprived masses in the developing world. In research on the law, one objective would be to support the rights of the powerless, those who traditionally have not been able to "deploy an army of 100+ Ph.Ds." as consultants (Cox, 1989).

Concepts and Issues

Social psychological research has identified a variety of biases in the testimony of eyewitnesses and in the decisions made by juries. More general reviews of commonsense law suggest that ordinary people make fairly sound judgements in deciding guilt and innocence. Of course, in many instances interpretations of the correctness and even legality of a behavior depend on culture. A broader and more fundamental criticism of the law has been raised by scholars who argue that the law often serves as an instrument in the hands of the powerful.

1. Give three examples of biases found in eyewitness testimony.
2. "Jury biases are less likely on issues that are more ambiguous." Do you agree? Explain with reference to research.
3. What is commonsense law? Give examples.

Conclusion

Social psychologists have applied their professional skills to achieve better solutions in a number of important domains, particularly conflict resolution, national development, and the law. They have become influential in these applied domains, and are increasingly sought as consultants in situations involving intergroup conflict, policy development at regional and national levels, and legal cases. Because the challenges people face in these domains are so complex, social psychologists have often relied on simplified simulations of the real world in order to test their ideas. Complex conflict situations involving groups with long histories are reduced to brief interactions between strangers in laboratory simulations, weeks-long jury debates on decisions with serious consequences by members of the general public are reduced to hour-long discussions among undergraduate students making decisions with no actual consequences. This type of simplification means that we must be cautious in how we extrapolate from social psychological research to applied settings. But with this caution in mind, social psychologists can continue to be of enormous practical help in applied domains.

For Review

Social psychologists have used their knowledge to solve problems in many applied domains, including conflict resolution, national development, and the law. One approach to conflict resolution has been the rationalist perspective, that people will try to maximize their own profits once they overcome misunderstandings and misperceptions.

Gaming research has been used to provide insight into how conflicts can best be managed outside the laboratory. Such conflicts often involve groups with long and complex histories, plus what seem to be senseless acts of destruction. The assumption that conflict between individuals and between groups is essentially the same underlies the work of applied and research social psychologists; this assumption is invalid in many situations.

Applied social psychology in Western societies has a history of helping people cope with rapid change, whereas in developing societies it faces the challenge of generating change. There are differences in the speed of change possible at macro political–economic levels and micro social psychological levels. Macro-level changes can sometimes be brought about overnight, but changes in everyday social behavior typically come about far more slowly.

Social psychologists working in law have demonstrated an array of biases that can influence the outcome of court cases and that creep into the stories of events constructed by judges, lawyers, jurors, police officers, and the general public. Eyewitness testimony plays a very important role in legal process in Western societies, but research has shown that eyewitness testimony can become biased in many ways. Jurors construct stories of the events by exchanging ideas and information, and negotiating a generally acceptable story. Ethnic and gender biases creep in, particularly in ambiguous cases.

Some scholars argue that in real court cases people in general make sound decisions and that research has focused too heavily on the biases that can occur in laboratory simulations. A few researchers have proposed that social psychologists should be more critical of the entire legal system. The law, they argue, is not neutral but serves to protect the position of the powerful.

For Discussion

1. Provide examples of how social psychologists have furthered a better understanding of biases in the justice system.

2. "Applied social psychologists inevitably influence relationships between the more and the less powerful." Discuss this statement, using examples from conflict resolution, national development, and the law to support your point of view.

Key Terms

Applied social psychology *512*

Community social psychology *524*

Conflict *513*

Conflict resolution *513*

Gaming research *515*

Generative psychology *524*

Modulative psychology *522*

Non-zero-sum game *516*

Personal space *524*

Reconstructive memory *532*

Sexual harassment *535*

Social memory *533*

Zero-sum game *516*

Annotated Readings

Leading researchers discuss conflict resolution research in D. J. D. Sandole and H. van der Merwe, eds., *Conflict resolution theory and practice: Integration and application* (Manchester, England: Manchester University Press, 1993).

A critical overview of social psychology and conflict resolution is provided by R. Fisher, *The social psychology of intergroup relations and international conflict resolution* (New York: Springer, 1989).

A model of how conflicts arise and can be resolved at micro and macro levels is discussed in J. Z. Rubin, D. G. Pruitt, and S. H. Kim, *Social conflict: Escalation, statement, and settlement* (New York: McGraw-Hill, 1994).

The major issues revolving around psychology and developing nations are covered in a set of discussions in S. C. Carr and J. F. Schumaker, eds., *Psychology and the developing world* (Westport, CT: Praeger, 1996).

For a lively and in-depth discussion of commonsense law, see N. Finkel *Commonsense justice: Jurors' notions of the law* (Cambridge, MA: Harvard University Press, 1995).

D. N. Robinson discusses the insanity defense with wonderful skill in *Wild beasts and idle humours: The insanity defense from antiquity to the present* (Cambridge, MA: Harvard University Press, 1996).

Glossary

acceptance type of conformity in which a change in outward behavior is accompanied by a change in beliefs.

actor-observer effect the tendency for observers to attribute others' actions to dispositional factors and for actors to attribute their actions to situational factors.

aggression behavior intended to harm another human being.

altruism behavior intended to help another, without regard for benefit to oneself.

androgynous an individual who shows little difference between his or her scores on feminine and masculine items in a test designed to measure masculinity and femininity.

angry aggression emotional behavior intended to harm, such as murder in the heat of passion.

applied social psychology the application of social psychological knowledge to the solution of practical problems.

arousal cost-reward model theory that people are aroused by the suffering and distress of others and will try to relieve that arousal by helping the distressed person using the least costly and most rewarding means.

assimilation the abandonment of heritage cultures by minorities in an attempt to "melt into" mainstream society.

attitude evaluation of oneself, other people, events, issues, and material things, with some degree of favor and disfavor.

attitude inoculation exposing people to mild attacks on their attitudes on particular topics to help them build up resistance to strong attacks.

attribution how people identify causes.

attributional style the tendency to make attributions in a consistent manner across different situations and times.

authoritarian personality a personality type that is submissive and obedient to authority, but repressive and vindictive toward those who violate conventional values.

availability heuristic a rule of thumb leading to estimates of the likelihood of an event on the basis of how readily instances come to mind.

balance theory proposition that people find inconsistency in relationships distressing and will change some aspect of a situation to achieve balance.

Bem Sex-Role Inventory a test that provides independent measures of masculinity and femininity.

"bowling alone" decline in league bowling as indicative of a decline in group life in the United States.

bystander effect the fact that the presence of others can actually decrease the likelihood of one person acting, because each person is looking to the others in the situation for guidance.

categorization the grouping of phenomena.

causal (explanation) explanations that assume human behavior to be causally determined by factors within persons or within the environment.

causal schema idea a person has about how different factors combine to produce certain kinds of effects.

central route route to persuasion taken by messages that engage the recipient in serious thought.

channel how the message is being delivered to try to persuade.

charisma exceptional personality characteristics that set a person apart from others.

charismatic leadership a leadership style that relies on exceptional personality characteristics.

coercion social influence in which the recipient experiences no choice.

cognitive dissonance a state of discomfort that arises when a person is aware of having incongruent cognitions and is motivated to change one or the other to make them congruent.

cognitive neoassociationist model model of aggression which proposes that cognitive associations are learned through rewards and punishments.

cognitive psychology a branch of psychology that focuses on thinking and on mental processes inside the person.

commonsense psychology a set of beliefs that people share about the world which may not necessarily be true.

community social psychology the application of social psychological knowledge to strengthen and mobilize communities.

compliance type of conformity in which a change in outward behavior is not accompanied by a change in beliefs.

computer simulation an attempt to program the computer to behave in a way analogous to human behavior.

conflict a perceived incompatibility of interests.

conflict model model of social influence which assumes that both majorities and minorities are sources and targets of persuasion.

conflict resolution the application of psychological knowledge to achieve peaceful relations between individuals and groups.

conformity changes in behavior that arise from real or imagined group pressure.

contact hypothesis under certain conditions, the more the members of different groups interact, the more they will grow to have favorable attitudes toward one another.

content what is being said to try to persuade.

contingency theory proposition that the effectiveness of a leader in achieving group goals depends on the characteristics of the leader and of the situation.

control the regulation of variables in a situation so that the hypothesized causal factors can be unambiguously identified.

correlational method social psychological method involving examination of associations between variables.

correspondent inference theory that specifies the conditions under which we are more likely to attribute causes to the dispositional characteristics of others.

covariation model the assumption that individuals make attributions by assessing the relationship among three types of information: distinctiveness, consistency, and consensus.

cultural realism the ability of participants to experience the laboratory situation as realistic and to believe that behavior in this context should be guided by certain norms and rules.

cultural relativism the viewpoint that all phenomena can be assessed only from the perspective of the culture in which they exist.

cultural set a whole package of variables that are normally experienced together in the real world, within a given society.

culture a normative system that prescribes how individuals should behave in a given context.

deindividuation the loss of one's sense of identity as an individual person, associated with lower self-awareness and decreased personal responsibility in group settings.

dependence model model of social influence which assumes that minorities are targets but not sources of persuasion.

dependent variable the variable that is measured by experimental research.

diffusion of responsibility a decrease in the sense of responsibility felt by each person in association with the number of people present in a situation.

discourse all kinds of communication, including spoken language.

discrimination actual behavior directed at others on the basis of category membership.

discursive psychology the study of how people construct reality, generate their version of events, and make inferences about causes in everyday life.

dispositional factors characteristics of a person.

dissimilarity-repulsion hypothesis hypothesis which asserts that people are repulsed by dissimilarity.

dramaturgical model a model of self-presentation, based on a metaphor of life as *drama*, which holds that we perform or present ourselves in different ways in different contexts, according to the norms of that context.

dramaturgical role expectation about how people in a specific social situation will behave.

ego-involvement effect better retrieval of material associated with an ongoing task than with a completed task.

elaboration likelihood model an information-processing approach which proposes that central rather than peripheral routes to persuasion lead to more enduring change.

emic a characteristic specific to one or a few cultural groups and not universal.

empathy-altruism hypothesis hypothesis that when people feel empathy, they become motivated to act, with the ultimate goal of helping the person for whom the empathy is felt.

empathy-joy hypothesis hypothesis that people are less likely to offer help when they will not be able to share the joy of the needy person's relief, or when the likelihood of improvement is low.

encodings internal representations of external phenomena.

equity theory theory that conceptualizes human relationships as a form of economic exchange and assumes that people are motivated to achieve equitable relationships and will be unhappy with inequity even when they benefit from the situation.

etics behaviors that are found in all or most societies.

exchange theory proposition that we assess the contributions of each person in social relationships, including intimate friendship and love relations.

experimental method in traditional terms, social psychological method concerned with manipulating causes to test for effects.

experimental realism the realism of the experimental situation for participants.

external factors characteristics of a situation.

external validity the relationship between the results of the laboratory study and the external world.

extrinsic motivation behavior motivated by external rewards.

face-ism a tendency for public photographs of men to focus on their faces and for those of women to focus on their bodies.

false-consensus effect overestimating the extent to which others agree with certain of our opinions.

false gender consciousness tendency for some individuals to misperceive the characteristics and interests of their gender.

false-uniqueness effect overestimating the extent to which we can differentiate ourselves from others in a positive way.

field experiment studies involving the manipulation of independent variables in the field.

field research   any study conducted outside the laboratory.

five-stage model   proposition that all intergroup relations pass through the same five stages in the same order, and that the most capable disadvantaged group members will first attempt to move into the advantaged group individually.

flashbulb memory   vivid and essentially permanent image of an event that has importance for a person.

frustration-aggression hypothesis   idea that frustration evokes a state of instigation to act aggressively and that aggression is always preceded by some kind of frustration.

fundamental attribution error   the tendency for observers to underestimate the influence of situational factors and overestimate the influence of dispositional factors when assessing the behavior of others.

gaming research   research that examines decision-making which takes into account the actions of others whose interests may conflict with those of the participant.

gender   the social role ascribed to people who fall into either the male or the female sex category.

generalized personal/group discrepancy   a tendency for individuals to rate the effect of a phenomenon as less on themselves than on their group.

generative psychology   psychology intended to generate positive social change through direct intervention.

genotype   genetic makeup.

gestalt   idea that the whole is more than the sum of its parts.

great person theory   proposition that leaders have certain personality traits that set them apart and make them uniquely suitable for positions of authority.

group   entity that exists when two or more people define themselves as members of it and its existence is recognized by at least one other person.

group polarization   the finding that group interaction tends to lead to a more extreme position on an already existing orientation.

groupthink   the tendency for people in groups to converge on unwise courses of action they would have avoided if were making the decision individually.

halo effect   tendency for a few outstanding characteristics to influence the overall assessment of a person.

hate crimes   crimes motivated by racial, religious, ethnic, or sexual orientation hatred or bias.

hermaphrodite   individual born with some organs of both sexes.

heroic altruism   altruism that is often short term, requires physical action, and is public, or "visible."

hypothesis   a proposition that serves as a tentative explanation of certain facts.

image-repair hypothesis   hypothesis that people want to have a positive self-image, that their social image is damaged when they harm someone, and that they will do good deeds to repair their image.

independent self   a concept of the self that emphasizes separateness, internal characteristics, and uniqueness of individuals.

independent variable   hypothesized cause in experimental research.

in-group   group to which a person belongs.

instrumental aggression   a calculated, premeditated attack designed to gain material benefit for the aggressor.

interdependent self   a concept of the self that emphasizes dependence on social relations and group characteristics, and that has fuzzier boundaries.

intergroup attribution   a causal inference on the part of group members about the members of their own or other groups.

internal validity   the degree of control achieved in a laboratory setting.

intrinsic motivation   the pleasure a person gets from performing an activity without receiving any external reward.

just-world hypothesis the hypothesis that people are motivated to see the world as just, and that this can lead to a lack of helping, as when a victim is seen as not deserving help.

kin selection choosing to help or save one's own child or a close relative to increase the chances of one's own genes being passed on.

laboratory a separate space, such as a room or set of rooms, where all the variables in the context can be controlled by the experimenters.

leadership process by which one person directs group members toward the attainment of specific goals.

learned helplessness situation that occurs when individuals come to believe they are incapable of influencing the environment, so they give up trying.

learned script information learned about a normative sequence of events for given social situations.

libido the energy of those instincts that have to do with all that may be included under the term *love*.

locus of control people who believe they control their own destiny versus people who believe their destiny is determined by external factors.

looking-glass self the self as an outcome of people's assumptions about how others view them.

majority influence how a majority maintains control by pressuring a minority to conform.

manipulated norm norm explicitly brought about by design.

melting-pot assimilation situation in which both majority and minority groups contribute to the formation of a new and common culture.

memory structure a set of interconnected memories.

mere exposure effect the positive association found between liking for and repeated exposure to novel stimuli.

meta-analysis technique for statistically combining and integrating findings from many different studies.

minimal group paradigm an experimental demonstration of intergroup bias using arbitrary and apparently trivial criteria for group formation.

minority assimilation abandonment of their heritage cultures by minorities and adoption of the majority way of life.

minority influence how a minority brings about change through the process of interactions and social conflict.

modulative psychology psychology that has evolved by psychologists reacting to problems created by rapid change and attempting to modulate their consequences.

multiculturalism the retention and further development of heritage cultures, with the goal of achieving a cultural mosaic.

mundane realism the similarity of events in an experiment to those in the world outside the laboratory.

natural experiment an experiment that involves the manipulation of variables, but under the control of nature rather than experimenters.

negative correlation relationship that exists when two or more factors change in opposite directions.

negative-state relief hypothesis hypothesis that feeling empathy for someone in distress involves a temporary feeling of sadness and that people are motivated to relieve that sadness by mood-enhancing experiences, like helping others and feeling good about doing it.

non-zero-sum game game in which both players can win if they act cooperatively.

norm a guide to correct behavior in a given setting.

normative explanation explanations of behavior that assume people are intentional agents who behave in a manner they see as correct in a given context.

normative system networks of related norms and rules.

norm of trust the norm that others should generally be trusted.

norm of truth the norm that people should generally tell the truth.

norm of turn-taking in dialogue the norm that parties in a dialogue should display a minimal level of respect by taking turns to listen to the other as well as to respond to what is being said by the other.

nuisance variable a variable that if not controlled may influence the dependent variables and prevent researchers from isolating the influence of independent variables.

nurturant altruism altruism that requires long-term involvement, tends to be private rather than public, and is passive rather than active.

obedience changes in behavior that arise when people follow the instructions of persons in authority.

objective self-awareness the state of self-focused attention.

opposites-attract hypothesis the hypothesis that we are attracted to people who are different from us.

optimal distinctiveness theory proposition that individuals are motivated to achieve equilibrium between opposing needs for assimilation and differentiation.

out-group group to which a person does not belong.

participant subject in psychological research.

performance style the manner in which individuals present themselves.

peripheral route route to persuasion taken by messages that lead to acceptance without engaging the recipient in thought.

personal/group discrimination discrepancy tendency for minority group members to perceive a higher level of discrimination directed at their group as a whole than at themselves as individual members of that group.

personal space a portable, invisible boundary that surrounds each person, into which others may not trespass.

persuasion communication designed to influence another's cognition or overt behavior in which the recipient has some measure of free choice.

phenotype physical features.

pluralistic ignorance when bystanders assume nothing is wrong because other people present seem to see nothing wrong.

population all those who could possibly be included in social psychological research.

positive correlation relationship that exists when two or more factors change in the same direction.

power majority group that has most control over how important resources are distributed; may be the numerical minority.

power minority group that has little control over the distribution of important resources; may be the numerical majority.

prejudice an attitude toward others solely on the basis of group membership.

primacy effect information presented first has greater impact.

primary group group that has a small membership and frequent face-to-face interaction, is marked by strong ties of affection, and exists for a long time.

priming the activation of thoughts and experiences that are applicable to presently experienced stimuli.

prisoner's dilemma game gaming research situation in which two accomplices in crime confront a dilemma: If one betrays the other, the betrayer gets off free and the other gets a heavy sentence; but if both keep quiet, both get light sentences.

racism prejudice toward ethnic minorities.

rape myth false but pervasive beliefs about the sexual desires of women that excuse sexual aggression against them.

realistic conflict model idea that competition for scarce resources is the root cause of conflict.

recency effect information presented last has greater impact.

reconstructive memory the biased re-creation of an earlier experience.

reference group a group to which a person does not belong but with which she or he identifies.

relative deprivation a belief that one is worse off than others with whom one compares oneself.

reliability consistency in measurement.

replication a subsequent study that attempts to reproduce an earlier study.

resource mobilization theory theory that conflicts arise when those with resources mobilize people to take collective action.

risky shift the proposition that people in groups make riskier decisions.

rule prescription for how people in particular role relationships should behave.

sample the group selected for study from among the population.

schema a cognitive structure that serves to organize experiences in a given domain.

scientific method the systematic procedures social psychologists try to follow to gather and analyze data in order to test hypotheses about social behavior.

secondary group group with opposite characteristics to primary group: little face-to-face interaction, weak group identification, weak ties of affection, and short-term existence.

self the totality of personal experiences.

self-centered bias the taking of more than one's fair share of responsibility for a jointly produced outcome.

self-complexity the number of ways in which people think of themselves.

self-confrontational method a research method in which a pattern of relationships is revealed and used to identify motives central to the life of the participant.

self-generation effect better retrieval of material actively generated by the person than material that is only passively encountered.

self-handicapping an attempt to explain poor performance as due to shortcomings rather than lack of ability.

selfish gene term used to describe helping behavior as part of a complex pattern of competition between genes rather than between individuals.

self-monitoring being aware of how to present the self in a given situation and changing self-presentation to fit the situation.

self-perception theory theory that when cues about their internal states seem confused, people explain how they feel and think by observing their own behavior.

self-reference effect the idea that people have more accurate recall of material that has been memorized with reference to the self.

self-schema the self as a memory structure composed of a collection of schemata.

self-serving bias basking in the glory of our self-made positive illusions; taking more credit for success than for failure.

sex biological category to which a person belongs.

sexism prejudice toward women.

sexual harassment uninvited sexually oriented behavior.

similarity-attraction hypothesis hypothesis that asserts a positive association between similarity and attraction.

situational variable an aspect of culture selected from all possible cultural characteristics, usually to serve as an independent variable in laboratory studies.

sleeper effect conditions under which the characteristics of the source have less influence, so that a message from a low credibility source increases in persuasiveness.

social capital societal resource composed of informal networks, organizations, and norms.

social change change in the relative power and status of majority and minority groups.

social comparison theory   theory that holds that when no objective measures are available, we compare ourselves with others in order to make more accurate self-evaluations.

social exchange theory   theory of social behavior based on the assumption that during social interactions people keep track of inputs and outcomes and attempt to maximize their profits.

social facilitation   increased performance as a result of the mere presence of others.

social identity theory   proposition that people strive to achieve a positive social identity and will take steps to remedy the situation if they feel they have an inadequate social identity.

social impact theory   theory that each additional confederate in a group will have less influence than the first.

social influence model   theory that the second and third additional confederates should have more influence than the first.

social learning theory   theory that behavior is learned through observation and imitation and by being rewarded and punished.

social loafing   a tendency for people to exert more effort when working on a task individually than as part of a group.

social memory   an agreed-upon version of the past.

social mobility   attempt to exit from the minority group and gain entrance to a higher-status group.

social psychology   the scientific study of individuals in social contexts.

social representations   the ideas and explanations that exist in society and are used by people to think about and interpret the world.

sociobiology   the scientific study of the biological basis of behavior.

source   who is trying to do the persuading.

spoiled identity   identity derived from group membership that puts a person at a disadvantage.

spontaneous norm   norm that evolves naturally within a group without any effort to control norm formation.

stereotype   culturally based but often unfounded generalization about groups.

subculture   distinct norms, rules, values, and other human-made characteristics used to distinguish a group from the dominant culture.

superordinate goals   goals that both conflicting groups desire, but that neither can achieve without the cooperation of the other.

target   who the communication is trying to persuade.

theory of planned behavior   theory that people form attitudes through a rational two-step process in which three factors combine to influence intent, and intent then influences behavior.

theory of reasoned action   theory that specific behavioral intentions are good predictors of specific behaviors.

tokenism   the practice of appearing to implement equality of opportunity by including or hiring a representative of a minority group.

transsexuals   those born anatomically of one sex and socialized as such, but who feel they belong to the other sex.

transvestites   those who take on the dress and appearance of the opposite sex.

triangular model of love   model that assumes three components to love relationships: intimacy, passion, and decision/commitment.

two-component model of emotion   theory which suggests that common to most emotional experiences, such as romantic love, are at least two steps: physiological changes in the person and interpreting such physiological changes according to the norms and rules of the culture.

ultimate attribution error   perceiving desirable actions by one's own group as arising from factors internal to the group, but those of out-groups as arising from factors external to the group. Similarly, seeing undesirable actions by one's own group as arising from external factors, and by other groups as arising from group characteristics.

validity the inferences that can be made on the basis of a measurement.

variable any characteristic that can have different values for a group of people or category of events, but only has one value at a given time.

zero-sum game game in which each player necessarily wins at the expense of the other.

Abdalla, R. (1982). *Sisters in affliction.* London: Zed Press.

Abeles, R. P. (1976). Relative deprivation, rising expectations, and black militancy. *Journal of Social Issues, 32,* 119–137.

Abelson, R. P., Aronson, E., McGuire, W. J., Newcomb, T. M., Rosenberg, M. J., & Tannenbaum, P. H. (Eds.) (1968). *Theories of cognitive consistency: A sourcebook.* Chicago: Rand McNally.

Abrahamian, E. (1993). *Khomeinism: Essays on the Islamic Republic.* Berkeley: University of California Press.

Abrams, D., & Hogg, M. A. (Eds.) (1990). *Social identity theory: Constructive and critical advances.* London: Harvester Wheatsheaf.

Abramson, L. Y., Seligman, M. E. P., & Teasdale, J. D. (1978). Learned helplessness in humans: Critique and reformulation. *Journal of Abnormal Psychology, 87,* 49–74.

Abroms, E. M. (1993). *The freedom of the self: The bio-existential treatment of character problems.* New York: Plenum Press.

Achenbach, J. (1995, March 19). Critique of pure O. J. *Washington Post Magazine,* p. 3.

Adair, G., Dushenko, T. W., & Lindsay, R. C. L. (1985). Ethical regulations and their impact on research practice. *American Psychologist, 40,* 59–72.

Adler, A. (1956). *The individual psychology of Alfred Adler.* New York: Basic Books.

Adler, N. J. (1986). *International dimensions of organizational behavior.* Boston: Kent.

Adorno, T. W., Frenkel-Brunswik, E., Levinson, D. J., & Sanford, B. W. (1950). *The authoritarian personality.* New York: Harper & Row.

Aiello, J. R. (1987). Human spatial behavior. In D. Stokols & I. Altman (Eds.), *Handbook of environmental psychology* (Vol. 1, pp. 505–531). New York: Wiley-Interscience.

Ajzen, I. (1988). *Attitudes, personality and behavior.* Chicago: Dorsey Press.

Ajzen, I. (1991). The theory of planned behavior. *Organizational Behavior and Human Decision Processes, 50,* 179–211.

Ajzen, I., & Fishbein, M. (1977). Attitude–behavior relations: A theoretical analysis and review of empirical research. *Psychological Bulletin, 84,* 888–918.

Allen, F. (1994). *Secret formula: How brilliant marketing and relentless salesmanship made Coca-Cola the best-known product in the world.* New York: Harper Business.

Allen, J. B., Kendrick, D. T., Linder, D. E., & McCall, M. A. (1989). Arousal and attraction: A response facilitation alternative to misattribution and negative-reinforcement models. *Journal of Personality and Social Psychology, 57,* 261–270.

Allen, V. L. (1975). Social support for nonconformity. In L. Berkowitz (Ed.), *Advances in experimental social psychology* (Vol. 2, pp. 133–175). New York: Academic Press.

Allen, V. L., & Levine, J. M. (1969). Consensus and conformity. *Journal of Experimental Social Psychology, 4,* 389–399.

Allison, J. A., & Wrightsman, L. S. (1993). *Rape: The misunderstood crime.* Newbury Park, CA: Sage.

Allon, N. (1982). The stigma of overweight in everyday life. In B. B. Woldman (Ed.), *Psychological aspects of obesity* (pp. 130–174). New York: Van Nostrand Reinhold.

Allport, G. W. (1954). *The nature of prejudice.* Garden City, NY: Doubleday/Anchor.

Allport, G. W. (1985). The historical background of social psychology. In D. Lindzey & E. Aronson (Eds.), *Handbook of social psychology* (pp. 1–46). New York: Random House.

Alper, J. (1993). The pipeline is leaking women all the way along. *Science, 260,* 409–411.

Altemeyer, B. (1981). *Right-wing authoritarianism.* Winnipeg: University of Manitoba Press.

Altemeyer, B. (1988a). *Enemies of freedom: Understanding right- wing authoritarianism.* San Francisco: Jossey-Bass.

Altemeyer, B. (1988b). The good soldier, marching in step: A psychological explanation of state terror. *Sciences,* March/April, 30–38.

Altemeyer, B. (1994). Reducing prejudice in right-wing authoritarians. In M. P. Zanna & J. M. Olson (Eds.), *The psychology of prejudice: The Ontario Symposium* (Vol. 7, pp. 131–148). Hillsdale, NJ: Lawrence Erlbaum.

Ameisen, E. R. (1990). Exclusivity in an ethnic elite: Racial prejudice as boundary maintenance. In P. L. Kilbride, J. C. Goodale, & E. R. Ameisen (Eds.), *Encounters with American ethnic cultures* (pp. 25–76). Tuscaloosa: University of Alabama Press.

American Psychological Association (1992). Ethical principles of psychologists and code of conduct. *American Psychologist, 47,* 1597–1611.

Amir, Y. (1969). Contact hypothesis in ethnic relations. *Psychological Bulletin, 71,* 319–342.

Amir, Y. (1976). The role of intergroup contact in change of prejudice and ethnic relations. In P. A. Katz (Ed.), *Toward the elimination of racism* (pp. 245–308). Elmsford, NY: Pergamon Press.

Anant, S. S. (1977). The changing intercaste attitudes in India: A follow-up after four years. *European Journal of Social Psychology, 5,* 49–59.

Anant, S. S. (1978). Caste attitudes of college students in India. *European Journal of Social Psychology, 8,* 193–202.

Ancona, L., & Pareyson, R. (1968). Contributo allo studie della aggressione: la dinamica della obbedienza distruttiva. *Archivadi psicologia, neurologia e psichiatria, 29,* 340–372.

Anderson, C. A. (1987). Temperature and aggression: Effects on quarterly, yearly, and city rates of violent and nonviolent crime. *Journal of Personality and Social Psychology, 52,* 1161–1173.

Anderson, C. A. (1989). Temperature and aggression: Ubiquitous effects of heat on occurrence of human violence. *Psychological Bulletin, 106,* 74–96.

Anderson, C. A., Anderson, K. B., & Deuser, W. E. (1996). Examining an affective aggression framework: Weapon and temperature effects on aggressive thoughts, affects, and attitudes. *Personality and Social Psychology Bulletin, 22,* 366–376.

Anderson, C. A., Deuser, W. E., & DeNeve, K. M. (1995). Hot temperatures, hostile affect, hostile cognition, and arousal: Tests of a general model of affective aggression. *Personality and Social Psychology Bulletin, 21,* 434–448.

Anderson, S. M. (1987). The role of cultural assumptions in self-concept development. In K. Yardley & T. Honess (Eds.), *Self and identity: Psychosocial perspectives* (pp. 231–246). New York: Wiley.

Anderson, S. M., & Ross, L. (1984). Self knowledge and social inference: I. The social impact of cognitive/affective and behavioral data. *Journal of Personality and Social Psychology, 46,* 280–293.

Anthony, T., Copper, C., & Mullen, B. (1992). Cross-racial facial identification: A social cognitive integration. *Personality and Social Psychology Bulletin, 18,* 296–301.

Aral, A. O., & Sunar, D. G. (1977). Interaction and justice norms: A cross-national comparison. *Journal of Social Psychology, 101,* 175–186.

Archer, D., & Gartner, R. (1984). *Violence and crime in cross-national perspective.* New Haven, CT: Yale University Press.

Archer, D., Iritani, B., Kimes, D. D., & Barrios, M. (1983). Face-ism: Five studies of sex differences in facial prominence. *Journal of Personality and Social Psychology, 45,* 725–735.

Archer, J. (1991). The influence of testosterone on human aggression. *British Journal of Psychology, 82,* 1–28.

Archer, J. (1996). Sex differences in social behavior: Are the social role and evolutionary explanations compatible? *American Psychologist, 51,* 909–917.

Archer, J., & Huntingford, F. (1994). Game theory models and escalation of animal fights. In M. Potegal & J. F. Knutson (Eds.), *The dynamics of aggression: Biological and social processes in dyads and groups* (pp. 3–31). Hillsdale, NJ: Lawrence Erlbaum.

Argyle, M. (1994). *The social psychology of social class.* New York: Routledge.

Aristotle. (1952). *The rhetoric.* (L. Cooper, Trans.). New York: D. Appleton.

Aronson, E. (1969). The theory of cognitive dissonance: A current perspective. In L. Berkowitz (Ed.), *Advances in experimental social psychology* (Vol. 4, pp. 1–34). New York: Academic Press.

Aronson, E. (1988). Persuasion via self-justification: Large commitments for small rewards. In E. Aronson (Ed.), *Readings about the social animal* (pp. 151–167). New York: W. H. Freeman.

Aronson, E. (1992). *The social animal* (6th ed.). New York: W. H. Freeman.

Aronson, E. (1995). *The social animal* (7th ed.). New York: W. H. Freeman.

Aronson, E., Brewer, M. B., & Carlsmith, J. M. (1985). Experimentation in social psychology. In G. Lindzey & E. Aronson (Eds.), *Handbook of social psychology* (3rd ed., Vol. I, pp. 441–486). New York: Random House.

Aronson, E., & Carlsmith, J. M. (1968). Experimentation in social psychology. In G. Lindzey & E. Aronson (Eds.), *The handbook of social psychology* (Vol. 2, pp. 1–79). Reading, MA: Addison-Wesley.

Aronson, E., Ellsworth, P. C., Carlsmith, J. M., & Gonzales, M. H. (1990). *Methods of research in social psychology* (2nd ed.). New York: McGraw-Hill.

Aronson, E., & Mills, J. (1959). The effect of severity of initiation on liking for a group. *Journal of Abnormal and Social Psychology, 59,* 177–181.

Aronson, E., Stephan, C., Sikes, J., Blaney, N., & Snapp, M. (1978). *The jigsaw classroom.* Beverly Hills, CA: Sage.

Asch, S. E. (1951). Effects of group pressure upon the modification and distortion of judgments. In H. Guetzkow (Ed.), *Groups, leadership, and men.* Pittsburgh: Carnegie Press.

Asch, S. E. (1955, November). Opinions and social pressure. *Scientific American,* pp. 31–35.

Asch, S. E. (1956). Studies of independence and conformity: A minority of one against a unanimous majority. *Psychological Monographs, 70* (9, Whole No. 416).

Ashmore, R. D. (1990). Sex, gender, and the individual. In L. A. Pervin (Ed.), *Handbook of personality: Theory and research* (pp. 486–526). New York: Guilford Press.

Astin, A. W., & Astin, H. S. (1993). *Undergraduate science education: The impact of different college environments on the educational pipeline in the sciences.* Higher Education Research Institute, University of California, Los Angeles.

Averill, J. R. (1982). *Anger and aggression: An essay on emotion.* New York: Springer-Verlag.

Averill, J. R. (1983). Studies on anger and aggression: Implications for theories of emotion. *American Psychologist, 38,* 1145–1160.

Avineri, S., & de-Shalit, A. (Eds.) (1992). *Communitarianism and individualism.* Oxford: Oxford University Press.

Ayres, I. (1991). Fair driving: Gender and race discrimination in retail car negotiations. *Harvard Law Review, 104,* 817–872.

Ayres, I., & Waldfogel, J. (1994). A market test for race discrimination in bail setting. *Stanford Law Review, 46,* 987–1047.

Bachman, J. G., Johnston, L. D., O'Malley, P. M., & Humphrey, R. N. (1988). Explaining the recent decline in marijuana use: Differentiating the effects of perceived risks, disapproval, and general lifestyle factors. *Journal of Health and Social Behavior, 29,* 92–112.

Baenninger, R. (Ed.) (1991). *Targets of violence and aggression.* Amsterdam: Elsevier/North-Holland.

Bainbridge, W. S., & Stark, R. (1980). Scientology: To be perfectly clear. *Sociological Analysis, 41,* 128–136.

Baldus, D. C., Woodworth, G., & Pulaski, C. A. (1985). Monitoring and evaluating contemporary death sentencing systems: Lessons from Georgia. *University of California, Davis, Law Review, 18,* 1375–1407.

Baldus, D. C., Woodworth, G., & Pulaski, C. A. (1994). Reflections on the "inevitability" of racial discrimination in capital sentencing and the "impossibility" of its prevention, detection, and correction. *Washington and Lee Law Review, 51,* 359–430.

Baldwin, M. W., Keelan, J. P. R., Fehr, B., & Enns, V. (1996). Social–cognitive conceptualization of attachment working models: Availability and accessibility effects. *Journal of Personality and Social Psychology, 71,* 94–109.

Bandura, A. (1965). Influence of models' reinforcement contingencies on the acquisition of imitative responses. *Journal of Personality and Social Psychology, 1,* 589–595.

Bandura, A. (1973). *Aggression: A social learning analysis.* Englewood Cliffs, NJ: Prentice Hall.

Bandura, A. (1986). *The social foundations of thought and action: A social cognitive theory.* Englewood Cliffs, NJ: Prentice Hall.

Bandura, A., & Walters, R. (1963). *Social learning and personality development.* New York: Holt, Rinehart & Winston.

Barbaree, H. E., & Marshall, W. L. (1991). The role of male sexual arousal in rape: Six models. *Journal of Consulting and Clinical Psychology, 59,* 621–630.

Bargh, J. A., Chaiken, S., Covender, R., & Pratto, F. (1992). The generality of the automatic attitude activation effect. *Journal of Personality and Social Psychology, 62,* 893–912.

Bargh, J. A., Raymond, P., Pryor, J. B., & Strack, F. (1995). Attractiveness of the underling: An automatic power–sex association and its consequences for sexual harassment and aggression. *Journal of Personality and Social Psychology, 68,* 768–781.

Barinaga, M. (1993). Feminists find gender everywhere in science. *Science, 260,* 392–393.

Barnett, R. C., Raudenbush, S. W., Brennan, R. T., Pleck, J. H., & Marshall, N. C. (1995). Change in job and marital experiences and change in psychological distress: A longitudinal study of dual–earner couples. *Journal of Personality and Social Psychology, 69,* 839–850.

Barnett, S. (Ed.) (1993). *Concepts of person: Kinship, caste, & marriage in India.* New York: Oxford University Press.

Barnlund, D. C. (1975). *Public and private self in Japan and the United States.* Tokyo: Simul Press.

Baron, R. A. (1972). Aggression as a function of ambient temperature and prior anger arousal. *Journal of Personality and Social Psychology, 21,* 183–189.

Baron, R. A. (1979). Aggression, empathy, and race: Effects of victim's pain cues, victim's race, and level of instigation on physical aggression. *Journal of Applied Social Psychology, 9,* 103–114.

Baron, R. A. (1987). Effects of negative air ions on interpersonal attraction: Evidence for intensification. *Journal of Personality and Social Psychology, 52,* 547–553.

Baron, R. A., & Bell, P. A. (1975). Aggression and heat: Mediating effect of prior provocation and exposure to an aggressive model. *Journal of Personality and Social Psychology, 31,* 825–832.

Baron, R. A., & Bell, P. A. (1976). Aggression and heat: The influence of ambient temperature, negative affect, and a cooling drink on physical aggression. *Journal of Personality and Social Psychology, 33,* 245–255.

Baron, R. A., & Richardson, D. R. (1994). *Human aggression* (2nd ed.). New York: Plenum Press.

Baron, R. A., Russell, G. W., & Arms, R. I. (1985). Negative ions and behavior: Impact of mood, memory, and aggression among Type A and Type B persons. *Journal of Personality and Social Psychology, 48,* 746–754.

Baron, R. S. (1986). Distraction–conflict theory: Progress and problems. In L. Berkowitz (Ed.), *Advances in experimental social psychology* (pp. 1–40). Orlando, FL: Academic Press.

Baron, R. S., Burgess, M. L., & Kao, C. F. (1991). Detecting and labeling prejudice: Do female perpetrators go undetected? *Personality and Social Psychology Bulletin, 17,* 115–123.

Baron, W. S., & Kennedy, W. L. (1993). Routine activities and a sub–culture of violence: A study of violence on the streets. *Journal of Research on Crime and Delinquency, 30,* 88–112.

Barry, H., Child, I., & Bacon, M. (1959). Relationship of child training to subsistence economy. *American Anthropologist, 61,* 51–63.

Bar–Tal, D., Goldberg, M., & Knaani, A. (1984). Causes of success and failure and their dimensions as a function of SES and gender: A phenomenological analysis. *British Journal of Educational Psychology, 54,* 51–61.

Bartlett, F. (1932). *Remembering.* Cambridge: Cambridge University Press.

Batson, C. D. (1987). Prosocial motivation: Is it ever altruistic? In L. Berkowitz (Ed.), *Advances in experimental social psychology* (Vol. 20, pp. 65–122). New York: Academic Press.

Batson, C. D. (1990). How social an animal? The human capacity for caring. *American Psychologist, 45,* 336–346.

Batson, C. D. (1991). *The altruism question: Toward a social psychological answer.* Hillsdale, NJ: Lawrence Erlbaum.

Batson, C. D. (1994). Why act for the public good? Four answers. *Personality and Social Psychology Bulletin, 20,* 603–610.

Batson, C. D. (1995). Prosocial motivation: Why do we help others? In A. Tesser (Ed.), *Advanced social psychology* (pp. 333–381). Boston: McGraw–Hill.

Batson, C. D., Batson, J. G., Slingsby, J. K., Harrell, K. L., Peekna, H. M., & Todd, R. M. (1991). Empathy–joy and the empathy–altruism hypothesis. *Journal of Personality and Social Psychology, 61,* 413–426.

Batson, C. D., Batson, J. G., Todd, R. M., & Brummett, B. H. (1995). Empathy and the collective good: Caring for one of the others in a social dilemma. *Journal of Personality and Social Psychology, 68,* 619–631.

Batson, C. D., Klein, T. R., Highberger, L., & Shaw, L. L. (1995). Immorality from empathy–induced altruism: When compassion and justice conflict. *Journal of Personality and Social Psychology, 68,* 1042–1054.

Batson, C. D., & Oleson, K. C. (1991). Current status of the empathy–altruism hypothesis. In M. S. Clark (Ed.), *Prosocial behavior* (pp. 62–85). Newbury Park, CA: Sage.

Batson, C. D., & Weeks, J. L. (1996). Mood effects of unsuccessful helping: Another test of the empathy–altruism hypothesis. *Personality and Social Psychology Bulletin, 22,* 148–157.

Baumeister, R. F. (1986). *Public self and private self.* New York: Springer–Verlag.

Baumeister, R. F. (Ed.) (1993). *Self–esteem: The puzzle of low self–regard.* New York: Plenum Press.

Baumeister, R. F. (1995). Self and identity: An introduction. In A. Tesser (Ed.), *Advanced social psychology* (pp. 51–98). New York: McGraw–Hill.

Baxter, T. L., & Goldberg, L. R. (1988). Perceived behavioral consistency underlying trait attributions to oneself and another: An extension of the actor–observer effect. *Personality and Social Psychology Bulletin, 13,* 437–447.

Beall, A. E., & Sternberg, R. J. (Eds.) (1995). *The psychology of gender.* New York: Guilford Press.

Beattie, J. (1980). Review article: Representations of the self in traditional Africa. *Africa, 50,* 313–320.

Beck, K. H., & Lund, A. L. (1981). The effects of health seriousness and personal efficacy upon intentions and behavior. *Journal of Applied Social Psychology, 11,* 401–415.

Beijing Review (1988). Changing attitudes toward marriage. *31,* 40.

Belanger, S., & Pinard, M. (1991). Ethnic movements and the competition model: Some missing links. *American Sociological Review, 56,* 446–457.

Belknap, P., & Leonard, W. M. II. (1991). A conceptual replication and extension of Erving Goffman's study of gender advertisements. *Sex Roles, 25,* 103–118.

Bell, B. E., & Loftus, E. F. (1985). Vivid persuasion in the courtroom. *Journal of Personality Assessment, 49,* 659–664.

Bell, C. C., & Jenkins, J. E. (1993). Community violence and children on Chicago's Southside. *Psychiatry, 56,* 46–55.

Bell, P. A. (1980). Effects of heat, noise, and provocation in retaliatory evaluative behavior. *Journal of Social Psychology, 110,* 97–100.

Bell, P. A., & Baron, R. A. (1977). Aggression and ambient temperature: The faciliating and inhibiting effects of hot and cold environments. *Bulletin of the Psychonomic Society, 9,* 443–445.

Bell, P. A., Fisher, J. D., Baum, A., & Greene, T. E. (1990). Environmental psychology. (3rd ed.). Fort Worth, TX: Holt, Rinehart & Winston.

Bell, P. R., & Jamieson, B. D. (1970). Publicity of the initial decisions and the risky shift phenomenon. *Journal of Experimental Social Psychology, 6,* 329–345.

Bell, R. P. (1981). *Worlds of friendship.* Beverly Hills, CA: Sage.

Bem, D. B. (1965). *Beliefs, attitudes, and human affairs.* Belmont, CA: Brooks/Cole.

Bem, D. B. (1970). *Beliefs, attitudes, and human affairs.* Belmont, CA: Brooks/Cole.

Bem, D. J. (1972). Self-perception theory. In L. Berkowitz (Ed.), *Advances in experimental social psychology* (Vol. 6, pp. 1–62). New York: Academic Press.

Bem, S. L. (1974). The measurement of psychological androgyny. *Journal of Consulting and Clinical Psychology, 42,* 155–162.

Benbow, C. P., & Lubinski, D. (1993). Consequences of gender differences in mathematical reasoning ability and some biological linkages. In M. Haug, R. E. Whalen, C. Aron, & K. L. Olsen (Eds.), *The development of sex differences and similarities in behaviour* (pp. 87–109). London: Kluwer Academic.

Bennett, P. G. (1995). Modeling decisions in international relations: Game theory and beyond. *Mershon International Studies Review, 39,* 19–52.

Benokraitis, N. V. (Ed.) (1997). *Subtle sexism: Current practices and prospects for change.* Thousand Oaks, CA: Sage.

Benson, P. L., Karabenick, S. A., & Lerner, R. M. (1976). Pretty pleases: The effects of physical attractiveness, sex, and race on receiving help. *Journal of Experimental Social Psychology, 12,* 409–415.

Bergen, R. K. (1996). *Wife rape: Understanding the responses of survivors and service providers.* Thousand Oaks, CA: Sage.

Bergmann, B. R. (1996). *In defense of affirmative action.* New York: New Republic/Basic Books.

Berkowitz, L. (1962). *Aggression: A social psychological analysis.* New York: McGraw-Hill.

Berkowitz, L. (1989). Frustration–aggression hypothesis: Examination and reformulation. *Psychological Bulletin, 106,* 59–73.

Berkowitz, L. (1993). *Aggression: Its causes, consequences, and control.* New York: McGraw-Hill.

Berkowitz, L. (1994). On the escalation of aggression. In M. Potegal & J. F. Knutson (Eds.), *The dynamics of aggression: Biological and social processes in dyads and groups* (pp. 33–41). Hillsdale, NJ: Lawrence Erlbaum.

Berlin, B., & Kay, P. (1969). *Basic color terms: Their universality and evolution.* Berkeley: University of California Press.

Berman, J. J., Murphy-Berman, V., & Pachauri, A. (1988). Sex differences in friendship patterns in India and in the United States. *Basic and Applied Social Psychology, 9,* 61–71.

Berman, J. J., & Singh, P. (1985). Cross-cultural similarities and differences in perceptions of fairness. *Journal of Cross-Cultural Psychology, 16,* 55–67.

Bernstein, M., & Crosby, F. (1980). An empirical examination of relative deprivation theory. *Journal of Experimental Social Psychology, 16,* 442–456.

Berry, J. W. (1966). Temne and Eskimo perceptual skills. *International Journal of Psychology, 1,* 207–229.

Berry, J. W. (1967). Independence and conformity in subsistence-level societies. *Journal of Personality and Social Psychology, 7,* 415–418.

Berry, J. W. (1984). Multicultural policy in Canada: A social psychological analysis. *Canadian Journal of Behavioural Science, 16,* 353–370.

Berry, J. W. (1991). *Sociopsychological costs and benefits of multiculturalism.* Working paper No. 24. Ottawa: Economic Council of Canada.

Berry, J. W. (1997). Individual and group relations in plural societies. In C. S. Granrose & S. Oskamp (Eds.), *Cross-cultural work groups* (pp. 17–35). Thousand Oaks, CA: Sage.

Berry, J. W., Kalin, R., & Taylor, D. M. (1977). *Multiculturalism and ethnic attitudes in Canada.* Ottawa: Supply and Services Canada.

Berscheid, E. (1985). Interpersonal attraction. In G. Lindzey & E. Aronson (Eds.), *Handbook of social psychology* (3rd ed., Vol. II, pp. 413–484). New York: Random House.

Bersoff, D. M., & Miller, J. G. (1993). Culture, context and the development of moral accountability judgments. *Developmental Psychology, 29,* 664–676.

Bertcher, H. J., & Maple, F. F. (1996). *Creating groups* (2nd ed.). Thousand Oaks, CA: Sage.

Bertenthal, B. I., & Fischer, K. W. (1978). Development of self recognition in the infant. *Developmental Psychology, 14,* 44–50.

Betancourt, H., & Weiner, B. (1982). Attributions of achievement related events, expectancy, and sentiments: A study of success and failure in Chile and the United States. *Journal of Cross-Cultural Psychology, 13,* 362–374.

Bethlehem, D. W. (1975). The effect of westernization on cooperative behavior in Central Africa. *International Journal of Psychology, 10,* 219–224.

Bharati, A. (1983). India: South Asian perspectives on aggression. In A. P. Goldstein & M. H. Segall (Eds.),

Aggression in global perspective (pp. 237–260). New York: Pergamon Press.

Bickman, L. (1974). The social power of a uniform. *Journal of Applied Social Psychology, 4,* 47–61.

Billig, M. G. (1976). *Social psychology and intergroup relations.* London: Academic Press.

Billig, M. G. (1978). *Fascists: A social psychological view of the National Front.* London: Academic Press.

Billig, M. (1995). *Banal nationalism.* Thousand Oaks, CA: Sage.

Birt, C. M., & Dion, K. L. (1987). Relative deprivation theory and responses to discrimination in a gay male and lesbian sample. *British Journal of Social Psychology, 26,* 139–145.

Bjorkqvist, K., Lagerspetz, K. M. J., & Kaukiainen, A. (1993). Do girls manipulate and boys fight? Developmental trends in regard to direct and indirect aggression. *Aggressive Behavior, 18,* 117–127.

Bjorkqvist, K., Osterman, K., & Lagerspetz, K. M. J. (1994). Sex differences in covert aggression among adults. *Aggressive Behavior, 20,* 27–33.

Blackler, F. (Ed.) (1983). *Social psychology and developing countries.* Chichester, England: Wiley.

Blair, I. V., & Banaji, M. R. (1996). Automatic and controlled processes in stereotype priming. *Journal of Personality and Social Psychology, 70,* 1142–1163.

Blair, S. L., & Lichter, D. T. (1991). Measuring the division of household labor: Gender segregation of housework among American couples. *Journal of Family Issues, 12,* 91–113.

Blake, R. R., & Mouton, J. S. (1962). The intergroup dynamics of win–loss conflict and problem–solving collaboration in union–management relations. In M. Sherif (Ed.), *Intergroup relations and leadership* (pp. 94–141). New York: Wiley.

Blasovich, J., Ernst, J. M., Tomaka, J., Kelsey, R. M., Salomon, K. L., & Fazio, R. H. (1993). Attitude accessibility as a moderator of autonomic reactivity during decision making. *Journal of Personality and Social Psychology, 64,* 165–176.

Blau, P. M. (1964). *Exchange and power in social life.* New York: Wiley.

Bleier, R. (Ed.) (1986). *Feminist approaches to science.* New York: Pergamon Press.

Block, J. H. (1973). Conceptions of sex role: Some cross–cultural and longitudinal perspectives. *American Psychologist, 28,* 512–526.

Blunt, P., & Jones, M. L. (1992). *Managing organizations in Africa.* Berlin: De Gruyter.

Bogdanich, W. (1991). *The great white lie: Dishonesty, waste, and incompetence in the medical community.* New York: Touchstone.

Bolaria, B. S., & Li, P. S. (1988). *Racial oppression in Canada* (2nd ed.). Toronto: Garamond Press.

Bond, M. H. (1983). A proposal for cross–cultural studies of attribution. In M. Hewstone (Ed.), *Attribution theory: Social and functional extensions.* Oxford: Blackwell.

Bond, M. H. (1986). *The psychology of the Chinese people.* New York: Oxford University Press.

Bond, M. H. (Ed.) (1988). *The cross-cultural challenge to social psychology.* Beverly Hills, CA: Sage.

Bond, M. (Ed.). (1997). *Working at the interface of cultures: 20 lives in social science.* London: Routledge.

Bond, M., Leung, K., & Wan, K. C. (1982). The social impact of self–effacing attributions: The Chinese case. *Journal of Social Psychology, 118,* 157–166.

Boothe, J. W., Bradley, L. H., Keough, K. K., & Kirk, S. P. (1993). The violence at your door. *The Executive Educator, 15,* 16–21.

Borgida, E., & Brekke, N. (1985). Psychological research on rape trials. In A. Burgess (Ed.), *Rape and sexual assault* (pp. 313–342). New York: Garland.

Borgida, E., & Campbell, B. (1982). Belief relevance and attitude–behavior consistency: The moderating role of personal experience. *Journal of Personality and Social Psychology, 42,* 239–247.

Bornstein, R. F. (1989). Exposure and affect. Overview and meta–analysis of research, 1968–1987. *Psychological Bulletin, 106,* 265–289.

Bossard, J. H. S. (1932). Residential propinquity as a factor in marriage selection. *American Journal of Sociology, 38,* 219–224.

Boster, F. J., & Mongeau, P. (1984). Fear-arousing persuasive messages. In R. N. Bostrom (Ed.), *Communication yearbook* (Vol. 8, pp. 330–375). Beverly Hills, CA: Sage.

Bothwell, R. K., Bringham, J. C., & Malpass, R. S. (1989). Cross-racial identification. *Psychology and Personality Bulletin, 15,* 19–25.

Boucher, J., Landis, D., & Clark, K. A. (1987). *Ethnic conflict: International perspectives.* Newbury Park, CA: Sage.

Bower, G. H., & Gilligan, S. G. (1979). Remembering information related to one's self. *Journal of Research in Personality, 13,* 420–432.

Bowser, B. P. (Ed.) (1995). *Racism and antiracism in world perspective.* Thousand Oaks, CA: Sage.

Bowser, B. P., & Hunt, R. G. (Eds.) (1996). *Impacts of racism on white Americans* (2nd ed.). Beverly Hills, CA: Sage.

Boyanowsky, E. O., Calvert, J., Young, J., & Brideau, L. (1981–1982). Toward a thermoregulatory model of violence. *Journal of Environmental Systems, 1,* 81–87.

Bradac, J. J., Hemphill, M. E., & Tardy, C. H. (1981). Language style on trial: Effects of "powerful" and "powerless" speech upon judgments of victims and villains. *Western Journal of Speech Communication, 45,* 327–341.

Brandon, R., & Davies, C. (1973). *Wrongful imprisonment.* London: Allen & Unwin.

Braunstein, P. (1988). Toward intimacy: The fourteenth and fifteenth centuries. In P. Aries & G. Duby (Eds.), *A history of private life: Revelations of the medieval world* (pp. 535–630). Cambridge, MA: Belknap Press.

Breakwell, M. B. (Ed.) (1991). *Social psychology of identity and the self concept.* London: Academic/Surrey University Press.

Brearley, H. C. (1932). *Homicide in the United States.* Montclair, NJ: Patterson-Smith.

Brehm, J. W., & Cohen, A. R. (1962). *Explorations in cognitive dissonance.* New York: Wiley.

Brehm, S. (1992). *Intimate relationships* (2nd ed.). New York: McGraw-Hill.

Brennan, M. B. (1996, June 10). Women chemists reconsidering careers at research universities. *Chemical & Engineering News,* pp. 8–15.

Brewer, M. B. (1991). The social self: On being the same and different at the same time. *Personality and Social Psychology Bulletin, 17,* 475–482.

Brewer, M. B. (1993). The role of distinctiveness in social identity and group behavior. In M. Hogg & D. Abrams (Eds.), *Group motivation: Social psychological perspectives.* London: Harvester Wheatsheaf.

Brewer, M. B., Manzi, J. M., & Shaw, J. S. (1993). In-group identification as a function of depersonalization, distinctiveness, and status. *Psychological Science, 4,* 88–92.

Brewer, M. B., & Miller, N. (1997). *Intergroup relations.* Pacific Grove, CA: Brooks/Cole.

Brewer, M. B. & Weber, J. G. (1994). Self-evaluation effects of interpersonal versus intergroup social comparison. *Journal of Personality and Social Psychology, 66,* 268–275.

Bright, S. B. (1995). Discrimination, death and denial: The tolerance of racial discrimination in infliction of the death penalty. *Santa Clara Law Review,* February, 107–113.

Bromley, D. G., & Shupe, A. D., Jr. (1979). *"Moonies" in America: Cult, church, and crusade.* Beverly Hills, CA: Sage.

Bronfenbrener, U. (1986). The ecology of the family as a context for human development. *Developmental Psychology, 22,* 723–742.

Broverman, I. K., Vogel, S. R., Broverman, D. M., Clarkson, F. E., & Rosenkrantz, P. S. (1972). Sex-role stereotypes: A current appraisal. *Journal of Social Issues, 28,* 59–78.

Brown, B. (1987). Territoriality. In D. Stokols & I. Altman (Eds.), *Handbook of environmental psychology* (Vol. 1, pp. 505–531). New York: Wiley-Interscience.

Brown, D. E. (1991). *Human universals.* Philadelphia: Temple University Press.

Brown, I., & Hullin, R. (1993). Contested bail applications: The treatment of ethnic minority and white offenders. *Criminal Law Review,* February, 107–113.

Brown, J. D., & Dutton, K. A. (1995). Truth and consequences: The costs and benefits of accurate self-knowledge. *Personality and Social Psychology Bulletin, 21,* 1288–1296.

Brown, L., Kane, H., & Ayres, E. (1993). *Vital signs: The trends that are shaping our future.* New York: Norton and the Worldwatch Institute.

Brown, L. B. (1987). *The psychology of religious belief.* London: Academic Press.

Brown, R. (1966). *Social psychology.* New York: Free Press.

Brown, R., & Kulik, J. (1977). Flashbulb memories. *Cognition, 5,* 73–99.

Brown, R. J. (1984). The effects of intergroup similarity and cooperation vs. competitive orientation on intergroup discrimination. *British Journal of Social Psychology, 23,* 21–33.

Brown, R. J. (1988). *Group processes: Dynamics within and between groups.* Oxford: Blackwell.

Brown, R. J. (1995). *Prejudice: Its social psychology.* Oxford: Blackwell.

Brown, R. J., & Smith, A. (1989). Perceptions of and by minority groups: The case of women in academia. *European Journal of Social Psychology, 19,* 61–75.

Bruner, J. S. (1990). *Acts of meaning.* Cambridge, MA: Harvard University Press.

Brush, S. (1984). *Men: An owner's manual. A comprehensive guide to having a man underfoot.* New York: Simon & Schuster.

Bryan, J. H., & Test, M. A. (1967). Models of helping: Naturalistic studies in helping behavior. *Journal of Personality and Social Psychology, 6,* 400–407.

Buck, R., & Ginsburg, B. (1991). Spontaneous communication and altruism: The communicative gene hypothesis. In M. C. Clark (Ed.), *Prosocial behavior* (pp. 142–173). Newbury Park, CA: Sage.

Burgoon, M. (1989). Messages and persuasive effects. In J. J. Bradac (Ed.), *Message effects in communication science* (pp. 129–164). Newbury Park, CA: Sage.

Burgoon, M., Dillard, J. P., & Miller, M. D. (1982). Cultural and situational influences on the process of persuasion strategy selection. *International Journal of Intercultural Relations, 6,* 85–100.

Burn, S. M. (1996). *The social psychology of gender.* New York: McGraw-Hill.

Burnett, A. L., Sr. (1994). Permeation of race, national origin and gender issues from initial law enforcement through sentencing: The need for sensitivity, equalitarianism and vigilance in the criminal justice system. *American Criminal Law Review, 31,* 1153–1175.

Burnstein, E., Crandall, C., & Kitayama, S. (1994). Some neo-Darwinian decision rules for altruism: Weighing cues for inclusive fitness as a function of the biological importance of the decision. *Journal of Personality and Social Psychology, 67,* 773–789.

Burtless, G., & Smeeding, T. (1995, June 25). America's tide: Lifting the yachts, swamping the row boats. *Washington Post,* p. C3.

Bushman, B. (1984). Perceived symbols of authority and their influence on compliance. *Journal of Applied Social Psychology, 14,* 501–508.

Bushman, B. J. (1996). Individual differences in the extent and development of aggressive cognitive-association networks. *Personality and Social Psychology Bulletin, 22,* 811–819.

Buss, D. M. (1981). Sex differences in the evaluation and performance of dominant acts. *Journal of Personality and Social Psychology, 40,* 147–154.

Buss, D. M. (1985). Human mate selection. *American Scientist, 73,* 47–51.

Buss, D. M. (1989). Sex differences in human mate preferences: Evolutionary hypothesis tested in 37 cultures. *Behavioral and Brain Sciences, 12,* 1–49.

Buss, D. M. (1994a). *The evolution of desire: Strategies of human mating.* New York: Basic Books.

Buss, D. M. (1994b). The strategies of human mating. *American Scientist, 82,* 238–249.

Buss, D. M., Gomes, M., Higgins, D. S., & Lauterbach, K. (1987). Tactics of persuasion. *Journal of Personality and Social Psychology, 52,* 1219–1229.

Buss, D. M., Larsen, R., Westen, D., & Semmelroth, J. (1992). Sex differences in jealousy: Evolution, physiology, and psychology. *Psychological Science, 3,* 251–255.

Buss, D. M., & Schmitt, D. P. (1993). Sexual strategies theory: An evolutionary perspective on human mating. *Psychological Review, 100,* 204–232.

Buunk, B. P., & Van Yperen, N. W. (1991). Referential comparisons, relational comparisons, and exchange orientation: Their relation to marital satisfaction. *Personality and Social Psychology Bulletin, 17,* 709–717.

Byrne, D. (1961). Interpersonal attraction and attitude similarity. *Journal of Abnormal Social Psychology, 62,* 713–715.

Byrne, D. (1971). *The attraction paradigm.* New York: Academic Press.

Byrne, D., Clore, G, L., & Worchel, P. (1966). The effect of economic similarity–dissimilarity on interpersonal attraction. *Journal of Personality and Social Psychology, 4,* 220–224.

Cadenhead, C., Durant, H. R., Pendergrast, A. R., & Salvens, G. (1994). Factors associated with the use of violence among urban black adolescents. *American Journal of Public Health, 84,* 612–617.

Callaghan, K. A. (Ed.) (1994). *Ideals in feminine beauty.* Westport, CT: Greenwood Press.

Calvert, J. D. (1988). Physical attractiveness: A review and reevalaution of its role in social skill research. *Behavioral Assessment, 10,* 29–42.

Campbell, D. T. (1957). Factors relevant to validity of experiments in social settings. *Psychological Bulletin, 54,* 297–312.

Campbell, J. D., Tesser, A., & Fairey, P. J. (1986). Conformity and attention to stimuli: Some temporal and contextual dynamics. *Journal of Personality and Social Psychology, 51,* 315–324.

Campbell, J. D., Trapnell, P. D., Heine, S. J., & Katz, L. M. (1996). Self-concept clarity: Measurement, personality correlates, and cultural boundaries. *Journal of Personality and Social Psychology, 70,* 141–156.

Cantor, J. R., Alfonso, H., & Zillmann, D. (1976). The persuasive effectiveness of the peer appeal and the communicator's first-hand experience. *Communication Research, 3,* 293–310.

Caplan, N., Choy, M. H., & Whitmore, J. K. (1992). Indochinese refugee families and academic achievement. *Scientific American, 266,* 36–42.

Carli, L. L. (1989). Gender differences in interaction style and influence. *Journal of Personality and Social Psychology, 56,* 565–576.

Carlson, J., & Davis, D. M. (1971). Cultural values and the risky shift: A cross-cultural test in Uganda and the United States. *Journal of Personality and Social Psychology, 20,* 392–399.

Carr, S. C., & Schumaker, J. F. (Eds.) (1996). *Psychology and the developing world.* Westport, CT: Praeger.

Carrasco, S. (1996, October 17). Scores killed in soccer stampede. *Washington Post,* p. A25.

Cartwright, D. (1979). Contemporary social psychology in historical perspective. *Social Psychology Quarterly, 42,* 82–93.

Carver, C. S., & Scheier, M. F. (1981). *Attention and self-regulation: Control theory approach to human behavior.* New York: Springer-Verlag.

Cash, T. F., Gillen, B., & Burns, D. S. (1977). Sexism and "beautyism" in personnel consultant decision making. *Journal of Applied Psychology, 62,* 301–310.

Castro, M. A. C. (1974). Reactions to receiving aid as a function of cost to donor and opportunity to aid. *Journal of Applied Social Psychology, 4,* 194–209.

Ceci, S., Ross, D., & Toglia, M. (Eds.) (1989). *New directions in child witness research.* New York: Springer-Verlag.

Cerbus, G. (1970). Seasonal variation in some mental health statistics: Suicides, homicides, psychiatric admissions, and institutional placement of the retarded. *Journal of Clinical Psychology, 26,* 60–63.

Chagnon, N. A. (1992). *Yanomamo* (4th ed.). New York: Harcourt Brace Jovanovich.

Chaiken, S. (1979). Communicator's physical attractiveness and persuasion. *Journal of Personality and Social Psychology, 37,* 1387–1397.

Chaiken, S. (1986). Physical appearance and social influence. In C. P. Herman, M. P. Zanna, & E. T. Higgins (Eds.), *Physical appearance, stigma, and social behavior: The Ontario Symposium* (Vol. 3, pp. 143–177). Hillsdale, NJ: Lawrence Erlbaum.

Chaiken, S., & Eagly, A. H. (1976). Communication modality as a determinant of message persuasiveness and message comprehensibility. *Journal of Personality and Social Psychology, 34,* 605–614.

Chaiken, S., & Stangor, C. (1987). Attitudes and attitude change. *Annual Review of Psychology, 38,* 575–630.

Chandler, T. A., Shama, D. D., & Wolf, F. M. (1983). Gender differences in affiliation and attributions: A five-nation study. *Journal of Cross-Cultural Psychology, 14,* 241–256.

Chandra, S. (1973). The effects of group pressure in perception: A cross-cultural conformity study in Fiji. *International Journal of Psychology, 8,* 37–39.

Charry, J. M., & Hawkinshire, F. B. W. (1981). Effects of atmospheric electricity on some substrates of disordered social behavior. *Journal of Personality and Social Psychology, 41,* 185–197.

Chemical and Engineering News (1996, June 3). Birth control research, "second contraceptive revolution" urged, p. 6.

Chen, H., Yates, B. T., & McGinnies, E. (1988). Effects of involvement on observers' estimates of consensus, distinctiveness, and consistency. *Personality and Social Psychology Bulletin, 14,* 468–478.

Christie, R. (1965). Some implications of research trends in social psychology. In O. Klienberg and R. Christie (Eds.), *Perspectives in social psychology* (pp. 141–152). New York: Holt, Rinehart & Winston.

Christie, R. (1991). Authoritarianism and related constructs. In J. P. Robinson, P. R. Shaver, & L. S. Wrightsman (Eds.), *Measures of personality and social psychological attitudes* (pp. 501–571). New York: Academic Press.

Christie, R., & Geis, F. L. (1970). *Studies in Machiavellianism.* New York: Academic Press.

Cialdini, R. B. (1988). *Influence: Science and practice.* Glenview, IL: Scott, Foresman/Little, Brown.

Cialdini, R. B., & Richardson, K. D. (1980). Two indirect tactics of image management: Basking and blasting. *Journal of Personality and Social Psychology, 39,* 406–415.

Cialdini, R. B., Schaller, M., Houlihan, D., Arps, K., Fultz, J., & Beaman, A. L. (1987). Empathy-based helping: Is it selflessly or selfishly motivated? *Journal of Personality and Social Psychology, 52,* 749–758.

Clark, K. B. (1992). Candor about Negro-Jewish relations. In I. Howe (Ed.), *Bridges and boundaries: African-Americans and Jewish Americans.* New York: Jewish Museum.

Clark, K. B., & Clark, M. P. (1947). Racial identification and preferences in Negro children. In T. M. Newcomb & E. L. Hartley (Eds.), *Readings in social psychology* (pp. 169–178). New York: Holt.

Clark, M. S. (Ed.) (1991). *Prosocial behavior.* Newbury Park, CA: Sage.

Clark, M. S., Gotay, G. C., & Mills, J. (1974). Acceptance of help as a function of the potential helper and opportunity to repay. *Journal of Applied Social Psychology, 4,* 224–229.

Clark, M. S., Mills, J., & Corcoran, D. (1989). Keeping track of needs and inputs of friends and strangers. *Personality and Social Psychology Bulletin, 15,* 533–542.

Clémence, A., Doise, W., de Rosa, A. S., & Gonzalez, L. (1995). La représentation sociale des droits de l'homme: Une recherche internationale sur l'étendue et les limites de l'universalité. *Journal International de Psychologie, 30,* 181–212.

Clement, R., & Noels, K. A. (1992). Toward a situated approach to ethnolinguistic identity: The effects of status on individuals and groups. *Journal of Language and Social Psychology, 11,* 202–232.

Cogan, J. C., Bhalla, S. K., Sefa-Dedeh, A., & Rothblum, E. D. (1996). A comparison study of United States and African students on perceptions of obesity and thinness. *Journal of Cross-Cultural Psychology, 27,* 98–113.

Cohen, D. (1996). Law, social policy, and violence: The impact of regional cultures. *Journal of Personality and Social Psychology, 70,* 961–978.

Cohen, D., & Nisbett, R. E. (1994). Self-protection and the culture of honor: Explaining Southern homicide. *Personality and Social Psychology Bulletin, 20,* 551–567.

Cohen, L. L., & Swim, J. K. (1995). The differential impact of gender ratios on women and men: Tokenism, self-confidence, and expectations. *Personality and Social Psychology Bulletin, 21,* 976–991.

Cole, J. R., & Zuckerman, H. (1987). Marriage, motherhood and research performance in science. *Scientific American, 256,* 119–125.

Cole, M., & Cole, S. R. (1993). *The development of children* (2nd ed.). New York: W. H. Freeman.

Collier, G., Minton, H. L., & Reynolds, G. (1991). *Currents of thought in American social psychology.* New York: Oxford University Press.

Condry, J., & Condry, S. (1976). Sex differences: A study of the eye of the beholder. *Child Development, 47,* 812–819.

Conger, J. A. (1991). Inspiring others: The language of leadership. *The Executive: An Academy of Management Publication, 5,* 31–45.

Conger, J. A., & Kanungo, R. N. (Eds.) (1988). *Charismatic leadership: The elusive factor in organizational effectiveness.* San Francisco: Jossey-Bass.

Connor, R. C., Smolker, R. A., & Richards, A. F. (1992). Two levels of alliance formation among male bottlenose dolphins. *Proceedings of the National Academy of Science, 89,* 987–990.

Constantinople, A. (1973). Masculinity-femininity: An exception to a famous dictum? *Psychological Bulletin, 80,* 389–407.

Cook, E. A., Thomas, S., & Wilcox, C. (Eds.) (1994). *The year of the woman: Myths and realities.* Boulder, CO: Westview Press.

Cooley, C. H. (1902). *Human nature and the social order.* New York: Scribner's.

Coon, C. S. (1946). The universality of natural groupings in human societies. *Journal of Educational Sociology, 20,* 163–168.

Cooper, H. M. (1979). Statistically combining independent studies: A meta-analysis of sex differences in conformity research. *Journal of Personality and Social Psychology, 37,* 131–146.

Corter, C., Trehub, S., Boukydis, C., Ford, L., Clehoffer, L., & Minde, K. (1978). Nurses' judgments of the attractiveness of premature infants. *Infant Behavior Development, 1,* 373–380.

Costa, J. A. (Ed.) (1994). *Gender issues and consumer behavior.* Thousand Oaks, CA: Sage.

Cotton, J. L. (1986). Ambient temperature and violent crime. *Journal of Applied Social Psychology, 16,* 786–801.

Courneya, K. S., & Carron, A. V. (1992). The home advantage in sport competitions: A literature review. *Journal of Sport and Exercise Psychology, 14,* 13–27.

Cousins, S. D. (1989). Culture and self-perception in Japan and the United States. *Journal of Personality and Social Psychology, 56,* 124–131.

Cox, G. D. (1989, May 29). Consultants to the stars, they deploy an army of 100+ Ph.Ds. *National Law Journal,* pp. 26–27.

Crandall, C. S. (1994). Prejudice against fat people: Ideology and self-interest. *Journal of Personality and Social Psychology, 66,* 882–894.

Crawford, M., & Marecek, J. (1989). Psychology reconstructs the female. *Psychology of Women Quarterly, 13,* 147–165.

Crèvecoeur, M. G. J. de (1782/1985). Letters from an American farmer. In G. McMichael (Ed.), *Anthology of American literature* (pp. 392–406). New York: Macmillan.

Critchfield, R. (1983). *Villages.* New York: Anchor Books.

Crocker, J., Cronwell, B., & Major, B. (1993). The stigma of overweight: Affective consequences of attributional ambiguity. *Journal of Personality and Social Psychology, 64,* 60–70.

Crocker, J., & Luhtanen, R. (1990). Collective self-esteem and in-group bias. *Journal of Personality and Social Psychology, 58,* 60–67.

Crocker, J., & Major, B. (1989). Social stigma and self-esteem: The self-protective properties of stigma. *Psychological Review, 96,* 608–630.

Crosby, F. (1982). *Relative deprivation and working women.* New York: Oxford University Press.

Crosby, F. (1984a). The denial of personal discrimination. *American Behavioral Scientist, 27,* 371–386.

Crosby, F. (1984b). Relative deprivation in organizational settings. In B. M. Staw & L. L. Cummings (Eds.), *Research in organizational behavior: An annual series of analytic essays and critical reviews* (pp. 51–93). Greenwich, CT: JAI Press.

Crosby, F., Bromley, S., & Saxe, L. (1980). Recent unobtrusive studies of black and white discrimination and prejudice: A literature review. *Psychological Bulletin, 87,* 546–563.

Cross, W. E. (1991). *Shades of black: Diversity in African-American identity.* Philadelphia: Temple University Press.

Crystal, D. S., & Watanabe, H. (1997). Intolerance of human differences: A cross-cultural and developmental study of American, Japanese, and Chinese children. *Journal of Applied Developmental Psychology, 18,* 149–167.

Culbertson, F. M. (1997). Depression and gender: An international review. *American Psychologist, 52,* 25–31.

Cummins, H. J. (1993, November 14). Brokers may see women differently. *Washington Post,* p. H10.

Cunningham, M. R. (1986). Measuring the physical in physical attractiveness: Quasi-experiments in the sociobiology of female beauty. *Journal of Personality and Social Psychology, 50,* 925–935.

Cunningham, M. R., Shaffer, D. R., Barbee, P. L., & Kelley, D. J. (1990). Separate processes in the relation of elation and depression to helping: Social versus personal concerns. *Journal of Experimental Social Psychology, 26,* 13–33.

Cunningham, M. R., Steinberg, J., & Grev, R. (1980). Wanting to and having to help: Separate motivations for positive mood and guilt-induced helping. *Journal of Personality and Social Psychology, 38,* 181–192.

Cunnison, I. (1960). Headmanship and the ritual of Luapula villages. In S. Ottenberg & P. Ottenberg (Eds.), *Cultures and societies of Africa* (pp. 284–302). New York: Random House.

Curtin, K. (1975). *Women in China*. New York: Pathfinder Press.

Cyrus, V. (Ed.) (1993). *Experiencing race, class, and gender in the United States*. Mountain View, CA: Mayfield.

Daly, M., & Wilson, M. (1988a). *Homicide*. New York: Aldine de Gruyter.

Daly, M., & Wilson, M. (1988b). Evolutionary social psychology and family homicide. *Science, 242*, 519–524.

Daly, M., & Wilson, M. (1990). Killing the competition: Female/female and male/male homicide. *Human Nature, 1*, 81–107.

Darley, J. M. (1991). Altruism and prosocial behavior research: Reflections and prospects. In M. C. Clark (Ed.), *Prosocial behavior* (pp. 322–327). Newbury Park, CA: Sage.

Darley, J. M., & Latané, B. (1968). Bystander intervention in emergencies: Diffusion of responsibility. *Journal of Personality and Social Psychology, 8*, 377–383.

Darwin, C. (1859/1993). *The origin of species by natural selection or the preservation of favored races in the struggle for life*. New York: Modern Library.

Davis, D. M. (1991). Portrayals of women in prime-time network television: Some demographic characteristics. *Sex Roles, 23*, 325–332.

Davis, M. H., Conklin, L., Smith, A., & Luce, C. (1996). Effect of perspective taking on the cognitive representation of persons: A merging of self and other. *Journal of Personality and Social Psychology, 70*, 713–726.

Davis, M. H., & Harvey, J. C. (1992). Declines in major league batting performance as a function of game pressure: A drive theory analysis. *Journal of Applied Social Psychology, 22*, 714–735.

Davis, M. H., & Stephan, W. G. (1980). Attributions for exam performance. *Journal of Applied Social Psychology, 10*, 235–248.

Davis, S. (1990). Men as success objects and women as sex objects: A study of personal advertisements. *Sex Roles, 23*, 43–51.

Dawes, R. M. (1991). Social dilemmas, economic self-interest, and evolutionary theory. In D. R. Brown & J. E. K. Smith (Eds.), *Frontiers of mathematical psychology: Essays in honor of Clyde Coombs* (pp. 53–79). New York: Springer-Verlag.

Dawkins, R. (1976). *The selfish gene*. New York: Oxford University Press.

Dawkins, R. (1982). *The extended phenotype*. San Francisco: W. H. Freeman.

DeAngelis, T. (1996, November). Women in construction more often harassed. *APA Monitor*, p. 43.

Deaux, K., & Emswiller, T. (1974). Explanations of successful performance on sex-linked tasks: What is skill for the male is luck for the female. *Journal of Personality and Social Psychology, 29*, 80–85.

de Bary, W. T. (1970). *Self and society in Ming thought*. New York: Columbia University Press.

Deci, E. L., & Ryan, R. M. (1985). *Intrinsic motivation and self-determination in human behavior*. New York: Plenum Press.

deFronzo, J. (1984). Climate and crime. *Environment and Behavior, 16*, 185–210.

Delgado, J. M. R. (1969). *Physical control of the mind*. New York: Harper & Row.

Denmark, F. (1994). Engendering psychology. *American Psychology, 49*, 329–334.

Deutsch, M. (1949). An experimental study of the effects of cooperation and competition upon group process. *Human Relations, 2*, 199–231.

Deutsch, M. (1962). Psychological alternatives to war. *Journal of Social Issues, 18*, 97–119.

Deutsch, M. (1969). Socially relevant science: Reflections on some studies of interpersonal conflict. *American Psychologist, 24*, 1076–1092.

Deutsch, M. (1973). *The resolution of conflict*. New Haven, CT: Yale University Press.

Deutsch, M. (1975). Equity, equality, and need: What determines which value will be used as the basis of distributive justice? *Journal of Social Issues, 31*, 137–149.

Deutsch, M. (1985). *Distributive justice: A social psychological perspective*. New Haven, CT: Yale University Press.

Deutsch, M. (1993). Educating for a peaceful world. *American Psychologist, 48*, 510–517.

Deutsch, M. (1994). Constructive conflict resolution: Principles, training, and research. *Journal of Social Issues, 50*, 13–32.

Deutsch, M., & Gerard, H. B. (1955). A study of normative and informational social influence upon individual judgment. *Journal of Abnormal and Social Psychology, 51*, 629–636.

Devine, P. G. (1995). Prejudice and out-group perception. In A. Tesser (Ed.), *Advanced social psychology* (pp. 467–524). New York: McGraw-Hill.

Devine, P. G., & Elliot, A. J. (1995). Are racial stereotypes really fading? The Princeton trilogy revisited. *Personality and Social Psychology Bulletin, 21*, 1139–1150.

De Vos, G. A. (1985). Dimensions of the self in Japanese culture. In A. Marsella, G. De Vos, & F. L. K. Hsu (Eds.), *Culture and self* (pp. 149–184). London: Tavistock.

De Vos, G. A. (1992). *Social cohesion and alienation: Minorities in the U.S. and Japan*. Boulder, CO: Westview Press.

De Vos, G. A., & Wetherall, W. O. (1983). *Japan's minorities: Burakumin, Koreans, Ainu, and Okinawans*. London: Minority Rights Group.

Dew, M. A., Dunn, L. O., Bromet, E. J., & Shulberg, H. C. (1988). Factors affecting help-seeking during depression in a community sample. *Journal of Affective Disorders, 14*, 223–234.

Dhawan, N., Roseman, I. J., Naidu, R. K., & Rettek, S. I. (1995). Self-concepts across two cultures: India and the United States. *Journal of Cross-Cultural Psychology, 26*, 606–621.

Diab, L. N. (1970). A study of intragroup and intergroup relations among experimentally produced groups. *Genetic Psychology Monographs, 82*, 49–82.

Diamond, S. A. (1996). *Anger, madness, and the daimonic*. Albany: SUNY Press.

Dibble, U. (1981). Socially shared deprivation and the approval of violence: Another look at the experience of American blacks during the 1960s. *Ethnicity, 8*, 149–168.

Dickens, C. (1854/1977). *A tale of two cities*. New York: Amsco.

Dion, K. K., & Berscheid, E. (1974). Physical attractiveness and peer perception among children. *Sociometry, 37*, 1–12.

Dion, K. K., Berscheid, E., & Walster, E. (1972). What is beautiful is good. *Journal of Personality and Social Psychology, 24*, 285–290.

Dion, K. K., & Dion, K. L. (1996). Cultural perspectives on romantic love. *Personal Relationships, 3*, 5–17.

Dion, K. L. (1986). Responses to perceived discrimination and relative deprivation. In J. M. Olson, C. P. Herman, & M. P.

Zanna (Eds.), *Relative deprivation and social comparison: The Ontario Symposium* (Vol. 4, pp. 159–180). Hillsdale, NJ: Lawrence Erlbaum.

Dion, K. L., & Dion, K. K. (1987). Belief in a just world and physical attractiveness stereotype. *Journal of Personality and Social Psychology, 52,* 775–780.

Dion, K. L., & Dion, K. K. (1993). Gender and ethnocultural comparisons in styles of love. *Psychology of Women Quarterly, 17,* 463–473.

Dipboye, R. L. (1977). Alternative approaches to deindividuation. *Psychological Bulletin, 84,* 1057–1075.

Doherty, W. J., & Baldwin, C. (1985). Shifts and stability in locus of control during the 1970s: Divergence of sexes. *Journal of Personality and Social Psychology, 48,* 1048–1053.

Doise, W. (1978). *Groups and individuals: Explanations in social psychology.* Cambridge: Cambridge University Press.

Doise, W. (1986). *Levels of explanation in social psychology.* Cambridge: Cambridge University Press.

Doise, W., Dell'Ambrogio, P., & Spini, D. (1991). Psychologie sociale et droits de l'homme. *Revue Internationale de Psychologie Sociale, 4,* 259–277

Doise, W., & Herrera, M. (1994). Déclaration universelle et représentations sociales des droits de l'homme: Une étude à Genève. *Revue Internationale de Psychologie Sociale, 7,* 87–107.

Doise, W., Spini, D., & Clémence, A. (1997). *Human rights studies as social representations in cross-cultural context.* Unpublished manuscript, Psychology Department, University of Geneva.

Dollard, J., Doob, L. W., Miller, N. E., Mowrer, O. H., & Sears, R. R. (1939). *Frustration and aggression.* New Haven, CT: Yale University Press.

Domino, G., & Takahashi, Y. (1991). Attitudes toward suicide in Japanese and American medical students. *Suicide and life-threatening behavior, 21,* 345–359.

Donne, J. (1624/1975). *Devotions upon emergent occasions* (A. Raspa, Ed.). Montreal: McGill-Queen's University Press.

Dovidio, J. F. (1984). Helping behavior and altruism: An empirical and conceptual overview. In L. Berkowitz (Ed.), *Advances in experimental social psychology* (Vol. 17, pp. 361–427). New York: Academic Press.

Dovidio, J. F., Evans, N., & Tyler, R. B. (1986). Racial stereotypes: The contents of their cognitive representations. *Journal of Experimental Social Psychology, 22,* 22–37.

Dovidio, J. F., & Fazio, R. H. (1992). New techniques for the direct and indirect assessment of attitudes. In J. M. Tanur (Ed.), *Questions about questions: Inquiries into the cognitive bases of surveys* (pp. 204–237). New York: Russell Sage Foundation.

Dovidio, J. F., & Gaertner, S. L. (1986). Prejudice, discrimination, and racism: Historical trends and contemporary approaches. In J. F. Dovidio & S. L. Gaertner (Eds.), *Prejudice, discrimination, and racism* (pp. 1–34). London: Academic Press.

Dovidio, J. F., Gaertner, S. L., Isen, A. M., & Lowrance, R. (1995). Group representations and intergroup bias: Positive affect, similarity, and group size. *Personality and Social Psychology Bulletin, 21,* 856–865.

Downing, J., Mohammadi, A., & Sreberny-Mohammadi, A. (Eds.) (1995). *Questioning the media: A critical introduction.* Thousand Oaks, CA: Sage.

Drigotas, S. M. (1993). Similarity re-visited: A comparison of similarity-attraction versus dissimilarity-repulsion. *British Journal of Social Psychology, 32,* 365–377.

Drout, C. E., & Kataoka, Y. (1997). *Japanese and American perceptions of the 1995 rape of an Okinawan girl.* Paper presented at the annual meeting of the Society for Cross-Cultural Research, San Antonio, TX.

Druckman, D., Benton, A. A., Ali, F., & Bager, J. S. (1976). Cultural differences in bargaining behavior: India, Argentina, and the United States. *Journal of Conflict Resolution, 20,* 413–452.

Duckitt, J. (1992). Psychology and prejudice: A historical analysis and integrative framework. *American Psychologist, 47,* 1182–1193.

Dudycha, G. J. (1936). An objective study of punctuality in relation to personality and achievement. *Archives of Psychology, 29,* 1–53.

Durkheim, E. (1898/1974). *Sociology and philosophy.* New York: Free Press.

Dutton, D. G., & Aron, A. P. (1974). Some evidence for heightened sexual attraction under conditions of high anxiety. *Journal of Personality and Social Psychology, 30,* 510–517.

d'Ydewalle, G., Degryse, M., & DeCorte, E. (1981). Expected time of test and acquisition of knowledge. *British Journal of Educational Psychology, 51,* 23–31.

Eagly, A. H. (1978). Sex differences in influenceability. *Psychological Bulletin, 85,* 86–116.

Eagly, A. H. (1983). Gender and social influence: A social psychological analysis. *American Psychologist, 38,* 971–981.

Eagly, A. H. (1987). *Sex differences in social behavior: A social role interpretation.* Hillsdale, NJ: Lawrence Erlbaum.

Eagly, A. H. (1995). The science and politics of comparing women and men. *American Psychologist, 50,* 145–158.

Eagly, A. H., Ashmore, R. D., Makhijani, M. G., & Longo, L. C. (1991). What is beautiful is good, but . . . : A meta-analytic review of research on the physical attractiveness stereotype. *Psychological Bulletin, 110,* 109–128.

Eagly, A. H., & Carli, L. L. (1981). Sex of researchers and sextyped communications as determinants of sex differences in influenceability: A meta-analysis of social influence studies. *Psychological Bulletin, 90,* 1–20.

Eagly, A. H., & Chaiken, S. (1992). *The psychology of attitudes.* San Diego: Harcourt Brace Javonovich.

Eagly, A. H., & Crowley, M. (1986). Gender and helping behavior: A meta-analytic view of the social psychological literature. *Psychological Bulletin, 100,* 283–308.

Eagly, A. H., & Kite, M. E. (1987). Are stereotypes of nationalities applied to both women and men? *Journal of Personality and Social Psychology, 53,* 451–462.

Eagly, A. H., & Steffen, V. J. (1986). Gender and aggressive behavior: A meta-analytic review of the social psychological literature. *Psychological Bulletin, 100,* 309–329.

Eagly, A. H., & Wood, W. (1991). Explaining sex differences in social behavior: A meta-analytic perspective. *Personality and Social Psychology Bulletin, 17,* 306–315.

Eagly, A. H., Wood, W., & Chaiken, S. (1978). Causal inferences about communicators and their effect on opinion change. *Journal of Personality and Social Psychology, 36,* 424–435.

Eagly, A. H., Wood, W., & Fishbaugh, L. (1981). Sex differences in conformity: Surveillance by the group as a determinant of male non-conformity. *Journal of Personality and Social Psychology, 40,* 384–394.

Eastland, T. (1996). *Ending affirmative action: The case for colorblind justice.* New York: Basic Books.

Eccles, S., & Jacobs, J. E. (1986). Social forces shape math attitudes and performance. *Signs, 11,* 367–389.

Eckert, P. (1982). Clothing and geography in a suburban high school. In C. P. Kottak (Ed.), *Researching American culture* (pp. 139–145). Ann Arbor: University of Michigan Press.

Edwards, A. L. (1941). Unlabeled fascist attitudes. *Journal of Abnormal and Social Psychology, 36,* 579–582.

Edwards, D., & Potter, J. (1992). *Discursive psychology.* London: Sage.

Edwards, D., & Potter, J. (1993). Language and causation: A discursive action model of description and attribution. *Psychological Review, 100,* 23–41.

Ehrlich, H. J. (1973). *The social psychology of prejudice.* New York: Wiley.

Eibl-Eibesfeldt, I. (1989). *Human ethology.* New York: Aldine de Gruyter.

Eisenberg, G. J. (1980). Children and aggression after observed film aggression with sanctioning adults. *Annals of the New York Academy of Science, 347,* 304–318.

Eiser, J. R., & Bhavnani, K. K. (1974). The effect of situational meaning on the behavior of subjects in the Prisoner's Dilemma game. *European Journal of Social Psychology, 4,* 93–97.

Elkin, R. A., & Leippe, M. R. (1986). Physiological arousal, dissonance, and attitude change: Evidence for a dissonance–arousal link and a "Don't remind me" effect. *Journal of Personality and Social Psychology, 51,* 55–65.

Ellickson, R. C. (1991). *Law without order: How neighbors settle disputes.* Cambridge, MA: Harvard University Press.

Elliot, A. J., & Devine, P. G. (1993). *On the motivational nature of cognitive dissonance: Dissonance as psychological discomfort.* Unpublished manuscript, Department of Psychology, University of Wisconsin–Madison.

Elms, A. C., & Milgram, S. (1966). Personality characteristics associated with obedience and defiance toward authority command. *Journal of Experimental Research in Personality, 1,* 282–289.

Emerson, R. W. (1974). Self-reliance. In G. McMichael (Ed.), *Anthology of American literature* (3rd ed., pp. 1061–1077). New York: Macmillan.

Emler, N., & Reicher, S. (1995). *Adolescence and delinquency: The collective management of reputation.* Oxford: Blackwell.

Emler, N. P. (1983). Morality and politics: The ideological dimension in the theory of moral development. In H. Weinreich-Haste & D. Locke (Eds.), *Morality in the making: Thought, action and social context* (pp. 47–71). Chichester, England: Wiley.

Emler, N. P., & Hogan, R. (1981). Developing attitudes to law and justice: An integrative view. In A. A. Brehm, S. M. Kassin, & F. X. Gibbons (Eds.), *Developmental social psychology* (pp. 298–314). New York: Oxford University Press.

Emler, N. P., Renwick, S., & Malone, B. (1983). The relationship between moral reasoning and political orientation. *Journal of Personality and Social Psychology, 45,* 1073–1080.

Engle, P. L., & Breaux, C. (1994). *Is there a father instinct?* Report for the Population Council and the International Center for Research on Women, Washington, DC.

Entwisle, D. R., & Baker, D. P. (1983). Gender and young children's expectations for performance in arithmetic. *Developmental Psychology, 19,* 200–209.

Equal Employment Opportunity Commission (1990). *Sex discrimination guidelines.* Washington, DC.

Erdelyi, M., Buschke, H., & Finkelstein, S. (1977). Hyperamnesia for Socratic stimuli: The growth of recall for an internally generated memory list abstracted from a series of riddles. *Memory and Cognition, 5,* 283–286.

Esses, V. M., & Zanna, M. P. (1995). Mood and the expression of ethnic stereotypes. *Journal of Personality and Social Psychology, 69,* 1052–1068.

Esware, H. S. (1972). Administration of rewards and punishment in relation to ability. *Journal of Social Psychology, 87,* 139–140.

Etzioni, A. (1993). *The spirit of community: Rights, responsibilities, and the communitarian agenda.* New York: Crown.

Etzkowitz, H., Kemelgor, C., Neuschatz, M., Uzzi, B., & Alonzo, J. (1994). The paradox of critical mass for women in science. *Science, 266,* 51–54.

Evans, H. M. (1981). Internal–external locus of control and word association: Research with Japanese and American students. *Journal of Cross-Cultural Psychology, 12,* 372–382.

Evans, J. L. (1975). Learning to classify by color and by class: A study of concept discovery within Colombia, South America. *Journal of Social Psychology, 97,* 3–14.

Evans, M. C., & Wilson, M. (1949). Friendship choices of university women students. *Educational and Psychological Measurement, 9,* 307–312.

Evans, R. I. (Ed.) (1980). *The making of social psychology.* New York: Gardner Press.

Eysenck, H. J. (1978). An excercise in mega–silliness. *American Psychologist, 33,* 517.

Falbo, T. (1977). Multidimensional scaling of power strategies. *Journal of Personality and Social Psychology, 35,* 537–547.

Falbo, T., & Peplau, L. A. (1980). Power strategies in intimate relationships. *Journal of Personality and Social Psychology, 38,* 618–628.

Fallon, A. E., & Rozin, P. (1985). Sex differences in perceptions of desirable body shape. *Journal of Abnormal Psychology, 94,* 102–105.

Farr, R. M., & Moscovici, S. (Eds.) (1984). *Social representations.* Cambridge: Cambridge University Press.

Fazio, R. H. (1987). Self-perception theory: A current perspective. In M. P. Zanna, J. M. Olson, & C. P. Herman (Eds.), *Social influence: The Ontario Symposium* (Vol. 5, pp. 129–149). Hillsdale, NJ: Lawrence Erlbaum.

Fazio, R. H. (1990). Multiple processes by which attitudes guide behavior: The MODE model as an integrative framework. *Advances in Experimental Social Psychology, 23,* 75–109.

Fazio, R. H., & Cooper, J. (1983). Arousal in the dissonance process. In J. T. Cacioppo & R. E. Petty (Eds.), *Social psychophysiology* (pp. 122–152). New York: Guilford Press.

Fazio, R. H., Jackson, J. R., Dunton, B. C., & Williams, C. J. (1995). Variability in automatic activation as an unobstrusive measure of racial attitudes: A bona fide pipeline? *Journal of Personality and Social Psychology, 69,* 1013–1027.

Fazio, R. H., & Zanna, M. P. (1981). Direct experience and attitude–behavior consistency. In L. Berkowitz (Ed.), *Advances in experimental social psychology* (Vol. 14, pp. 161–202). New York: Academic Press.

Feagin, P. L. (1991). The continuing significance of race: Antiblack discrimination in public places. *American Sociological Review, 56,* 101–116.

Feather, N. T. (1985). Attitudes, values, and attributions: Explanations of unemployment. *Journal of Personality and Social Psychology, 48,* 876–889.

Federal Bureau of Investigation (1994). *Uniform crime reports for the United States, 1993.* Washington, DC: U.S. Government Printing Office.

Feingold, A. (1990). Gender differences in physical attractiveness on romantic attraction: A comparison across five research domains. *Journal of Personality and Social Psychology, 59,* 981–993.

Feingold, A. (1992). Gender differences in mate selection differences: A test of the parental investment model. *Psychological Bulletin, 112,* 125–139.

Feinman, S. (1980). Infant response to race, size, proximity, and movement of strangers. *Infant Behavior Development, 3,* 187–204.

Feldman, R. (1968). Responses to compatriots and foreigners who seek assistance. *Journal of Personality and Social Psychology, 10,* 202–214.

Feldman-Summers, S., & Kiesler, S. B. (1974). Those who are number two try harder: The effect of sex on attributions of causality. *Journal of Personality and Social Psychology, 30,* 846–855.

Felson, R. B., & Tedeschi, J. T. (Eds.) (1993). *Aggression and violence: Social interaction perspectives.* Washington, DC: American Psychological Association.

Fentress, J., & Wickham, C. (Eds.) (1992). *Social memory: New perspectives on the past.* Oxford: Blackwell.

Festinger, L. (1954). A theory of social comparison processes. *Human Relations, 7,* 117–140.

Festinger, L. (1957). *A theory of cognitive dissonance.* Stanford, CA: Stanford University Press.

Festinger, L., Pepitone, A., & Newcomb, T. (1952). Some consequences of deindividuation in a group. *Journal of Abnormal and Social Psychology, 47,* 382–389.

Festinger, L., Schachter, S., & Back, K. (1950). *Social pressures in informal groups: A study of a housing community.* New York: Harper.

Fiedler, F. E., & Garcia, J. E. (1987). *Leadership: Cognitive resources and performance.* New York: Wiley.

Fiedler, K., Semin, G. R., Finkenauer, D., & Berkel, I. (1995). Actor-observer bias in close relationships. *Personality and Social Psychology Bulletin, 21,* 525–538.

Filardo, E. K. (1996). Gender patterns in African American and white adolescents' social interactions in same-race, mixed-gender groups. *Journal of Personality and Social Psychology, 71,* 71–82.

Fine, M., & Bowers, C. (1984). Racial self-identification: The effects of social history and gender. *Journal of Applied Social Psychology, 14,* 136–146.

Finkel, N. (1995). *Commonsense justice: Jurors' notions of the law.* Cambridge, MA: Harvard University Press.

Finn, J. D., Dulberg, L., & Reis, J. (1979). Sex differences in educational attainment: A cross-national perspective. *Harvard Educational Review, 49,* 477–503.

Fischer, K. P. (1995). *Nazi Germany: A new history.* New York: Continuum.

Fishbein, M., & Ajzen, I. (1974). Attitudes toward objects as predictive of single and multiple behavioral criteria. *Psychological Review, 81,* 59–74.

Fishbein, M., & Ajzen, I. (1975). *Belief, attitude, intention, and behavior: An introduction to theory and research.* Reading, MA: Addison-Wesley.

Fisher, C. B., & Fyrberg, D. (1994). Participant partners: College students weigh the costs and benefits of deceptive research. *American Psychologist, 49,* 417–427.

Fisher, R. (1989). *The social psychology of intergroup relations and international conflict resolution.* New York: Springer.

Fiske, A. P. (1990). Relativity within Moose ("Mossi") culture: Four incommensurable models for social relationships. *Ethos, 18,* 180–204.

Fiske, A. P. (1991). The cultural relativity of selfish individualism. In M. C. Clark (Ed.), *Prosocial behavior* (pp. 176–214). Newbury Park, CA: Sage.

Fiske, S. T. (1993a). Controlling other people: The impact of power on stereotyping. *American Psychologist, 48,* 621–628.

Fiske, S. T. (1993b). Social cognition and social perception. *Annual Review of Psychology, 44,* 155–194.

Fiske, S. T., & Neuberg, S. L. (1990). A continuum of impression formation, from category-based to individuating processes: Influences of information and motivation on attention and interpretation. In M. P. Zanna (Ed.), *Advances in Experimental Social Psychology* (Vol. 23, pp. 1–74). New York: Academic Press.

Fiske, S. T., & Taylor, S. E. (1991). *Social cognition* (2nd ed.). New York: McGraw-Hill.

Fletcher, G. J. O., & Ward, C. (1988). Attribution theory and processes: A cross-cultural perspective. In M. H. Bond (Ed.), *The cross-cultural challenge to social psychology.* Newbury Park, CA: Sage.

Flowers, B. J., & Richardson, F. C. (1996). Why is multiculturalism good? *American Psychologist, 51,* 609–621.

Forbes, H. D. (1985). *Nationalism, ethnocentrism and personality.* Chicago: University of Chicago Press.

Ford, M. R., & Lowery, C. R. (1986). Gender differences in moral reasoning: A comparison of the use of justice and care orientations. *Journal of Personality and Social Psychology, 50,* 777–783.

Fox, D. R. (1993). Psychological jurisprudence and radical social change. *American Psychologist, 48,* 234–241.

Fox, D. R., & Prilleltensky, I. (Eds.) (1997). *Critical psychology.* Thousand Oaks, CA: Sage.

Frager, R. (1970). Conformity and anti-conformity in Japan. *Journal of Personality and Social Psychology, 15,* 203–210.

Frank, R., & Cook, P. (1995). *The winner-takes-all society.* New York: Simon & Schuster.

Fraser, C., Gouge, C., & Billig, M. (1970). Risky shifts, cautious shifts and group polarization. *European Journal of Social Psychology, 1,* 7–30.

Freedman, J. L., & Fraser, S. C. (1966). Compliance without pressure: The foot in the door technique. *Journal of Personality and Social Psychology, 4,* 195–202.

Freire, P. (1985). *The politics of education: Culture, power, and liberation.* New York: Bergin and Garvey.

French, D., & Richards, M. (Eds.) (1996). *Contemporary television.* Thousand Oaks, CA: Sage.

Freud, S. (1921/1953–1964). Group psychology and the analysis of the ego. In J. Strachey (Ed. & Trans.), *The standard edition of the complete works of Sigmund Freud* (Vols. 1–24). London: Hogarth Press.

Freud, S. (1930). Civilization and its discontents. In J. Strachey (Ed. & Trans.), *The standard edition of the complete works of Sigmund Freud* (Vol. 21). London: Hogarth Press.

Frey, D. L., & Gaertner, S. L. (1986). Helping and the avoidance of inappropriate interracial behavior: A strategy that perpetuates a nonprejudiced self-image. *Journal of Personality and Social Psychology, 50*, 1083–1090.

Friedan, B. (1963). *The feminine mystique.* New York: Norton.

Friedlander, Z. B. (1993). Community violence, children's development, and mass media: In pursuit of new insights, new goals, new strategies. *Psychiatry, 56*, 66–81.

Friedrich, W. N. (1995). *Psychotherapy with sexually abused boys: An integrated approach.* Thousand Oaks, CA: Sage.

Friestad, M., & Wright, P. (1995). Persuasion knowledge: Lay people's and researchers' beliefs about the psychology of advertising. *Journal of Consumer Research, 22*, 62–74.

Frieze, I. H., Olson, J. E., & Russell, J. (1991). Attractiveness and income for men and women in management. *Journal of Applied Social Psychology, 21*, 1039–1057.

Fudenberg, D., & Tirole, J. (1991). *Game theory.* Cambridge, MA: MIT Press.

Funder, D. C. (1987). Errors and mistakes: Evaluating the accuracy of social judgment. *Psychological Bulletin, 101*, 75–90.

Gabrenya, W. K., Jr., Latané, B., & Wang, Y. E. (1983). Social loafing in cross-cultural perspective: Chinese in Taiwan. *Journal of Cross-Cultural Psychology, 14*, 368–384.

Gabrenya, W. K., Jr., Wang, Y. E., & Latané, B. (1985). Social loafing on an optimizing task: Cross-cultural differences among Chinese and Americans. *Journal of Cross-Cultural Psychology, 16*, 223–242.

Gaertner, S. L., & Bickman, L. (1971). Effects of race on elicitation of helping behavior: The wrong number technique. *Journal of Personality and Social Psychology, 20*, 218–222.

Gaertner, S. L., & Dovidio, J. F. (1986). The aversive form of racism. In J. F. Dovidio & S. L. Gaertner (Eds.), *Prejudice, discrimination, and racism* (pp. 61–89). San Diego: Academic Press.

Gagnon, J., Laumann, E., Michael, R. T., & Michaels, S. (1994). *The social organization of sexuality.* Chicago: University of Chicago Press.

Gaines, S. O., Jr., & Reed, E. S. (1995). Prejudice: From Allport to DuBois. *American Psychologist, 50*, 96–103.

Galdue, B. (1991). Qualitative and quantitative sex differences in self-reported aggressive behavioral characteristics. *Psychological Reports, 68*, 675–684.

Gallois, C., Barker, M., Jones, E., & Callan, V. J. (1990). Intercultural communications: Evaluations of lecturers and Australian and Chinese students. In S. Iwawaki, Y. Kashima, & K. Leung (Eds.), *Innovations in cross-cultural psychology* (pp. 86–102). Amsterdam: Swets & Zeitlinger.

Gallup, G. G., Jr. (1977). Chimpanzees: Self-recognition. *Science, 167*, 86–87.

Galton, F. J. (1878). Composite portraits. *Nature, 18*, 97–100.

Garland, H., & Price, K. H. (1977). Attitudes toward women in management and attributions for their success and failure in a managerial position. *Journal of Applied Psychology, 62*, 29–33.

Garner, D. M., Garfinkel, P. E., Schwartz, D., & Thompson, M. (1980). Cultural expectations of thinness in women. *Psychological Reports, 47*, 183–191.

Geen, R. G. (1990). *Human aggression.* Pacific Grove, CA: Brooks/Cole.

Geen, R. G. (1995). Human aggression. In A. Tesser (Ed.), *Advanced social psychology* (pp. 383–417). New York: McGraw-Hill.

Geen, R. G., & Donnerstein, E. I. (Eds.) (1983). *Aggression: Theoretical and empirical reviews* (Vols. 1–2). New York: Academic Press.

Geertz, C. (1984). From the native's point of view: On the nature of anthropological understanding. In R. A. Shweder & R. A. LeVine (Eds.), *Culture theory: Essays on mind, self, and emotion* (pp. 123–136). Cambridge: Cambridge University Press.

Geis, F. L. (1993). Self-fulfilling prophecies: A social psychological view of gender. In A. E. Beall & R. J. Sternberg (Eds.), *The psychology of gender* (pp. 9–54). New York: Guilford Press.

Geis, F. L., Brown, V., Jennings, J., & Porter, N. (1984). TV commercials as achievement scripts for women. *Sex Roles, 10*, 513–525.

George, S. A. (1989). Evolution and family homicide. *Science, 243*, 462.

Gergen, K. J. (1973). Social psychology as history. *Journal of Personality and Social Psychology, 26*, 309–320.

Gergen, K. J. (1991). *The saturated self: Dilemmas of identity in everyday life.* New York: Basic Books.

Gergen, K. J., & Gergen, M. M. (1974). Understanding foreign assistance through public opinion. *Yearbook of World Affairs, 28*, 125–140.

Gergen, K. J., Morse, S. J., & Bode, K. A. (1974). Overpaid or overworked? Cognitive and behavioral reactions to inequitable rewards. *Journal of Applied Social Psychology, 4*, 259–274.

Gibbons, J. L., Lynn, M., & Stiles, D. A. (1997). Cross-national gender differences in adolescents' preferences for free-time activities. *Cross-Cultural Research, 31*, 55–69.

Gibbons, J. L., Stiles, D. A., Perez-Prada, E., Shkodriani, G. M., & Medina, J. (1996). *Adolescents' gender role ideology in four countries.* Paper presented at the annual meeting of the Society for Cross-Cultural Research, Pittsburgh.

Gibbons, J. L., Stiles, D. A., & Shkodriani, G. M. (1991). Adolescents' attitudes toward family and gender roles: An international comparison. *Sex Roles, 25*, 625–643.

Gibbons, R. (1992). *Game theory for economists.* Princeton, NJ: Princeton University Press.

Gibbs, J. T. (1984). Black adolescents and youth: An endangered species. *American Journal of Orthopsychiatry, 54*, 6–22.

Gibbs, J. T. (1996). *Race and justice: Rodney King and O. J. Simpson in a house divided.* San Francisco: Jossey-Bass.

Giele, J. Z., & Smock, A. C. (Eds.) (1977). *Women: Role and status in eight countries.* New York: Wiley.

Gielen, U. P. (1994). American mainstream psychology and its relationship to international and cross-cultural psychology. In A. L. Comunian & U. P. Gielen (Eds.), *Advancing psychology and its applications: International perspectives* (pp. 26–40). Milan: Franco Angeli.

Gilbert, D. T., & Hixon, J. G. (1991). The trouble of thinking: Activation and application of stereotypic beliefs. *Journal of Personality and Social Psychology, 60,* 509–517.

Gilbert, D. T., & Jones, E. E. (1986). Perceiver-induced constraint: Interpretations of self-generated reality. *Journal of Personality and Social Psychology, 50,* 269–280.

Gilbert, D. T., & Malone, P. S. (1995). The correspondence bias. *Psychological Bulletin, 117,* 21–38.

Giles, H., Bourhis, R. Y., & Taylor, D. M. (1977). Toward a theory of language in ethnic relations. In H. Giles (Ed.), *Language, ethnicity, and intergroup relations* (pp. 307–348). London: Academic Press.

Giles, H., & Coupland, N. (1991). *Language: Contexts and consequences.* Pacific Grove, CA: Brooks/Cole.

Giles, H., Williams, A., Mackie, D. M., & Rosselli, F. (1995). Reactions to Anglo- and Hispanic-accented speakers: Affect, identity, persuasion, and the English-only controversy. *Language and Communication, 15,* 107–120.

Gillig, P. M., & Greenwald, A. G. (1974). Is it time to lay the sleeper effect to rest? *Journal of Personality and Social Psychology, 29,* 132–139.

Gilligan, C. (1977). In a different voice: Women's conception of the self and morality. *Harvard Educational Review, 47,* 481–517.

Gilligan, C. (1982). *In a different voice.* Cambridge, MA: Harvard University Press.

Gladwell, M. (1997, February 24 & March 3). Damaged: Why do some people turn into violent criminals? New evidence suggests that it may all be in the brain. *The New Yorker,* pp. 132–147.

Glass, G. V., McGraw, B., & Smith, M. L. (1981). *Meta-analysis in social research.* Beverly Hills, CA: Sage.

Gleick, E. (1997, April 7). The marker we've been waiting for. *Time,* pp. 28–36.

Glock, C. V., Wuthnow, R., Piliavin, J. A., & Spencer, M. (1975). *Adolescent prejudice.* New York: Harper & Row.

Godfrey, D., Jones, E. E., & Lord, C. G. (1986). Self-promotion is not ingratiation. *Journal of Personality and Social Psychology, 50,* 106–115.

Goethals, G. R., Messick, D. M., & Allison, S. T. (1991). The uniqueness bias: Studies of constructive social comparison. In J. Suls & T. A. Wills (Eds.), *Social comparison: Contemporary theory and research.* Hillsdale, NJ: Lawrence Erlbaum.

Goffman, E. (1956). *The presentation of the self in everyday life.* Edinburgh: University of Edinburgh Social Sciences Research Centre, Monograph No. 2.

Goffman, E. (1959). *The presentation of the self in everyday life.* New York: Doubleday/Anchor.

Goffman, E. (1961). *Asylums.* Harmondsworth: Penguin.

Goffman, E. (1963). *Stigma: Notes on the management of spoiled identity.* Englewood Cliffs, NJ: Prentice Hall.

Goffman, E. (1971). *Relations in public.* New York: Harper & Row.

Goffman, E. (1976). *Gender advertising.* New York: Harper & Row.

Goldberg, L. R. (1981). Unconfounding situational attributions from uncertain, neutral and ambiguous ones: A psychometric analysis of the descriptions of oneself and various types of others. *Journal of Personality and Social Psychology, 41,* 517–552.

Goldman, W., & Lewis, P. (1977). Beautiful is good: Evidence that the physically attractive are more socially skillful. *Journal of Experimental Social Psychology, 13,* 125–130.

Goldstein, A. P., & Segall, M. H. (Eds.) (1983). *Aggression in global perspective* (pp. 237–260). New York: Pergamon Press.

Gologor, E. (1977). Group polarization in a non-risk taking culture. *Journal of Cross-Cultural Psychology, 8,* 331–346.

Government of Canada (1971). Statement by the Prime Minister (Response to the report of the Royal Commission on Bilingualism and Biculturalism, Book Four, House of Commons). Ottawa Press Release.

Gowan, M. A., & Zimmermann, R. A. (1996). Impact of ethnicity, gender, and previous experience on jury judgments in sexual harassment cases. *Journal of Applied Social Psychology, 26,* 596–617.

Graham, J. L. (1985). The influence of culture on the process of business negotiations: An exploratory study. *Journal of International Business Studies,* Spring, 81–96.

Graham, S. (1992). "Most of the subjects were white and middle class": Trends in published research on African Americans in selected APA journals, 1970–1989. *American Psychologist, 47,* 629–639.

Graham, S., & Folkes, V. S. (Eds.) (1990). *Attribution theory: Applications to achievement, mental health, and interpersonal conflict.* Hillsdale, NJ: Lawrence Erlbaum.

Graham, S., & Long, A. (1986). Race, class, and the attributional process. *Journal of Educational Psychology, 78,* 4–13.

Graves, N. B., & Graves, T. D. (1983). The cultural context of prosocial development: An ecological model. In D. L. Bridgeman (Ed.), *The nature of prosocial development: Interdisciplinary theories and strategies* (pp. 243–264). New York: Academic Press.

Graziano, W. G., Jensen-Campbell, L. A., Shebilske, L. J., & Lundgren, S. R. (1993). Social influence, sex differences, and judgments of beauty: Putting the *interpersonal* back in interpersonal attraction. *Journal of Personality and Social Psychology, 65,* 522–531.

Green, B. L., & Kendrick, D. T. (1994). The attractiveness of gender-typed traits in different relationship levels: Androgynous characteristics may be desirable after all. *Personality and Social Psychology Bulletin, 20,* 244–253.

Green, S. K., Buchanan, D. R., & Heuer, S. K. (1984). Winners, losers, and choosers: A field investigation of dating initiation. *Personality and Social Psychology Bulletin, 10,* 502–511.

Greenberg, J., & Rosenfield, D. (1979). Whites' ethnocentrism and their attributions for the behavior of blacks: A motivational bias. *Journal of Personality,* 643–657.

Greenwald, A. G. (1980). The totalitarian ego: Fabrication and revision of personal history. *American Psychologist, 35,* 603–618.

Greenwald, A. G. (1981). Self and memory. In G. H. Bower (Ed.), *The psychology of learning and motivation* (Vol. 15, pp. 201–236). New York: Academic Press.

Greenwald, A. G., & Banaji, M. R. (1995). Implicit social cognition: Attitudes, self-esteem, and stereotypes. *Psychological Review, 102,* 4–27

Greenwald, A. G., & Pratkanis, A. R. (1984). The self. In R. S. Wyer & T. K. Srull (Eds.), *Handbook of social cognition* (pp. 129–178). Hillsdale, NJ: Lawrence Erlbaum.

Greenwald, A. G., & Schuh, A. S. (1994). An ethnic bias in scientific citations. *European Journal of Social Psychology, 24,* 623–639.

Gregor, J. A. (1974). *Interpretations of fascism*. Morristown, NJ: General Learning Press.

Grimsley, K. D. (1996, August 25). Learning where to draw the line. *Washington Post*, p. H1.

Grinker, R. R. (1994). *Houses in the rainforest: Ethnicity and inequality among the farmers and foragers in Central Africa*. Berkeley: University of California Press.

Grodin, D., & Lindlof, T. R. (Eds.) (1996). *Constructing the self in a mediated world*. Thousand Oaks, CA: Sage.

Groebel, J., & Hinde, R. (Eds.) (1988). *Aggression and war: Their biological and social bases*. New York: Cambridge University Press.

Grossman, D. (1995). *On killing: The psychological cost of learning to kill in war and society*. New York: Little, Brown.

Grove, J. R., Hanrahan, S. J., & McInman, A. (1991). Success/failure bias in attributions across involvement categories in sport. *Personality and Social Psychology Bulletin, 17*, 93–97.

Guerin, B. (1993). *Social facilitation*. Cambridge: Cambridge University Press.

Guimond, S., & Dube-Simard, L. (1983). Relative deprivation theory and the Quebec nationalist movement: The cognition–emotion distinction and the person–group deprivation issue. *Journal of Personality and Social Psychology, 44*, 526–535.

Gurr, T. R. (1981). Historical trends in violent crime: A critical review of the evidence. *Crime and Justice: An Annual Review of Research, 3*, 295–353.

Gurr, T. R. (1994). Peoples against states: Ethnopolitical conflict and the changing world system. *International Studies Quarterly, 38*, 347–377.

Haeri, S. (1989). *Law of desire: Temporary marriage in Shi'i Iran*. Syracuse, NY: Syracuse University Press.

Hafer, C. L., & Olson, J. M. (1993). Beliefs in a just world, discontent, and assertive actions by working women. *Personality and Social Psychology Bulletin, 19*, 30–38.

Hafer, C. L., & Olson, J. M. (in press). Individual differences in the belief in a just world and responses to personal misfortune. In M. J. Lerner & L. Montada (Eds.), *The motivational impact of the belief in a just world*. New York: Plenum Press.

Halberstadt, A. G., & Ellyson, S. L. (Eds.) (1990). *Social psychology readings: A century of research*. New York: McGraw-Hill.

Hall, G. C. N. (1996). *Theory-based assessment, treatment, and prevention of sexual aggression*. New York: Oxford University Press.

Hall, G. C. N., & Barongan, C. (1997). Prevention of sexual aggression: Sociocultural risk and protective factors. *American Psychologist, 52*, 5–14.

Hall, G. S. (1904). *Adolescence: Its psychology and its relation to physiology, anthropology, sociology, sex, crime, religion and education*. New York: Appleton.

Hall, V. C., Howe, A., Merkel, S., & Lederman, N. (1986). Behavior, motivation, and achievement in desegregated junior high school science classes. *Journal of Educational Psychology, 78*, 108–115.

Halpern, D. F. (1992). *Sex differences in cognitive abilities* (2nd ed.). Hillsdale, NJ: Lawrence Erlbaum.

Hamilton, D. L., & Sherman, J. W. (1994). Stereotypes. In R. S. Wyer & T. K. Srull (Eds.), *Handbook of social cognition* (2nd ed., Vol. 2., pp. 1–68). Hillsdale, NJ: Lawrence Erlbaum.

Hamilton, V. L. (Ed.) (1992). *Social psychological approaches to responsibility and justice: A view across cultures*. Mahwah, NJ: Lawrence Erlbaum.

Hamilton, V. L., & Sanders, J. (1983). Universals in judging wrongdoing: Japanese and Americans compared. *American Sociological Review, 48*, 199–211.

Hamilton, V. L., & Sanders, J. (1995). Crimes of obedience and conformity in the workplace: Surveys of Americans, Russians, and Japanese. *Journal of Social Issues, 51*, 67–88.

Hamilton, W. D. (1964). The genetical evolution of social behavior. *Journal of Theoretical Biology, 7*, 1–52.

Hammer, R. (1971). *The court-martial of Lt. Calley*. New York: Coward, McCann, & Geoghegan.

Han, S.-P., & Shavitt, S. (1994). Persuasion and culture: Advertising appeals in individualistic and collectivistic societies. *Journal of Experimental Social Psychology, 30*, 326–350.

Hannover, B. (1995). Self-serving biases and self-satisfaction in East versus West German students. *Journal of Cross-Cultural Psychology, 26*, 176–188.

Hardin, G. (1968). The tragedy of the commons. *Science, 162*, 1243–1248.

Hare-Mustin, R. T., & Marecek, J. (1988). The meaning of difference: Gender theory, postmodernism, and psychology. *American Psychologist, 43*, 455–464.

Harré, R. (1991). The discursive production of selves. *Theory and Psychology, 1*, 51–63.

Harré, R. (1993). *Social being* (2nd ed.). Oxford: Blackwell.

Harré, R. (1997). *Singularities of self*. London: Sage.

Harris, P. R., & Moran, R. T. (1991). *Managing cultural differences* (3rd ed.). Houston: Gulf.

Hart, C. W. M., Pilling, A. R., & Goodale, J. C. (1988). *The Tiwi of North Australia* (3rd ed.). New York: Holt, Rinehart & Winston.

Harvey, L., Burnham, R. W., Kendall, K., & Pease, K. (1992). Gender differences in criminal justice: An international comparison. *British Journal of Criminology, 32*, 208–217.

Hastie, R., Penrod, S. D., & Pennington, N. (1983). *Inside the jury*. Cambridge, MA: Harvard University Press.

Hatfield, E., & Rapson, R. L. (1993). *Love, sex, and intimacy: Their psychology, biology, and history*. New York: HarperCollins.

Hatfield, E., & Sprecher, S. (1986). *Mirror, mirror . . . : The importance of looks in everyday life*. Albany: SUNY Press.

Hatfield, E., & Sprecher, S. (1995). Men's and women's preferences in marital partners in the United States, Russia, and Japan. *Journal of Cross-Cultural Psychology, 26*, 728–750.

Hatfield, E., & Walster, G. W. (1981). *A new look at love*. Reading, MA: Addison-Wesley.

Haug, M., Whalen, R. E., Aron, C., & Olsen, K. L. (Eds.) (1993). *The development of sex differences and similarities in behaviour*. London: Kluwer Academic.

Haugtvedt, C. P., & Petty, R. E. (1992). Personality and persuasion: Need for cognition moderates the persistence and resistance of attitude change. *Journal of Personality and Social Psychology, 63*, 308–319.

Haugtvedt, C. P., & Wegener, D. T. (1994). Message order effects in persuasion: An attitude strength perspective. *Journal of Consumer Research, 21*, 205–218.

Hawkins, J. N. (1986). Japan. *Education and Urban Society, 18*, 412–422.

Hawthorne, N. (1850/1961). *The scarlet letter.* New York: Holt, Rinehart & Winston.

Healy, B. (1995). *A new prescription for women's health: Getting the best medical care in a man's world.* New York: Penguin.

Heath, R. G. (1963). Electrical self-stimulation of the brain in man. *American Journal of Psychiatry, 120*, 571–577.

Heidensohn, F. M. (1991). Women as perpetrators and victims of crime: A sociological perspective. *British Journal of Psychiatry, 158*, 50–54.

Heider, F. (1944). Social perception and phenomenal causality. *Psychological Review, 51*, 385–374.

Heider, F. (1958). *The psychology of interpersonal relations.* New York: Wiley.

Hendrick, C., & Hendrick, S. S. (1993). *Romantic love.* Newbury Park, CA: Sage.

Hendrick, S. S., & Hendrick, C. (1992). *Liking, loving, and relating.* Pacific Grove, CA: Brooks/Cole.

Hendrick, S., Hendrick, C., Slapion-Foote, M. J., & Foote, F. H. (1985). Gender differences in sexual attitudes. *Journal of Personality and Social Psychology, 48*, 1630–1642.

Herdt, G. (1990). Mistaken gender: 5-Alpha reductase hermaphroditism and biological reductionism in sexual identity reconsidered. *American Anthropologist, 92*, 433–446.

Hermans, H. J. M. (1987). The dream in the process of valuation: A method of interpretation. *Journal of Personality and Social Psychology, 53*, 163–175.

Hermans, H. J. M. (1989). The meaning of life as an organized process. *Psychotherapy, 26*, 11–22.

Hermans, H. J. M. (1991). The person as co-investigator in self-research: Valuation theory. *European Journal of Personality, 5*, 217–234.

Hermans, H. J. M., & Bonarius, H. (1991). The person as co-investigator in personality research. *European Journal of Personality, 5*, 199–216.

Hermans, H. J. M., Kempen, H. J. G., & van Loon, R. J. P. (1992). The dialogical self: Beyond individualism and rationalism. *American Psychologist, 47*, 23–33.

Herodotus (1954). *The histories* (Aubrey de Selincourt, Trans.). Baltimore, MD: Penguin.

Herzlich, C. (1873). *Health and illness: A social psychological analysis* (D. Graham, Trans.). London: Academic Press.

Hewstone, M. (1990). *Causal attributions: From cognitive processes to collective beliefs.* Oxford: Blackwell.

Hewstone, M., Bond, M. H., & Wan, K. C. (1983). Social facts and social attributions: The explanation of intergroup differences in Hong Kong. *Social Cognition, 2*, 142–157.

Hewstone, M., & Jaspers, J. M. F. (1982). Explanations for racial discrimination: The effect of group discussion on intergroup attributions. *European Journal of Social Psychology, 12*, 1–16.

Hewstone, M., Jaspers, J. M. F., & Lalljee, M. (1982). Social representations, social attributions and social identity: The intergroup images of "public" and "comprehensive" schoolboys. *European Journal of Social Psychology, 12*, 241–269.

Hewstone, M., & Ward, C. (1985). Ethnocentrism and causal attribution in Southeast Asia. *Journal of Personality and Social Psychology, 48*, 614–623.

Higgins, E. T. (1987). Self-discrepancy: A theory relating self and affect. *Psychological Review, 94*, 319–340.

Higgins, E. T. (1989). Continuities and discontinuities in self-regulatory and self-evaluative processes: A developmental theory relating self and affect. *Journal of Personality, 57*, 407–444.

Higgins, E. T., & Bryant, S. L. (1982). Consensus information and the fundamental attribution error: The role of development and in-group versus out-group knowledge. *Journal of Personality and Social Psychology, 43*, 889–900.

Higgins, E. T., Tykocinski, O., & Vookles, J. (1990). Patterns of self beliefs: The psychological significance of relations among the actual, ideal, ought, can, and future selves. In J. M. Olson & M. P. Zanna (Eds.), *Processes in self-perception: The Ontario Symposium* (Vol. 7, pp. 153–190). Hillsdale, NJ: Lawrence Erlbaum.

Hilsman, R., & Garber, J. (1995). A test of the cognitive diathesis-stress model of depression in children: Academic stressors, attributional style, perceived competence, and control. *Journal of Personality and Social Psychology, 69*, 70–380.

Hilton, D. J., Smith, R. H., & Kin, S. H. (1995). Processes of causal explanation and dispositional attribution. *Journal of Personality and Social Psychology, 68*, 377–387.

Himmelstein, P. & Moore, J. C. (1963). Racial attitudes and the action of Negro- and white-background figures as factors in petition signing. *Journal of Social Psychology, 61*, 267–272.

Hines, H. J., & Fry, D. P. (1994). Indirect modes of aggression among women of Buenos Aires. *Sex Roles, 30*, 213–236.

Hirschman, A. O. (1970). *Exit, voice and loyalty: Responses to decline in forms, organizations and states.* Cambridge, MA: Harvard University Press.

Hirschman, A. O. (1984). *Getting ahead collectively: Grassroots experiences in Latin America.* New York: Pergamon Press.

Hochschild, A. (1990). *The second shift.* New York: Avon.

Hochschild, A. R. (1997). *The time bind: When work becomes home & home becomes work.* New York: Metropolitan Books/Henry Holt.

Hochschild, J. L., & Herk, M. (1990). "Yes, but . . . ": Principles and caveats in American racial attitudes. In J. W. Chapman & A. W. Wertheirmer (Eds.), *Majorities and minorities* (pp. 308–335). New York: New York University Press.

Hoffman, C., & Hurst, N. (1990). Gender stereotypes: Perception or rationalization? *Journal of Personality and Social Psychology, 58*, 197–208.

Hofstede, G. (1980). *Culture's consequences.* Beverly Hills, CA: Sage.

Hogan, R., Curphy, G. J., & Hogan, J. (1994). What we know about leadership: Effectiveness and personality. *American Psychologist, 49*, 493–504.

Hogg, M. A., & Abrams, D. (1990). Social motivation, self-esteem, and social identity. In D. Abrams & M. A. Hogg (Eds.), *Social identity theory: Constructive and critical advances* (pp. 28–47). London: Harvester Wheatsheaf.

Hogg, M. A., & Hardie, E. A. (1992). Prototypicality, conformity and depersonalized attraction: A self-categorization analysis of group processes. *British Journal of Social Psychology, 31*, 41–56.

Hogg, M. A., & Sunderland, J. (1991). Self-esteem and intergroup discrimination in the minimal group paradigm. *British Journal of Social Psychology, 30*, 51–62.

Hollander, E. P., & Hunt, R. G. (Eds.) (1972). *Classic contributions to social psychology.* New York: Oxford University Press.

Holliday, A. (1988). *Moral powers: Normative necessity in language and history.* London: Routledge.

Holmes, D. S. (1968). Dimensions of projection. *Psychological Bulletin, 69,* 248–268.

Holmes, S. A. (1994, March 3). Survey finds minorities resent one another almost as much as they do whites. *New York Times,* p. B8.

Homans, G. C. (1961). *Social behavior: Its elementary forms.* New York: Harcourt, Brace and World.

Homans, G. C. (1974). *Social behavior: Its elementary forms* (rev. ed.). New York: Harcourt Brace Jovanovich.

Homer-Dixon, T. F., Boutwell, J. H., & Rathjens, G. W. (1993, February). Environmental change and violent conflict. *Scientific American,* pp. 38–45.

Hong, G. Y. (1992). *Contributions of "culture absent" cross- cultural psychology to mainstream psychology.* Paper presented at the annual meeting of the Society for Cross–Cultural Research, Santa Fe, NM.

Hong, G. Y. (1997). *Cultural representations and uses of non-material beliefs in Korea.* Paper presented at the annual meeting of the Society for Cross–Cultural Research, San Antonio, TX.

Hong, G. Y. (1997). Just-world beliefs and attributions of causal responsibility among Korean adolescents. *Cross-Cultural Research, 31,* 121–136.

Horowitz, E. L. (1936). The development of attitudes toward the negro. *Archives of Psychology, 194.*

Hostetler, J. A. (1980). *Amish society* (3rd ed.). Baltimore, MD: Johns Hopkins University Press.

Hovland, C. I., Janis, I. K., & Kelley, H. H. (1953). *Communication and persuasion.* New Haven, CT: Yale University Press.

Hovland, C. I., Lumsdaine, A. A., & Sheffield, F. D. (1949). *Experiments on mass communications.* Princeton, NJ: Princeton University Press.

Hovland, C. I., & Mandell, W. (1952). An experimental comparison of conclusion–drawing by the communicator and by the audience. *Journal of Abnormal and Social Psychology, 47,* 581–588.

Howard, G. S. (1991). Culture tales: A narrative approach to thinking, cross–cultural psychology, and psychotherapy. *American Psychologist, 46,* 187–197.

Howard, J. A. (1985). Further appraisal of correspondence inference theory. *Personality and Social Psychology Bulletin, 11,* 467–477.

Howard, J. A., Blumstein, P., & Schwartz, P. (1986). Sex, power, and influence tactics in intimate relationships. *Journal of Personality and Social Psychology, 51,* 102–109.

Howard, J. A., & Hollander, J. A. (1996). Gendered situations, gendered selves. Thousand Oaks, CA: Sage.

Howard, W., & Crano, W. D. (1974). Effects of sex, conversation, location, and size of observer group on bystander intervention in a high risk situation. *Sociometry, 37,* 491–507.

Hoyenga, K. B., & Hoyenga, K. T. (1993). *A manual to accompany gender-related differences: Origins and outcomes.* Boston: Allyn & Bacon.

Hsu, F. L. K. (1953). *Americans and Chinese: Two ways of life.* New York: Abelard-Schuman.

Hsu, F. L. K. (1981). *Americans and Chinese: Passage to differences.* Honolulu: University of Hawaii Press.

Hsu, F. L. K. (1985). The self in cross–cultural perspective. In A. J. Marsella, G. De Vos, & F. L. K. Hsu (Eds.), *Culture and self* (pp. 24–55). London: Tavistock.

Huesmann, L. R. (1986). Psychological processes promoting the relation between exposure to media violence and aggressive behavior by the viewer. *Journal of Social Issues, 42,* 125–139.

Huesmann, L. R., & Eron, L. D. (Eds.) (1986). *Television and the aggressive child: A cross-national comparison.* Mahwah, NJ: Lawrence Erlbaum.

Hughes, R. (1986). *The fatal shore: The epic of Australia's founding.* New York: Knopf.

Hui, C. H., & Ip, K. C. (1989). The control of social role bias: Effects of question preparation and subsequent feedback in a quiz game. *British Journal of Social Psychology, 28,* 31–38.

Hull, J. G., & Levy, A. S. (1979). The organizational functions of the self: An alternative to the Duval and Wicklund model of awareness. *Journal of Personality and Social Psychology, 37,* 756–768.

Hupka, R. B., & Bank, A. L. (1996). Sex differences in jealousy: Evolution or social construction? *Cross-Cultural Research, 30,* 24–59.

Hyde, J. S., Fennema, E., & Lamon, S. J. (1990). Gender differences in mathematical performance: A meta-analysis. *Psychological Bulletin, 107,* 139–155.

Hymes, R. W., Leinart, M., Rowe, S., & Rogers, W. (1993). Acquaintance rape: The effect of race of defendent and race of victim on white juror decisions. *Journal of Social Psychology, 133,* 627–634.

Iacocca, L. (1984). *Iacocca: An autobiography.* New York: Bantam.

Ingham, A. G., Levinger, G., Graves, J., & Peckham, V. (1974). The Ringelmann effect: Studies of group size and group performance. *Journal of Experimental Social Psychology, 10,* 371–384.

Inkeles, A. (1983). *Exploring individual modernity.* New York: Columbia University Press.

Inman, M. L., & Baron, R. S. (1996). Influence of prototypes on perceptions of prejudice. *Journal of Personality and Social Psychology, 70,* 727–739.

Innes, J. M. (1974). The semantics of asking a favour: An attempt to replicate cross-culturally. *International Journal of Psychology, 9,* 57–61.

Insko, C. A., & Wilson, M. (1977). Interpersonal attraction as a function of social interaction. *Journal of Personality and Social Psychology, 35,* 903–911.

International Development Research Centre. (1991). *Our common bowl: Global food interdependence.* Ottawa.

Iwao, S. (1988). *Social psychology's model of social behavior: Is it not time for West to meet East?* Paper presented at the 24th International Congress of Psychology, Sydney, Australia.

Jacklin, C. N. (1989). Female and male: Issues of gender. *American Psychologist, 44,* 127–133.

Jacklin, C. N., & Maccoby, E. E. (1978). Social behavior at 33 months in same–sex and mixed–sex dyads. *Child Development, 49,* 557–569.

Jackson, C. (1981). *Color me beautiful.* New York: Ballantine.

Jackson, J. M. (1988). *Social psychology, past and present.* Hillsdale, NJ: Lawrence Erlbaum.

Jackson, L. A. (1992). *Physical appearance and gender.* Albany: SUNY Press.

Jacobs, R. C., & Campbell, D. T. (1961). The perpetuation of an arbitrary tradition through several generations of a laboratory microculture. *Journal of Abnormal and Social Psychology, 62,* 649–658.

James, K. (1997) *Illusions of reality: A history of deception in social psychology.* Albany: SUNY Press.

James, W. (1890/1983). *The principles of psychology.* Cambridge, MA: Harvard University Press.

Jamieson, K. H. (1988). *Eloquence in an electronic age: The transformation of political speechmaking.* New York: Oxford University Press.

Janis, I. L. (1971, November). Groupthink. *Psychology Today,* pp. 43–46.

Janis, I. L. (1972). *Victims of groupthink: A psychological study of foreign-policy decisions and fiascoes.* Boston: Houghton Mifflin.

Janis, I. L. (1982). *Groupthink* (2nd ed.). Boston: Houghton Mifflin.

Janis, I. L., & Mann, L. (1977). *Decision-making: A psychological analysis of conflict, choice and commitment.* New York: Free Press.

Jankowiak, W. R., & Fischer, E. F. (1992). A cross-cultural perspective on romantic love. *Ethnology, 31,* 149–155.

Jelen, T. G., Thomas, S., & Wilcox, C. (1994). The gender gap in comparative perspective: Gender differences in abstract ideology and concrete issues in Western Europe. *European Journal of Political Research, 25,* 171–186.

Jenkins, S. R. (1996). Self-definition in thought, action, and life path choices. *Personality and Social Psychology Bulletin, 22,* 99–111.

Jensen-Cambell, L. A., Graziano, W. G., & West, S. G. (1995). Dominance, prosocial orientation, and female preferences: Do nice guys really finish last? *Journal of Personality and Social Psychology, 68,* 427–440.

Johnson, D. W., Johnson, R., Dudley, B., & Acikgoz, K. (1994). Effects of conflict resolution training on elementary school children. *Journal of Social Psychology, 134,* 803–817.

Johnson, F. (1985). The Western concept of self. In A. Marsella, G. De Vos, & F. L. K. Hsu (Eds.), *Culture and self* (pp. 91–138). London: Tavistock.

Johnson, G. B. (1941). The Negro and crime. *Annals of the American Academy of Political and Social Science, 217,* 93–104.

Jones, E. E. (1985). Major developments in social psychology during the past five decades. In D. Lindzey & E. Aronson (Eds.), *Handbook of social psychology* (pp. 47–107). New York: Random House.

Jones, E. E. (1990). *Interpersonal perception.* New York: W. H. Freeman.

Jones, E. E., & Berglas, S. (1978). Control of attributions about the self through self-handicapping strategies: The role of alcohol and underachievement. *Personality and Social Psychology Bulletin, 4,* 200–206.

Jones, E. E., & Davis, K. E. (1965). From acts to dispositions: The attribution process in person perception. In L. Berkowitz (Ed.), *Advances in Experimental Social Psychology* (Vol. 2, pp. 220–266). New York: Academic Press.

Jones, E. E., & Harris, V. A. (1967). The attribution of attitudes. *Journal of Experimental Social Psychology, 3,* 2–24.

Jones, E. E., & Nisbett, R. E. (1972). The actor and the observer: Divergent perceptions of the causes of behavior. In E. E. Jones, D. E. Kenouse, H. H. Kelley, R. E. Nisbett, S. Valins, & B. Weiner (Eds.), *Attribution: Perceiving the causes of behavior.* Morristown, NJ: General Learning Press.

Jones, E. E., & Pittman, T. S. (1982). Toward a general theory of strategic self-presentation. In J. M. Suls (Ed.), *Psychological perspectives on the self* (Vol. 1, pp. 231–262). Hillsdale, NJ: Lawrence Erlbaum.

Jones, E. E., & Sigall, H. (1971). The bogus pipeline: A new paradigm for measuring affect and attitude. *Psychological Bulletin, 76,* 349–364.

Jones, J. M. (1983). The concept of race in social psychology. In L. Wheeler & P. Shaver (Eds.), *Review of Personality and Social Psychology* (Vol. 4, pp. 117–150). Beverly Hills, CA: Sage.

Jones, T. S., & Remland, M. S. (1992). Sources of variability in perceptions of and responses to sexual harassment. *Sex Roles, 27,* 121–142.

Jost, J. T., & Banaji, M. R. (1994). The role of stereotyping in system-justification and the production of false consciousness. *British Journal of Social Psychology, 33,* 1–27.

Joyce, P. (Ed.) (1995). *Class.* Oxford: Oxford University Press.

Judd, C. M., & Park, B. (1988). Out-group homogeneity: Judgments of variability at the individual and group levels. *Journal of Personality and Social Psychology, 54,* 778–788.

Judd, C. M., & Park, B. (1993). Definition and assessment of accuracy in social stereotypes. *Psychological Review, 100,* 109–128.

Judd, C. M., Park, B., Ryan, C. S., Brauer, M., & Kraus, S. (1995). Stereotypes and ethnocentrism: Diverging interethnic perceptions of African American and White American youth. *Journal of Personality and Social Psychology, 69,* 460–481.

Jussim, L. (1993). Accuracy in interpersonal expectations: A reflection-construction analysis of current and classic research. *Journal of Personality, 61,* 638–668.

Kagan, S., & Knight, G. P. (1979). Cooperation–competition and self-esteem: A case of cultural relativism. *Journal of Cross-Cultural Psychology, 10,* 457–467.

Kağitçibaşi, Ç. C. (1984). Socialization in traditional society: A challenge to psychology. *International Journal of Psychology, 19,* 145–157.

Kağitçibaşi, Ç. (1996). *Family and human development across cultures: A view from the other side.* Mahwah, NJ: Lawrence Erlbaum.

Kalin, R. (1996). Ethnic attitudes as a function of ethnic presence. *Canadian Journal of Behavioural Science, 28,* 171–179.

Kallgren, C. A., & Wood, W. (1986). Access to attitude relevant information in memory as a determinant of attitude-behavior consistency. *Journal of Experimental Social Psychology, 22,* 328–338.

Kanungo, R. N., & Conger, J. A. (1989). *Charismatic leadership: A behavioral theory and its cross-cultural implications.* Paper presented at the 2nd Regional Conference of the International Association for Cross-Cultural Psychology, Amsterdam.

Kaplan, H. B. (1986). *Social psychology of self-referent behavior.* New York: Plenum Press.

Kaplan, R. D. (1994, February). The coming anarchy. *Atlantic Monthly,* pp. 44–75.

Karabenick, S. A., & Knapp, J. R. (1988). Effects of computer privacy on help seeking. *Journal of Applied Social Psychology, 18,* 461–472.

Karau, S. J., & Williams, K. (1993). Social loafing: A meta-analytic review and theoretical integration. *Journal of Personality and Social Psychology, 65,* 681–706.

Kashima, Y. (1995). Introduction to the special section on culture and self. *Journal of Cross-Cultural Psychology, 26,* 698–713.

Kashima, Y., Siegel, M., Tanaka, K., & Isaka, H. (1988).

Universalism in lay conceptions of distributive justice: A cross-cultural examination. *International Journal of Psychology, 23,* 51–64.

Kassin, S. M. (1997). The psychology of confession evidence. *American Psychologist, 52,* 221–233.

Kassin, S. M., Ellsworth, P. C., & Smith, V. L. (1989). The "general acceptance" of psychological research on eyewitness testimony: A survey of the experts. *American Psychologist, 44,* 1089–1098.

Kasson, J. F. (1990). *Rudeness & civility.* New York: Noonday Press.

Katz, A. M., & Hill, R. (1958). Residential propinquity and marital selection: A review of theory, method, and fact. *Marriage and Family Living, 20,* 237–335.

Katz, I., & Hass, R. G. (1988). Racial ambivalence and American value conflict: Correlational and priming studies of dual cognitive structures. *Journal of Personality and Social Psychology, 55,* 893–905.

Katz, P. A. & Taylor, D. (1988). *Eliminating racism: Profiles in controversy.* New York: Plenum Press.

Keegan, J. (1993). *A history of human warfare.* New York: Knopf.

Kegan, J. (1996). Three pleasing ideas. *American Psychologist, 51,* 901–908.

Keller, E. F. (1986). *Reflections on gender and science.* New Haven, CT: Yale University Press.

Kelley, H. H. (1967). Attribution theory in social psychology. In D. Levine (Ed.), *Nebraska Symposium on motivation* (Vol. 15, pp. 192–240). Lincoln: University of Nebraska Press.

Kelley, H. H. (1972). *Causal schemata and the attribution process.* Morristown, NJ: General Learning.

Kelley, H. H. (1973). The process of causal attribution. *American Psychologist, 28,* 107–128.

Kelley, H. H. (1979). *Personal relationships: Their structures and processes.* Hillsdale, NJ: Lawrence Erlbaum.

Kelly, G. (1955). *The psychology of personal constructs* (Vols. 1–2). New York: Norton.

Kelman, H. C. (1997). Group processes in the resolution of international conflicts: Experiences from the Israeli-Palestinian case. *American Psychologist, 52,* 212–220.

Kelman, H. C., & Hamilton, V. L. (1989). *Crimes of obedience: Toward a social psychology of authority and responsibility.* New Haven, CT: Yale University Press.

Kendrick, D. T., Cialdini, R. B., & Linder, D. E. (1979). Misattribution under fear-producing circumstances: Four failures to replicate. *Personality and Social Psychology Bulletin, 5,* 392–334.

Kendrick, D. T., & Keefe, R. C. (1992). Age preferences in mates reflect sex differences in reproductive strategies. *Behavioral and Brain Sciences, 15,* 75–91.

Kennedy, J. F. (1956). *Profiles in courage.* New York: Harper.

Kephart, W. M. (1967). Some correlates of romantic love. *Journal of Marriage and Family, 29,* 470–474.

Kessler, S. J. (1990). The medical construction of gender: Case management of intersexed infants. *Signs, 16,* 3–26.

Kihlstrom, J. F., Cantor, N., Albright, J. S., Chew, B. R., Klein, S. B., & Niedenthal, P. M. (1988). Information processing and the study of the self. In L. Berkowitz (Ed.), *Advances in experimental social psychology* (Vol. 21, pp. 145–180). New York: Academic Press.

Kilham, W., & Mann, L. (1974). Level of destructive obedience as a function of transmitter and executant roles in the Milgram obedience paradigm. *Journal of Personality and Social Psychology, 29,* 696–702.

Kilmartin, C. T. (1994). *The masculine self.* New York: Macmillan.

Kim, K. I., Park, H. J., & Suzuki, N. (1990). Reward allocations in the United States, Japan, and Korea: A comparison of individualistic and collectivistic cultures. *Academy of Management Journal, 33,* 188–198.

King, M. L. (1963). Letter from a Birmingham city jail. In *A testament of hope* (pp. 289–302). New York: Harper & Row.

Kingdon, J. W. (1967). Politicians' beliefs about voters. *American Political Science Review, 61,* 137–145.

Kipnis, D. (1997). Ghosts, taxonomies, and social psychology. *American Psychologist, 52,* 205–211.

Kirkpatrick, S. A., & Locke, E. A. (1991). Leadership: Do traits matter? *Academy of Management Executive, 5,* 48–60.

Klein, S. B., Loftus, J., & Burton, H. A. (1989). Two self-reference effects: The importance of distinguishing between self-descriptiveness judgments and autobiographical retrieval in self-referent encoding. *Journal of Personality and Social Psychology, 56,* 853–865.

Kluckholm, F. & Strodtbeck, F. (1961). *Variations in value orientations.* Evanston, IL: Row, Peterson.

Kogan, N., & Doise, W. (1969). Effects of anticipated delegate status on level of risk taking in small decision making groups. *Acta Psychologica, 29,* 228–243.

Kogan, N., & Wallach, M. (1967). Risk taking as a function of the situation, the person, and the group. In G. Mandler (Ed.), *New directions in psychology* (Vol. 3, pp. 111–278). New York: Holt, Rinehart & Winston.

Kohlberg, L. (1963). Moral development and identification. In H. W. Stevenson (Ed.), *Year-book of the National Society for the Study of Children: Part I. Child Psychology* (pp. 277–332). Chicago: University of Chicago Press.

Kohlberg, L. (1976). Moral stages and moralization: The cognitive-developmental approach. In T. Lickona (Ed.), *Moral development and behavior* (pp. 31–53). New York: Holt.

Kohn, M. L. (1969). *Class and conformity.* Homewood, IL: Dorsey Press.

Kohn, M. L. (1977). *Class and conformity* (2nd ed.). Chicago: University of Chicago Press.

Korn, J. (1997). *Illusions of Reality: A History of Deception in Social Psychology* Albany: State University of New York Press.

Koss, M. P., Gidycz, C. A., & Wisniewski, N. (1987). The scope of rape: Incidence and prevalence of sexual aggression and victimization in a national sample of higher education students. *Journal of Consulting and Clinical Psychology, 55,* 162–170.

Koss, M. P., Goodman, L. A., Browne, A., Fitzgerald, L. F., Keita, G. P., & Russo, N. F. (1994). *No safe haven: Male violence against women at home, at work, and in the community.* Washington, DC: American Psychological Association.

Koss, M. P., Huse, L., & Russo, N. F. (1994). The global health burden of rape. *Psychology of Women Quarterly, 18,* 1509–1537.

Kotre, J. (1992). Experiments as parables. *American Psychologist, 47,* 672–673.

Kraut, R. E., & Lewis, S. H. (1982). Person perception and self-awareness: Knowledge of one's influences on one's own judgments. *Journal of Personality and Social Psychology, 42,* 448–460.

Kristof, N. D. (1996, July 13). In sexist South Korea, schoolgirls even the score. *New York Times International Edition,* p. 4.

Krosnick, J. A., & Alwin, D. F. (1989). Aging and susceptivity to attitude change. *Journal of Personality and Social Psychology, 57,* 416–425.

Kruglanski, A. W., & Mayseless, O. (1990). *Psychological Bulletin, 108,* 195–208.

Kumar, P., & Gairola, L. (1983). Attitudinal and motivational factors in contraception usage among women. *Perspectives in Psychological Researches, 6,* 27–31.

Kunst-Wilson, W. R., & Zajonc, R. B. (1980). Affective discrimination of stimuli that cannot be recognized. *Science, 207,* 557–558.

LaFree, G. D. (1980). The effect of sexual stratification by race on official reactions to rape. *American Sociological Review, 45,* 842–854.

Lalonde, R. N., & Cameron, J. E. (1994). Behavioral responses to discrimination: A focus on action. In M. P. Zanna & J. M. Olson (Eds.), *The psychology of prejudice: The Ontario Symposium* (Vol. 7, pp. 257–288). Hillsdale, NJ: Lawrence Erlbaum.

Lalonde, R. N., Majumder, S., & Parris, R. D. (1995). Preferred responses to situations of housing and employment discrimination. *Journal of Applied Social Psychology, 25,* 1105–1119.

Lalonde, R. N., & Silverman, R. A. (1994). Behavioral preferences in response to social injustice: The effects of group permeability and social identity salience. *Journal of Personality and Social Psychology, 66,* 78–85.

Lambert, W. E. (1969). A social psychology of bilingualism. *Journal of Social Issues, 23,* 91–109.

Lambert, W. E. (1978). Cognitive and socio-cultural consequences of bilingualism. *Canadian Modern Language Review, 34,* 537–547.

Lambert, W. E. (1987). The fate of old-country values in a new land: A cross-cultural study of child (rearing/reasoning?) *Canadian Psychologist, 28,* 9–20.

Lambert, W. E., Mermegis, L., & Taylor, D. M. (1986). Greek Canadians' attitudes towards own group and other Canadian ethnic groups: A test of the multiculturalism hypothesis. *Canadian Journal of Behavioural Science, 18,* 35–51.

Lambert, W. E., Moghaddam, F. M., Sorin, J., & Sorin, S. (1990). Assimilation vs. multiculturalism: Views from a community in France. *Sociological Forum, 5,* 387–411.

Lambert, W. E., & Taylor, D. M. (1990). *Coping with cultural and racial diversity in urban America.* New York: Praeger.

Lambert, W. E., & Taylor, D. M. (1996). Language in the lives of ethnic minorities: Cuban American families in Miami. *Applied Linguistics, 17,* 477–500.

Landau, S. F. (1984). Trends in violence and aggression: A cross-cultural analysis. *International Journal of Comparative Sociology, 25,* 133–158.

Lane, S. T. M., & Sawaia, B. (1991). Community social psychology in Brazil. *Applied Psychology: An International Review, 40,* 119–142.

Langlois, J. H., Ritter, J. M., Casey, R. J., & Sawin, D. S. (1995). Infant attractiveness predicts maternal behaviors and attitudes. *Developmental Psychology, 31,* 464–472.

Langlois, J. H., & Roggman, L. A. (1990). Attractive faces are only average. *Psychological Science, 1,* 115–121.

Langlois, J. H., Roggman, L. A., Casey, R. J., Ritter, J. M.,

Rieser-Danner, L. A., & Jenkins, V. Y. (1987). Infant preferences for attractive faces: Rudiments of a stereotype? *Developmental Psychology, 23,* 363–369.

Langlois, J. H., Roggman, L. A., & Rieser-Danner, A. (1990). Infants' differential social responses to attractive and unattractive faces. *Developmental Psychology, 26,* 153–159.

LaPiere, R. T. (1934). Attitude and actions. *Social Forces, 13,* 230–237.

LaPiere, R. T. (1936). Type-rationalizations of group antiplay. *Social Forces, 15,* 232–237.

L'Armand, K., & Pepitone, A. (1975). Helping to reward another person: A cross-cultural analysis. *Journal of Personality and Social Psychology, 31,* 189–198.

Larson, C. U. (1995). *Persuasion: Reception and responsibility.* (7th ed.). Belmont, CA: Wadsworth.

Latané, B. (1981). The psychology of social impact. *American Psychologist, 36,* 343–356.

Latané, B., & Dabbs, J. M., (1975). Sex, group size and helping in three cities. *Sociometry, 38,* 180–194.

Latané, B., & Darley, J. M. (1970). *The unresponsive bystander: Why doesn't he help?* Englewood Cliffs, NJ: Prentice Hall.

Latané, B., & Rodin, J. (1969). A lady in distress: Inhibiting effects of friends and strangers on bystander intervention. *Journal of Experimental Social Psychology, 5,* 189–202.

Latané, B., Williams, K., & Harkins, S. (1979). Many hands make light the work: Causes and consequences of social loafing. *Journal of Personality and Social Psychology, 37,* 822–832.

Latour, B., & Woolgar, S. (1979). *Laboratory life: The social construction of scientific facts.* Beverly Hills, CA: Sage.

Lau, S., & Gruen, G. E. (1992). The social stigma of loneliness: Effect of target person's and perceiver's sex. *Personality and Social Psychology Bulletin, 18,* 182–189.

Lawrence, D. H. (1928/1959). *Lady Chatterley's lover.* New York: Grove Press.

Lazarus, R. S., & Folkman, S. (1984). *Stress, appraisal, and coping.* New York: Springer.

Leary, M. R., & Shepperd, J. A. (1986). Behavioral self-handicaps versus self-reported handicaps: A conceptual note. *Journal of Personality and Social Psychology, 51,* 1265–1268.

Leary, T. (1957). *Interpersonal diagnosis of personality.* New York: Ronald Press.

LeBon, G. (1897). *The crowd: A study of the popular mind.* London: T. Fisher Unwin.

Lebra, T. S. (1992). Self in Japanese culture. In N. R. Rosenberger (Ed.), *Japanese sense of self* (pp. 105–120). Cambridge: Cambridge University Press.

Lebra, T. S., & Lebra, W. P. (1986). *Japanese culture and behavior: Selected readings.* Honolulu: University of Hawaii Press.

Lee, J. A. (1976). *The colors of love.* New York: Bantam.

Lee, R. B. (1979). *The !Kung San: Men, women and work in a foraging society.* Cambridge: Cambridge University Press.

Lee, Y. T. (1993). Ingroup preference and homogeneity among African American and Chinese American students. *Journal of Social Psychology, 132,* 225–235.

Lee, Y. T. (1995). A comparison of politics and personality in China and in the U.S.: Testing a "kernel of truth" hypothesis. *Journal of Contemporary China, 9,* 56–68.

Lee, Y. T., Albright, L., & Malloy, T. E. (in press). Social perception and stereotyping. In U. P. Gielen & A. L. Comunian (Eds.), *Cross-cultural and international dimensions of psychology.* Trieste, Italy: Edizioni Lint Trieste.

Lee, Y. T., & Jussim, L., & McCauley, C. (1995). Stereotype accuracy: *Toward appreciating group differences.* Washington, DC: American Psychological Association.

Lee, Y. T., & Ottati, V. (1993). Determinants of ingroup and outgroup perceptions of heterogeneity: An investigation of Sino–American stereotypes. *Journal of Cross-Cultural Psychology, 24,* 298–318.

Lee, Y. T., & Ottati, V. (1995). Perceived in-group homogeneity as a function of group membership salience and stereotype threat. *Personality and Social Psychology Bulletin, 21,* 610–619.

Lee, Y. T., Pepitone, A., & Albright, L. (1997). Descriptive and prescriptive beliefs about justice: A Sino–U.S. comparison. *Cross-Cultural Research, 31,* 101–120.

Leippe, M. R., & Eisenstadt, D. (1994). Generalizations of dissonance reduction: Decreasing prejudice through induced compliance. *Journal of Personality and Social Psychology, 67,* 395–413.

Lemain, G., & Kasterszstein, J. (1971–1972). Recherches sur l'originalité sociale et l'incomparabilité. *Bulletin de Psychologie, 25,* 673–693.

Lenihan, J. H. (1980). *Showdown: Confronting modern America in the Western film.* Urbana: University of Illinois Press.

Lenney, E. (1991). Sex roles: The measurement of masculinity, femininity, and androgyny. In J. P. Robinson, P. R. Shaver, & L. S. Wrightsman (Eds.), *Measures of personality and social psychological attitudes* (pp. 573–660). New York: Academic Press.

Lerner, M. J. (1977). The justice motive: Some hypotheses as to its origins and forms. *Journal of Personality, 45,* 1–52.

Lerner, M. J. (1980). *The belief in a just world: A fundamental delusion.* New York: Plenum Press.

Lerner, M. J. (1991). Interpreting societal and psychological rules of entitlement. In R. Vermunt & H. Steensma (eds.), *Social justice in human relations* (Vol. 1, pp. 13–32). New York: Plenum Press.

Lester, D. (1979). Temporal variation in suicide and homicide. *American Journal of Epidemiology, 109,* 517–520.

Leung, K., & Bond, M. H. (1984). The impact of cultural collectivism on reward allocation. *Journal of Personality and Social Psychology, 47,* 793–804.

Leung, K., & Lind, E. A. (1986). Procedural justice and culture: Effects of culture, gender, and investigator status on procedural preferences. *Journal of Personality and Social Psychology, 50,* 1134–1140.

Leung, K., & Wu, P. G. (1990). Dispute processing: A cross-cultural analysis. In R. W. Brislin (Ed.), *Applied cross-cultural psychology* (pp. 209–231). Newbury Park, CA: Sage.

Leventhal, G. S., & Lane, D. W. (1970). Sex, age, and equity behavior. *Journal of Personality and Social Psychology, 15,* 312–316.

Levine, M. (1996). *Viewing violence: How media violence affects your child's and adolescent's development.* New York: Doubleday.

LeVine, R. A. (1990). The pace of life. *American Scientist, 78,* 450–459.

LeVine, R. A., & Campbell, D. T. (1972). *Ethnocentrism: Theories of conflict, ethnic attitudes, and group behavior.* New York: Wiley.

LeVine, R., Sato, S., Hashimoto, T., & Verma, J. (1995). Love and marriage in eleven cultures. *Journal of Cross-Cultural Psychology, 26,* 554–571.

Lewin, K. (1935). *A dynamic theory of personality.* New York: McGraw–Hill.

Lewin, K. (1948). *Resolving social conflicts.* New York: Harper & Row.

Lewin, K. (1952). *Field theory in social science.* New York: Harper & Row.

Lewis, M., & Brooks-Gunn, J. (1979). *Social cognition and the acquisition of self.* New York: Plenum Press.

Lewis, M., & Michalson, L. (1983). *Children's emotions and moods: Developmental theory and measurement.* New York: Plenum Press.

Leyens, J. P., Herman, G., & Dunand, M. (1982). The influence of an audience upon the reactions to filmed violence. *European Journal of Social Psychology, 12,* 131–142.

Leyens, J. P., Yzerbyt, V., & Schadron, G. (1994). *Stereotypes and social cognition.* Thousand Oaks, CA: Sage.

Lieberman, M. A., & Tobin, S. S. (1983). *The experience of old age: Stress, coping, and survival.* New York: Basic Books.

Lieberson, W., & Waters, M. C. (1987). The location of racial and ethnic groups in the United States. *Sociological Forum, 2,* 780–810.

Liebling, B. A., Seiler, M., & Shaver, P. (1975). Unsolved problems for self-awareness theory: A reply to Wicklund. *Journal of Experimental Social Psychology, 11,* 82–85.

Liebrand, W. B. G., & van Run, G. J. (1985). The effects of social motives on behavior in social dilemmas in two cultures. *Journal of Experimental Social Psychology, 21,* 86–102.

Lightdale, J. R. & Prentice, D. A. (1994). Rethinking sex differences in aggression: Aggressive behavior in the absence of social roles. *Personality and Social Psychology Bulletin, 20,* 34–44.

Lindsay, R. C. L., Wells, G. L., & Rumpel, C. M. (1981). Can people detect eyewitness-identification accuracy within and across situations? *Journal of Applied Psychology, 66,* 79–89.

Ling, W. Q. (1989). Pattern of leadership behavior assessment in China. *Psychologia, 32,* 129–134.

Linville, P. W. (1985). Self-complexity and affective extremity: Don't put all your eggs in one cognitive basket. *Social Cognition, 3,* 94–120.

Linville, P. W. (1987). Self-complexity as a cognitive buffer against stress-related depression and illness. *Journal of Personality and Social Psychology, 52,* 663–676.

Linville, P. W., Fischer, G. W., & Salovey, P. (1989). Perceived distributions of the characteristics of in-group and out-group members: Empirical evidence and a computer simulation. *Journal of Personality and Social Psychology, 57,* 165–188.

Little, A. (1987). Attributions in cross-cultural context. *Genetic, Social, and General Psychology Monographs, 113,* 61–79.

Llewelyn-Davies, M. (1981). Women, warriers, and patriarchs. In S. B. Ortner & H. Whitehead (Eds.), *Sexual meanings: The cultural construction of gender and sexuality* (pp. 330–358). Cambridge: Cambridge University Press.

Loftus, E. F. (1979). *Eyewitness testimony.* Cambridge, MA: Harvard University Press.

Lombroso, C. (1899/1911). *Crime: Its causes and remedies.* Boston: Little, Brown.

Lont, C. M. (Ed.) (1995). *Women and media: Content, careers, and criticism.* Belmont, CA: Wadsworth.

Lorber, J. (1994). *Paradoxes of gender.* New Haven, CT: Yale University Press.

Lord, C. G. (1980). Schemas and images as memory aids: Two modes of processing social information. *Journal of Personality and Social Psychology, 38,* 257–269.

Lorenz, K. (1966). *On aggression* (M. Wilson, Trans.). New York: Harcourt, Brace & World.

Losch, M. E., & Cacioppo, J. T. (1990). Cognitive dissonance may enhance sympathetic tonus, but attitudes are changed to reduce negative affect rather than arousal. *Journal of Experimental Social Psychology, 26,* 289–304.

Lott, B., & Maluso, D. (Eds.) (1995). *The social psychology of interpersonal discrimination.* New York: Guilford Press.

Louis, W. R., & Taylor, D. M. (1997). *From acceptance to collective action: Toward an understanding of behavioral responses to discrimination.* Unpublished manuscript, Psychology Department, McGill University, Montreal.

Louw, J., & Louw-Potgieter, J. (1986). Achievement related causal attributions: A South-African cross-cultural study. *Journal of Cross-Cultural Psychology, 17,* 269–282.

Lovdal, L. T. (1989). Sex role messages in television commercials: An unpdate. *Sex Roles, 21,* 715–724.

Lummis, M., & Stevenson, H. W. (1990). Gender differences in beliefs and achievement: A cross-cultural study. *Developmental Psychology, 26,* 254–263.

Luria, A. R. (1974/1976). *Cognitive development: Its cultural and social foundations* (M. Lopez-Morillas & L. Solotaroff, Trans.). Cambridge, MA: Harvard University Press.

Luus, C. A. E., & Wells, G. L. (1994). Eyewitness identification confidence. In D. F. Ross, J. D. Read, & M. P. Toglia (Eds.), *Adult eyewitness testimony: Current trends and developments.* Cambridge: Cambridge University Press.

Maas, A., & Clark, R. D. III (1984). Hidden impact of minorities: Fifteen years of minority influence research. *Psychological Bulletin, 95,* 428–450.

Maas, A., West, S. G., & Cialdini, R. B. (1987). Minority influence and conversion. In C. Hendrick (Ed.), *Group processes* (pp. 55–79). London: Sage.

Macbeth, T. M. (Ed.) (1996). *Tuning in to young viewers: Social science perspectives on television.* Thousand Oaks, CA: Sage.

Maccoby, E. E. (1988). Gender as a social category. *Developmental Psychology, 26,* 755–765.

Maccoby, E. E. (1990). Gender and relationships: A developmental account. *American Psychologist, 45,* 513–520.

Maccoby, E. E., & Jacklin, C. N. (1974). *The psychology of sex differences.* Stanford, CA: Stanford University Press.

Maccoby, E. E., & Jacklin, C. N. (1987). Gender segregation in childhood. In H. W. Reese (Ed.), *Advances in child development and behavior* (Vol. 20, pp. 239–288). New York: Academic Press.

Mackie, D. M., & Hamilton, D. L. (1993). *Affect, cognition and stereotyping: Interactive processes in group perception.* San Diego: Academic Press.

MacNeil, M. K., & Sherif, M. (1976). Norm change over subject generations as a function of arbitrariness of prescribed norms. *Journal of Personality and Social Psychology, 34,* 762–773.

Macrae, C. N., Stangor, C., & Hewstone, M. (Eds.) (1995). *Stereotypes and stereotyping.* New York: Guilford Press.

Madden, T. J., Ellen, P. S., & Ajzen, I (1992). A comparison of the theory of planned behavior and the theory of reasoned action. *Personality and Social Psychology Bulletin, 18,* 3–9.

Mahler, I., Greenberg, L., & Hayashi, H. (1981). A comparative study of rules of justice: Japanese versus American. *Psychologia, 24,* 1–8.

Majeed, A., & Ghosh, E. S. K. (1981). Ingroup and outgroup evaluation in intergroup context. *Psychological Reports, 26,* 34–40.

Major, B. (1994). From social inequality to personal entitlement: The role of social comparisons, legitimacy appraisals, and group membership. In M. Zanna (Ed.), *Advances in experimental psychology* (Vol. 26, pp. 293–355). New York: Academic Press.

Majors, R. G., & Gordon, J. U. (Eds.) (1994). *The American Black male.* Chicago: Nelson-Hall.

Malamuth, N. M. (1981). Rape proclivity among males. *Journal of Social Issues, 37,* 138–157.

Malamuth, N. M., Linz, D., Heavy, C. L., Barnes, G., & Acker, M. (1995). Using the confluence model of sexual aggression to predict men's conflict with women: A 10-year follow-up study. *Journal of Personality and Psychology, 69,* 353–369.

Mandelbaum, D. G. (1970). *Society in India, Vol. 2: Change and continuity.* Berkeley: University of California Press.

Manson, J. H., & Wrangham, R. W. (1991). Intergroup aggression in chimpanzees and humans. *Current Anthropology, 32,* 369–377, 385–390.

Mantell, D. M. (1971). The potential for violence in Germany. *Journal of Social Issues, 27,* 101–112.

Maquet, J. J. (1961). *The premise of inquality in Rwanda: A study of political relations in a Central African kingdom.* London: Oxford University Press.

Marecek, J. (1995). Gender, politics, and psychology's ways of knowing. *American Psychologist, 50,* 162–163.

Marin, G. (1981). Perceiving justice across cultures: Equity vs. equality in Colombia and in the United States. *International Journal of Psychology, 16,* 153–159.

Markus, H. (1977). Self-schemata and processing information about the self. *Journal of Personality and Social Psychology, 35,* 63–78.

Markus, H. R., & Kitayama, S. (1991). Culture and the self: Implications for cognition, emotion, and motivation. *Psychological Review, 98,* 224–253.

Markus, H., & Zajonc, R. B. (1985). The cognitive perspective in social psychology. In G. Lindzey & E. Aronson (Eds.), *The handbook of social psychology* (3rd ed., Vol. 1, pp. 137–230). New York: Random House.

Marrow, A. J. (1969). *The practical theorist: The life and work of Kurt Lewin.* New York: Basic Books.

Marshall, D. S., & Suggs, R. C. (Eds.) (1971). *Human sexual behavior: Variations in the ethnographic spectrum.* New York: Basic Books.

Martinez, P., & Richters, E. J. (1993a). The NIMH community violence project: I. Children as victims of and witnesses to violence. *Psychiatry, 53,* 7–21.

Martinez, P., & Richters, E. J. (1993b). The NIMH community violence project: II. Children's distress symptoms associated with violent exposure. *Psychiatry, 53,* 22–35.

Marwell, G., & Schmitt, D. (1967). Dimensions of compliance gaining behavior: An empirical analysis. *Sociometry, 30,* 350–364.

Marx, K. (1852/1979). The eighteenth brumaire of Louis Bonaparte. In *Collected works* (Vol. 11, pp. 99–197). London: Lawrence and Wishart.

Marx, K., & Engels, F. (1848/1967). *Communist manifesto.* New York: Pantheon.

Maslow, A. (1987). *Motivation and personality* (3rd ed.). New York: Harper & Row.

Masters, M. S., & Sanders, B. (1993). Is the gender difference in tal rotation disappearing? *Behavior Genetics, 23,* 337–341.

Matsuda, N. (1985). Strong, quasi-, and weak conformity among Japanese in the modified Asch procedure. *Journal of Cross-Cultural Psychology, 16,* 83–97.

Matsumoto, M. (1990). *The unspoken way.* Tokyo: Kodansha International.

McCarthy, T. D., & Zald, M. N. (1977). Resource mobilization and social movements: A partial theory. *American Journal of Sociology, 82,* 1212–1241.

McCauley, C. (1989). The nature of social influence in groupthink: Compliance and internalization. *Journal of Personality and Social Psychology, 57,* 250–260.

McClelland, D. C. (1961). *The achieving society.* Princeton, NJ: Van Nostrand.

McClelland, D. C., Atkinson, J. W., Clark, R. A., & Lowell, E. L. (1953). *The achievement motive.* New York: Appleton-Century-Crofts.

McClelland, D. C., & Winter, D. G. (1969). *Motivating economic achievement.* Glencoe, IL: Free Press.

McClintock, C. G., & McNeel, C. P. (1966). Cross-cultural comparisons of interpersonal motives. *Sociometry, 29,* 406–427.

McClintock, C. G., & Nuttin, J. M. Jr. (1969). Development of competetive game behavior in children across two cultures. *Journal of Experimental Social Psychology, 5,* 203–218.

McCloskey, M., Wible, C. G., & Cohen, N. J. (1988). Is there a special flashbulb–memory mechanism? *Journal of Experimental Psychology: General, 117,* 171–181.

McConahay, J. B. (1986). Modern racism, ambivalence, and the Modern Racism Scale. In J. F. Dovidio & S. L. Gaertner (Eds.), *Prejudice, discrimination, and racism* (pp. 91–125). San Diego: Academic Press.

McDonald, K. A. (1993). Kansas physicist finds consistency in life as minister and cosmologist. *Chronicle of Higher Education,* May 12, pp. A7, A9.

McDougall, W. (1908). *Introduction to social psychology.* London: Methuen.

McDougall, W. (1920). *The group mind.* Cambridge: Cambridge University Press.

McGraw, K. O., & Wong, S. P. (1992). A common language effect size statistic. *Psychological Bulletin, 111,* 361–365.

McGuire, W. J. (1962). Persistence of the resistance to persuasion induced by various types of prior belief defences. *Journal of Abnormal and Social Psychology, 64,* 241–248.

McGuire, W. J. (1969). Nature of attitudes and attitude change. In G. Lindzey & E. Aronson (Eds.), *The handbook of social psychology* (2nd ed., Vol. 3, pp. 233–346). New York: Addison-Wesley.

McGuire, W. J. (1970). A vaccine for brainwash. *Psychology Today, 3,* 36–39, 63–64.

McGuire, W. J. (1985). Attitudes and attitude change. In G. Lindzey & E. Aronson (Eds.), *The handbook of social psychology* (3rd ed., Vol. 2, pp. 233–346). New York: Random House.

McGuire, W. J. (1989). Theoretical foundations of campaigns. In R. E. Rice & C. E. Atkins (Eds.), *Public communication campaigns* (pp. 43–66). Newbury Park, CA: Sage.

McGuire, W. J., & McGuire, C. V. (1981). The spontaneous self concept as affected by personal distinctiveness. In A. Norem-Hebeisen, M. D. Lynch, & K. Gergen (Eds.), *The self concept: Advances in theory and research* (pp. 147–171). New York: Ballinger.

McGuire, W. J., & McGuire, C. V. (1991). The content, structure, and operation of thought systems. In R. S. Wyer, Jr., & T. Srull (Eds.), *Advances in social cognition* (Vol. 4, pp. 1–78). Hillsdale, NJ: Lawrence Erlbaum.

McGuire, W. J., McGuire, C. V., & Cheever, J. (1986). The self in society: Effects of social contexts on the sense of self. *British Journal of Social Psychology, 25,* 259–270.

McGuire, W. J., & Padawer-Singer, A. (1976). Trait salience in the spontaneous self concept. *Journal of Personality and Social Psychology, 33,* 743–754.

McInerney, D. M. (1995). Achievement motivation and indigenous minorities: Can research be psychometric? *Cross-Cultural Research, 29,* 211–239.

McLoyd, V. C., & Randolph, S. M. (1984). The conduct and publication of research on Afro-American children. *Human Development, 27,* 65–75.

McLoyd, V. C., & Randolph, S. M. (1985). Secular trends in the study of Afro-American children: A review of *Child Development, 1936-1980. Monographs of the Society for Research in Child Development, 50,* 78–92.

McMaster, H. R. (1997). *Dereliction of duty: Lyndon Johnson, Robert McNamara, The Joint Chiefs of Staff, and the lies that led to Vietnam.* New York: HarperCollins.

McNeel, C. P., McClintock, C. G., & Nuttin, J. M. Jr. (1972). Effect of sex-role in a two-person mixed-motive game. *Journal of Personality and Social Psychology, 24,* 372–378.

Mead, G. H. (1934). *Mind, self, and society.* Chicago: University of Chicago Press.

Meeker, B. F. (1970). An experimental study of cooperation and competition in West Africa. *International Journal of Psychology, 5,* 11–19.

Meeus, V. H. J., & Raaijmakers, Q. A. W. (1986). Administrative obedience carrying out orders to use psychological–administrative violence. *European Journal of Social Psychology, 16,* 311–324.

Meltzoff, A. N., & Gopnik, A. (1997). *Words, thoughts, and theories.* Cambridge, MA: MIT Press.

Messick, D. M., & Cook, K. S. (Eds.) (1983). *Equity theory: Psychological and sociological perspectives.* New York: Praeger.

Messick, D. M., & Mackie, D. M. (1989). Intergroup relations. *Annual Review of Psychology, 40,* 45–81.

Messner, S. F. (1980). Income inequality and murder rates: Some cross-national findings. In R. F. Tomasson (Ed.), *Comparative social research* (Vol. 3, pp. 185–198). Greenwich, CT: JAI Press.

Meyer, J., & Jesilow, P. (1996). Research on bias in judicial sentencing. *New Mexico Law Review, 26,* 107–131.

Michael, R. P., & Zumpe, D. (1983). Annual rhythms in human violence and sexual aggression in the United States and the role of temperature. *Social Biology, 30,* 263–278.

Middlebrook, K. J. (1995). *The paradox of revolution: Labor, state, and authoritarianism in Mexico.* Baltimore, MD: Johns Hopkins University Press.

Miles, J. (1992, October). Blacks vs. browns. *Atlantic Monthly,* pp. 41–68.

Milgram, S. (1961). Nationality and conformity. *Scientific American, 205,* 45–51.

Milgram, S. (1972a). The lost-letter technique. In L. Bickman & T. Henchy (Eds.), *Beyond the laboratory: Field research in social psychology* (pp. 245–255). New York: McGraw–Hill.

Milgram, S. (1972b). The small-world problem. In L. Bickman & T. Henchy (Eds.), *Beyond the laboratory: Field research in social psychology* (pp. 290–299). New York: McGraw–Hill.

Milgram, S. (1974). *Obedience to authority: An experimental view.* New York: Harper & Row.

Milgram, S. (1977). *The individual in a social world.* Reading, MA: Addison–Wesley.

Miller, A. (1983). *For your own good: Hidden cruelty in child-rearing and the roots of violence.* New York: Farrar, Straus, & Giroux.

Miller, B. D. (Ed.) (1993). *Sex and gender hierarchies.* New York: Cambridge University Press.

Miller, C. T., Rothblum, E. D., Felicio, D., Brand, P. (1995). Compensating for stigma: Obese and nonobese women's reactions to being visible. *Personality and Social Psychology Bulletin, 21,* 1093–1106.

Miller, G. R. (1987). Persuasion. In C. R. Berger & S. H. Chaffee (Eds), *Handbook of communication science* (pp. 446–483). Newbury Park, CA: Sage.

Miller, J. G. (1984). Culture and the development of everyday social explanation. *Journal of Personality and Social Psychology, 46,* 961–978.

Miller, J. G. (1986). Early cross-cultural commonalities in social explanation. *Developmental Psychology, 22,* 514–520.

Miller, J. G. (1987). Cultural influences on the development of conceptual differentiation in person description. *British Journal of Developmental Psychology, 5,* 309–319.

Miller, J. G. (in press). Taking culture into account in social cognitive development. In G. Misra (Ed.), *Socialization and social development in India.* New Delhi, India: Sage.

Miller, J. G., & Bersoff, D. M. (1992). Culture and moral judgement: How are conflicts between justice and friendship resolves? *Journal of Personality and Social Psychology, 62,* 541–554.

Miller, J. G., & Bersoff, D. M. (1994). Cultural influences on the moral status of reciprocity and the discounting of endogenous motivation. *Personality and Social Psychology Bulletin, 20,* 592–602.

Miller, J. G., Bersoff, D. M., & Harwood, R. L. (1990). Perceptions of social responsibility in India and in the United States: Moral imperatives or personal decisions? *Journal of Personality and Social Psychology, 58,* 33–47.

Miller, N., & Campbell, D. T (1959). Recency and primacy in persuasion as a function of the timing of speeches and measurements. *Journal of Abnormal and Social Psychology, 59,* 1–9.

Miller, R. L. (1977). Preferences for social vs. non-social comparison as a means of self-evaluation. *Journal of Personality, 36,* 1221–1223.

Mischel, W. (1968). *Personality assessment.* New York: Wiley.

Misumi, J. (1985). *The behavioral science of leadership: An interdisciplinary Japanese research program.* Ann Arbor: University of Michigan Press.

Mitchell, A. A. (Ed.) (1993). *Advertising exposure, memory, and choice.* Hillsdale, NJ: Lawrence Erlbaum.

Moghaddam, F. M. (1987). Psychology in the third world: As reflected by the "crisis" in social psychology and the move towards indigenous third world psychology. *American Psychologist, 47,* 912–920.

Moghaddam, F. M. (1990). Modulative and generative orientations in psychology: Implications for psychology in the third world. *Journal of Social Issues, 56,* 21–41.

Moghaddam, F. M. (1992a). Assimilation et multiculturalisme: Le cas de minorités au Quebec. *La Revue Québécoise de Psychologie, 13,* 140–157.

Moghaddam, F. M. (1992b). There can be a just and moral social constructionist psychology, but only in a social world that is homogeneous and/or static. In D. N. Robinson (Ed.), *Social discourse and moral judgment* (pp. 167–179). New York: Academic Press.

Moghaddam, F. M. (1993). Managing cultural diversity: North-American experiences and suggestions for the German unification process. *International Journal of Psychology, 28,* 727–741.

Moghaddam, F. M. (1994). Ethnic segregation in a multicultural society: A review of recent trends in Montreal and Toronto and reconceptualization of "causal factors." In F. Frisken (Ed.), *The changing Canadian metropolis* (pp. 237–258). Berkeley and Toronto: University of California Press and Canadian Urban Studies Institute.

Moghaddam, F. M. (1996). Training for developing world psychologists: Can the training be better than the psychology? In S. C. Carr & J. F. Schumaker (Eds.), *Psychology and the developing world* (pp. 49–59). New York: Praeger.

Moghaddam, F. M. (1997a). *The specialized society: The plight of the individual in an age of individualism.* Westport, CT: Praeger.

Moghaddam, F. M. (1997b). Change and continuity in organizations: Assessing intergroup relations through social reduction theory. In C. Granrose & S. Oskamp (Eds.), *Cross-cultural work groups* (pp. 36–58). Newbury Park, CA: Sage.

Moghaddam, F. M., & Crystal, D. (1997). Reductons, Samurai, and revolutions: The paradoxes of change and continuity in Iran and Japan. *Journal of Political Psychology, 18,* 355–384.

Moghaddam, F. M., Ditto, B., & Taylor, D. M. (1990). Attitudes and attributions related to psychological symptomatology in Indian immigrant women. *Journal of Cross-Cultural Psychology, 21,* 335–350.

Moghaddam, F. M., & Harré, R. (1992). Rethinking the laboratory experiment. *American Behavioral Scientist, 36,* 22–38.

Moghaddam, F. M., & Harré, R. (1995). But is it science? Traditional and alternative approaches to the study of social behavior. *World Psychology, 1,* 47–78.

Moghaddam, F. M., & Perreault, S. (1992). Individual and collective mobility strategies among minority group members. *Journal of Social Psychology, 132,* 343–357.

Moghaddam, F. M., & Solliday, E. A. (1991). "Balanced multiculturalism" and the challenge of peaceful coexistence in pluralistic societies. *Psychology and Developing Societies, 3,* 51–72.

Moghaddam, F. M., Stolkin, A. J., & Hutcheson, L. S. (1997). A generalized personal/group discrepancy: Testing the domain specificity of a perceived higher effect of events on my groups than on myself. *Personality and Social Psychology Bulletin, 23,* 743–750.

Moghaddam, F. M., & Stringer, P. (1986). "Trivial" and "important" criteria for social categorization in the minimal group paradigm. *Journal of Social Psychology, 126,* 345–354.

Moghaddam, F. M., & Studer, C. (1997a). Cross-cultural psychology: The frustrated gadfly's promises, potentialities, and failures. In D. Fox & I. Prilleltensky (Eds.), *Handbook of critical psychology* (pp. 185–201). Newbury Park, CA: Sage.

Moghaddam, F. M., & Studer, C. (1997b). The sky is falling, but not on me: A cautionary tale of illusions of control, in four acts. *Cross-Cultural Research, 31,* 155–167.

Moghaddam, F. M., & Taylor, D. M. (1987). The meaning of multiculturalism for visible minority immigrant women. *Canadian Journal of Behavioural Science, 19,* 121–136.

Moghaddam, F. M., Taylor, D. M., & Lalonde, R. N. (1987). Individual and collective integration strategies among Iranians in Canada. *International Journal of Psychology, 22,* 301–313.

Moghaddam, F. M., Taylor, D. M., & Lalonde, R. N. (1989). Integration strategies and attitudes toward the built environment: A study of Haitian and Indian immigrant women in Montreal. *Canadian Journal of Behavioural Science, 21,* 160–173.

Moghaddam, F. M., Taylor, D. M., Lambert, W. E., & Schmidt, A. E. (1995). Attributions and discrimination: A study of attributions to the self, the group, and external factors among whites, blacks, and Cubans in Miami. *Journal of Cross-Cultural Psychology, 26,* 209–220.

Moghaddam, F. M., Taylor, D. M., Pelletier, P. T., & Shepanek, M. (1994). The warped looking glass: How minorities perceive themselves, believe they are perceived, and are actually perceived by majority group members. *Canadian Ethnic Studies, 26,* 112–123.

Moghaddam, F. M., Taylor, D. M., & Wright, S. C. (1993). *Social psychology in cross-cultural perspective.* New York: W. H. Freeman.

Moghaddam, F. M., & Vuksanovic, V. (1990). Attitudes and behavior toward human rights across different contexts: The role of right–wing authoritarianism, political ideology, and religiosity. *International Journal of Psychology, 25,* 455–474.

Money, J. (1986). *Venuses penuses: Sexology, sexosophy, and exigency theory.* Buffalo, NY: Prometheus Books.

Money, J., & Ehrhardt, A. A. (1975). Rearing of sex-reassigned normal male infant after traumatic loss of penis. In J. Petras (Ed.), *Sex: Male/Gender: Masculine* (pp. 46–51). Port Washington, NY: Alfred.

Monteith, M. J., Devine, P. G., & Zuwerink, J. R. (1993). Self-directed versus other–directed affect as a consequence of prejudice–related discrepancies. *Journal of Personality and Social Psychology, 64,* 198–210.

Montgomery, P., & Davies, C. (1991). A woman's place in Northern Ireland. In P. Stringer & G. Robinson (Eds.), *Social attitudes in Northern Ireland* (pp. 74–95). Belfast: Blackstaff Press.

Moore, M. L. (1992). The family as portrayed on prime–time television, 1947-1990: Structure and characteristics. *Sex Roles, 26,* 41–61.

Morain, R., & Balz, D. (1996, January 28). Americans losing trust in each other and institutions. *Washington Post,* pp. A1, A6–A7.

Morell, V. (1993). Called "Trimates," three bold women shaped their field. *Science, 260,* 420–429.

Morgan, S. (Ed.) (1989). *Critical reviews of gender and anthropology: Implications for teaching and research.* Washington, DC: American Anthropological Association.

Morrin, R., & Berry, J. M. (1996, October 13). A nation that poor-mouths its good times. *Washington Post,* pp. A1, A38.

Morris, C. W. (1956). *Varieties of human values.* Chicago: University of Chicago Press.

Morris, M., & Peng, R. (1994). Culture and cause: American and Chinese sttributions for social and physical events. *Journal of Personality and Social Psychology, 67,* 949–971.

Morrison, D. M. (1989). Predicting contraceptive efficacy: A discriminant analysis of three groups of adolescent women. *Journal of Applied Social Psychology, 19,* 1431–1452.

Morrow, J. D. (1994). *Game theory for political scientists.* Princeton, NJ: Princeton University Press.

Moscovici, S. (1972). Society and theory in social psychology. In J. Israel & H. Tajfel (Eds.), *The context of social psychology* (pp. 17–68). London: Academic Press.

Moscovici, S. (1974). Social influence I: Conformity and social control. In C. Nemeth (Ed.), *Social psychology: Classic and contemporary integrations* (pp. 179–216). Chicago: Rand–McNally.

Moscovici, S. (1976a). *La psychoanalyse, son image et son public.* Paris: Presses Universitaires de France.

Moscovici, S. (1976b). *Social influence and social change.* New York: Academic Press.

Moscovici, S. (1980). Toward a theory of conversion behavior. In L. Berkowitz (Ed.), *Advances in experimental social psychology* (Vol. 13, pp. 209–239). New York: Academic Press.

Moscovici, S. (1984). The phenomenon of social representations. In R. Farr & S. Moscovici (Eds.), *Social representations* (pp. 3–69). Cambridge: Cambridge University Press.

Moscovici, S. (1985a). Innovation and minority influence. In S. Moscovici, G. Mugny, & E. Van Avermaet (Eds.), *Perspectives on minority influence* (pp. 9–51). Cambridge: Cambridge University Press.

Moscovici, S. (1985b). Social influence and conformity. In G. Lindzey & E. Aronson (Eds.), *The handbook of social psychology* (Vol. 2, pp. 347–412). New York: Random House.

Moscovici, S. (1988a). Notes towards a description of social representations. *European Journal of Social Psychology, 18,* 211–250.

Moscovici, S. (1988b). The origin of social representations: A response to Micheal. *New Ideas in Psychology, 8,* 383–388.

Moscovici, S., Lage, E., & Naffrechoux, M. (1969). Influence of a consistent minority on the responses of a majority in a color perception task. *Sociometry, 32,* 365–380.

Moscovici, S., Mucchi-Faina, A., & Maas, A. (Eds.) (1994). *Minority influence.* Chicago: Nelson-Hall.

Moscovici, S., & Zavalloni, M. (1969). The group as a polarizer of attitudes. *Journal of Personality and Social Psychology, 12,* 124–135.

Moskowitz, G. B. (1996). The mediational effects of attributions and information processing in minority social influence. *British Journal of Social Psychology, 35,* 47–66.

Moyer, K. E. (1976). *The psychobiology of aggression.* New York: Harper & Row.

Mugny, G. (1982). *The power of minorities.* New York: Academic Press.

Mugny, G. (1984). Compliance, conversion, and the Asch paradigm. *European Journal of Social Psychology, 14,* 353–368.

Mugny, G., & Carugati, F. (1989). *Social representations of intelligence.* Cambridge: Cambridge University Press.

Muhlhauser, P., & Harré, R. (1990). *Pronouns and people.* Oxford: Blackwell.

Mullen, B., & Goethals, G. R. (1990). Social projection, actual consensus and valence. *British Journal of Social Psychology, 29,* 279–282.

Mullen, B., & Riordan, C. A. (1988). Self-serving attributions for performance in naturalistic settings: A meta-analytical review. *Journal of Applied Social Psychology, 18,* 3–22.

Mummendey, A. (1984). *Social psychology of aggression: From individual behavior to social interaction.* New York: Springer-Verlag.

Munene, J. C. (1995). "Not-on-seat": An investigation of some correlates of organizational citizenship behavior in Nigeria. *Applied Psychology, 44,* 111–122.

Munroe, R. L., Munroe, R. H., & Whiting, B. B. (Eds.) (1981). *Handbook of cross-cultural human development.* Monterey, CA: Brooks/Cole.

Murdock, G. P. (1949). *Social structure.* New York: Macmillan.

Murphy, P. L., & Miller, C. T. (1997). Postdecisional dissonance and the commodified self-concept: A cross-cultural examination. *Personality and Social Psychology Bulletin, 23,* 50–62.

Murstein, B. (1986). *Paths to marriage.* Newbury Park, CA: Sage.

Mussen, P. H. (1977). *Roots of caring, sharing and helping: The development of prosocial behavior in children.* San Francisco: W. H. Freeman.

Myers, D. G., & Bishop, G. D. (1970). Discussion effects on racial attitudes. *Science, 169,* 778–789.

Myers, D. G., & Lamm, H. (1976). The group polarization phenomenon. *Psychological Bulletin, 83,* 602–627.

Nadler, A. (1986). Help seeking as a cultural phenomenon: Differences between city and Kibbutz dwellers. *Journal of Personality and Social Psychology, 51,* 976–982.

Nadler, A. (1991). Help-seeking behavior: Psychological costs and instrumental benefits. In M. S. Clark (Ed.) *Prosocial behavior* (pp. 290–311). Newbury Park, CA: Sage.

Nadler, A., Shapira, R., & Ben-Itzhak, S. (1982). Good looks may help: Effect of helper's physical attractiveness and sex of helper on males' and females' help seeking behavior. *Journal of Personality and Social Psychology, 42,* 90–99.

Nash, J. (1979). *We eat the mines and the mines eat us: Dependency and exploitation in Bolivian tin mines.* New York: Columbia University Press.

National Advisory and Co-ordinating Committee on Multicultural Education (1987). *Education in and for a multicultural society: Issues and strategies for policy making.* Canberra, Australia: Derek Kelly & Sons.

National Research Council (1991). *Women in science and engineering: Increasing their numbers in the 1990s, a statement on policy and strategy.* Washington, DC.

National Victims Center. (1992). *Rape in America: A report to the nation.* Arlington, VA.

Neimeyer, R. A., & Mitchell, K. A. (1988). Similarity and attraction: A longitudinal study. *Journal of Social and Personality Relationships, 5,* 131–148.

Nelson, R. J., Demas, G. E., Huang, P. L., Fishman, M. C., Dawson, V. L., Dawson, T. M., & Snyder, S. H. (1995). Behavioural abnormalities in male mice lacking neuronal nitric oxide synthase. *Nature, 378,* 383–386.

Nelson-Le Gall, S., & Glor-Scheib, S. (1985). Academic help seeking and peer relations in school. *Contemporary Educational Psychology, 11,* 187–193.

Nemeth, C. (1972). A critical analysis of research utilizing the Prisoner's Dilemma paradigm for the study of bargaining. In L. Berkowitz (Ed.), Advances in social psychology (Vol. 6, 203–234). New York: Academic Press.

Nemeth, C. (1986). Differential contributions of majority and minority influence. *Psychological Review, 93,* 23–32.

Nemeth, C. (1992). Minority dissent as a stimulant to group performance. In S. P. Worchel, W. Wood, & J. L. Simpson (Eds.), *Group process and productivity.* Newbury Park, CA: Sage.

Nemeth, C., & Staw, B. M. (1989). The tradeoffs of social control and innovation in groups and organizations. In L. Berkowitz (Ed.), *Advances in experimental social psychology* (Vol. 22, pp. 175–210). New York: Academic Press.

Newcomb, M. D., Rabow, J., & Hernandez, A. C. R. (1992). A cross-national study of nuclear attitudes, normative support, and activist behavior: Additive and interactive effects. *Journal of Applied Social Psychology, 22,* 780–800.

Newcomb, T. M. (1943). *Personality and social change.* New York: Dryden Press.

Newcomb, T. M. (1961). *The acquaintance process.* New York: Holt, Rinehart & Winston.

Newsweek. (1993, August 2). Wild in the streets, pp. 40–46.

Nicholson, N., Cole, S. G., & Rocklin, T. (1985). Conformity in the Asch situation: A comparison between contemporary British and US university students. *British Journal of Social Psychology, 24,* 59–63.

Nisbett, R. E. (1993). Violence and U.S. regional culture. *American Psychologist, 48,* 441–449.

Nisbett, R. E., & Cohen, D. (1996). *Culture of honor: Violence and the U.S. South.* Boulder, CO: Westview Press.

Nisbett, R. E., & Wilson, T. D. (1977). Telling more than we know: Verbal reports on mental processes. *Psychological Review, 84,* 231–259.

Nishiyama, K. (1971). Interpersonal persuasion in a vertical society—The case of Japan. *Speech Monographs, 38,* 148–154.

Noels, K. A., & Clement, R. (1996). Communicating across cultures: Social determinants and acculturative consequences. *Canadian Journal of Behavioural Science, 28,* 214–228.

Nord, W. R. (1969). Social exchange theory: An integrative approach to social conformity. *Psychological Bulletin, 71,* 171–208.

Northouse, P. G. (1997). *Leadership: Theory and practice.* Thousand Oaks, CA: Sage.

Nowicki, S., Jr., & Manheim, S. (1991). Interpersonal complementarity and time of interaction in female relationships. *Journal of Research in Personality, 25,* 322–333.

Nuckolls, C. W. (1992, March 13). *Ethno-dissonance.* Paper presented at the Department of Anthropology, University of Tulsa.

Nuckolls, C. W. (1993). The anthropology of explanation. *Anthropological Quarterly,* January, 1–21.

Oakes, P. J., Haslam, S. A., & Turner, J. C. (1994). *Stereotyping and social reality.* Oxford: Blackwell.

Obeyesekere, G. (1975). Sorcery, premeditated murder, and the canalization of aggression in Sri Lanka. *Ethnology, 14/1.*

Ogletree, S. M., Coffee, M. C., & May, S. A. (1992). Perceptions of male/female presidential candidates. *Psychology of Women Quarterly, 16,* 21–29.

Oliner, S. P., Oliner, P. M. (1988). *The altruistic personality: Rescuers of Jews in Nazi Europe.* New York: Free Press.

Oliver, M. B., & Hyde, J. S. (1993). Gender differences in sexuality: A meta-analysis. *Psychological Bulletin, 114,* 29–51.

Olsak, L., Perreault, S., & Moghaddam, F. M. (1997). Similarity and intergroup relations. *International Journal of Intercultural Relations, 21,* 113–123.

Olson, J. M., & Hafer, C. L. (1996). Affect, motivation, and cognition in relative deprivation research. In R. M. Sorrentino & E. T. Higgins (Eds.), *Handbook of motivation and cognition* (Vol. 3, pp. 85–117). New York: Guilford Press.

Olson, J. M., Herman, C. P., & Zanna, M. P. (Eds.) (1986). *Relative deprivation and social comparison: The Ontario symposium* (Vol. 4). Hillsdale, NJ: Lawrence Erlbaum.

Olson, J. M., & Zanna, M. P. (1993). Attitudes and attitude change. *Annual Review of Psychology, 44,* 117–154.

O'Reilly, K. (1995). *Nixon's piano: Presidents and racial politics from Washington to Clinton.* New York: Free Press.

Ornstein, N. J., Mann, T. E., & Malbin, M. J. (Eds.) (1994). *Vital statistics on Congress 1993–1994.* Washington, DC: Congressional Quarterly.

Ortner, S. B., & Whitehead, H., (Eds.) (1981). *Sexual meanings: The cultural construction of gender and sexuality.* Cambridge: Cambridge University Press.

Osbeck, L., Moghaddam, F. M., & Perreault, S. (1997). Similarity and attraction among majority and minority groups in a multicultural context. *International Journal of Intercultural Relations, 21,* 113–123.

Otten, C. A., Penner, L. A., & Waugh, G. (1988). That's what friends are for: The determinants of psychological helping. *Journal of Social and Clinical Psychology, 7,* 34–41.

Palamarek, D. L., & Rule, B. G. (1979). The effects of ambient temperature and insult on the motivation to retaliate or escape. *Motivation and Emotion, 3,* 83–92.

Pandey, J. (1980). Ingratiation as expected and manipulative behavior in Indian society. *Social Change, 10,* 15–17.

Pandey, J. (1986). Cross-cultural perspectives on ingratiation. In B. Maher & W. Maher (Eds.), *Progress in experimental personality research.* New York: Academic Press.

Pandey, J., & Rastogi, R. (1979). Machiavellianism and ingratiation. *Journal of Social Psychology, 108,* 221–225.

Pareto, V. (1935). *The mind and society: A treatise in general sociology* (Vols. 1–4). New York: Dover.

Park, B., & Rothbart, M. (1982). Perception of out-group homogeneity and levels of social categorization: Memory for the subordinate attributes of in-group and out-group members. *Journal of Personality and Social Psychology, 42,* 1051–1068.

Park, R. E., (1950). *Race and culture.* Glencoe, IL: Free Press.

Parrott, W. G. (1993). Beyond hedonism: Motives for inhibiting or maintaining good and bad moods. In D. M. Wegner & J. W. Pennebaker (Eds.), *Handbook of mental control* (pp. 278–305). Englewood Clifs, NJ: Prentice Hall.

Parrott, W. G. (1994). An association between emotional self-control and mood-incongruent recall. *Proceedings of the Eighth Conference of the International Society for Research on Emotions* (pp. 313–317). Storrs, CT: ISRE Publications.

Parrott, W. G., & Sabini, J. (1990). Mood and memory under natural conditions: Evidence for mood incongruent recall. *Journal of Personality and Social Psychology, 59,* 321–336.

Parrott, W. G., & Smith, R. H. (1993). Distinguishing the experiences of envy and jealousy. *Journal of Personality and Social Psychology, 64,* 906–920.

Paulus, P. B. (Ed.) (1989). *The psychology of group influence.* (2nd ed.). Hillsdale, NJ: Lawrence Erlbaum.

Payer, L. (1988). *Medicine and culture.* New York: Penguin.

Pelto, P. J. (1968). The differences between "tight" and "loose" societies. *Transaction,* April, 37–40.

Pennington, N., & Hastie, R. (1986). Evidence evaluation in complex decision making. *Journal of Personality and Social Psychology, 51,* 242–258.

Pennington, N., & Hastie, R. (1992). Explaining the evidence: Tests of the story model for juror decision making. *Journal of Personality and Social Psychology, 62,* 189–206.

Pepitone, A., & L'Armand, K. (1996). The justice and injustice of life events. *European Journal of Social Psychology, 26,* 581–597.

Pepitone, A., & L'Armand, K. (1997). Justice in cross-cultural context: A social-psychological perspective. *Cross-Cultural Research, 31,* 83–100.

Perloff, R. M. (1993). *The dynamics of persuasion.* Hillsdale, NJ: Lawrence Erlbaum.

Perrett, D. I., May, K. A., & Yoshikana, S. (1994). Facial shapes and judgements of female attractiveness. *Nature, 368,* 293–242.

Perrin, S., & Spencer, C. (1981). Independence or conformity in the Asch experiment as a reflection of cultural and situational factors. *British Journal of Social Psychology, 20,* 205–209.

Perry, D. G., White, A. J., & Perry, L. C. (1984). Does early sex typing result from children's attempts to match their behavior to sex role stereotypes? *Child Development, 55,* 2114–2121.

Peters, L. H., Hartke, D. D., & Pohlman, J. R. (1985). Fiedler's contingency theory of leadership: An application of the meta-analysis procedures of Schmidt and Hunter. *Psychological Bulletin, 97,* 274–285.

Peterson, C., & Barrett, L. C. (1987). Explanatory style and academic performance among university freshmen. *Journal of Personality and Social Psychology, 53,* 603–607.

Peterson, C., Seligman, M. E. P., & Vaillant, G. E. (1988). Pessimistic explanatory style is a risk factor for physical illness: A thirty-five-year longitudinal study. *Journal of Personality and Social Psychology, 55,* 23–27.

Pettigrew, T. F. (1979). The ultimate attribution error: Extending Allport's cognitive analysis of prejudice. *Personality and Social Psychology Bulletin, 5,* 461–476.

Pettigrew, T. F. (1986). The intergroup contact hypothesis reconsidered. In M. Hewstone & R. Brown (Eds.), *Contact and conflict in intergroup encounters* (pp. 169–195). Oxford: Blackwell.

Pettigrew, T. F. (1988). Integration and pluralism. In P. A. Katz & D. A. Taylor (Eds.), *Eliminating racism: Profiles in controversy* (pp. 19–30). New York: Plenum Press.

Pettigrew, T. F., Allport, G. W., & Barnett, E. O. (1958). Binocular resolution and perception of race in South Africa. *British Journal of Psychology, 49*, 265–278.

Petty, R. E. (1995). Attitude change. In A. Tesser (Ed.), *Advanced social psychology* (pp. 195–255). New York: McGraw-Hill.

Petty, R. E., & Cacioppo, J. T. (1986a). *Attitudes and persuasion: Classic and contemporary approaches.* Dubuque, IA: Brown.

Petty, R. E., & Cacioppo, J. T. (1986b). The elaboration likelihood model of persuasion. In L. Berkowitz (Ed.), *Advances in experimental social psychology* (Vol. 19, pp. 123–205). New York: Academic Press.

Petty, R. E., & Cacioppo, J. T. (1996). *Attitudes and persuasion: Classic and contemporary approaches.* Boulder, CO: Westview Press.

Petty, R. E., & Krosnick, J. A. (Eds.) (1995). *Attitude strength: Antecedents and consequences.* Hillsdale, NJ: Lawrence Erlbaum.

Pfau, M., & Kenski, H. C. (1990). *Attack politics: Strategy and defense.* New York: Praeger.

Pfeifer, J. E., & Ogloff, J. R. (1991). Ambiguity and guilt determinations: A modern racist perspective. *Journal of Applied Social Psychology, 21*, 1713–1725.

Pham, M. T. (1995). Cue representation and selection effects of arousal on persuasion. *Journal of Consumer Research, 22*, 373–387.

Phares, E. J. (1976). *Locus of control in personality.* Morristown, NJ: General Learning Press.

Philipchalk, R. P. (1995). *Invitation to social psychology.* Fort Worth, TX: Harcourt Brace.

Piaget, J., & Inhelder, B. (1969). *The psychology of the child.* New York: Basic Books.

Piliavin, J. A., Dovidio, J. F., Gaertner, S. L., & Clark, R. D. III. (1981). *Emergency intervention.* New York: Academic Press.

Pilkington, N. W., & Lydon, J. E. (1997). The relative effect of attitude similarity and attitude dissimilarity on interpersonal attraction: Investigating the moderating roles of prejudice and group membership. *Personality and Social Psychology Bulletin, 23*, 107–122.

Plato (1984). *The last days of Socrates: Euthyphro, The Apology, Crito, Phaedo* (H. Tredennick, Trans.). Baltimore, MD: Penguin.

Platz, S. G., & Hosch, H. M. (1988). Cross-racial/ethnic eyewitness identification: A field study. *Journal of Applied Social Psychology, 13*, 972–984.

Pliner, P., & Chaiken, S. (1990). Eating, social motives, and self-presentation in women and men. *Journal of Experimental Social Psychology, 26*, 240–254.

Pliner, P., Chaiken, S., & Flett, G. L. (1990). Gender differences in concern with body weight and physical appearance over the lifespan. *Personality and Social Psychology Bullletin, 16*, 263–273.

Poggie, J. J. (1995). Food resource periodicity and cooperation values: A cross-cultural consideration. *Cross-Cultural Research, 29*, 276–296.

Polivy, J., Herman, C. P., Hackett, R., & Kuleshnyk, I. (1986). The effects of self-attention and public attention on eating in restrained and unrestrained subjects. *Journal of Personality and Social Psychology, 50*, 1253–1260.

Pomazal, R. A., & Clore, G. L. (1973). Helping on the highway: The effects of dependency and sex. *Journal of Applied Social psychology, 3*, 150–164.

Ponterotto, J. G. (1988). Racial/ethnic minority research in the *Journal of Counselling Psychology*: A content analysis and methodological critique. *Journal of Counselling Psychology, 35*, 410–418.

Poole, M. E., De Lacy, R., & Randhawa, B. B. (Eds.) (1985). *Australia in transition: Culture and life possibilities.* Sydney, Australia: Harcourt Brace Jovanovich.

Popovich, P. M., Gehlauf, D. N., Jolton, J. A., Somers, J. M., & Godinho, R. M. (1992). Perceptions of sexual harassment as a function of sex of rater and incident form and consequence. *Sex Roles, 27*, 609–625.

Potegal, M., & Knutson, J. F. (Eds.) (1994). *The dynamics of aggression: Biological and social processes in dyads and groups.* Hillsdale, NJ: Lawrence Erlbaum.

Pratkanis, A. R., & Aronson, E. (1991). *The age of propaganda: The everyday use and abuse of persuasion.* New York: W. H. Freeman.

Pratkanis, A. R., Breckler, S. J., & Greenwald, A. G. (Eds.) (1989). *Attitude structure and function.* Hillsdale, NJ: Lawrence Erlbaum.

Pratkanis, A. R., Greenwald, A. G., Leippe, M. R., & Baumgardner, M. H. (1988). In search of reliable persuasion effects: III. The sleeper effect is dead, long live the sleeper effect. *Journal of Personality and Social Psychology, 54*, 203–218.

Pratto, F., Stallworth, L. M., Sidanius, J., & Siers, B. (1997). The gender gap in occupational role attainment: A social dominance approach. *Journal of Personality and Social Psychology, 72*, 37–53.

Pressler, M. W. (1997, March 23). Clothes sizes to fit a wider clientele. *Washington Post*, pp. A1, A18.

Priester, J. R., & Petty, R. E. (1995). Source attributions and persuasion: Perceived honesty as a determinant of message scrutiny. *Personality and Social Psychology Bulletin, 21*, 637–654.

Prilleltensky, I. (1989). Psychology and the status quo. *American Psychologist, 44*, 795–802.

Prince, M. (1905/1968). *The dissociation of personality.* New York: Johnson.

Proust, M. (1970). *Remembrance of things past* (A. Mayor, Trans.). New York: Vintage Books.

Pruitt, D. G., & Rubin, J. Z. (1986). *Social conflict: Escalation, stalemate, and settlement.* New York: Random House.

Punch, M. (1996). *Dirty business: Exploring corporate misconduct.* Thousand Oaks, CA: Sage.

Putnam, R. D. (1995). Bowling alone: America's declining social capital. *Journal of Democracy, 6*, 65–78.

Quattrone, G. A. (1985). On the congruity between internal states and action. *Psychological Bulletin, 98*, 3–40.

Quattrone, G. A., & Jones, E. E. (1980). The perception of variability within ingroups and outgroups: Implications for the law of small numbers. *Journal of Personality and Social Psychology, 38*, 141–152.

Radcliffe, S. G., Masera, N., Pan, H., & McKie, M. (1994). Head circumference and IQ of children with sex chromosome abnormalities. *Developmental Medicine and Child Neurology, 36,* 533–544.

Ransford, E. H. (1972). Blue–collar anger: Reactions to student and black protest. *American Sociological Review, 37,* 333–346.

Raushenbush, C. (1937). *Fordism: Ford and the workers, Ford and the community.* New York: League of Industrial Democracy.

Raviv, A., Raviv, A., & Yunovitz, R. (1989). Radio psychology and psychotherapy: A comparison of client attitudes and expectations. *Professional Psychology: Research and Practice, 20,* 1–7.

Rector, N. A., & Bagby, R. M. (1995). Criminal sentence recommendations in a simulated rape trial: Examining juror prejudice in Canada. *Behavioral Sciences and the Law, 13,* 113–121.

Reicher, S. (1984a). The St. Paul's riot: An explanation of the limits of crowd action in terms of a social identity model. *European Journal of Social Psychology, 14,* 1–21.

Reicher, S. (1984b). Social influence in the crowd: Attitudinal and behavioural effects of deindividuation in conditions of high and low group salience. *British Journal of Social Psychology, 23,* 341–350.

Reinard, J. C. (1988). The empirical study of the persuasive effects of evidence: The status after fifty years of research. *Human Communication Research, 15,* 3–59.

Reis, H. T., Nezlek, J., & Wheeler, L. (1980). Physical attractiveness in social interaction. *Journal of Personality and Social Psychology, 38,* 604–617.

Rest, R., Nierenberg, R., Weiner, B., & Heckhausen, H. (1973). Further evidence concerning the effects of perceptions of effort and ability on achievement evaluation. *Journal of Personality and Social Psychology, 28,* 187–191.

Rhodes, N., & Wood, W. (1992). Self-esteem and intelligence affect influenceability: The mediating role of message reception. *Psychological Bulletin, 111,* 156–171.

Rhodewalt, F., & Agustsdottir, S. (1986). Effects of self-presentation on the phenomenal self. *Journal of Personality and Social Psychology, 50,* 47–53.

Rim, Y. (1963). Risk–taking and need for achievement. *Acta Psychologica, 21,* 108–115.

Robbins, M. C., DeWalt, E. R., & Pelto, P. J. (1972). Climate and behavior: A biocultural study. *Journal of Cross-Cultural Psychology,* 331–344.

Robertson, M. F. (1988). Differential use by male and female students of the counseling services design and counseling models. *International Journal for the Advancement of Counseling, 11,* 231–240.

Robinson, D., & Beauchamp, T. (1978). Personal identity: Reid's answer to Hume. *The Monist, 61,* 326–339.

Robinson, D. N. (1989). *Aristotle's psychology.* New York: Columbia University Press.

Robinson, D. N. (1995). *An intellectual history of psychology* (3rd ed.). Madison: University of Wisconsin Press.

Robinson, J. P., Shaver, P. R., & Wrightsman, L. S. (Eds.) (1991). *Measures of personality and social psychological attitudes.* New York: Academic Press.

Rodgers, J. L., Billy, J. O. B., & Udry, J. R. (1984). A model of friendship similarity in mildly deviant behaviors. *Journal of Applied Social Psychology, 14,* 413–425.

Rodriguez, A. (1980). Causal ascription and evaluation of achievement related outcomes: A cross-cultural comparison. *International Journal of Intercultural Relations, 4,* 379–389.

Rogers, C. G. (1980). The development of sex differences in evaluation of others' successes and failures. *British Journal of Educational Psychology, 50,* 243–252.

Rogers, C. R. (1971). *Client-centered therapy: Its current practice, implications, and theory* (2nd ed.). Boston: Houghton Mifflin.

Rogers, R. S., Stenne, P., Gleeson, K., & Rogers, W. S. (1995). *Social psychology: A critical agenda.* Oxford: Polity Press.

Rogers, T. B. (1981). A model of the self as an aspect of the human information processing system. In N. Cantor & J. Kihlstrom (Eds.), *Personality, cognition, and social interaction* (pp. 193–214). Hillsdale, NJ: Lawrence Erlbaum.

Rogers, T. B., Kuiper, N. A., & Kirker, W. S. (1977). Self-reference and the encoding of personal information. *Journal of Personality and Social Psychology, 35,* 677–688.

Rohrer, J. H., Baron, S. H., Hoffman, E. L., & Swander, D. V. (1954). The stability of autokinetic judgments. *Journal of Abnormal and Social Psychology, 49,* 595–597.

Rokeach, M. (1973). *The nature of human values.* New York: Free Press.

Roland, A. (1988). *In search of the self in India and Japan: Toward a cross-cultural psychology.* Princeton, NJ: Princeton University Press.

Romero, G. J., & Garza, R. T. (1986). Attributions for the occupational success/failure of ethnic minority and nonminority women. *Sex Roles, 14,* 445–452.

Rose, H. M. (1971). The development of the urban subsystem. In L. S. Bourne (Ed.), *Internal strucure of the city* (pp. 316–320). New York: Oxford University Press.

Rosen, L. (1989). Islamic "case law" and the logic of consequence. In J. Starr & J. F. Collier (Eds.), *History and power in the study of law: New directions in legal anthropology* (pp. 302–319). Ithaca, NY: Cornell University Press.

Rosenbaum, M. E. (1986a). The repulsion hypothesis: On the nondevelopment of relationships. *Journal of Personality and Social Psychology, 6,* 1156–1166.

Rosenbaum, M. E. (1986b). Comment on a proposed two–stage theory of relationship formation: First, repulsion; then, attraction. *Journal of Personality and Social Psychology, 6,* 1171–1172.

Rosenbaum, M. E., Moore, D. L., Cotton, J. L., Cook, M. S., Hieser, R. A., Shover, M. N., & Gray, M. J. (1980). Group productivity and process: Pure and mixed reward structures and task interdependence. *Journal of Personality and Social Psychology, 39,* 626–42.

Rosenberg, S. W., & Wolfsfeld, G. (1977). International conflict and the problem of attribution. *Journal of Conflict Resolution, 21,* 75–103.

Rosenberger, N. R. (Ed.) (1992). *Japanese sense of self.* Cambridge: Cambridge University Press.

Rosenthal, R., & Rosnow, R. L. (1984). *Meta-analytic procedures for social research.* Beverly Hills, CA: Sage.

Roskies, E., & Carrier, S. (1992). *Marriage and children for professional women: Asset or liability?* Paper presented at the APA/NIOSH conference, "Stress in the '90's: A changing workforce in a changing workplace," Washington, DC.

Roslow, P., & Nicholls, J. A. F. (1996). Targeting the Hispanic market: Comparative persuasion of TV commercials in Spanish and English. *Journal of Advertising Research, 36,* 67–77.

Ross, E. A. (1908). *Social psychology.* New York: Macmillan.

Ross, L. D. (1977). The intuitive psychologist and his shortcomings: Distortions in the attribution process. In L. Berkowitz (Ed.), *Advances in Experimental Social Psychology* (Vol. 10). New York: Academic Press.

Ross, L. D., Amabile, T. M., & Steinmetz, J. L. (1977). Social roles, social control, and biases in social–perception processes. *Journal of Personality and Social Psychology, 35,* 485–494.

Ross, L., Greene, D., & House, P. (1977). The "false consensus effect": An egocentric bias in social perception and attribution processes. *Journal of Experimental Social Psychology, 13,* 279–301.

Ross, M., & Fletcher, G. J. O. (1985). Attribution and social perception. In G. Lindzey & E. Aronson (Eds.), *Handbook of social psychology* (3rd ed., Vol. 2). New York: Random House.

Ross, M., & Sicoly, F. (1977). Egocentric biases in availability and attribution. *Journal of Personality and Social Psychology, 37,* 322–336.

Ross, S. I., & Jackson, J. M. (1991). Teachers' expectations for black males' and females' academic achievement. *Personality and Social Psychology Bulletin, 17,* 78–82.

Rosselli, F., Skelly, J. J., & Mackie, D. M. (1995). Processing rational and emotional messages: The cognitive and affective mediation of persuasion. *Journal of Experimental Social Psychology, 31,* 163–190.

Rossiter, M. W. (1995). *Women scientists in America: Before affirmative action, 1940–1972.* Baltimore, MD: Johns Hopkins University Press.

Rothbart, M., Dawes, R., & Park, B. (1984). Stereotyping and sampling biases in intergroup perception. In J. R. Eiser (Ed.), *Attitudinal judgment* (pp. 109–134). New York: Springer-Verlag.

Rotter, J. B. (1966). Generalized expectancies for internal versus external control of reinforcement. *Psychological Monographs, 80* (1, Whole No. 609).

Rotter, J. B. (1971). External control and internal control. *Psychology Today, 5,* pp. 37–42, 58.

Rotter, J. B. (1973). Internal–external locus of control scale. In J. P. Robinson & R. P. Shaver (Eds.), *Measures of social psychological attitudes.* Ann Arbor, MI: Institute for Social Research.

Rotton, J. (1986). Determinism redux: Climate and cultural correlates of violence. *Environment and Behavior, 18,* 346–368.

Rotton, J., & Frey, J. (1985). Air pollution, weather, and violent crimes: Concomitant time–series analysis of archival data. *Journal of Personality and Social Psychology, 49,* 1207–1220.

Rousseau, J. J. (1947). *The social contract.* (Anonymous translation, 1791). New York: Hafner.

Rozee, P. D. (1993). Forbidden or forgiven? Rape in cross-cultural perspective. *Psychology of Women Quarterly, 17,* 499–514.

Rubin, J. Z., Pruitt, D. G., & Kim, S. H. (1994). *Social conflict: Escalation, stalemate, and settlement.* New York: McGraw-Hill.

Ruggiero, K. M., & Taylor, D. M. (1994). The personal/group discrimination discrepancy: Women talk about their experiences. *Journal of Applied Social Psychology, 24,* 1806–1826.

Ruggiero, K. M., & Taylor, D. M. (1995). Coping with discrimination: How disadvantaged group members perceive the discrimination that confronts them. *Journal of Personality and Social Psychology, 68,* 826–838.

Ruggiero, K. M., & Taylor, D. M. (1997). Why minority group members perceive or do not perceive the discrimination that confronts them: The role of self-esteem and perceived control. *Journal of Personality and Social Psychology, 72,* 373–389.

Runciman, W. G. (1966). *Relative deprivation and social justice: A study of attitudes to social inequality in twentieth-century England.* Berkeley: University of California Press.

Ruscher, J. B., & Hammer, E. Y. (1996). Choosing to sever or maintain association induced impression formation. *Journal of Personality and Social Psychology, 70,* 701–712.

Rushton, J. P. (1988). Epigenetic rules in moral development: Distal–proximal approaches to altruism and aggression. *Aggressive Behavior, 14,* 35–50.

Rushton, J. P. (1989). Genetic similarity, human altruism, and group selection. *Behavioral and Brain Sciences, 12,* 503–559.

Rushton, J. P. (1991). Is altruism innate? *Psychological Inquiry, 2,* 141–143.

Rushton, J. P., & Campbell, A. C. (1977). Modeling, vicarious reinforcement and extraversion on blood donating in adults: Immediate and long–term effects. *European Journal of Social Psychology, 7,* 297–306.

Russell, K., Wilson, M., & Hall, R. (1992). *The color complex: The politics of skin color among African Americans.* New York: Harcourt Brace Jovanovich.

Rutter, P. (1996). *Sex, power, & boundaries: Understanding & preventing sexual harassment.* New York: Bantam.

Sabo, D., & Jansen, S. C. (1992). Images of men in sport media: The social reproduction of gender order. In S. Craig (Ed.), *Men, masculinity, and the media* (pp. 169–186). Thousand Oaks, CA: Sage.

Sadock, B. J. (1975). Group psychotherapy. In A. M. Freedman, H. I. Kaplan, & B. J. Sadock (Eds.), *Comprehensive textbook of psychiatry* (Vol. 2, pp. 1850–1876). Baltimore, MD: Williams & Wilkins.

Saenz, D. S., & Lord, C. G., (1989). Reversing roles: A cognitive strategy for undoing memory deficits associated with token status. *Journal of Personality and Social Psychology, 56,* 698–708.

Salili, F., Maehr, M. J., & Gillmore, G. (1976). Achievement and morality: A cross–cultural analysis of causal attribution and evaluation. *Journal of Personality and Social Psychology, 33,* 327–337.

Salisbury, H. E. (1992). *The new emperors: China in the era of Mao and Deng.* New York: Avon.

Sampson, E. E. (1975), On justice as equality. *Journal of Social Issues, 31,* 45–63.

Sampson, E. E. (1977). Psychology and the American ideal. *Journal of Personality and Social Psychology, 35,* 767–782.

Sampson, E. E. (1989). The challenge of social change for psychology: Globalization and psychology's theory of the person. *American Psychologist, 44,* 914–921.

Sampson, E. E. (1993). Identity politics: Challenges to psychology's understanding. *American Psychologist, 48,* 1219–1230.

Sanchez, E. (1996). The Latin American experience in community social psychology. In S. C. Carr &

J. F. Schumaker (Eds.), *Psychology and the developing world* (pp. 119–129). Westport, CT: Praeger.

Sanders, W. B. (1994). *Gangbangs and drive-bys: Grounded culture and juvenile gang violence.* Hawthorne, NY: Aldine de Gruyter.

Sandole, D. J. D., & van der Merwe, H. (Eds.) (1993) *Conflict resolution theory and practice: Integration and application.* Manchester, England: Manchester University Press.

Sansone, C. (1986). A question of competence: The effects of competence and task feedback on intrinsic interest. *Journal of Personality and Social Psychology, 51,* 918–931.

Saraswathi, T. S., & Dutta, R. (1990). Poverty and human development: Socialization of girls among the urban and rural poor. In G. Misra (Ed.), *Applied social psychology in India* (pp. 141–169). New Delhi, India: Sage.

Sato, K. (1987). Distribution of the cost of maintaining common resources. *Journal of Experimental Social Psychology, 23,* 19–31.

Sawyer, A. G. (1988). Can there be effective advertising without explicit conclusions? Decide for yourself. In S. Hecker & D. W. Stewart (Eds.), *Nonverbal communication in advertising* (pp. 159–184). Lexington, MA: D. C. Heath.

Scarr, S. (1988). Race and gender as psychological variables. *American Psychologist, 43,* 56–59.

Schachter, S. (1964). The interaction of cognitive and physiological determinants of emotional state. In L. Berkowitz (Ed.), *Advances in experimental social psychology* (Vol. 1, pp. 48–81). New York: Academic Press.

Schachter, S. (1971). *Emotion, obesity, and crime.* New York: Academic Press.

Schachter, S., & Singer, J. E. (1962). Cognitive, social, and physiological determinants of emotional state. *Psychological Review, 69,* 379–399.

Schafer, M., & Crichlow, S. (1996). Antecedents of groupthink. *Journal of Conflict Resolution, 40,* 415–435.

Schaller, M., & Cialdini, R. (1988). The economics of empathic helping: Support for a mood management motive. *Journal of Experimental Social Psychology, 24,* 163–181.

Schenck-Hamlin, W. J., Wiseman, R. L., & Georgacarakos, G. N. (1982). A model of properties of compliance-gaining strategies. *Communication Quarterly, 30,* 92–100.

Scheper-Hughes, N. (1990). Mother love and child death in northeast Brazil. In J. W. Stigler, R. A. Shweder, & G. Herdt (Eds.), *Cultural psychology: Essays on comparative human development* (pp. 542–565). Cambridge: Cambridge University Press.

Schlegel, A., & Barry, H. III (1986). The cultural consequences of female contribution to subsistence. *American Anthropologist,* 142–150.

Schlenker, B. (Ed.) (1985). *The self and social life.* New York: McGraw-Hill.

Schlenker, B. R., & Trudeau, J. V. (1990). The impact of self-presentations on private self-beliefs: Effects of prior self-beliefs and misattribution. *Journal of Personality and Social Psychology, 58,* 22–32.

Schmidt, F. L. (1992). What do data really mean? Research findings, meta-analysis, and cumulative knowledge in psychology. *American Psychologist, 47,* 1173–1181.

Schmitt, B., Gilovich, T., Goore, H., & Joseph, L. (1986). Mere presence and social facilitation: One more time. *Journal of Experimental Social Psychology, 22,* 242–248.

Schmitt, D. P., & Buss, D. M. (1996). Strategic self-promotion and competitor derogation: Sex and context effects on the perceived effectiveness of mate attraction tactics. *Journal of Personality and Social Psychology, 70,* 1185–1204.

Schoeneman, T. J., & Rubanowitz, D. E. (1985). Attributions in the advice columns: Actors and observers, causes and reasons. *Personality and Social Psychology Bulletin, 11,* 315–325.

Schroder, J., De La Chapelle, A., Hakola, P., & Virkkunen, M. (1981). The frequency of XYY and XXY men among criminal offenders. *Acta Psychiatrica Scandinavica, 63,* 272–276.

Schroeder, D. A., Dovidio, J. F., Sibicky, M. E., Mathews, L. L., & Allen, J. L. (1988). Empathy and helping behavior: Egoism or altruism. *Journal of Experimental Social Psychology, 24,* 333–353.

Schroeder, D. A., Penner, L. A., Dovidio, J. F., & Piliavin, J. F. (1995). *The social psychology of helping and altruism: Problems and puzzles.* New York: McGraw-Hill.

Schuman, H., & Scott, J. (1989). Generations and collective memories. *American Sociological Review, 54,* 359–381.

Schuman, H., Steeh, C., & Bobo, L. (1985). *Racial attitudes in America: Trends and interpretation.* Cambridge, MA: Harvard University Press.

Schumann, D. W., Petty, R. E., & Clemons, D. S. (1990). Predicting the effectiveness of different strategies for advertising variation: A test of the repetition-variation hypothesis. *Journal of Consumer Research, 17,* 192–202.

Schuster, B., Forsterling, F., & Weiner, B. (1989). Perceiving the causes of success and failure: A cross-cultural examination of attributional concepts. *Journal of Cross-Cultural Psychology, 20,* 191–213.

Schwartz, D. C. (1968). On the ecology of political violence: "The long hot summer" as a hypothesis. *American Behavioral Scientist, 11,* 24–28.

Schwartz, M. D., & DeKeseredy, W. S. (1997). *Sexual assault on the college campus: The role of male peer support.* Thousand Oaks, CA: Sage.

Schwartz, S. H. (1992). Universals in the content and structure of values: Theoretical advances and empirical tests in 20 countries. In M. Zanna (Ed.), *Advances in experimental social psychology.* New York: Academic Press.

Searcy, E., & Eisenberg, N. (1992). Defensiveness in response to aid from a sibling. *Journal of Personality and Social Psychology, 62,* 422–433.

Sears, D. O. (1986). College sophomores in the laboratory: Influences of a narrow data base on social psychology's view of human nature. *Journal of Personality and Social Psychology, 51,* 515–530.

Sears, D. O. (1988). Symbolic racism. In P. A. Katz & D. A. Taylor (Eds.), *Eliminating racism* (pp. 53–84). New York: Plenum Press.

Sedekides, C., & Strube, M. J. (1995). The multiply motivated self. *Personality and Social Psychology Bulletin, 21,* 1330–1335.

Seligman, M. E. P. (1975). *Helplessness: On depression, development and death.* San Francisco: W. H. Freeman.

Seligman, M. E. P. (1991). *Learned optimism.* New York: Knopf.

Seligman, M. E. P., & Maier, S. F. (1967). Failure to escape traumatic shock. *Journal of Experimental Psychology, 74,* 1–9.

Shain, B. A. (1994). *The myth of American individualism: The Protestant origins of American political thought.* Princeton, NJ: Princeton University Press.

Shanab, M. E., & Yahya, K. A. (1977). A behavioral study of obedience in children. *Journal of Personality and Social Psychology, 35,* 530–536.

Shaughnessy, J. J., & Zechmeister, E. B. (1997). *Research methods in psychology* (4th ed.). New York: McGraw–Hill.

Shaw, M. E., & Costanzo, P. R. (1982). *Theories of social psychology* (2nd ed.). New York: McGraw–Hill.

Sheldon, R. G., Tracy, S. K., & Brown, W. B. (1997). *Youth gangs in American society.* New York: Wadsworth.

Shelton, B. A., & John, D. (1993). Ethnicity, race, and difference: A comparison of white, black, and Hispanic men's household labor time. In J. C. Hood (Ed.), *Men, work, and family* (pp. 131–150). Newbury Park, CA: Sage.

Sheppard, B. H., Hartwick, J., & Warshaw, P. R. (1988). The theory of reasoned action: A meta–analysis of past research with recommendations for modifications and future research. *Journal of Consumer Research, 15,* 325–343.

Sherif, M. (1935). A study of some social factors in perception. *Archives of Psychology, 27,* No. 187.

Sherif, M. (1936). *The psychology of social norms.* New York: Harper.

Sherif, M. (1951). A preliminary experimental study of inter-group relations. In J. H. Rohrer & M. Sherif (Eds.), *Social psychology at the cross-roads* (pp. 388–424). New York: Harper.

Sherif, M. (1966). *Group conflict and co-operation: Their social psychology.* London: Routledge and Kegan Paul.

Sherif, M., Harvey, O. J., White, B. J., Hood, W. R., & Sherif, C. W. (1961). *Intergroup conflict and cooperation: The Robber's Cave experiment.* Norman: University of Oklahoma Book Exchange.

Sherif, M., & Sherif, C. W. (1953). *Groups in harmony and tension.* New York: Harper.

Sherman, S. P. (1921). Introductory note. In *Essays and Poems of Emerson.* New York: Harcourt Brace.

Shikanai, K. (1978). Effects of self-esteem on attribution of success and failure. *Japanese Journal of Experimental Social Psychology, 18,* 47–55.

Shikanai, K. (1984). Effects of self-esteem and one's own performance on attribution of others' success and failure. *Japanese Journal of Experimental Social Psychology, 24,* 37–46.

Shinagawa, L. H. (1997). *Atlas of American diversity.* Thousand Oaks, CA: Sage.

Shweder, R. A., & Bourne, E. J. (1984). Does the concept of the person vary cross-culturally? In R. A. Shweder & R. A. LeVine (Eds.), *Culture theory: Essays on mind, self, and emotion* (pp. 158–199). Cambridge: Cambridge University Press.

Si, G., Rethorst, S., & Willimczik, K. (1995). Causal atribution perception in sports achievement: A cross–cultural study on attributional concepts in Germany and China. *Journal of Cross-Cultural Psychology, 26,* 537–553.

Sidanius, J. (1993). The psychology of group conflict and the dynamics of oppression: A social dominance perspective. In W. McGuire & S. Iyengar (Eds.), *Current approaches to political psychology* (pp. 183–219). Durham, NC: Duke University Press.

Sidanius, J., Pratto, F., & Bobo, L. (1994). Social dominance orientation and the political psychology of gender: A case of invariance? *Journal of Personality and Social Psychology, 67,* 998–1011.

Sidanius, J., Pratto, F., & Brief, D. (1995). Group dominance and the political psychology of gender: A cross–cultural comparison. *Political Psychology, 16,* 381–396.

Sidanius, J., Pratto, F., & Rabinowitz, J. L. (1994). Gender, ethnic status, and ideological symmetry: A social dominance interpretation. *Journal of Cross-Cultural Psychology, 25,* 194–216.

Sigall, H., & Michela, J. (1976). I'll bet you say that to all the girls: Physical attractiveness and reaction to praise. *Journal of Personality, 44,* 611–626.

Signorielli, N. (1989). Television and conceptions about sex roles: Maintaining conventionality and the status quo. *Sex Roles, 21,* 341–360.

Silverberg, J. (Ed.) (1968). *Social mobility in the caste system in India.* The Hague: Mouton.

Simpson, J., A., Campbell, B., & Berscheid, E. (1986). The association between romantic love and marriage: Kephart (1967) twice revisited. *Personality and Social Psychology Bulletin, 12,* 363–372.

Sinclair, R. C., Mark, M. M., & Clore, G. L. (1994). Mood–related persuasion depends on (mis) attributions. *Social Cognition, 12,* 309–326.

Singelis, T. M. (1994). The measurement of independent and interdependent self-construals. *Personality and Social Psychology Bulletin, 20,* 580–591.

Singelis, T. M., & Brown, W. J. (1995). Culture, self, and collective communication: Linking culture to individual behavior. *Human Communication Research, 21,* 354–389.

Singh, A. K. (1988). Intergroup relations and social tensions. In J. Pandey (Ed.), *Psychology in India: The state-of-the-art* (Vol. 2, pp. 159–223). New Delhi: Sage.

Singh, D. (1993). Adaptive significance of female physical attractiveness: Role of waist–to–hip ratio. *Journal of Personality and Social Psychology, 65,* 293–307.

Singh, R., Gupta, M., & Dalal, A. K. (1979). Cultural differences in attribution of performance: An integration of theoretical analysis. *Journal of Personality and Social Psychology, 37,* 1342–1351.

Singh, R., & Tan, L. S. (1992). Attitudes and attraction: A test of the similarity–repulsion hypothesis. *British Journal of Social Psychology, 31,* 227–238.

Singh, S. (1977). Achievement motivation and economic growth. *Indian Psychological Review, 14,* 52–56.

Sinha, J. B. P. (1980). *Nurturant task leader.* New Delhi: Concept

Sistrunk, F., & McDavid, J. W. (1971). Sex variable in conforming behavior. *Journal of Personality and Social Psychology, 17,* 200–207.

Sivacek, J., & Crano, W. D. (1982). Vested interest as a moderator of attitude-behavior consistency. *Journal of Personality and Social Psychology, 43,* 210–221.

Slack, A. (1988). Female circumcision: A critical appraisal. *Human Rights Quarterly, 10,* 439–479.

Slamecka, N. J., & Graf, P. (1978). The generation effect: Delineation of a phenomenon. *Journal of Experimental Psychology: Human Language and Memory, 4,* 592–604.

Sloan, T. (Ed.) (1990). [Special issue] *Journal of Social Issues.*

Smetana, J. G., Killen, M., & Turiel, E. (1991). Children's reasoning about interpersonal and moral conflicts. *Child Development, 62,* 629–644.

Smith, K. D., Keating, J. P., & Stotland, E. (1989). Altruism revisited: The effect of denying feedback on a victim's status to empathic witnesses. *Journal of Personality and Social Psychology, 57,* 641–650.

Smith, M. J. (1982). *Persuasion and human action: A review and critique of social influence theories.* Belmont, CA: Wadsworth.

Smith, P. A., & Midlarsky, E. (1985). Empirically derived conceptions of femaleness and maleness: A current view. *Sex Roles, 12,* 313–328.

Smith, P. B., & Peterson, M. F. (1988). *Leadership, organizations, and culture.* London: Sage.

Smith, P. B., Peterson, M. F., Bond, M., & Misumi, J. (1990). Leadership style and leader behaviour in individualistic and collectivist cultures. In S. Iwawaki, Y. Kashima, & K. Leung (Eds.), *Innovations in cross-cultural psychology* (pp. 76–85). Amsterdam: Swets & Zeitlinger.

Smith, S., & Whitehead, G. (1984). Attributions for promotion and demotion in the United States and India. *Journal of Social Psychology, 124,* 27–34.

Smith, S. M., & Shaffer, D. R. (1995). Speed of speech and persuasion: Evidence for multiple effects. *Personality and Social Psychology Bulletin, 21,* 1051–1060.

Snyder, M. (1974). The self-monitoring of expressive behavior. *Journal of Personality and Social Psychology, 30,* 526–537.

Snyder, M. (1987). *Public appearances/Private realities.* New York: W. H. Freeman.

Snyder, M., & DeBono, K. G. (1985). Appeals to images and claims about quality: Understanding the psychology of advertising. *Journal of Personality and Social Psychology, 49,* 586–597.

Snyder, M., & Gangestad, S. (1986). On the nature of self-monitoring: Matters of assessment, matters of validity. *Journal of Personality and Social Psychology, 51,* 125–139.

Snyder, M., & Jones, E. E. (1974). Attitude attribution when behavior is constrained. *Journal of Experimental Social Psychology, 10,* 585–600.

Snyder, M., & Monson, T. C. (1975). Persons, situations, and the control of social behavior. *Journal of Personality and Social Psychology, 32,* 637–644.

Snyder, M., & Simpson, J. A. (1984). Self-monitoring and dating relationships. *Journal of Personality and Social Psychology, 47,* 1281–1291.

Solomon, L. Z., Solomon, H., & Stone, R. (1978). Helping as a function of number of bystanders and ambiguity of emergency. *Personality and Social Psychology Bulletin, 4,* 318–321.

Sonnert, G., & Holton, G. (1995). *Gender differences in science careers: The project access study.* New Brunswick, NJ: Rutgers University Press.

Sorenson, S. B., & Siegel, J. M. (1992). Gender, ethnicity, and sexual assault: Findings from a Los Angeles study. *Journal of Social Issues, 48,* 93–104.

Sorrentino, R. M., & Roney, C. J. R. (1986). Uncertainty orientation, achievement–related motivation, and task–diagnosticity as determinants of task performance. *Social Cognition, 4,* 420–436.

Spacaman, S., & Oskamp, S. (Ed.) (1992). *Helping and being helped: Naturalistic Studies.* Newbury Park, CA: Sage.

Sparks, P., & Durkin, K. (1987). Moral reasoning and political orientation: The context sensitivity of individual rights and democratic principles. *Journal of Personality and Social Psychology, 52,* 931–936.

Spears, R., Oakes, P. J., Ellemers, N., & Haslam, S. A. (Eds.). (1996). *The social psychology of stereotyping and group life.* Oxford: Blackwell.

Spence, J. T., Helmreich, R., & Stapp, J. (1974). The Personal Attributes Questionnaire: A measure of sex role stereotypes and masculinity–femininity. *JSAS Catalog of Selected Documents in Psychology, 4,* 43–44.

Spencer, H. (1893/1978). *The principles of ethics.* Indianapolis: Liberty Classics.

Spencer, S., Steele, C. M., & Quinn, D. (1997). *Under suspicion of inability: Stereotype threat and women's math performance.* Unpublished manuscript, Psychology Department, Stanford University.

Sperber, D. (1985). Anthropology and psychology: Toward an epidemiology of representations. *Man, 20,* 73–89.

Sprecher, S., & Duck, S. (1994). Sweet talk: The importance of perceived communication for romantic and friendship attraction experienced during a get-acquainted date. *Personality and Social Psychology Bulletin, 20,* 391–400.

Stagner, R. (1936). Fascist attitudes: An exploratory study. *Journal of Social Psychology, 6,* 309–319.

Stalans, L. (1993). Citizens' crime stereotypes, biased recall, and punishment preferences in abstract cases: The educative role of interpersonal sources. *Law and Human Behavior, 17,* 451–470.

Stangor, C., Sullivan, L. A., & Ford, T. E. (1991). Affective and cognitive determinants of prejudice. *Social Cognition, 9,* 359–380.

Starr, B. J., Sloan, L. R., & Kudrick, T. R. (1997). Just desserts: African American judgments of justice in stories of varying cultural relevance. *Cross-Cultural Research, 1,* 137–154.

Starr, J., & Collier, J. F. (Eds.) (1989). *History and power in the study of law: New directions in legal anthropology.* Ithaca, NY: Cornell University Press.

Stasser, G. (1992). Pooling of unshared information during group discussions. In S. Worchel, W. Wood, & J. A. Simpson (Eds.), *Group process and productivity* (pp. 48–67). Newbury Park, CA: Sage.

Stasson, M., & Fishbein, M. (1990). The relation between perceived and preventive action: A within–subject analysis of perceived driving risk and intentions to wear seatbelts. *Journal of Applied Social Psychology, 20,* 1541–1557.

Staub, E. (1989). *The roots of evil: The origins of genocide and other group violence.* Cambridge: Cambridge University Press.

Staub, E. (1996). Cultural–societal roots of violence: The examples of genocidal violence and of contemporary youth violence in the United States. *American Psychologist, 51,* 117–132.

Steele, C. M. (1992, April). Race and schooling of Black Americans. *Atlantic Monthly,* pp. 68–78.

Steele, C. M. (1997). A threat in the air: How stereotypes shape intellectual identity and performance. *American Psychologist, 52,* 613–629.

Stephan, W. G. (1977). Stereotyping: The role of ingroup–outgroup differences in causal attribution for behavior. *Journal of Social Psychology, 101,* 255–266.

Stephan, W. G., Ageyev, V., Coates-Shrider, L., Stephan, C. W., & Abalakina, M. (1994). On the relationship between stereotypes and prejudice: An international study. *Personality and Social Psychology Bulletin, 20,* 277–284.

Stephenson, G. M., & Brotherton, C. J. (1975). Social progression and polarization: A study of discussion and negotiation in groups of mining supervisors. *British Journal of Social and Clinical Psychology, 14,* 241–252.

Stern, P. C., & Aronson, E. (Eds.) (1984). *Energy use: The human dimension.* New York: W. H. Freeman.

Sternberg, R. J. (1986). A triangular theory of love. *Psychological Review, 93,* 119–135.

Sternberg, R. J. (1988). Triangulating love. In R. J. Sternberg & M. L. Barnes (Eds.), *The psychology of love* (pp. 119–138). New Haven, CT: Yale University Press.

Stevens, G. (1986). Bias in the attribution of hyperkinetic behavior as a function of ethnic identification and socioeconomic status. *Psychology in the Schools, 18,* 99–106.

Stevenson, H. W., Chen, C., & Lee, S. Y. (1993). Mathematics achievement of Chinese, Japanese, and American children: Ten years later. *Science, 259,* 53–58.

Stiles, D. A., Gibbons, J. L., & Peters, E. (1993). Adolescents' views of work and leisure in the Netherlands and the United States. *Adolescence, 28,* 473–489.

Stiles, D. S., Gibbons, J. L., & Schnellmann, J. De La Garza (1990). Opposite-sex ideal in the U.S.A. and Mexico as perceived by young adolescents. *Journal of Cross-Cultural Psychology, 21,* 180–199.

Stomberg, A. H. (Ed.) (1981). *Women, health and medicine.* Palo Alto, CA: Mayfield.

Stoner, J. A. F. (1961). *A comparison of individual and group decisions including risk.* Unpublished master's thesis, Massachusetts Institute of Technology, School of Management.

Stover, E., & Nightingale, E. O. (Eds.) (1985). *The breaking of bodies and minds: Torture, psychiatric abuse, and the health professions.* New York: W. H. Freeman.

Strack, F., Martin, L. L., & Stepper, S. (1988). Inhibiting and facilitating conditions of the human smile: A nonobtrusive test of the facial feedback hypothesis. *Journal of Personality and Social Psychology, 54,* 768–777.

Strader, M. K., & Katz, B. M. (1990). Effects of a persuasive communication on beliefs, attitudes, and career choice. *Journal of Social Psychology, 130,* 141–150.

Straubhaar, J., & LaRose, R. (1995). *Communications media in the information society.* Belmont, CA: Wadsworth.

Strauman, T. J., & Higgins, E. T. (1987). Automatic activation of self-discrepancies and emotional syndromes: When cognitive structures influence affect. *Journal of Personality and Social Psychology, 53,* 1004–1014.

Strickland, B. R. (1988). Internal–external expectancies and health-related behaviors. *Journal of Consulting and Clinical Psychology, 46,* 1192–1211.

Stringer, P., & Robinson, G. (Eds.) (1991). *Social attitudes in Northern Ireland.* Belfast: Blackstaff Press.

Suedfeld, P., Rank, D., & Borrie, R. (1975). Frequency of exposure and evaluation of candidates and campaign speeches. *Journal of Applied Social Psychology, 5,* 118–126.

Suls, J., & Greenwald, A. J. (Eds.) (1986). *Psychological perspectives on the self.* Hillsdale, NJ: Lawrence Erlbaum.

Suls, J., & Wills, T. A. (Eds.) (1991). *Social comparison: Contemporary theory and research.* Hillsdale, NJ: Lawrence Erlbaum.

Sumner, R. (1906). *Folkways.* Boston: Ginn.

Sundstrom, E. (1986). *Work places: The psychology of the physical environment in offices and factories.* New York: Cambridge University Press.

Swann, J. B., Jr. (1990). To be adored or to be known: The interplay of self-enhancement and self-verification. In R. M. Sorrentino & E. T. Higgins (Eds.), *Motivation and cognition* (Vol. 2, pp. 408–448). New York: Guilford Press.

Swann, J. B., Jr., Hixon, J. G., & De La Ronde, C. (1992). Embracing the bitter "truth": Negative self-concepts and marital commitment. *Psychological Science, 3,* 118–121.

Swann, J. B. Jr., Hixon, J. G., Stein-Seroussi, A., & Gilbert, D. T. (1990). The fleeting gleam of praise: Behavioral reactions to self-relevant feedback. *Journal of Personality and Social Psychology, 59,* 17–26.

Sweeney, L. T., & Haney, C. (1992). The influence of race on sentencing: A meta-analytic review of experimental studies. *Behavioral Sciences and the Law, 10,* 179–195.

Sweeney, P. D., Anderson, K., & Bailey, S. (1986). Attributional style in depression: A meta-analytic review. *Journal of Personality and Social Psychology, 50,* 974–991.

Sweeny, J., & Bradbard, M. R. (1988). Mothers' and fathers' changing perceptions of their male and female infants over the course of pregnancy. *Journal of Genetic Psychology, 149,* 393–404.

Swim, J. K., Aikin, K. J., Hall, W. S., & Hunter, B. A. (1995). Sexism and racism: Old-fashioned and modern prejudices. *Journal of Personality and Social Psychology, 68,* 199–214.

Tajfel, H. (1957). Value and the perceptual judgment of magnitude. *Psychological Review, 64,* 192–204.

Tajfel, H. (1959). Quantitative judgement in social perception. *British Journal of Psychology, 50,* 16–29.

Tajfel, H. (Ed.) (1978). *Differentiation between social groups.* London: Academic Press.

Tajfel, H. (Ed.) (1982). *Social identity and intergroup relations.* Cambridge: Cambridge University Press.

Tajfel, H. (Ed.) (1984). *The social dimension* (Vols. 1–2). Cambridge: Cambridge University Press.

Tajfel, H., Flament, C., Billig, M. G., & Bundy, R. F. (1971). Social categorization and intergroup behaviour. *European Journal of Social Psychology, 1,* 149–177.

Tajfel, H., & Turner, J. C. (1979). An integrative theory of intergroup conflict. In W. G. Austin & S. Worchel (Eds.), *The social psychology of intergroup relations* (pp. 33–47). Monterey, CA: Brooks/Cole.

Tajfel, H., & Wilkes, A. L. (1963). Classification and quantitative judgement. *British Journal of Psychology, 54,* 101–113.

Talapessy, L. (Ed.) (1993). *Women in science/technology research in the European Community.* Brussels: Directorate-General for Science, Research & Development of the European Union.

Tan, S., & Moghaddam, F. M. (1995). Reflexive positioning and culture. *Journal for the Theory of Social Behavior, 25,* 387–400.

Tan, S., & Moghaddam, F. M. (in press). Positioning and intergroup relations. In R. Harré & L. Van Langenhove (Eds.), *Positioning theory.* Oxford: Blackwell.

Tanford, S., & Penrod, S. (1984). Social influence model: A formal integration of research on majority and minority influence processes. *Psychological Bulletin, 95,* 189–225.

Tang, C. S., Critelli, J. W., & Porter, J. F. (1995). Sexual aggression and victimization in dating relationships among Chinese college students. *Archives of Sexual Behavior, 24,* 47–53.

Tangri, S. S., Burt, M. R., & Johnson, L. B. (1982). Sexual harassment at work: Three explanatory models. *Journal of Social Issues, 38,* 33–54.

Tata, J. (1993). The structure and phenomenon of sexual harassment: Impact of category of sexually harassing behavior, gender, and hierarchical level. *Journal of Applied Social Psychology, 23,* 199–211.

Taylor, D. M., & Brown, R. J. (1979). Toward a more social social psychology? *British Journal of Social and Clinical Psychology, 18,* 173–180.

Taylor, D. M., Doria, J., & Tyler, J. K. (1983). Group performance and cohesiveness: An attribution analysis. *Journal of Social Psychology, 119,* 187–198.

Taylor, D. M., & Jaggi, V. (1974). Ethnocentrism in a South Indian context. *Journal of Cross-Cultural Psychology, 5,* 162–172.

Taylor, D. M., & Lambert, W. E. (1996). The meaning of multiculturalism in a culturally diverse urban American area. *Journal of Social Psychology, 136,* 727–740.

Taylor, D. M., & McKirnan, D. J. (1984). A five-stage model of intergroup relations. *British Journal of Social Psychology, 23,* 291–300.

Taylor, D. M., & Moghaddam, F. M. (1987). *Theories of intergroup relations: International social psychological perspectives.* New York: Praeger.

Taylor, D. M., & Moghaddam, F. M. (1994). *Theories of intergroup relations: International social psychological perspectives* (2nd ed.). Westport, CT: Praeger.

Taylor, D. M., Moghaddam, F. M., & Bellerose, J. (1989). Social comparison in an intergroup context. *Journal of Social Psychology, 129,* 499–515.

Taylor, D. M., Moghaddam, F. M., Gamble, I., Zellerer, E. (1987). Disadvantaged group responses to perceived inequality: From passive acceptance to collective action. *Journal of Social Psychology, 127,* 259–272.

Taylor, D. M., Ruggiero, K. M., & Louis, W. R. (1996). Personal/group discrimination discrepancy: Toward a two-factor explanation. *Canadian Journal of Behavioural Science, 28,* 193–202.

Taylor, D. M., Wong–Rieger, D., McKirnan, D. J., & Bercusson, T. (1982). Interpreting and coping with threat in the context of intergroup relations. *Journal of Social Psychology, 117,* 257–269.

Taylor, D. M., Wright, S. C., Moghaddam, F. M., & Lalonde, R. N. (1990). The personal/group discrimination discrepancy: Perceiving my group, but not myself, to be a target for discrimination. *Personality and Social Psychology Bulletin, 16,* 254–262.

Taylor, D. M., Wright, S. C., & Porter, L. E. (1994). Dimensions of perceived discrimination: The personal/group discrimination discrepancy. In M. P. Zanna & J. M. Olson (Eds.), *The psychology of prejudice: The Ontario Symposium* (pp. 233–255). Hillsdale, NJ: Lawrence Erlbaum.

Taylor, D. M., Wright, S. C., & Ruggiero, K. M. (1991). The personal/group discrimination discrepancy. *Journal of Social Psychology, 131,* 847–858.

Taylor, S. E. (1989). *Positive illusions: Creative self-deception and the healthy mind.* New York: Basic Books.

Taylor, S. E., Fiske, S. T., Etcoff, N. L., & Ruderman, A. J. (1978). Categorical and contextual bases of person memory and stereotyping. *Journal of Personality and Social Psychology, 36,* 778–793.

Taylor, S. E., & Thompson, S. C. (1982). Stalking the elusive "vividness" effect. *Psychological Review, 89,* 155–181.

Taylor, T. (1996). *The prehistory of sex: Four million years of human sexual culture.* New York: Bantam.

Tedeschi, J. T., & Felson, R. B. (1994). *Violence, aggression, and coercive actions.* Washington, DC: American Psychological Association.

Teixeira, R. A. (1992). *The disappearing American voter.* Washington, DC: Brookings Institution.

Terkel, S. (1985). *Working: People talk about what they do all day and how they feel about what they do.* New York: Ballantine.

Tesser, A., & Shaffer, P. (1990). Attitudes and attitude change. *Annual Review of Psychology, 41,* 479–523.

Testa, M., Crocker, J., & Major, B. M. (1988). *The self-protective function of prejudice: Effects of negative feedback and evaluator prejudice on mood and self-esteem.* Paper presentation, Midwestern Psychological Association, Chicago.

Tetlock, P. E., & Levi, A. (1982). Attributional bias: On the inconclusiveness of the cognitive–motivation debate. *Journal of Experimental Social Psychology, 18,* 68–88.

Tetlock, P. E., & Manstead, A. S. R. (1985). Impression management versus intrapsychic explanations in social psychology: A useful dichotomy? *Psychological Review, 92,* 59–77.

Tetlock, P. E., Peterson, R. S., McGuire, C., & Feld, P. (1992). Assessing political group dynamics: A test of the groupthink model. *Journal of Personality and Social Psychology, 63,* 403–425.

Thatcher, M. (1993). *The Downing Street years.* New York: HarperCollins.

Thibaut, J. T., & Kelley, H. H. (1959). *The social psychology of groups.* New York: Wiley.

Thoma, S. J. (1986). Estimating gender differences in the comprehension and preference of moral issues. *Developmental Review, 6,* 165–180.

Thomas, S. (1991). The impact of women on state legislative policies. *Journal of Politics, 53,* 958–976.

Thomas, S. (1997). Why gender matters: The perceptions of women officeholders. *Women & Politics, 17,* 27–53.

Thompson, S. C., & Kelley, J. J. (1981). Judgments of responsibility for activities in close relationships. *Journal of Personality and Social Psychology, 41,* 469–477.

Thompson, S. C., & Pitts, J. S. (1992). In sickness and in health: Chronic illness, marriage, and spousal caregiving. In S. Spacaman & S. Oskamp (Eds.), *Helping and being helped: Naturalistic studies* (pp. 115–151). Newbury Park, CA: Sage.

Thoreau, H. D. (1849/1985). Civil disobedience. In G. McMichael (Ed.), *Anthology of American literature* (pp. 1481–1496). New York: Macmillan.

Thornton, B. (1992). Repression and its mediating influence on the defensive attribution of responsibility. *Journal of Research in Personality, 26,* 44–57.

Thucydides (1951). *The Peloponnesian War.* New York: Modern Library.

Timaeus, E. (1968). Untersuchungen zum sogenannten konformen Verhalten. *Zeitschrift für Experimentelle und Angewandte Psychologie, 15,* 176–194.

Time. (1994, September 19). Murder in miniature, pp. 54–59.

Tobin, G. A. (1987). *Divided neighborhoods: Changing patterns of racial segregation.* Newbury Park, CA: Sage.

Tocqueville, Alexis de (1845). *Democracy in America* (Vol. 1) (H. Reeve, Trans.). New York: Henry G. Langley.

Tolstoy, L. (1955). *War and peace.* (C. Garnett, Trans.). New York: Dell.

Tougas, F., Brown, R., Beaton, A. M., & Joly, S. (1995). Neosexism: Plus ça change, plus c'est pareil. *Personality and Social Psychology Bulletin, 21,* 842–849.

Triandis, H. (1972). *The analysis of subjective culture.* New York: Wiley-Interscience.

Triandis, H. C. (1984). Toward a psychological theory of economic development. *International Journal of Psychology, 19,* 79–95.

Triandis, H. C. (1989). The self and social behavior in differing cultural contexts. *Psychological Review, 96,* 506–520.

Triandis, H. (1994). *Culture and social behavior.* New York: McGraw-Hill.

Triandis, H. (1995). *Individualism & collectivism.* Boulder, CO: Westview Press.

Triandis, H., & Vassiliou, V. (1967). Frequency of contact and stereotyping. *Journal of Personality and Social Psychology, 7,* 316–328.

Tripathi, R. C., & Srivastava, R. (1981). Relative deprivation and intergroup attitudes. *European Journal of Social Psychology, 11,* 313–318.

Triplett, H. (1898). The dynamogenic factors in pace making and competition. *American Journal of Psychology, 9,* 507–533.

Trope, Y. (1980). Self-assessment, self-enhancement, and taste preference. *Journal of Experimental Social Psychology, 16,* 116–129.

Trope, Y. (1983). Self-assessment in achievement behavior. In J. M. Suls & A. A. Greenwald (Eds.), *Psychological perspectives on the self* (Vol. 2, pp. 93–122). Hillsdale, NJ: Lawrence Erlbaum.

Tucker, B. M., & Mitchell-Kernan, C. (1990). New trends in Black American interracial marriage: The social structural context. *Journal of Marriage and the Family, 52,* 209–217.

Tulis, J. K. (1987). *The rhetorical presidency.* Princeton, NJ: Princeton University Press.

Turnbull, C. M. (1972). *The mountain people.* New York: Simon & Schuster.

Turner, F. J. (1920). *The frontier in American life.* New York: Holt.

Turner, F. J. (1921). *The frontier in American history.* New York: Holt.

Turner, J. C., Hogg, M. A., Oakes, P. J., Reicher, S. D., & Wetherell, M. S. (1987). *Rediscovering the social group: A self-categorization theory.* Oxford: Blackwell.

Tversky, A., & Kahneman, D. (1974). Judgment under uncertainty: Heuristics and biases. *Science, 185,* 1123–1131.

Twain, M. (1974). *Letters from the earth* (B. De Voto, Ed.). New York: Perennial Library.

Tyler, A., & Davies, C. (1990). Cross-linguistic communication missteps. *Text, 10,* 385–411.

Ueda, K. (1974). Sixteen ways to avoid saying "no" in Japan. In J. C. Condon & M. Saito (Eds.), *Intercultural encounters in Japan.* Tokyo: Simul Press.

Unger, R., & Crawford, M. (1992). *Women and gender: A feminist psychology.* New York: McGraw-Hill.

Unger, R., & Crawford, M. (1996). *Women and gender: A feminist psychology* (2nd ed.). New York: McGraw-Hill.

Uniform Crime Reports for the United States. (1993). Washington, DC, Federal Bureau of Investigation, U.S. Department of Justice.

United Nations (1991). *The world's women 1970–1990: Trends and statistics.* New York: United Nations Publications.

United Nations (1994). *World social situation in the 1990s.* New York: United Nations Publications.

United Nations Development Programme (UNDP) (1990). *Human development report.* Oxford: Oxford University Press.

United Nations Development Programme (UNDP) (1993). *Human development report.* Oxford: Oxford University Press.

U.S. Bureau of the Census. (1990). *Current population reports: Series P-20.* Washington, DC: U.S. Government Printing Office.

U.S. Department of Justice (1992). *Hate crime statistics.* Uniform Crime Reports, FBI, Criminal Justice Information Services Division.

U.S. Department of Justice (1993). *Hate crime statistics.* Uniform Crime Reports, FBI, Criminal Justice Information Services Division.

Vaidyanathan, P., & Naidoo, J. (1991). Asian Indians in Western countries: Cultural identity and the arranged marriage. In N. Bleichrodt & P. Drenth (Eds.), *Contemporary issues in cross-cultural psychology* (pp. 37–49). Amsterdam: Swets & Zeitlinger.

Vallacher, R. R., & Wegner, D. M. (1985). *A theory of action identification.* Hillsdale, NJ: Lawrence Erlbaum.

Vallacher, R. R., & Wegner, D. M. (1987). What do people think they are doing? Action identification and human behavior. *Psychological Review, 94,* 3–15.

VandeBerg, L. R., & Streckfuss, D. (1992). Prime-time television's portrayal of women and the world of work: A demographic profile. *Journal of Broadcasting and Electronic Media, 36,* 195–208.

Van den Berghe, P. (1987). *The ethnic phenomenon.* New York: Praeger.

Vanneman, R. D., & Pettigrew, T. F. (1972). Race and relative deprivation in the United States. *Race, 13,* 461–486.

Van Overwalle, F., Segebarth, K., & Goldchstein, M. (1989). Improving performance of freshmen through attributional testimonies from fellow students. *British Journal of Educational Psychology, 59,* 75–85.

Vasta, R., & Copitch, P. (1981). Simulating conditions of child abuse in the laboratory. *Child Development, 52,* 164–170.

Venkatesan, M., & Losco, J. (1975). Women in magazine ads: 1959-1971. *Journal of Advertising Research, 15,* 49–54.

Vidmar, N. (1970). Group composition and the risky shift. *Journal of Experimental Social Psychology, 6,* 153–166.

Vigil, J. D. (1988). *Barrio boys.* Austin: University of Texas Press.

Vygotsky, L. S. (1978). *Mind in society.* Cambridge, MA: Harvard University Press.

Wachter, K. W., & Straf, M. L. (1990). *The future of meta-analysis.* New York: Russell Sage Foundation.

Wagner, U., & Schonbach, P. (1984). Links between educational status and prejudice: Ethnic attitudes in West Germany. In N. Miller & M. Brewer (Eds.), *Groups in contact: The psychology of desegregation* (pp. 29–52). New York: Academic Press.

Walker, L., Thibaut, J. T., & Andreoli, V. (1972). Order of presentation at trial. *Yale Law Journal, 82,* 216–226.

Walsh, A. (1991). *The science of love: Understanding love and its effects on mind and body.* Westport, CT: Prometheus.

Walsh, E. (1993, November 29). Chicago street gang study shows fearful toll of powerful weapons. *Washington Post,* p. A4.

Walster, E., Walster, G. W., & Berscheid, E. (1978). *Equity: Theory and research.* Boston: Allyn & Bacon.

Walt Disney (n.d.). *Snow White and the seven dwarfs.* New York: Twin Books.

Warren, R. L., & Lyon, L. (Eds.) (1988). *New perspectives on the American community* (5th ed.). Belmont, CA: Wadsworth.

Warshaw, R. (1962). *The immediate experience: Movies, comics, theater and other aspects of popular culture.* New York: Doubleday.

Washington Post. (1993, November 8). M. Asher. *Survey shows unrealistic hopes by black athletes: High schoolers living pro lie,* p. C5.

Watson, D. (1982). The actor and the observer: How are their perceptions of causality divergent? *Psychological Bulletin, 92,* 682–700.

Watson, G. (1985). *Social factors in justice evaluation.* Doctoral dissertation, Oxford University.

Watson, J. B. (1913). Psychology as the behaviorist views it. *Psychological Review, 20,* 158–177.

Watts, B. L. (1982). Individual differences in circadian activity rhythms and their effects on roommate relationships. *Journal of Personality, 50,* 374–384.

Weber, M. (1930). *The Protestant ethic and the spirit of capitalism.* (T. Parsons, Trans.). New York: Scribner's.

Weber, M. (1968). *On charisma and institution building.* Chicago: University of Chicago Press.

Wegner, D. M., Lane, J. D., & Dimitri, S. (1994). The allure of secret relationships. *Journal of Personality and Social Psychology, 66,* 287–300.

Weigert, S. L. (1996). *Traditional religion and guerrilla warfare in modern Africa.* New York: St. Martin's Press.

Weiner, B. (1980). A cognitive (attribution)–emotion–action model of motivated behavior: An analysis of judgments of help-giving. *Journal of Personality and Social Psychology, 59,* 281–312.

Weiner, B. (1985). An attributional theory of achievement-related motivation and emotion. *Psychological Review, 29,* 548–573.

Weiner, B. (1986). *An attributional theory of motivation and emotion.* New York: Springer-Verlag.

Weiner, B. (1988). An attributional analysis of changing reactions to persons with AIDS. In R. A. Berk (Ed.), *The social impact of AIDS in the U.S.* (pp. 139–169). Cambridge, MA: Abt.

Weiner, B. (1991). Metaphors in motivation and attribution. *American Psychologist, 46,* 921–930.

Weiner, B. (1993). On sin versus sickness: A theory of perceived social responsibility and social motivation. *American Psychologist, 48,* 957–965.

Weiner, B., Perry, R. P., & Magnusson, J. (1988). An attributional analysis of reactions to stigma. *Journal of Personality and Social Psychology, 55,* 738–748.

Weinstein, N. D. (1980). Unrealistic optimism about future life events. *Journal of Personality and Social Psychology, 39,* 806–820.

Weisz, J. R., Rothbaum, F. M., & Blackburn, T. C. (1984). Standing out and standing in: The psychology of control in America and Japan. *American Psychologist, 39,* 955–969.

Wells, G. L. (1981). Lay analyses of causal forces on behavior. In J. H. Harvey (Ed.), *Cognition, social behavior and the environment.* Hillsdale, NJ: Lawrence Erlbaum.

Wells, G. L. (1982). Attribution and reconstructive memory. *Journal of Experimental Social Psychology, 18,* 447–463.

Wetherell, M. S. (1982). Cross-cultural studies of minimal groups: Implications for social identity theory and intergroup relations. In H. Tajfel (Ed.), *Social identity and intergroup relations* (pp. 207–240). Cambridge: Cambridge University Press.

Wheatley, J. J., & Oshikawa, S. (1970). The relationship between anxiety and positive and negative anxiety appeals. *Journal of Marketing Research, 7,* 85–89.

Wheeler, J. O. (1971). Residential location by occupational status. In L.S. Bourne (Ed.), *Internal structure of the city* (pp. 309–315). New York: Oxford University Press.

White, G. L., Fishbein, S., & Rutstein, J. (1981). Romantic attraction: Misattribution of arousal on secondary reinforcement. *Journal of Personality and Social Psychology, 41,* 56–62.

Whiting, B. B., & Edwards, C. P. (1973). A cross-cultural analysis of sex differences in the behavior of children aged three to eleven. *Journal of Social Psychology, 91,* 171–188.

Whiting, B. B., & Edwards, C. P. (1988). *Children of different worlds: The foundations of social behavior.* Cambridge, MA: Harvard University Press.

Whiting, B. B., & Whiting, J. W. (1975). *Children of six countries: A psychological analysis.* Cambridge, MA: Harvard University Press.

Whitley, B. E. (1983). Sex role orientation and self-esteem: A critical meta-analytic review. *Journal of Personality and Social Psychology, 44,* 756–778.

Whitley, B. E. (1985). Sex-role orientation and psychological well-being: Two meta-analyses. *Sex Roles, 12,* 207–225.

Whitley, B. E., & Kite, M. E. (1995). Sex differences in attitudes toward homosexuality: A comment on Oliver and Hyde (1993). *Psychological Bulletin, 117,* 146–154.

Whittaker, J. O., & Meade, R. D. (1967). Social pressure on the modification and distortion of judgment: A cross-cultural study. *International Journal of Psychology, 2,* 109–113.

Whittler, T. E., & DiMeo, J. (1991). Viewers' reactions to racial cues in advertising stimuli. *Journal of Advertising Research,* December, 37–45.

Wicker, A. W. (1969). Attitudes versus actions: The relationship of verbal and overt behavioral responses to attitude objects. *Journal of Social Issues, 25,* 41–78.

Wicklund, R. A. (1975). Objective self-awareness. In L. Berkowitz (Ed.), *Advances in experimental social psychology* (Vol. 8, pp. 233–275). New York: Academic Press.

Wicklund, R. A., & Brehm, J. W. (1976). *Perspectives on cognitive dissonance.* New York: Wiley.

Wicklund, R. A., & Eckert, M. (1992). *The self-knower: A hero under control.* New York: Plenum Press.

Wicklund, R. A., & Frey, D. (1980). Self-awareness theory: When the self makes a difference. In D. M. Wegner & R. R. Vallacher (Eds.), *The self in social psychology* (pp. 31–54). New York: Oxford University Press.

Wiederman, M. W., & Allgeier, E. R. (1993). Gender differences in sexual jealousy: Adaptational or social learning explanations? *Ethology and Sociobiology, 14,* 115–140.

Wiehe, V. R., & Richards, A. L. (1995). *Intimate betrayal: Understanding and responding to the trauma of acquaintance rape.* Thousand Oaks, CA: Sage.

Wierda, H. J. (1992). *The Dominican Republic: A Caribbean crucible.* San Francisco: Westview Press.

Wilder, D. A. (1977). Perception of groups, size of opposition, and social influence. *Journal of Experimental Social Psychology, 13,* 253–268.

Wilder, D. A. (1978). Homogeneity of jurors: The majority's influence depends upon their perceived independence. *Law and Human Behavior, 2,* 253–268.

Wilder, G. Z., & Powell, K. (1989). *Sex differences in test performance: A survey of the literature.* College Board Report #89-3. New York: College Entrance Examination Board.

Wilkinson, S. (1997). Feminist psychology. In D. Fox & I. Prilleltensky (Eds.), *Critical psychology: An introduction* (pp. 247–264). Thousand Oaks, CA: Sage.

Wilkinson, S., & Kitzinger, C. (Eds.) (1996). Representing the other: *A feminist & psychology reader.* Thousand Oaks, CA: Sage.

Williams, J. E., & Best, D. L. (1982). *Measuring sex stereotypes: A thirty-nation study.* Beverly Hills, CA: Sage.

Williams, J. E., & Best, D. L. (1990a). *Measuring sex stereotypes: A multi-nation study.* Newbury Park, CA: Sage.

Williams, J. E., & Best, D. L. (1990b). *Sex and psyche: Gender and self viewed cross-culturally.* Newbury Park, CA: Sage.

Williams, K., Harkins, S., & Latané, B. (1981). Identifiability as a deterrent to social loafing: Two cheering experiments. *Journal of Personality and Social Psychology, 40,* 303–311.

Williams, K., & Karau, S. J. (1991). Social loafing and social compensation: The effects of expectations of co-worker performance. *Journal of Personality and Social Psychology, 61,* 570–580.

Williams, W. F. (1992). *The spirit and the flesh.* Boston: Beacon Press.

Williams–Meyers, A. J. (1995). *Destructive impulses.* New York: University Press of America.

Wills, T. A. (1992). The helping process in the context of personal relationships. In S. Spacaman & S. Oskamp (Eds.), *Helping and being helped: Naturalistic studies* (pp. 17–48). Newbury Park, CA: Sage.

Wilson, E., & Katayani, M. (1968). Intergroup attitudes and strategies in games between opponents of the same or different race. *Journal of Personality and Social Psychology, 9,* 24–30.

Wilson, E. O. (1975). *Sociobiology: The new synthesis.* Cambridge, MA: Belknap Press.

Wilson, K., & Gallois, C. (1993). *Assertion and its social context.* Oxford: Pergamon.

Wilson, T. D. (1985). Strangers to ourselves: The origins and accuracy of beliefs about one's own mental states. In J. H. Harvey & G. Weary (Eds.), *Attribution: Basic issues and applications* (pp. 9–36). New York: Academic Press.

Wilson, T. D. (1990). Self-persuasion via self-reflection. In J. Olson & M. P. Zanna (Eds.), *Self-inference processes: The Ontario Symposium* (Vol. 6, pp. 43–67). Hillsdale, NJ: Lawrence Erlbaum.

Wilson, T. D., & Hodges, S. D. (1992). Attitudes as temporal constructions. In L. L. Martin & A. Tesser (Eds.), *The construction of social judgments* (pp. 37–65). Hillsdale, NJ: Lawrence Erlbaum.

Wilson, T. D., Hodges, S. D., & LaFleur, S. J. (1995). Effects of introspecting about reasons: Inferring attitudes from accessible thoughts. *Journal of Personality and Social Psychology, 69,* 16–28.

Wilson, T. D., Hull, J. G., & Johnson, J. (1981). Awareness and self-perception: Verbal reports on internal states. *Journal of Personality and Social Psychology, 40,* 53–70.

Wilson, T. D., & Nisbett, R. E. (1978). The accuracy of verbal reports about the effects of stimuli on evaluations and behavior. *Social Psychology, 41,* 118–131.

Wilson, T. D., & Schooler, J. W. (1991). Thinking too much: Introspection can reduce the quality of preferences and decisions. *Journal of Personality and Social Psychology, 60,* 181–192.

Wilson, W., & Wong, J. (1968). Intergroup attitudes toward cooperative vs. competitive opponents in a modified prisoner's dilemma game. *Perception and Motor Skills, 27,* 1059–1066.

Winn, M. (1985). *The plug-in drug: Television, children, and the family.* New York: Penguin.

Witkin, H. A., Mednick, S. A., Schulsinger, F., Bakkestrom, E., Christiansen, K. O., Goodenough, D. R., Hirschhorn, K., Lundsteen, C., Owen, D. R., Philip, J., Rubin, D. B., & Stocking, M. (1976). Criminality in XYY and XXY men. *Science, 193,* 547–555.

Wober, M. (1975). *Psychology in Africa.* London: International African Institute.

Wojciszke, B. (1987). Ideal-self, self-focus, and value-behavior consistency. *European Journal of Social Psychology, 17,* 187–198.

Wolf, N. (1991). *The beauty myth: How images of beauty are used against women.* New York: Morrow.

Wolf, S., & Bugaj, A. M. (1990). The social impact of courtroom witnesses. *Social Behaviour, 5,* 1–13.

Wong, P. T. P., Derlega, V. J., & Colson, W. (1988). The effects of race on expectancies and performance attributions. *Canadian Journal of Behavioural Science, 20,* 29–39.

Wood, J. V. (1989). Theory and research concerning social comparisons of personal attributes. *Psychological Bulletin, 106,* 231–248.

Worchel, S., & Austin, W. G. (Eds.) (1986). *Psychology of intergroup relations.* Monterey, CA: Brooks/Cole.

Wormser, M. D. (Ed.), with Moore, J. L., & Tan, D. R. (Assoc. Eds.) (1982). *Congressional Quarterly's Guide to Congress* (3rd ed.). Washington, DC: Congressional Quarterly.

Wright, S. C., & Taylor, D. M. (1995). Identity and the language of the classroom: Investigating the impact of heritage versus second language instruction in personal and collective self-esteem. *Journal of Educational Psychology, 87,* 241–252.

Wright, S. C., Taylor, D. M., & Moghaddam, F. M. (1990). The relationship of perceptions and emotions to behaviour in the face of collective inequality. *Social Justice Research, 4,* 229–250.

Wright, W. (1975). *Six guns and society: A structural study of the Western.* Berkeley, CA: University of California Press.

Wylie, R. C. (1979). *The self concept* (Vol. 2). Lincoln: University of Nebraska Press.

Yang, K. (1988). Will societal modernization eventually eliminate cross-cultural psychological differences? In M. Bond (Ed.), *The cross-cultural challenge to social psychology* (pp. 67–85). Newbury Park, CA: Sage.

Yang, M. M. (1994). *Gifts, favors, and banquets: The art of social relationships in China.* Ithaca, NY: Cornell University Press.

Yarkin, K. L., Town, J. P., & Wallston, B. S. (1982). Blacks and women must try harder: Stimulus persons' race and sex attributions of causality. *Personality and Social Psychology Bulletin, 8*, 21–24.

Yoshika, T., Kojo, K., & Kaku, H. (1982). A study in the development of social presentation in children. *Japanese Journal of Educational Psychology, 30*, 120–127.

Zajonc, R. B. (1965). Social facilitation. *Science, 149*, 269–274.

Zajonc, R. B. (1970, February). Brainwash: Familiarity breeds comfort. *Psychology Today*, pp. 32–35, 60–62.

Zajonc, R. B. (1980). Feeling and thinking: Preferences need no inferences. *American Psychologist, 35*, 151–175.

Zangwill, I. (1909). *The melting pot*. New York: Macmillan.

Zanna, M. P., Crosby, F., & Loewenstein, G. (1986). Male reference groups and discontent among female professionals. In B. A. Gutek & L. Larwood (Eds.), *Women's career development* (pp. 28–41). Newbury Park, CA: Sage.

Zarbatany, L., Hartmann, D. P., Gelfand, D. M., & Vinciguerra, P. (1985). Gender differences in altruistic reputation: Are they artifactual? *Developmental Psychology, 21*, 97–101.

Zeager, L. A., & Bascom, J. B. (1996). Strategic behavior in refugee repatriation. *Journal of Conflict Resolution, 40*, 460–485.

Zern, D. S. (1984). Relationships among selected child-rearing variables in a cross-cultural sample of 110 societies. *Developmental Psychology, 20*, 683–690.

Zilboorg, G., & Henry, G. W. (1941). *A history of medical psychology*. New York: Norton.

Ziller, R. C. (1990). *Photographing the self: Methods for observing personal orientations*. Newbury Park, CA: Sage.

Zimbardo, P. (1972). Pathology of imprisonment. *Transactional/Society, 4*–8 (a).

Zimbardo, P. (1973, April 8). The mind is a formidable jailer: A Pirandellian prison. *New York Times*, p. 38.

Zuckerman, H., Cole, J. R., & Bruer, J. T. (Eds.) (1991). The outer circle: *Women in the scientific community*. New York: Norton.

Zuckerman, M. (1979). Attribution of success and failure revisited, or: The motivational bias is alive and well in attribution theory. *Journal of Personality, 47*, 245–287.

Zuckerman, M. (1987). Affect of the game player. *Personality and Social Psychology Bulletin, 12*, 390–402.

Zullow, H. M., & Seligman, M. E. P. (1990). Pessimistic rumination predicts electoral defeat of Presidential candidates. *Psychology Inquiry, 1*, 52–61.

Zuwerink, J. R., & Devine, P. G. (1996). Attitude importance and resistance to persuasion: It's not just the thought that counts. *Journal of Personality and Social Psychology, 70*, 931–944.

Photograph Credits

Chapter 1 *Opposite 1*: Michael Schumann/SABA.   *4: Left*, P. Howell/Gamma Liaison; *right*, William Taufic/The Stock Market.   *6*: Wesley Bocxe/Photo Researchers.   *10*: Mark A. Johnson/The Stock Market.   *11: Left*, Fonseca/Contrasto/ SABA; *center*, Underwood & Underwood/Corbis–Bettmann; *right*, W. Stone/Gamma Liaison.   *14: Left*, Bulcao/Gamma Liaison; *right*, Charlyn Zlotnik/Woodfin Camp & Associates.   *19*: David Strickler/The Picture Cube.

Chapter 2 *24*: Chuck Savage/The Stock Market.   *30*: A. Ramey/Woodfin Camp & Associates.   *33*: L. Dematteis/ The Image Works.   *39*: Gale Zucker/Stock, Boston.   *42*: Jonathan Elderfield/Gamma Liaison.   *44*: Francekevich/The Stock Market.   *50*: Springer/Corbis–Bettmann.

Chapter 3 *56*: Chris Noble/Tony Stone Images.   *61*: Frank Herholdt/Tony Stone Worldwde.   *65*: Paul Chesley/ Photographers/Aspen.   *71*: Stan Ries/The Picture Cube.   *72*: Paul Chesley/Photographers/Aspen.   *78*: Camerique/The Picture Cube.   *80*: John Neubauer/PhotoEdit.   *85*: Spooner/Gamma Liaison.   *89*: Cynthia Johnson/Gamma Liaison.

Photo Essay: The Self *94*: Bob Daemmrich/The Image Works.   *95: Top left*, Fatin Philippe/Gamma Liaison; *bottom left*, Daniele Pellegrini/Photo Researchers. *bottom right*, Victor Englebert/Photo Researchers.   *96: Above*, Bachmann/Stock, Boston; *below*, Gary A. Conner/PhotoEdit.   *97: Left*, Jeff Greenberg/Photo Researchers; *right*, Noboru Komine/Photo Researchers.

Chapter 4 *98*: Jonathan Nourok/Tony Stone Images.   *105: Left*, Michael Newman/PhotoEdit; *right*, Barry Iverson/Woodfin Camp & Associates.   *113*: R. Lord/The Image Works.   *119: Left*, John Annerino/Gamma Liaison; *right*, Greg Meadors/Stock, Boston.   *127*: Everett Collection.

Chapter 5 *138*: Jeff Chrjeo Christensen/Gamma Liaison.   *141*: William McCoy/The Stock Market.   *148*: Simon Jauncey/Tony Stone Images.   *150*: Tony Freeman/PhotoEdit.   *153*: A. Sussman/The Image Works.   *157*: Archive Photos.   *166*: Bob Daemmrich/The Image Works.   *169*: Hulton Getty Images/Tony Stone Images.

Chapter 6 *176*: Fritz Hoffman/The Image Works.   *179: Above*, David Burnett/The Stock Market; *below*, Bettina Cirone/Photo Researchers.   *184*: Steven Rubin/The Image Works.   *188*: Dinodia/The Image Works.   *195*: A. Ramey/ Stock, Boston.   *199*: John Eastcott, Yva Momatiuk/The Image Works.   *208*: S. Freedman/Spooner/Gamma Liaison.

Photo Essay: Conformity *214: Above*, D. Young–Wolff/ PhotoEdit; *below*, John Henley/The Stock Market.   *215: Above*, Ulrike Welsch/Photo Researchers; *below*, Greenberg/PhotoEdit.   *216: Above*, Mark Peterson/SABA; *below*, Blair Seitz/Photo Researchers.   *217: Above*, Ken Straiton/The Stock Market; *below*, Alain Evrard/Photo Researchers.

Chapter 7 *218*: Alain Evrard/Photo Researchers.   *225*: Esaias Baitel/Gamma Liaison.   *231*: William Vandivert/ Scientific American.   *236*: UPI/Corbis–Bettmann.   *237*: Rod Lamkey, Jr./Gamma Liaison.   *241*: Viviane Moos/The Stock Market.   *244: Left*, UPI/Corbis–Bettmann; *right*, Shone/ Gamma Liaison.   *246*: Milgram.   *252*: UPI/Corbis–Bettmann.

Chapter 8 *258*: Frank Siteman/Stock, Boston.   *267*: Lefkir–Laffitte Naima/Gamma Liaison.   *273: Above*, J. Polleross/The Stock Market; *below*, Andrew Holbrooke/The Stock Market.   *277*: Tom Stewart/The Stock Market.   *280*: Ann States/SABA.   *283: Left*, Fujifotos/The Image Works; *right*, Lori Grinker/The Stock Market.   *288*: Jay Dickman, Littleton, Colorado.

Chapter 9 *294*: Job Roger/Gamma Liaison.   *299: Above*, Margaret Miller/Photo Researchers; *below*, Alan Oddie/ PhotoEdit.   *301: Left*, Frank Siteman/Tony Stone Images; *right*, Viviane Moos/The Stock Market.   *315: Left*, Eastcott/The Image Works; *right*, Spencer Grant/Photo Researchers.   *319*: George Holz/The Image Works.

Photo Essay: Altruism *324: Above*, Neale Haynes/Tony Stone Images; *below*, Kenneth Murray/Photo Researchers.   *325: Above*, Jose L. Pelaez/The Stock Market; *below*, John Barr/Gamma Liaison.   *326: Above*, Randy Taylor/Gamma Liaison; *below*, Bruce Brander/Photo Researchers.   *327: Above*, Wesley Bocxe/Photo Researchers; *below*, Robert Semeniuk/The Stock Market.

Chapter 10 *328*: Christopher Brown/Stock, Boston.   *333: Left*, Charles Gupto/The Stock Market; *right*, A. Ramey/Stock, Boston.   *340*: Katsuyoshi Tanaka/Woodfin Camp & Associates.   *343*: Ben Simmons/The Stock Market.   *348*: Bob Daemmrich/Stock, Boston.   *355*: Craig Filipacchi/ Gamma Liaison.   *359*: AP/Wide World Photos/Michael S. Green.

Chapter 11 *364*: Kevin Jacobus © The Syracuse Newspapers/ The Image Works.   *368*: Frank Fournier/Contact Press/The Stock Market.   *374*: Petit (Nikon) Agence Vandystadt/Photo Researchers.   *379*: J. Barr/Gamma Liaison.   *383*: Victor Englebert/Photo Researchers.   *389*: A. Ramey/Stock, Boston.

Name Index

Page numbers in *italics* indicate figure captions.

Subject Index

Page numbers in *italics* indicate figure captions.